COLUMBIA COLLEGE
848.91409S251C0 C1 V1
S0-IWZ-989
3 2711 00006 9102

848.91409 S251co v.1

ENTERED SEP 2 1 1992

A Bibliographical Life

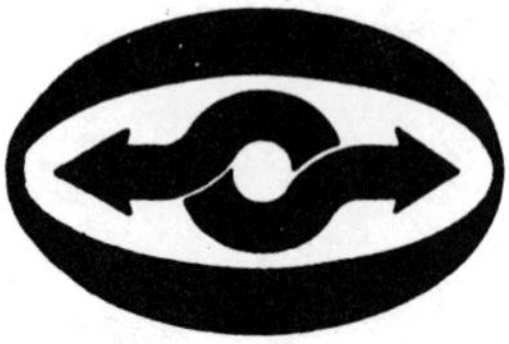

Northwestern University

STUDIES IN *Phenomenology & Existential Philosophy*

COLUMBIA COLLEGE LIBRARY

GENERAL EDITOR
James M. Edie

CONSULTING EDITORS
Hubert L. Dreyfus
William Earle
J. N. Findlay
Dagfinn Føllesdal
Marjorie Grene
Aron Gurwitsch
Emmanuel Levinas
Alphonso Lingis
Maurice Natanson
Paul Ricoeur
George Schrader
Calvin O. Schrag
Herbert Spiegelberg
Charles Taylor

The Writings of Jean-Paul Sartre

Compiled by

Translated by

Volume 1
A Bibliographical Life

MICHEL CONTAT
and MICHEL RYBALKA

COLUMBIA COLLEGE LIBRARY

RICHARD C. McCLEARY

NORTHWESTERN UNIVERSITY PRESS
EVANSTON 1974

Copyright © 1974 by Northwestern University Press
All rights reserved
Library of Congress Catalog Card Number: 73–85750
ISBN 0–8101–0430–X (Vol. 1)
ISBN 0–8101–0439–3 (Vols. 1 and 2 as a set)
First clothbound printing, 1974
Second clothbound printing, 1985

This is volume 1 of a two-volume translation, with revisions and additions, of a one-volume work originally published in French as *Les Ecrits de Sartre: Chronologie, bibliographie commentée*, copyright © 1970 by Editions Gallimard.

Michel Contat is associated with *Les Temps modernes* in Paris. Michel Rybalka is Professor of Romance Languages, Washington University, St. Louis, Missouri. Richard C. McCleary is Professor of Philosophy at Old Dominion University, Norfolk, Virginia.

Grateful acknowledgment is made to the following for permission to quote from published sources: Simone de Beauvoir and Malcolm Cowley for excerpt from Simone de Beauvoir, "Jean-Paul Sartre: Strictly Personal," translated by Malcolm Cowley, *Harper's Bazaar* (January, 1946); G. P. Putnam's Sons for excerpts from Simone de Beauvoir, *Force of Circumstance*, translated by Richard Howard, copyright © 1964, 1965 by G. P. Putnam's Sons, original copyright © 1963 by Librairie Gallimard; Atheneum Publishers and Penguin Books Ltd. (for Longmans) for excerpts from Kenneth Tynan, *Tynan Right and Left*, copyright © 1953, 1954, 1957, 1958, 1959, 1960, 1961, 1962, 1963, 1964, 1965, 1966, 1967 by Kenneth Tynan.

848.91409 S251co v.1

Contat, Michel.

The writings of Jean-Paul
Sartre

To Bouvard and Pécuchet

Contents

Prefacing Letter

Dear Friends,

You have done a remarkable piece of work. I know that authors are not qualified to judge the value of the bibliographies devoted to them: bibliographical investigations require a discipline and rigor we are scarcely capable of, and cannot really be justly appreciated by anyone except bibliographers. But just because I recognized my own incompetence, I appreciated your book from a purely personal point of view for being a Boswell to my memory. I not only found in it all the writings, without exception, that I remembered; you also resurrected the ones I had forgotten. I rediscover them with a certain astonishment, and at times a feeling of uneasiness: most of them are witnesses for the prosecution. But it is nice to be able, in spite of everything, to never disown them. More generally speaking, you have the unusual merit of having given life to what without you would have been no more than a posthumous inventory. Thanks to your brief and rich analyses, you have transformed this numbered list into a portrait: you have restored the movement through which any writer, good or bad, gives himself objective form in his works. If it is true that one is nothing but what one has done, then this portrait, whatever feelings it evokes, is undeniably true. I come back to myself as a stranger who is sometimes hard to recognize. But there is nothing I can take exception to. Thanks to your good offices, the subject of this painting is in a certain sense the author's self-portrait; and the reason why I am no more than half in love with your depiction is clearly that it's true.

J.-P. Sartre

Introduction

From whatever angle you look at his thought and works, Jean-Paul Sartre is uncontestably the most outstanding philosopher and writer of our time. "An enormous pieceworker, a night-patrolman on all the battlefronts of intelligence," as Jacques Audiberti already defined him in 1953, he has been able, with exemplary lucidity and throughout the different stages of an extremely lively intellectual life, to speak to us in always timely language and to make us understand our time. And yet around 1965, when the two of us independently began our research, there was (in spite of several praiseworthy attempts) no systematic inventory of his writings and no strict analysis of his work as a whole. A great number of texts, even well-known ones, were inaccessible. Like it or not, one had to be satisfied with a partial picture and with incomplete and often approximate information. At the start, it was this sense of an unmet need and this concern for the whole which led us to undertake what is ordinarily a dull and inglorious task. One of us, after having finished a study of Boris Vian, found himself quite naturally in the role of Chick in THE FROTH OF PASSING DAYS; the other, after having written about THE CONDEMNED OF ALTONA, chose to try out for three years that refined form of voluntary imprisonment, writing bibliographies.

Whatever its Freudian implications, this volume, which is conceived of as essentially a *documentary work*, aspires to reconstruct a sort of "bibliographical life" of Sartre and sets itself the following goals:

1. to provide a well-constructed tool which will enable students and the general public to get an overall view of Sartre's *oeuvre*, and to enable investigators to stop wasting their time in bio-bibliographical research. In this sense we can claim, with a certain immodesty, that this volume, precisely because it is documentary, sums up, corrects, and sharpens much of what has been written about Sartre up till now;

2. to put a certain number of unpublished, rare, or hard-to-find texts at the disposition of the general public;

3. to promote a new kind of bibliography which is both rigorous and supple, which avoids the purism and formalism of traditional bibliographies, and which tries instead to communicate a certain amount of information in the most effective way possible.

In order to accomplish these aims, we have decided--

1. not to use symbols or abbreviations;

2. to reduce the number of references to the minimum necessary;

3. to give little space to purely bibliophilic information;

4. to accompany each reference with an annotation in which we try to provide, as concisely as possible, information about the nature and content of the texts as well as about the circumstances under which they first appeared.

This work must obviously be *provisional* and cannot claim to be *exhaustive*, in spite of our continuing ambition to make it so. We have just about doubled the number of known references, and we are more or less certain that we have not overlooked any essential text. Yet given the variety and the geographical and historical dispersion of Sartre's activities, and given too that there seems to be no coherent file of his writings, there is no doubt that we have missed a certain number of references, above all among those which have to do with interviews in little magazines or abroad (systematic research needs to be done in Italy, for example). We have been able to locate quite a few of these manuscripts, but we have scarcely taken them into account within the framework of this study.

The biographical references we have given in our chronology are of uneven value. Most of the biographical articles we have looked at lack precision, and some are just downright capricious. Anyone who wants livelier and more solid information should refer to Simone de Beauvoir's memoirs and Sartre's autobiographical writings.

The annotations are inevitably the most subjective part of the book and therefore most open to criticism. They are intended to inform and guide the reader of Sartre's *oeuvre* rather than to express a critical viewpoint. We are also aware that our own commentaries would lend themselves especially well to a semeiology of the academic style, which is a rhetoric of prudence. No one should expect to find any sort of definitive statement in our annotations; our judgments are hasty and our analyses are usually limited to the most striking points. Whenever we had Sartre's commentaries on his own works at our disposal, we chose them over those we could have suggested ourselves. Thus we have chosen to look at his works from *within*, and that is why we are presenting our work as an *annotated bibliography* rather than a critical bibliography. The annotations are in all cases the result of our collaboration; but in general the political and philosophical part has been drafted by Michel Contat, and the literary and theatrical part by Michel Rybalka.

As a result of our basic concern with giving the reader the completest possible information about Sartre's least known interviews and writings, the length of the annotations is in almost inverse proportion to the notoriety of the texts and is not indicative of their worth. We have accepted the various forms of presentation which the diversity of the texts themselves often demanded. We saw in fact, as we went about writing this book, that it was impossible to stick to an absolutely uniform system, and that if there is one literary genre in which flexibility is imperative, it is surely bibliography. We eliminated summaries of all texts easily accessible in bookstores or libraries: the reader will find good summaries of all Sartre's major works in the *Dictionnaire des oeuvres contemporaines* published by Laffont-Bompiani.

There could be no question of including the enormous mass of works, studies, and articles devoted to Sartre, and we have mentioned them only in exceptional cases. Let us hope, however, that a critical list of writings on Sartre will soon appear in print: two or three checklists are now in preparation.

Although some of the limitations of our work were the result of our own choice, others have been imposed upon us by the very nature of the subject and by that state of bibliographical underdevelopment which makes most research done in Parisian libraries extremely long, arduous, and incomplete.

The Rondel Fund of the Arsenal library, and also the newspaper files at Gallimard, have been invaluable; but we have been greatly handicapped by the lack of an author-subject index for French and Italian periodicals; the 1967-68 period suffers somewhat from this lack.

There is no doubt that the best tool for studying contemporary French literature is *French XX Bibliography*, which is published each year by the French Institute of New York. Original references may also be found in:

Marguerite L. Drevet. *Bibliographie de la littérature française 1940-1949* ⟨Bibliography of French Literature, 1940-1949⟩. Geneva: Droz, and Lille: Giard, 1954.

Otto Klapp. *Bibliographie der französischen Literaturwissenschaft* ⟨Bibliography of French Literature⟩. Frankfurt am Main: V. Klostermann. 10 volumes.

Among the bibliographies about Sartre which have been the most useful to us, we should like to cite those of:

Kenneth Douglas. *A Critical Bibliography of Existentialism (The Paris School).* Yale French Studies Special Monograph, no. 1, 1950. Republished by Kraus (New York) in 1966. Pleasant to read and by far the most complete at that date.

Karl Kohut. *Was ist Literatur? Die Theorie der "littérature engagée" bei Jean-Paul Sartre* ⟨What is Literature? The Theory of "Committed Literature" in Jean-Paul Sartre⟩. Inaugural dissertation. Marburg, 1965. The most complete of recent bibliographies: gives 219 references to writings by Sartre and more than 1300 to writings about Sartre. Not critical.

Dina Dreyfus and Pierre Trotignon. "Bibliographie de Jean-Paul Sartre." *Revue de l'enseignement philosophique*, 16th Year, no. 2 (December, 1965-January, 1966), pp. 16-38. Supplements in the following issues: 16th Year, no. 6 (August-September, 1966); 17th Year, no. 1 (October-November, 1966); 17th Year, no. 3 (February-March, 1967). A noncritical bibliography which is well-documented from a political point of view, although it has gaps and guesswork.

Jacques Prunair. An unpublished bibliography of one hundred pages from which we have taken several references.

Michel-Antoine Burnier. *Les Existentialistes et la politique.* Idées series. Gallimard, [1966]. English translation, *Choice of Action: The French Existentialists on the Political Front Line.* New York: Random House, Vintage Books, 1969. This excellent study includes numerous references to Sartre's political writings in its footnotes.

Allen Belkind. *Jean-Paul Sartre: Sartre and Existentialism in English, a Biographical Guide.* Kent State University Press, 1970. Incomplete, mediocre in many ways, but nevertheless useful.

Philip Thody. *Jean-Paul Sartre: A Literary and Political Study.* London: Hamish Hamilton, 1960.

Biblio, 1st Year, no. 5 (May-June, 1950), pp. 13-14; *Livres de France*, 17th Year, no. 1 (January, 1966), pp. 24-27.
Yale French Studies, nos. 1, 10, 16. 30.

This volume would not have been possible without the constant, friendly, and generous support of Jean-Paul Sartre. The many indispensable items of information he gave us, both during our several interviews with him and indirectly, enabled us to find many texts he had no particular reason to want to see dug up. In the case of an author whose extremely abundant writings have already been welling forth for half a century and were often closely connected to circumstances which led to a profound change in the author himself, such generosity needs to be stressed. For it testifies to his strict intellectual honesty: more than any other, perhaps, Sartre is a writer who takes responsibility for all his texts. Those he has been kind enough to give us permission to reproduce, leaving us complete freedom of choice, are for the most part minor writings, and this is why he did not reprint them in the SITUATIONS volumes. Yet all of them, we thought, have some sort of interest, and some of them are of high quality.

We owe Sartre much more than our thanks. Yet in order to avoid any misunderstanding, we would like to point out that the information and the judgments in our annotations are entirely our own responsibility and in no way commit Sartre.

We received invaluable aid from the people around Sartre. For two years Arlette El Kaïm helped us with her unflagging willingness to pass on the questions which sprang up as our research went forward. A good bit of unpublished information was provided by Michelle Vian, who also gave us valuable help. Our debt to Simone de Beauvoir is shown by the quantity of information we owe to her memoirs; our frequent quotations from the *Memoirs of a Dutiful Daughter* (translated by James Kirkup [Cleveland: World Publishing, 1959]), *The Prime of Life* (translated by Peter Green [Cleveland: World Publishing, 1962], and *Force of Circumstance* (translated by Richard Howard [New York: Putnam, 1965]) will remind the reader that without these essential books a work like ours could not have been completed.

It is impossible to mention all the people who contributed to this volume. But we especially thank Freddy Buache, who pointed out certain very little known texts to us and made the resources of the Swiss Cinémathèque available to us, thereby enabling us to complete the bibliography with an appendix on writing about movies; Michel-Antoine Burnier, who gave us efficient help throughout our research, especially by getting several hard-to-find texts for us; Georges Michel, who let us see his collection of articles on Sartre; and Michel Thévoz, whose useful suggestions enabled us to profit from his profound knowledge of Sartre's thought.

We thank MM. Gilbert Guisan, professor at the University of Lausanne,[1] and Oreste F. Pucciani, professor at the University of California at Los Angeles, whose teaching and encouragement are the immediate source of this work.

And finally, each of the following persons merits our thanks: Luc Chessex, Stanko Lasič, Kaspar Locher, Jacqueline Pace, André Puig, Phillipe Schwed, Dominique Spinetta, Katrina Streiff.

In a work as long as this a certain number of errors is inevitable. We would be very grateful to our readers if they would let us know about them and would write to Michel Contat in care of Editions Gallimard, 5 rue Sébastien-Bottin, 75007 Paris, or to Michel Rybalka, Department of Romance Languages,

Washington University, Saint Louis, Mo. 63130, if they know of any texts or information we may have left out.

MICHEL CONTAT

MICHEL RYBALKA

---

1. My half of this work was carried out thanks to the material aid of the Swiss National Foundation for Scientific Investigation, to which I express my warmest thanks. M.C.

Note to the English Translation

Au cours des ans au cours des ans
il est pareil et non le même.

(Raymond Queneau in *Fendre les flots* [Gallimard], p. 104)

Since 1968, our knowledge of Sartre has evolved considerably, but it is clear, however, that the directions indicated in his early works as well as in CRITIQUE OF DIALECTICAL REASON and THE WORDS have been followed and reaffirmed. If the impact of his new political commitments and of his huge study on Flaubert is yet to be measured and if most of the recent advances in Sartrian scholarship have not yet been made public, it appears nevertheless that we have today a deeper and more coherent understanding of a man who has made it a point to function inseparably as a philosopher, writer, and militant and who has given thus a new meaning to the word *intellectual*.

The following translation of *Les Ecrits de Sartre* has been revised for the period 1923-69 and updated to cover all Sartre's writings and activities till Spring, 1973. A number of approximations and minor mistakes have been corrected and more than two hundred new references and notes have been added. It should be noted also that with most of the recent political writings the notion of authorship has--to confirm Michel Foucault's view--become problematical.

To make the work more useful for the Anglo-American public, a concise bibliography of Sartre's translations into English has been integrated in the reference section of the book. My aim here has not been to attempt original and thorough bibliographical research (in small or little-known periodicals, for instance), but to indicate to the reader what corpus of English translations seems to be available at present. One will thus realize, with some astonishment, that a number of Sartre's texts, sometimes major, have been left untranslated.

For the revision and updating, I wish to acknowledge, above all, Michel Contat's collaboration: we have published together two supplements to *Les Ecrits de Sartre*, the first one in *Adam* (nos. 343-45 [1970]), the second, under the able editorship of Jean-Jacques Brochier, in *Magazine littéraire* (no. 55

[September, 1971]). Simone de Beauvoir, Arlette El Kaïm, and Michelle Vian have been of much assistance. Wanda Kosakiewicz has communicated several very important manuscripts, as have Marc Benard, George Bauer, and André Gorz. Takeshi Ebisaka (who is the author, with Michihiko Suzuki and Kinuko Urano, of the excellent study *Sartre et son temps: Bibliographie synthétique* ⟨*Sartre and His Times: A Synthetic Bibliography*⟩, published in Tokyo, 1971, by Jimbun Shoin) has contributed much information about Sartre in Japan and has brought new material to my attention. Lena Zonina, who translated THE WORDS and has done much for French literature in her country, has provided invaluable information about Sartre in the U.S.S.R.

On the other hand, I wish to thank the following persons: Father Paul Feller, Paul A. Fortier (who has done a much-needed IBM concordance to NAUSEA), Stepha Gerassi, Fernando Gerassi and John Gerassi (who is now engaged in writing a political biography of Sartre), P. S. Hambly, Peter Hoy (who is preparing a study on Sartre's bibliographies), François H. Lapointe (who has compiled an extensive bibliography of French existentialism), Abbé Milet, Jacques Prunair, and Georges Raillard.

I have also received much help from the following: Service de presse des éditions Gallimard, Direction of *Borba*, Théâtre Antoine, Lycée Louis-le-Grand, Lycée de la Rochelle, Office de la Radiodiffusion-Télévision Française, Bibliothèque Jacques Doucet, University of Rochester Library (especially Interlibrary Loan Office), Centre de Documentation Juive Contemporaine, Agence de Presse Libération, *L'Humanité*, *Le Monde*, and *La Cause du peuple-J'accuse*.

My special thanks, finally, to the John Simon Guggenheim Foundation for granting me a fellowship during the 1970-71 academic year.

A last word: conditions of work at the Bibliothèque Nationale have to a degree improved.

MICHEL RYBALKA

J.-P. SARTRE'S CHRONOLOGY

(based on the autobiographical writings of Sartre and Simone de Beauvoir and completed by information from various sources)

1904

Marriage, on May 3, of Jean-Baptiste Sartre, country doctor's son and naval officer, to Anne-Marie Schweitzer, daughter of Charles Schweitzer and Louise Guillemin.

1905

Birth of Jean-Paul-Charles-Aymard Sartre in Paris (2, rue Mignard, XVIe) on June 21, 1905.

1906

Death of Jean-Baptiste Sartre on September 17.

1908

Birth of Simone de Beauvoir and Maurice Merleau-Ponty.

1905-15

"Up till the age of ten, I lived alone with an old man and two women." For this period, see THE WORDS.

From 1905 to 1911, Sartre lives with his mother and his grandparents in Meudon. In 1911, Charles Schweitzer moves to Paris, 1 rue Le Goff, where he founds a modern language institute.

Toward 1909, learns to read on Hector Malot's *Nobody's Boy*.

Toward 1912-13, reads *Madame Bovary, Michel Strogoff,* Corneille, Michel Zévaco; he is deeply impressed by the movies; makes a collection of picture books; rewrites the fables of La Fontaine in alexandrines, writes "novels": "Pour un papillon" ⟨For a Butterfly⟩, "Le Marchand de bananes" ⟨The Banana Man⟩; sends a letter to Courteline on January 26, 1912.

1912-13

Put in the eighth form and then in the tenth at the Lycée Montaigne; private lessons, school at Arcachon and the Institution Poupon.

1915

October: Enters sixth A-II form at the Lycée Henri-IV as a day student. One of his teachers, M. Olivier, evaluaates him at the end of the first trimester in this way: "Excellent little boy, but very thoughtless. Almost never gets the answer right the first time. Should get used to thinking more." He makes a lot of progress and his teachers grade him "excellent in all respects" at the end of the year.

1916

He is joined in the fifth form by Paul-Yves Nizan. His French teacher, M. Noël, says in grading him, "Among the best in the class for French. Openness of mind--already has his little kit of literary tools, and a very ready memory."

During the school year, his mother remarries to a naval engineer, M. Mancy. The young couple take up residence in an apartment of their own, while "Poulou" stays at his grandparents', having now become a supervised day student at Henri-IV. The end of his year in the fifth form is upset by this shake-up in the family.

1917-20

M. and Mme Mancy go to live in La Rochelle. Sartre goes through fourth, third, and second form at the *lycée* in La Rochelle.

Adolescence is a rather unhappy time for Sartre, mainly because of the psychological and cultural differences between him and his stepfather. He undergoes a sort of "inward alienation" from his mother, establishes a counterculture in his personal relations with his parents, and burns his bridges behind him. He is at this time a mediocre student, not accepted by his schoolmates, and, in the third form, two years after his mother's remarriage, he systematically steals money and books (which he resells) from his parents. Sartre describes the years 1916-20 as "the three or four worst years in my life. In his preface to *Aden Arabie*, he asserts, "I lived ten years of my life under the thumb of an *Ecole polytechnique* man."

In the second form, he starts making satisfactory grades again. A few years later he will get material for a novel, *Jesus the Owl*, from his experience as a *lycée* student.

1920

Comes back for the first form to the Lycée Henri-IV, where he meets Nizan again, and stays till 1922. His teacher, M. Georgin, says in his comment, "Definitely has what it takes."

1921-22

According to one of his fellow students, he is supposed to have written an Ubuesque play, "Vaticiner sans pouvoir" ⟨Prophesy without Power⟩, which was a grotesque description of Rodin's *The Thinker*. Sartre has no recollection of it whatsoever today.

1921

June: Competes in the *Concours général* and takes the first part of his *baccalauréat* exam.

1922

After he has completed his philosophy course, M. Chabrier evaluates him in these terms: "Excellent student: mind already lively, good at discussing questions, but needs to depend a little less on himself."

June: Second part of *baccalauréat* exam.

1922-24

Studies at the Lycée Louis-le-Grand to compete for admission to the Ecole normale supérieure, where he will be a schoolmate of Nizan.

1923

Publishes a short story, *The Angel of Morbidity*, in *La Revue sans titre*, and (under the pen name of Jacques Guillemin) several chapters of a novel, *Jesus the Owl, Small-Town Schoolteacher*.

1924

June: Passes the entrance exam to the Ecole normale supérieure along with Nizan, Raymond Aron, Daniel Lagache, etc.

1924-29

Takes mainly courses in philosophy and psychology, and studies for the *agrégation* in philosophy.

1925

Meets "Camille," real name, Camille-Simone Sans, later

known as Simone Jolivet. In two long (unpublished) letters to her, sets forth his idea of a contingency and of consciousness as a void in being.

March 28: Plays the part of Langson in *Langson's Disaster*, show put on at the Ecole normale supérieure. Subsequently takes part in several shows of this sort.

1926

According to Lagache, "We planned--Sartre, Nizan, Aron, and I--to make a script from *Carrot Top*. [...] Sartre had quite rightly said, 'What we have to stress is the need for tenderness.'"

Writes, under the direction of Professor H. Delacroix, a thesis on the imagination for his diploma in advanced studies (grade of Excellent. This work will be published in a different version in 1936.

1927-28

Writes "Une Défaite" ⟨A Defeat⟩, a novel inspired by the loves of Nietzsche and Cosima Wagner and "judiciously" rejected by Gallimard, "Er l'Arménien" ⟨Er, the Armenian⟩, and an article on law for the *Revue universitaire internationale*. Takes part along with Nizan in the translation of Karl Jaspers' *General Psychopathology*.

1928

To everyone's surprise, fails the written exam for the *agrégation*.

1929

Answers a survey made by *Les Nouvelles littéraires*. Meets Simone de Beauvoir, who in her memoirs sketches a vivid and attractive portrait of Sartre as he was then: "'He never stops thinking,' Herbaud had told me. That didn't mean that formulas and theories came leaking out of him at every pore; he hated pedantry. But his mind was always on the alert. He did not know torpor, somnolence, evasions, dodges, truces, prudence, respect. He was interested in everything and never took anything for granted."

He studies with Simone de Beauvoir for the oral for the *agrégation* and suggests to her a little later that they take "a two-year lease" on one another. Both will pass the competitive exam; he in first place, she in second.

Toward 1929-30, has fun making little amateur movies with Simone de Beauvoir and the Nizans, one of which is called "Le Vautour de la sierra" ⟨The Vulture of the

Sierra⟩.

Applies for a job lecturing in Japan beginning in October, 1931, a job which in the end he will not get.

November: Begins his eighteen months of military service in meteorology at Fort Saint-Cyr. Is transferred in January, 1930, to Saint-Symphorien, near Tours. While he is in service, having a measure of freedom, he writes poems, the first chapter of a novel, and then *The Legend of Truth* as well as *Epimetheus*, a one-act play, inspired by Pirandello, about a character who is getting ready for his burial. There are three characters in the play: Prometheus the Engineer, Epimetheus the Truckster, and Pandora.

1931

February: Having refused to apply for O.C.S., he is discharged as a buck sergeant. He is appointed professor of philosophy at Le Havre for the last trimester of 1931 and for 1931-32 and 1932-33.

June: *The Legend of Truth* appears in *Bifur*. Nizan presents him in the following way: "Young philosopher. Is writing a volume of destructive philosophy."

July 12: Sartre gives a talk on the movies at the awarding of honors at the *lycée* in Le Havre.

Summer: Trip to Spain with Simone de Beauvoir. Goes often to the Prado, where he likes Bosch and hates Titian.

October: The volume of essays *The Legend of Truth* is rejected by Rieder.

End of Year: Begins a "pamphlet on contingence" which will become, in a considerably modified form, NAUSEA.

1931-33

Gives lectures, at the Salle de la Lyre in Le Havre, on literary subjects: "The Stream-of-Consciousness: Joyce" and "Moral Problems and Contemporary Writers."

1932

Louis-Ferdinand Céline's *Voyage to the End of the Night*: "Sartre took it as his model."

Easter: Trip to Brittany.

Summer: Trip to Spanish Morocco and to Spain.

Discovers the yo-yo about this time: "Sartre practiced it relentlessly and somberly from morning till night."

1933

Easter: Vacation in London; slight falling out with Simone de Beauvoir.

Summer: Italy, Venice, and Tintoretto.

September: Sartre has a grant to the French Institute in Berlin, where he succeeds Aron and discovers phenomenology.

Christmas vacation in France.

1934

Reads William Faulkner, Franz Kafka, and Edmund Husserl.

In Berlin, finishes a second version of NAUSEA and writes *The Transcendence of the Ego*.

Easter: Vacation in Paris.

July-August: Rendezvous with Simone de Beauvoir in Hamburg, then a trip to Germany, Austria, and Prague.

1934-36

Professor at the *lycée* in Le Havre. According to one of his students, "Sartre came into his first class wearing a sport jacket, black shirt, and no tie. We knew immediately he wouldn't be a prof like the others. The vice-principal knew it too and raised his eyebrows. Sartre won over his students immediately with his cordial authority and his nonconformism. In fact, he didn't teach; he talked to young friends; and what he said seemed so evident, so certain that we felt we were discovering the Truth."

"Sartre was vaguely tempted more than once during these years to join the P.C." ⟨Communist Party⟩.

1935

Partially represented in the character Lange in Nizan's *The Trojan Horse*.

February: Has his old schoolmate, Dr. Lagache, give him a shot of mescaline. It leads to depression accompanied by hallucinations which last more than six months: "He had seen umbrellas become vultures, shoes turn into skeletons, and faces take on monstrous characteristics, while behind him, just past the corner of his eye, swarmed crabs and polyps and grimacing Things."

Summer: Cruise to Norway with his parents, which will be the inspiration for the unpublished short story, "Soleil de minuit" ⟨Midnight Sun⟩, and the excursion with Simone de Beauvoir in central France. "Sartre suddenly declared that he was tired of being crazy."

1936

Publishes *Imagination* (the first part of a work which was to have been entitled "The Image" or "Imaginary Worlds") at Alcan.

Sartre and Simone de Beauvoir integrate Olga Kosakiewicz into their life together: "From now on we would be a trio instead of a couple. We believed that human relationships are a matter of constant new discovery, and that no particular kind is a priori especially privileged or beyond the pale: our own seemed to have come about by itself." The failure of this trial will be the inspiration for Simone de Beauvoir's novel *She Came to Stay*.

Submits "Melancholia" (NAUSEA) to Gallimard; favorable criticism, but rejection, by Jean Paulhan.

Writes the short story *Erostratus*. At Easter, sees the movie *Modern Times*.

Does not vote in the elections. Is offered a *khâgne* in Lyon, but takes a job in Laon instead.

July: Beginning of the Spanish Civil War, "a drama which dominated our whole life for two and a half years."

Summer: Trip to Italy--Naples, Rome, Venice. After this trip writes the short story "Homelessness," a modified section of which will later be published with the title *Foods*.

1936-37

Professor at Laon.

1937

Thanks to the help of Charles Dullin and Pierre Bost, "Melancholia" is finally accepted by Gaston Gallimard, who suggests NAUSEA as a title for the book.

Summer: Vacation in Greece with Simone de Beauvoir and Jacques Bost. The village of Embrosio will be the inspiration for the sets in THE FLIES.

Autumn: Is appointed to the Lycée Pasteur in Paris.

1938

Finishes a 400-page work of psychology, "The Psyche,"

a segment of which will constitute in 1939 THE EMOTIONS: OUTLINE OF A THEORY.

In April, publishes NAUSEA, which will be a rather big critical success.

Articles on John Dos Passos and Nizan.

Easter: Vacation in Basque country.

July: Finishes *Childhood of a Leader*, the last of the narratives in THE WALL. Plans a novel in two parts, "Lucifer," which will subsequently become *Roads to Freedom*.

Summer: Vacation in Morocco; will be the inspiration for the script "Typhus," which, worked over during 1943-44 and then changed, will be used for the movie *The Beautiful and the Damned* (1953).

1939

Publishes THE WALL in January and THE EMOTIONS: OUTLINE OF A THEORY in December.

Collaborates in an issue of *Verve* on the human face.

Articles on Husserl, François Mauriac, Vladimir Nabokov, Denis de Rougemont, Charles Morgan, Faulkner.

September 2: Called up, joins the Seventieth Division at Nancy, and then is transferred to Brumath and Morsbronn, in Alsace, where he works on THE AGE OF REASON and BEING AND NOTHINGNESS.

Period of intense work: Sartre fills a series of notebooks he subsequently misplaces.

November 1: Simone de Beauvoir visits Sartre at Brumath.

Les Nouvelles littéraires, in their December 30 issue, announce that the N.R.F. 〈*La Nouvelle Revue française*〉 will publish THE AGE OF REASON in 1940.

1940

PSYCHOLOGY OF THE IMAGINATION published in March.

Beginning of February: On leave in Paris; Simone de Beauvoir notices a serious change in him: he begins to develop the idea of commitment.

April: Sartre gets a second leave and wins the *Roman populiste* prize for THE WALL.

May 23: Death of Nizan, killed at the front.

June 21: Without having been under fire, Sartre is captured at Padoux, in Lorraine, then sent to the *gardes mobiles* barracks at Nancy, where he is kept until mid-August. He is then transferred to Stalag XII D at Trèves.

Gives a course on Heidegger to a group of imprisoned priests.

December: Writes and produces for his comrades a Christmas play, BARIONA, OR THE SON OF THUNDER, in which he himself plays the role of one of the Three Wise Men.

1941

End of March: Liberated by passing himself off as a civilian. Simone de Beauvoir is struck by the rigidity of his moralism. "The war had taught me that you have to commit yourself."

After Easter vacation, professor at the Lycée Pasteur. Meets Alberto Giacometti.

Founds (with Maurice Merleau-Ponty) the intellectuals' Resistance group, "Socialism and Liberty." Seeks in vain to make contact with the Communists, who spread the rumor that he is an *agent provocateur*. Finishes THE AGE OF REASON.

Article on *Moby Dick* in the June 21 issue of *Comoedia*.

Summer: Bicycle trip to Free France to organize a Resistance movement; meets André Gide, André Malraux.

September: *Khâgne* professor at the Lycée Condorcet, where he will teach until 1944.

October: Makes up his mind to break up the "Socialism and Freedom" group. "At that time he settled down obstinately to the play he had begun [THE FLIES]: it represented the only form of resistance available to him."

1942

Writes copiously (above all at the Flore) and finishes THE FLIES. Publishes excerpts from his journal.

On Sartre's day-to-day life during this year of the Occupation, see *The Prime of Life*, pp. 398-424.

1943

Publishes THE FLIES in April and, at the beginning of the summer, BEING AND NOTHINGNESS, which passes almost unnoticed.

Articles on Albert Camus, Pierre Drieu la Rochelle, Maurice Blanchot, and Georges Bataille.

Beginning: Joins the C.N.E. ⟨National Writers Committee⟩ and the C.N.Th. ⟨National Theater Committee⟩, and collaborates with the underground magazine *Les Lettres françaises*.

June 2: Premiere of THE FLIES at the Théâtre de la

Cité. Production by Dullin. The play will run for twenty-five performances, and then will reopen in the fall.

Summer: Vacation in central France.

Hired by the Maison Pathé, thanks to Jean Delannoy, writes several scenarios in 1943-44: THE CHIPS ARE DOWN, "Typhus," "The End of the World," etc.

Interrupts THE REPRIEVE to write a play which will be entitled "The Others," and then NO EXIT. Asks Camus to play the role of Garcin and take charge of the production.

Dullin has him give a course in the history of the theater, which is mainly concerned with Greek dramaturgy.

Decides to found a magazine after the war.

From 1943, is one of the people collaborating with the clandestine *Combat*, although he does not do any writing for it.

The word *existentialism* is introduced by Gabriel Marcel.

1944

Articles on Brice Parain, Francis Ponge.

February: Pays tribute to Jean Giraudoux when he dies.

March 5: Participates in a discussion of sin with Marcel Moré.

March 19: Plays *le Bout rond* in Pablo Picasso's *Desire Caught by the Tail* at Michel Leiris'. Takes part during this time in a number of "celebrations."

May: Meets Jean Genet at the Flore with Camus.

May 27: Premiere of NO EXIT at the Vieux-Colombier. Production by Raymond Rouleau. The play will be revived after the Liberation, in September.

June 10: Debate on the theater with Jean Vilar, Jean Cocteau, Camus.

August-September: Articles on the days of the Liberation in *Combat*, with the help of Simone de Beauvoir.

September: The editorial board of *Les Temps modernes* is established; Malraux will not agree to be on it.

Meets Ernest Hemingway at the Ritz.

December: Camus offers him a job representing *Combat* in the U.S.A. He publishes a clarification of the existentialist position in response to Communist attacks.

1945

Publication of NO EXIT in March, and of THE AGE OF REA-

SON and THE REPRIEVE in September.
Turns down (as does Camus) the Legion of Honor.

January 12: Leaves by plane for the United States as special correspondent for *Combat* and *Le Figaro*. Stays in America till May. Meets M. (Dolores) and President Franklin Roosevelt, and visits Hollywood.

January 21: Death of Sartre's stepfather, M. Mancy.

Summer: Travels in Belgium with Simone de Beauvoir and takes part in a discussion organized by Les Editions du Cerf.

September-October: Beginning of the rage for existentialism and of Sartre's notoriety.

October 15: First number of *Les Temps modernes* comes out.

October 29: Famous lecture, "Existentialism Is a Humanism," given at the Club Maintenant.

End of 1945: Writes THE VICTORS.

December 12: Goes back to the United States for a series of lectures at American universities.

1946

Publication of EXISTENTIALISM IS A HUMANISM, THE VICTORS, THE RESPECTFUL PROSTITUTE, ANTI-SEMITE AND JEW, and THE CHIPS ARE DOWN.
Prefaces to selections from Descartes and from Charles Baudelaire's *Intimate Writings*.

April: Has the mumps.

May-June: Lectures in Switzerland: Geneva, May 20; Zurich, May 22 and 23; Lausanne (where he meets André Gorz), June 1.

June: Travels and lectures in Italy.

June: Unsuccessfully backs Vian for the Pléiade Prize (Sartre had met Boris and Michelle Vian at the beginning of the year).

June: First shake-up of the *Temps modernes* staff when Aron and Albert Ollivier quit.

October: Program notes to an Alexander Calder show.

November 1: Sorbonne lecture, on the occasion of the forming of UNESCO, about the responsibility of the writer.

November 8: Premiere of THE VICTORS and THE RESPECT-

FUL PROSTITUTE at the Théâtre Antoine. The title of the second play is censored. Big headline in the November 17 *France-Dimanche*, "Scandal in Paris."

November: Trip to Holland, where he works on WHAT IS LITERATURE? First falling out with Camus, till March, 1947.

1947

Publication of SITUATIONS, I, BAUDELAIRE, and THEATRE, I.

February: Begins publication of WHAT IS LITERATURE? in *Les Temps modernes*.

February: Helps the committee for the defense of Henry Miller.

April-June: Takes up the defense of Nizan, whose name is being defamed by the Communists.

May 31: Lecture on Kafka.

June 2: Talk, "Consciousness of Self and Knowledge of Self," to the French Philosophical Society.

July: Trip to London and press conference for the production of THE VICTORS and THE RESPECTFUL PROSTITUTE.
Backs Genet for the Pléiade Prize.

Summer: Trip to Sweden and Lapland with Simone de Beauvoir.

September 19: Statement to a meeting of movie buffs to whom he shows THE CHIPS ARE DOWN.

October-November: *Les Temps modernes*'s radio tribune (dates: October 6, 20, 27; November 10, 17, and 24). After having provoked lively reactions, the program is cut out.
Sartre quarrels with Aron and Arthur Koestler.

November: An appeal to world opinion signed by *Esprit*, *Les Temps modernes*, Camus, Sartre, David Rousset, etc.

1948

Publication of DIRTY HANDS, SITUATIONS, II, IN THE MESH.

February: Trip to Berlin; lecture and discussion about THE FLIES.
Sartre joins the group which started the R.D.R. (Revolutionary Peoples' Assembly) and signs the appeal which announces the birth of the movement.

February 13: Testifies in the Misrahi trial.

March 10: Takes part in an R.D.R. press conference with Rousset.

March 12: General assembly of the R.D.R. at the Scientific Society.

March 19: Short speech at an R.D.R. meeting in the Salle Wagram. Works with the paper *La Gauche R.D.R.*

April 2: Premiere of DIRTY HANDS at the Théâtre Antoine. Very great success. Communist campaign against the play.

April 2: Lecture in a Masonic lodge.

May: Takes a stand in favor of the creation of the State of Israel.

June 11: Takes part in the discussion at an R.D.R. meeting.

June 18: Conversation on politics with Rousset and Gérard Rosenthal; second conversation November 24. The book, DISCUSSIONS OF POLITICS, will come out in March, 1949.

Summer: Trip to Algeria with Simone de Beauvoir.

October 30: The Holy Office decrees that Sartre's whole *oeuvre* be placed on the Index.

November 18: Takes part in the discussion at a meeting on Morocco.

End of November: Protests the adaptation of DIRTY HANDS staged in New York, and presses charges against the publisher, Nagel, about it.

Beginning of December: Russians take steps to have the Helsinki authorities stop the performance of DIRTY HANDS, which they consider "propaganda hostile to the U.S.S.R."

About this time, Konstantin Fadeev calls him a "fountain-pen hyena."

December 13: Meeting at the Salle Pleyel with Richard Wright, Carlo Levi, etc.

End of 1948: *Les Temps modernes* leaves Gallimard and is taken over by Julliard (see *Force of Circumstance,* pp. 168-69).

Sartre works on his "Ethics" and begins a long study of Stéphane Mallarmé.

1949

Publishes: SICK AT HEART, SITUATIONS, III, DISCUSSIONS OF POLITICS.

January-February: Polemic with Georges Lukács, who is visiting Paris.

April 24: Lecture at the Centre d'Etudes de Politique Etrangère: "Defending French Culture with European Culture."

April 30: Disagreeing with the positions which are beginning to take shape, refuses to take part in an R.D.R. meeting.

May: Controversy with Mauriac.

June 30: Instigates the calling of a special meeting of the R.D.R.

Summer: Visits Guatemala, Panama, Curaçao, Haiti, and Cuba. Pays a visit to Hemingway in Havana.

October 4: Sends a telegram to the Gary Davis trial.

October 15: Officially resigns from the R.D.R. Has a part and a text in Nicole Védrès's movie *Life Begins Tomorrow* (which is to come out in 1950).

Sartre breaks up with M.

Works on a preface to the works of Genet and brings out a part of Volume IV of *Roads to Freedom* in the November and December *Temps modernes*.

1950

According to Simone de Beauvoir, "Sartre had practically given up all political activity." He gives up his "Ethics," concerns himself with history and economics, rereads Marx, and undertakes to write a book on Italy, "Queen Albemarle and the Last Tourist." The preface to Genet takes on the dimensions of a big work and is published in part in *Les Temps modernes*.

Writes several prefaces.

Conversations with the Marxist philosopher Tran Duc Thao (not published).

Beginning of 1950: Gives a lecture on the theater to a club of autodidacts on rue Mouffetard.

January: Takes a stand with Merleau-Ponty against the existence of Soviet concentration camps.

February: Supports a committee for the review of the Tananarive trials.

February: Has a tribute to Dullin read at the Théâtre

de l'Atelier.

Spring: Trip to the Sahara and Black Africa. Return by way of Morocco.

May-June: Does not sign the Stockholm appeal.

June: Beginning of the Korean War, which brings out major differences between Sartre and Merleau-Ponty. Politically, Sartre "drifts in uncertainty."

1951

Beginning: Puts together THE DEVIL AND THE GOOD LORD, which he will complete while some tumultuous rehearsals are going on.

Writes an article on Gide, on the occasion of his death.

June 7: Premiere of the play at the Théâtre Antoine. Production by Louis Jouvet.

Summer: Starting in mid-July, travels with Simone de Beauvoir in Norway, Iceland, Scotland.

DIRTY HANDS, a movie by Fernand Rivers.

1952

Publication of SAINT GENET, ACTOR AND MARTYR.

January: Is received by President Vincent Auriol, to whom he presents a demand that Henri Martin be pardoned. Agrees to collaborate on a book about the Henri Martin affair.

Spring-Summer: Trip to the south of France and Italy; works on his study of Mallarmé.

"Revising his political positions, he carried on at the same time an exacting inner reworking of his ideas and studies which consumed his days."

June: Writes the first part of THE COMMUNISTS AND PEACE, which appears in the July issue of *Les Temps modernes*. The second part is published in October-November. For four years, with the exception of KEAN, Sartre's activities are going to be almost entirely dominated by politics.

August: *Reply to Albert Camus*. Sartre is permanently estranged from Camus.

November 15: Signs the C.N.E.'s ⟨National Writers' Committee⟩ "Manifesto against the Cold War."

November 19: Forbids the performance of DIRTY HANDS in

Vienna.

December 12: Sartre takes part in the discussion at the opening session of the Peoples' Peace Congress in Vienna.

December 23: Talks about the Vienna Congress at a meeting in the Vel' d'Hiv' organized by the Peace Movement.

Conversation on R.T.F. ⟨French Radio-Television⟩ during a program about Pierre Brasseur.

Gives a long lecture at Fribourg-am-Brisgau and pays a visit to Heidegger.

THE RESPECTFUL PROSTITUTE, a movie by Marcel Pagliero.

1953

"Sartre is absorbed in politics and his writings."

January 15: Attends Merleau-Ponty's inaugural lecture at the Collège de France.

March: Brasseur asks Sartre to adapt KEAN.

March: New controversy with Mauriac.

April: *Reply to Claude Lefort.*

May 5: Participates in the discussion at a Peace Movement meeting at the Mutualité.

June: Protests violently against the execution of the Rosenbergs, which took place on June 19.

July: Adapts KEAN in Rome. From 1953 on, Sartre spends every summer (except the summer of 1960) in this city.

October 24: Dedication of THE HENRI MARTIN AFFAIR at the sale given by the C.N.E. (whose governing board he had become a member of at the beginning of the year).

November 14: Premiere of KEAN at the Théâtre Sarah-Bernhardt. Plan for a movie on the same subject.

The Beautiful and the Damned, movie by Yves Allégret.

Toward the end of the year, plans to write an autobiography. "Thrown into an atmosphere of action, I suddenly had a clear insight into the sort of neurosis which had dominated my previous work."

1954

January 27: Lecture in which Sartre protests the C.E.D. ⟨European Defense Committee⟩ and the Bonn-Paris agreements. Later, short speech at a meeting against the C.E.D.

February: Takes part in the meeting of East and West writers at Knokke-le-Zoute.

February 28: "Executes" Kanapa.

April-June: Finishes the preface for the book of photographs by Henri Cartier-Bresson, *From One China to the Other*.

April: Lecture in Berlin: "The Universality of History and Its Paradox."

May: Protests the prohibition of the Russian ballet after the defeat at Dien Bien Phu.

May 24-25: Takes part in a special session of the World Peace Council in Berlin.

May 26-June 23: First trip to the U.S.S.R.--Moscow, Leningrad, Uzbekistan. While he is there he is taken to the hospital, where he is treated for ten days following a crisis of hypertension.

June 24: Back in Paris. Sartre will be very weak for several months.

July: Publishes a report on his trip to the U.S.S.R. in *Libération* and *L'Unità*. Controversy with the Lazareffs.

Summer: Stay in Italy, where he meets Palmiro Togliatti.

End of August-September: Travels with Simone de Beauvoir in Germany, Austria, and Czechoslovakia, then back to Italy.

September 23: Press conference in Vienna to oppose the staging of DIRTY HANDS.

December: Sartre is named vice-president of the France-U.S.S.R. Association.

Publication of *The Mandarins*, by Simone de Beauvoir.

NO EXIT, a movie by Jacqueline Audry.

1955

February 20: Short speech at a France-U.S.S.R. meeting commemorating the victory at Stalingrad.

June 8: Premiere of NEKRASSOV at the Théâtre Antoine, after many delays as a result of changes in the script and the cast as well as of difficult rehearsals. The play, supported by the Communists, runs into a violent newspaper campaign against it and is only a minor success.

June 26: Takes part in the discussion at the Congress of the Peace Movement in Helsinki, where he meets Lukács.

June: Publication of Merleau-Ponty's *Adventures of the Dialectic*, which makes the difference between the two philosophers clear. Sartre holds his peace, but Simone de Beauvoir replies in her article, "Merleau-Ponty and Pseudo-Sartrianism."

September-November: Sartre spends two months in China with Simone de Beauvoir. Arriving September 6, he attends the parade in Peking on October 1 and then comes home by way of the U.S.S.R., spending a week in Moscow and taking part in a meeting of critics.
Signs a tract asking people to vote for Roger Garaudy.

November: Begins the script for a movie of Arthur Miller's *The Crucible* (French title translates as *The Salem Witches*).

1956

Keeps working on his autobiography and the script for *The Salem Witches*.
Decides with Garaudy to compare the existentialist and Marxist methods as applied to Gustave Flaubert.

January 27: Meeting at the Salle Wagram against the Algerian War.

February 2: Chairs a meeting on China.

February: Polemics against Pierre Hervé and Pierre Naville.

March 26-31: Takes an active part in the meeting of the European Cultural Society in Venice (where he meets Merleau-Ponty).

May 16: Lecture at the Sorbonne: "Ideology and History."

July: Sartre meets Arlette El Kaïm. A native of Constantine, Algeria, the girl was studying at Versailles for the entrance exams for the Ecole normale supérieure at Sèvres. She had written to him in relation to academic work she had done in reference to Sartre's philosophy which had been criticized by her philosophy teacher. Sartre will adopt her in March, 1965.

Summer-Fall: Trip to Italy, Yugoslavia, and Greece; then a long stay in Italy, where he hears about the Hungarian uprising.

November 9: In an interview granted to *L'Express*, Sartre condemns the Soviet intervention in Hungary. He signs several appeals, resigns from France-U.S.S.R., but stays in the C.N.E. and the Peace Movement. Writes *The Ghost of Stalin*, and publishes a special issue of *Les Temps modernes*. November and December dominated by the Hungarian affair.

1957

Feels sympathetic to the Polish Communists and the Communists in the opposition.

Publishes "Existentialism and Marxism" in a Polish magazine (see *Search for a Method*). Study of Tintoretto.

Begins CRITIQUE OF DIALECTICAL REASON. During a stay in Rome, writes the preface to Gorz's *Traitor*.

Makes many protests against torture and war in Algeria.

January: Trip to Poland for the Polish premiere of THE FLIES.

April 4: Tribute to Bertolt Brecht at the Théâtre des Nations.

April 7-16: Writes "A Project of Demoralization," first version of *You Are Really Something*, rejected by *Le Monde*.

June 1: Takes part in the discussion of Algeria at the Peace Movement.

Summer: Stay in Italy.

December 10: Testimony at the Ben Sadok trial.
The Salem Witches, a movie by Rouleau.

1958

Works on a play which was to become THE CONDEMNED OF ALTONA and which was to have been staged in the fall of 1958.

Writes "furiously" on his CRITIQUE.

February: Writes a commentary on Henri Alleg's *The Question* for *L'Express* which provokes a confiscation of the magazine. From this time on, the confiscations--especially of *Les Temps modernes*--multiply.

Spring: Reopens contact with the Italian Communists.

Lecture, "Dialectic and Alienation," at Jean Wahl's request.

May 30: Takes part in the anti-Gaullist demonstration at the Place de la Nation.

May 30: Press conference on "the violations of human rights in Algeria."

June 2: Takes part in another demonstration.

June: Agrees to write a script on Freud for John

Huston; first version completed in December.

June 16-September 15: Stay in Italy, where he meets Alberto Moravia, Merleau-Ponty, etc.

September: Articles in *L'Express* calling on people to vote no to the September 28 referendum.

September 22: Short speech at an antifascist meeting.

September-October: Profound disillusionment at the results of the September 28 referendum.

October: Sartre barely misses having a heart attack: his health is of very great concern to the people around him. The play scheduled for the fall of 1958 is set back to the fall of 1959.

1959

Grants Francis Jeanson an interview for the underground magazine *Vérités pour. . . .*

Summer: Stay in Rome, where he completes THE CONDEMNED OF ALTONA.
As usual, the writing and above all the rehearsals of the play keep him extremely busy.

September 24: Premiere of THE CONDEMNED at the Théâtre de la Renaissance. Great success.

September: Short stay in Ireland to work on the movie *Freud* with Huston.

1960

Publication of CRITIQUE OF DIALECTICAL REASON.

January 4: Death of Camus.

Mid-February: Leaves for Cuba with Simone de Beauvoir; meets Fidel Castro, Che Guevara; speaks on television; attends funeral for the victims of the explosion of the ship La Coubre on March 5. On his return trip, stops in New York, where he holds a press conference on Cuba. Starts the work from which he excerpts *Storm over Sugar*, published in *France Soir* (June 28-July 15).

March: During his stay in Cuba, finishes his preface to Nizan's *Aden Arabie*.

March 29: Important lecture on the theater at the Sorbonne.

March 31: Sartre and Simone de Beauvoir attend the reception Nikita Khrushchev gives at the Soviet embassy in Paris.

May 11: Arrives in Belgrade, to which he and Simone de Beauvoir have been invited by the Yugoslavian Writers' Union. He is received by Tito on the thirteenth. Attends performances of THE CONDEMNED OF ALTONA and NO EXIT. Gives a lecture at the Belgrade University College of Liberal Arts.

June 10: Takes part in the discussion at the National Congress for a negotiated peace in Algeria. Takes part in the June 11 and 12 debates.

June 17: Testifies at the Georges Arnaud trial.

Mid-August-November: Trip to Brazil with Simone de Beauvoir. Visits all Brazil and especially the Amazon; gives numerous interviews and lectures (on literature, colonialism, dialectic); dedicates the Brazilian translation of *Storm over Sugar*.

August: Signs the Manifesto of the 121.

September 20: Has a deposition read at the trial of the Jeanson network.

October: *Les Temps modernes* is confiscated. Veterans parade on the Champs-Elysées shouting, "Execute Sartre." *Paris-Match* entitles an editorial, "Sartre, a Civil War Machine."

End of October-November: Return from Brazil by way of Cuba (where he holds a press conference and discussions) and Spain. Is not arrested, as it had been rumored he would be, but demands that he and Simone de Beauvoir be indicted for the 121 Affair. Returning to France November 4, he has a hearing at the police court on November 8.

December 1: Sartre holds a press conference at which he recommends a no vote for the January 6, 1961, referendum.

1961

Winter: Death of Richard Wright.
Stay in Antibes. Sartre writes a second version of his study of Tintoretto.

March: Lecture at the Ecole normale supérieure which Merleau-Ponty attends.

May: Program notes to the Lapoujade show.

May 4: Death of Merleau-Ponty. A special issue of *Les Temps modernes* is devoted to him in October.

July 19: Sartre's apartment on rue Bonaparte is hit

by a plastic bomb explosion.

End of July-October: Stay in Rome, where he writes his article on Merleau-Ponty and has a long conversation with Frantz Fanon, shortly before the latter's death. Writes a preface to *The Wretched of the Earth* in September.

November 1: Silent demonstration at the Place Maubert.

November 18: New demonstration, followed by a press conference at the Hôtel Lutétia.

December 7: Takes part in Marxist Thought Week at the Mutualité (controversy about dialectic with Garaudy, Jean-Pierre Vigier, Jean Hyppolite).

December: Stay in Rome, where he gives a lecture at the Gramsci Institute ("Subjectivity and Marxism") and holds a meeting on Algeria (December 13).

Elected a member of the International Institute of Philosophy (part of UNESCO).

December 19: Takes part in a demonstration against the O.A.S. 〈Underground Army of Algeria〉.

Starts working again on "Flaubert," which he had begun in 1957.

1962

January 7: Second plastic bomb attempt against 42, rue Bonaparte. Sartre had been living in an apartment on the boulevard Saint-Germain for a month; he left it to live for a while on the quai Blériot.

January: Testifies in favor of the abbé Robert Davezies.

February 11: Takes part in the discussion at the sessions of the F.A.C. (an antifascist group).

February 13: Takes part in the march protesting the massacre at the Charonne subway stop.

March 12: Meeting in Brussels about Algeria; short television interview, "Fascism in France."

March 14: Sartre is elected vice-president of the Congress of the European Writers' Community.

March 15: Meeting of the F.A.C. at the Mutualité.

June: Marcel Péju has to retire from the *Temps modernes* team.

June-July: Trip to Poland and the U.S.S.R. Sartre is received by Khrushchev and has a discussion with the *Inostranaia Literatura* staff.

July 10-16: Takes part in a writers' congress in Moscow and gives a speech on the demilitarization of culture. Comes back from the U.S.S.R. by way of Poland.

October 31: Authorizes the noncommercial publication of BARIONA.

End of 1962: Stay in Rome, where he plans a new play.
Freud, a movie by Huston. Sartre has his name withdrawn from the credits.
THE CONDEMNED OF ALTONA, a movie by Vittorio de Sica.
No Exit, an Argentine movie by Pedro Escudero and Tad Danielewski, after Sartre's NO EXIT.
L'Uomo Sartre ⟨Sartre, the Man⟩, a short by Leonardo Autera and Gregorio Lo Cascio.

1963

Beginning of January: During a stay in Moscow (December 28-January 13), makes contacts with the idea of creating an International Writers' Community.

January 21: Press conference on the fate of condemned AWOLs and deserters.

February 20: Does not testify at the Bastien-Thiry trial.

April: Praises Nico Papatakis' movie, *Les Abysses*.

June 24: Lecture against apartheid.

August 5-8: C.O.M.E.S. ⟨European Writers' Community⟩ Congress in Leningrad, where Sartre says something about the novel.

August 9: Press conference in Leningrad.
Finishes and publishes THE WORDS.

November 12-24: Stay in Czechoslovakia, to which he and Simone de Beauvoir have been invited by the Writers' Union. Discussion in Prague of the idea of decadence. Short speech on the Czechoslovakian broadcasting system. Attends the Prague premiere of THE CONDEMNED OF ALTONA.

1964

Publication of IL FILOSOFO E LA POLITICA ⟨The Philosopher and Politics⟩ in Italy and SITUATIONS, IV, V, and VI in France.

March: After twelve years of refusals, Sartre authorizes the staging of DIRTY HANDS in Turin.

Spring: Interviews with Jacqueline Piatier and Yves

Buin.

April 21: Lecture at the conference on Sören Kierkegaard organized by UNESCO in Paris.

May 23: Very important speech at a conference on ethics and society organized by the Gramsci Institute in Rome.

June 1-July 10: Trip to the U.S.S.R. Sartre writes a short preface to the Russian translation of THE WORDS.

July-August: Stay in Rome, where he writes THE TROJAN WOMEN.

August: Writes an article in memory of Togliatti.

October 15: Sartre hears that they are thinking about giving him the Nobel Prize. Sends a letter on the sixteenth saying that he will refuse to accept it. The reception of the letter is officially confirmed on October 21.

October 22: The Swedish Academy nevertheless gives Sartre the prize (which includes an award of 250,000 kröner or 260,000 new francs). That very evening Sartre sends a communiqué to the Swedish press in which he sets forth his reasons for refusing. A great many articles in the French and world press.

December 9: Takes part in a debate at the Mutualité: "What Can Literature Do?"

End of 1964: Records an introduction to the recorded version of NO EXIT.

1965

Publication of SITUATIONS, VII. Conversation with Pierre Verstraeten.

January 26: Petitions to adopt Arlette El Kaïm. Petition granted, March 18, 1965.

March 10: Premiere of THE TROJAN WOMEN at the T.N.P. (Théâtre National Populaire). Produced by Michel Cacoyannis.

March: Refusal to go to Cornell University in the U.S. to give a series of lectures.

June: Political articles in opposition to Gaston Deferre's concept of an alliance of Western socialist powers.

July 1-August 5: Trip to the U.S.S.R.

September: Revival of THE CONDEMNED OF ALTONA at the

Athénée.

October 6: Speaks about the idea of the avant-garde at a congress of the C.O.M.E.S.

October: NO EXIT is shown on television in a production by Michel Mitrani, who had previously adapted *The Room* to television.

December: After having expressed his reservations about him, backs, *in extremis*, François Mitterand.

1966

Selections from "Flaubert" in *Les Temps modernes*.

February: Preface to Georges Michel's *Sunday Stroll*.

May 2-June 6: Stay in the U.S.S.R.

July: At Bertrand Russell's request, agrees to take part in a "tribunal" charged with investigating American war crimes in Vietnam.

July-August: Trip to Greece.

September-October: Trip and lectures in Japan. Return through Moscow.

October: Special issue of *L'Arc* on Sartre, which reprints another part of "Tintoretto" and an interview.

November 9: Chairs a meeting on apartheid in Paris.

November 13-15: Meeting of the "Russell Tribunal" in London to establish its rules and objectives.

December 4: Lecture on the theater in Bonn.

1967

February 25-March 13: Trip and lectures in Egypt. Conversation with Gamal Abdel Nasser, visit to refugee camps.

March 14-30: Trip and lectures in Israel; conversation with Levi Eshkol.

April 13: Letter from Sartre to General Charles de Gaulle about the Russell Tribunal.

April 19: De Gaulle's reply, followed by Sartre's at the end of April.

May 2-10: Session of the Russell Tribunal in

Stockholm; Sartre, executive president.

May 2: Takes part in the opening session.

May 10: Sends letter to Dean Rusk.
Sartre declines (as does Louis Aragon) an invitation to participate in the Tenth Soviet Writers' Conference in order to indicate his disagreement with the organization and with the verdict of the Siniavsky-Daniel trial.

End of May: Writes the preface to a special issue of *Les Temps modernes* on the Israeli-Arab conflict.

May 30: Meeting for Régis Debray at the Mutualité.

May 30: Takes Israel's side concerning the opening of the Gulf of Akaba. Violent reaction in the Arab countries.

July-August: Individual trip to Spain.

September 5: Press conference at the Venice Festival on Serge Roullet's movie, THE WALL.

October 23: Simultaneous showing of THE WALL in Paris and New York.

October 27: Lecture on Vietnam in Brussels.

November 20-December 1: Second session of the Russell Tribunal in Roskilde, near Copenhagen.

1968

January: Is unable, because of his health, to attend the Havana Cultural Congress.

February 27: Testifies at the trial of the Guadaloupians.

March 23: Takes part in a teach-in on Vietnam.

April: Trip to Yugoslavia.

May 6: Takes a stand in favor of the student movement and against police repression.

May 12: Interview on Radio-Luxembourg about the student rebellion.

May 20: Takes part in a debate with the students at the Sorbonne during the uprising.

May 20: Conversation with Daniel Cohn-Bendit.

June: In two interviews, draws out the meaning of the Days in May.

July: In an interview for *Der Spiegel*, accuses the Communist Party of having betrayed the May Revolution.

July: Individual trip to Yugoslavia. Long interview broadcast on the National Television Network.

Summer: Italy. Supports the protest against the Venice Film Festival.

August 24: In an interview in *Paese Sera*, condemns the intervention of Soviet troops in Czechoslovakia.

October: Revival of NEKRASSOV in Strasbourg in a production by Hubert Gignoux.

November 14: Revival of THE DEVIL AND THE GOOD LORD at the T.N.P. with François Périer, in a production by Georges Wilson.

November 28-December 1: Short stay in Czechoslovakia to attend the premiere of THE FLIES in Prague, where DIRTY HANDS is also produced (first performance in a socialist state).

1969

January 30: Death of Mme Mancy, Sartre's mother.

February 10: Takes part, with Michel Foucault especially, in a meeting at the Mutualité protesting the expulsion of thirty-four students from the University of Paris. Takes a stand against the guidelines for university reform.

March-April: Favors the boycott of the referendum to regionalize France.

May: Signs a petition in favor of the Communist League candidate, Alain Krivine, but does not actively support his candidacy for the presidency of the Republic.

Summer: Trip to Yugoslavia and Italy; works on the editing of "Flaubert."

November: Demands, along with Malraux and Mauriac, that Debray be liberated. Denounces the repression in Czechoslovakia.

December 11: Is interviewed on television by Olivier Todd about the Vietnam War and the Song-My ⟨My Lai⟩ massacre. It is the first time he has agreed to appear on O.R.T.F. ⟨French Radio-Television⟩.

December 19: Presides over a press conference on the Vietnam massacres.

December: Televised interview for the Quebec Liberation Front.

1970

Publishes two important prefaces, one to Antonin J. Liehm's *Three Generations*, the other to André Puig's *The Uncompleted*.

January 10: Attends the removal of the bodies of five African workers suffocated by gas leaks in their barracks.

January 15: Talk on Brazil at the Mutualité.

January 27: Takes part in a press conference on what is happening to soldiers held in prison.

February 23: Testifies at Roland Castro's trial.

March: Joins the Israel-Palestine Committee.

April: Becomes editor of *La Cause du peuple* and enters a stage of militant action which will bring him close to the Maoists.

May 25: Presides over a meeting at the Mutualité in which Alain Geismar also takes part.

May 27: Makes a deposition at the trial of the former editors of *La Cause du peuple*, Jean-Pierre Le Dantec and Michel Le Bris.

June 4: Announces the formation of the Association of Friends of *La Cause du peuple*.

June 11: Takes part in the founding of the Secours Rouge ⟨Red Aid⟩.

June 13: Takes part in a debate on African workers.

June 20 and 26: Hands out *La Cause du peuple* in the marketplace on rue Daguerre and on the *grands boulevards*; is issued a summons by the police.

July: Trip to Norway and the Scandinavian countries.

August: Customary stay in Rome.

September: Becomes editor of the newspaper *Tout!*.

September 11 and 29: Testifies at the trial of those selling *La Cause du peuple*.

September 18: Secours Rouge meeting at the Mutualité.

October: Preface to a show by Paul Rébeyrolle.

October 16: Takes a direct role in the distribution of *La Cause du peuple*.

October 21: Refuses to testify at Geismar's trial and goes to talk to the workers at the Renault plant.

November 5: Speaks at the Maison du Maroc in the Cité Universitaire.

1971

Publication of the first two volumes of THE FAMILY IDIOT, a study of Flaubert, and of a preface on the Basque problem.

January 7: Brief talk at the Mutualité in behalf of the Jews in the U.S.S.R.

January 15: Publication of the first issue of *J'accuse*, a journal Sartre will write for regularly.

February 13: Occupation of the Sacré-Coeur.

April: Break with Castro over the Padilla affair.

May 3: Debate about the movie *The Sorrow and the Pity.*

May 12: Investigation at Ivry concerning the Behar Rehala affair.

May 25: Overworked, suffers a mild attack he quickly recovers from.

End of May: Merger of *La Cause du peuple* and *J'accuse.*

June: Becomes editor of *Révolution!*
Founds, with Maurice Clavel, the *Libération* news agency.

June 19: Is charged with libel for the articles he published in *La Cause du peuple* and *Tout!*.
Calls for a people's trial of the police, which will be forbidden.

Summer and fall: Completes Volume III of THE FAMILY IDIOT.

November 7 and 27: Takes part in the demonstrations against racism in the Goutte d'Or section.

December 24: Welcomes Geismar when he gets out of jail.

1972

Publication of SITUATIONS, VIII and IX, of Volume III of THE FAMILY IDIOT, and of a preface of the Maoists.

January: Makes talks about prison uprisings.

February-March: Alexandre Astruc begins shooting a

film on Sartre in which Simone de Beauvoir and Sartre take part; script by Michel Contat.

February 14: Is kicked out, along with a group of militants, of the Renault plant.

February 25: Lecture, "Justice and the State," in Brussels.

February 28: Investigation at Boulogne-Billancourt of the murder of the militant Maoist Pierre Overney. Takes part in a Leftist march.

March 4: Attends the funeral of Overney.
Subsequently signs a declaration protesting the Communist Party's stand.

April 11: Press conference on squatters.

May: Article about the Bruay-en-Artois affair.

June: Writes a letter in support of an Israeli conscientious objector.
Opens a debate on *La Cause du peuple*.

September: Publication of the sequel to the memoirs of Simone de Beauvoir.

Fall: Attacks President Pompidou and takes part in the Aranda affair. Publishes interviews in *Libre*, *Gulliver*, and *Esquire*.

1973

Publication of UN THEATRE DE SITUATIONS and preface to Olivier Todd's *Les Paumés* ⟨The Mixed-up Ones⟩. Interview in *Actuel*.

In March, Sartre has very serious trouble with his health, and his eyesight is failing. From then on, he discontinues some of his political activities but keeps working on Volume IV of THE FAMILY IDIOT.

BIBLIOGRAPHY

Directions for Use of the Bibliography

The texts are numbered by year and in the order of their publication. For example: 38/11 for NAUSEA indicates that this text was published in 1938 and that it is the eleventh we have listed. The volumes (with their titles in capitals) are placed at the beginning of the year, and are followed by the articles (with their titles in italics) and the interviews (with their titles in quotation marks) in chronological order. The notes are placed together at the end of each year through 1969. Thereafter they are integrated chronologically with the texts. A certain number of annotations pertaining to the same subject (for example the Russell Tribunal or the Israeli-Arab conflict) are placed together without consideration for the order in which they were published. Thus the spoken preface to the recording of NO EXIT, done in 1965, immediately follows the main title (44/47) and bears the number 65/48. Let us remind you at this point that the titles of the articles or interviews have not always been chosen by Sartre himself.

The references do not indicate pages or issues of dailies or weeklies except when such indications seem necessary to us. There may be a slight variation, above all in the case of Gallimard publications, in the page numbers and format of the different volumes. Following French bibliographical practice, unbracketed publication dates are taken from the title pages of volumes; when the date is not stated on the title page but is known, it is enclosed in brackets. Unless otherwise indicated, the place of publication is Paris.

In the body of the annotations, quotations from Sartre are always in italics, and any others in quotation marks. Out of a concern for clarity and coherence, and without making it an absolute rule, we have standardized titles as well as certain typographical signs. An asterisk * preceding a title means that the text referred to is reproduced, *in extenso*, in volume II.

An appendix detailing the movies with which Sartre has been involved immediately follows the body of the Bibliography. A general index and an index of works by Sartre will be found at the end of the book.

1923

23/1

* *L'Ange du morbide* ⟨The Angel of Morbidity⟩, short story.

-- *La Revue sans titre* (journal for the defense of youth, review of the general association of young writers and artists; edited by Charle Fraval), no. 1 [January 15, 1923].

This short story, which is reprinted almost in its entirety in Marc Beigbeder's *L'Homme Sartre* ⟨Sartre, the Man⟩ (Bordas, 1947), and is often quoted for all its foreshadowings of Sartre's obsessed world, is the first work Sartre had published, at the age of eighteen. It tells, in a violently satirical tone, the escapade which a mediocre small-town schoolteacher (who foreshadows the "scum" ⟨salaude⟩ in Sartre's future work) has with a young tubercular woman.

In volume II we give the complete text of it, which we were able to procure thanks to the kindness of M. Jean Gaulmier, professor of humanities at the University of Strasbourg,who has a collection of this exceedingly rare journal.

23/2

* *Jésus la Chouette, professeur de province* ⟨Jesus the Owl, Small-Town Schoolteacher⟩, excerpts from a novel, under the pen name of Jacques Guillemin.

-- *Le Revue sans titre*, no. 2 [February 10, 1923]; no. 3 [February 25, 1923]; no. 4 [March 10, 1923]; no. 5 [March 25, 1923]. None of the issues is paginated. B.N. listing: Jo. 72736.

The Bibliothèque Nationale has only issues nos. 3 and 4 of the *Revue sans titre*. No. 2 was shown to us by Jean Gaulmier. In his interesting article, "Quand Sartre avait dix-huit ans . . ." ⟨When Sartre Was Eighteen⟩ (*Le Figaro littéraire*, July 5, 1958), there are a great number of details about the short history of this journal, which stopped with issue no. 5. There were three hundred printed copies of the first issue, which was sufficiently successful to indicate the need for a second edition. *La Revue sans titre* also published the first literary efforts of two of Sartre's fellow students who were destined to be famous. In it we find a criticism of Jean Giraudoux's *Siegfried*, as well as some poems by René Maheu, the present director general of UNESCO, and two texts by Paul Nizan, the second of which is nicely titled "Lament of the Medical Student Who Dissected His Girl Friend While Smoking Two Packs of Marylands." We should point out too that in the Letters to the Editor column there is a letter in which the student Pierre Mendès-France enthusiastically supports the journal's aims as stated on the cover of its second issue: "The Republic of Letters should not be a Republic of Friends. *La Revue sans titre* is open to all."

The four installments of *Jesus the Owl* are the only remaining fragments of a youthful novel whose manuscript is lost. Sartre told us that this novel was inspired by the real case of one of his professors at the *lycée* in La Rochelle, a poor, second-rate teacher whose students mocked him and who ended by committing suicide. This is what explains his using a pseudonym (his grandmother's maiden name) for the only time in his career.

The title might suggest a novel in the style of Francis Carco, whom the young Sartre greatly admired at the time. But Carco's influence stops with the title. The chapters which follow, written in an already established if rather scholarly classical style, paint the Balzacian portrait of a grotesque professor nicknamed Jesus the Owl, and describe satirically the shabby milieu of small-town teachers, seemingly the young writer's favorite target. These fragments are too short to permit one to judge the novel's worth; all that seems evident in it is a gift for writing which it is undoubtedly all too easy to judge promising in retrospect. Their principal interest lies in the indirect light they throw on the least-known period of Sartre's life. Along with *The Angel of Morbidity*, these are the only remaining traces of the great number of adolescent writings.

1927

27/3

* *La Théorie de l'état dans la pensée française d'aujourd'hui* ⟨The Theory of State in Modern French Thought⟩, essay.

-- *Revue universitaire internationale*, no. 1 (January, 1927), pp. 25-37.

The Theory of State in Modern French Thought.

-- *New Ambassador* (an International University Review, official organ of the International University Federation; English edition, Paris), no. 1 (January, 1927), pp. 29-41. British Museum listing: P.P. 3555, al. The translation is anonymous and poor.

Sartre's fellow student at the Ecole normale supérieure, Daniel Lagache, had asked Sartre to write this article for a journal he was editing at the time for a university association connected with the League of Nations and published simultaneously in Paris in French, English, and German (see on this subject Lagache's interview in Claude Bonnefoy's article, "Rien ne laissait prévoir que Sartre deviendrait 'Sartre': Enquête sur la jeunesse du grand écrivain" ⟨Nothing Foretold that Sartre Would Become "Sartre": An Investigation of a Great Writer's Youth⟩, *Arts*, January 11-17, 1961.

This is a brilliant and solidly documented study in which Sartre, making use of the intellectual virtuosity of a well-trained *normalien*, examines the legal philosophy of several French theorists of international law, especially that of René Hauriou, Georges Davy, and Léon Duguit.

1928

28/4

Proofreading, in collaboration with Paul Nizan, of the French translation of Karl Jaspers' *General Psychopathology* by A. Kastler and J. Mendousse. Librairie Félix Alcan, 1928.

A note on p. III points out: "We thank MM. Sartre and Nizan, students at the Ecole normale supérieure, for having been kind enough to put the manuscript in shape and take part in the correction of the proofs."

It seems, as Sartre remembers it, that they did far more than simply proofread. We know that before Sartre approached German phenomenology he had studied psychology extensively, and that his 1926 thesis for advanced studies was devoted to the imagination.

1929

29/5

Excerpt from a letter in "Enquête auprès des étudiants" ⟨Investigation of Today's Students⟩, carried out by Roland Alix.

-- *Les Nouvelles littéraires*, February 2, 1929, p. 10.

This text has been reprinted by Simone de Beauvoir in her *Memoirs of a Dutiful Daughter* (p. 363).

It is a fragment of a long letter Sartre wrote to *Les Nouvelles littéraires* in response to an investigation about students. (The weekly had previously published, in its December 8, 1928, issue, an interview with Paul Nizan.) Sartre tried to give a systematic exposition of his philosophical ideas, some of which will appear in BEING AND NOTHINGNESS. The fragment published ends with the following sentence, in which, comparing his generation to the previous one, Sartre concludes, *We are less happy, but more likable.*

1931

31/6

* *Légende de la vérité* ⟨The Legend of Truth⟩.

-- *Bifur*, no. 8 (June, 1931), pp. 77-96.

This is the only published fragment of a work written in 1929 and entitled *The Legend of Truth*. There were three parts to this work: "The Legend of the Certain," "The Legend of the Probable," and "The Legend of the Solitary Man." The certain represents science and its social counterpart, democracy; the probable defines the field of abstract philosophy and corresponds to the aristocracy; and finally, "the solitary man" is clearly Sartre himself trying to go beyond the certain and the probable to discover the truth through an individual, concrete investigation which led to a social anarchist attitude.

Simone de Beauvoir presents *The Legend of Truth* in the following way: "Once again [Sartre] put forth his ideas in story form. He could hardly present them in a straightforward way: in denying the validity of universal statements, he denied himself the right to state even this denial as a universal. Instead of saying, he had to show. He admired those myths to which Plato, for similar reasons, had had recourse, and was not ashamed to imitate them. But this outmoded device imposed various irksome restrictions on his aggressive mind which were reflected in the stiffness of his style. And yet some new ideas did manage to show through this rusty armor. *The Legend of Truth* displayed some of Sartre's latest theories. He was already relating different ways of thinking to different social structures. *Truth,* he wrote, *is a by-product of commerce*, and commerce he linked to democracy: when citizens consider themselves interchangeable, they have to judge the world in the same way, and science is an expression of this intellectual consensus. Such universality is despised by the elite, who hammer out for their own private use so-called general ideas which are never more than probable. Sartre detested these closet ideologies even more than the scientists' consensus. His sympathies went to the wonder workers who, shut off from the City with its logic and mathematics, wander about by themselves in the wilderness and only trust their eyes to teach them what there is to know. Thus it was only to the artist, the writer, or the philosopher--those whom he called the *solitaries*--that he granted the privilege of grasping living reality" (*The Prime of Life*, p. 41).

Paul Nizan submitted the manuscript of *The Legend of Truth* to Europe Press, which rejected it (see *The Prime of Life*, p. 68). Henceforth Sartre gave up trying to publish it. Thanks to Nizan, however, a fragment of it appeared in *Bifur*,[1] a journal that he helped put out and that Georges Ribemont-Dessaignes edited. The chief interest of this text, which gives no stylistic indication whatsoever of the work to come, is that it gives us an idea about the way Sartre originally planned to unite philosophy and literature.

The complete manuscript of the work is preserved, and will be the object of a coming study which ought to give, particularly, a more precise idea of the beginnings of Sartre's political thought. More generally, the work is probably the most finished expression of what the Sartre of THE WORDS (see pp. 249-55) will call his *imposture* or his *neurosis*: the certainty that he is *chosen*, has been given a mandate to save the world through literature.

31/7

* *L'Art cinématographique* ⟨Motion Picture Art⟩.

a) In a brochure published by the *lycée* in Le Havre (*Grand Lycée*). *Public Distribution of Awards* (presided over by M. Albert Dubosc), Sunday, July 12, 1931. Le Havre: Press of the newspaper *Le Petit Havre*, 1931. Pp. 25-31.

b) Reprinted as *Le Cinéma n'est pas une mauvaise école* ⟨The Movies Are Not a Bad School⟩. *Gazette du cinéma*, no. 2 (June, 1950), no. 3 (September, 1950).

---

1. This same issue of *Bifur*, which was the last to come out, also published the translation of a fragment of Martin Heidegger's *What Is Metaphysics?*

This is a speech Sartre gave at the distribution of awards when he held his first teaching job at the *lycée* in Le Havre. This speech, whose interest is above all retrospective, nevertheless shows the importance Sartre saw very early in the movies. He sees them from the start as the art which *by its very nature reflects the civilization of our time*, and he does so in a time when many cultivated people scorned the movies as a minor art if they did not categorically condemn them.

An account of Sartre's first contacts with the movies is found in THE WORDS: *In the egalitarian discomfort of the neighborhood movie theaters, I had learned that this new art belonged to me as it belonged to everyone. We were the same mental age: I was seven and knew how to read; it was twelve and did not know how to talk. People said it was just beginning, that it still had progress to make; I thought we would grow up together* (p. 122). Here the young professor is trying nineteen years later to prove to his students that the movies are indeed an art.

1936

36/8

L'IMAGINATION ⟨Imagination⟩.

a) Librairie Félix Alcan, 1936. 162 pages. The author is identified as "*lycée* professor in Le Havre."

*b)*Presses universitaires de France. Nouvelle Encyclopédie philosophique series. Librairie Félix Alcan, 1949. Several reprintings, the latest of which (1969) has a new cover.

IMAGINATION: A PSYCHOLOGICAL CRITIQUE, translated and with an introduction by Forrest Williams.

-- Ann Arbor: University of Michigan Press, 1962; London: Cresset Press [1962]. Paperback edition, 1972.

This book was requested of Sartre by Professor Henri Delacroix, under whose supervision he had written his thesis for his diploma in advanced studies, and who was editor of the Nouvelle Encyclopédie philosophique series at Alcan. In his thesis, which had earned the grade of "excellent," Sartre had tried to sum up his investigations of imagination. Interrupting the writing of what was going to become NAUSEA, Sartre took up the work of his thesis again to develop it into a work called "The Image." Alcan kept only the first part of this work and published it under the title IMAGINATION. As such the book is the critical introduction to PSYCHOLOGY OF THE IMAGINATION, which Sartre will subsequently elaborate when he starts working again on the part Alcan rejected.

Reviewing the different theories of the imagination which have been developed since Descartes, Sartre subjects them to rigorous criticism and ends his second chapter with an exposition of Edmund Husserl's ideas.

Maurice Merleau-Ponty, in his review of IMAGINATION for the *Journal de psychologie normale et pathologique* (XXXIII, nos. 9-10 [November-December, 1936], 756-61), speaks favorably of the book but suggests that its criticisms of Henri Bergson are too harsh.

1937

37/9

La Transcendance de l'ego: Esquisse d'une description phénoménologique ⟨The Transcendence of the Ego: An Existentialist Theory of Consciousness⟩.

a) Recherches philosophiques, VI (1936-37), 85-123. Printed August, 1937.

This periodical, published annually by Boivin, had Henri Delacroix on its advisory committee and was greatly interested in phenomenology. Volume VI includes, among other things, a study of "being-in-situation" by Gabriel Marcel, an article on ideology by Raymond Aron, and a report on IMAGINATION by Michel Souriau (pp. 398-99).

b) Republished as a book. LA TRANSCENDANCE DE L'EGO: ESQUISSE D'UNE DESCRIPTION PHÉNOMÉNOLOGIQUE. Introduction, notes, and appendixes by Sylvie Le Bon. Librairie philosophique Vrin, 1965. 134 pages.

THE TRANSCENDENCE OF THE EGO: AN EXISTENTIALIST THEORY OF CONSCIOUSNESS, translated and annotated and with an introduction by Forrest Williams and Robert Kirkpatrick.

-- New York: The Noonday Press, Farrar, Straus and Cudahy, 1957; London: Vision Press, 1958.

> Written in 1934 during Sartre's stay in Berlin, and for almost thirty years practically impossible for French readers to find, this first important philosophical essay has been republished with great care and competence by a friend of Sartre and Simone de Beauvoir, Sylvie Le Bon. In her Introduction, Sylvie Le Bon points out this essay's continuity with subsequent works, and she reprints the excellent presentation of it Simone de Beauvoir gives in *The Prime of Life* (pp. 147-48), so that we need not reprint it here.

37/9

The Transcendence of the Ego contains, in rudimentary form, most of the philosophical positions which will be developed in BEING AND NOTHINGNESS and ends with what might be called the program of the whole philosophical *oeuvre* to come, including the CRITIQUE OF DIALECTICAL REASON and the "Ethics" which is still being developed:

Nothing is more unfair than to call phenomenologists "idealists." On the contrary, for centuries we have not felt in philosophy so realistic a trend. The phenomenologists have plunged man back in the world, have given full weight to his anguish, his sufferings, and to his revolts. . . . I have always thought that a working hypothesis as fruitful as historical materialism stands in no need whatsoever of so absurd a foundation as a materialist metaphysic. In fact it is not necessary for the object *to precede the* subject *for spiritual pseudo-values to vanish and for ethics to find its foundation in reality. It is sufficient that the Me be contemporary with the World and that the subject-object dualism, which is purely logical, finally disappear from the preoccupations of philosophers. The World has not created the Me, the Me has not created the World. They are two objects for the absolute, impersonal consciousness, and it is by this consciousness that they are linked together. . . . And the relation of interdependence established by this absolute consciousness between the Me and the World is sufficient for the Me to appear as "in jeopardy" before the World, for the Me (indirectly through the mediation of its "states") to draw the whole of its content from the world. No more is needed in the way of a philosophical foundation for an ethics and a politics which are absolutely positive.*

37/10

Le Mur ⟨The Wall⟩, short story.

a) La Nouvelle Revue française, no. 286 (July, 1937), pp. 38-62.

b) Reprinted unchanged in LE MUR.

c) Textbook edition presented and annotated by W. Peeters. Anvers: Editions de Sikkel,[1964]. Third edition with photographs from Serge Roullet's film, 1969.

The Wall.

t1) Abridged and bowdlerized translation by Lucy Cores. *Three Who Died. Living Age*, no. 353 (October, 1937), pp. 135-40.

t2) Reprinted in Alfred Brant and Frederick H. Law, eds. *War or Peace*. New York: Harper, 1938.

t3) Translated by Maria Jolas. In *Chimera*, III, no. 4 (summer, 1945), 15-36.

t4) Reprinted in Belle Becker and Robert N. Linscott, eds. *Bedside Book of Famous French Short Stories*. New York: Random House, 1945. Pp. 397-414.

t5) Translated by Phyllis Duveen. In John Lehmann, ed. *Modern French Stories*. New York: New Directions, [1948]. Pp. 42-62.

t6) Translated by Lloyd Alexander. In THE WALL AND OTHER STORIES.

This short story, the first Sartre published as an adult, was accepted by Jean Paulhan at the same time as *The Room* and seems to have been written in 1936. It was an immediate and continuing success: more "absurdist," more political, and less erotic than the other short stories in THE WALL, it has been reprinted in many anthologies. Let us point out besides a faithful movie adaptation in 1967 by Serge Roullet (see Appendix).

A recent interview in *Jeune Cinéma* (see 67/476) gives much information about the story and clarifies the author's intentions. Sartre says especially, The Wall *is not a work of philosophy but a spontaneous emotional reaction to the Spanish Civil War*. And the source of the plot of the story is in fact as follows:

I happened to be friends with some men . . . who were connected with Malraux, and Malraux was organizing volunteers for Spain. And one of my friends, one of my former students, a very young man, had asked me after he had suffered some personal disappointments to get him into Spain, and I was very upset because it seemed to me on the one hand that he was not militarily or even biologically prepared to stand up under tough conditions, and on the other hand that I could not refuse a man who asked me privately for permission--if he could get it--to go fight.

According to *The Prime of Life* (p. 232), the former student is Jacques-Laurent Bost. The Belgian doctor is a real person who was mentioned in a text Sartre no longer recalls: *He was a doctor who had asked to see those who were condemned to death; they were soldiers who had run, and the real person was not, by the way, actually Belgian. He had noted down with great precision the premonitory symptoms of death.*

But this *personal meditation on the possible death of a friend* is put into a more general context: *When I wrote* The Wall, *I had no real knowledge of Marxian thought, I was simply in complete opposition to the existence of Spanish fascism, and since the Spanish people were about to be defeated at that time, I was much more sensitive to the absurdity of these deaths than to the positive elements to be found in a struggle against fascism.* The main character in *The Wall,* Pablo, is not a positive hero: he is not *really and completely involved in the struggle* and is not *devoted enough to a cause for his death not to seem absurd to him.*

The Wall has often been used to compare Sartre and Albert Camus; the more precise information Sartre gave in his interview should enable us to avoid too hasty conclusions in the future.

1938

38/11

LA NAUSÉE ⟨Nausea⟩, novel.

a) First edition. Gallimard, [1938]. 223 pages.

Dedication: *Au Castor* ⟨To the Beaver⟩ [Simone de Beauvoir]. 23 copies on wood-free finish, 40 on esparto grass. Date of press-proof: March 21, 1938. Printing date: April 5, 1938.

Many new printings, whose format and number of pages vary only slightly. The latest (printing date: May 3, 1968) has 243 pages and has on the inside of the cover the insert which we reprint below.

b) Bound according to Mario Prassinos' model. Gallimard, [1944]. 550 copies Héliona finish.

c) Pourpre series. Gallimard, [1950].

d) Grand Prix des meilleurs romans du demi-siècle series, no. 11. Sauret, [1951].

e) With twelve gouaches by Mario Prassinos. Le Rayon d'or series. Gallimard, [1951]. 3600 copies printed on bound parchment.

f) Novels series. Le Club du Meilleur Livre, [1954].

g) Le Livre de poche series, no. 160. Gallimard, [1956].

h) Soleil series. Gallimard, [1960]. 243 pages.

i) *Oeuvre romanesque*. Vol. I. Illustrated by W. Spitzer. Lidis, [1965].

j) With a study and notes by Georges Raillard. Le Livre de poche université series. Gallimard, [1966].

Text of edition *(g)* followed by 70 pages of notes.

k) Club edition with notes by André Gérel. Culture, Arts, Loisirs, [1967].

l) Folio pocketbook series, no. 46. Gallimard, [1972].

NAUSEA or THE DIARY OF ANTOINE ROQUENTIN.

t1) Excerpt. *The Root of the Chestnut Tree*, translated by Frances A. Lippman. *Partisan Review*, XIII, no. 1 (winter, 1946), 25-33.

t2) Excerpt. *The Provincial Portrait Gallery*, translated by Juliette Bigney. *Partisan Review*, XIII, no. 2 (spring, 1946), 215-27.

t3) NAUSEA, translated by Lloyd Alexander. New York: New Directions, 1949.

t4) THE DIARY OF ANTOINE ROQUENTIN, translated by Lloyd Alexander. London: John Lehmann, 1949.

t5) Same as *(t3)* in paperback. With an introduction by Hayden Carruth. New York: New Directions, 1959.

t6) Ibid. London: Hamish Hamilton, 1962.

This translation, which is rather mediocre, includes a certain number of paraphrases and misinterpretations.

t7) Translated by Robert Baldick. Penguin Books, 1965.

The insert for the first edition, which was drafted by Sartre, reads as follows:

> *After lengthy travels, Antoine Roquentin has settled in Bouville among ferociously good people. He lives near the railway station in a hotel for traveling salesmen and is writing a thesis in history about an eighteenth-century adventurer, M. de Rollebon. His work takes him frequently to the municipal library, where his friend the Autodidact, a humanist, is instructing himself by reading the books in alphabetical order. In the evening, Roquentin goes and sits at a table in the Railwaymen's Cafe and listens to a record--always the same one--*"Some of These Days." *And sometimes he goes upstairs with the woman who runs the place. Anny, the woman he loves, left four years ago. She always wanted there to be "perfect moments," and she constantly exhausted herself in minute and vain attempts to reconstruct the world around herself. She and Roquentin broke up. Now Roquentin is losing his past drop by drop; every day he sinks more deeply into a strange and suspicious present. His life itself no longer makes any sense: he thought he had had great adventures; but there aren't any adventures, there are only "stories." He clings to M. de Rollebon: death is to justify life.*

It is then that his real adventure--an insinuating, softly horrible metamorphosis of all his sensations--begins; it is Nausea, it grabs you from behind and then you drift in a tepid sea of time. Is it Roquentin who has changed? Is it the world? Walls, gardens, cafes are abruptly overcome by nausea. Another time he wakes up to a baleful day: something is rotten in the air, the light, people's gestures. M. de Rollebon dies a second time: the dead can never justify the living. Roquentin wanders the streets, voluminous and unjustifiable. And then, on the first day of spring, he grasps the meaning of his adventure: Nausea is Existence revealing itself--and Existence is not pleasant to see. Roquentin still clings to a feeble hope: Anny has written to him; he is going to see her again. But Anny has become a sedentary woman, fat and desperate. She has given up her perfect moments just as Roquentin has given up his Adventures. She too, in her own way, has discovered Existence. The two of them have nothing more to say to one another. Roquentin goes back to his solitude at the depths of this enormous Nature which is oozing suffocation on the town and which he senses will soon be rent by cataclysmic upheavals. What is to be done? Call to other men for help? But the other men are good people: they tip their hats to one another without knowing they exist. He is going to leave Bouville; he goes to the Railwaymen's Cafe to listen one last time to "Some of These Days," *and while the record is playing, he catches sight of a chance, a slim chance of accepting himself.*

This insert, with its half-ironic, half-serious tone, seems to be a compromise between the anecdotal content and the philosophic meaning of the book; but there are several possible ways of interpreting it, none of which has so far really been explored.

Today the genesis of NAUSEA is well known, thanks to Simone de Beauvoir, who herself played an intimate part in the novel's development (see the whole first part of *The Prime of Life*, and especially pages 37, 89-90, 121-22, 147, 163, 227-28, 236-39). While he had been doing his military service, Sartre had composed or completed three works which would in varying degrees provide him with a starting point for the "pamphlet on contingency" he had begun in the fall of 1931: a poem entitled *The Tree*, the play *Epimetheus*, and a volume of essays, *The Legend of Truth*, which had been rejected by a number of publishers. Simone de Beauvoir, after quoting a letter from Sartre which speaks at length of a chestnut tree, describes this first attempt in the following words (pp. 89-90):

"In its very first draft the new pamphlet was still very much like *The Legend of Truth*, being a lengthy, abstract dissertation on contingency. I insisted that Sartre should give Roquantin's [Roquentin's] discovery some fictional depth, and infuse his narrative with a little of that suspense which we enjoyed in detective novels. He agreed."

A second version of the work was completed during a stay in Berlin in 1934: this time Sartre had "overdone his adjectives and comparisons" (p. 163). He stopped revising a third version to plunge back into psychology and write IMAGINATION, but the final manuscript, entitled "Melancholia" after Dürer's engraving, was ready in the first months of 1936. Setting out from a reflection on absurdity and adventure, it was in a sense the sum of Sartre's experiences the past four years set down on paper, and it reflected his teaching years at Le Havre, his discovery of phenomenology and Franz Kafka, the depression he had been a victim of after he had had himself injected with mescaline in February, 1935, and so on. Although the work, which was finished before the Popular Front and the beginning of the Spanish Civil War, seemed uncommitted and paid practically no attention to the political events of the time, Sartre had nevertheless been struck by the rise of fascism in Europe and had been present in person at the Nazi victory in Germany. He had even been "vaguely tempted" to join the Communist Party.

The manuscript of "Melancholia" was first submitted to a reader at Gallimard by Paul Nizan, and Sartre subsequently "received a note from Paulhan telling him that, in spite of certain favorable qualities, the book had not been accepted" (p. 227). In the fall of 1936, the manuscript was again recommended to Gaston Gallimard by Charles Dullin and Pierre Bost, and it was definitively accepted in April or May, 1937. In a long letter which appears in *The Prime of Life* (pp. 236-39), Sartre himself tells about his call at Gallimard and his conversations with Jean Paulhan and Brice Parain. It turned out that Paulhan had only refused to publish "Melancholia" serially in *La Nouvelle Revue française* because it was too long. We will not go over the details here.

Sartre made certain changes in the original manuscript, but it is hard to tell precisely what they were. On the other hand, we do know that the title was changed from "Melancholia" to NAUSEA at Gaston Gallimard's suggestion.

First published in the spring of 1938, the novel was well received by the critics, had a rather big success without becoming a best seller, and above all established Sartre as a writer to be reckoned with in the future. Among the thirty criticisms we have been able to locate, we shall cite only those of:

-- Paul Nizan (*Ce Soir*, May 16, 1938): "M. Sartre could be a French Kafka . . . if his thinking . . . were not entirely unconcerned with moral problems";

-- Edmond Jaloux (*Les Nouvelles littéraires*, June 18, 1938): perceptive and extremely favorable report;

-- Armand Robin (*Esprit*, no. 70 [July, 1938], pp. 574-75): "*Nausea* is undoubtedly one of the distinctive works of our time. . . . It is a novel in search of a life";

-- Jean Daniélou (*Etudes*, CCXXVII [October, 1938], 140-41): "It seems to me that Antoine Roquentin's disgust goes beyond [the estheticism of Valéry and Proust], and that we cannot really overcome it except by a difficult reinvention of the need for man himself";

-- Albert Camus (*Alger républicain*, October 20, 1938; reprinted in Albert Camus, *Essais*, with an Introduction by R. Quillot, pp. 1417-19. Bibliothèque de la Pléiade series, Gallimard, [1965]).

Sartre's chief aim was to "express metaphysical truths and feelings in literary form" (*The Prime of Life*, p. 227). The critics apparently took him too much at his word, because they constantly stressed the philosophical aspect of NAUSEA at the expense of other possible approaches. It seems to us today, however, that the images and metaphors of the work are not always there to illustrate a system, but that on the contrary, Sartre is inventing a philosophy to unite these images and report his own obsessions. NAUSEA is on the one hand an exploratory work in which Sartre completely reveals himself, and on the other hand a transitional work which, even before it came out in 1938, marked a stage in the development of his thinking which he had already gone beyond.

Sartre has never rejected what he wrote in NAUSEA, but his attitude toward his novel, and toward Antoine Roquentin in particular, has changed considerably as the years have gone by. To begin with, if we compare Roquentin (a name which Sartre may have found in Flaubert) with what Sartre calls the "scum," and above all with the character of Lucien Fleurier in *The Childhood of a Leader*, we have to grant that he is a character who is, if not positive, at least authentic and lucid. In *Materialism and Revolution* (see SITUATIONS, III, p. 184 ff.), moreover, Sartre sets up an implicit and rather extended parallel between Roquentin's situation and that of a revolutionary. Subsequently, however, Sartre will attack this image of himself and will attribute it to his *neurosis:*

> *I couldn't see things the way they really were; and as long as I kept up the illusion, I thought I was out of trouble. At the age of thirty, I had pulled off the masterstroke of writing* [describing] *in* NAUSEA--*quite sincerely, believe me--about the bitter, unjustified existence of my fellowmen while justifying my own.* I was *Roquentin; I used him to show, without complacency, the texture of my life. At the same time, I was* I, *the elect, chronicler of Hell, a glass and steel photomicroscope peering at my*

own protoplasmic juices. . . . Fake to the marrow of my bones and mystified, I wrote joyfully about our unhappy lot. Dogmatically, I doubted everything except that I was the elected doubter. I built with one hand what I destroyed with the other, and I took my uneasiness to be the guarantee of my security. I was happy (THE WORDS, pp. 251-52).

In an interview he granted to Jacqueline Piatier (see 64/405), Sartre says, in the same connection:

What I regret about NAUSEA *is not having completely involved myself in it. I stayed outside my hero's suffering, protected by my neurosis, which brought me happiness through writing. . . . I have always been happy. Even if I had been more honest with myself at the time, I still would have written* NAUSEA. *What I lacked was a sense of reality. I've changed since then. I have slowly come to learn about reality. I have seen children die of hunger. Balanced against a dying child,* NAUSEA *has no weight.*

Reactions to this last sentence will be found at 64/405. Our comments on NAUSEA stop here: an extensive documentation will soon be found in the forthcoming Pléiade edition of Sartre's fictional works and a special study by Michel Rybalka will propose a new interpretation of the novel.

Two short studies on NAUSEA, for school use, have recently appeared in book form.

-- Georges Raillard. *"La Nausée" de J.-P. Sartre* 〈NAUSEA, by J.-P. Sartre〉. Poche critique series. Hachette, 1972. Perceptive and stimulating.

-- Geneviève Idt. *"La Nausée," analyse critique* 〈NAUSEA, a Critical Analysis〉. Profil d'une oeuvre series. Hatier, 1972. More conventional.

On the other hand, a very useful and thorough IBM concordance of the book has been compiled by Professor Paul A. Fortier (University of Manitoba, Winnipeg).

See also 38/12 and 38/13.

38/12

"Jean-Paul Sartre, romancier philosophe" 〈Jean-Paul Sartre, Philosopher-Novelist〉, interview-article by Claudine Chonez.

-- *Marianne*, November 23, 1938.

38/13

"A qui les lauriers Goncourt, Fémina, Renaudot, Interallié?" ⟨Who Will Win the Goncourt, Fémina, Renaudot, Interallié Prizes?"⟩, interview-article by Claudine Chonez.

-- *Marianne*, December 7, 1938.

Claudine Chonez made two articles out of the interview Sartre granted her during the literary prize competitions, in which NAUSEA, which had come out a few months before, had a good chance along with Paul Nizan's *The Conspiracy*. According to Sartre's own recollection, it was the first interview anyone had ever asked him for.

Claudine Chonez presents Sartre as a "pure spirit," tries to explain phenomenology, briefly describes NAUSEA, and sets forth Sartre's projects, including an essay called "Les Mondes imaginaires" ⟨Imaginary Worlds⟩. Sartre says: *I dreamed of expressing my ideas in nothing but a beautiful form--I mean in a work of art, a novel, or a short story. But I came to realize that this was impossible. There are things which are so technical they require a philosophical vocabulary. Thus I saw that I had to duplicate, so to speak, each novel with an essay. So at the same time I was writing* NAUSEA *I was writing* The Psyche, *a work which will soon come out and which will deal with psychology from a phenomenological point of view.* Then the article describes the novel Sartre is writing. Here Sartre's remarks are not quoted directly, and it may be that he was having fun fooling his interviewer. For the interviewer does speak in the following way of what will become *Roads to Freedom*: "In the next novel Roquentin will discover that he is free, but it will take a great upheaval in the world to let him do it. Jean-Paul Sartre, making use as a good novelist of what is at hand, makes his hero live the recent days when we thought everything was going to be swept into war. He imagines him called up and discovering in this break with his past his total and intoxicating freedom. Antoine, on the other hand, is ripe for the gratuitous act, in the footsteps of Lafcadio and the surrealists. But Sartre is at pains to point out that the precursors of his hero have ordinarily had to work very hard to perfect their gratuitous act, whereas Antoine cannot help committing his.

"Naturally he rapes a woman and causes a crime to be committed. For it is in fact essential to gratuitous acts, which are aimed against all shackles and all utilitarianism, to direct themselves toward realms

38/13

condemned by the ethics of established society. Yet it is nevertheless a profound moral reconstruction of the individual which is involved here, a true resurrection--from nausea to zeal, from suicide to a taste for life, for unique, irreversible, free life."

Of course we have to be careful not to take these claims literally, and not to draw too precise conclusions about the first stages of *Roads to Freedom*. But just the same you will notice that by the time Sartre had finished NAUSEA he was thinking of Mathieu as one of Roquentin's possibilities, and that he had even managed to think about continuing to develop the character. And in fact Claudine Chonez, in her second article, reports the following relevant comment of Sartre's: NAUSEA *has been accused of being too pessimistic. But let's wait for the end. In a future novel, which will be a sequel to this one, the hero will straighten things out--you'll see existence reinstated, and my hero act, get a taste of action."* This clearly indicates Sartre's first intention of embodying the passage to a positive ethic in the character of Mathieu (see also 49/191 and 49/192).

38/14

La Chambre ⟨The Room⟩, short story.

a) Mesures, 3d Year, no. 1 (January 15, 1938), pp. 119-49.

b) Reprinted without major alterations in THE WALL.

The Room.

t1) Translated by John Rodker. In *New Writing*, n.s., II (spring, 1939), 6-28.

t2) Translated by John Rodker. In *French Stories from New Writing*. London: Lehmann, 1947. Pp. 13-41. In John Lehmann, ed. *Modern French Stories*. New York: New Directions, 1948. Pp. 13-41.

t3) Translated by Lloyd Alexander. In THE WALL AND OTHER STORIES.

This short story was accepted by Jean Paulhan for the quarterly *Mesures*. It takes up the theme of sequestration again, a theme which will characterize most of Sartre's work. An excellent adaptation of the story for television was made by Michel Mitrani in 1964.

According to Simone de Beauvoir (*The Prime of Life*, pp. 139-40), *The Room* originated in an atrocious sexual experience one of her friends underwent.

38/15

"Sartoris" par William Faulkner ⟨*Sartoris*, by William Faulkner⟩.

a) La Nouvelle Revue française, no. 293 (February, 1938), pp. 323-28.

b) Reprinted in SITUATIONS, I.

William Faulkner's "Sartoris."

t1) Translated by Melvin Friedman. In *Yale French Studies*, no. 10 (fall, 1952), pp. 95-99.

t2) Translated by Annette Michelson. In LITERARY AND PHILOSOPHICAL ESSAYS. New York: Criterion Books, 1966; London: Rider, 1955. Reprinted in several other volumes.

This first article of literary criticism contributed to establishing Faulkner's reputation in France and indicates the lively interest Sartre had from the beginning of the thirties for the American novel and its technical innovations.

See also, concerning Faulkner, 39/26.

38/16

Intimité ⟨Intimacy⟩, a short story.

a) La Nouvelle Revue française, no. 299 (August, 1938), pp. 187-200; no. 300 (September, 1938), pp. 381-406.

b) Reprinted in LE MUR with one change: the *Hôtel du Globe* in the magazine story becomes the *Hôtel du Théâtre* in the book.

Intimacy, translated by Lloyd Alexander.

-- in THE WALL AND OTHER STORIES.

Under the ironic title of *Intimacy*, Sartre describes another case of alienation, based this time on the main character's hatred for his body. It is on the basis of this story and *Erostratus* that people have been able to talk about Sartre's dread of incarnation and his "erotic resentment"[1] by attributing to personal obsessions what is above all a writer's interest in existential borderline cases.

---

1. See Suzanne Lilar, *A propos de Sartre et de l'amour* ⟨On Sartre and Love⟩ (Grasset, 1967).

38/17

A propos de John Dos Passos et de "1919" ⟨John Dos Passos and *1919*⟩, essay.

a) La Nouvelle Revue française, no. 299 (August, 1938), pp. 292-301.

b) Reprinted with no major changes in SITUATIONS, I. Only a note mentioning that *1919* is a work translated by Maurice Rémond for Editions sociales internationales has been omitted.

John Dos Passos and "1919," translated by Annette Michelson.

-- In LITERARY AND PHILOSOPHICAL ESSAYS (1955) and other volumes.

> This important piece of criticism devoted to an author to whom Sartre owes the method of simultaneity he uses in THE REPRIEVE is one of the most enthusiastic articles he ever wrote. There is probably no need to add that it has been a long time since Sartre considered Dos Passos *the greatest writer of our time*.

38/18

Structure intentionnelle de l'image ⟨The Intentional Structure of the Image⟩.

a) Revue de métaphysique et de morale, 45th Year, no. 4 (October, 1938), pp. 543-609.

b) Text incorporated in PSYCHOLOGY OF THE IMAGINATION as its first part and entitled "The Certain" (pp. 9-76 of the Gallimard edition).

The article has a few extra introductory lines and does not have the sketches found on pages 46, 48, and 50 of the book.

38/19

"La Conspiration" par Paul Nizan ⟨*The Conspiracy*, by Paul Nizan⟩.

a) La Nouvelle Revue française, no. 302 (November, 1938), pp. 842-45.

b) Reprinted in SITUATIONS, I.

> *The Conspiracy* won the Interallié prize in 1938. This is the novel in which Nizan calls a detective Sartre. Undoubtedly Sartre wanted to pay him back in kind when he put a "General Nizan" in *The Childhood of a Leader*.

Concerning the relationship between Sartre and Nizan, see 47/128, 60/333, and 71/560.

38/20

* *Nourritures* ⟨Foods⟩.

a) Verve, no. 4 [1938], pp. 115-16.

Published on November 15, 1938.

b) Reprinted without change in NOURRITURES. Jacques Damase, 1949.

In this volume the text is dated "Naples, 1935."

Food, anonymous translation.

-- *Verve* (English edition), I, no. 4 (January-March, 1939), 115-16.

Foods is a fragment from a story called "Dépaysement" ⟨"Homelessness"⟩ which has never been published. "Homelessness" was written after a stay in Naples during the summer of 1936. In it, Sartre was inspired by his own experience during a night of barhopping with a sailor and a pimp (the same episode appears in a different form in THE REPRIEVE, in the scene in which Gros-Louis, the shepherd, is attacked by his buddies in Marseilles).

In this text, which is reminiscent of certain pages of NAUSEA, Sartre tries to show both the *truth* and the *horror* of the food. Let us point out here that the culinary theme, though it is not always very evident, has an important place in Sartre's *oeuvre* and would warrant an in-depth study.

1939

39/21

LE MUR ⟨The Wall⟩.

Volume containing *The Wall* (see 37/10), *The Room*, (see 38/14), *Erostratus* (previously unpublished; written in 1936), *Intimacy* (see 38/16), *The Childhood of a Leader* (previously unpublished; completed in July, 1938).

a) First edition. Gallimard, [1939]. Printing date: January 26, 1939. Sold by subscription beginning October, 1938. Includes 70 copies on esparto grass and 40 copies on pur fil. Dedicated to Olga Kosakiewicz.

b) Illustrated edition with 33 copperplate engravings by Mario Prassinos. Gallimard, [1945].

c) Le Livre de poche series, no. 33. Gallimard, [1953]. By the end of 1971, 1,100,000 copies of this edition had been printed.

d) Pourpre series. Gallimard, [1954].

e) Récits series. Le Club du Meilleur Livre, [1958].

f) Soleil series. Gallimard, [1961].

g) With a preface by Jean-Louis Curtis. Lausanne: Rencontre, [1965].

h) Oeuvre romanesque. Vol. II. Illustrated by W. Spitzer. Lidis, [1965].

i) Republished by Gallimard (1967) with an illustrated jacket because the film was coming out. On the back of the jacket there is a letter from Sartre to Serge Roullet dated January 10, 1967.

j) Folio series, no. 68. Gallimard, [1972].

THE WALL [or INTIMACY] AND OTHER STORIES, translated by Lloyd Alexander.

t1) THE WALL AND OTHER STORIES. Limited edition. New York: New Directions, 1948.

t2) INTIMACY AND OTHER STORIES. London: Peter Nevill, 1949; New York: New Directions, 1952.

t3) THE WALL AND OTHER STORIES. London: Neville Spearman, 1956.

t4) Paperback. INTIMACY. New York: Berkley Books, [1956]. Continued by Berkley Medallion Books, [1960].

t5) Paperback. THE WALL AND OTHER STORIES. London, Panther Books, [1960].

t6) Paperback. THE WALL (INTIMACY) AND OTHER STORIES. New York: New Directions, [1969].

NOTE: One of the tales in THE WALL, *Erostratus*, was first translated by Eleanor Clark in *Decision*, II, nos. 5-6 (November-December, 1941), 60-73.

The first pages of *The Childhood of a Leader* were translated as *Boy into Man* by Constance Coolidge in *Portfolio* (Washington, D.C.: Black Sun Press), Vol. III (spring, 1946), on 4 pages.

The insert, drawn up by Sartre, reads as follows:

> *No one wants to look Existence in the face. Here are five little failures--tragic or comic--confronting it, five lives. Pablo, who is to be shot, wants to cast his thoughts beyond Existence and conceive of his own death. In vain. Eve tries to join Pierre in the unreal, closed world of madness. In vain; this world is only a sham and madmen are liars. Erostratus intends to scandalize everyone by a striking rejection of the human condition, by a crime. In vain: the crime is committed, the crime exists, and Erostratus no longer recognizes it; it's a big filthy bag with blood running out of it. Lola* [Lulu] *lies to herself: she tries to slip a thin mist between herself and the glance she can't help casting at herself. In vain; the mist immediately becomes transparent. We don't lie to ourselves; we believe we do. Lucien Fleurier is the closest to feeling he exists, but he doesn't want to; he evades himself and takes refuge in thinking of his rights; for rights do not exist, they ought to. In vain. All these efforts to escape are blocked by a Wall; to flee Existence is still to exist. Existence is a plenum man cannot leave.*

The book was rather successful: it was designated the "book of the month" for March, 1939, and even won Sartre the *Roman populiste* prize in April,

39/21

1940. The book was violently attacked by Robert Brasillach in the April 13, 1939, *Action française* and defended in a paragraph in *La Nouvelle Revue française*, no. 308 (May, 1939), p. 808, entitled "Concerning *Intimacy*."

Let us note, among the first reviews, the one by Albert Camus in the *Alger républicain* of March 12, 1939 (reprinted in the Pléiade volume, *Essais*, pp. 1419-22).

The short stories in THE WALL helped give Sartre a reputation for obscenity. Yet many consider the collection his best work of fiction. On the other hand, stories like *The Room* or *The Childhood of a Leader* help us understand NAUSEA better: Is not Lucien Fleurier up to a certain point an anti-Roquentin? Is not Paul Hilbert's letter to writers in *Erostratus* Sartre's most radical condemnation of humanism?

Judging by a passage in SITUATIONS, II (pp. 212-13), Lucien Fleurier corresponds to a person who had a place in Sartre's life: *Around 1924 I knew a young man from a good family who was crazy about literature, and contemporary writers in particular. He was really crazy when it suited him to be, stuffed himself with barroom poetry when it was fashionable, noisily displayed a mistress, and then, when his father died, went back to the family factory and the straight and narrow like a good boy. He has since married an heiress. . . . Around the time he got married he drew from his readings the formula which was to justify his life. "We have to act like everybody else," he wrote me one day, "and be like nobody else."*

A more general definition of this type of person is found in SITUATIONS, III (pp. 184 ff.): *Every member of the ruling class is a man by divine right. Born in a circle of leaders, he is convinced from birth that he is born to rule. . . . There is a certain social function waiting for him in the future, a role that he will step into when he is old enough, and that is, so to speak, the metaphysical reality of his individuality.*

Concerning THE WALL, see also 69/503.

39/22

ESQUISSE D'UNE THÉORIE DES ÉMOTIONS ⟨Sketch for a Theory of the Emotions⟩.

a) Actualités scientifiques et industrielles series, no. 838. Hermann, 1939. Philosophical essays published by Jean Cavaillès. 52 pages. Printed December, 1939. Copyright February 23, 1940.

b) New edition, 1960. Text the same as *(a)*, but with a new cover and a new format.

THE EMOTIONS: OUTLINE OF A THEORY or SKETCH FOR A THEORY OF THE EMOTIONS.

t1) THE EMOTIONS: OUTLINE OF A THEORY, translated by Bernard Frechtman. New York: Philosophical Library, [1948].

t2) Ibid. in paperback. New York: Citadel Press, [1971].

t3) SKETCH FOR A THEORY OF THE EMOTIONS, translated by Philip Mairet. With an introduction by Mary Warnock. London: Methuen, [1962].

Simone de Beauvoir tells us on page 253 of *The Prime of Life* that this is the only published part of a big treatise on phenomenological psychology called "The Psyche." When it is almost finished Sartre will give it up in order to complete the collection of stories INTIMACY AND OTHER STORIES.

In spite of its brevity, THE EMOTIONS: OUTLINE OF A THEORY is the best introduction to a study of BEING AND NOTHINGNESS because it is rigorous yet accessible.

39/23

Une Idée fondamentale de la phénoménologie de Husserl: l'intentionnalité 〈A Fundamental Idea of Husserl's Phenomenology: Intentionality〉, essay.

a) La Nouvelle Revue française, no. 304 (January, 1939), pp. 129-31.

b) Reprinted in SITUATIONS, I.

Intentionality: A Fundamental Idea of Husserl's Phenomenology, translated by Joseph P. Fell.

-- *Journal of the British Society for Phenomenology*, I no. 2 (May, 1970), 4-5. In special number on Sartre, in honor of his sixty-fifth birthday.

This article, written during Sartre's stay in Berlin in 1933-34, at the time he was enthusiastically discovering Edmund Husserl's phenomenology, is undoubtedly one of his best.

Compared to *The Legend of Truth*, this text marks not only a major development of his thought but also the first expression of his philosophical originality. Sartre attacks traditional psychology, condemns

39/23

alimentary philosophy, and then gives an interpretation of the complex Husserlian idea of intentionality which is personal yet comprehensible to a nonspecialized public.

39/24

M. François Mauriac et la liberté ⟨M. François Mauriac and Freedom⟩, essay.

a) *La Nouvelle Revue française*, no. 305 (February, 1939), pp. 212-32. There is also a published offprint of this article.

b) Reprinted in SITUATIONS, I.

François Mauriac and Freedom, translated by Annette Michelson.

-- In LITERARY AND PHILOSOPHICAL ESSAYS (1955) and other volumes.

This knock-down, drag-out attack is without a doubt the most famous literary criticism Sartre ever wrote. In it he shows, in connection with *The End of the Night*, that every narrative technique involves an ethic and a metaphysic. This will turn out to be a very fruitful idea which will be adopted by most modern criticism.

Sartre's article raised quite a row at the time. Let us cite as a reminder André Rousseaux's scandalized reaction in the February 15, 1939, *Revue universelle*. The editors of *La Nouvelle Revue française* came to Sartre's defense in a note published in their March, 1939, issue (no. 306) entitled "Concerning François Mauriac and Sartre." The latter kept one of his most stinging barbs in reserve for André Rousseaux, writing thirteen years later in SAINT GENET: *Even if you were pure as the driven snow, free of all repression, even though you were naturally turned toward virtue like the moth to the flame and M. Rousseaux to error, Genet would still disgust you, and thus compromise you.*

As for the relations between Sartre and Mauriac, they have since the article increasingly taken on the air of a local polemic, Sartre never missing a chance to vent his spleen on Mauriac; whereas Mauriac, on the contrary, seems to be overcome by an irresistible fascination for this man he calls the "providential atheist."

In an interview in 1960 (see 60/321), Sartre was asked whether he still stood by his claim that Mauriac was no novelist. Here is his answer: *I think I'd be more flexible now, considering the essential characteristic of the novel to be to intrigue or interest, and I'd be a lot less finicky about its techniques of doing so. That's because I have come to realize that all techniques--including those of the American novel--are tricks. We always manage to say what we think to the reader--the author is always present. The American novel's trickery is more subtle, but it's still there. Having said this, I must also say that I don't think that making oneself too visible is the best technique for writing a good novel. If I had to write* Roads to Freedom *over again, I'd try to present each character without comment, without revealing my feelings.*

Mauriac recently gave an interview on the occasion of the publication of his new novel, *An Adolescent in the Olden Days*, in which he holds Sartre responsible in a sense for his long silence as a novelist: "I was wounded, if you like, by Sartre's attack. One of my novels, called *The End of the Night*, had been torn apart by Sartre, who was not only a very young author but the glory of his generation. I won't say that this demoralized me, but just the same it made me think" (*France-Soir*, February 28, 1969).

39/24 A

Elsa Triolet, review.

-- *Europe*, February 15, 1939, pp. 281-83.

This review of Triolet's novel *Goodnight Thérèse* marks the beginning of Sartre's collaboration with the review *Europe* (see below). Paul Nizan had asked Sartre to replace him because he did not have time to do his usual article; the piece pleased Louis Aragon, and that is how it happened that Jean Cassou asked Sartre to contribute a regular chronicle.

This piece is rather closely connected to NAUSEA and several of the short stories in THE WALL. In Sartre's view, Triolet's novel is of interest because it shows *the being-in-the-world of a solitary woman. When you are reading* Goodnight Thérèse, *you seem to feel a woman's body from within--sick and tired, rebellious, and voluptuous. Through this suffocating, sensual sweetness of a body which never forgets itself, we see Thérèse's world--this "world-for-a-woman" which is so compelling, so threatening, and yet kept at a respectful distance, in suspense in this solitude and freedom.*

39/25

La Chronique de J.-P. Sartre ⟨Sartre's Chronicle⟩.

a) Europe, June 15, 1939, pp. 240-51.

In this chronicle, Sartre reviews the following three works: Vladimir Nabokov's *Mistrust*, Denis de Rougemont's *Love and the Western World*, and Charles Morgan's *The Sparkling Stream.* This review is followed by *Memento*, signed J.-P. Sartre, which rapidly examines three works: Jean Giraudoux's *Duel of Angels*, Marguerite Steen's *L'Etalon*, and Katherine Mansfield's *German Boarding House.*

b) The criticisms of Nabokov and Denis de Rougemont have been reprinted without any major revisions as separate chapters of SITUATIONS, I. We reproduce the integral text about Charles Morgan below.

> *After* Fontaine *and* Sparkenbrooke, *people could speak of M. Morgan's Platonism*[1] *and compare his heroes to Tristan and Isolde.*[2] *He thus provided a strange confirmation of M. de Rougemont's claims. But now we have a work which has a wholly different ring. Certainly Fevrers and Karen, who love and desire one another, do not give themselves to one another immediately. They erect barriers between one another, and here again we have the obstacle love requires, the King Mark's sword M. de Rougemont talks about. But the obstacles are in no way intended to intensify the passion, they are in no way a symbolic representation of death:* [Karen and Fevrers] *subordinate their personal desires to the work they have undertaken in common, and as long as the nature of this work and circumstances demand an absolute devotion, a personal ardor, and a perfect unity of spirit, they will not give themselves to one another. Thus the basic source of the obstacle is what they have to live, doing their job as human beings. On this basis, M. Morgan outlines something like a humanism of love. The essential thing for man is to realize and keep his unity of spirit, although this is not an end but a means of creating and acting. Doing so may sometimes involve a provisional chastity: "The writer at the high point of his labors or the minister of God come to grips with his faith or the scientist confronting his toughest problems can have a glimpse of the moment in which renunciation of the sexual act will preserve his unity of spirit, and then he will deliberately abstain." Here is Tristan the hermit again, wandering alone in the forest. But this chastity is in no way an end in itself; on the contrary, what is of primary importance is to accept our body, to "revive" sexual desire--to take it up anew as we revive a play--and integrate it into our unity of spirit. (By means of a rather striking parallel which would warm the cockles of M. de Rougemont's heart, M. Morgan also accepts war.) So love becomes an affirmation of the unity of*

---

1. Maxime Chastaing, "De l'imagination chez Charles Morgan" ⟨Imagination in the Works of Charles Morgan⟩, *Vie intellectuelle*, April 25, 1939.

2. P.-H. Simon, "Essai d'une critique chrétienne de Morgan" ⟨An Attempt at a Christian Critique of Morgan⟩, in *ibid.*

personality, almost a challenge to time and to the forces of destruction. When I read this admirable dialogue from The Sparkling Stream:

KAREN: *"We'll always love each other, through all follies, infidelities, all failures and denials. Through all the separations, always, till the very end.*
FEVRERS: *"Karen, this is the hope of a madwoman.*
KAREN: *"It's like the love of God,"*

I can't help thinking of the marital fidelity extolled by M. de Rougemont (which is also a challenge), of his definition of Christian union as an attempt to "live with" rather than to "die together," of the "mad virtue" he offers us--in short, of his personalism. *Only M. Morgan's virtue is less harsh; it's a sparkling stream.*

Reread M. Fernandez's The Wager, *read* Love and the Western World *by M. de Rougement and* The Sparkling Stream*: you will see emerging, through all the dissimilarities and contrasts, a curious and laudable* love ethic. *But is love susceptible to ethical considerations? Is it susceptible to them* in our society? (*Europe*, June 15, 1939, pp. 248-49).

Jean Cassou was the one who had asked Sartre to provide *Europe* with a regular chronicle. But since war came shortly afterward, Sartre's collaboration was limited to a single issue of the journal.

Let us point out, on the other hand, that Sartre alludes rather frequently to Denis de Rougemont and attacks him in *The Ghost of Stalin.*

39/26

A propos de "Le Bruit et la fureur": La Temporalité chez Faulkner ⟨On *The Sound and the Fury*: Time in the Work of Faulkner⟩.

a) La Nouvelle Revue française, no. 309 (June, 1939), pp. 1056-61; no. 310 (July, 1939), pp. 147-51.

b) Reprinted with minor changes in SITUATIONS, I.

On "The Sound and the Fury": Time in the Work of Faulkner.

t1) In Frederick J. Hoffman and Olga W. Vickery, eds. *William Faulkner: Two Decades of Criticism.* Ann Arbor: University of Michigan Press, 1951. Pp. 180-88.

Also in *William Faulkner: Three Decades of Criticism.* 1960. Pp. 180-88.

t2) Translated by Annette Michelson. In LITERARY AND PHILOSOPHICAL ESSAYS (1955).

39/26

This study goes beyond Faulkner's works to foreshadow already the chapter on temporality in BEING AND NOTHINGNESS.

39/27

* *Portraits officiels* ⟨Official Portraits⟩.

a) Verve, nos. 5-6 [1939], pp. 9-12. An unsigned text in a special issue devoted to the human face.

b) Reprinted in VISAGES. Seghers, 1948.

Official Portraits.

t1) Anonymous translation in *Verve* (English edition), II,nos. 5-6 (July-October, 1939), 9-12.

t2) Translated by Anne P. Jones (see 39/28).

This piece, originally anonymous, serves to introduce a series of texts and illustrations whose general theme is the human face. It constitutes an original commentary on four portraits reproduced in the volume, those of Francis I, Louis XIV, Charles the Bald, and Napoleon Bonaparte.

This commentary should be compared to the famous description of the portraits in the Bouville museum in NAUSEA.

39/28

* *Visages* ⟨Faces⟩.

a) Verve, nos. 5-6 [1939], pp. 43-44.

b) Reprinted in VISAGES. Seghers, 1948.

Faces.

t1) Anonymous translation in *Verve* (English edition), II, nos. 5-6 (July-October, 1939), 43-44.

t2) Translated by Anne P. Jones. *Faces*, preceded by *Official Portraits*. In Maurice Natanson, ed. *Essays in Phenomenology*. The Hague: M. Nijhoff, 1966. Pp. 157-63.

One of Sartre's finest pieces of writing. In it, he undertakes to describe phenomenologically (*I simply say what I see*) those special beings called faces, which are not things. What Sartre is trying to do is to bring to light their essence in the phenomenological sense of the truth of the face. This intuition of

> the essence of the human face is summed up in the idea that . . . *the meaning of a face is to be* visible *transcendence*.

39/NOTE 1.

The notice set into the February-June, 1939, *La Nouvelle Revue française* announces a study by Sartre called "The Novels of André Malraux." This projected article never got any farther than that.

1940

40/29

L'IMAGINAIRE, *psychologie phénoménologique de l'imagination* ⟨The Imaginary, Phenomenological Psychology of the Imagination⟩.

a) The first part, called "The Certain," first appeared as *Structure intentionnelle de l'image* ⟨The Intentional Structure of the Image⟩. *Revue de métaphysique et de morale*, 45th Year, no. 4 (October, 1938), pp. 543-609. (See 38/18.)

b) Bibliothèque des Idées series. Gallimard, 1940. 247 pages.

Volume was offered to subscribers beginning September, 1939. Published February 15, 1940. This edition includes 20 numbered copies Lafuma finish. Dedicated to Albert Morel (Sartre's former student and the son of the Mme Louis Morel whom Simone de Beauvoir talks about in her memoirs under the name of Mme Lemaire).

c) Idées series. Gallimard, [1966].

Text the same as *(b)*.

PSYCHOLOGY OF THE IMAGINATION, translated by Bernard Frechtman.

t1) New York: Philosophical Library, [1948]. London: Rider, [1949].

t2) Paperback. New York: Citadel Press, [1961].

t3) Paperback. New York: Washington Square Press, [1966].

Mediocre translation; sometimes even unreadable.

t4) With an introduction by Mary Warnock. London: Methuen, 1972.

The insert for the 1940 edition, drawn up by Sartre, reads as follows:

Faculty Psychology, as it fell beneath the criticisms of scientific psychology, took Imagination, or the faculty of forming images, along with it as it fell. All that was left was sensation. In an effort to explain our imaginative life, people then tried to group certain sensations together as images, but they failed completely to distinguish them from the other sensations. And it is in fact absolutely impossible to base the distinction between images and sensations on an ontological *difference. Only a phenomenology of consciousness and Being was capable of taking up the problem of imagination from scratch and making an* existential *distinction between the "imaged" and the perceived object. In this book I have tried to describe by means of the phenomenological method certain special objects which are present to consciousness at every instant, which are distinguished from real "things" by the fact that their being is a nothingness of being, and which I have called "imaginaries" to avoid using the old term "image," which is still so muddied by empiricism and positivism. Studying them led me to try to examine the* imaginary life *phenomenologically, for as soon as consciousness "meets"* one *of its objects it undergoes remarkable changes as a consequence, as we see in the case of schizophrenia, dreaming, and hallucination. And finally, I was led through a rational progression to ask myself what consciousness had to be in its intrinsic nature for* imaginaries *to be able to be given to it in general. Then I saw that there could not possibly be anything* imaginary *except against a ground of nihilating the World, and I showed that "the imaging function of consciousness would have its origin in the nihilating power of Mind, which is another word for its total Freedom."*

This work, which Sartre first thought of calling "The Imaginary World" or "Imaginary Worlds," is the sequel to IMAGINATION: A PSYCHOLOGICAL CRITIQUE (see 36/8) and the upshot of investigations carried out since the twenties.

Sartre examines the structure of the image by using the phenomenological method and in particular the Husserlian concept of intentionality, according to which consciousness is not the mental record of an external reality but an act which constitutes consciousness in projecting itself toward its objects. This projection may take two essentially distinct forms depending on whether consciousness posits its object as existent and present (perception) or as absent and unreal (imagination). According to Sartre, these are two comprehensive, contrasting, and incompatible attitudes: we can imagine and perceive only alternatively.

Such a dichotomy presents certain difficulties, even from a phenomenological point of view. Thus Merleau-Ponty set about showing in *Le Visible et l'Invisible* ⟨The Visible and the Invisible⟩ (Gallimard, 1964; Evanston, Illinois: Northwestern University Press, 1969) that things always exceed what we observe about them, and that there would be no objectivity if the visible did not extend uninterruptedly toward an inexhaustible latent content springing from the imaginary. From another perspective, the psychoanalysts are trying to bring to light the acts of fantasy which are genetically the source of all cognitive functions and which continue to operate secretly in adult perception. From a psychiatric point of view, Henri Faure protests in his *Hallucinations et réalité perceptive* ⟨Hallucinations and Perceptual Reality⟩ (P.U.F., Bibliothèque de psychiatrie, 1965) against Sartre's "restrictive" interpretation of hallucination, which the author interprets as a specific organization of the spatial field in which real and imaginary indissolubly overlap. And finally, in stressing "the essential poverty of the image," Sartre has gone against all the psychologies of imagination which have come out of the work of Gaston Bachelard and Mircea Eliade; thus, Gilbert Durand devotes many pages of his voluminous work *Les Structures anthropologiques de l'Imaginaire* ⟨The Anthropological Structures of the Imaginary⟩ (P.U.F., Bibliothèque de philosophie contemporaine, 1963) to Sartre in order to denounce what he calls an "ontological devaluation of the image" (in the same perspective, see Maurice-Jean Lefebve, *L'Image fascinante et le surréel* ⟨The Fascinating Image and the Surreal⟩ [Plon, 1965]).

Sartre's aesthetic analyses, especially in the realms of literature and the plastic arts, are based upon the principles defined in PSYCHOLOGY OF THE IMAGINATION. But it must be added that the few pages he devotes to determining the status of the work of art may seem simplistic in respect to the analyses he will subsequently give of the works of Francis Ponge, Giacometti, Jean Genet, or Tintoretto.

One of the first reviews of PSYCHOLOGY OF THE IMAGINATION was Daniel Lagache's in *Bulletin de la Faculté des lettres de Strasbourg*, XIX, no. 8 (June, 1941), 309-25.

40/30

M. Jean Giraudoux et la philosophie d'Aristote: A propos de "Choix des élues" ⟨M. Jean Giraudoux and the Philosophy of Artistotle: Concerning "Duel of Angels"⟩, essay.

a) La Nouvelle Revue française, no. 318 (March, 1940), pp. 339-54.

This article, with the title *On Jean Giraudoux*, was first announced for publication in the journal in July, 1939.

b) Reprinted in SITUATIONS, I.

Jean Giraudoux and the Philosophy of Aristotle, translated by Annette Michelson.

-- In LITERARY AND PHILOSOPHICAL ESSAYS (1955) and other volumes.

Continuing his critique of established values, Sartre this time spiritedly but unmaliciously attacks an author who at the time was considered untouchable, and takes advantage of the opportunity to show the anti-Aristotelian side of his own philosophy.

This critical essay has been ceaselessly commented on ever since it came out: see particularly Claude-Edmonde Magny in *Précieux Giraudoux* ⟨Precious Giraudoux⟩ (Seuil, 1945) and Oreste F. Pucciani ("The 'Infernal Dialogue' of Giraudoux and Sartre," *Tulane Drama Review*, no. 4 [1959], pp. 57-75). It has often been reprinted, notably in *Cahiers de la Compagnie Madeleine Renaud-Jean-Louis Barrault* ⟨Workbooks of the Madeleine Renaud-Jean-Louis Barrault Company⟩ (no. 36 [November, 1961], pp. 53-58).

See at 44/43 the text of the tribute Sartre wrote to Giraudoux when he died.

40/NOTE 1.

For BARIONA, the Christmas play Sartre wrote and had put on when he was a prisoner of war in Trèves, look under the date of publication (62/368).

40/NOTE 2.

In *The Prime of Life*, p. 340, Simone de Beauvoir reproduces a very interesting fragment of a letter in which Sartre talks about his army life and THE AGE OF REASON, and she adds in a note, "Paulhan sent this letter on to Adrienne Monnier, who wanted to publish the fragment I quote in some bulletin or other." This refers to a letter dated February 23, 1940, and addressed directly to Adrienne Monnier to thank her for sending issue 9 of *La Gazette des amis des livres* (a bulletin she published in her bookstore, "Aux Amis des Livres," 7, rue de l'Odéon). Adrienne Monnier asked Sartre to publish part of the letter in a coming issue of *La Gazette*, but Sartre for obvious reasons refused.

Sartre sent several other letters to Adrienne Monnier

40/NOTE 2.

and had dedicated copies of NAUSEA and THE WALL sent to her when they came out. All of these documents are preserved in the Jacques Doucet Library.

40/NOTE 3.

In April, 1940, a jury consisting of Georges Duhamel, Daniel Halévy, Léon Lemonnier, Jules Romains, André Thérive, etc., awarded--on the second ballot and by a nine-to-four majority--the Roman Populiste prize to Sartre for THE WALL and his work as a whole. With the prize money (5000 francs), Sartre bought himself (they say) a suit.

1941

41/31

Sartre wrote two or three pieces in the underground report put out by the "Socialism and Liberty" group in 1941. This report, which had only a few issues, seems to have been lost beyond recall. The *Catalogue des périodiques clandestins diffusés en France de 1939 à 1945*, published by the Bibliothèque Nationale, does not mention it. It has no connection with the journal, *Socialisme et liberté*, an S.F.I.O. ⟨French Branch of the Workers' International⟩ organ, which was circulated in the Northern Zone after December, 1941, and which subsequently became *Le Populaire*.

In an article entitled "Le Sartre que je connais" ⟨The Sartre I Knew⟩ (*Jeune Afrique*, November 8, 1964), Dominique Desanti, who was active in the group, speaks about it by the name of "Liberty and Socialism" and provides some interesting information. She reveals particularly that the group included Marxists like herself and non-Marxists, and that Sartre let the representatives of the two tendencies take turns editing the journal.

Simone de Beauvoir told in *The Prime of Life* (pp. 382-83, 396) about the ephemeral existence of this intellectuals' resistance group which Sartre had started in the spring of 1941 along with (among others) Maurice Merleau-Ponty, Jacques-Laurent Bost, Jean Pouillon, and herself. She says of the first editorial Sartre wrote, " . . . The possibility of a defeat also had to be considered, and in his first report Sartre claimed that if Germany won the war, we would have to see to it that she lost the peace."

In the fall, Sartre made contact with the Communists but met with their suspicion. Shortly afterward they started the rumor that the Germans had freed him so that he could be their *agent provocateur*. The group found itself completely isolated, and Sartre took it upon himself to break it up, judging that its real importance was completely out of proportion with the risks its members were running (see also DISCUSSIONS OF POLITICS, Gallimard edition, p. 70).

41/31

Sartre has told us that it was during the time of "Socialism and Liberty" that he set down his ideas concerning the postwar future of Europe, even drawing up a proposed constitution.

41/32

* *"Moby Dick" d'Herman Melville: Plus qu'un chef-d'oeuvre, un formidable monument* ⟨Herman Melville's *Moby Dick*: More Than a Masterpiece, An Imposing Monument⟩, essay.

-- *Comoedia*, n.s., no. 1 (June 21, 1941).

Moby Dick, translated by Martin Noble.

-- *Adam International Review*, nos. 343-45 (1970), pp. 86-88.

The first article Sartre wrote after his return from captivity for the new *Comoedia*, whose literary column he had agreed to write. That was the end of his collaboration, because "the basic rule which all the intellectuals of the Resistance were agreed upon was 'No writing for Occupied Zone publications'" (*The Prime of Life*, p. 385).

This is an introduction to Melville's great novel, whose French translation by Jean Giono was the major literary event of 1941. Sartre picks holes in Giono's preface in the process.

1942

42/33

* *La Mort dans l'âme* ⟨Sick at Heart⟩, pages from a journal.

-- In *Exercice du silence* ⟨Studied Silences⟩. Brussels, 1942. Published December 10, 1942. Publisher, Jean Annotiau, rue Marché-aux-Herbes, 61, Brussels. Copyright by Librairie du Centre. Nonpaginated work (Sartre's text covers 15 pages).

B.N. listing: *Messages* 8° z. 29291 (1942, III).

In addition to Sartre's text, *Studied Silences* contains pages from, among others, Gaston Bachelard, Paul Eluard, Jean Tardieu, Gabriel Audisio, Raymond Queneau, André Frénaud, Arthur Adamov, Michel Leiris, Jean Lescure, and Georges Bataille. Although it does not say so anywhere, this volume is the fifth in the new series of the journal *Messages* (Cahiers de la poésie française), edited by Jean Lescure. The first were printed in Paris at the outset of the war, *Studied Silences* in Brussels, and the following, *French Territory*, in Geneva.

This totally unknown text, which bears the same title as the last published volume of *Roads to Freedom*,[1] is very valuable. It consists of two extracts from Sartre's war diary, dated June 10 and June 11, 1940. They describe his direct experience of the rout of the French Army. What is fascinating about this text, as compared to the novel, is that it is the only autobiographical one which allows us to study the way in which a personal experience is transformed into

---

1. For the novel that is also entitled LA MORT DANS L'ÂME see 49/179.

literature. The quality of these pages gives us a good idea of the worth of the war notebooks lost by Jacques-Laurent Bost, to whom Sartre had given them after his unit had been put to flight. Sartre had tried to come to terms with his past life in them, as well as beginning the first draft of what was to become BEING AND NOTHINGNESS. A certain number of these notebooks were found by a doctor who wrote to Sartre in 1950 to tell him that he had them, but Sartre forgot to get them back. Later other notebooks which had been found were offered him for money, and Sartre, finding the business distasteful, did not follow up the offer.

1943

43/34

L'ÊTRE ET LE NÉANT: *Essai d'ontologie phénoménologique* ⟨Being and Nothingness: An Essay on Phenomenological Ontology⟩.

a) Bibliothèque des idées series. Gallimard,[1943]. 724 pages. Dedicated "Au Castor" ⟨To the Beaver⟩ [Simone de Beauvoir]. Published June 25, 1943. Several reprintings since 1947.

In 1945, the volume was sold in bookstores encircled by a band advertising it, for which Sartre had found the following catch phrase: "What counts in a vase is the hollow at the heart of it."

b) Gallimard,[1947]. Edition bound according to Colette Duhamel's maquette. Limited to 1040 copies on esparto grass.

BEING AND NOTHINGNESS: *An Essay on Phenomenological Ontology*, translated by Hazel E. Barnes.

t1) Major section published under the title EXISTENTIAL PSYCHOANALYSIS. With an introduction by Hazel E. Barnes. New York: Philosophical Library, 1953.

t2) *Ibid.* With an introduction by Rollo May. New York: Gateway Books, 1962.

t3) Excerpt. "The Caress," translated by Kenneth Douglas. *Yale French Studies*, no. 16 (1955-56), pp. 96-99.

t4) Complete version. With an introduction by Hazel E. Barnes. New York: Philosophical Library, 1956; London: Methuen, 1957. Index.

t5) *Ibid.* in paperback. New York: Washington Square Press, 1966; London: Methuen, 1966.

t6) Special abridged edition. With an introduction by Hazel E. Barnes. New York: Citadel Press, 1964.

Numerous excerpts from BEING AND NOTHINGNESS have appeared in other publications, for instance in the very useful anthology *The Philosophy of Jean-Paul Sartre*, edited and with an introduction by Robert Denoon Cumming (New York: Random House, 1965; Vintage Books, 1972; London: Methuen, 1968).

The translation by Hazel E. Barnes is probably the best that could be done under the circumstances.

BEING AND NOTHINGNESS is the upshot of philosophical investigations Sartre had begun in 1933. This explains how he was able to draft this monumental work in less than two years and, it seems, with great ease. The pages in Simone de Beauvoir's memoirs which tell about the period during which it was being written make only brief allusions to Sartre's labors, and it must be stressed that during this same period he wrote THE REPRIEVE and THE FLIES, all the while teaching at the Lycée Condorcet, which is a rather stupefying performance and gives us an idea of what Sartre means by the *full use of oneself.*

The project to write BEING AND NOTHINGNESS seems to have been formed in 1939, during the "phony" war when Sartre, who had been called up, used his long periods of free time to fill notebooks which were subsequently lost (see 42/33). He had in particular outlined a philosophy book whose broad dimensions he set forth to Simone de Beauvoir while he was on leave in April, 1940 (see *The Prime of Life*, p. 346). He continued to think about it during his captivity by giving a course on Heidegger (whose works he had been able to get) to a group of priests. After he was released, the first thing he did was to finish THE AGE OF REASON, and it was only in the fall of 1941 that he began to write BEING AND NOTHINGNESS. Sartre has told us that he used certain analyses from his psychological treatise "The Psyche" (see 39/22), but that he had, as always, rewritten and recast them completely for BEING AND NOTHINGNESS.

Finished at the beginning of 1943, the book came out during the summer and, given the circumstances, went more or less unnoticed. It was not until 1945, the year when the sudden fad for Sartre called more attention to his master work than any previous philosophical work had ever known, that the commentators seized on the book--and even then it was generally misunderstood. Yet the book had had since it first came out a small number of devoted readers who were aware from the start of its importance and novelty. Witness, for example, André Gorz in *Le Traître* ⟨The Traitor⟩ (Seuil, 1959, pp. 245-46) or the following lines from Michel Tournier: "One fall day in 1943 a book fell on our workdesks: BEING AND NOTHINGNESS. There was a moment of stupefaction, then a long period of reflection. The work was massive, hirsute, overflowing, irresistible in its strength, filled with exquisite subtleties, encyclopedic, superbly technical, and characterized throughout by an insight of diamantine simplicity. The antiphilosophical riffraff was already starting to raise a hue and cry in the papers. There could be no doubt about it: a new system had been born" (*Les Nouvelles littéraires*, October 29, 1964).

It is obviously out of the question to try here to give a general introduction to a work which has been the object of innumerable studies and which has been relatively well commented on. And even though there are still misunderstandings about it, we could not hope to clear them up in a short note. So we shall limit ourselves to a few summary comments.

The first thing we might point out is that BEING AND NOTHINGNESS has the (we think mistaken) reputation of being a book which is unapproachable for the nonspecialized reader. Although the book does require a certain effort, once the terminological difficulties have been overcome, it is perfectly easy to read and soon becomes intriguing, above all because of its numerous concrete analyses of situations from everyday life. Just reading the book will, moreover, provide the minimum familiarity with philosophical technique which is necessary to understand it fully. So it is much more preferable to read BEING AND NOTHINGNESS (perhaps using THE EMOTIONS: OUTLINE OF A THEORY for an introduction) than to curry second-hand works for information which will be partial at best and, at worst, misleading.

On the other hand, the subsequent development of Sartre's thought enables us to put the book into proper perspective by situating it in his overall work as a fundamental stage on the basis of which he was subsequently able to go dialectically beyond it. Thus a prior reading of *Search for a Method* can illuminate the implicit horizon of BEING AND NOTHINGNESS by adding the almost completely lacking dimension of history and class struggle. Thus we can avoid the frequent mistake of seeing this book as an expression of radical pessimism and particularly of taking its analysis of our originally conflicting relationships with others to be a universal and necessary condition stemming from a tragic vision of human existence.

Sartre has only rarely and always incidentally come back to BEING AND NOTHINGNESS; he has never doubted its essential conclusions. A footnote to his CRITIQUE OF DIALECTICAL REASON (Gallimard edition pp. 285-86), moreoever, explicitly links the problem of his second great philosophical work to that of his first, at the

43/34

same time clearly pointing out the way in which he has enlarged upon and developed it, and warning us about the mistaken interpretation BEING AND NOTHINGNESS can give rise to. In an important discussion in 1965 (see 65/430), he addressed himself to the criticism that he had used a too literary language in BEING AND NOTHINGNESS, and had thereby laid himself open to misunderstanding. We must also call attention to the expression *eidetic of bad faith*, which Sartre used to characterize BEING AND NOTHINGNESS in 1961 (see SITUATIONS, IV, p. 196). This expression clearly indicates the limitations of the work: in this first step, Sartre is basing his phenomenology of consciousness on an analysis of the patterns of behavior in which individuals viewed in a psychological and intellectual perspective manifest their basic alienation, but he is not yet aware of the historical and social causes of that alienation, and this is precisely what he will try with increasing precision to do in all of his subsequent work.

In reference to the "Ethics" announced at the close of this work, see 49/179, 49/187, and 49/192.

43/35

LES MOUCHES ⟨The Flies⟩, a play in three acts.

a) First edition. Gallimard, [1943]. 145 pages. Printing date: December, 1942. Placed on sale in April, 1943. 18 copies on wood-free finish and 550 copies on Héliona finish. Dedication: "To Charles Dullin in witness to his recognition and his friendship."

b) Excerpt (act 2, tableau 1, complete and unchanged) in *Confluences*, 3d Year, no. 19 (April-May, 1943), pp. 371-91.

c) Reprinted in THÉÂTRE, I (1947).

d) Reprinted in THÉÂTRE (1962).

e) Edition intended to go with the foreign performances of the Tréteau de Paris. Gallimard, [1962]. 121 pages.

f) American textbook edition. Annotated and with a good introduction by F. C. St.-Aubyn and Robert G. Marshall. New York: Harper & Row, [1963].

g) British textbook edition. Well-documented introduction and notes by Robert J. North. London: George G. Harrap, [1963].

h) Reprinted in HUIS CLOS ⟨No Exit⟩, followed by LES MOUCHES. Le Livre de poche series, no. 1132. Gallimard, [1964].

i) Edition *(h)* supplanted by HUIS CLOS, followed by LES MOUCHES. Folio series, no. 3. Gallimard, [1972].

THE FLIES, translated by Stuart Gilbert.

t1) THE FLIES *and* IN CAMERA. London: Hamish Hamilton, [1946].

t2) NO EXIT *and* THE FLIES. New York: Alfred A. Knopf, [1947].

t3) Paperback. NO EXIT *and Three Other Plays* [THE FLIES; DIRTY HANDS; THE RESPECTFUL PROSTITUTE]. New York: Vintage Books, [1955].

t4) Paperback. ALTONA; MEN WITHOUT SHADOWS; THE FLIES. Penguin Books, [1962].

The request to publish edition *(b)*, drawn up by Sartre, reads:

Tragedy is the mirror of Destiny. I have not found it impossible to write a tragedy of freedom, since the classical Fatum is only freedom turned inside out-- Orestes is free to commit a crime and free beyond his crime: I showed him stalked by freedom as Oedipus is stalked by destiny. He struggles in its steely grip, but he has to end by killing, hoisting his murder onto his own shoulders, and carrying it to the other side. For freedom is not some abstract power to fly high above the human condition; it's our most absurd and inexorable human commitment. Orestes will go down that road of his, unjustifiable, without excuses, without recourse, alone. Like a hero. Like anybody.

THE FLIES is the only play Sartre called a "drama." It was first staged on June 3, 1943, at the Théâtre de la Cité (which before the Occupation had been the Théâtre Sarah-Bernhardt) with a production by Charles Dullin and settings by Henri-Georges Adam. Principal roles:

JUPITER	Charles Dullin
ORESTES	Jean Lannier
AEGISTHUS	H. Norbert
ELECTRA	Olga Dominique

It was during a production of the *Choephori* (produced by Jean-Louis Barrault, music by Honegger, and settings by Labisse) during the summer of 1941 that Sartre, encouraged by Olga Kosakiewicz and other friends, got the idea for the play. In a letter to Adrienne Monnier, dated July, 1942, he writes: *I'd also be happy if you'd come to the dress rehearsal of that play you read and I have finally decided to set my name to. That will be at the beginning of November, I hope.* Jean-Louis Barrault, who originally

43/35

had been sounded out for the production, backed out, and it was Charles Dullin who, in spite of the twists and turns of the Néron business (see *The Prime of Life*, pp. 408-41), assumed responsibility for the play and succeeded in getting it going.

THE FLIES was announced in an interview with Sartre in *Comoedia* (see below) and in an article by Dullin in *La Gerbe* (June 3, 1943). The twenty-five performances scheduled had a rather ambiguous success, and the *Comoedia* of June 19, 1943, was able to note:

"The production of *The Flies* at the Théâtre de la Cité provoked 'varied stirrings' of artistic opinion. The great majority of critics judged Jean-Paul Sartre's work harshly. . . .

"Yet the repercussions of *The Flies* have been deep, not only in intellectual circles but among the young who saw it as making contact with a new world and had a feeling of discovery.

"So we shall begin a debate about *The Flies* in the near future."

Because of the censor, the anticipated debate was never published, but the play was put on again in the fall in 1943 and reprinted in January, 1944. Most critics at the time ignored the political meaning of the work and tackled it on the aesthetic level, especially reproaching it for being second-rate Giraudoux. The most unfavorable reviews were those by Alain Laubreaux (*Le Petit Parisien*, June 5, 1943; *L'Oeuvre*, June 7; *Je suis partout*, June 11), by Roland Purnal (*Comoedia*, June 12) and above all by André Castelot (*La Gerbe*, June 17). The review by Frédérique Straub in the French section of the *Pariser Zeitung* (June 17) was not hostile and mainly stressed the formal defects of the play. The most perceptive reviews were written by Michel Leiris (the underground edition of *Les Lettres françaises*, no. 12, reprinted with some revisions in *Brisées* ⟨Spoor⟩ [Mercure de France, pp. 74-78]) and by Maurice Merleau-Ponty (*Confluences*, no. 25 [September-October, 1943], pp. 514-16).

Sartre himself has made many statements about the play which enable us to be more precise about his intentions:

43/36

"Ce que nous dit Jean-Paul Sartre de sa première pièce" ⟨What Jean-Paul Sartre Says about His First Play⟩, interview by Yvon Novy.

-- *Comoedia*, April 24, 1943.

I wanted to deal with the tragedy of freedom as contrasted to the tragedy of fate. In other words, the subject of my play could be summed up this way: "How does a man behave when he has committed an act whose consequences and responsibilities he fully accepts, yet which still horrifies him? . . . It is clear that when the problem is put this way it is incompatible with the principle that man is only inwardly free, which certain philosophers--and not the least important--such as Bergson sought to make the source of all our successful efforts to liberate ourselves from fate. Such a freedom is still theoretical and spiritual. . . . The man who has risen above himself to the point of being free in his consciousness will not become free in his actual situation unless he establishes freedom for others, unless his act results in the disappearance of an existing state of things and the reestablishment of what ought to be. . . .

If I had invented my hero, the horror he would have provoked would have condemned him unmercifully to being misunderstood. That is why I fell back on a character who was already situated in our theatrical tradition. I had no choice!

Much of this interview must be read between the lines. Sartre avoids speaking directly of the political content of the play, but he nevertheless alludes to it very clearly.

In an interview he gave to *Carrefour* a few days after the liberation of Paris (see 44/52), Sartre attacks plays with mythological subjects (*These plays are of an inferior type, symbolic plays*) and adds: *Why make the Greeks speak . . . if not to disguise one's real thinking under a fascist regime? . . . The real drama, the one I would have liked to write, is that of the terrorist who shoots Germans down in the street and causes fifty hostages to be shot.*

From June, 1940, the Vichy regime had tried to impose its policy of contrition on the French. Addressing himself to the nation, Philippe Pétain-Egisthe declared on June 17, 1941: "You are suffering now and you will continue to suffer for a long time yet because we have not yet paid for all our sins." (*La France nouvelle* ⟨The New France⟩ [Fasquelle, 1941, p. 167]). During a discussion of THE FLIES held in Berlin (see 48/161), Sartre confirms that he wrote his play in order to *extirpate somewhat this sickness of repenting, this complacency of repentance and shame*, and he goes on:

At that time the French people needed to be put back on their feet again, encouraged.

43/36

Orestes is that small group of Frenchmen who carried out attacks on the Germans and subsequently bore this anguish of repentance within themselves, but resisted the temptation to go turn themselves in.

When THE FLIES was revived at the Vieux-Colombier in January, 1951, Sartre drew up the following text:

51/37

Ce que fut la création des "Mouches" ⟨What the Staging of THE FLIES Was Like⟩.

-- *Le Figaro*, January 11, 1951.

Complete text:

For me, my play THE FLIES *is wrapped up with my memories of Charles Dullin. He had to have a lot of courage to agree to put this play on. To begin with, I was an unknown author, and then among its other meanings* THE FLIES *was a "political play." It was 1943 and Vichy wanted to mire us deeper in repentance and shame. In writing* THE FLIES, *I tried with the small means available to me to help extirpate somewhat this sickness of repenting, this giving in to shame that they were trying to get out of us.*

The collaborators were not deceived by the play. Violent press campaigns quickly obliged the Théâtre Sarah-Bernhardt to remove the play from the playbill, and the man who was our greatest director got no compensation for his remarkable labors. But the interest Charles Dullin was to show in my first play was to be the most precious encouragement to me.

It is not impossible that this text-- which gives an approximate version of several facts--was the one read during a tribute to Charles Dullin at the Atelier in February, 1950. Sartre has associated THE FLIES and Dullin in many texts (see 47/129 and 66/443), and in particular in a recent interview (see 68/487):

My dialogue was wordy. Dullin, without reproaching me for it or even advising cuts at first, made me understand by simply talking to the actors that a play should be just the opposite of an orgy of eloquence--that is, the smallest possible number of words cemented irresistibly by an irreversible action and a restless passion.

Like BEING AND NOTHINGNESS, the work could be defined as an *eidetic of bad faith* (see 43/34). This seems to be the perspective in which we should interpret the character of Orestes today and clear up the ambiguity hovering about the end of the play. Orestes does in fact represent the *prise de conscience* of a freedom which chooses to escape bad faith. But the solitary act of heroism in which this freedom is affirmed is a means to personal salvation rather than to practical liberation. This attitude corresponds to Sartre's at a time when he still thought of commitment as an individual moral problem. Sartre did not really get beyond this conception until later on when he realized that the ethic he was developing threatened to be no more than a *writer's ethic*.

The best documented study of THE FLIES is that of the Swede Thure Stenström, pp. 190-260 of the volume *Existentialismen* ⟨Existentialism⟩ (Stockholm: Natur och Kultur, 1966). Stenström gives much unpublished information he got from conversations he had with Sartre and Simone de Beauvoir in June, 1965, and points out that the historical sources of the play might be two works which came out in 1942: *Archaic Roman Religion* by Georges Dumézil, and *The Etruscans and Their Civilization* by V. Basanoff.

Sartre himself went to Czechoslovakia at the beginning of December, 1968, to attend a performance of THE FLIES and thereby express his solidarity with the Czech people. It should be pointed out, however, that this performance had already been scheduled before the Russian troops intervened.

See also 47/130 and 48/161.

43/38

L'Age de raison ⟨The Age of Reason⟩, excerpt from THE AGE OF REASON, novel to be published by Gallimard.

-- In *Domaine français, "Messages,"* ⟨French Territory, *Messages*⟩. Geneva and Paris: Trois Collines, [August], 1943. Pp. 51-60.

Published in Geneva by Jean Lescure and François Lachenal, who was the Swiss publisher of some of the most important writings of the Resistance, this collection of writings by most of the French antifascist writers contains the episode in THE AGE OF REASON in which Brunet suggests that Mathieu join the Communist Party (pp. 126-32 of the future Gallimard edition). *Domaine français* cites on its cover the previous publications of the journal *Messages*, including the *Pages from a Journal* in *Studied Silences* (see 42/33), which explains why this text sometimes appears under the wrong title in bibliographies. The volume also contains an article "Signification de Sartre" ⟨The Significance of Sartre⟩ (pp. 415-26), written by one of Sartre's former students, the future filmmaker Alexandre Astruc.

43/39

Explication de "L'Etranger" ⟨An Analysis of *The Stranger*⟩, essay.

a) *Cahiers du Sud*, no. 253 (February, 1943), pp. 189-206.

b) Book. Sceaux: Le Palimugre, 1946. See 46/97.

c) Reprinted in SITUATIONS, I.

Camus's "The Outsider," translated by Annette Michelson.

-- In LITERARY AND PHILOSOPHICAL ESSAYS (1955) and other volumes.

This text, which is basic to an understanding of Albert Camus, was written in September, 1942. Note that Sartre will not meet Camus until a few months later, at the dress rehearsal of THE FLIES (see 52/223).

43/40

* *Drieu la Rochelle ou la haine de soi* ⟨Drieu la Rochelle, or Self-Hatred⟩.

a) *Les Lettres françaises* (clandestine), no. 6 (April, 1943). Mimeographed. Unsigned.

b) Excerpt in Frédéric Grover. *Drieu la Rochelle.* Bibliothèque idéale series. Gallimard,[1962]. P. 224.

The unsigned articles Sartre wrote for the underground issues of *Les Lettres françaises* are authenticated in the *Lettres françaises clandestines* album (B.N. listing: Rés. Gr. Z. 200), which in 1947 reproduced a facsimile of the twenty issues published during the Occupation by the C.N.E. ⟨National Writers' Union⟩, whose organ was *Les Lettres françaises* and which Sartre belonged to beginning in January, 1943 (for Sartre's collaboration with the underground *Lettres françaises*, see DISCUSSIONS OF POLITICS, Gallimard edition, pp. 71-74).

Sartre shows the logic of the choice which led Drieu la Rochelle to collaboration. Some of the ideas in this article will be taken up again in *What Is Literature?* (SITUATIONS, II, p. 228).

43/41

"Aminadab" ou du fantastique considéré comme un langage ⟨*Aminadab*, or The Fantastic Considered as a Language⟩, essay.

a) Cahiers du Sud, no. 255 (April, 1943), pp. 299-305; no. 256 (May, 1943), pp. 361-71.

b) Reprinted in SITUATIONS, I.

"Aminadab," or The Fantastic Considered as a Language, translated by Annette Michelson.

-- In LITERARY AND PHILOSOPHICAL ESSAYS (1955) and other volumes.

Important critical study in which Sartre reaches a general definition of the fantastic in comparing Maurice Blanchot to Franz Kafka.

43/41 A

Les Chats ⟨The Cats⟩, excerpt from THE AGE OF REASON, novel to be published by Gallimard.

-- *L'Arbalète* (Lyon), no. 7 (summer, 1943). 14 pages.

Issue printed in August, 1943, with 425 copies.

This excerpt is one of the best passages in THE AGE OF REASON, the one in which Daniel is going to drown his cats (pp. 89-98 of the Gallimard edition; see 45/60).

43/42

Un Nouveau Mystique ⟨A New Mystic⟩.

a) Cahiers du Sud, no. 260 (October, 1943), pp. 782-90; no. 261 (November, 1943), pp. 866-86; no. 262 (December, 1943), pp. 988-94.

b) Reprinted in SITUATIONS, I.

Another major study. In analyzing Georges Bataille's *The Experience Within*, Sartre attacks the author's faithless mysticism and challenges in passing Emile Durkheim's sociology and Freud's psychoanalysis.

On Bataille, see 45/62.

1944

44/43

Tribute to Jean Giraudoux.

a) Comoedia, February 5, 1944.

b) Reprinted in *Voici la France de ce mois*, no. 49 (March, 1944), pp. 10-11.

c) L'Esprit créateur, IX, no. 2 (summer, 1969), 71.

On the occasion of Giraudoux's death on January 31, 1944, *Comoedia* gathered together, under the general title "Tributes to Giraudoux," brief texts by Colette, Paul Valéry, Marcel Arland, Alexandre Arnoux, Jacques Audiberti, Fernand Crommelynck, Edouard Bourdet, Jean Cocteau, Léon-Paul Fargue, Daniel Halévy, Jean Grenier, Marcel Jouhandeau, Henri Mondor, Jean-Louis Vaudoyer, and Sartre.

We reprint below the complete (and up till now practically unknown) text, in which Sartre pays tribute to a writer he felt affection for in spite of the distance between them. And yet the influence of Giraudoux's style is evident in his first two plays, BARIONA and THE FLIES.

Somebody said about someone else, in Giraudoux's presence, "He's a fair-weather friend"; and he replied, "We have to hold firm, and then he'll become a real friend." Somebody asked him how to make a good movie without losing sight of the needs of the movie business and he answered, "Don't think about anything except doing a good job; a good movie is always a commercial success." I don't know whether he was right, but his ideas of what was right came from the depths of his being, from that metaphysical optimism which holds that every really efficacious force can only produce good and that "the worst is not sure to happen." But if it was hard to do wrong in Giraudoux's pagan world,

> *it wasn't because an all-powerful God kept men from it, but because things took care of themselves. A rare harmony united men and stones, animals, and other men. Each was concerned only with realizing his own essence, but at the same time he realized the essence of the world. And this equilibrium of human nature and the forces of the earth, the sun, and the water was called happiness. Events seemed to prove Giraudoux wrong and he stepped aside, taking with him the keys to this useless world which men no longer wished to enter. And yet his "vacation time" books, which were written in happiness ("I write," he said, "to have a good time"), don't speak to us of happiness in vain. Nothing is lost. They are still there, anachronistic yet bearing witness to the time. The old values of measure, order, reason, and humanism which he rediscovered are still--now that he is dead--"offered." All the violence we are doing won't stop them from existing and from being called Bella, Fontranges, Eglantine, and from still being--whatever the road we choose tomorrow--like an opportunity which is still possible or a regret which is still beautiful--or maybe like a twinge of remorse.*

44/44

Aller et retour ⟨Departure and Return⟩.

a) Les Cahiers du Sud, no. 264 (February, 1944), pp. 117-33; no. 265 (March, 1944), pp. 248-70.

b) Reprinted in SITUATIONS, I.

The Journey and the Return or *Departure and Return*.

t1) The Journey and the Return. In J. L. Hevesi, ed. *Essays on Language and Literature.* London: Allan Wingate, 1947; Port Washington, N.Y.: Kennikat Press, 1967. Pp. 143-206.

t2) Departure and Return, translated by Annette Michelson. In LITERARY AND PHILOSOPHICAL ESSAYS (1955).

> Devoted to the works of Brice Parain, whose *The Metaphysics of Language* had come out two years earlier, this long article may be considered a sort of outline of Sartre's subsequent applications of existential method to the study of a way of thinking. In it he describes Brice Parain's itinerary and relates it both to the personal history of this *paysan déraciné* and to literary progress between the two wars. After an exposition which shows his evident ability to grasp someone else's thought thoroughly and sympathetically, Sartre subjects Brice Parain to basic criticism in the closing pages. He accuses him of misunderstanding the nature of language as "being-for-others" (let us remember the phrase, *Language is nothing but existing in the presence of others*) and of basing his doctrine

44/44

on outmoded theoretical principles. He says in conclusion that it is above all Brice Parain's ethic, which is close to Albert Camus's, which touches the younger generation.

Sartre had known Brice Parain since 1934 and, in the words of this article, had carried on *a long and friendly dialogue* with him. We know the decisive role Parain played in Gallimard's publication of NAUSEA. After the war, the relationship between the two grew more remote for political reasons, and Brice Parain attacked Sartre violently in 1956 for having pulled his punches for political reasons in denouncing the Russian intervention in Hungary (see his article, "Sartre a parlé,"*Monde nouveau*, December, 1956).

44/45

La Littérature, cette liberté ⟨Literature, That Freedom⟩.

--*Les Lettres françaises* (clandestine), no. 15 (April, 1944), p. 8. Unsigned.

Here Sartre tries to show why the writers who are collaborators do not and cannot have talent (an idea we will find again in *What Is Literature?*): literature, being an act of communication, requires and assumes the reader's freedom. *Literature is not an innocent and facile lyric capable of accommodating itself to any sort of régime, but by its very nature confronts us with the political problem: to write is to demand that all men be free, and if a work is not the act of a freedom which wants to get itself recognized by other freedoms, it is nothing but infamous gossip.* Now the paradox of pro-German writers is that they write for a muzzled audience whom they want to enslave still further yet could not possibly do without: . . . *it is clear that they do not like to write, that they even hate literature, because in their hearts they know they have no talent.*

The implicit example again seems to be Drieu la Rochelle.

44/46

Un Film pour l'après-guerre ⟨The Kind of Movie that We Need When the War is Over⟩.

-- *L'Ecran français,* incorporated in *Les Lettres françaises* (clandestine), no. 15 (April, 1944), pp. 3-4. Unsigned.

We know how much Sartre admired the movies of D. W. Griffith and King Vidor. Referring to these examples as evidence that the privileged calling of the movies is to be mass art, the sole art capable of showing the individual in his whole social situation, Sartre deplores the mystifying intimacy the movies have strayed into (*They've confined this giant to painting miniatures*) and hopes that after the war there will be great social frescoes on the Occupation and Resistance which will renew the deepest calling of the movies: *In this way the liberation of the movies will go hand in hand with the liberation of territory.*

44/47

HUIS CLOS, *pièce en un acte* ⟨No Exit, a Play in One Act⟩.

a) Published under the title *Les Autres* ⟨The Others⟩. *L'Arbalète*, no. 8 (spring, 1944), pp. 37-80.

This issue of *L'Arbalète*, published in Lyon by Marc Barbezat, had 1,100 copies printed in April, 1944; it also includes texts by Jean Genet (selections from *Our Lady of the Flowers*) and Mouloudji (*In Remembrance of Barbary*). *The Others* is dedicated to Mme Louis Morel (who appears as Mme Lemaire in Simone de Beauvoir's memoirs).

The text is from the Gallimard edition, with a few changes in punctuation and the substitution of *want* for *can* in one of Garcin's lines (see THÉÂTRE, I, p. 178). Let us point out in this connection that Inez' question preceding this line does read, "*Do you really want to convince me?*" and not, "*You really can convince me,*" as in the Livre de poche edition, p. 71.

b) HUIS CLOS, *pièce en un acte.* Gallimard,[1945]. 125 pages.

Printing date: March 19, 1945. Dedicated enigmatically "To that Lady." 24 copies on Madagascar and 2,250 on *châtaignier* finish.

c) London edition with a French text. Horizon French Texts, 1945. 59 pages. 500 copies printed in October, 1945.

d) Text *(b)* reprinted in THÉÂTRE,I (1947).

e) Text *(b)* reprinted in THÉÂTRE (1962).

f) American textbook edition, annotated by Jacques Hardré and George B. Daniel. New York: Appleton-Century-Crofts, [1962]; London: Methuen, [1962].

g) Edition to accompany the Trêteau de Paris performances abroad. Gallimard, [1962]. 62 pages.

h) HUIS CLOS, followed by LES MOUCHES ⟨The Flies⟩.

Le Livre de poche series, no. 1132. Gallimard, [1964].

i) Dutch textbook edition. Sketchily presented by Aldert Walrecht. Zutphen: W. J. Thieme, [1969].

j) Edition *(h)* supplanted by HUIS CLOS, followed by LES MOUCHES. Folio series, no. 3. Gallimard, [1972].

NO EXIT, or IN CAMERA.

t1) Adapted as *Vicious Circle* for the London stage by Marjorie Gabain and Joan Swinstead, 1946.

t2) Adapted as *Vicious Circle* for the New York stage by Paul Bowles, 1946.

Book. New York: Samuel French, [1958].

t3) For translation by Stuart Gilbert, see THE FLIES (43/35).

t4) NO EXIT *and Three Other Plays* [THE FLIES; DIRTY HANDS; THE RESPECTFUL PROSTITUTE], translated by Lionel Abel. New York: Vintage Books, [1955].

The play led, furthermore, to:

-- A movie by Jacqueline Audry (1954). Adaptation and additional dialogues by Pierre Laroche. There is a 214-page script covering 166 shots (see Appendix);

-- *No Exit*, an Argentine movie by Pedro Escudero and Tad Danielewski (1962);

-- A televised version by Michel Mitrani, with Michel Auclair, Judith Magre, and Evelyne Rey in the leading roles, which the O.R.T.F. ⟨French Radio-Television⟩ broadcast in October, 1965;

-- A recording by Deutsche Grammophon Gesellschaft (no. 43902/03, 1965) with the voices of Michel Vitold, Christiane Lenier, Gaby Sylvia and R.-J. Chauffard as well as a preface by Jean-Paul Sartre read by the author (see below).

And finally, let us point out that a certain J. C. P. Alberts felt the imperious need to complete Sartre's work with additional scenes in a brochure appropriately entitled *The Open Door/De Open Hel* (The Hague, 1949).

> NO EXIT was first performed at the Théâtre du Vieux-Colombier on May 27, 1944, under the direction of Raymond Rouleau, with settings by Max Douy. The first reviews do not begin till June 4, and Simone de Beauvoir gives June 10 as the date of the dress rehearsal. Cast:
>
> INEZ Tania Balachova
> ESTELLE Gaby Sylvia

GARCIN	Michel Vitold
THE WAITER	R.-J. Chauffard

The play, which was put on along with P.-J. Toulet's *The Interrupted Meal*, was an immediate and great success, and was revived beginning at the end of August, 1944, along with André Roussin's *Achilles' Tomb*. Today it is considered a classic and has had numerous revivals on Parisian stages. In September, 1946, it was banned by the censor in Britain (where it was nevertheless performed in private clubs under the title *Vicious Circle*) but it was a success in the United States, where it received the Donaldson Prize for the best play performed in New York in 1946-47.

According to Simone de Beauvoir (*The Prime of Life*, pp. 438-39), it was Marc Barbezat who suggested that Sartre write a play for his future wife, Olga, and for Wanda Kosakiewicz that would be "easy to stage and could be taken on tour all over the country. . . . The idea of writing a short play, with a single set and two or three characters only, intrigued Sartre. He at once thought of a situation *in camera*, as it were: a group of people shut up in a cellar during a long bombardment. Then he had the inspired notion of placing his characters in Hell, for all eternity."

In the early fall of 1943, Sartre stopped editing THE REPRIEVE and wrote the play very quickly in a fortnight. Originally, NO EXIT was to be the curtain-raiser for a road show organized in the Free Zone by Marc Barbezat and Marc Beigbeder. After having sounded out Sylvain Itkine, Sartre then suggested to Albert Camus--whom he had met at the dress rehearsal of THE FLIES--that he handle the directing and play the role of Garcin himself. Camus agreed to, and the first rehearsals took place in Simone de Beauvoir's room with Wanda Kosakiewicz, Olga Barbezat, and Chauffard, a former student of Sartre. The project to go on tour fell through after they ran into financial difficulty and Olga Barbezat was arrested. The play was then accepted by Annet Badel, an industrialist who had just become the director of the Théâtre du Vieux-Colombier. After Camus had withdrawn, Badel entrusted the directing to Raymond Rouleau and hired professional actors; only Chauffard was left from the original group.

NO EXIT obviously illustrates the ideas Sartre developed in the chapter of BEING AND NOTHINGNESS "Concrete Relationships with the Other." People have also seen in it the possible influence of Sutton Vane's *Outward Bound* on the beginning and of Strindberg's *Dance of Death* on the denouement. The problems of interpretation presented by the play have not always been satisfactorily resolved. Catholic criticism, especially, has taken the expression *Hell is other people* too literally and interpreting it in a doggedly nondialectical sense, has attributed to Sartre a

44/47

pessimism he was far from having. It has frequently been overlooked that the characters in NO EXIT are dead consciousnesses and that their existence is above all theatrical. In this respect the play may be compared to another work written at the same time, THE CHIPS ARE DOWN (see 47/118).

Let us select, from among the clarifications Sartre has made of his work, the most recent (see also 68/487):

I began writing NO EXIT *with a concern for both its matter and its form. Its matter: although I had wanted to dramatize certain aspects of inexistentialism, I was not forgetting the feeling I had had at the Stalag of living constantly and totally beneath the eyes of others, and the Hell which naturally set in under such circumstances. Its form: I wanted to take account of the demands of actors who cannot bear having their fellow actors have more lines than they do. Thus the idea of leaving the characters together the whole time.*

It could be pointed out here that the theme of being *in camera* or in solitary does not date from Sartre's stay in the Stalag but runs in various forms throughout his entire work (see in this connection the study by Marie-Denise Boros, *Un séquestré: L'Homme sartrien* 〈Solitary Confinement: The Sartrean Man〉 [Nizet, 1968]).

There is a second, more important clarification Sartre has made concerning NO EXIT. (See 65/48.)

65/48

Spoken preface to the recording of NO EXIT (Deutsche Grammophon Gesellschaft).

a) Excerpts. *Sartre donne les clefs de "L'Enfer, c'est les Autres"* 〈Sartre Gives the Keys to *Hell Is Other People*〉. *Le Figaro littéraire*, January 7-13, 1965.

b) Excerpts. *"Huis clos" sur le petit écran* 〈NO EXIT on Television〉. *L'Express*, October 11-17, 1965.

In this preface to a remarkably successful recording, Sartre says among other things:

When one writes a play, there are always immediate explanations and underlying concerns.

The immediate explanation of NO EXIT *is that when I was writing it around 1943 and the beginning of 1944 I had three friends and I wanted them to act in a play, my play, without any one of them having any special advantage--that is, I wanted them to be on stage together the whole time--because I said to myself, "If one of them goes off he'll think the others are getting a better role. . . ." So I wanted to keep them together. And I said to myself, "How can you put three people together without ever having any one of them leave and keep them on stage right to the end, as if for eternity?" . . .*

"Hell is other people" has always been misunderstood. People thought that what I meant by it is that our relations with others are always rotten or illicit. But I mean something entirely different. I mean that if our relations with others are twisted or corrupted, then others have to be hell. . . . Fundamentally, others are what is most important in us for our understanding of ourselves. . . .

Then Sartre stresses the fact that the characters in NO EXIT are dead and we are living, and he goes on: *Of course "dead" in this context is symbolic. What I wanted to suggest is precisely that many people are encrusted in a series of habits and customs, and that they are suffering from judgments made about them, but that they don't even try to change. . . . It's a living death to be surrounded by an endless concern for judgments and actions you don't want to change. So the fact of the matter is, that since we are alive, I wanted to show by way of the absurd the importance freedom has for us, that is, the importance of changing our actions by acting differently. No matter what circle of Hell we're living in, I think we're free to break out of it. And if people don't break out of it, they still stay there freely. So that they condemn themselves freely to Hell.*

Before paying tribute to the actors who played NO EXIT, when it was first staged and in subsequent revivals, Sartre sums up what he is saying in the following way: *Relations with others, encrustation, and freedom--freedom as the barely suggested other side of things--these are the three themes in the play.*

The song *Rue des Blancs-Manteaux* ⟨White Mantle Street⟩, whose words were written by Sartre in the thirties, was set to music by Joseph Kosma and published by Enoch publications in 1949.

44/49

L'Espoir fait homme ⟨Hope Makes a Man of You⟩.

-- *Les Lettres françaises* (underground), no. 18 (July, 1944), p. 2. Unsigned article.

Under this ironic title Sartre talks about Marcel Aymé's play *Let's Run the Risk*, which pro-German

44/49

reviews had greeted as "the first play to be directly inspired by the principles of national socialism." Now this work claims to show that human nature is irremediably evil. Sartre takes off from this point to compare the unhealthy pessimism of collaborationist writers, *all-powerful and handsomely rewarded*, with the generous optimism of Resistance writers who are on the contrary being hunted after and constantly tracked down. Although Sartre is hard on Marcel Aymé, he nevertheless distinguishes him from collaborationist writers: *He is surely guilty, but he is not a criminal like Brasillach and Châteaubriant.*

44/50

A propos du "Parti pris des choses" ⟨Concerning *A Prejudice for Things*⟩.

a) Poésie 44, no. 20 (July-October, 1944), pp. 58-77; no. 21 (November-December, 1944), pp. 74-92.

b) Reprinted as *L'Homme et les choses* ⟨Man and Things⟩ and dated December, 1944. In SITUATIONS, I.

c) Reprinted in L'HOMME ET LES CHOSES. Seghers, 1947. See 47/120.

A basic article about Francis Ponge. Ponge was the only Communist during the postwar period whom Sartre associated with as a friend. In SITUATIONS, II (p. 329), he is called *the only real Communist writer.*

44/51

UN PROMENEUR DANS PARIS INSURGÉ

(série de sept articles sur la libération de Paris)

⟨Walking around Paris During the Uprising (a series of seven articles about the Liberation of Paris)⟩

Written at Albert Camus's request and published as the events happened, this very vivid report gives a detailed description of what Sartre saw by walking and bicycling around the streets of the capital during the uprising. Note that in spite of the opening sentence, *I am only telling what I saw*, Simone de Beauvoir's collaboration gave Sartre a certain ubiquity. Her parallel but more concise account may be found in *The Prime of Life*, pp. 470-72. The quotations given below are not intended to replace the entire report but only to stress some of its main traits.

I. L'Insurrection ⟨The Uprising⟩. Tuesday, August 22.

-- *Combat*, August 28, 1944.

> *I am only telling what I saw. What everyone walking around the way I was could see. . . .*
>
> *It begins like a festival, and even today the Boulevard Saint-Germain, deserted and swept intermittently by machine-gun fire, keeps its air of tragic solemnity. . . .*
>
> *The street has once again become--as it did in 1789 and 1848--the theater for great collective movements and social life. . . .*
>
> *In this time of drunkenness and joy everybody feels the need to plunge back into the collective life. . . .*
>
> *In the middle of the road an enormous truck lay dying, turned over on its back like a crab.*

In this first article, Sartre concentrates above all on describing the reactions of civilians and crowds.

II. Naissance d'une insurrection ⟨Birth of an Uprising⟩. Saturday morning.

-- *Combat*, August 29, 1944.

Sartre establishes *the geography of the uprising* and then shows how the civilians gradually become rebels.

> *Already, along with the noonday heat, there is something sinister weighing on the morning's joy. The Senate, enormous and dark at the very end of its empty street, seems venomous with its unbearable flag which you look at in spite of yourself.*

III. Colère d'une ville ⟨A City's Wrath⟩. Sunday. Monday.

-- *Combat*, August 30, 1944.

> *All morning long wrath has breathed through the city. This crowd has finally decided to take its destiny into its own hands.*

Sartre tells about a number of skirmishes and incidents, especially the following:

> *They've just pointed out to the F.F.I.* ⟨Domestic French Forces⟩ *a group of Darnand's militia who are trying to fire into the street from a hotel on the rue de Buci. The F.F.I. men go into the hotel and soon*

come down again with a dozen little yellow guys with anxious but inscrutable faces and hands up. Japanese. *So these are the men who make up Vichy's "real French" militia. The laughter suddenly becomes Homeric: some people have grabbed hold of a few of these assassins, taken their pants down, and energetically spanked them; and here they are now with their pants at their heels getting into the recently arrived paddy wagon in little hops, like a sack race. At the windows there are laughs, flowers, already a few flags, women's faces.*

IV. *Toute la ville tire* ⟨The Whole City Is Shooting⟩.

-- *Combat*, August 31, 1944.

We know the order: knock out a German and take his pistol, take over a rifle, with the rifle get hold of a car, with the car take an armored car and a tank. More than one of the people who are skeptical about the Resistance smiled at it. And yet I saw this program carried out point by point beneath my eyes. One of my friends fought with a musket he requisitioned from an antique dealer. He didn't keep it very long either. After half an hour an F.F.I. man who had no weapon grabbed it away from him: "Give it to me; I can shoot better than you can." . . .

A first German truck went by, heading east. Big blond, rather handsome men, not distrusting us, were standing in the back of it. The Parisians hanging over their balconies knew they only had to make a gesture, call out, and these men would be saved from death. But they did not want to, could *not do it. They let the truck roll on toward its destiny, with the obscure feeling of taking part in a tragic and mortal festival, a bullfight. At bullfights too you wait, hanging over the ring, for the fated death of the beast in the sun, "death in the afternoon."*

V. *Espoirs et angoisses de l'insurrection* ⟨Hopes and Fears of the Uprising⟩.

-- *Combat*, September 1, 1944.

Sartre stresses the fear which preceded the Allied troops' entry into Paris and then tells about his encountering, with Armand Salacrou, a German spy pretending to be a Canadian parachutist.

VI. *La Délivrance est à nos portes* ⟨The Rescuers Are at Our Gate⟩.

-- *Combat*, September 2, 1944.

Sartre describes the crowd's enthusiasm and joy at the arrival of the soldiers of Leclerc's division.

For four years the war had shown us an inhuman face: the soldiers we came across seemed, with their tense faces and hollow eyes, to be branded by a merciless fate; they belonged to an alien world, fantastic and desolate. And now suddenly, beneath their khaki uniforms, these warriors we are greeting, these conquerors, are men to us. They look at us, cry out, smile. They salute us with their fingers spread in V for Victory signs, and we are aware that their hearts and ours beat in a common rhythm.

Later on in his article, Sartre regrets the vengeance which has overcome certain Parisians, and is touched by the sight of an old woman whose head has been shaved.

It seemed to me the faces of the men escorting her were drained of gaiety: a sort of shameful weariness weighed upon them. Was their victim guilty? Was she more so than the ones who had denounced her, the ones who were insulting her? Even if she had been a criminal, this medieval sadism would have been no less worthy of disgust. . . . It is regrettable [that the crowd] has frequently chosen to express its joy and patriotic zeal by thoughtlessly gratifying its base desire for vengeance.

VII. *Un Jour de victoire parmi les balles* ⟨A Victorious Day under Fire⟩.

-- *Combat*, September 4, 1944.

Sartre gives a very fine description of Parisians parading through the streets at the Liberation, characterizing it as follows:

Never in human memory have rebels been so friendly and fraternal toward the army. Never before have civilian fighters--armed for guerilla warfare and ambushes, for rebellion and the barricade's unequal struggle--and impeccable soldiers and their leaders been seen parading to the same approving cheers. The crowd applauded both, obscurely understanding the dual character of this patriotic and revolutionary procession. They sensed all the promise of this extraordinary ceremony--that it was not simply a matter of booting the Germans out of France but of beginning a tougher and more patient struggle to establish a new order.

The procession is interrupted by shots. From his place on a rue de Rivoli balcony, Sartre sees General de Gaulle's car go by and watches the crowd stampede up to the point when well meaning F.F.I. men *gallantly*

44/51

open fire on him and the people with him. Sartre then tells how an innocent bellhop (who subsequently declares he is a homosexual) barely escapes death. The report concludes with these words: *A few more shots and it's all over. So is the big festival, the week of glory. Tomorrow will be a very bleak and empty Sunday; a real day after. And Monday shops and offices will open up again: Paris will go back to work.*

44/52

"Pour un théâtre d'engagement--Je ferai une pièce cette année et deux films" ⟨For a Committed Theater--This Year I'll Do One Play and Two Movies⟩, interview by Jacques Baratier.

-- *Carrefour*, no. 3 (September 9, 1944).

The day after the Liberation of Paris, Sartre comes back to his first plays (THE FLIES, NO EXIT, BARIONA) and talks above all about his projects:

This year I'll write a play on a contemporary subject. . . . Through present events we'll try to bring out the unchanging relations between men. The eternal ought to struggle free of the everyday. . . . I have just written two scripts: THE CHIPS ARE DOWN *and* "Typhus."

44/53

La République du silence ⟨The Republic of Silence⟩.

a) Les Lettres françaises, no. 20 (first legal issue) (September 9, 1944), p. 1.

b) Reprinted in *L'Eternelle Revue*, n.s., no. 1 (December 1, 1944), pp. 2-5.

The piece called "La Voix de Robespierre" ⟨The Voice of Robespierre⟩ and attributed to Sartre in the table of contents of the same issue is obviously not by him.

c) Reprinted in French in a textbook. Abbot Joseph Liebling and Eugene Jay Sheffer. *The Republic of Silence: The Story of the French Resistance*. New York: Harcourt, Brace, 1946. Pp. 442-45.

This book owes its title to Sartre and was also published in a solely English-language edition (see below).

d) Reprinted in SITUATIONS, III.

The Republic of Silence.

t1) Translated by Lincoln Kirstein. In *Atlantic Monthly*, CLXXIV (December, 1944), 39-40.

t2) Translated by Ramon Guthrie. In A. J. Liebling, ed. *The Republic of Silence*. New York: Harcourt, Brace, 1947. Pp. 498-500.

t3) Playboy, January, 1966.

This fine piece of writing has been widely distributed and often quoted and translated.

44/54

23 septembre 1938 ⟨September 23, 1938⟩, a selection from THE REPRIEVE.

-- *Les Lettres françaises*, October 28, 1944. This selection corresponds to the opening pages of the volume published in 1945.

44/55

Dullin et l'Espagne ⟨Dullin and Spain⟩.

-- *Combat*, November 8, 1944.

Charles Dullin's productions of Calderón's *Life Is a Dream* and *The Doctor of His Honor*, as well as of Lope de Vega's *The Galician Lovers*, had met with a complete lack of understanding by the critics. Sartre defends the productions, comparing *these three austere and pure works* to the tragedy of the Greeks or Corneille and contrasting them to the tragedy of Racine, in which passion is *mechanical*.

44/56

Paris sous l'occupation ⟨Paris During the Occupation⟩.

a) La France libre (London), no. 49 (November 15, 1944), pp. 9-18.

b) Reprinted in *La France libre*, anthology issue, September, 1945, pp. 56-68.

c) Reprinted in SITUATIONS, III.

In this article, which is without a doubt one of the best accounts we have of the Occupation years,

44/56

Sartre undertakes to reconstruct the atmosphere of the 1940-44 period for readers who did not live through them in France: *For four whole years they took our future away from us. We had to count on other people.*

See also 45/64.

44/57

"Lectures de prisonniers" ⟨Prisoners' Reading⟩, article by Claire Vervin including interviews with many writers, among them Sartre.

-- *Les Lettres françaises*, December 2, 1944, p. 3.

Sartre said that he read a little bit of everything according to what he happened to lay his hands on. At Baccarat, during the "phoney" war and after the *gardes mobiles* library had been looted, he read Blaise de Montluc's *Mémoires*, Vaulabelle's *History of the Two Restorations* (in which he found a parallel with the Vichy restoration) and *Around the World in Eighty Days*.

In Stalag XII D in Trèves, he found a *ridicule* novel by Dekobra gripping reading because it was an escape. But he also read Gérard de Nerval's *Daughters of Fire*, Sophocles' plays, *The Cid*, *Mithridate*, Bossuet's *Sermons*, and some poems by Rainer Maria Rilke and Hans Carossa in German. He made two major discoveries: *Diary of a Country Priest* and, especially, *Satin Slipper*, selections from which he would have liked to stage in the Stalag Theater.

These were all happenstance readings: *I never found any works there I would have brought along if I had known I was going to live there. During those terribly inactive days when daydreaming helped us escape and yet we avoided thinking about the past too much, reading had a charm and magic I had only felt in it when I was just a child.*

44/58

"Jean-Paul Sartre ou l'interview sans interview" ⟨Jean-Paul Sartre, or The Interview without an Interview⟩, interview-article by Pierre Lorquet.

-- *Mondes nouveaux*, no. 2 (December 21, 1944), p. 3. B.N. listing: Gr. Fol. Z196.

This interview was published in a weekly which stopped coming out after three issues and became afterwards *Mondes* and then *Le Rouge et le Noir*. In it, Sartre talks primarily about literature and shows what he is concerned with right after the Liberation:

My main interest now is what it always has been--ethics. . . . I have scarcely been concerned with the beautiful. When I write a book I don't want people to say it's beautiful; I want them to say it exists. . . . What is important is to tell about what exists!

All things considered, Frenchmen haven't helped me much. As much as I admire Proust, he's just the opposite of me: he likes to analyze, and I tend to simply synthesize. No doubt Valéry says more to me, but I don't like his rationalism. No really, there's only one of our people who has had any profound effect on my mind, and that's Descartes. I consider myself a descendant of his and appeal to the old Cartesian tradition which has been maintained in France.

. . . The war taught me I had to commit myself.

44/59

* *A propos de l'existentialisme: Mise au point* ⟨A More Precise Characterization of Existentialism⟩, essay.

a) Action, no. 17 (December 29, 1944), p. 11.

b) Long excerpts in *Lettres* (Geneva), no. 1 (1945), pp. 82-85.

c) Excerpts in Gaëtan Picon. *Panorama de la nouvelle littérature*. Gallimard, [1960]. Pp. 654-57.

What Is Existentialism? translated by André Du Bouchet.

-- *Foreground* (Cambridge, Mass.), I, no. 2 (spring-summer, 1946), 117-23.

Just as soon as the euphoria of the Liberation which had brought Sartre and the Communists together had been dissipated, the latter began to attack existentialism harshly by accusing it of being a philosophy which diverted people from the class struggle. The Communist weekly *Action*, whose cultural section was at that time edited by Francis Ponge, had especially opened its columns to such accusations, but had given Sartre an opportunity to answer them. This is the origin of this *More Precise Characterization of Existentialism*, which in spite of its moderation did not succeed in stopping the continuing deterioration of relations between Sartre and official communism. Some months later in fact, *Action* (no. 40, [June 8, 1945]) published "Existentialisme et marxisme: Réponse à une mise au point" ⟨Existentialism or Marxism, a Reply to a More Precise Characterization⟩, in which Henri Lefebvre "while pretending to no longer condemn Sartre 'for having been a disciple of the Nazi Heidegger,' called him an idealist and subjectivist who was building a war machine

44/59

against Marxism" (Michel-Antoine Burnier, *Choice of Action* [Gallimard edition, p. 53]). (It would be worth everyone's while to refer to Burnier's valuable study, especially chapter 3, for everything which has to do with Sartre's relationship to the P.C. ⟨Communist Party⟩ during the immediate postwar years. See also *Force of Circumstance*, pp. 14 and 45, where Simone de Beauvoir points out that the Communists' animosity seemed painfully unjust to Sartre.)

For non-Communist reactions to this article see Pierre Emmanuel, "Réflexions sur une mise au point" ⟨Thoughts on a More Precise Characterization⟩, *Fontaine*, no. 41 (April, 1945), pp. 111-17; and Jean Beaufret, "A propos de l'existentialisme (III): Jean-Paul Sartre" ⟨On Existentialism (III): Jean-Paul Sartre⟩, *Confluences*, no. 5 (June-July, 1945), pp. 531-38, no. 6 (August, 1945), pp. 637-42.

And in the last place, see Sartre's own comments in DISCUSSIONS OF POLITICS (Gallimard edition, p. 72).

44/NOTE 1.

Sartre remembers having written an editorial about Germany for *Combat*; but in spite of all our investigations, we have not been able to identify it.

44/NOTE 2.

Henri Michel, in his book *Les Courants de pensée de la Résistance* ⟨Currents of Thought in the Resistance⟩ ([P.U.F., 1962], p. 421), quotes the following lines which he attributes to Sartre: "We have often been told that the Europe of the future could not possibly do without France. I don't think that this is so at all. Four years of Occupation have infected us with a sort of laziness and fatalism." The reference given is "*Study* by a philosopher, sent to Algiers in May of 1944, the Oudard papers, C.H.G. archives."

This interesting document raises problems we have not been able to solve. It is preserved in the Archives du Comité d'Histoire de la Seconde Guerre mondiale (32, rue de Léningrad, Paris-8ᵉ) among the papers left there by M. Georges Oudard. Thanks to the cooperation of Oudard and of M. Henri Michel, director of the C.H.G., we have been able to look at it. The document bears the number CCD/D.I. and is "addressed personally to M. Woliner. Received: May, 1944. Source: Alain." The heading is stamped "TOP SECRET," and also bears the handwritten note, "Jean-Paul Sartre, *normalien*, supports the National Front." The text is entitled "*The Resistance: France and Tomorrow's World*, by a philosopher." It covers five large typed pages. We give a broad summary of it here:

The study begins with a very pessimistic description of the state of mind and effective role of the Resistance in Occupied France. The struggle is taking place under disastrous material, and above all psychological, conditions. Except for the Communists and the conservative Resistants, the majority of patriots have an ideology which is confused, hesitant, purely negative, or concerned solely with private morality. Then comes a historical analysis of the cause of this state of affairs; that is to say that France is no longer a major power. There is at present a profound hesitancy in French thinking, a spiritual crisis.

The main part of the study is then devoted to describing this crisis from a philosophical point of view. The author contrasts the spirit of analysis underlying the reasoning and individualistic behavior of the French to the synthetic thinking which gave birth elsewhere to different modes of totalitarianism, especially national socialism. This synthetic thinking represents a great step forward, for it alone enables us to account for the diversity and interaction of particular or collective situations. Although totalitarianism must be overcome by defeating the Fascist powers, it must also in a certain sense be absorbed. The French are beginning to see that they exist in society and that you change man by changing the society in which he lives. This requirement would lead most of them to communism if it did not meet resistance from their bias for analysis and individualism. This inner conflict may explain the exclusively negative character of the Resistance. The drama of occupied France is its inability to choose between a program which would subordinate man to society and a pure and simple return to democratic isolation. The way to resolve this conflict is to build a socialism whose goal would be the liberation of the person--"A government in exile which took account of the difficulties we are struggling through, and which took the realization of concrete freedom through collectivization of the means of production as its watchword, would rally the majority of Frenchmen around it. It would give the Resistance a positive faith. Strengthened with such a message, France would find a policy and dignity again; she would make a new place for herself in the world."

We showed this document to Sartre; he could only admit to being perplexed and a little astounded. Although he recognizes to a great extent the ideas and even the style he had at the time, he has no recollection of having written this text and does not see how it could have come from Algiers. He never sent a report to the government in Algiers, and above all he no longer had such a pessimistic view of the Resistance at the date mentioned on the document.

We are persuaded for our part that this text is either by Sartre or directly inspired by him. The main problem, in our view, is that of the date at which this study was written. The only internal evidence for determining it is the allusion in the text to "four years of Occupation," which seems to confirm the date it was received in Algiers. Yet it seems more likely to us that the text was drafted long before that, perhaps even at the time of "Socialism and Liberty" (see 41/31), and that its date was changed by someone who had it in his possession and had it sent to Algiers. It is also possible that it was based on previous notes by Sartre or drawn up by someone around him who knew or shared his ideas enough to adopt his style and familiar turns of phrase.

Henri Michel told us in a letter about the hypothesis which seemed most likely to him: "It's the one which would group this study with the works carried out by the General Committee of Experts (C.G.E.). This committee, created by Jean Moulin, undertook a great number of investigations. Only some of these were published in the *Political Notebooks*. Others were sent unpublished to London or Algiers, naturally, for security reasons, without any precise indication of their author's name. At times the author of these studies did not even know that they were working for the C.G.E."

We hope that new information will enable us to determine in the future just where this letter came from. If it turns out that Sartre is its author, this would be a very important document for establishing the date of a major stage in the evolution of his philosophical and political thinking. We could especially see Sartre using in it for the first time the term *totalitarian* in reference to dialectical thinking--an idea he will give precise expression to in *Search for a Method* and CRITIQUE OF DIALECTICAL REASON. Furthermore, and more generally, we would find in this text the first deeper formulation of an idea Sartre has never abandoned, that of the necessary alliance of socialism and liberty.

NOTE: Recently acquired information allows us to specify that this text was originally drawn up toward the end of 1941 by Maurice Merleau-Ponty, after discussions with Sartre and Jean Desanti. For the time being we prefer not to change our annotation, for it seems to us that it is still of documentary interest.

1945

45/60

L'ÂGE DE RAISON ⟨The Age of Reason⟩, Vol. I of *Les Chemins de la liberté* ⟨Roads to Freedom⟩, novel.

a) Excerpt. *L'Age de raison.* In *Domaine français, "Messages"* ⟨French Territory, *Messages*⟩, pp. 51-60. (See 43/38.)

b) Another excerpt. *Les Chats.* *L'Arbalète* (Lyon), no. 7 (summer, 1943). (See 43/41 A.)

c) Published as a book. Gallimard, [1945]. 309 pages.

Printing date: March 15, 1945. Put on sale with LE SURSIS ⟨The Reprieve⟩ in September, 1945. Dedicated to Wanda Kosakiewicz. 8 copies on laid antique paper; 1000 on *châtaignier* finish, bound.

Reset in 1949, the volume was also published in the Soleil series in 1962.

d) Le Livre de poche series, nos. 522-23. Gallimard, [1960].

e) *Oeuvre romanesque.* Vol. III. Illustrated by W. Spitzer. Lidis, [1965].

f) Folio series, no. 14. Gallimard, [1972].

THE AGE OF REASON, Volume I of *Roads to Freedom*, translated by Eric Sutton.

t1) New York: Alfred A. Knopf, 1967; London: Hamish Hamilton, 1947.

t2) Paperback. New York: Bantam Books, [1959]. With an introduction by Henri Peyre taken from his *French*

45/60

Novelists of Today (New York: Oxford University Press, 1967).

t3) Revised translation. Paperback. Penguin Books, [1961].

t4) New York: Modern Library, [1963].

t5) London: Heron Press, [1970]. With an introduction and appreciation by Maurice Cranston. Original illustrations by Rachel.

45/61

LE SURSIS ⟨The Reprieve⟩, Vol. II of *Les Chemins de la liberté* ⟨Roads to Freedom⟩, novel.

a) Excerpt. *La nuit du 29 septembre 1938* ⟨The Night of September 29, 1938⟩. *Les Etoiles* (a journal edited by Pierre Emmanuel and G. Sadoul), no. 6 (June 19, 1945).

This excerpt constitutes pages 349-55 of the reset Gallimard edition.

b) Book. Gallimard, [1945]. 350 pages.

Printing date: August 31, 1945. 8 copies on laid antique paper; 1000 on *châtaignier* finish, bound.

Reset in 1949, the volume was also published in the Soleil series in 1962.

c) Le Livre de poche series, nos. 654-55. Gallimard, [1961].

d) *Oeuvre romanesque*. Vol. IV. Lidis, [1965].

e) Folio series, no. 36. Gallimard, [1972].

THE REPRIEVE, Volume II of *Roads to Freedom*, translated by Eric Sutton.

t1) New York: Alfred A. Knopf, 1947; London: Hamish Hamilton, 1947.

t2) Paperback. New York: Bantam Books, [1960].

t3) Paperback. Penguin Books, [1963].

t4) New York: Modern Library, [1963].

Sartre drafted the following insert for THE AGE OF REASON and THE REPRIEVE:

My intention is to write a novel about freedom. I wanted to recall the road some individuals and social groups took between 1938 and 1944. This road will take them up to the Liberation of Paris, but not perhaps up to their own. Yet I hope to give at least a hint of the conditions which will be necessary, beyond this point at which I must stop, for a complete liberation. In this novel, which will consist of three volumes, I have not felt obliged to use the same technique throughout. During the deceptive calm of 1937-38, there were people in certain circles who could still maintain the illusion of having their neatly walled-off and impenetrable individual histories. That's why I chose to narrate THE AGE OF REASON *in the conventional manner, showing only the relations between a few individuals. But when the days of September, 1938, came, the walls came tumbling down. The individual, without ceasing to be a monad, becomes aware that he is playing in a more than individual game. He is still a window on the world, but he discovers unexpectedly that his life is taking on a general meaning and coming apart at the seams. It's a monad which has sprung a leak, and which will always keep on leaking even though it will not sink. To account for the ambiguity of this condition, I had to resort to the "wide screen" technique. All the characters in* THE AGE OF REASON *will reappear in* THE REPRIEVE, *only this time as lost people thwarted by a crowd of other people. I wanted to avoid talking about a crowd or a nation as a single person by attributing tastes, wishes, and ideas to it the way Zola does in* Germinal; *and at the same time I wanted to avoid reducing it to the sum of its constituent parts. I tried to profit from technical investigations of simultaneity made by certain novelists such as Dos Passos and Virginia Woolf. I took up the question where they had left it and tried to find new things along this road. It will be up to the reader to decide whether I have succeeded.*

I ask that my characters not be judged on the basis of these first two volumes, one of which tried to describe France's stagnation during the interwar period and the other of which aims to bring back the sense of disarray which seized so many people at the time of the derisory reprieve that Munich offered. Many of my creatures, even those who now seem to be the most cowardly, will later prove to be heroic, and what I want to write is certainly a novel about heroes. But unlike our solid citizens, I do not think that it is easy to be a hero.

The plan for *Roads to Freedom* seems to date back to the summer of 1938. After having completed *The Childhood of a Leader*, Sartre writes to Simone de Beauvoir (*The Prime of Life*, pp. 261-62): *I have, quite suddenly, found the theme, scope, and title of this book: as you will probably guess, the theme is freedom.* And Simone de Beauvoir adds: "The title, which he printed in capital letters, was *Lucifer*. Volume I was to be called *The Revolt*, and Volume II, *The Oath*.

The epigraph read: 'The pity of it is, we are free.'"

The two interviews by Claudine Chonez (see 38/12 and 38/13) give a better glimpse of Sartre's original intentions; he presents his next novel as a sequel to NAUSEA and thinks of Mathieu as a continuation of Roquentin. The latter will *discover freedom, get things going again; we shall see existence rehabilitated, and my hero act, have a taste of action.*

By the beginning of 1939 the work is no longer called "Lucifer" but has its final title, *Roads to Freedom.* Sartre goes on writing the first volume in Alsace after he is called up. An advertising space in the December 30, 1939, *Nouvelles littéraires* (p. 3) announces: "The N.R.F. will publish in 1940 . . . THE AGE OF REASON, a novel by Jean-Paul Sartre." *La Nouvelle Revue française* will subsequently announce, from March to June, 1940, as one of its coming articles: "*The Age of Reason* (excerpts)."

Sartre will put the finishing touches on his novel upon his return from captivity in the spring of 1941. Considered too scandalous to be published under Marshal Pétain's regime, the manuscript will be kept in reserve till the end of 1944, at which date it will be resubmitted to Gallimard along with the text of THE REPRIEVE.

THE AGE OF REASON centers on the personal problems of a group of individuals who have been identified, to a certain extent, with people Sartre knew. The novel ends before Munich.

The second volume covers the Munich crisis up to the abdications of Neville Chamberlain and Edouard Daladier (September 23-30, 1938), and tries this time to describe a "detotalized totality." THE REPRIEVE was written in 1943-44.

The two volumes published together in September, 1945, created a sensation, if not a scandal, in the literary world. In spite of the precise clarifications given in the insert, the critics were rare who did not pillory Sartre for his morals and deplore, in a more or less shocked tone, what they considered his complacency concerning filth. Raymond Las Vergnas's little volume, *L'Affaire Sartre* ⟨The Sartre Affair⟩ (Hautmont, 1946), constitutes a (quite involuntary) treasury of these unwarranted and foolish reactions. Among the few perceptive reviews published here and there, let us cite those of C.-E. Magny (*Clartés*, October 19, 1945, and *Poésie 46*, January, 1946) and Maurice Blanchot (*L'Arche*, October, 1945).

Sartre himself undertook to justify his two novels in an interview he granted to Christian Grisoli in October, 1945 (see 45/87):

I think that the main thing which makes my characters disturbing is their lucidity. Whatever they are they know they are and they choose to be. If they were hypocrites or blind they would be more acceptable. People got upset because there was a story of abortion at the center of THE AGE OF REASON. *Quite unjustifiably. For after all in 1938 people got abortions; so it follows they existed. Why put out your eyes voluntarily? . . . Yes, Mathieu is guilty. But his real sin isn't what people thought. It lies less in the abortion he suggests Marcelle get than in his having committed himself eight years earlier to living with her without loving her. Or rather, Mathieu hasn't really committed himself in respect to Marcelle. Not because he did not marry her: marriage in my view is an unimportant act, nothing more than the social form of commitment. But because he knew very well that the affair was not really a shared undertaking. They see one another four times a week. They say they tell each other everything: in truth they never stop lying to one another, because their relationship is false and deceitful.*

After having alluded to the evacuation of the patients in THE REPRIEVE and analyzed Charles as a character, Sartre goes on:

THE AGE OF REASON *and* THE REPRIEVE *are still no more than an inventory of false, mutilated, incomplete freedoms, a description of the vagaries of freedom. It's only in "The Last Chance" that the conditions for a true freedom will be defined. . . .*

Mathieu is the embodiment of that total availability which Hegel calls terroristic freedom and which is practically the opposite of freedom. He is like Orestes at the outset of THE FLIES, *weightless, rootless, with no connections with the world. He is not free because he has not been able to commit himself. . . . He feels excluded from the undertaking which is taking place. . . . Mathieu is the freedom of indifference, abstract freedom, freedom for nothing. Mathieu is not free, he is nothing, because he is always an outsider. . . .*

Brunet embodies the spirit of seriousness, which believes in transcendent values written in the sky for all to read and understand, like things with no relation to our human subjectivity. For him the world and history have an absolute meaning which governs his undertakings. Brunet commits himself because he needs a certainty in order to live. His commitment is not more than his passive obedience to that need. He frees himself at little cost from anguish. He is not free. Man is free to commit himself, but he is not free unless he commits himself to being free. There is a militant life which is different from Brunet's. But Brunet is a militant who fails his freedom.

45/61

It is in writing THE REPRIEVE that Sartre gets the idea for a third volume of *Roads to Freedom*. This volume was originally to be called "The Last Chance" but it became TROUBLED SLEEP in 1949, and the original title was then transferred to a fourth volume, half of which was published in *Les Temps modernes* and the rest never published.

See 49/179, 49/191, and 49/192.

45/61 A

HUIS CLOS ⟨No Exit⟩.

See 44/47.

45/62

Participation in "Discussion of Sin."

a) Dieu vivant, no. 4 (1945), pp. 83-133.

b) Le Nouveau Commerce, no. 20 (fall, 1972), pp. 103-51.

Shorthand account of a debate which took place at Marcel Moré's on March 5, 1944, after a lecture by Georges Bataille on the problem of Good and Evil (subsequently reproduced in *Sur Nietzsche* ⟨On Nietzsche⟩ [Gallimard, 1945] with a further elaboration provoked in part by Sartre's objections). Participating were, among others, the Reverend Jean Daniélou, Pierre Klossowski, Arthur Adamov, Maurice de Gandillac, Jacques Madaule, Jean Hyppolite, Louis Massignon, and Gabriel Marcel.

Sartre's contributions have to do mainly with logic, and bring out the difficulties of the position Bataille has adopted. These difficulties stem from the use which the author of *The Experience Within* has made of Christian concepts and terminology while rejecting the values of the Christian ethic. Bataille will subsequently respond, quoting Nietzsche: "We want to be the inheritors of Christian meditation and breakthroughs . . . to go beyond all Christianity by means of a *hyper-Christianity*, and not be satisfied to simply do away with it." Sartre says he sees in Bataille an ethic of investigation for its own sake. (See also 43/42.)

45/63

Un Collège spirituel ⟨A Spiritual School⟩, excerpt from a study of Baudelaire.

-- *Confluences*, n.s., no. 1 (January-February, 1945), pp. 9-18.

This excerpt corresponds to pages 153-69 of the Gallimard edition (1947) and gets its title from an expression on page 166.

See 46/101 and 47/115.

45/64

Une Grande Revue française à Londres ⟨A Major French Magazine in London⟩.

-- *Combat*, January 7-8, 1945.

Short article giving a very favorable account of *La France libre*, a magazine published in London by André Labarthe and Raymond Aron beginning in November, 1940.

REPORTS FROM THE UNITED STATES, 1945

Toward the end of November, 1944, the Office of War Information in Washington, wanting to make the American war effort known, invited a group of French journalists to visit the United States. Albert Camus asked Sartre to represent *Combat*. Sartre accepted enthusiastically (see concerning this subject *Force of Circumstance*, p. 17) and it was subsequently agreed that he would also be the special correspondent for *Le Figaro*. Sartre left France by plane with six other journalists on January 12, 1945, and stayed several months in the United States.

We have been able to enumerate thirty-two articles written alternately for *Le Figaro* and *Combat* and falling into eight different series (which we group together here in order to facilitate their classification). The articles for *Combat* are generally more technical and less literary than the ones for *Le Figaro*, which, by the way, distressed Camus. (See *Force of Circumstance*, p. 18.)

NOTE: The article titles usually are not by Sartre but by the newspaper editorial staffs.

45/65

Series called *Les Journalistes français aux Etats-Unis* ⟨The French Journalists in the United States⟩.

I. La France vue d'Amérique ⟨France in American Eyes⟩.

45/65

-- *Le Figaro*, January 24, 1945.

Cable dated New York, January 22. This first article emphasizes the extremely warm welcome they received in New York, and then stresses the struggles between supporters of Philippe Pétain, Henri Giraud, and Charles de Gaulle which marked the life of the French colony during the war years. Sartre takes a clear stand in favor of the Gaullists, and in a passage which was to cause a scandal, accuses certain journalists (without naming them) of having used money from high finance or the State Department to bring out a newspaper which did much harm to the French cause.

The January 25 *New York Times* publishes a dispatch from its Paris correspondent which calls attention to this passage and condemns Sartre for attacking the very foundations of Franco-American friendship. A letter from Geneviève Tabouis, which appears in the same newspaper on January 31, claims to refute Sartre's charges and identifies the newspaper in question as *Pour la Victoire*.

These different reactions led Sartre to write a more precise statement under the title:

45/66

Mr. Sartre Explains Article.

-- *New York Times*, February 1, 1945.

A letter, dated New York, January 30, in which Sartre condemns the Paris correspondent of the *New York Times* for having distorted the spirit of his first article by incomplete quotations, and says that he believes in Franco-American friendship and that he in no way intended to question it.

II. Victoire du gaullisme ⟨The Victory of Gaullism⟩.

-- *Le Figaro*, January 25, 1945.

Sartre attacks *the petty bourgeois France of the Girauds and Pétains* and, using Malraux's expression, says that *the blood which flowed in Paris in August was the blood of the Left.*

45/67

Le Président Roosevelt dit aux journalistes français son amour de notre pays ⟨President Roosevelt Tells the French Journalists of His Love for Our Country⟩.

-- *Le Figaro*, March 11-12, 1945.

This article reports an interview French journalists had with President Roosevelt in Washington on March 10. Roosevelt is described in these terms:

> *What strikes you first of all is the deeply human charm of this long face, hard and delicate at the same time, with its eyes shining with intelligence. You find a sort of generous warmth in it: something open and communicative intermingled curiously with the slightly savage harshness of the jaws.*

45/68

Series for *Combat*:

Un Français à New York ⟨A Frenchman in New York⟩.

-- *Combat*, February 2, 1945.

Jamais les Américains n'ont eu tant d'argent ⟨The Americans Never Had So Much Money⟩.

-- *Combat*, February 3, 1945.

Les Américains dans le souci ⟨The Americans Worrying⟩.

-- *Combat*, February 4-5, 1945.

This series describes the conditions of life in the United States. Sartre sees above all a *contrast between wealth and pennypinching, pleasures and profound sadness, comfort and anguish.*

45/69

Series for *Combat:*

Déséquilibre aux U.S.A. ⟨Disequilibrium in the U.S.A.⟩.

-- *Combat*, March 4-5, 1945.

Deux courants politiques dans les U.S.A. de demain: Isolationnisme contre intervention ⟨Two Political Currents in Tomorrow's U.S.A.: Isolationism vs. Intervention⟩.

-- *Combat*, March 6, 1945.

Roosevelt et son "brain-trust" envisagent de réformer demain la géographie industrielle des Etats-Unis ⟨Roosevelt and His "Brain Trust" Plan to Reform the Industrial Geography of the United States after the War⟩.

-- *Combat*, March 7, 1945.

45/69

La Vallée du miracle ⟨The Valley of the Miracle⟩.

-- *Combat*, March 8, 1945.

L'Echec ou la réussite de l'expérience tentée aux U.S.A. dans le Tennessee influera demain sur la politique américaine ⟨The Success or Failure of the Experiment Being Tried Out in Tennessee Will Have an Influence on Tomorrow's Politics in America⟩.

-- *Combat*, March 9, 1945.

These last three articles bear more specifically on the Tennessee Valley Authority.

45/70

Series on Hollywood for *Combat*:

Hollywood 1945.

-- *Combat*, March 27, 1945.

Hollywood 1945: Comment les Américains font leurs films ⟨Hollywood 1945: How the Americans Make Their Movies⟩.

-- *Combat*, March 30, 1945.

Hollywood évolue ⟨Changing Hollywood⟩.

-- *Combat*, April 1-2, 1945.

Deals with unions, the struggle against fascism, and war movies; and welcomes the birth of the "thinking picture."

Un Film sur Wilson a apporté des voix à Roosevelt ⟨A Movie about Wilson Won Votes for Roosevelt⟩.

-- *Combat*, April 5, 1945.

Hollywood aura demain un concurrent de plus: Le Mexique ⟨Tomorrow Hollywood Will Have One More Competitor: Mexico⟩.

-- *Combat*, April 7, 1945.

45/71

Series for *Le Figaro:*
"En cherchant l'âme de l'Amérique" ⟨Looking for America's Soul⟩.

I. Un Pays où l'on n'est jamais seul ⟨A Country Where One Is Never Alone⟩.

-- *Le Figaro*, March 29, 1945.

II. Comment on fait un bon Américain ⟨How To Make a Good American⟩.

-- *Le Figaro*, March 30, 1945.

III. Hors des ligues, point de salut ⟨If You Aren't a Member of a Club You Can't Be Saved⟩.

-- *Le Figaro*, March 31, 1945.

This series of reports was reprinted as *Individualisme et conformisme aux Etats-Unis* in SITUATIONS, III, where it is dated February, 1945 (translated by Annette Michelson as *Individualism and Conformism in the United States* in LITERARY AND PHILOSOPHICAL ESSAYS [1955]).

45/72

Series for *Le Figaro*:
"Villes d'Amérique" ⟨American Cities⟩.

I. Chaque jour, naît une cité. Chaque Jour, meurt un village ⟨Each Day a City Is Born; Each Day a Town Dies⟩.

-- *Le Figaro*, April 6, 1945.

II. La Cité. Pour nous c'est un passé, pour eux c'est un avenir ⟨The City. For Us It's a Past; For Them It's a Future⟩.

-- *Le Figaro*, April 13, 1945.

III. Le Passé, ici, ne laisse pas de monuments mais seulement des résidus ⟨Here the Past Leaves No Monuments, Only Remains⟩.

-- *Le Figaro*, April 14, 1945.

IV. Seuls quelques Noirs, ici, ont le temp de rêver ⟨Only a Few Blacks Have Time to Dream Here⟩.

-- *Le Figaro*, April 23, 1945.

This series of reports was reprinted under the title *Villes d'Amérique* ⟨American Cities⟩. In SITUATIONS, III.

American Cities, translated by Annette Michelson.

t1) In LITERARY AND PHILOSOPHICAL ESSAYS (1955).

t2) In Leslie A. Fiedler, ed. *The Art of the Essay*. New York: Crowell, 1958.

45/73

Series of seven articles on American workers for *Combat*:

Les Travailleurs américains ne sont pas encore des prolétaires ⟨American Workers Are Not Proletarians Yet⟩.

-- *Combat*, June 6, 1945.

Les Etats-Unis pays de colons ⟨The United States, a Land of Colonists⟩.

-- *Combat*, June 7, 1945.

La Table de l'ouvrier américain n'est pas moins bien garnie que celle de son patron ⟨The American Worker's Table Is No Less Well Provided Than His Boss's⟩.

-- *Combat*, June 9, 1945.

> Sartre describes in detail the American worker's standard of living, menu, and budget, but he adds: *It must be said that their standard of living, above all at present, tends to hide the real problems from them.*

Hello Jim! dit l'évêque de Chicago au balayeur d'école.--Hello évêque! répond le balayeur ⟨Hello Jim! Says the Bishop of Chicago to the School Janitor; Hello Bishop! the Janitor Replies⟩.

-- *Combat*, June 10-11, 1945.

> Sartre notices *this truly human kindness which governs class relationships* and says that *the external signs of class do not exist.*

Un Tristesse faite de fatigue et d'ennui pèse sur les travailleurs des usines américaines ⟨A Sadness Which Comes from Weariness and Boredom Weighs upon the American Factory Workers⟩.

-- *Combat*, June 12, 1945.

> Sartre stresses the mechanization of labor and the fear of Marxism.

Depuis la crise de 1930, la travailleur américain vit dans la crainte de redevenir un jour chômeur ⟨Since the Depression, the American Worker Has Lived in Fear of Becoming Unemployed Again Some Day⟩.

-- *Combat*, June 14, 1945.

> *. . . That profound American contradiction: America is the most optimistic country--the one whose people have always considered war an avoidable accident and the use of force never justifiable, but it is also the country in which one finds, in a latent state, the greatest possibility of violence.*

Deux grandes organisations groupent aux U.S.A. un tiers des travailleurs: l'A.F.L. avec 5 800 000, le C.I.O. avec 5 200 000 adhérents ⟨Two Great Unions Include a Third of the American Workers: The A.F.L. with 5,800,000, the C.I.O. with 5,200,000 Members⟩.

-- *Combat*, June 30, 1945.

Sartre's sympathy goes to the C.I.O., which includes Communists and blacks and which is more aware of the limits of political liberalism.

In the same issue of *Combat* a series of reports by Jacques-Laurent Bost, "Across the U.S.A.," begins.

45/74

A two-part series for *Le Figaro* entitled: *Retour des Etats-Unis. Ce que j'ai appris du problème noir* ⟨Return from the United States. What I Learned about the Black Problem⟩.

-- *Le Figaro*, June 16, 1945, and July 30, 1945.

An objective report which takes into account both general facts and statistics and personal contacts. Its conclusion is as follows: *The black problem is neither a political problem nor a cultural problem: the blacks are a part of the American proletariat and their cause is the same as that of the white workers. . . . There seems to be only one solution to the black problem--and it is not near at hand: when the American proletariat--black and white--recognize that their interests in opposition to the ruling class are the same, the Negroes will struggle as equals alongside the white workers for the recognition of their rights. . . . All progress in America depends, at bottom, on the development of working-class consciousness.*

In July, 1945, Sartre gave a lecture at the Centre d'études on the rue de Varenne entitled "Les Américains tels que je les ai vus" ⟨The Americans As I Saw Them⟩ (see report in *L'Ordre de Paris*, July 14, 1945).

45/75

L'Homme ligoté: Notes sur le "Journal" de Jules Renard ⟨Man in Chains: Notes on Jules Renard's *Journal*⟩.

a) Messages II, 1944, [non-paginated].

1513 copies printed. Printing date: April 15, 1945. *L'Homme ligoté* takes up twelve pages of this issue, which is

45/75

subtitled *Risques, Travaux, Modes* ⟨Risks, Works, Fashions⟩, and in which there is also Pablo Picasso's *Desire Caught By the Tail,* Raymond Queneau's "Stylistic Exercises," and a short story by Mouloudji.

b) Reprinted in SITUATIONS, I, with no indication of its source but dated 1945.

This study seems to have been written at the same time as BAUDELAIRE: Sartre tries to show with precise examples that human alienation and the writer's are the same.

He stopped speaking; he did nothing. His project was to destroy himself. Suffocated, gagged by his family, his times and his surroundings, his penchant for psychological analysis, and his marriage, and sterilized by his Journal, *he found strength only in dreams.*

The expression *man in chains* occurs quite often in Sartre's writings of 1944-45.

45/76

New Writing in France: The Resistance "Taught That Literature Is No Fancy Activity Independent of Politics."

a) Vogue, July 1945, pp. 84-85.

b) Translated from English as "Neue Literatur in Frankreich." *Neue Rundschau*, no. 2 (January, 1946), pp. 248-53.

Taking bearings on the course of French literature in 1945, Sartre distinguishes two generations of writers: the one which, with men like Georges Bataille, Maurice Blanchot, and Jean Anouilh, is producing interesting works but is tied to the prewar period and has no followers, and the one which, with men like Michel Leiris, Jean Cassou, and above all Albert Camus, came out of the Resistance and represents the future. André Malraux is the prewar writer who, although he has not published anything for five years, has best adapted himself to the present and *will of course resume his place of honor in our eyes.*

A good half of the article is devoted to Camus, who Sartre thinks represents the opportunity for a new classicism in France. Sartre does not cease to praise the man and the writer, analyzes his works, and even summarizes the plot of *The Plague* (which was not to come out for two more years).

45/77

Quand Hollywood veut faire penser . . . "Citizen Kane" d'Orson Welles ⟨When Hollywood Wants to Make Us Think . . . Orson Welles' *Citizen Kane*⟩.

-- *L'Ecran français*, no. 5 (August 1, 1945).

In re-reading this article, which he did not remember at all, Sartre hardly recognized his style and expressed some doubt about the authenticity of his signature. On the other hand, he did find in it the ideas *Citizen Kane* had suggested to him when he first saw it in the United States. After he saw the film again in France, Sartre had a slightly more favorable opinion of it, but he still thinks it is undoubtedly no masterpiece.

The article grants Welles' mastery of technique and the ideological rightness of the film; yet it expresses serious reservations about the worth of *Citizen Kane* and doubts that it can serve as an example to French moviemaking. The film is reproached for being an *intellectual work, an intellectual's work* which is not suited to the peculiar genius of the movies. Then comes a long and ingenious analysis of the narrative techniques of the film--especially its deliberate disruption of the temporal order. These techniques are said to constitute an American avatar of "artistic writing." The conclusion of the article: *In* Citizen Kane *the chips are down. We are not dealing with a novel, but with a narrative in the* past tense. . . . *Everything is analyzed, dissected, and presented in the intellectual realm, in a false disorder constituted by subordinating events to the causal order--everything is dead. . . . In my opinion Orson Welles' work is a fine illustration of the drama of the American intelligentsia, which is rootless and entirely cut off from the masses.*

The only reference to this article we know of is in a review by André Bazin, "La technique de *Citizen Kane*" ⟨The Technique of *Citizen Kane*⟩, which appeared in *Les Temps modernes* (no. 17 [February, 1947], pp. 943-49) and which quotes at length from Sartre's analysis.

45/78

* *La Libération de Paris: Une Semaine d'apocalypse* ⟨The Liberation of Paris: An Apocalyptic Week⟩.

-- *Clartés*, no. 9 (August 24, 1945), p. 1.

This important article has never to our knowledge been mentioned. It commemorates the first anniversary of the Liberation of Paris. Denouncing

45/78

the vanity of the a posteriori claim that Paris liberated itself, Sartre writes that the rebels' struggle *owes its greatness to its limitations: . . . they wanted to affirm the sovereignty of the French people; and they understood that the only means they had of legitimizing the power of the people was to shed their own blood.*

He relates the Parisian uprising to the taking of the Bastille, and shows that the two events had the same character of a festival or an apocalypse. Borrowing the term *apocalypse* from André Malraux's *Man's Hope*, Sartre defines it as *a spontaneous organization of revolutionary forces*, and says more precisely: *So what we're going to commemorate each year, officially and in good order, is the explosion of freedom, the rupture of the established order, and the invention of a spontaneous and effective order.* You will recognize here the outline of the description of the "group becoming fused together" which Sartre will give in the CRITIQUE OF DIALECTICAL REASON, and you will recall that during these days of August, 1944, he himself lived through this exalting victory over the "serial order," and that this experience marked him deeply. (See also 44/51.)

45/79

Qu'est-ce qu'un collaborateur? ⟨What Is a Collaborator?⟩.

a) La République française, 2d Year, no. 8 (August, 1945), pp. 5-6; 2d Year, no. 9 (September, 1945), pp. 14-17.

b) Reprinted in SITUATIONS, III.

La République française was a French magazine put out in New York.

In this article Sartre draws a psychological and social portrait of the collaborator, taking Drieu la Rochelle especially as an example. He notes the following characteristics in him: *Realism, rejection of law and the universal, anarchy and the dream of an iron rule, justification of violence and deception, hatred of man.* (See also 43/40.)

45/80

Présentation ⟨Introduction⟩ [to *Les Temps modernes*].

a) First French publication. *Les Temps modernes*, no. 1 (October, 1945), pp. 1-21. Dedication: "To Dolores."

b) Reprinted as *Présentation des "Temps modernes."* In SITUATIONS, II.

The Case for Responsible Literature, translated by Natalie Galitzine.

t1) Horizon, IX, no. 65 (May, 1945), 307-12. Later collected in Cyril Connolly, ed. *The Golden Horizon*. London: Weidenfeld and Nicolson, 1943. Pp. 90-91.

t2) Abridged version in *Partisan Review*, XII, no. 3 (summer, 1945), 304-8.

> This text, in which Sartre characterizes in a striking way the kind of editorship he plans to give to his magazine as well as his idea of committed literature, excited universal interest at the time and elicited many commentaries--most of them expressing consternation--in literary circles. André Gide in particular was one of the first to attack the concept of commitment (in *Terre des hommes*, no. 8 [November 17, 1945]): "The manifesto of *Les Temps modernes* is disturbing. . . . Existentialism despises duration. Great progress, that is certain; great progress toward barbarity."

45/81

La Fin de la guerre ⟨The End of the War⟩.

a) Les Temps modernes, no. 1 (October, 1945), pp. 163-67.

b) Reprinted in SITUATIONS, III.

The End of the War, translated by Constance Coolidge.

-- *Portfolio* (Paris: Black Sun Press), Vol. II (December, 1945).

> In this disillusioned text he wrote after Japan had surrendered, Sartre seems to foresee the problems of the cold war and already gives an indication of what the main lines of his political action in the years to come will be: *Today, August 20, 1945, in this deserted, starving Paris, the war has come to an end. Peace has not begun. . . . The end of the war is no more than the end of* that *war.*

45/82

A la Kafka.

-- *Les Temps modernes*, no. 1 (October 1, 1945), p. 191. Unsigned text.

> Several witnesses justify our being certain that Sartre wrote this short piece in which he protests the

45/82

indefinite suspension of certain directors who worked during the war at the Continental film company and for Italian firms.

45/83

La Nationalisation de la littérature ⟨The Nationalization of Literature⟩.

a) Les Temps modernes, no. 2 (November 1, 1945), pp. 193-211.

b) Reprinted in SITUATIONS, II.

The Nationalization of Literature.

-- *View* (New York), nos. 6-7 (1946-47), pp. 9, 29, 34, 36-40.

This article includes quite a large number of autobiographical elements (allusions to Paul Nizan, Charles Dullin, NAUSEA, etc.) and might well have been inspired by the publicity given Sartre's name after 1945. (*It is not pleasant to be taken for a public monument while one is still alive* [SITUATIONS, II, p. 43].)

45/84

La Liberté cartésienne ⟨Cartesian Freedom⟩, selection from an introduction to Descartes.

a) Labyrinthe (Geneva), no. 14 (November 15, 1945), p. 7.

b) Reprinted in SITUATIONS, I.

This selection is the end of the introduction to the Traits edition (see 46/102).

Cartesian Freedom, translated by Annette Michelson.

-- In LITERARY AND PHILOSOPHICAL ESSAYS (1955).

45/85

"Qu'est-ce que l'existentialisme? Bilan d'une offensive" ⟨What Is Existentialism? The Balance of an Offensive⟩, interview-article by Dominique Aury.

-- *Les Lettres françaises*, November 24, 1945.

The first part of an investigation by Dominique Aury which includes short interviews with Sartre, Pierre Emmanuel, and Henri Lefebvre.

Sartre speaks of problems of the novel, particularly of the freedom of its characters:

In Zola's works everything is strictly determined. Zola's books are written in the past, whereas my characters have a future. . . . Mathieu's childhood . . . does not count. . . . He tied himself down with his mistress, his culture.

Let us stress too, as curiosities, Pierre Emmanuel's statements: "I do not want to talk about [existentialism]. It's foul. . . . Existentialism seems to me to be a sickness of the soul and thus beyond cure. Why do they want to make us think that man is an abominable running sore on the face of nature?"

As for Henri Lefebvre, he sees existentialism as "a phenomenon of decay which is wholly in keeping with the decomposition of bourgeois culture." For him, "humanism is fighting to make human beings healthy again. To say *Hell is other people* is to deny humanism."

Aury's investigation is continued in the December, 1945, *Lettres françaises* with interviews with Simone de Beauvoir, Gabriel Marcel, and Francis Ponge. Ponge has a favorable opinion of Sartre: "A certain taste I find in the man and in his works leads me to give credit to a philosophy which has not yet put forth its ethics." As for Gabriel Marcel, he says without subtlety: "Sartre's existentialism is negative. Now there is Christian existentialism which is positive."

45/86

Portrait de l'antisémite ⟨Portrait of the Anti-Semite⟩.

-- *Les Temps modernes*, no. 3 (December 1, 1945), pp. 442-70.

Portrait of the Anti-Semite, translated by Mary Guggenheim.

-- Abridged version in *Partisan Review*, XIII, no. 2 (spring, 1946), 163-78.

Published also as a *Partisan Review* pamphlet the same year.

First part of ANTI-SEMITE AND JEW (Gallimard edition, pp. 7-65--see 46/98). This entire essay was written in October, 1944, as a note in the book makes clear (p. 86, Gallimard edition). But a letter Sartre wrote to a progressive Jewish intellectual (see 46/99) tells us that just as he was publishing it in *Les Temps modernes* he agreed to cut out fifty pages of it which were devoted to Jewish authenticity and inauthenticity, giving in thereby to the request of Jewish friends who were afraid that these elaborations would do their

45/86

cause a disservice. These pages, which apparently make up Part III of the essay, were finally published in ANTI-SEMITE AND JEW. Thus it is not impossible that the positive reaction in progressive Jewish circles encouraged Sartre to publish the entire study.

Let us recall that a phrase in *Portrait of the Antisemite (The reason why Céline could support the Nazis' socialist theses was that he was paid off)* led the author of *Bagatelles for a Massacre*, and also of the *Journey to the Bottom of the Night*, to which NAUSEA owes so much, to write the most violent broadside against Sartre that has ever been written: *A l'agité du bocal* ⟨To the Restless Fellow in the Glass Jar⟩ (P. Lanauve de Tartas, [1948]). Céline complains that Sartre wrote this sentence to get him killed: "So this is what this little mucker wrote while I was in prison and in great risk of being hanged. You devilish little shit-crammed piece of filth, you poke yourself out of the crack of my ass to dirty me behind my back!"

45/87

"Entretien avec Jean-Paul Sartre" ⟨Interview with Jean-Paul Sartre⟩, by Christian Grisoli.

-- *Paru* (Monaco), no. 13 (December, 1945), pp. 5-10.

An interview which took place the day after Sartre's lecture at the Club Maintenant in October, 1945 (see 46/88). Sartre goes over the main themes of the lecture; talks about the response to *Roads to Freedom* and analyzes several of its main characters (Mathieu, Brunet, Charles); justifies the scene in THE REPRIEVE about the evacuees from Berck; makes the meaning of the profound difference between him and Camus more precise; defines his position in respect to Marxism (it is the one found in *Materialism and Revolution*); and finally says he does not want any disciples.

45/NOTE 1.

Most bibliographies, following the Bibliothèque Nationale catalogue, attribute the preface to Suzanne Normand's *Liberté Ship* (Nagel, 1945) to Sartre. This is a big mistake which is, however, explained by the book's being headed by a short text (untitled but probably by the author) which has a truncated phrase of Sartre's inscribed below it.

45/NOTE 2.

An article by Sartre entitled "Nationalism and Revolution" and "Revolutionary Nationalism," in turn, is announced on the back cover of the November and December, 1945, *Les Temps modernes* cover. This article was never published, at least not under either of these titles. The December issue also announces "Vie d'un Allemand" ⟨"The Life of a German"⟩ for publication.

45/NOTE 3.

The files of the weekly *Terre des hommes* do not contain any text by Sartre. They do, however, hold many articles devoted to Sartre and existentialism, particularly (in no. 8 [November 17, 1945]) an attack by André Gide on the ideas put forth in the *Introduction to "Les Temps modernes."*

45/NOTE 4.

As a joke, Sartre was called a translator of the following work:

Lilian White (pseudonym). *Midi à 14h* (Here forever). Translated by Jean-Paul Sartre. NRF Gallimard.

"Edition illustrated by Savignac. Work awarded prizes by the Académie Française and the Society for the Advancement of Good. Volume IV of the Shock Literature series published by the *Nouvelle Revue française* under the direction of Maurice Thorez." Printing date: April 25, 1945.

An introductory page signed J.-P. S. points out that Lilian White spent her whole youth in France. The "translation" is the work of Pierre Bettencourt, who printed and published the book in 1946.

1946

46/88

L'EXISTENTIALISME EST UN HUMANISME ⟨Existentialism Is a Humanism⟩.

-- Pensées series. Nagel, [1946]. 143 pages. Printed in February, 1946, and put on sale the following month. 500 copies on vellum superior. Many reprintings.

EXISTENTIALISM or EXISTENTIALISM AND HUMANISM.

t1) EXISTENTIALISM, translated by Bernard Frechtman. New York: Philosophical Library, [1947].

This rather free adaptation of Sartre's text has been reprinted in its entirety or in excerpts in a number of volumes, and more particularly in EXISTENTIALISM AND HUMAN EMOTIONS (New York: Philosophical Library, 1957).

t2) EXISTENTIALISM AND HUMANISM, translated and with an introduction by Philip Mairet. London: Methuen, [1948].

The slightly altered text of a lecture given at the Club Maintenant on Monday, October 28, 1945, at Centraux Hall, rue Jean-Goujon. This lecture marks an unforgettable day in the anecdotal history of existentialism: so many people came that women fainted and the lecturer could scarcely make himself understood (see the reports in the October 29 *Combat*, the November 3 *Terre des hommes*, etc., as well as the burlesque version by Boris Vian in chapter 28 of *The Froth of Passing Days*). It was impossible to discuss what Sartre had said; to allow discussion the lecture was repeated in private before a few critics. Part of the discussion, that in which the Marxist Pierre Naville takes part, is reprinted at the end of the Nagel volume.

During the lecture, Sartre caused some astonishment by calling T. E. Lawrence an existentialist; all reference to Lawrence vanishes in the final version.

EXISTENTIALISM IS A HUMANISM was one of the most read and most criticized of Sartre's works and led to considerable misunderstanding. As Michel-Antoine Burnier saw quite well in *Choice of Action* (Gallimard edition, p. 31), "the importance these pages assumed seems due to the laziness of a good number of critics who hesitated to read BEING AND NOTHINGNESS and were happy to be able to attack Sartre without too much effort and with a good conscience after having skimmed through 141 pages." It is worth recalling, however, that the work constitutes a rather poor introduction to Sartre's philosophy, above all for readers who have not been forewarned. Focused primarily on ethical questions, it popularizes the outstanding claims of existentialism at the price of making a sort of moralistic travesty of them. This is, moreover, the only work Sartre has largely rejected.

NOTE: Although the lecture was announced in the papers as "Existentialism Is a Humanism," it is entitled "L'Existentialisme est-il un humanisme?" ⟨Is Existentialism a Humanism?⟩ by Sartre himself in the text of the book, and by Simone de Beauvoir in *Force of Circumstance* (p. 38).

46/89

MORTS SANS SÉPULTURE ⟨usually translated as THE VICTORS⟩.

a) Complete text of tableau 1, with variations, published as *Les Vainqueurs* ⟨The Victors⟩. *Valeurs* (Alexandria), no. 4 (January, 1946), pp. 6-23.

b) Text of act 1, tableau 2, in *Spectateur*, November 12, 1946.

c) First edition. Lausanne: Marguerat, [1946]. 195 pages. Printing date: November 30, 1946. Volume printed with 60 copies on Marais vellum and 6000 copies on esparto grass. Dedication: "To Dolores."

THE VICTORS is described here as a "play in three acts," act 3 being divided into two tableaux. As the result of a confusion, scene 2 of the final tableau is called scene 5.

The text differs from that of the Gallimard edition (which gives the version used for the staging of the play). The differences are almost all minor ones, with the exception of the ones in scene 3 of tableau 4 (pp. 181-91 of the Marguerat edition, pp. 244-49 of the Gallimard edition), which we shall comment upon briefly at the close of this annotation.

d) A modified text presented as "a play in four acts"

in *France-Illustration, Supplément littéraire et théâtral*, no. 1 (March, 1947), pp. 15-38. With photographs of the play and a photograph of Sartre taken during rehearsals.

e) Modified text, in "four tableaux." Reprinted in THÉÂTRE, I (1947).

In the cast of the play there appears an enigmatic Corbier, played by Maïk.

f) Text in "two acts, four tableaux." In LA P... RESPECTUEUSE ⟨The Respectful Prostitute⟩, followed by MORTS SANS SÉPULTURE. Le Livre de poche series, no. 55. Gallimard, [1954].

g) Reprinted in THÉÂTRE (1962).

h) Similar to *(f)*. Folio series, no. 109. Gallimard, [1972].

THE VICTORS or MEN WITHOUT SHADOWS.

t1) THE VICTORS, translated for the New York stage by Thornton Wilder, 1949.

t2) Translated under the same title by Lionel Abel. In *Three Plays*. New York: Alfred A. Knopf, 1949. Volume includes also THE RESPECTFUL PROSTITUTE and DIRTY HANDS.

t3) MEN WITHOUT SHADOWS, translated by Kitty Black. In *Three Plays*. London: Hamish Hamilton, 1949. Volume includes also THE RESPECTABLE PROSTITUTE and CRIME PASSIONNEL.

t4) Same as *(t2)*, in paperback, with addition of NO EXIT. Vintage Books, [1955].

t5) Same as *(t3)*. London: Methuen, [1961]. Also Methuen paperback.

t6) Paperback. Kitty Black's translation. ALTONA; MEN WITHOUT SHADOWS; THE FLIES. Penguin Books, [1962].

THE VICTORS and THE RESPECTFUL PROSTITUTE are listed in the registry of authors as being by Sartre and Simone de Beauvoir.

The play was staged for the first time in France on November 8, 1946, at the Théâtre Antoine in a double bill with THE RESPECTFUL PROSTITUTE. It had been produced in Swedish at Göteborg on October 26, 1946, and then in Copenhagen (see *Le Figaro*, November 6, 1946).

Directed by Michel Vitold. Settings by André Masson. Leading roles:

LUCIE	Marie-Olivier
SORBIER	R.-J. Chauffard
CANORIS	François Vibert
HENRI	Michel Vitold
JEAN	Alain Cuny
LANDRIEU	Yves Vincent

The first performance caused a scandal, primarily as a result of the torture scenes in the second tableau. Cries of "Take it to the Grand-Guignol!" and "Murderers!" were heard, and Mme Stève Passeur was seen walking out (see *Le Monde*, November 9, 1946). The November 17, 1946, *France-Dimanche* had "Scandal in Paris" in big headlines and printed photographs of faintings. The day after the first performance, before the opening curtain, Sartre had a notice read in which he said he was not trying to cause a scandal, that he had carefully avoided an *inferior realism*, and that he had only wanted to show *human grandeur*. Moreover, cuts were made in the torture scene and instead of tearing Sorbier's fingernails out on stage they simply beat him with clubs. There were 180 performances.

Sartre had said since 1944 that he intended to write a play on a contemporary subject. He finally chose a Resistance episode and took a theme which reappears constantly in his work--torture. The play was written at the end of 1945 and was apparently called "Les Vainqueurs" ⟨The Victors⟩ to start with; Sartre talks about it this way in an interview he gave in October, 1945 (see 45/87): *The characters themselves have already been down the road to freedom. The action takes place in an underground unit, and the theme of the play is what I'll call, for the lack of a better word, heroism. I'll try to show what is total about heroism, as I shall show in a coming issue of* Les Temps modernes *what is total about antisemitism.* The play was announced in *Les Temps modernes* (no. 3 [December 1, 1945]) with its final title.

In *Force of Circumstance* (p. 112), Simone de Beauvoir describes Sartre's intentions in the following manner: "In November, THE VICTORS opened. Sartre had written this play a year before; at the time when the ex-collaborators were beginning to show themselves again, he had wanted to refresh people's memories. He had thought a great deal about torture for four whole years; alone, and among friends, he asked himself: Should I not speak about it too? What would be the best way to handle it? He had also pondered a great deal on the relation between the torturer and his victim. All these thoughts that haunted him he threw into his play. Once more he confronted ethics and *praxis*: Lucie retreats stubbornly into her individualistic pride, while the militant Communist, presented by Sartre as in the right, aims at effectiveness."

46/89

THE VICTORS was badly received by the critics and has never been revived on a Parisian stage. Sartre could say about it in 1960 (see 60/346):

It's a failure. Broadly speaking, I dealt with a subject which gave no breathing room: the victims' fate was absolutely determined ahead of time, no one could suppose they would talk, and so, as they say nowadays, there was no suspense. I put people with a clearly established destiny on the stage. In the theater, there are two possibilities: to give in or to escape. The cards were already on the table. It is a very somber play with no surprises. It would have been better to make a novel or a movie out of it.

This judgment is a little too strict: the play is not attractive, but it has a severity and toughness which end by becoming strange and giving the play a special place in Sartre's theatrical works.

The variations mentioned under *(c)* above are interesting because they draw our attention to another special characteristic of the play. In the first version of one of the final scenes, Lucie, who wants only to die because she feels irremediably debased by the tortures she has been subjected to, gives way before the arguments of first Canoris and then Henri, who have decided to make false confessions in order to save their lives. They convince her by appealing to the duty of solidarity with all those to whom their lives could still be useful. In the second version of this scene, Lucie remains deaf to these same arguments (which, by the way, are presented this time in a less extended form: some of the most moralizing sentences, in particular, disappear), and it is the sound of falling rain and her memory of the smell of wet earth which finally revive in her the urge to live. These changes do not, in spite of what has been said (see Roger Garaudy in *Perspectives for Man*), involve any change in the meaning of the play; they are better explained by a concern for psychological plausibility than by some ideological intention. They do not prevent THE VICTORS from being the only play of Sartre's in which there is an explicit affirmation of positive values close to a certain "socialist-realist" humanism, embodied in the character of the Communist Canoris. In spite of his apparently tragic end and his extremely harsh character, the play is definitely optimistic.

For interviews concerning THE VICTORS, see 46/91-46/96 A.

46/90

LA PUTAIN RESPECTUEUSE ⟨The Respectful Prostitute⟩, play in one act and two tableaux.

a) Nagel, [1946]. 164 pages.

Printing date: October 29, 1946. Dedication: "To Michel and Zette Leiris." 500 copies on Alma vellum.

b) Reprinted in THÉÂTRE, I (1947).

c) LA P... RESPECTUEUSE, followed by L'ENGRENAGE ⟨In the Mesh⟩. Le Livre de poche series, no. 55. Gallimard, [1954].

d) LA P... RESPECTUEUSE, followed by MORTS SANS SÉPULTURE ⟨The Victors⟩. Le Livre de poche series, no. 55. Gallimard, [1954].

e) Reprinted in THÉÂTRE (1962).

f) Reprinted in *L'Avant-Scène Théâtre*, nos. 402-3 (May 1-15, 1966), pp. 19-31.

g) Similar to *(d)*. Folio series, no. 109. Gallimard, [1972].

THE RESPECTFUL PROSTITUTE.

t1) Adaptation for the New York stage by E. Wolas.

t2) First translated by Lionel Abel. In *Art and Action*, 10th anniversary issue, twice a year 1938-48. New York: Twice a Year Press, [1948]. Pp. 18-64. (See 48/160.)

For publication in book form, see 46/89.

t3) THE RESPECTABLE PROSTITUTE, translated by Kitty Black. (See 46/89.)

The play also led to:

-- a movie version by Marcel Pagliero (1952), with Barbara Laage and Ivan Desny (see Appendix);
-- a complete LP recording by the troupe Les Tréteaux de Paris, on L'Avant-Scène, 1968;
-- a "musical comedy," with a score by Olivier Bernard, first staged in October, 1967, at the Théâtre-Maison de la Culture in Caen.

The play was first performed on November 8, 1946, at the Théâtre Antoine (directed by Simone Berriau) in a double bill with THE VICTORS. The producer's name is not given, but he was Sartre, assisted by Michel Vitold. Settings by André Masson.

Leading roles:

LIZZIE	Héléna Bossis
THE NEGRO	Habib Benglia
FRED	Yves Vincent
THE SENATOR	Robert Moor

Sartre wrote the play in a few days to complete the bill scheduled for the Théâtre Antoine. The Negro problem was in the news in 1946 in connection with Senator Bilbo's racist politics and with a series of lynchings in the United States South, and it would not be long before it was exploited in literature (see Boris Vian [Vernon Sullivan], *I'll Spit on Your Graves*). Sartre gets his inspiration from a famous case reported in a partisan fashion by Vladimir Pozner in *Les États désunis* ⟨The Dis-United States⟩ ([Denoël, 1938]; the chapter called "Le Viol" ⟨The Rape⟩, pp. 97-109): at Scottsboro, Alabama, in 1931, nine Negroes were accused of raping two prostitutes, Victoria Price and Ruby Bates, and were condemned as a result of their testimony to death in the electric chair. The affair had international repercussions; it was complicated by the fact that the two prostitutes, giving in to the various pressures put on them, changed their testimony several times.

Already before the war Sartre had found it deplorable that the title of John Ford's play, *'Tis a Pity She's a Whore*, had been translated as *Dommage qu'elle soit une prostituée* ⟨'Tis a Pity She's a Prostitute⟩. The title he gave to his play was considered by some people to be an outrage to good morals, and led Fréderic Dupont, town councilor, in particular to demand that the chief of police ban the play. In the November 21, 1946, *Figaro*, Dupont declared: "This already controversial title is a vulgar defamation of the great American democracy." The management of the subways, which had let titles like *Le Cocu magnifique* ⟨The Magnificent Cuckold⟩ and *Une femme dans son lit* ⟨A Woman in His Bed⟩ be posted, insisted that the word *putain* ⟨whore⟩ be censored, and the play ran its course under the title *La P... respectueuse*, giving this last word a meaning it was far from having had till then and making Sartre a neologian in spite of himself.

Sartre took much more seriously the charge of anti-Americanism which had been brought against him from many sides, notably by Thierry Maulnier in the November 19, 1946, *Spectateur*:

"This play in which, only two years after the Liberation of Paris, we are shown Americans with the face of the most repulsive ferocity, imposture, and hypocrisy, produces an almost intolerable discomfort. If there had been an American soldier in the theater, I would not have dared to look at him."

Sartre gave the following reply to an American reader who had accused him in the November 13 *New York Herald Tribune* of being anti-American as well:

46/91

A Letter from M. Sartre, letter dated November 18, 1946.

-- *New York Herald Tribune* (European edition), November 20, 1946, p. 2.

Excerpts:

I am not anti-American. I don't even know what the word means. . . . It is true that if I had shown only the unsavory aspects of your civilization, it could have been said that I was against it. But I haven't. I have just devoted two whole issues of my review, Les Temps modernes, *to the United States. . . .*

The writer's duty, and his special mission to his readers, is to denounce injustice everywhere, and all the more so when he loves the country which lets this injustice happen.

Sartre took the same line of argument in his preface to the American version of THE RESPECTFUL PROSTITUTE in 1948 (see 48/160), and in an answer to Frédéric Dupont's attempt to get the play closed down:

46/91 A

M. J.-P. Sartre répond à M. Frédéric Dupont ⟨M. J.-P. Sartre Replies to M. Frédéric Dupont⟩.

-- *Une Semaine dans le monde*, November 23, 1946.

Text: *I have learned that M. Frédéric Dupont is asking the Conseil Municipal to ban my play,* Le P... respectueuse ⟨The Respectful P[rostitute]⟩. *The reason he gives for this strange request is that I allegedly insulted our American friends.*

Criticizing a certain racism which is found not only in some regions of the United States but also here in France can in no way be considered, if one is in good faith, an act of hostility toward our American allies.

Following a debate which took place on December 5, 1946, the Municipal Council of Paris rejected Frédéric Dupont's request while paying tribute to America.

From the progressive camp came another sort of criticism which is well summarized by Simone de Beauvoir (*Force of Circumstance*, p. 114): "The Communists thought it a pity Sartre had shown his public a Negro trembling with fear and respect, instead of a real fighter. *That's because my play reflects the present impossibility of solving the color problem in the U.S.*, Sartre replied.

46/91 A

THE RESPECTFUL PROSTITUTE, produced by the "Respectful Company" in a mutilated translation, had a pretty big success in the U.S.A., and had wrangles with the censors of many towns, especially Chicago. This adaptation was indirectly the source of serious financial difficulties for Sartre. One clause of the contract, signed in a rush with the Respectful Company, specified that the company reserved the rights to a movie version. In 1951, Sartre, wanting to do a favor to one of his friends, Marcel Pagliero, authorized him to film a French version of the play. Arguing on the basis of its contract, the Respectful Company brought a suit against Sartre, succeeded in blocking his American rights, and had him condemned to paying them a very large sum.

Let us point out here that Sartre let Pagliero give his movie (1952) an optimistic ending, and that he also agreed in 1954 that the Soviet version of his play be changed in the same way. This version was performed with great success in Moscow under the chaste title of *Lizzie MacKay*, the heroine of the play, and was published in *Inostranaia Literatura* (no. 1 [January, 1955]; translation by N. Ignatieva and V. Fink).

In an interview he gave to *Libération* (July 16, 1954), Sartre says more specifically that the Russians will use the movie ending and not the play ending: *They cannot accept the idea that the girl could have a glimmer of awareness and then be completely taken in. I don't have any objection to this change since I wrote the two versions.* In a subsequent interview (*The Observer*, June 25, 1961), he gives the following justification: *I've known too many young workers who had seen the play and had been discouraged to see it end sadly. And I realized that those who are really pushed to the limit, those who hang on to life the best they can, these people need to have hope.*

Along with NEKRASSOV, THE RESPECTFUL PROSTITUTE is one of the two dramatic works of Sartre which have been performed publicly in the U.S.S.R. (see 67/NOTE 3).

The play was also put on in Havana in February-March, 1960, during the stay which Sartre and Simone de Beauvoir made in Cuba. Generally speaking, its success has been much greater than that of THE VICTORS.

On October 29, 1946, Sartre individually received the representatives of the Parisian newspapers in order to talk to them about THE VICTORS and THE RESPECTFUL PROSTITUTE. We have been able to cull out the following interviews, all of which say more or less the same thing.

46/92

"Morts san sépulture" n'est pas une pièce sur la Résistance" ⟨THE VICTORS Is Not a Play about the Resistance⟩.

-- *Combat*, October 30, 1946.

What interests me are borderline situations and the reactions of those who find themselves thrust into them. For a while I thought about having my play take place during the Spanish Civil War. It could just as well take place in China. . . .

I especially wanted to show that sort of intimacy which comes to grow up between the executioner and his victim.

46/93

"Jean-Paul Sartre va faire ses débuts de metteur en scène avec *La Putain respectueuse*" ⟨Jean-Paul Sartre Will Make His Debut as a Producer with THE RESPECTFUL PROSTITUTE⟩, interview by Jacques Marcerou.

-- *Libération*, October 30, 1946.

46/94

"'*La Torture pose le problème de la liberté humaine*,' nous dit Jean-Paul Sartre" ⟨"Torture Confronts Us with the Problem of Human Freedom," Jean-Paul Sartre Says⟩, interview by André Warnod.

-- *Le Figaro*, November 1, 1946.

Here Sartre characterizes THE RESPECTFUL PROSTITUTE as "comic opera."

46/94 A

"L'Homo Sartrius chez Antoine" ⟨*Homo Sartrius* at the Antoine⟩, interview-article by René Laborde.

-- *Paysage*, November 1, 1946.

46/94 B

Interview-article by P. S.

-- *L'Aurore*, November 3, 1946.

Speaking of THE RESPECTFUL PROSTITUTE, Sartre says, *People who go looking for a scandal are wasting their time.*

46/95

"Les deux pièces de M. Jean-Paul Sartre" ⟨M. Jean-Paul Sartre's Two Plays⟩, interview by H. K.

-- *Le Monde*, November 5, 1946.

46/96

"Jean-Paul Sartre installe l'existentialisme chez Antoine" ⟨Jean-Paul Sartre Moves Existentialism into the Antoine⟩, interview by Marc Blanquet.

-- *Opéra*, November 6, 1946.

Concerning THE RESPECTFUL PROSTITUTE, Sartre says, *In it I took . . . my timid first steps--for which I beg indulgence--as a producer.*

46/96 A

"La Défense de J.-P. Sartre" ⟨J.-P. Sartre's Defense⟩, interview by Simone Chevallier.

a) Paris-Spectacles, November 15, 1946.

b) Reprinted in *Une Semaine de Paris*, November 19-25, 1946.

Sartre justifies representing the torture of Resistants on the stage as follows: *If the theater . . . is only a distraction, it keeps men from thinking about what they are. The theater is above all a means of showing the human situation to the public.*

And he adds: *I don't believe in characters. Men are free. They take good and bad stands in relation to a given situation. Man chooses his destiny up till the moment he is crossed out by death, the borderline case of human freedom.*

46/97

EXPLICATION DE "L'ÉTRANGER" ⟨Analysis of *The Stranger*⟩.

-- Sceaux: Le Palimugre, 1946. 31 pages.

Although this little booklet printed in January, 1946, was in principle not for sale, it was widely disseminated and seems to have been the origin of Jean-Jacques Pauvert's career as a publisher.

See also 43/39.

46/98

RÉFLEXIONS SUR LA QUESTION JUIVE ⟨Reflections on the Jewish Question (referred to hereafter by American edition title, ANTI-SEMITE AND JEW)⟩.

a) Excerpt. *Portrait de l'antisémite* ⟨Portrait of the Anti-Semite⟩. *Les Temps modernes*, no. 3 (December, 1945), pp. 442-70. (See 45/86.)

b) Book. Paul Morihien, [1946]. 198 pages. 120 copies on wood-free Lafuma and 3000 on esparto grass. Printing date: November 20, 1946. New edition, 1947.

c) Republished. Gallimard, [1954]. 189 pages.

d) Idées series. Gallimard, [1961].

ANTI-SEMITE AND JEW or PORTRAIT OF THE ANTI-SEMITE.

t1) About three-fourths of the book first translated by George J. Becker. *Reflections on the Jewish Question-- 1. The Situation of the Jew--2. Portrait of the Inauthentic Jew--3. Gentile and Jew. Commentary*, V, no. 4 (April, 1948), 306-16; V, no. 5 (May, 1948), 389-97; V, no. 6 (June, 1948), 522-31.

t2) ANTI-SEMITE AND JEW, translated by George J. Becker. New York: Schocken, [1948]. Same in paperback, [1965].

t3) PORTRAIT OF THE ANTI-SEMITE, translated by Eric de Mauny. London: Secker and Warburg, [1948].

t4) Same as *(t1)*. New York: Grove Press, Black Cat paperback, [1962].

This essay, one of Sartre's most famous, has become a classic for anyone concerned with the Jewish problem, and it has undoubtedly helped make us more clearly conscious of this problem (see also 46/99 and 47/132; on Israel, see 48/164, 49/185, 65/457 to 67/463, and 69/504). Yet today Sartre judges the book incomplete in several respects, and said in a 1966 interview (see 66/458):

> *Its shortcomings leap out at me. I had to deal with the problem from a twin point of view, historical and economic. I kept myself to a phenomenological description. If I were to redo my essay today, I would base it on a series of remarkable works--like Poliakoff's* History of Antisemitism*--which have since appeared, and I would try to deepen it in the two directions I mentioned. But I don't think my conclusions would have changed very much. The relation between the Jew and antisemitism is as virulent as ever. And I would retain my distinction between the authentic and the inauthentic Jew. Being authentic*

46/98

does not necessarily mean committing oneself to Israel: a Jew is authentic when he has become conscious of his Jewish condition and feels his solidarity with all other Jews.

See also *Force of Circumstance*, p. 45, where Simone de Beauvoir writes: "ANTI-SEMITE AND JEW . . . shows how the phenomenological method can be enriched and made flexible by constant recourse to the social; but the concrete factual basis necessary to a history of anti-Semitism is not there."

Jewish reactions to this essay have been in general rather divided. They are well summed up in the following opinion expressed by Arnold Mandel: "ANTI-SEMITE AND JEW is both the worst and best of things. . . . [The best is the portrait of the anti-Semite], which is drawn with admirable perspicacity. . . . [The worst is] the categorical refusal to consider the nevertheless real dimension in which Judaism represents for the Jews something more than and different from a nickname pinned on them which they defiantly adopt. . . . Sartre's great defect, in the circumstances, is his almost total lack of experience of an organic and thus truly authentic dimension of Jewish life" (*L'Arche*, February, 1962, p. 48). The reception from traditionalist Jewish circles was much harsher (see, for example, Josué Jéhouda, *L'Antisémitisme, miroir du monde* ⟨Antisemitism, a Reflection of the World⟩ [Geneva, 1958], pp. 261-64).

Let us recall, finally, Albert Memmi's book dedicated to Sartre, *Portrait d'un Juif* ⟨Portrait of a Jew⟩ (Gallimard, 1962), which although close to Sartre's main ideas, is a sort of protest against them in the name of the "fact of being Jewish."

46/99

Une Lettre de Jean-Paul Sartre ⟨A Letter from Jean-Paul Sartre⟩.

-- *Hillel* (organ of the World Union of Jewish Students; Paris), no. 3 (December 1946-January 1947), p. 29.

This letter concerning ANTI-SEMITE AND JEW, which is undated but was apparently written in December, 1945, and which is addressed to someone (probably Robert Misrahi or Albert Memmi) who works for *Hillel*, is presented this way by the magazine: "Coming from an outsider, this view of the Jewish problem could be of use in teaching certain of our fellow believers."

We reproduce below the published passage in its entirety:

. . . I have just found your letter and I want you to know what a pleasure it was to read it: I am in

complete *agreement with you about the Jewish problem . . . at the moment your letter arrived, a study I had called "Portrait of the Anti-Semite" was appearing in the* Temps modernes. *Now this study included a long sequel in which I painted the portrait of the inauthentic Jew (who is like the worker who wished to deny his condition as a worker by acting like a bourgeois instead of demanding to be liberated as a* worker, *that is, instead of going beyond his situation through a revolutionary attitude which involves recognition of this situation). I ended by showing what the authentic Jew could demand--that is, his full rights* as a Jew *and as a man--instead of trying to conceal his peculiar characteristics. In my judgment these characteristics are neither ethnic nor physiological nor religious. It's just that the Jew's situation is to be the man other men treat as a Jew. And it really is his situation, that is, it is not a matter of a Jew's declaring that this attitude is absurd or criminal (although it is both) but of his struggling to go beyond this condition others constitute for him by fully recognizing the condition. I sincerely believe that for a Jew authenticity begins from the moment he says, I am a Jew, that is, from the moment he takes responsibility, through a proud and resolute decision, for the characteristics which the others sought to impose upon him externally and which end, like the look another person subjects us to, by piercing him to the marrow. It is as a Jew and not just as a man (that is, insofar as this age-old situation has led to your own culture, your own conception of the world, and your own particular virtues) that you should claim your absolute equality with non-Jews. When one is not oneself in danger, and has not oneself known the humiliation and anguish of persecutions, it is always hard to give advice and make judgments. So when my Jewish friends asked me to cut out the 50 pages in which I set forth this opinion, it was for them and not for me to decide what was best for them. (I think most of them are hesitating between assimilation and authenticity.) But I am especially happy to find a Jew who thinks the same as I do about this subject and who has the right himself to say what he thinks.*

46/100

Les Mobiles de Calder ⟨Calder's Mobiles⟩.

a) Text dated 1946 which was listed in show catalogue. *Alexander Calder: Mobiles Stabiles Constellations* ⟨Alexander Calder: Mobiles, Stabiles, Constellations⟩. Louis-Carré Gallery, 10, avenue de Messine, Paris-VIIIe. Pp. 7-19.

Published for a show which was held from October 25 to November 16, 1946, and distributed by the Hune bookstore.

46/100

Printing date: October 22, 1946.

In addition to Sartre's article and the list of works on show, the catalogue includes a text by James Johnson Sweeney.

b) Incomplete translation. In *Art News*, December, 1947.

c) Complete translation by Wade Baskin. In Wade Baskin, trans. ESSAYS IN AESTHETICS. New York: Philosophical Library, 1963.

d) Reprinted in SITUATIONS, III.

An attempt to define and describe, in an almost poetic way, these "strange beings, halfway between matter and life" that mobiles are.

Sartre had met Calder in America; he was at the opening of his show at the Louis Carré Gallery (see *Force of Circumstance*, p. 118).

46/101

Study of Baudelaire.

a) Excerpt. *Un Collège spirituel* ⟨A Spiritual School⟩. *Confluences*, n.s., no. 1 (January-February, 1945), pp. 9-18. (See 45/63.)

b) Fragment d'un portrait de Baudelaire ⟨Excerpt from a Portrait of Baudelaire⟩. *Les Temps modernes*, no. 8 (May, 1946), pp. 1345-77.

This excerpt, dedicated to Jean Genet, corresponds to pages 58-114 of the Gallimard edition and does not involve any modifications.

c) Published as Introduction. In Charles Baudelaire. *Ecrits intimes: Fusées, Mon coeur mis a nu, Carnet, Correspondance* ⟨Intimate Writings: Rockets, My Heart Laid Bare, Notebook, Correspondence⟩. Point du Jour, 1946. Pp. I-CLXV.

Printing date: November 3, 1946. This volume, the fourth in the Incidences series, had a printing of 2040 numbered copies and 50 noncommercial copies. The selections were chosen by the publisher, R. B. [René Bertelé], and Jean-Paul Sartre.

d) The introduction was reprinted as an independent volume. BAUDELAIRE. Point du Jour, 1946. 166 pages. This edition, which is exceedingly hard to find, was a separate printing of volume *(c)*; its pages are numbered in Arabic rather than Roman numerals.

e) Book. Gallimard, [1947]. (See 47/115.)

NOTE: We have not been able to uncover any trace of the "D.A.C., Monaco" edition which one or two bibliographies mention. (For English translations, see 47/115.)

This essay on Baudelaire, which was originally conceived of as an introduction to his *Intimate Writings* (a fact which needs stressing), was written in 1944, that is to say at a time when, on the one hand, Sartre was bent on stressing the writer's need to commit himself and be morally responsible, and, on the other, according to Simone de Beauvoir (*Force of Circumstance*, p. 44), he was "still far from having understood the fecundity of the dialectical idea and of Marxist materialism."

Trying to reconstruct Baudelaire's experience, Sartre makes use of the idea of *original choice* and says in conclusion: *The free choice man makes of himself is absolutely identical to what is called his destiny.* For Sartre, Baudelaire *is the man who has chosen to see himself as if he were another--his life is nothing but the story of that failure.*

Since Baudelaire had become a national institution and the very symbol of poetry, the essay caused a scandal and was violently attacked on all sides. What Sartre was above all condemned for--in spite of the limits he himself had set to his study--was having spoken only of the man and ignored the "fact of being a poet." Subsequently, people did not fail to challenge the ethical distinction Sartre had made between Baudelaire and Jean Genet. Although Sartre himself recognized the inadequacies of his method (he thinks he did not explain Baudelaire enough in terms of his body and the facts of his life history), the fact remains that his study, and the violent reactions it provoked, marked a date in Baudelairian criticism.

In spite of several superficial likenesses, especially the mother's remarriage, it does not seem to us that there is any basis for establishing too close a parallel between the case of the infant Baudelaire and that of the infant Sartre. On the other hand, the character of Philippe in *Roads to Freedom* seems to be directly inspired by Baudelaire as Sartre described him.

46/102

La Liberté cartésienne ⟨Cartesian Freedom⟩, introduction to a volume of selections from Descartes.

a) Excerpt in *Labyrinthe* (Geneva), no. 14 (November 15, 1945), p. 7.

This selection is the end of the introduction to the Traits edition.

46/102

b) Published in *Descartes, 1596-1650*. Introduction and selections by J.-P. Sartre. Les Classiques de la Liberté series. Geneva and Paris: Traits, Trois Collines, [1946]. Pp. 9-52.

This is the first volume in the Classiques de la Liberté series supervised by Bernard Groethuysen. Printing date: May 30, MCMIVL (1946 and not 1944, as some read it). The text is the same as that in SITUATIONS, I, with the exception of certain minor changes in punctuation and of the final note, which was added following an article by Simone Pétrement, "La Liberté selon Descartes et selon Sartre" ⟨Freedom According to Descartes and Sartre⟩, which came out in *Critique* (no. 7 [December, 1946], pp. 612-20).

c) Reprinted in SITUATIONS, I.

Cartesian Freedom, translated by Annette Michelson.

-- In LITERARY AND PHILOSOPHICAL ESSAYS (1955).

In an interview he gave in 1944 (see 44/58) Sartre said that Descartes was the only Frenchman who had had a great effect on his mind. In this essay he gives a clear and precise statement of what he thinks Descartes's originality and limitations consist of: Descartes understood, well before Heidegger, that *freedom was the sole basis of being*, and that free will was bound to negativity, but he had not been able to *conceive of this negativity as productive*, and so he had attributed to God the role which properly belongs to man.

Several developments, particularly those concerning responsibility and commitment, allow us to understand Sartre's position in 1945 better. Let us point out the formula, *To be free is by no means to be able to do what one wants but to want what one is able to do.*

46/103

Conversation with Roger Troisfontaines.

-- Excerpts in Roger Troisfontaines. *Le Choix de J.-P. Sartre* ⟨J.-P. Sartre's Choice⟩. 2d ed. Aubier-Montaigne, [1946]. Pp. 52-53, 85-87.

This conversation took place in Brussels on October 23, 1945, and bore on several of the criticisms developed by Father Troisfontaines in the first edition of his study of Sartre (same publisher, 1945).

Troisfontaines had written the following passage (pp. 51-52):

"What kind of man is a man under forty who hangs out in cafes? Look at him flopped down any old place in a moleskin booth. The reason why he ordinarily lives in this public hall is that he has no 'home,' no hearth around which his family might gather or at which he might greet his close friends. The people he calls his friends are really just passing acquaintances, and love for him is what he 'makes with' women he happens to run into. Politics? Oh! He talks a lot about it, but without really committing himself except to criticize and scheme: social service, civic life, job, everything which might be effective and constructive dies at the frosted door. Not to speak of the religious life. . . . Or of love of nature. . . . What is left of it in these adulterated circles where the very products of the earth themselves are drunk, in an advanced state of fermentation, from little glasses? . . .

"'The cafe man,' with all his anchors broken, cut off from his organic ties with the world, other men, and God, life's river has cast up in solitude upon her banks."

Sartre objects that Troisfontaines presents the cafe as an intrinsically evil place, and says more specifically (pp. 52-53):

It's true I spend my days there, and from morning to night. But your interpretation of this is wrong, because I'm more "committed" there than I am at home. In my room I feel like stretching out on my bed. In the cafe I work: that's where I've written all my books. . . . What draws me to the cafe? It's an indifferent atmosphere where other people exist without caring about me and without my bothering about them. The anonymous customers who dispute noisily at the neighboring table bother me less than a wife and children who creep around so as not to bother me. The weight of a family would be unbearable to me. Whereas in the cafe the others are there, and that's that. The door opens. A pretty woman walks through the room and sits down. I watch her go by and then go back effortlessly to my blank page. She has gone by like a movement of my consciousness, and nothing more.

The second theme broached in the conversation is that of the existence of God. Sartre says in this respect (p. 86):

The world is obviously absurd and ends for us in death. It is because men are afraid of this gratuitous existence, it is in order to guarantee that they will be rewarded in the great beyond, that they have invented a God. But for us, who look life in the face, there's no need to bother about these chimeras. You are mistaken when you accuse me of being against *God: how could one be against what does not exist? I am* without *God and I'm proud of it.*

Naturally, Troisfontaines sees this attitude as Lucifer's.

46/104

Text on *Miracle de la rose* ⟨Miracle of the Rose⟩, by Jean Genet.

-- Publicity inset for the first edition of *Miracle de la rose*. Lyon: Barbezat. Edition limited to 475 copies and printed on March 30, 1946. B.N. listing: Enfer 1479.

This text seems to be the first Sartre wrote about Genet. We reproduce it below *in extenso* (as translated by Philip Thody in his book *Jean Genet: A Study of His Novels and Plays* [London: Hamish Hamilton, 1968]):

"Since you are not a homosexual, how can you like my books?" asks Genet with his feigned naivety. It is because I am not a homosexual that I like them: pederasts are afraid of this violent, ceremonious work, in which Genet, using long, magnificent, highly decorated sentences, follows his vice right through to the end, making it into an instrument with which to explore the world, and, at the end of this haughty confession, into a passion. Proust presented homosexuality as a fate imposed upon men, Genet demands it as a choice. Everything is choice, in Miracle of the Rose, *the events and the surprising order of the narration: the author has chosen theft and prison, he has chosen love and chosen to maintain awareness in the midst of Evil* [la conscience dans le Mal]. *He touches lightly on his subject, he flaunts his own nature, and yet never abandons himself completely: his art lies in holding his readers at a distance. Thanks to this, what we find in the depths of this far-off world, in the hell of warders, cracksmen and punishment cells, is a man.*

Philip Thody also points out, on the other hand, that a publicity inset for *Our Lady of the Flowers*, the translation of *Notre-Dame des Fleurs*, which was published in Paris in 1949 by Paul Morihien, includes the following lines from Sartre:

French literature is known abroad chiefly in its universalistic, rationalist and humanistic aspect. But it should not be forgotten that it has been marked since its origins with works that are secret and black--in the sense of black magic--and these are perhaps its most beautiful. From the poems of Villon to the works of Sade, Rimbaud and Lautréamont they bear witness of our guilty conscience. It is not sure whether Jean Genet, the latest of these "magicians," is not also the greatest.

46/104 A

"Existentialist," anonymous interview-article.

-- *New Yorker*, March 16, 1946, pp. 24-25.

This article gives a vivid picture of Sartre on the occasion of a lecture he gave at the beginning of March, 1946, at Carnegie Hall under the auspices of the avant-garde magazine *View*, and it relates some of his comments on life in New York: *The hotels have the very good custom of throwing out the guests after a sojourn of three or five days. I prefer three. If one takes the precaution of leaving no forwarding address, it is impossible for anybody interested in literature to find one. One is free to promenade oneself in the streets but relieved of the necessity of conversation. That is, if one has taken the precaution not to learn spoken English. Two phrases only are necessary for a whole evening of English conversation, I have found: "Scotch-and-soda?" and "Why not?" By alternating them, it is impossible to make a mistake.*

46/105

"A la recherche de l'existentialisme: M. Jean-Paul Sartre s'explique" ⟨In Quest of Existentialism: M. Jean-Paul Sartre Explains Himself⟩, interview by Jean Duché.

a) Le Littéraire, April 13, 1946.

b) Reprinted as "Assumer pleinement sa condition d'homme" ⟨To Fully Assume One's Human Condition⟩. In Jean Duché. *Liberté européenne*. Flammarion, 1949. Pp. 133-40.

Jean Duché adopts a frivolous tone and questions Sartre about what he alleges is his complacency about filth. Sartre explains himself in good grace and then takes up the defense of Mathieu: *There is in him that constant effort to be lucid, that pride in questioning everything, in fully assuming his human condition, . . . the man who seeks is already ethical.*

Concerning Marxism, Sartre states, *I think there is a contradiction in terms between materialism and dialectic*, but he says he shares the Communists' will to realize concrete freedom. He adds, however, *But what would the liberation of a man whose actions were determined mean? If man were not free, it wouldn't be worth moving a finger for him.*

He announces the appearance of an atheistic humanism which will take its place alongside Christian humanism and Communist society. The final volume of *Roads to Freedom* should help to base an ethics on lucidity, freedom, and responsibility (see 49/191 and 49/192).

46/106

Manhattan: The Great American Desert.

46/106

a) Town and Country, May, 1946, pp. 65 ff.

b) Excerpts in *Time*, May 13, 1946, pp. 25-26.

c) Reprinted in Alexander Klein, ed. *Empire City*. New York, Rinehart, 1955. Pp. 451-57.

d) Reprinted as *New York, the Colonial City*. In LITERARY AND PHILOSOPHICAL ESSAYS (1955).

e) Retranslated into French as *Ville coloniale* ⟨Colonial City⟩. *Spectateur*, July 2, 1946.

The text is preceded by the following note: " . . . *Here is an article which appeared in an American magazine and which I don't have the French original of. Have it translated and I'll touch it up.* It is this article, retranslated and then revised by the author, that we are publishing."

f) Original version under the title *New York, ville coloniale*. In SITUATIONS, III.

> In this engaging, melancholy text, Sartre defines what he calls "New York sickness." His hasty judgment of jazz is to be understood in terms of this melancholy (SITUATIONS, III, p. 123).

46/107

Forgers of Myths: The Young Playwrights of France.

a) Theatre Arts (New York), XXX, no. 6 (June, 1946), 324-35. Reprinted in:

b) Rosamond Gilder, ed. *Theatre Arts Anthology*. New York: Theatre Arts Books, 1950. Pp. 135-42.

c) Toby Cole, ed. *Playwrights on Playwriting*. New York: Hill and Wang, 1960. Pp. 117-24.

d) J. Gassner and R. C. Allen, eds. *Theatre and Drama in the Making*. New York: Houghton-Mifflin, 1964. Pp. 806-13.

> This article, translated into English by Rosamond Gilder, has no French version extant. There is, however, a résumé with numerous quotations in an article entitled "Jean-Paul Sartre déclare la guerre à la psychologie et se fait l'apôtre du mythe" ⟨Jean-Paul Sartre Declares War on Psychology and Declares Himself the Apostle of Myth⟩, in *La Voix de Paris*, June 26, 1946, and another shorter one entitled "Sartre et le théâtre"⟨Sartre and the Theater⟩, in *Juin*, July 23, 1946.
>
> The fullest statement of Sartre's ideas about what has been called "existential theater" is found in this article. Sartre explains to the American public the intentions of postwar French theater. The presentation

of Jean Anouilh's *Antigone* in New York had led to a certain number of misunderstandings among the critics which this article tries to clear up. Sartre rejects the idea of a "return to tragedy" or a "renaissance of philosophic theater," but recognizes that the new playwrights are *less concerned with innovation than with going back to a tradition.* He then analyzes the meaning of the break with a "theater of characters" and sets forth the aims of a "theater of situations": he justifies the rejection of psychology, gives his reasons for preferring Corneille to Racine, extols a theater that is "ethical" in the sense of "representing conflicts of rights"; refutes the claim that the works of the new playwrights are problem plays, explains that they resort to myths because myths take account of the human situation in its entirety, evokes his own experience of having the power of the theater revealed to him in staging BARIONA, justifies the austerity and the recourse to extreme situations of the new playwrights' plays, and extols a theater that keeps the air of a rite and expresses itself in a language which is simple, sober, and concise. The examples he cites are Anouilh's *Antigone*, Camus's *Misunderstanding* and *Caligula*, and Simone de Beauvoir's *The Useless Mouths*, as well as his own plays.

46/108

Matérialisme et révolution ⟨Materialism and Revolution⟩.

a) *Les Temps modernes*, no. 9 (June, 1946), pp. 1537-63; no. 10 (July, 1946), pp. 1-32.

b) Reprinted in *France-Asie* (Saigon), 2d Year; nos. 15 (June 15, 1947) to 18 (September 15, 1947).

c) Reprinted in SITUATIONS, III. The notes to pages 135, 184, 193, 210, and 215 have been added; the one on page 206 is modified.

There are several translations in independent volumes abroad.

Materialism and Revolution.

t1) Large excerpts translated by Ralph Manheim. *Materialism and Revolution.* *Politics*, IV, no. 4 (July-August, 1947), 161-72. In a special number entitled "French Political Writing," edited by Lionel Abel and with texts by Simone de Beauvoir, Georges Bataille, Albert Camus, Maurice Merleau-Ponty, etc.

t2) Translated by Annette Michelson. In LITERARY AND PHILOSOPHICAL ESSAYS (1955) and other volumes.

46/108

This article, which was announced in the first issue of *Les Temps modernes* under the title "Revolutionary Materialism," formulates Sartre's basic objections to dialectical materialism--or rather, as a note added in SITUATIONS, III, makes clear, *to the Marxist scholasticism of 1949. Or, if you wish, to Marx* seen through *Stalinist neo-Marxism.* Written at a time when Sartre, as Simone de Beauvoir puts it, "was still far from having grasped the fruitfulness of the Marxian conception of the dialectic and materialism," this article has obvious weaknesses on the intellectual level: "[Sartre] pointed out the place that revolution actually and necessarily gives to the idea of freedom. At this time his thinking fell short because it was uncertain about the freedom-situation relation, and even more so about history." Sartre's criticism here of the idea of a dialectic of nature and of materialism as a *revolutionary myth*, as well as his affirmation of freedom as the constituent structure of action, will be taken up again, deepened and developed, superseded at several points, and backed up by new and more valid arguments in various writings in the fifties, and will find their most complete expression in *Search for a Method* and (above all) CRITIQUE OF DIALECTICAL REASON.

Let us note that although Sartre concedes nothing concerning the main point of his polemic with orthodox Marxism, his tone is moderate. Only Roger Garaudy, who had attacked Sartre very violently the year before (see "Un faux prophète: Jean-Paul Sartre" ⟨Jean-Paul Sartre, False Prophet⟩, *Les Lettres françaises*, December 28, 1945), is singled out personally.

In Georges Lukács, *Existentialisme ou Marxisme?* ⟨Existentialism or Marxism?⟩ ([Nagel, 1948], pp. 141-60 and *passim*), there is a Marxist criticism, made without excessive good faith, of this article. See also André Lentin, "Sartre, le marxisme et la science" ⟨Sartre, Marxism, and Science⟩, *La Pensée*, no. 9 (October-December, 1946), pp. 112-15.

46/109

"Alcune domande a Jean-Paul Sartre e a Simone de Beauvoir" ⟨Some Questions Put to Jean-Paul Sartre and Simone de Beauvoir⟩, interview by Franco Fortini.

-- *Il Politecnico* (Milan), nos. 31-32 (July-August, 1946), pp. 33-35.

This interview, which was given during a trip Sartre made to Italy, is part of a work entitled "Esistenzialismo, l'uomo e la realta" ⟨Existentialism, Man, and Reality⟩, which also includes an article by Simone de Beauvoir, "Idealismo morale e realismo politico" ⟨Ethical Idealism and Political Realism⟩.

Il Politecnico, edited by Elio Vittorini, had already published Sartre's manifesto on committed literature (see 45/80), and Franco Fortini subsequently published a text entitled "Biographie d'un jeune bourgeois intellectuel" ⟨Biography of a Young Bourgeois Intellectual⟩ in a special issue of *Les Temps modernes* devoted to Italy (nos. 23-24 [August-September, 1947], pp. 418-30).

Although short, the interview is interesting in many respects: Sartre first analyzes religious feeling *(In Christ we have a God who sacrifices himself in order that man may live; but in reality man's passion is to sacrifice himself perpetually in order that God may exist. A useless, ruinous sacrifice* ⟨from French translation by Rybalka and Contat⟩); he then talks about psychoanalysis and goes on to say that he believes it is necessary to collaborate *laterally* with the Communists on the level of action.

46/110

American Novelists in French Eyes, translation by Evelyn de Solis of a lecture given at Yale in 1946.

a) Atlantic Monthly, CLXXVIII, no. 2 (August, 1946), 114-18.

b) In William M. Gibson, ed. *Twelve American Writers*. New York: Macmillan, 1962. Pp. 781-86.

Sartre gives the reasons for the infatuation of young French novelists such as Albert Camus, Simone de Beauvoir, and himself, as well as Mouloudji and Jean Jeansion, for writers like William Faulkner, Ernest Hemingway, John Dos Passos, John Steinbeck, and John Erskine Caldwell, whom the educated public in the United States frequently consider second-rate authors. The Occupation increased the fascination which American life, with its violence, proliferation, and mobility, had for French intellectuals. But the main reason for the influence of the American novel stems from its revolutionary narrative techniques. *We have not sought with morose delight stories of murder and rape, but lessons in a renewal of the art of writing. We were weighted down, without being aware of it, by our traditions and our culture. These American novelists, without such traditions, without help, have forged, with barbaric brutality, tools of inestimable value. . . . We have treated consciously and intellectually what was the fruit of a talented and unconscious spontaneity. . . . Soon the first French novels written during the Occupation will appear in the United States. We shall give back to you these techniques which you have lent us. We shall return them digested, intellectualized, less effective, and less brutal--consciously adapted to French taste. Because of that incessant exchange which makes nations rediscover in other nations what they have invented first and then*

46/110

rejected, perhaps you will rediscover in these foreign books the eternal youth of that "old" Faulkner.

46/111

Présentation ⟨Introduction⟩ (to a special issue of *Les Temps modernes* on the United States).

a) Les Temps modernes, nos. 11-12 (August-September, 1946), pp. 193-98.

b) Reprinted in SITUATIONS, III.

Americans and Their Myths, anonymous translation.

-- *The Nation*, October 18, 1947, pp. 402-3.

In the *Introduction*, Sartre rapidly makes a survey of the United States and briefly comments on some of the articles published in this issue.

46/111 A

Jean-Paul Sartre présente Gjon Mili ⟨Jean-Paul Sartre Presents Gjon Mili⟩.

a) Text written for the first Gjon Mili photography show held at the Galerie du Bac from October 1 to 10, 1946.

b) Reprinted in facsimile in the catalog for the Gjon Mili show held at the Musée des Arts Décoratifs from June 3 to July 26, 1971.

[Mili] makes each photograph a test: according to him, there are as many ways to get photographed as there are men. If you take his test, he will not only have pinned you alive into his collection but observed you. He will know you: you will have put yourself doubly in his hands. The primitives of the South Seas refuse, they say, to let themselves be photographed; it seems to them they're being captured and locked up forever. Look at Mili's photograph of Molotov and you will understand their wisdom.

46/112

"Sartre dans Paris et dans le monde" ⟨Sartre in Paris and the World⟩, interview-article by Pierre Berger.

-- *Spectateur*, October 1, 1946.

Text of no interest. In it Sartre gives a few details about his youth.

46/113

La Guerre et la peur ⟨War and Fear⟩.

-- *Franchise* (Notebooks of a France Reborn), no. 3 (November-December, 1946).

A special issue, "Le Temps des assassins" ⟨The Age of Assassins⟩, including among others an article by Albert Camus entitled "Nous autres meurtriers" ⟨We Murderers⟩.

The first of a number of articles that Sartre wrote during this period to denounce belief in the inevitability of war. We reproduce it below in its entirety:

This war will be the war of fear. It is in fear that it is being readied. People are letting it come on softly, with a sort of ecstasy. They believe in it the way they do in fortune-telling, or in their confessor, or in anything which rids them of the responsibility of forging their own destiny. They love their fear. It reconciles them with themselves, and like a sneeze or diarrhea, puts the mind to sleep. And this threat hanging over their heads conceals the empty heaven from them--it's a roof. Yet in their terror governments are watching one another. When one nation, out of panic, makes too quick a move, the others, out of panic, will leap for its throat.

Then the abstract massacre will start. In other times one risked his life against the lives of others, one saw his dead enemy up close, one could touch his wounds; this time one will fire with no further risk and will die for nothing. Technicians off in Washington and Texas will set up a slaughterhouse in Baku or in Leningrad and never even see it. Never even imagine it. No heroes; no martyrs: just a cataclysm coming down on panic-stricken animals.

I do not believe in the end of the world and I do not even know whether I believe in this war. Twenty, maybe fifty years will pass before it does take place. But if we keep on waiting for it all this time, if we have to souse ourselves in fear for fifty years, if we convince ourselves that we must wait until the coming war is over before we can start living, then we will have made the Bomb three-quarters useless: there will not be any men left to kill; that will have been done already.

46/114

* *Ecrire pour son époque* ⟨We Write for Our Own Time⟩.

This excerpt from *What is Literature?* has been widely disseminated even though it has never been reprinted in a book.

46/114

a) French version. *Erasme* (The Hague), nos. 11-12 (1946), pp. 454-60.

b) French version. *Valeurs* (Alexandria), nos. 7-8 (October, 1946-January, 1947), pp. 105-12.

Issue published in January, 1947.

c) Excerpt in French. In *Adam International Review*, no. 166 (January, 1947), pp. 1-5.

d) Italian version. *Srivere per il proprio tempo. Nuova Antologia* (January, 1947), pp. 51-56.

e) Reprinted in *Les Temps modernes*, no. 33 (June, 1948), pp. 2113-21.

We Write for Our Own Time, translated by Sylvia Glass.

t1) Virginia Quarterly Review, XXIII (April, 1947), 236-43.

t2) Meanjin, VI (summer, 1947), 222-26.

t3) In Haskell M. Block and Herman Salinger, eds. *Creative Vision*. New York: Grove Press, 1960; Gloucester, Mass.: Peter Smith, 1968. Pp. 187-94.

> This excellent text seems to be a reply to the criticisms evoked by the *Introduction* to *Les Temps modernes* and has the marks of a manifesto. It is undoubtedly for this reason that the text was not included in the final version of *What Is Literature?*

46/114 A

Prose et langage ⟨Prose and Language⟩.

a) Vrai (Brussels), no. 51 (December 21, 1946).

b) Adam International Review, nos. 169-70 (April-May, 1947), pp. 3-6.

> Concentrated version of pages 70-76 of SITUATIONS, II, with an unpublished passage in which Sartre talks about puns.

46/114 B

Une Conférence de Jean-Paul Sartre ⟨A Lecture by Jean-Paul Sartre⟩.

-- *Fraternité*, December 31, 1946.

46/NOTE 3.

Excerpts from a lecture given under the auspices of *Fraternité* and the Alliance Against Racism and dealing with racial minorities in the United States. Sartre shows the sexual and economic aspects of the Negro problem, stressing, like Boris Vian [Vernon Sullivan] in *I'll Spit on Your Graves* (published in November, 1946), the problem of white blood for the blacks and the sexual obsession of the whites with the blacks.

46/NOTE 1

In Lausanne, on June 1, 1946, Sartre gave a lecture entitled "What is Existentialism?" (there is a report of it in *La Gazette de Lausanne*, June 3, 1946). It was after this lecture that André Gorz met "Morel"-Sartre (see *Le Traître* ⟨The Traitor⟩ [Seuil, (1958)], pp. 245-48). The portrait Gorz draws of Sartre at that time is one of the most vivid ones we have of him.

46/NOTE 2.

An announced but never published article, "Interim Report" (*Les Temps modernes*, no. 10 [July, 1946]), was reduced to "Report" (*Les Temps modernes*, no. 15 [December, 1946]).

46/NOTE 3.

According to the July 4, 1946, *Humanité*, which sees the following statement as a proof of hostility toward the new Yugoslavia, Sartre allegedly said during his trip to Italy: *I did not want to sign the manifesto of the French Leftist intellectuals demanding that Venezia Giulia be given to Yugoslavia, for I admire the new democratic Italy.*

1947

47/115

BAUDELAIRE.

a) Current edition preceded by a note by Michel Leiris. Les Essais series, no. 24. Gallimard, [1947]. 224 pages.

The book is dedicated to Jean Genet. The original edition includes 30 copies on wood-free vellum and 1040 copies on esparto grass.

b) New edition. Idées N.R.F. series, no. 31. Gallimard, [1963]. 245 pages. As far as content is concerned, this volume is the same as the earlier one.

c) Pages 25-33 of edition *(a)* were reprinted as Introduction to Charles Baudelaire. *Les Fleurs du mal* ⟨The Flowers of Evil⟩. Le Livre de poche series, no. 677. Gallimard, [1961]. Pp. 5-9.

BAUDELAIRE, translated by Martin Turnell.

t1) With a foreword by translator. London: Horizon Press, 1949; New York: New Directions, 1950.

t2) *Ibid.* London: Hamish Hamilton, [1964].

t3) *Ibid.* in paperback. New York: New Directions, [1947].

See also 46/101

47/116

THÉÂTRE: LES MOUCHES, HUIS CLOS, MORTS SANS SÉPULTURE, LA PUTAIN RESPECTUEUSE ⟨Theater: The Flies, No Exit, The Victors, The Respectful Prostitute⟩.

-- Gallimard, [1947]. 301 pages. Printing date: March 20, 1947.

The volume was subsequently reset to have 317 pages, and it was published in 1960 in the Soleil series. Throughout this book, it is designated as THÉÂTRE, I.

The text of THE VICTORS involves major variations from that of the Marguerat edition. (See 46/89.)

Translation: No English-language volume includes the selection of plays noted above. For translations, see under individual play titles.

> In the July, 1947, *Bulletin N.R.F.*, Sartre himself presents this work in these terms:
>
> *No matter what the circumstances, no matter what the time or place, man is free to choose himself a traitor or a hero, a coward or a conqueror. In choosing either slavery or freedom for himself, he will at the same time choose a world where man is free or enslaved--and the drama will arise from his attempts to justify this free choice. Whether we are face to face with gods, with tyranny or death, there is one thing that we are sure of: we are free.*

47/117

SITUATIONS, I.

-- Gallimard, [1947]. 337 pages. Printing date: October 20, 1947.

This volume, which had been in the offing since 1945, was originally to be called "Significations." It includes, in French, sixteen critical essays arranged in order of publication:

-- *"Sartoris," by William Faulkner*	see ## 38/15
-- *John Dos Passos and "1919"*	## 38/17
-- *"The Conspiracy," by Paul Nizan*	38/19
-- *A Fundamental Idea of Husserl's Phenomenology: Intentionality*	39/23
-- *M. François Mauriac and Freedom*	## 39/24
-- *Vladimir Nabokov: "Mistrust"*	39/25
-- *Denis de Rougemont: "Love and the Western World"*	39/25
-- *On "The Sound and the Fury": Time in the Work of Faulkner*	## 39/26

47/117

-- *M. Jean Giraudoux and the Philosophy of Aristotle: Concerning "Duel of Angels"* ## 40/30

-- *An Analysis of "The Stranger"* ## 43/39

-- *"Aminadab," or The Fantastic Considered as a Language* (on Maurice Blanchot) ## 43/41

-- *A New Mystic* (on Georges Bataille) 43/42

-- *Departure and Return* (on Brice Parain) # 44/44

-- *Man and Things* (on Francis Ponge) 44/50

-- *Man in Chains: Notes on Jules Renard's "Journal"* 45/75

-- *Cartesian Freedom* # 45/84

There is no major change in any of these texts.

Parts of SITUATIONS, I, translated by Annette Michelson.

t1) Essays marked # in LITERARY AND PHILOSOPHICAL ESSAYS. New York: Criterion Books; London: Rider, 1955.

The essays included in this volume were selected by Sartre himself.

t2) *Ibid.* in paperback. New York: Collier Books, [1962].

t3) *Ibid.* London: Hutchinson, 1968.

t4) Essays marked ## reprinted also in LITERARY ESSAYS. New York: Philosophical Library, [1957]. Issued later in paperback (Wisdom).

With the exception of the article on Husserl, the other essays apparently have not yet been published in English.

47/118

LES JEUX SONT FAITS ⟨The Chips Are Down⟩, movie script.

a) Nagel, [1947]. 198 pages.

Printing date: September, 1947. 500 copies on wood-free vellum. There is a complete technical index of the movie at the end of the volume.

b) Published as a serial in *Le Courrier de l'Ouest* from May 26 to June 15, 1948. Eighteen-part narrative illustrated with photographs from the movie and adapted by Georges Emmanuel.

c) Anglo-Saxon textbook edition. Presented and annotated by Mary E. Storer. New York: Appleton-Century-Crofts, 1952; London: Methuen, [1952].

Today Mary E. Storer's introduction and notes seem very inadequate.

d) Textbook editions with French text:

-- Copenhagen: Gyldendal, [1964].

-- Groningen: Wolters-Noordhoff, 1965.

-- Stockholm: Läromedelsförlagen, [1966]. This edition is slightly abridged and illustrated with photographs from the movie.

e) The script of Jean Delannoy's movie (194 pages, 518 shots, unpublished) is slightly different from the Nagel edition. The adaptation is by Jean Delannoy and J.-L. Bost.

THE CHIPS ARE DOWN, translated by Louise Varese.

-- New York: Lear, 1948; London: Rider, 1951.

According to Simone de Beauvoir, this is the first film script Sartre submitted to Pathé, toward the end of 1943. It takes up elements of the story *The Room* again (characters' names, theme of sequestration, etc.) and presents, in a more poetic and less realistic way, the same problems of interpretation as NO EXIT, a play written at approximately the same time.

Sartre's text is reproduced faithfully but without genius in Jean Delannoy's adaptation (see Appendix). At a showing of the movie in September, 1947, during the First International Congress of Filmology being held at the Sorbonne, Sartre said a few words about the language of the movies (see *Samedi-Soir*, September 27, 1945, and *Le Figaro*, September 28, 1947).

47/119

"*Les Jeux sont faits?* Tout le contraire d'une pièce existentialiste, nous dit Jean-Paul Sartre" ⟨THE CHIPS ARE DOWN? Just the Opposite of an Existentialist Play,Jean-Paul Sartre Says⟩, interview by Paul Carrière.

-- *Le Figaro*, April 29, 1947.

Excerpts: *My first film,* THE CHIPS ARE DOWN, *will not be existentialist. . . . On the contrary, existentialism never admits that the chips are ever*

47/119

down. Even after death our acts pursue us. We outlive ourselves in our acts, even though they often develop contrary to our intentions and in directions we did not want them to. . . .

My script is bathed in determinism, because I thought that I was allowed to have fun too.

47/120

L'HOMME ET LES CHOSES ⟨Man and Things⟩.

-- Seghers, [1947]. 76 pages.

Date of printing: January, 1947. This edition consists of 100 copies of vélin Johannot, 880 numbered copies on alfa Marais, and 100 copies marked H.C. (See 44/50.)

47/121

La Responsabilité de l'écrivain ⟨The Writer's Responsibility⟩, lecture.

a) Les Conférences de l'U.N.E.S.C.O. ⟨UNESCO Conferences⟩. Fontaine, [1947]. Pp. 57-73.

The Responsibility of the Writer, translated by Betty Askwith.

t1) In *Reflections on Our Age*. London: Allan Wingate, 1948; New York: Columbia University Press, 1949. Pp. 67-83.

t2) In Haskell M. Block and Herman Salinger, eds. *Creative Vision*. New York: Grove Press, 1960; Gloucester, Mass.: Peter Smith, 1968. Pp. 165-85.

Text of a lecture given at the Sorbonne on November 1, 1946, to commemorate the founding of UNESCO (see reports in the November 2 *Franc-Tireur* and *Combat*, as well as in *Travaux et Documents*, nos. 5-6 [May-June, 1947], pp. 37-40). In *Force of Circumstance* (p. 109), there is an account of the rather quaint circumstances under which Sartre prepared for his speech. This account sums up, in a direct, effective way, most of the themes which *What Is Literature?* will subsequently consider: the responsibility of the writer, the difference between prose and poetry, literature as "perpetual affirmation of human freedom," the historical situation of the writer, the function of the bourgeois writer in the present time, etc.

Toward the end of his lecture, Sartre raises the problem of violence:

. . . A writer ought not to condemn violence a priori; he ought to condemn it in its framework and as a means. Above all, he has to understand that we must make an effort not to condemn violence generally and abstractly, but to try in each case to determine the minimum of violence that's necessary. For we can do nothing today without violence, since everything is violent. Thus there is no question of condemning all violence but only of condemning useless violence (p. 71).

And consequently he defines the responsibility of the writer:

-- His task is to create a positive theory of liberty and liberation.

-- His task in every case is to put himself in a position to condemn violence from the viewpoint of oppressed men and classes.

-- His task is, finally, to establish a true relationship of means and ends.

-- His task is to immediately reject, in his own name--which of course will not prevent it--any violent means of establishing or upholding a regime.

-- His task, basically, is to reflect untiringly, always, unceasingly upon the means-end problem or the problem of the relation between ethics and politics (p. 72).

We can see in the conclusion both the Sartre of THE FLIES and the one who, starting in 1946, will constantly take stands against the war:

What we writers must avoid is having our responsibility turn into guilt because, fifty years from now, people can say: They saw the biggest catastrophe the world has ever known coming on and they kept silent (p. 72).

47/122

Prefacing letter to *Le Problème moral et la pensée de Sartre* ⟨Sartre's Thinking and the Moral Question⟩, by Francis Jeanson.

a) Pensées et Civilisations series. Editions du Myrte, [1947]. Pp. 13-14.

b) New edition. *Le Problème moral et la pensée de Sartre*, with a postscript entitled *Un Quidam nommé Sartre (1965)* ⟨A Certain Man Named Sartre (1965)⟩. Seuil, [1965]. Pp. 11-12.

47/122

In this extremely laudatory prefacing letter, Sartre wrote to Jeanson: *If there were any need to show the excellence of your method and your strict honesty in applying it, I would say this in proof: you have caught the spirit of my thought so well that you have managed to move beyond the position I had taken in my books at the same time I was moving beyond it, and to ask yourself the same questions about the relations of ethics and history, of the universal and concrete transcendence, that I was simultaneously asking myself.* This recommendation helped establish Jeanson's reputation as the most reliable commentator on Sartre's thinking. Let us remember that Jeanson was only twenty-five when he wrote this book which was long considered the best philosophical study of the Sartre of BEING AND NOTHINGNESS and those works stemming directly from it. Jeanson's profound understanding of this fundamental stage of Sartre's thought is also evident in the pertinent exegesis of Sartre's theater he gives in his *Sartre par lui-même* ⟨Sartre by Himself⟩ (Seuil, 1955). In spite of the perhaps excessive importance this work gives to the theme of "bastardy," it is often considered the best introduction to Sartre's work. On the other hand, Jeanson does not seem to have followed in any such precise fashion the subsequent development of Sartre's thinking in *Search for a Method* and CRITIQUE OF DIALECTICAL REASON, so that what Colette Audry and André Gorz have written about this stage of Sartre's thinking is preferable to what Jeanson has written about it.

(Concerning the relationship between Sartre and Jeanson, see also 59/329 and 68/484.)

47/123

* *Sculptures à n dimensions* ⟨N-Dimensional Sculpture⟩, introduction to a show by David Hare.

a) Exposition David Hare : Catalogue ⟨The David Hare Show Catalogue⟩. Maeght Gallery, 13, rue de Téhéran, Paris-VIIIe: "Editions Pierre à feu," [1947]. Four in-folio pages.

b) Excerpts under the same title in *Arts*, December 12, 1947.

N-Dimensional Sculpture.

-- Anonymous translation in *Women : A Collaboration of Artists and Writers*. New York: Samuel M. Kootz, [1948].

During the war, David Hare had published a New York review called *VVV* backed by André Breton. During his stay in France, Hare was an active member of the surrealist group and published several pieces in *Les*

Temps modernes. Sartre, who had met him through Jacqueline Breton, agreed out of friendship to write an introduction to his show. The show was held from December 19, 1947, to January 18, 1948.

David Hare at present lives in New York, and it is thanks to him that we are able to reprint here in its entirety a text which up till now has been practically inaccessible.

47/124

"'Vous nous embêtez avec Faulkner le vieux,' disent les Américains" ⟨"You Give Us a Pain Talking about Old Faulkner All the Time," the Americans Say⟩, interview by Jean Desternes.

-- *Combat*, January 3, 1947.

Here Sartre opens an investigation of a subject which was fashionable at the time, the influence of the American novel. Albert Camus's response is to be found in the January 17 *Combat* and François Mauriac's in that of January 26-27.

Sartre adds nothing new or striking to what he has said elsewhere.

47/125

Qu'est-ce que la littérature? ⟨What Is Literature?⟩.

a) Les Temps modernes, no. 17 (February, 1947), pp. 769-805; no. 18 (March, 1947), pp. 961-88; no. 19 (April, 1947), pp. 1194-1218; no. 20 (May, 1947), pp. 1410-29; no. 21 (June, 1947), pp. 1607-41; no. 22 (July, 1947), pp. 77-114.

The first version was published in a more-or-less complete form in SITUATIONS, II. There are important changes in the final version: a certain number of notes have been added (in particular notes 2 and 4, pp. 85-88; note 3, p. 115; notes 5-11, pp. 198-201; and note 6, pp. 316-26), as well as a twenty-six line passage on pages 265-66; another passage (pp. 177-85) has been transferred from the chapter "Situation de l'écrivain en 1947" ⟨The Writer's Situation in 1947⟩; and a sentence has been omitted on page 315, line 11: "Puisque nous sommes écrivains, c'est notre devoir d'aider à faire l'Europe *par nos écrits*," ⟨Since we are writers, it's our duty to help create Europe by our writings⟩, etc.

There are several uncorrected errors, especially the one on page 68 where Sartre puts together the second and fourteenth lines of Stéphane Mallarmé's "Brise marine" ⟨Sea Breeze⟩:

> *Fuir, là-bas fuir, je sens que des oiseaux sont ivres,*
> *Mais ô mon coeur entends le chant des matelots.*
> ⟨If only I could flee, flee far away, to where the birds themselves, I feel, are drunken, / But oh my heart just listen to the song the sailors sing.⟩

and adds: *This "mais"* ⟨but⟩, *which looms like a monolith at the mouth of the phrase, does not tie the last verse to the first.* Let us point out, however, that this mistaken quotation does not have any real effect on Sartre's line of reasoning.

b) Final version in SITUATIONS, II.

c) Book. Idées series, no. 58. Gallimard, [1964].

On page 370, a typographical error transforms *Drieu* into *Dieu.*

What is Literature?, excerpts translated by Bernard Frechtman.

t1) In four parts. *Partisan Review,* Vol. XV (January, March, May, and June, 1948).

t2) Transition 48, nos. 1-4 (1948).

For publication in volume, see 48/155.

To be better understood, this manifesto in favor of committed literature should be put back into the atmosphere of the years 1945-48, and into its polemical context.

In his *Introduction* to *Les Temps modernes* and his article *The Nationalization of Literature,* Sartre had made a certain number of claims which he had not had the time to expand on and which had been violently attacked. By taking issue here with the traditional conception of literature, he tries to reply to his critics and at the same time to show how art is actually *a free person's assumption of his responsibility for the world.* To do this, he does not devote his efforts to defining any sort of essence of literature or to emphasizing "the achievement of literature"; he tries, on the contrary, to establish the theoretical and practical foundations for a committed literature by answering the questions What does it mean to write? Why does one write? For whom does one write? and by analyzing the situation of the writer in 1947.

In spite of the rather large number of rough approximations and some actual errors of detail in its historical part, and in spite of the obvious rigidity of certain stands it takes, *What Is Literature?* is still one of the most stimulating books one can read, and it has been recognized for a long time now as a classic of criticism. The questions Sartre raises were topical in 1947; although the historical situation has changed considerably, they are just as topical today.

Theoretically, most of the interpretive limitations of the work derive from the fact that Sartre does not hesitate to use the terms *freedom* and *commitment* in a simultaneously philosophical and political (or moralizing) sense, and that he does not always take the trouble to distinguish (as he will later concerning Gustave Flaubert) between political commitment and *literary commitment* (the expression used in CRITIQUE OF DIALECTICAL REASON, Gallimard edition, p. 72). In his concern with giving the idea of commitment a greater complexity, Sartre has moreover *constantly* corrected certain ideas he formulated in *What Is Literature?*, although he has never rejected his basic position.

47/126

* *Le Processus historique* 〈The Historical Process〉.

a) La Gazette de Lausanne, February 8, 1947.

b) Excerpts in *Le Figaro littéraire*, April 19, 1947.

In an article in *Pravda* (January 23, 1947) entitled "The Smertchiakines in France," which *Les Temps modernes* (no. 20 [May, 1947], pp. 1531-36) ironically reprinted, a Soviet critic called D. Zaslavski had made a violent attack on the "nauseating, putrid concoctions which bourgeois advertising is trying to pass off as the latest thing and the most original expression in philosophical fashion." Obviously, Sartre's existentialism was meant. Zaslavski also provided this strong definition: "'Existentialism', from the French, 'existence', teaches that all historical processes are absurd and fortuitous, and every ethic a lie. It's the doctrine of spiritual emptiness. For it there neither are nor can be laws or norms. There is no History; only 'historification'. There is no ethics; only a 'life style'. There are neither peoples nor society; only personal interest and profit according to the principle, *Carpe diem.*"

Sartre replies to these attacks in an article which we note as appearing in *La Gazette de Lausanne* but which undoubtedly appeared first in some French publication.

47/127

Les Faux Nez 〈The False Noses〉, script.

-- *La Revue du cinéma*, n.s., no. 6 (spring, 1947), pp. 3-27.

The crown prince of the poverty-stricken kingdom of Moravia is afflicted with an enormous nose. In order to keep this deformity from giving him an inferiority complex, which will make him an inept ruler, the king and queen have rigged themselves out in false noses and have required that all their subjects never appear in court without wearing them too. Up till now their stratagem has succeeded. But the prince's coming marriage presents problems. The royal coffers are desperately empty, and only his marriage to the youngest daughter of the king of the Caucasus can replenish them. So this ravishing person has to disfigure herself with a false nose. Now the young prince manifests a lively repugnance for women which is unaccountably centered on their faces, and the princess experiences nothing but disgust for the unfortunate appearance of her future spouse. So the two of them decide to make the marriage which has been arranged for them fail without its seeming to be their fault that it has. Some plotters led by the king's brother, who covets both the princess and the throne, are also in league against this marriage. They have made up their minds to reveal the truth on the wedding day. The day before it, the prince surprises his fiancée without her false nose and, to the young woman's astonishment, takes off his own, to reveal a perfectly normal and even attractive face. He thinks that he is abnormal, and has, since he was very young, suffered in silence this lack of nose which makes him different from the others. Discovering this woman with an abnormality just like his own, he immediately falls in love with her. The princess, charmed by this, does not straighten him out, for she has always dreamed of a husband who has eyes only for her. So they keep on wearing their masks when they are with others and, when they are alone together, loving one another openly. But at just the moment when the marriage vows are ready to be signed, the conspirators take off their noses: are the people going to let the kingdom be ruled by a monster? The prince, not put out in the least, takes off his false nose in turn. Everyone is astounded. Then the old nurse confesses: *The real crown prince died when he was ten months old. Her majesty the queen, since she could have no more children and feared that the younger line would inherit the throne, had another child hidden in the cradle and outfitted with a false nose to make him look like the dead child. Fearing that he might betray the secret, they brought him up thinking that he was a monster and must hide his abnormality from every eye. The queen died five years later, making the old nurse swear that she would never tell the truth to a soul, not even the king. Thus the court kept on wearing false noses so that the prince would not become aware of his alleged infirmity, whereas the prince kept on wearing his in order to hide his alleged abnormality from the court.*

All ends well: the king adopts the prince, and the princess' dowry goes to the throne.

Such is, in a very condensed version, the ingenious plot of this comedy done for sheer amusement in which not a single one of Sartre's characteristic themes appears--although those who love serious meanings cannot of course be prevented from interpreting the false noses as the outward and visible sign of "bad faith" and the spirit of seriousness. This script simply represents an uncharacteristic and (it seems) unique moment of pure fantasy in Sartre's works, and as such it probably did not fail to surprise those at the time who saw him as a melancholy writer of exclusively dark and solemn works.

Given the bad luck Sartre has always had with movies, there is probably no need to regret that this script was never filmed. On the other hand, it was adapted to the theater in 1948 at Lausanne by a Swiss amateur troupe led by Charles Apothéloz and Freddy Buache, who staged their play in Paris on June 22 and 23, 1949, at the Théâtre de l'Atelier as an entry in the Concours des jeunes compagnies. The troupe, which became professional although it no longer exists today, took the name of the Compagnie des Faux-Nez ⟨Company of False Noses⟩, and the theater in Lausanne which housed them still bears this name.

The program for the Lausanne premiere of the play by the Belletrien troupe includes an excerpt from *Faces*--the complete text of *Official Portraits*--and a short anonymous piece which was written by André Gorz. The latter is entitled "Nehmt Euch selbst an der Nase" ⟨Pull Your Own Nose⟩, and uncovers very perspicaciously in *Les Faux Nez* an idea close to what Sartre will later call *seriality*.

47/128

Le Cas Nizan ⟨The Nizan Case⟩.

-- *Les Temps modernes*, no. 22 (July, 1947), pp. 181-84.

This article consists of a protest against the attacks on Paul Nizan's good name, which is signed by Sartre and others (originally published in *Carrefour* and *Le Littéraire* for March 29, 1947; also published in the April 4, 1947, *Combat*, and elsewhere), as well as a letter from Sartre to the C.N.E. ⟨National Writers' Committee⟩.

The Nizan Case, documents translated and with a comment by Cyril Connolly.

t1) Horizon, XV, no. 89 (June, 1947), 305-9.

47/128

t2) Cyril Connolly. *Ideas and Places.* New York: Harpers, [1953]. Pp. 153-58.

The above-mentioned protest challenged the Communists (and especially Henri Lefebvre) to prove their allegations against Nizan. It reveals in particular that Louis Aragon had told one of the signatories that Nizan "gave the minister of the interior information about the Communist Party." Without committing itself on the basic issue, the Editorial Board of the C.N.E. objected to "this kind of personal attack" on one of its members. In his reply to the C.N.E., Sartre said that he was the one Aragon had made the incriminating remark to and asked if the latter denied it: *In that case, it is his word against mine. Let him say it and each man may judge for himself.* Ultimately, the signatories to the protest published an official statement noting that those who had vilified Nizan had never responded to their challenge. It must be noted that the strong reaction of Nizan's defenders made short work of the Communists' accusations, and that no one today seems to claim that Nizan was a police spy.

On Nizan, see also 38/19, 60/333.

47/129

Déclaration ⟨Declaration⟩ (concerning the Paris Municipal Council's decision to take Charles Dullin's theater away from him).

-- *Combat*, May 24, 1957.

Text that was part of a series of protests entitled "Paris chasse Dullin" ⟨Paris Is Kicking Dullin Out⟩.

I have known Dullin for twenty years. I have never stopped admiring his talent, his intelligence, his probity, and his courage. He is the man who brought me into the theater. He is the man who gave me good advice when I was starting out, the man who put on my first play, THE FLIES, *a flawed and violently attacked work which, in spite of a magnificent production, was a financial failure. Dullin backed the play for almost a year in the face of the critics, the city council, and the Germans. All he got for his efforts were debts and mud.*

Many other authors could say as much as I. Almost all of our contemporary playwrights were discovered by Dullin. In order to get them started, he went bankrupt over and over again. Sometimes, to console them for a temporary failure, he even asked for a second play when the first had just bombed. We are indebted to him for his Julius Caesar, The Doctor of His Honor, *Pirandello's plays, and* King Lear. *Above all, we are indebted to*

Dullin for a theatrical style which today's young producers are trying in vain to imitate.

This retirement is far more than an injustice, far more than ungratefulness. It's a blunder. Before you fired a man full of life and in full possession of his talent, maybe you should have made sure there was someone who could take his place. Otherwise you simply made French theater the poorer.

47/130

A propos de la représentation des "Mouches" en Allemagne ⟨Concerning the Performance of THE FLIES in Germany⟩.

a) Verger (literary and theatrical review for the French Zone, Baden-Baden/Paris), 1st Year, no. 2 (June, 1947), pp. 12-13.

b) Text in German. "Der Dichter über sein Werk." Preceding a translation of the play by Gritta Baerlocher. *Die Quelle*, II (1947), 131.

Short announcement written for the performances of THE FLIES given in Germany by the Compagnie des Dix, directed by Claude Martin. Sartre returns to the circumstances in which he wrote the play:

The future--even though France was occupied by an enemy army--was open. We had a hold on it, we were free to make of it a future of defeated or--on the contrary--of free men who refused to believe that a defeat means that everything that makes men want to live a life fit for men is gone.

Today the Germans are confronted with the same situation. For Germans, too, I think remorse is sterile.

This piece is followed by an article by Alexandre Astruc, "Sartre, the Theater, and Freedom."

See 43/35 and 48/161.

47/131

* *Nick's Bar, New York City.*

a) America (Cahiers France-Amérique-Latinité), no. 5 (special issue, "Jazz 47"), Intercontinentale du Livre, pp. 11-13. Copyright date: June 25, 1947. "Jazz 47" includes pieces by Sartre, Jean Cocteau, Boris Vian, Hugues Panassié, etc., and illustrations by Fernand Léger, Jean Dubuffet, and Félix Labisse.

47/131

I Discovered Jazz in America, translation of modified version by Ralph de Toledano.

a) Saturday Review of Literature, November 29, 1947, pp. 48-49. Collected in *Saturday Review Treasury*. New York: Simon and Schuster, 1957. Pp. 315-17.

b) Reprinted with changes as "Au Nick's Bar à New York" ⟨Nick's Bar, New York City⟩. *Caliban*, no. 18 (July 15-August 15, 1948), pp. 13-15.

This article is famous above all for its opening sentence: *Jazz is like bananas; to get the taste of it you've got to be where it's at.* (Let us point out that in SITUATIONS, II, Sartre uses the same analogy for intellectual works.)

Sartre's description of Nick's Bar is reminiscent in some respects of NAUSEA: we find here the same mixture of humor, satire, and "existence," the same sense of gratuitousness and necessity, etc. The article as a whole has a certain impact but often borders on the commonplace.

Sartre's interest in jazz dates back to the twenties: we recall the important place he gave to "Some of These Days" in NAUSEA, and we know that later on, especially because of the Vians, he hung out at most of the main Parisian jazz joints and met Charlie Parker, Miles Davis, etc. In spite of this interest, which never died out (and it ought to be studied in greater depth some day), it would be a mistake to consider Sartre anything but a sympathetic and understanding jazz buff. His choice of "Some of These Days," his mistaking the identity of the woman who sang it (the Negro woman in NAUSEA is really the white Sophie Tucker), are proof of this. The fact remains that Sartre is undoubtedly the only writer of his generation to consider jazz so important.

47/132

Interview on the Jewish question.

-- *La Revue juive* (Geneva), 10th Year, nos. 6-7 (June-July, 1947), pp. 212-13.

This is a rather strange interview. It took place during the summer of 1939, that is, at a time when Sartre--an author who was known by the educated public but relatively unknown beyond that--had not yet shown any interest for the Jewish question beyond the passages in *The Childhood of a Leader* which attack anti-Semites. Is this why an editor of *La Revue juive* in Geneva questions him about the Jewish question? The fact that the review was not published during the war explains the delay in publishing Sartre's remarks. And it was the publication of ANTI-SEMITE AND JEW which led the editors to dig up the interview. The interview, published under the title "His 1939 Statement," precedes an article by Emile Biollay entitled "Jean-Paul Sartre, the Man Who Steals from Israel?" which challenges Sartre's view of what it means to be a Jew but has the highest praise for his portrayal of the anti-Semite in ANTI-SEMITE AND JEW.

We reproduce Sartre's comments in their entirety below. Their calm tone may be surprising if we forget their date, but they have the interest of presenting, albeit hastily, the first stage of his ideas about the Jewish question.

-- What do you think about antisemitism?

-- *To me, antisemitism is generally a normal social phenomenon, as crime according to Durkheim is normal. This seems to me to be completely unrelated to the character of the Jews against whom antisemitism is directed. From time to time a society needs to define itself as "against," and non-Jewish society is generally against the assimilation of the Jews. It seems to me though that the normal phenomenon I'm alluding to never exceeds certain proportions which may be established scientifically as constant. This constant antisemitism varies of course from country to country. It is more intense in Germany, for example, than in France. But in certain periods there is an abnormal increase in antisemitism as a compensatory phenomenon, a markedly pathological development. (For example: the Dreyfus and Boulanger cases after the defeat of 1871.) Last October and November, after the defeat at Munich, an abnormal increase in hostility toward Jews could be observed in France. As far as Germany is concerned, I think that antisemitism among the masses has reached its high point there, and I would not be surprised to see a split between the leaders and the populace developing out of it. Generally speaking, I refuse to see anything lasting in nazism. It's a temporary outbreak. I don't believe in the advent of the "Nazi man."*

-- What do you think the Jews have generally contributed to culture and civilization?

-- *I only believe in the contribution Jews have made as individuals. To me it seems dangerous to talk about a specific Jewish temperament. In doing so one saddles the Jew with a prosemitic, antisemitic argument about the good or bad effects of his peculiar mentality. Of course if it were established that Jews do have a specific temperament, then in spite of everything we would have to accept this postulate in the interest of truth. But it is not. My personal experience is that Jewish contributions to philosophy are contradictory.*

47/132

Perhaps the argument we're always hearing about the restless, critical, and uncreative Jew may apply to Brunschvicg, but not to Bergson or Spinoza. Jews undoubtedly have their distinguishing characteristics. But we are unable to establish them because it is impossible to determine the extent to which they are attributable to the times, the living conditions, or the ethnic origin. And every attempt to isolate and define these characteristics is a concession to antisemitism. Personally, I can find no particular distinguishing characteristics common to the Jews I know. I think then when we do find them, it's because we put them there ourselves. Today's violent anti-semitism does not prove that assimilation is impossible. We may be witnessing no more than the temporary interruption of a continuing evolution. In any case the meaning of History cannot be determined until it is all over. But assimilation will certainly be impossible unless society is profoundly changed. It is a mistake to seek an independent solution to the Jewish problem, which is integral to a whole series of different problems.

I have reasons for being opposed to antisemitism. I am suspicious of an "anti-antisemitism" based on "the spirit of tolerance" and "broadmindedness." As soon as there's trouble, the balance swings and the "broad-mindedness," which as they used to say is "false-mindedness," becomes narrow-mindedness.

47/133

"Existentialism: A New Philosophy--or Is It Only a Word?" interview by Vincent Brome.

-- *Picture Post* (London), XXXVI, no. 5 (August 2, 1947), 4, 31.

In this article, written to inform a mass public and having no great interest, existentialism is presented as a third way between Marxism and Thomism. Its author portrays Sartre in London on the occasion of the English performance of THE VICTORS and THE RESPECTFUL PROSTITUTE, and reports (very loosely it would seem) what Sartre has to say. Facing London's ruins, Sartre allegedly declared: *Everything I've seen and felt and heard in London has made me less stubborn and hasty about individual salvation. London brought a process which has long been growing in me into flower. I'm in a hurry now: I have no time for paradoxes any more; I have to be constructive.*

The article is illustrated with good pictures of Sartre and a very beautiful one of Simone de Beauvoir.

RADIO BROADCASTS: "LA TRIBUNE DES 'TEMPS MODERNES'" ⟨The *Temps modernes* Tribune⟩.

In the fall of 1947, at the initiative of Lucien Bonafé, a former colleague of Sartre's, the Paul Ramadier government suggested to Sartre that he hold a weekly forum on the radio. Sartre agreed to and, in spite of the many waves it caused, made a series of six broadcasts with the help of the *Temps modernes* staff and his friends. These broadcasts had a wide political audience and took place on the following dates: October 6, 20, and 27, and November 10, 17, and 24, 1947. "The *Temps modernes* Tribune" was cancelled at the beginning of December when Paul Ramadier was replaced as prime minister by Maurice Schuman (see, concerning the whole series of broadcasts, *Force of Circumstance*, pp. 137-38).

Although we expect to make a more complete study of the whole series, thanks especially to the recordings that Radiodiffusion Française has, let us list the following texts now:

47/134

"A la veille de reprendre ses émissions à la radio, Jean-Paul Sartre déclare à *Combat*: 'Il est nécessaire de faire campagne contre la croyance en la fatalité de la guerre russo-américaine'" ⟨On the Eve of His First Radio Broadcasts, Jean-Paul Sartre Tells *Combat*, "We Must Campaign against Believing that War between the U.S. and the U.S.S.R. Is Inevitable"⟩, interview by Louis Pauwels.

-- *Combat*, October 18, 1947.

Taking up the program he had defined at the conclusion of *What Is Literature?*, Sartre says that committed writers must *get into these relay station arts, the movies and the radio*, and that these media need not require popularization. After having stressed the total independence of his broadcast, Sartre develops the idea contained in its title:

The concept of historical necessity is still wending its way through people's minds. And we are entering its world bound hand and foot. Every political act, no matter what it may be, inevitably works to the advantage of one bloc or the other, and hastens the conflict. We are leaving the causal order of history, which justifies action, and entering the order of fate, which turns our acts against us. And we're doing it through a sort of mental muddling through, a sort of draining of our strength into a vague uneasiness which we ourselves are slowly changing into an enslavement to disaster which we shall soon see changed in turn, if we're not careful, into the disaster itself.

47/135

"De Gaulle et le 'gaullisme' vus par Jean-Paul Sartre (et par l'équipe des *Temps modernes*)" ⟨De Gaulle and "Gaullism" As Seen by Jean-Paul Sartre (and the *Temps modernes* Staff)⟩.

-- *L'Ordre de Paris* and *Franc-Tireur*, October 22, 1947.

Complete text of the October 20 "*Temps modernes* Tribune." The participants were Sartre, Simone de Beauvoir, Maurice Merleau-Ponty, Jean-Baptiste Pontalis, Lucien Bonafé, and R.-J. Chauffard, the last in the role of the "Gaullist."

Sartre denounces the belief in the inevitability of war which Gaullist politics is based on: there is nothing to choose from between the Americans and the Russians. Merleau-Ponty points out that Gaullism has no program and says: "A real French politics would not consist in choosing one of the two blocs or in trying in a completely artificial way to create a third bloc as powerful as the other two. A French politics would consist in appealing to whatever forces within these two great countries were opposed to a politics of war and big-power blocs."

Simone de Beauvoir expresses doubt about the Gaullist leftists who would like to have a national socialism. This term leads Bonafé to attack Charles de Gaulle violently by comparing him to Hitler. After Sartre calls for moderation, Pontalis recalls the Maurrasian past of the author of *Put to the Sword* and speaks of his scorn for the masses.

This broadcast evoked an immediate response from the general's supporters: a much decorated band of R.P.F. ⟨French Peoples' Assembly⟩ men set out in search of Sartre and tried to find him at the Tabou and the Flore. Two well-known Gaullists, Henry Torrès and General Guillain de Bénouville replied to Sartre on the radio (see below). For a whole week all sorts of insults appeared in the right-wing press. In an article in *Carrefour* (October 29, 1947), the former member of the *Temps modernes* staff, Albert Ollivier, called those who took part in the broadcast "virtual fascists"; and in the same issue, a fuming Paul Claudel let fly this clever phrase: "M. Sartre attacks General de Gaulle's looks; is he so proud of his own?"

The same issue of *L'Ordre* reproduces a few comments by Sartre gathered by Franck-Dominique: *I feel no hatred for M. de Gaulle as a person. How could I, since I don't know him? . . . M. Torrès has shown an unbelievable crudeness and violence which aren't worth responding to.*

47/136

"Tempête à la radio: J.-P. Sartre répond à Guillain de Bénouville et à Henry Torrès qui avaient refusé un débat contradictoire sur le R.P.F." ⟨Storm on the Airwaves: J.-P. Sartre Replies to Guillain de Bénouville and Henry Torrès, Who Had Refused to Debate the R.P.F. [French Peoples' Assembly] with Him⟩, interview-article by Louis Pauwels.

-- *Combat*, October 22, 1947; *Franc-Tireur* and *Le Populaire*, October 23, 1947.

This article begins by printing the Guillain de Bénouville-Henry Torrès protest: "M. J.-P. Sartre is talking about General de Gaulle in an indecent way, and his comparison of the liberator of our country, the restorer of our freedom and our republic, to Marshall Pétain, not even to speak of the comparison to Hitler, is impermissible and worthy of public scorn."

Sartre answers: *Many of those who support de Gaulle today condemned him during the Occupation. . . . People are claiming that I compared de Gaulle to Hitler. That is false. I compared the R.P.F.'s posters with certain Nazi propaganda posters.*

47/137

"Mis en cause pour son émission anti-gaulliste d'hier, Sartre m'a dit: 'Mon but: empêcher les auditeurs d'adhérer à l'un ou l'autre des blocs'" ⟨Criticized for His Anti-Gaullist Broadcast Yesterday, Sartre Told Me, "My Goal: to Keep the Listeners from Supporting Either One of the Two Blocs"⟩, interview.

-- *France-Soir*, October 22, 1947.

Short interview bearing on the same subject as the one described above.

47/138

Une Mise au point de Sartre ⟨A Correction by Sartre⟩.

a) Libération, October 23, 1947.

b) Selection from the same statement entitled *L'Affaire des "Temps modernes" à la radio* ⟨The *Temps modernes* Affair on the Radio⟩. *Combat*, October 23, 1947.

A text of the short statement Sartre made on the October 22 broadcast "The Paris Tribune," in which he expresses his regrets that Guillain de Bénouville and Henry Torrès refused to have a dialogue with him: *It is easier to drape oneself in an outraged sense of dignity than to answer precise questions about politics.*

47/139

47/139

J.-P. Sartre parle de l'anticommunisme à la Tribune des "Temps modernes" ⟨J.-P. Sartre Talks about Anticommunism at the "*Temps modernes* Tribune"⟩.

-- *Combat*, October 28, 1947.

Summary and quotations of Sartre's remarks during his October 27, 1947, broadcast. He says especially: *France has no powerful weapons, but she still has one weapon no one up till now has dared to use and yet whose use is more and more imperative: the weapon of truth.*

Sartre's moderate attack on the Communists calmed down the right-wing press a bit, but naturally evoked a lively response in the P.C. ⟨Communist Party⟩ press. Pierre Hervé, in an article published in *Action* (November 5, 1947), calls Sartre Ramadier's "court jester," accuses him of playing the S.F.I.O. ⟨French Branch of the Workers' International⟩ government's game, and concludes: "The broadcast devoted to de Gaulle was (like the one devoted to the P.C.) vulgar and of poor quality."

47/140

L'Emission des "Temps modernes" a été "interdite ou supprimée" ⟨The *Temps modernes* Broadcast Was "Either Forbidden or Cut off the Air"⟩.

-- *Combat*, December 3, 1947.

A statement in which Sartre protests the discontinuation of the "*Temps modernes* Tribune" and tells what he would have done during the December 1, 8, and 15 broadcasts:

In the first broadcast I would have interviewed David Rousset about his recent trip to Germany. In the second, I would have read and commented on an intellectuals' manifesto on the international situation [Sartre is undoubtedly referring to the "Premier appel à l'opinion internationale" ⟨First Call to International Opinion⟩, which was published in the November, 1947, *Esprit*]. *In the third, replying to one of my listeners, I would have tried to defend the working class against the charge of "sordid materialism" which is so often brought against it.*

Sartre will take up the theme of the third broadcast again in a speech he makes to an R.D.R. ⟨Revolutionary People's Assembly⟩ meeting on March 19, 1948, in the Salle Wagram (see 48/170).

48/141

Jean-Paul Sartre répond à ses détracteurs: L'Existentialisme et la politique ⟨Jean-Paul Sartre Replies to His Critics: Existentialism and Politics⟩.

-- In *Pour et contre l'existentialisme* ⟨For and Against Existentialism⟩. Major debate, with J. B. Pontalis, J. Pouillon, F. Jeanson, Julien Benda, Emmanuel Mounier, R. Vailland. Led by Colette Audry. Atlas, 1948. Pp. 181-90.

Text of one of the November, 1947, broadcasts of the "*Temps modernes* Tribune." Sartre examines the many letters he received after his broadcast on Gaullism, selects the most characteristic insults, and ends by defining his political position. The final three pages of the text give an idea of the themes Sartre will develop in 1948 while campaigning for the R.D.R. ⟨Revolutionary Peoples' Assembly⟩.

47/142

Gribouille.

-- *La Rue*, no. 12 (November, 1947), p. 1.

Develops the idea that our fear of war threatens to plunge us into one: *It was Gribouille, I think, who threw himself into the river for fear the rain would get him wet. Today they want to make us all Gribouilles: they are using our fear of war to plunge us into it. . . . They tell us we must choose between two roads to war because there is no other way. And this is true:* There is no other. *But that's precisely it: it's not a matter of putting our trust in an already existing way. Man has only himself to put his trust in. There is still time to* invent *the road a socialist Europe will take, the road to freedom and to peace.*

47/143

* *Pour un théâtre de situations* ⟨For a Theater of Situations⟩.

-- *La Rue*, no. 12 (November, 1947), p. 8.

The views expressed in this article are developed in greater detail in the article (unpublished in French) *Forgers of Myths* (see 46/107). The unidentified quotation which is given on page 12 of the Seuil edition of Francis Jeanson's *Sartre by Himself*, constantly reprinted afterward as a definition of Sartre's theater, comes from *For a Theater of Situations*.

47/144

* *Présence noire* ⟨Black Presence⟩.

-- *Présence africaine*, no. 1 (1947), pp. 28-29.

A piece written to greet the birth of the journal *Présence africaine*, edited by Alioune Diop. Sartre was one of its patrons (along with André Gide, Albert Camus, Emmanuel Mounier, Michel Leiris, etc.) and had promised to write more articles.

47/NOTE 1.

The anthology by Jean Paulhan and Dominique Aury, *La Patrie se fait tous les jours. Textes français 1939-1945* ⟨The Fatherland Is Being Made Every Day. French Writings, 1939-1945⟩ (Minuit, 1947) includes two pieces by Sartre: "Le silence de Jupiter" ⟨Jupiter's Silence⟩ (THE FLIES, act 2, tableau 2, scenes 4 and 5) and *La République du silence* ⟨The Republic of Silence⟩.

47/NOTE 2.

According to Maurice Merleau-Ponty (see *France-Observateur*, March 2, 1961, "Réponse à Olivier Todd" ⟨Reply to Olivier Todd⟩), Sartre wrote the *Temps modernes* editorial "Apprendre à lire" ⟨Learn to Read⟩ (no. 22 [July, 1947]). Sartre assures us that Merleau-Ponty wrote it.

47/NOTE 3.

On May 31, 1947, Sartre gave a lecture at the Salle Iéna, "Kafka, Jewish Writer," under the auspices of the French League for a Free Palestine. The most detailed report of it is Françoise Derins's "Une conférence de J.-P. Sartre" ⟨A Lecture by J.-P. Sartre⟩ (*La Nef*, no. 32 [July, 1947], pp. 165-66).

47/NOTE 4.

Philip Thody, in his book *Jean-Paul Sartre: A Literary and Political Study* (London: Hamish Hamilton, 1960), and in his textbook edition of THE CONDEMNED OF ALTONA (see 59/311 [*f*]), makes a mistake in citing as Sartre's an article about the film *Paris 1900* which appeared in the October 25, 1947, *Figaro littéraire*: "Sartre et Breton à une séance de *Paris 1900*" ⟨Sartre and Breton at a showing of *Paris 1900*⟩. The article was really written by Claude Mauriac, who in a brilliant pastiche plays on the ideas Sartre and André Breton may have had when they saw Nicole Vedrès's movie together at a private showing.

1948

48/145

LES MAINS SALES ⟨Dirty Hands⟩, play in seven tableaux.

a) Complete text in two parts in *Les Temps modernes*, no. 30 (March, 1948), pp. 1537-82; no. 31 (April, 1948), pp. 1754-1813.

In comparison to the Gallimard edition, the text has a wrong number in the second tableau as well as a certain number of minor differences.

b) Selections in French in *Yale French Studies*, I, no. 1 (spring-summer, 1948), 4-20.

c) Book. Gallimard, [1948]. 261 pages.

Dedication:"To Dolores" (who appears as M. in *Force of Circumstance*). Printing date: June 15, 1948.

15 copies on Holland vellum; 60 on wood-free Lafuma vellum Navarre; 210 on alfa mousse Navarre; 1040 on vellum superior.

Reprinted in the Soleil series in 1961.

d) Le Livre de poche series, no. 10. Gallimard, [1953].

e) Pourpre series. Gallimard, [1954].

f) Reprinted in THÉÂTRE (1962).

g) Textbook edition in English, with an introduction and notes by Geoffrey Brereton. London: Methuen, Methuen's Twentieth Century Texts, [1963].

Oreste F. Pucciani's introduction to the French text of DIRTY HANDS in the anthology *The French Theater Since 1930*

(New York: Blaisdell, 1954) is much better than Geoffrey Brereton's mediocre one even though it was published long before it.

h) An Italian translation, slightly modified with Sartre's approval and accompanied by an important interview with him (see 64/154). *Le Mani sporche.* Turin: Einaudi, 1964.

i) Folio series, no. 30. Gallimard, [1972].

j) French school edition, with introduction and notes by Gaston Meyer. Univers des Lettres series. Bordas, [1972].

Excerpts from the play, accompanied by mediocre introduction and notes.

DIRTY HANDS, RED GLOVES, or CRIME PASSIONNEL.

t1) RED GLOVES, adapted for the New York stage by Daniel Taradash, 1948.

t2) DIRTY HANDS, translated by Lionel Abel. In *Three Plays*. New York: Alfred A. Knopf, 1949.

t3) Ibid. In NO EXIT *and Three Other Plays* [THE FLIES; DIRTY HANDS; THE RESPECTFUL PROSTITUTE]. New York: Vintage Books, [1955].

t4) CRIME PASSIONNEL, translated by Kitty Black. In *Three Plays*. London: Hamish Hamilton, 1949.

t5) Ibid., but published separately in paperback. London: Methuen, [1961].

DIRTY HANDS led to a movie by Fernand Rivers in 1951 (see Appendix).

The play was performed for the first time on April 2, 1948, at the Théâtre Antoine (under the direction of Simone Berriau), staged by Pierre Valde ("supervised in a friendly way" by Jean Cocteau) and with settings by Emile and Jean Bertin (with the assistance of Christian Bérard). The main roles:

HOEDERER	André Luguet
HUGO	François Périer
OLGA	Paula Dehelly
JESSICA	Marie-Olivier

Attracted by the actors' names and by the play's apparently anti-Communist theme, and identifying itself readily with the character Hugo, the public made DIRTY HANDS a hit: the play was performed at the Théâtre Antoine from April 2, 1948, till September 20, 1949, and was much performed in roadshows. With 625 performances in Paris and 300 in the provinces, it is at this date the dramatic work by Sartre which has had the greatest public success. We shall come back later to its eventful history abroad.

The play was written toward the end of 1947 and prepared by the beginning of 1948, that is, during the time the R.D.R. ⟨Revolutionary Peoples' Assembly⟩ was being organized. The January, 1948, *Temps modernes* advertizes "Dirty Hands (excerpts)." Yet Sartre seems to have hesitated a while before deciding to keep this title (which, let it be remembered, had been given to the script, IN THE MESH, in 1946). In *La Semaine de Paris* for January and February, 1948, the play was advertised under the title "Les Biens de ce monde" ⟨The Goods of This World⟩, and we know, furthermore, that Sartre was thinking of several other possible titles, especially "Crime passionnel" ⟨Crime of Passion⟩ and "Les Gants rouges" ⟨Red Gloves⟩. The title which he finally adopted was subsequently to become famous.

According to the *Figaro littéraire* of April 3, 1948, the play allegedly originated in a situation on one August afternoon of 1944 when there was a question of declaring a truce during the Paris uprising. Sartre himself, in a recent interview (see 68/487), has established two other sources: *I got my inspiration for* DIRTY HANDS *from the difficulties some of my students, who were middle-class men of good will, had with the Communist Party. I was also thinking of Trotsky's assassination.* Simone de Beauvoir elaborates on the last sentence in the following way (see *Force of Circumstance*, pp. 149-50):

"I had met one of Trotsky's old secretaries in New York; he had told me that the murderer, having succeeded in getting himself hired as a secretary too, had lived for quite a time with his victim in a very closely guarded house. Sartre had mused about this sequestered situation. He had imagined the character of a young Communist born bourgeois and trying through his acts to wipe out his origins, but unable to tear himself free of his subjectivity, even through an assassination. He had put this character in conflict with a militant who was totally committed to his goals. (Once again, ethics confronts *praxis*) . . . Sartre's sympathy goes to Hoederer. . . . [Hugo] is so radically wrong that the play could be performed during the thaw, in a Communist country."

Let us note in passing that DIRTY HANDS has been staged in Yugoslavia and Czechoslovakia.

Refer to interviews about the play, and to 64/154 in particular, for what Sartre himself thinks about his play. Among the numerous criticisms at the time, we shall point out only the one by Jean Biermoz which appeared in letter form in *Les Temps modernes* (no. 36 [September, 1948], pp. 574-76), the very hostile one by Marguerite Duras ("Sartre et l'humour involontaire" ⟨Sartre and Involuntary Humor⟩, *Action*, April, 1948), and the one by Guy Leclerc, "Monsieur Sartre a les mains sales" ⟨Monsieur Sartre Has Dirty Hands⟩, in the April 7, 1948, *Humanité*: "Hermetic philosopher, nauseating writer, scandal-mongering playwright, and third-rate demagogue. These are the stages in M. Sartre's career."

WRITINGS AND INTERVIEWS ABOUT "DIRTY HANDS"

48/146

"Drame politique puis crime passionnel . . . Jean-Paul Sartre nous parle de sa prochaine pièce" ⟨First a Political Drama and Then a Crime of Passion . . . Jean-Paul Sartre Talks about His Coming Play⟩, interview by Guy Dornand.

-- *Franc-Tireur*, March 25, 1948.

Sartre explains that for a long time he hesitated to use the title "Dirty Hands" because he was afraid that, given the play's political setting, it would lend itself to a tendentious interpretation. The reason he finally decided to keep the title is that the play is *in no way a political play*. It is a play about politics whose epigraph could be the phrase from Saint-Just: "Nul ne gouverne innocemment" ⟨"No one governs innocently"⟩.

The work has no conclusion: *I justify everyone: the old realist leader of the proletarian party who finds opportunists labeling him a "social traitor" for his merely temporary compromise with the forces of reaction; and also his hopelessly idealistic young disciple, who has been ordered by the "tough guys" to execute the man who was his idol.*

An article by Henry Magnan, "Avec J.-P. Sartre avant la première de *Les Mains sales*" ⟨With J.-P. Sartre Before the Opening of *Dirty Hands*⟩ (*Le Monde*, March 25, 1948), includes a short statement by Sartre: *My play might just as well have been called "Pure Hands."*

Another article, "Le 'Crime passionnel' projeté par Jean-Paul Sartre" ⟨The 'Crime of Passion' Planned by Sartre⟩ which was published in the March 26, 1948, *Arts*, suggests that Hoederer might be compared to Jean Anouilh's Créon and relates: *I preferred having professional actors in my play so that it would be acted as simply as possible.*

There was a rehearsal of DIRTY HANDS held on March 21, 1948, for journalists, who were then received individually by Sartre. He seems on the whole to have told them the same things that were reported in

48/146

Franc-Tireur. There are probably other interviews which escaped our search.

48/147

"'Peut-on entrer dans un parti quelconque sans se salir les mains?' nous demande J.-P. Sartre, écrivain 'engagé'" ⟨"Can One Join Any Party without Getting One's Hands Dirty?" Asks J.-P. Sartre, a 'Committed' Writer⟩, interview by Claude Outié.

-- *L'Aurore*, March 30, 1948.

48/148

"Quand Cocteau, le poète, met en scène le philosophe J.-P. Sartre" ⟨When the Poet Cocteau Stages the Philosopher J.-P. Sartre⟩, interview by J.-B. Jeener.

-- *Le Figaro*, March 30, 1948.

Short interview with Sartre and Jean Cocteau, who had been kind enough to help Pierre Valde with the staging.

48/149

"Dans *Les Mains sales*, Jean-Paul Sartre pose le problème de la fin et des moyens" ⟨In DIRTY HANDS, Jean-Paul Sartre Poses the Problem of Means and Ends⟩, interview by René Guilly.

-- *Combat*, March 31, 1948.

Sartre says that Hoederer represents revolutionary realism and Hugo revolutionary idealism: *I don't take sides. A good play ought to present problems, not solve them.* Then he alludes to Lenin's "infantile disease of communism" as the first treatment of the problem of political realism and alliance with reformist bourgeois parties. In rejecting Hoederer's politics of compromise, Hugo *is still acting from the bourgeois idealism which was precisely what had made him rebel against his class and which he does not succeed in overcoming.*

48/150

"Avant la création de *Les Mains sales*, Jean-Paul Sartre nous dit" ⟨Before DIRTY HANDS Opens, Jean-Paul Sartre Says⟩, interview by René Gordon.

-- *L'Ordre de Paris*, March 31, 1948.

48/151

"Demain, au théâtre Antoine, Jean-Paul Sartre prendra position devant le problème de l'engagement politique" ⟨Tomorrow at the Théâtre Antoine, Jean-Paul Sartre Will Take a Stand on the Problem of Political Commitment⟩, interview by Pierre-André Baude.

-- *L'Aube*, April 1, 1948.

My hero is a young bourgeois who for ideological reasons has committed himself to a proletarian party but who is unable, when faced with the realism action requires, to rid himself of just the idealistic ways of thinking which have led him to break with his class in the first place. This is the source of his sickness, which can only end in death. . . . My own opinion is that politics requires us to "get our hands dirty," and that this is the way things have to be.

48/151 A

Jean-Paul Sartre nous écrit . . . ⟨Jean-Paul Sartre Writes . . . ⟩, letter.

-- *Opéra*, November 3, 1948.

Replying to an article by Nerin E. Gun on DIRTY HANDS which appeared in the October 20, 1948, *Opéra*, Sartre says especially: *People are trying to make the play a violent diatribe against communism of the "Senatorial Investigating Committee against Espionage" type.*

I would oppose, if need be, and by whatever means necessary, any politically tendentious production of DIRTY HANDS. *If anyone in any country were planning to make this play serve the aims of anti-Soviet propaganda, he would do so with my formal disavowal of it.*

48/152

"On joue en Amérique une pièce de moi dont j'ignore le texte" ⟨They're Performing One of My Plays in America in a Version I've Never Read⟩, interview by J.-P. Vivet.

-- *Combat*, November 27-28, 1948.

An American adaptation of DIRTY HANDS by Daniel Taradash, with Charles Boyer in the role of Hoederer,

48/152

had just been offered to the New York public under the title RED GLOVES. Sartre, who had not, in spite of his repeated requests, been able to get a copy of the adapted script, was warned by friends that strange things were being done in his name: *Hugo does not die. Jessica is no longer the same woman and . . . Hoederer has become the main character.* To please Charles Boyer, Hoederer--whom Sartre describes as "vulgar"--had been turned into an elegant, refined politician who at a certain moment gives Hugo a long speech on Abraham Lincoln.

In this interview, Sartre says that he is opposed to the play's being performed in these circumstances, and that he refuses to let it be given an anti-Soviet dimension. He also reproaches his publisher, Nagel--who held the rights to his plays--for having authorized RED GLOVES without his approval, and indicates that he is bringing suit against him. This business was the beginning of the apparently permanent estrangement of the two men.

48/153

"Author! Author?" interview by Roderick MacArthur.

-- *Theatre Arts* (New York), no. 33 (March, 1949), pp. 11-13.

This interview, conducted in Paris, gives numerous details about the RED GLOVES business and picks out most of the changes made by the American adapter. Sartre concludes that 90 percent of the text is not his. After having compared and summed up the two versions, the interviewer, MacArthur, says that Sartre is quite correct and stresses, furthermore, the poor quality of the adaptation.

The reviews of RED GLOVES were very bad. Gilbert W. Gabriel, for example, writing in *Theatre Arts* (January, 1949), regretted that Sartre's work had been "butchered," "sabotaged," by a mediocre, obtuse, limited translation which was slow from start to finish.

At the very moment Sartre was experiencing these disappointments from America, his play ran into a violent campaign by the Communists. At the beginning of December, 1948, the Soviets even took official steps to get the authorities in Helsinki to stop DIRTY HANDS, which the Soviets considered "propaganda hostile to the U.S.S.R.," from being performed. The February 10, 1949, *Lettres françaises* published a similar attack by Ilya Ehrenburg.

Sartre was very unhappy to see his work used as a cold war weapon. When he began to draw closer to the

Communists in 1952, he decided not to authorize any performance of DIRTY HANDS without the approval of the Communist parties concerned. The play was at first banned by Sartre in Spain, Greece, and Indochina. In November, 1952, refusing to turn it into a weapon against the Peace Congress he was about to take part in, he forbade its performance in Vienna (see *Le Monde*, November 19, 1952). Two years later, September 23, 1954, he held a press conference in the same city to protest the performing of DIRTY HANDS at the Volks-theater, and on this occasion said (see *Franc-Tireur* and *Le Monde* for September 25, 1954): *I do not disown* DIRTY HANDS, *but I regret the use to which it has been put. My play has become a political battlefield, an instrument of political propaganda. In the present atmosphere of tension, I do not think that performing it in sensitive key points like Berlin or Vienna can serve the cause of peace.*

It was not until after 1962 that Sartre authorized a new production of DIRTY HANDS in Yugoslavia, in Italy by the Teatro Stabile of Turin (see 64/154), and in Czechoslovakia (1968). As late as 1966, Sartre, afraid that the interpretation would be tendentious, had the performance of the play in Antwerp, where the Fakkel Teater had put it on without authorization, banned (see *Le Monde*, December 20, 1966). He brought suit against this theater, but he lost.

64/154

"Una intervista a Jean-Paul Sartre" ⟨An Interview with Jean-Paul Sartre⟩, interview by Paolo Caruso.

-- Jean-Paul Sartre. LE MANI SPORCHE ⟨Dirty Hands⟩, translated by Vittorio Sermonti. With an interview with J.-P. Sartre and an account by Simone de Beauvoir. Turin: Giulio Einaudi, 1964. Pp. 137-49.

An interview granted on March 4, 1964, to Paolo Caruso, the Italian translator of CRITIQUE OF DIALECTICAL REASON, to mark the staging of DIRTY HANDS by the Teatro Stabile of the city of Turin. Simone de Beauvoir's account (pp. 150-53) actually consists of a long selection from *Force of Circumstance* dealing with the play. The translator indicates that the work has undergone, with Sartre's approval, the following changes:

-- The action no longer unfolds in "a spectral Illyria" but in a precise way in Hungary from March, 1943 to the spring of 1945. The name of Hungary is never used, however, but is merely understood. It is in this perspective that the names of several characters have been changed: Louis becomes Walter; Georges, Lucas; etc. In this way the historical references are made more concrete.

-- Some "adventuresome" or "romantic" details are cut out.

-- The characterization of such characters as Slick and Georges-Lucas who make up the socio-economic "base" of the play is "thinned" for reasons of translation and to avoid an "at best equivocal plebeo-gangsterish" tone.

Sartre's statements to Paolo Caruso are essential to a good understanding of DIRTY HANDS. Here are some selections from them (from French translation by Rybalka and Contat):

The meaning of the drama and of Hugo's destiny are not the same. There were two things I wanted to say. On the one hand, I wanted to make a dialectical examination of the problem of the demands made by the praxis *of time. You are aware that we had a case like Hoederer's, the Doriot case, here in France, even though it did not end in an assassination. Doriot wanted the P.C.* (Communist Party) *to get closer to the S.F.I.O.* (French Branch of the Workers' International) *Social Democrats, and for that reason he was kicked out of the party. A year later, in order to stop the French situation from degenerating into fascism, and on the basis of specific Soviet directives, the P.C. took the precise path Doriot had suggested, but without ever recognizing that he had been correct--and this was the basis for the Popular Front. This is what interests me: the dialectical necessity within a* praxis.

There is another point I want to make clear: I have great understanding for Hugo's attitude, but you are wrong to think that he embodies me. Hoederer embodies me. Ideally, of course; don't think that I am claiming to be Hoederer. . . . Hoederer is the man I'd like to be if I were a revolutionary. . . .

Hugo is my students, my former students. It was the young who between 1945 and 1948 had the hardest time supporting communism because their bourgeois upbringing confronted them not with a party which might have helped them but with a party which, with its dogmatism, either used their shortcomings to make them radicals, extremists, etc., or rejected them and thereby put them in an untenable position. . . . Thus Hugo has my sympathies to the extent that I said to myself, Hoederer could have made something out of him. And it is clear that without the incident (the contingency) that I wanted to introduce on purpose with the Jessica-Hoederer scene, Hugo would have abandoned his undertaking, he would not have killed Hoederer; and if Hoederer had won his own battle, Hugo would not have continued to be his secretary but would have been trained by him and would somehow have become a real revolutionary. But Hugo joined the game, drawn in by Walter, by men like Walter, which means that at bottom

Walter's dogmatism, which is not a far-Left dogmatism, was translated into Hugo's "leftism."

Next Sartre compares Hugo to Hamlet and sees him as a *Musset-like* character. Although Sartre does not say specifically what he means, there are in fact great similarities between *Lorenzaccio* and DIRTY HANDS. Then Sartre tells a story which he says is characteristic of the mistaken judgments people have made of the play:

Camus had gone with me to one of the final rehearsals (he hadn't read the script yet), and as he was walking back with me after it was over, he said, "It's excellent, but there's one detail I don't approve of. Why does Hugo say, 'I don't love men for what they are but for what they ought to be' [an approximate quotation from scene 3 of tableau 5], *and why does Hoederer answer, 'And I love them for what they are?' The way I see it, it should have been just the opposite." In other words, he really thought that Hugo loved men for what they are since he didn't want to lie to them, whereas Hoederer, on the contrary, became in his eyes a dogmatic Communist who weighed men in terms of what they ought to be and who deceived them in the name of an ideal. This is just the opposite of what I meant to say.*

Then Sartre announces that he is going to try to clarify the problems raised by DIRTY HANDS in a paper he is writing for the colloquium "Ethics and Praxis," which is to be held at the Gramsci Institute in May, and he admits that there is a *profound thematic analogy* between THE CONDEMNED OF ALTONA and DIRTY HANDS. The interview concludes with the following words:

My real tendency is to be, as I said, a critical "fellow traveler." I have made many mistakes, but I think that the characteristic situation of the intellectual "fellow traveler" is one of tension between criticism and discipline. And I think it should be possible from now on to be one inside the party.

See also a short statement about the play in Francis Jeanson's *Sartre by Himself* (pp. 48-49 of the first Gallimard editions), as well as the following text.

67/154 A

Preface to the Czech translation of DIRTY HANDS.

-- In Jean-Paul Sartre. DRAMATA ⟨Plays⟩. Prague: Orbis, 1967.

The preface is dated Paris, April, 1965. The volume, whose printing was 6500 copies, includes

67/154 A

A. J. Liehm's translation of THE VICTORS, DIRTY HANDS, and THE TROJAN WOMEN, reprints (pp. 279-83) the interview about THE TROJAN WOMEN published in *Bref* (see 65/415), and concludes with a postscript by Milan Kundera.

Addressing himself directly to his Czechoslovakian audience, Sartre here again takes up many points of the interview granted to Paolo Caruso.

48/155

SITUATIONS, II.

-- Gallimard [1948]. 333 pages. Printing date: May 20, 1948. 14 copies on Holland vellum; 55 on wood-free Navarre vellum; 1040 copies on esparto grass, bound.

The volume includes, in French:

-- *Introduction to "Les Temps modernes"* see 45/80

-- *The Nationalization of Literature* 45/83

-- *What Is Literature?* 47/125

This last text is dedicated "To Dolores" (a friend of Sartre who appears as M. in *Force of Circumstance*) and contains a certain number of variations.

WHAT IS LITERATURE?, major part of SITUATIONS, II, translated by Bernard Frechtman.

t1) New York: Philosophical Library, [1949]; London: Methuen, [1950].

t2) Published under the title LITERATURE AND EXISTENTIALISM. New York: Citadel Press, [1962].

t3) With an introduction by Wallace Fowlie. New York: Harper Colophon Books, [1965].

t4) Ibid. Gloucester, Mass.: Peter Smith, 1966.

t5) Paperback. New York: Washington Square Press, 1966.

t6) With an introduction by David Caute. London: Methuen, 1967.

48/156

L'ENGRENAGE ⟨In the Mesh⟩, movie script.

a) Nagel, [1948]. 192 pages. Printing date: November, 1948. 500 copies on laid paper, 50 on esparto grass, and 20 on arches finish. Republished in the Pensées series in 1964.

b) L'Avant-Scène, no. 89 (1954).

c) LA P . . . RESPECTUEUSE ⟨The Respectful P[rostitute]⟩ followed by L'ENGRENAGE. Le Livre de poche series, no. 55. Gallimard, [1954].

d) La Petite Ourse series. Lausanne: La Guilde du livre, n.d.

e) Danish textbook edition. Copenhagen: Dansk Videnskab Forlag, 1968.

IN THE MESH, translated by Mervyn Savill.

-- London: Andrew Dakers, 1954.

A marginal note points out: "This script was written during the winter of 1946. It was originally entitled *Dirty Hands*. The play that fell heir to this title thus followed it by two years. The subject of the present work has nothing in common with that of the play."

The rights to IN THE MESH had been sold to the producer and director Bernard Borderie, and the script was to be shot around 1950. The project proved abortive *in extremis*. On the other hand, the text gave rise to several different theatrical adaptations, the first of which seems to have been that of the Zurich Schauspielhaus on November 30, 1952. IN THE MESH was staged by Erwin Piscator in Germany and Giorgio Strehler in Italy, at the Piccolo Teatro in Milan. And, finally, this script was staged by Jean Mercure at the Théâtre de Ville de Paris, the former Théâtre Sarah-Bernhardt, in February, 1969. On this occasion Sartre gave Bernard Pingaud an interview (see 68/499) in which he provides much interesting information about the meaning this script had for him in 1946 and the one it has taken on today:

. . . What I enjoyed doing at first was transposing to the screen a technique frequently used by Anglo-Saxon novelists before the war: the multiple point of view. As I imagined the movie, not only was the chronology disrupted but the same character, Hélène, appeared in exteriors which differed completely according to the viewpoint of the person speaking about her.

Nineteen forty-six was also the time when, without yet knowing the exact truth about the camps, we began to discover the ravages of Stalinism. But Stalinism itself was not at issue. I just set out from a very widespread, and in my view largely false, claim: "Stalin could not have done anything different from what he did." I thought of a country where people

48/156

really couldn't "do anything different." A little country rich in oil, for example, which lived completely dependent on other countries. . . .

In 1946, most of Latin America was in this sort of situation. Since then Castro has been able to break out of the circle. Castro understood that the problem was not to seize power but to create, at first through guerrilla warfare and then through a people's war, the conditions which make a real use of power possible. So the day Jean Mercure suggested that I adapt IN THE MESH my first tendency was to change the ending. . . .

But on top of Castro there have been the events we all know about in the East. Czechoslovakia has no oil, and Soviet imperialism follows different laws from American imperialism. But the situation is the same: a big country claims to impose its laws on smaller states which fall within its sphere of influence. . . .

In present circumstances, the important thing is to show the permanency and scandalousness of a power politics which is employed in the socialist as well as the capitalist camp. That's why I gave up the idea of changing my story.

Sartre further says that by introducing private motives into Jean's behavior, he touched on a problem which has always fascinated him: *knowing how the public and the private are conjoined in the statesman. . . . It should be possible to combine Marxist and psychoanalytic analyses in such a way as to show how a certain society and a certain childhood educate someone who will be capable of taking and using power in the name of his group.*

48/157

VISAGES ⟨Faces⟩.

-- VISAGES, preceded by PORTRAITS OFFICIELS ⟨Official Portraits⟩. With 4 dry-point etchings by Wols. Seghers, 1948. 41 pages.

Printed in January, 1948. 15 copies on China paper, 900 copies on Crèvecoeur du Marais, and 20 copies not for sale.

This volume consists of two pieces which had earlier appeared in the magazine *Verve* (see 39/27 and 39/28). See the same numbers for translations.

48/158

ORPHÉE NOIR ⟨Black Orpheus⟩.

a) Léopold Sedar Senghor. *Anthologie de la nouvelle poésie nègre et malgache de langue française* ⟨Anthology of New Black and Malgasy Poetry in the French Language⟩. Preceded by Jean-Paul Sartre. ORPHEE NOIR. Presses Universitaires de France, 1948. XLIV + 227 pages. Identical new edition, 1969.

Sartre's text is on pp. IX-XLIV. It is preceded by a foreword by Ch. André Julien which says particularly: "Not only did [Sartre] adapt himself to the worrisome requirements of hasty publication, but he enthusiastically wrote a profoundly original study whose breadth far exceeded our hopes. BLACK ORPHEUS will mark a date in the analysis of negritude."

b) Excerpts in *Les Temps modernes*, no. 37 (October, 1948), pp. 577-606.

These excerpts are followed, on pp. 607-25, by poems selected from Senghor's anthology. The omitted passages correspond to pages 247-51 and 257-61 of SITUATIONS, III.

c) Excerpt in *Présence africaine*, no. 6 (1949), pp. 9-14.

Let us point out the study by Francis Jeanson, "Sartre et le monde noir" ⟨Sartre and the Black World⟩. *Présence africaine*, no. 7 (1949), pp. 189-214.

d) Reprinted with two supplementary notes (pp. 265, 273) in SITUATIONS, III.

BLACK ORPHEUS.

t1) Translated by S. W. Allen. In *Présence africaine*, nos. 10-11 (1951), pp. 219-47.

t2) Ibid. in book form. Paris: Présence africaine, [1963]. Same volume distributed also from 1971 with imprint of Panther House, New York.

t3) Translated by Arthur Gilette. In *Stand*, V, no. 4 (1962), 2-12; VI, no. 1 (1963), 7-20.

t4) Ibid. in book form. New York: University Place Book Shop, [c. 1963].

t5) Translated by John MacCombie. In *Massachusetts Review*, VI (autumn-winter, 1964-65), 13-52.

> This superb, inspired piece ought to be reread by those who claim that Sartre has no understanding of poetry. After having stated that *black poetry in French is the only great revolutionary poetry of our time*, Sartre praises negritude and, taking the example of Aimé Césaire above all, shows how *in at least one instance the most authentic revolutionary project and the purest poetry spring from the same source.*

45/158 A

45/158 A

Jean-Paul Sartre répond à ses détracteurs ⟨Jean-Paul Sartre Replies to His Critics⟩. In *Pour et contre l'existentialisme* ⟨*For and Against Existentialism*⟩.

See 48/141.

48/159

Preface to *Portrait d'un inconnu* ⟨Portrait of a Man Unknown⟩, by Nathalie Sarraute.

a) Robert Marin, 1948. Pp. 7-16.

b) Reprinted by Gallimard, [1956].

c) New edition in Le Monde en 10/18 series. Union générale d'éditions, [1964].

d) Preface reprinted as *Portrait d'un inconnu.* In SITUATIONS, IV.

Preface to *Portrait of a Man Unknown*, by Nathalie Sarraute.

t1) Excerpt. *The Anti-Novel of Nathalie Sarraute*, translated by Beth Brombert. *Yale French Studies*, no. 16 (winter, 1955-56), pp. 40-44.

t2) Translated by Maria Jolas. In Nathalie Sarraute. *Portrait of a Man Unknown.* New York: George Braziller, 1958. Pp. VII-XIV.

t3) Same translation. "Nathalie Sarraute." In SITUATIONS, IV. New York: George Braziller, 1965.

> Three centuries after *The Extravagant Shepherd* (see, concerning this subject, J.-P. Faye's *A Topsail Yarn*), Sartre finds the term *anti-novel* to characterize this work of Nathalie Sarraute's as well as a whole tendency in the modern novel. He is sensitive to the *protoplasmic vision of our inner world* which is presented by *Portrait of a Man Unknown*, but doubts that the value of the book lies (as its author would have us believe) in its psychological investigations. Later, in 1963, Simone de Beauvoir will criticize Sarraute for reviving in her own way "the old French psychologism" (*Force of Circumstance*, p. 620).

48/160

Preface to THE RESPECTFUL PROSTITUTE.

a) Translated by Harold Clurman. In *Art and Action*, 10th anniversary issue, twice a year, 1938-48. New York: Twice a Year Press, [1948]. P. 17.

Art and Action was a committed American magazine which, beginning in 1945, published translations of Albert Camus, Simone de Beauvoir, etc.

b) Reprinted as *French Writer Answers His Varied Critics. New York Times* (March 21, 1948), section 2.

This short text precedes a translation of THE RESPECTFUL PROSTITUTE and follows an introductory note in which Richard Wright explains to the American reader the goals Sartre is trying to attain and recalls the celebrated case which was the source of the play (see 46/90).

We reprint about half of this preface below:

When I had this play produced it was said that I had shown myself rather ungrateful toward American hospitality [a reference to Sartre's trips to the United States, and to the criticisms of certain Frenchmen such as Thierry Maulnier]. *It was said I was anti-American. I am not anti-American. I don't even know what the word means. I am anti-racist because I do know what racism means. . . .*

It has been said that I saw the mote in my neighbor's eye and not the beam in my own. It is true that we French have colonies and we don't always behave well in them. But when it comes to oppression there is neither mote nor beam: one must denounce it wherever it exists. . . .

It would be peculiar if there were people in New York to accuse me of anti-Americanism at the moment when Pravda *in Moscow is energetically accusing me of being an agent for American propaganda. But if this were to happen it would only prove one of two things, either that I am pretty clumsy or that I am in the right.*

48/161

"Jean-Paul Sartre à Berlin: Discussion autour des *Mouches*" ⟨Jean-Paul Sartre in Berlin: Discussion of THE FLIES⟩.

-- *Verger* (Baden-Baden/Paris), I, no. 5 (1948), 109-23.

The complete report of a contentious meeting which took place at Berlin's Hebbel-Theater on February 1, 1948, on the occasion of a German performance of THE FLIES. The following participated in the discussion: M. Lusset, Sartre, Günther Weisenborn, Peter Theunissen, Edouard Roditi, Walter Karsch, Wolf Dieter Zimmermann, Peter A. Steinhoff, and the producer of THE FLIES, Jürgen Fehling.

A very good discussion in which Sartre first makes

48/161

clear the meaning he originally wanted his play to have, wonders if it applies just as much to Germany in 1948 as to France in 1943, and opens a discussion of more general themes--atheism, freedom, and human liberation:

It is not a question of knowing what we are free for but what are the roads to freedom. And on this score we agree completely with Hegel, who said, "No one, no man can be free unless all men are free." . . .

Our concrete goal--which is a very up-to-date, contemporary one--is human liberation. It has three aspects. To begin with, the metaphysical liberation of man: making him aware of his total freedom and his duty to struggle against everything which tends to limit his freedom. Second, his artistic freedom: making the free man's communication with other men easier thanks to works of art, and by this means immersing others in an atmosphere of freedom. Third, his political and social liberation: liberating the oppressed and other men. . . .

As soon as THE FLIES was performed in Berlin, the newspapers licensed by the Russians began a campaign against its "anti-humanism" and its "deformation of true freedom"; and the evangelical bishop of Berlin, Dr. Otto Dibelius, made the following comments during a Sunday sermon: "Christ can only answer Sartre's play with a categorical no. . . . Repentance is the way which leads to that reality [God], to grace, and to the true freedom of the children of God" (see *L'Ordre de Paris*, March 10, 1948).

48/162

La Recherche de l'absolu ⟨The Search for the Absolute⟩, article on Giacometti.

a) Article written on the occasion of a Giacometti show at the Pierre Matisse Gallery in New York in 1948. Translated as *The Search for the Absolute*, it constitutes the introduction to the catalogue for the exhibition (January 10-February 14).

b) Les Temps modernes, no. 28 (January, 1948), pp. 1153-63.

c) Included in SITUATIONS, III. See 49/180.

Search for [or *Quest of*] *the Absolute.*

t1) Anonymous translation. See *(a)* above.

t2) The Quest of the Absolute, translated by Wade Baskin. In *Essays in Aesthetics* (1963).

Sartre and Simone de Beauvoir had already noticed Giacometti at the Dôme toward 1936 ("He looked as solid as a rock and at the same time freer than an elf: it was too much." [*The Prime of Life*, p. 224]). They met him at Chez Lipp in the spring of 1941 and after that were regularly in touch with him and his wife Annette.

In the excellent passage in which she speaks of Giacometti (see *The Prime of Life*, pp. 386-88), Simone de Beauvoir outlines what his sculptures meant to her and says more precisely:

" . . . he was one of those very rare characters who can enrich your understanding simply by listening to what you say. There was a deep bond of understanding between him and Sartre: they had both staked everything on one obsession--literature in Sartre's case, art in Giacometti's--and it was hard to decide which of them was more fanatical. . . .

". . . [Giacometti's] attitude was comparable to that of the phenomenologists, since he claimed to sculpture a face *in its context*, as it existed at a distance for others, and by so doing to avoid the pitfalls of both subjective idealism and pseudo-objectivity."

This affinity is clearly evident in *The Search for the Absolute*: at the same time he brilliantly describes Giacometti's works (*these moving sketches always on the road between being and nothingness, always being changed, enhanced, destroyed, and undertaken once again, began to have their solitary, real existence)*, Sartre makes out in the Swiss sculptor's work an undertaking parallel to his own.

See 54/257 for an article about Giacometti.

48/163

Conscience de soi et connaissance de soi ⟨Consciousness of Self and Knowledge of Self⟩, paper read to the Société française de philosophie ⟨French Philosophical Society⟩ meeting on June 2, 1947.

-- *Bulletin de la Société française de philosophie*, 42d Year, no. 3 (April-June, 1948), pp. 49-91.

Consciousness of Self and Knowledge of Self, translated by Mary Ellen Lawrence and Nathaniel M. Lawrence.

-- In Nathaniel M. Lawrence and D. J. O'Connor, eds. *Readings in Existential Phenomenology*. Englewood Cliffs, New Jersey: Prentice-Hall, 1967. Pp. 113-42. Includes discussion.

This important paper, the only one Sartre has ever

48/163

given at the French Philosophical Society, of which he is still a member, is preceded according to custom by a summary of his arguments. The paper itself takes up the philosophical positions developed in BEING AND NOTHINGNESS without adding anything essential to them (see Introduction, par. 3; part 1, chapter 2; part 2, chapters 1, 2, par. 3, 3). Speaking of Husserl and Heidegger, Sartre, in order to situate his own philosophical project, concludes: *There has to be a synthesis of Husserl's contemplative and nondialectical consciousness, which leads us only to the contemplation of essences, with the activity of the dialectical but nonconscious and consequently unfounded project found in Heidegger's thought, whose basic element is seen to be, in contrast, transcendence* (p. 76).

Note that during the discussion which follows, Sartre is led in answering a psychoanalyst's objection to formulate his position concerning the unconscious in a rather crude way: ontologically, it is easy to demonstrate that there is no unconscious; instrumentally, the concept of the unconscious may be shown to be equally useless, for *in every case in which one appeals to the unconscious, one could appeal to different concepts* (p. 84). Sartre refers to Wilhelm Stekel to uphold his claim that there are psychoanalysts who are very well able to dispense with the concept of the unconscious.

48/164

Message addressed to the French League for a Free Palestine.

a) Published under the title *Un émouvant appel de J.-P. Sartre en faveur de la Palestine libre* ⟨A Moving Appeal by J.-P. Sartre for a Free Palestine⟩. *L'Ordre de Paris*, April 7, 1948.

b) Reprinted as *C'est pour nous tous que sonne le glas* ⟨The Bell Tolls for All of Us⟩. *Caliban*, no. 16 (May, 1948), pp. 13-16.

An article written shortly before the proclamation of the State of Israel on May 14, 1948. Sartre asks that the Hebrews be armed by the U.N. after the British troops leave and declares: *A Palestinian state, an independent, free, and peaceful state, will guarantee peace if it is strong enough to make itself respected.* Sartre concludes with a quotation: *"Do not ask," John Donne writes, "for whom the bell tolls; it tolls for thee."*

48/165

"Au Président de la République" ⟨To the President of the

Republic⟩, a letter signed by Jean Cocteau and Jean-Paul Sartre and written in favor of Jean Genet.

-- *Combat*, July 16, 1948.

"To the President of the Republic," translated by Richard N. Coe.

-- In Richard N. Coe, ed. *The Theater of Jean Genet: A Casebook*. New York: Grove Press, 1970. Pp. 40-41.

Complete text:

Dear Mr. President,

We have decided to appeal to your high authority to take exceptional measures in the case of a writer we all admire and respect--Jean Genet. We are not unaware of the fact that his work is on the fringe of literature proper and could not possibly be allowed to circulate freely. But the precedent of Villon and Verlaine has determined us to ask you to help this very great poet.

Moreover we have learned, without Jean Genet's having said a word to us about it, that the reason he received his final and irrevocable sentence was that he decided to take upon himself a wrong committed by Jean de Carnin, who died at the barricades during the Liberation, in order that his name might remain spotless.

This is yet another reason why he is entitled to our esteem, and it encourages us in our endeavor.

Jean Genet's whole work has torn him free from his past of flagrant wrongdoing, and an irrevocable sentence would plunge him back anew into the evil from which his work has managed to deliver him.

We beg you, Mr. President, to make, if it is possible, a quick decision and to save a man whose life henceforth is nothing but hard labor.

We beg you, Mr. President, to rest assured of our most humble gratitude and feelings of deepest respect.

Concerning Genet, see 49/189, 50/202, 52/215.

48/166

"Entrevistas Jean-Paul Sartre" ⟨An Interview with Jean-Paul Sartre⟩, interview in Spanish by Marcelo Saporta.

-- *Insula*, no. 32 (August 15, 1948).

48/166

A "timely" interview: politically, Sartre repeats the theses of the R.D.R. ⟨Revolutionary People's Assembly⟩, while literarily, he reaffirms some of the ideas expressed in *What Is Literature?* On the other hand he praises Camus's *The Plague* and says he is working above all on Stéphane Mallarmé.

See 54/251 for a different interview by Saporta in *Cuadernos Americanos*.

Ecrire pour son époque ⟨We Write for Our Own Time⟩.

See 46/114.

48/167

* Program notes for the ballet *La Rencontre ou Oedipe et le Sphinx* ⟨The Encounter, or Oedipus and the Sphinx⟩, by Boris Kochno, music by Henri Sanguet, choreography by David Lichine.

-- Ballet des Champs-Elysées, Théâtre des Champs-Elysées, album no. 8, November, 1948.

Written at the request of Jean Cocteau and Christian Bérard for a ballet which saw the debut of Leslie Caron, this piece has to our knowledge been mentioned only by Simone de Beauvoir in *Force of Circumstance* (p. 170). It seems to be the only one in which Sartre has spoken about the dance.

TEXTS RELATING TO THE REVOLUTIONARY PEOPLES' ASSEMBLY (R.D.R.)

As Michel-Antoine Burnier saw clearly in his *Choice of Action* (pp. 54-66), the R.D.R. episode marks an important step in Sartre's political life: it is the first time he throws himself into mass politics and direct action.

But it must be noted that Sartre was not part of the group (David Rousset, Jean Rous, Georges Altman, etc.) who originally conceived the R.D.R.; it was only in February, 1948, that he joined the managing committee of the movement (see, on this matter, *Force of Circumstance*, pp. 146-47). Yet the R.D.R. became very quickly identified as "Sartre's and David Rousset's party." Sartre's R.D.R. activities were many during 1948, but beginning with the following year he realized that the Revolutionary Peoples' Assembly did not correspond to any political reality and that he was on the wrong track. After many turnabouts, Sartre quit the movement in October, 1949.

We have succeeded in locating the following texts:

"Appel du Comité pour le Rassemblement Démocratique Révolutionnaire" ⟨A Call from the Committee of the Revolutionary Peoples' Assembly⟩.

a) Combat and *Franc-Tireur*, February 27, 1948.

b) Esprit, XVI, no. 3 (March, 1948), 464-66.

This call announcing the founding of the R.D.R. was signed by Sartre, David Rousset, Jean Rous, Paul Fraisse, etc. It was made public at the end of February 1948, and was widely reprinted in the newspapers.

Let us recall that its precursor was in some respects the "First Call to International Opinion," which had come out in November, 1947, and which we reprint here:

FIRST CALL TO INTERNATIONAL OPINION

Only a short time after the Armistice, the men of Europe have come to expect just a few years' or few months' respite before a new massacre. They have lost confidence in their own powers and no longer dare to undertake anything because skillful propaganda has convinced them they must wait for death with resignation and must for the time being place their fate in alien hands. When man allows himself to be convinced that he is powerless, the reign of fate begins and blood will soon begin to flow.

Those of us who in spite of differences of opinion are united here by such a pressing danger to make this call to you are not pacifists. On the contrary, we consider pacifism abstract and ineffectual, because it seeks to avoid war in general, and wrong because it wants to avoid it at any cost. We do not think that peace is more important than anything else. But we think that it is man who makes history, and that *this war*, since it is absurd and unjustifiable, *ought* to be avoided.

The war *ought* to be avoided because--

1. Its outcome is so uncertain and depends upon so many unknown circumstances that even if we had announced sympathies for one of the two camps, we could not bet reasonably on its winning. Moreover, preparations for this war involve in each bloc the undermining of the ideals which the war, it is claimed, will uphold. The winner, if there is one, and even if he is the one we want to win, would come to us as unrecognizable and as the bearer of the evils we most fear.

2. Although victory is uncertain, the consequences of a conflict are most clear: for Europe, war means occupation or battlefield ruins or both.

3. Preparation for war upsets the world's economic life and lessens its chances of getting on its feet again by paralyzing economic exchange.

4. Preparation for war retards social liberation; war would set it back indefinitely: unimaginable in its effects and its destructiveness, it would make any historical future unimaginable. To those, who whatever bloc they come from, claim that this war will be the final one before the liberation of mankind, or the only way mankind has of defending its freedom, we answer simply that they are making themselves accomplices to an enormous and criminal mystification. And do not let anyone try to tell us either that power-bloc politics is still a way of assuring peace by bringing about a balance of powers: armed peace is not peace; if it were to continue it would become the chief and perhaps insurmountable obstacle to the international organization without which peace is inconceivable.

The war *can* be avoided.

But only on condition that we men of France and Europe do not take ourselves for innocent victims. It is quite true that we are victims: before the war has even broken out, without anyone's even knowing whether it ever will break out, Europe is already a battlefield for the two great enemy powers. For both she is both prey and threat. Prey because her suffering and disunity leave her open to every sort of influence; threat because these influences divide her into two opposed camps and make of her the image of the conflict presently dividing the whole world. And since each bloc is trying to defend itself by subjugating Europe, it looks for supporters and soldiers on our soil, and by these undertakings it arouses the uneasiness and counter-undertakings of the other bloc. But if we submit, even through inertia, to this subjugation, we stop being victims and become accomplices. The cold war, tossing us about between the two camps and letting us be manipulated by them both, has caused our lack of unity; our lack of unity may cause a plain old war. As a result of this fact, there is no longer any country in Europe, there is not one citizen of any European country, who does not have the immense responsibility of becoming a factor determining war or peace by the decision he makes.

Yet even the most vibrant call for unity would not be effective if it were made from within a *single* country. No *national* organization, whether it call itself the middle way or the third force, can put an end to agitation and the rise of fascism as long as destitution, cold, and hunger continue to fan hatred, because no country is able by itself to conquer famine, destitution, or cold. Only a Europe which administered her resources herself and distributed them according to need and not just according to the interests of a few could regain an adequate standard of living and thereby overcome her internal disputes. Divided, Europe can be the source of war; united, of peace: it is not Europe that the U.S.S.R. fears but America's European policy; it is not Europe that America fears but the Kominform's influence on the European masses. The U.S.S.R. and the United States will have much less to fear from a continent which has managed to regain its sovereignty than from a shabby heap of nations whose sole remaining freedom is to choose the bloc they shall become the vassals of; and since the war which threatens is more a war of fear than of interests, such a radical change in the European situation could not fail to lead each bloc to change its policies.

But it is clear, on the other hand, that only a radical transformation of the existing social order will provide a definitive solution to the problems of the European economy, because it alone will provide for the liquidation of special interests. We have to know what we want: if we are determined to solve national problems, we have to do so within the framework of an international organization; and if we wish to establish such an organization, we have to recognize that it requires a socialist revolution and the replacing of private property by really collective property. Furthermore, since this Europe to be created includes several colonial empires, it is evident that the liberation of the working classes, which is both the goal of the revolution and the way to it, would make no sense whatsoever if it were not accompanied by the simultaneous emancipation of the colonized masses. Finally, the worst mistake would be to establish a third bloc whose existence would provoke a new sphere of scorn, mistrust, and isolation, and which would have the additional major inconvenience of being weaker than the weakest of the two existing blocs. We are not asking that Europe close in upon itself. The reason we consider it the starting point of a movement which should reach the proletariat of the whole world is that in the first place its situation allows it to know with certainty that it would in any case be the victim of the war without being, whatever the outcome may be, its beneficiary; and that in the second place we are neither Russians nor Americans but European citizens, and you have to work where you are. Thus our call is directed neither solely nor especially to Frenchmen, but beyond frontiers to all the world's democratic and social forces, to ask them to regroup and to take up again--beyond their divisions and these strained nationalisms which ill conceal the undercover action of foreign powers--the internationalist tradition which ought to be inseparable from socialism, and which is the only way of making sure there is peace.

A CALL FROM THE COMMITTEE OF THE REVOLUTIONARY PEOPLES' ASSEMBLY

There are millions of us here in France, in Europe, and throughout the world.

Millions who are looking for the same path.

Survivors of hell, escapees from the Resistance, and militants, sympathizers, or fellow-travelers in the great movements demanding social liberation, we think the world has paid dearly enough for its deliverance from nazism to look for its salvation--now that it is safe from the greatest attempt to enslave ever known to history--in nothing less than the respect for and assurance of the rights of man and freedom.

Between the corruptions of capitalist democracy, the flaws and weaknesses of a certain sort of social democracy, and the limitations of Stalinist communism, we think that a free peoples' assembly for revolutionary democracy is capable of giving new life to the principles of freedom and human dignity by linking them to the struggle for social revolution.

Neither violence for violence's sake, nor the illusoriness of stopgap organizations, nor the equivocacy of a confused parliamentary Third Force which has no goal or popular support can satisfy the great expectations of France and the world.

The peoples of the world are soaked with blood, death, charnel-houses, tortures, penitentiaries and prisons, wars, and at the same time they are sick at heart, bewildered by the bogged-down, bankrupt old systems of capitalist rule.

Are we, by missing our chance to join the principles of political democracy to the requirements of economic change, are we going to let the various neo-fascisms steal a march on us?

It is time to make socialism a reality which will attract the fearless and unqualified support of all who reject both the cowardly compromise of the one side and the blind subjection of the other.

We no more accept our present society's resignation to injustice and indignity than we do a social system which would unrestrictedly repress the individual. For us the means are just as important as the ends. And the end of socialism cannot be achieved by any means whatsoever. We could no more tolerate the double game of using means we know to be unworthy now in order to attain a noble end tomorrow than we can tolerate the double game of separating the party of the victims and the party of the executioners in the struggle.

IT IS ON THE BASIS OF THE JUSTICE WHICH HAS BEEN ACHIEVED ALREADY, of moral and civil law, of warrants won by all the peoples through the centuries who fought the lofty fight against all tyranny, it is on the basis of the heritage of political liberties common to all civilized peoples that we mean to define revolutionary democracy.

We are democrats in everything this term will always mean about the peoples' triumph over willfulness, arbitrariness, reasons of state, and obscurantism--in men or systems.

We are revolutionaries because capitalist democracy is no longer anything but the rule of the rich and the enslavement of the poor, because in becoming increasingly feeble it risks giving what is left of itself over to fascism, and thereby for a long time blocking all hopes for the future.

We have no intention of creating division in any democratic and proletarian forces. It is not for us to judge or criticize the fact that a great many militants stay with their party and others leave it; by calling upon all of them to come together in the international Revolutionary Peoples' Assembly, we are saying that we think the time has come to urge them to unite behind an immediate program of defense and republican, secular action which will take advantage of all the reformist and revolutionary experiences of History.

But it is also to that mass of citizens, republicans, democrats, unionists, and revolutionaries in France and in the world--to these millions of men, women, and young people who do not wish either to be nowhere or to choose between existing choices--it is to this immense mass of good will that we cry out:

Nothing is lost, but everything has to be redone, and done.

Together with all those who are working for European and world unity, we have to open up a wider field of action for workers and freemen, and loose a new spirit in it.

It is not true that a generation must be sacrificed in order to distribute the products of labor equitably.

It is not true that democracy cannot be grasped by clean, strong hands able to create within this country the conditions and the means for popular management in all sectors of the economy and public administration.

It is not true that power politics is the only way out we can offer to men.

It is not true that socialism must put on either an anemic or a savage mask.

Through the French Republic of 1848, whose hundredth anniversary we celebrate, and through the Russian Revolution, the socialist idea has descended unto earth.

Through the liberation from nazism, the democratic freedoms have proven irreplaceable.

Through the bankruptcies of capitalist democracy, defense and unity against fascism are once again becoming inescapable.

48/167

Through the failures of merely liberal remedies, the socialist solution is everywhere the order of the day.

Through the oppression and the awakening of the colonial peoples, freedom--complete freedom--must be proclaimed and instilled in the French Union.

Through the artificial exasperation of nationalisms, all the world's peoples are gaining a new international consciousness.

Revolutionary democracy means all these things.

It is up to France to hurl abroad again Saint-Just's cry of hope: "Happiness is a new idea in Europe."

And, to complete it, the call Marx made one hundred years ago:

"Workers and free men of all countries, unite!"

In 1948 as in 1848, let the call for a renewed freedom strengthened by social justice come from our country.

48/168

"La France peut proposer au monde une révolution à faire dans la liberté" ⟨France Can Offer the World a Revolution to Be Freely Made⟩, interview by Georges Altman.

-- *Franc-Tireur*, March 10, 1948.

Here, before the March 10 press conference begins, Sartre defines the R.D.R.'s ⟨Revolutionary Peoples' Assembly⟩ general aim.

48/169

"Les Fondateurs du R.D.R. aux représentants de la presse: 'Voici ce que nous sommes et ce que nous voulons . . .'" ⟨The Founders of the R.D.R. [Revolutionary Peoples' Assembly] Say to the Press: "This Is Who We Are and What We Want . . ."⟩.

-- *Franc-Tireur*, March 11, 1948.

Selections from the press conference given March 10 by Jean Rous, Sartre, and David Rousset to present the R.D.R. Sartre says among other things:

Most Europeans seem to have chosen their conquerors already. We are involved in a war we have not declared. The R.D.R. refuses to take one side out of fear of the other. It wants to sober up all the democratic European groups and make contact with their order to put Europe in the leadership for peace.

48/170

Le R.D.R. et le problème de la liberté ⟨The R.D.R. [Revolutionary Peoples' Assembly] and the Problem of Freedom⟩.

a) La Penseé socialiste, no. 19 (1st trimester, 1948), pp. 3-5.

b) Excerpts. *La faim au ventre, la liberté au coeur* ⟨Hunger in the Guts and Freedom in the Heart⟩. *La Gauche R.D.R.*, no. 1 (May 15-30, 1948), p. 1.

c) Modified version of *(b)*. *Avoir faim, c'est déjà vouloir être libre* ⟨To Be Hungry Is Already to Want to Be Free⟩. *Caliban*, no. 20 (October, 1948), pp. 11-14.

Speech given at the first meeting of the R.D.R. on March 19, 1948, in the Salle Wagram.

Taking up one of the themes he had not had time to deal with during the radio broadcasts, "Tribune of *Les Temps modernes*," Sartre attacks those who condemn workers for their "sordid materialism" and interprets hunger as *a demand for freedom* as well as an expression of solidarity: *A man is not hungry all alone; when that man is hungry, he is hungry with all the comrades of his class, with the people who are paid the same as he is.* And Sartre continues:

It is not a question of giving up freedom, not even the bourgeoisie's abstract freedoms, but of giving them a content, going back to their source to see how they spring from the most elementary requirements, the requirements of everyday life. . . . The primary aim of the Revolutionary Peoples' Assembly is to link revolutionary demands to the idea of freedom.

The modified version published in *Caliban* omits what directly concerns the R.D.R. and puts more stress on the relationships between freedom and hunger: [They tell the workers] *they will give them enough to eat, but they don't tell them what they want, which is not just to have enough to eat but to have enough to eat in order to be able to be free.* Let us also stress the following phrase: *The democracy that is practiced in bourgeois democracies is a hoax.*

48/171

"Revolutionary Democrats," interview by Mary Burnet.

48/171

-- *New York Herald Tribune* (Paris edition), June 2, 1948.

Here are some of the ideas Sartre develops:

-- The R.D.R. ⟨Revolutionary Peoples' Assembly⟩ is not a party but an assembly; it is addressed to individuals and not to established groups. Its immediate objective is to preserve the revolutionary ideal and to work to establish the conditions for an authentic socialism. It does not want reforms but a revolution which will be carried out without bloodshed and which will preserve the freedoms capitalism justifies itself by yet (unlike capitalism) extend them to all citizens. This revolution, which must be carried out on a European scale, should allow Europe to become an intervening force between the U.S.S.R. and the U.S.A.

Every objective, no matter how worthwhile, can only be compromised and betrayed if arbitrary means are used to reach it, etc.

48/172

Jeunes d'Europe, unissez-vous! Faites vous-mêmes votre destin ⟨Young People of Europe, Unite! Forge Your Own Destiny⟩.

-- *La Gauche R.D.R.*, no. 3 (June 16-30, 1948), p. 1.

The text of some remarks made on June 11, 1948, at an R.D.R. ⟨Revolutionary Peoples' Assembly⟩ meeting in the Salle des Sociétés Savantes. This meeting was marked by brawls with R.P.F. ⟨French Peoples' Assembly⟩ groups trying to sabotage the meeting.

After having attacked the R.P.F. (whose goal is *to prepare for tomorrow's war so that France may be on the side of the victors, that is, the Americans*), the Communist Party (which *since the Liberation has been bent on discouraging the most evident good will by the clumsiest of internal authoritarianism and the most rigid and inopportune of external activities*), and the Third Force (*out of date* and *without a program*), Sartre expresses the hope that *in creating Europe, the young will create democracy.*

The same issue of *La Gauche* quotes additional passages from Sartre's remarks in a report of the meeting: *Everywhere in Europe I have met young people who think the same as you. . . . Rise up against the false prophets who wish to drag you into bloody ventures.*

48/173

De partout, aujourd'hui, on veut nous mystifier ⟨People Everywhere Today are Trying to Mystify Us⟩.

-- *La Gauche R.D.R.*, no. 4 (July, 1948), p. 4.

A fragment from *What Is Literature?* which consists of pages 305-310 of SITUATIONS, II. The same issue of *La Gauche* includes a piece by Albert Camus: "Réflexions sur une démocratie sans catéchisme" ⟨Remarks on a Democracy without a Catechism⟩.

48/174

Entretien sur la politique ⟨A Discussion of Politics⟩ with David Rousset and Gérard Rosenthal.

a) *Les Temps modernes*, no. 36 (September, 1948), pp. 385-428.

b) Reprinted with many changes as *Premier entretien, 18 juin 1948* ⟨First Discussion, June 18, 1948⟩. In *Entretiens sur la politique* ⟨Discussions of Politics⟩. See 49/175.

This discussion, which took place June 18, 1948, is signed only by Rousset and Sartre.

Sartre reported some things Raymond Aron had said to him, and in a letter dated October 22, 1948, Aron criticized him for having twisted his ideas. This letter was published in *Les Temps modernes* (no. 38 [November, 1948], p. 957) with a short reply in which Sartre says that Aron said exactly what he said he said.

49/175

ENTRETIENS SUR LA POLITIQUE ⟨Discussions of Politics⟩.

-- J.-P. Sartre; David Rousset; and Gérard Rosenthal. ENTRETIENS SUR LA POLITIQUE. Gallimard, [1949].

The volume, which came out in March, 1949, includes "Second Discussion" dated November 24, 1948.

The insert, which was not drafted by Sartre, concludes as follows:

"The DISCUSSIONS OF POLITICS constitute a first 'summary' of the views of this 'Revolutionary Peoples' Assembly,' which was the result of the initiative of a handful of intellectuals and militant workers, and whose first demonstrations have already won it a large hearing among the masses and the young. . . .

49/175

"These free DISCUSSIONS--which constitute a critical dialogue, a manifesto, a program, a pamphlet--develop by subjecting the confessions of faith and the personalities of the opposing camps of Gaullism and Stalinism to an acrid dialectical analysis, and by hitting harshly in the process at the misadventures of Stalinist intellectuals, the acts of ministers, and the certainties of R.P.F. ⟨French Peoples' Assembly⟩ dignitaries."

Today the volume is of slight general interest; however, it does contain a good exposition of the R.D.R.'s ⟨Revolutionary Peoples' Assembly⟩ ideas and much information about Sartre's relations with the Communists (see especially pp. 70-78).

Among the leading responses, let us single out those of:

-- François Mauriac. See 49/184;

-- Raymond Aron ("Réponse à Jean-Paul Sartre" ⟨Reply to Jean-Paul Sartre⟩, *Liberté de l'esprit*, June, 1949);

-- Maurice Mouillaud ("Quand MM. Sartre, Rousset et Rosenthal parlent de politique" ⟨When MM. Sartre, Rousset, and Rosenthal Discuss Politics⟩, *La Nouvelle Critique*, November, 1949, pp. 15-24).

48/176

J.-P. Sartre aux Marocains: "Ceux qui vous oppriment, nous oppriment pour les mêmes raisons" ⟨J.-P. Sartre Tells the Moroccans: "Those Who Are Oppressing You Are Oppressing Us for the Same Reasons"⟩.

-- *La Gauche*, no. 8 (November, 1948), pp. 1, 3.

Excerpts from remarks made at a meeting on Morocco held at the Maison de la Chimie (Paris) on November 18, 1948.

As long as we cannot say to ourselves, "Not a single man on earth is oppressed as a result of our doing," we shall not even be able to imagine what it means to be free. . . . It is by fighting at your side against the class and the institutions which are oppressing you that we shall succeed in liberating ourselves.

48/177

* *Il nous faut la paix pour refaire le monde. Réponse à ceux qui nous appellent "munichois."* ⟨We Must Have Peace in order to Remake the World: Reply to Those Who Call Us "Men of Munich"⟩.

-- *Franc-Tireur*, December 10, 1948.

This piece is not tied directly to the R.D.R. ⟨Revolutionary Peoples' Assembly⟩, but it is undoubtedly the best thing Sartre wrote on politics during this period.

48/178

Il faut que nous menions cette lutte en commun ⟨We Have to Wage This Struggle Together⟩.

a) La Gauche, no. 10 (December 20, 1948), pp. 1-2.

Complete text of remarks made at a meeting for "the internationalism of the mind" which was held on December 13, 1948, at the Salle Pleyel, with the participation of Albert Camus, David Rousset, André Breton, Carlo Levi, Richard Wright, Theodor Plievier, etc.

b) Report of the meeting with quotations, in *Franc-Tireur*, December 14, 1948.

c) Excerpts. *Les Ecrivains de tous les pays ont en commun les mêmes craintes et les mêmes espoirs* ⟨Writers of All Countries Share the Same Fears and Hopes⟩. *Combat*, December 17, 1948.

Sartre points out what opposes him to Malraux:

A writer who is alas! far more distant from us in our own country than these foreigners who come from all parts of Europe, a writer of our own language who uses words which have a meaning we no longer give to them, once said: "Europe must think of herself in terms of destiny." And if I want to understand this word "destiny," I have to thumb through his books as I would a dictionary. Death changes our life into destiny: that's what destiny means. Europe's destiny comes from the fact that in the eyes of some she's dead. For this writer, hope is henceforth written somewhere else.

We writers gathered here tonight do not believe in destiny. We don't believe that Europe is a destiny. We still think that she can be an undertaking, the common undertaking of all Europeans.

Then Sartre says in conclusion:

Everywhere where men reject oppression, exploitation, colonialism, and a world of concentration camps, that's where our public is. . . . While waiting for her economy and politics to be unified, Europe intends to unify her literature herself.

In an interview in 1955 (see 55/267) Sartre sums up the R.D.R. ⟨Revolutionary Peoples' Assembly⟩

business in this way: *I had nothing to do with the founding of the R.D.R., which was the work of David Rousset and Altman. Its dissolution is another matter. Besides, the R.D.R. was only a tiny little group outside the main lines of historical development. In any case, personal conflicts would sooner or later have divided its few thousand supporters.*

48/NOTE 1.

Sartre was called as a character witness during the trial of one of his former students at the lycée Condorcet, Robert Misrahi, who was accused along with another student of concealing explosives (see "Le Problème juif? Un problème international, déclare Jean-Paul Sartre au procès des amis du Stern" 〈The Jewish Problem? An International Problem, Jean-Paul Sartre Declares at the Trial of the Friends of the Stern Gang〉, an observer's report by Madeleine Jacob, *Franc-Tireur*, February 14, 1948). After having praised the man he considered *his most brilliant student,* Sartre declared: *I consider it the non-Jew's duty to help the Jews and the Palestinian cause.*

48/NOTE 2.

The second issue of *Présence africaine* (1948) announced the future publication of two pieces by Sartre: "Du Paternalisme" 〈About Paternalism〉 and "Réponse à l'enquête sur le mythe du Nègre" 〈Reply to the Inquiry into the Myth of the Negro〉; and the sixth issue (1949): "A propos de l'esclavage" 〈Concerning Slavery〉. None of these articles was written.

The sixth issue also has the following advertisement: "Les Editions Africaines will soon inaugurate a new series, Leur Négritude: 50-page studies devoted to Aimé Césaire, Léopold Senghor, René Maran, Richard Wright, Louis Armstrong, Langston Hughes, etc., by Jean-Paul Sartre, Hugues Panassié, René Maran, etc.

Sartre may have been thinking of writing a study of Césaire.

1949

49/179

LA MORT DANS L'ÂME ⟨Sick at Heart[1]⟩, Vol. III of *Les Chemins de la liberté* ⟨Roads to Freedom⟩.

a) Complete text came out in six parts in *Les Temps modernes*:

No. 39 (December, 1948-January,1949), pp. 1-45.

No. 40 (February, 1949), pp. 230-78.

No. 41 (March, 1949), pp. 443-502.

No. 42 (April, 1949), pp. 626-66.

No. 43 (May, 1949), pp. 821-67.

No. 44 (June, 1949), pp. 1025-79.

b) Excerpts in a newspaper serial with the subtitle, *Le combat sans espoir* ⟨The Hopeless Battle⟩. *Combat*, October 21, 22-23, and 25, 1949.

The third part is marked "Continued."

c) Book. Gallimard, [1949]. 293 pages.

Printing date: August 24, 1949. Put on sale in September. 8 copies on laid antique paper; 105 on wood-free vellum; 2050 bound copies on esparto grass. Minor variations from *(a)*.

---

1. ["Sick at Heart" is one possible translation of LA MORT DANS L'ÂME. As indicated below, the novel was published under the title TROUBLED SLEEP in the U.S. and as IRON IN THE SOUL in the U.K. I prefer "Sick at Heart" and have used it throughout as the translation of the title of the French edition.--Trans.]

The volume came out in the Soleil series in 1962.

d) Le Livre de poche series, nos. 821-22. Gallimard, [1962], and the latest reprinting (1969) has on its cover the insert we reprint below.

e) *Oeuvre romanesque*, Vol. V. Lidis, [1965].

f) Folio series, no. 58. Gallimard, [1972].

IRON IN THE SOUL or TROUBLED SLEEP, translated by Gerard Hopkins.

t1) IRON IN THE SOUL. London: Hamish Hamilton, 1950.

t2) TROUBLED SLEEP. New York: Alfred A. Knopf, 1951.

t3) Paperback. TROUBLED SLEEP. New York: Bantam Books, [1961].

t4) Paperback. IRON IN THE SOUL. Penguin Books, [1963].

The insert for edition *(c)*, which was drawn up by Sartre, reads as follows:

They are still alive but death has touched them: something has come to an end; defeat has brought their shelf of values tumbling down from the wall. While Daniel is in Paris celebrating the triumph of bad conscience, Mathieu is in a village in Lorraine taking stock of damages: Peace, Progress, Reason, Law, Democracy, Country--all are in ruins and can never be put back together again.

But something is beginning too: without a road, without references or even a letter of introduction, without even having understood what has happened to them, by the mere fact that they have survived, they are on their way. Daniel, in the depths of his being, is (without knowing it) beginning the climb up the slope which will lead him to freedom and death. Brunet is getting involved in an undertaking which he is far from suspecting will break his armor of certainty and leave him naked and free. Boris, looking for the death he has been robbed of, is flying toward London: it is not death that he will find there. And Mathieu, above all, is having his first hesitant experience of solidarity. Among all these men who are being lost together, he learns that one never saves oneself alone. In the process he's the one who loses most: the others are duped by their principles; he is duped by his problem. But rest assured; he'll find another one.

Volume III of *Roads to Freedom* was first announced in 1945 under the title "The Last Chance," and excerpts from the novel were about to come out in *Les Temps modernes* (no. 26 [November, 1947]). In an interview he gave in October, 1945 (see 45/87), Sartre says that the roads to freedom are to lead the characters effectively to their freedom: *Mathieu will find his love and his undertaking. He will commit himself in a free commitment which will give the world a meaning for him. This will be the subject of "The Last Chance."* Sartre, finding subsequently that he could not do what he wanted in a single volume, decided to change the title and adopted "Troubled Sleep," which he had already used for some pages of his journal in 1942 (see 42/33).

The volume--undoubtedly the best in the series--was written in 1947-48, at the same time, let it be noted, as the rough draft of the existentialist ethics promised at the close of BEING AND NOTHINGNESS. The first part covers, chronologically, the period from June 15 to June 18, 1940, and concludes by leaving Mathieu in a particularly desperate situation. The second part describes the first days of captivity of a group of French soldiers which includes the Communist militant Brunet and a certain Schneider, who is suspected of being an informer.

See also 45/60, 45/61, 49/191, and 49/192.

49/180

SITUATIONS, III.

-- Gallimard, [1949]. 351 pages. Printing date: June 10, 1949. Dedicated to Jacques Bost. There is also a bound edition of 1119 copies.

This volume includes twelve pieces, in French, published between 1944 and 1948 and divided into five sections:

I. (On the War and the Occupation):

-- *The Republic of Silence*	see 44/53
-- *Paris during the Occupation*	44/56
-- *What Is a Collaborator?*	45/79
-- *The End of the War*	45/81

II. (On the United States):

-- *Individualism and Conformism in the United States*	# 45/71
-- *American Cities*	# 45/72
-- *New York, Colonial City*	# 46/106
-- *Introduction* (to a special issue of *Les Temps modernes* on the United States)	46/111

49/180

III. *Materialism and Revolution* # 46/108

IV. *Black Orpheus* 48/158

V. *The Search for* [or *Quest of*] *the Absolute* (on Giacometti) 48/162

-- *Calder's Mobiles* 46/100

None of these pieces has any major changes.

Translations of SITUATIONS, III.

t1) Essays marked # translated by Annette Michelson. In LITERARY AND PHILOSOPHICAL ESSAYS (1955).

t2) The Quest of the Absolute and *Calder's Mobiles*, translated by Wade Baskin. In *Essays in Aesthetics* (1963).

Paris during the Occupation, What Is a Collaborator? and *The End of the War* have not, to our knowledge, been translated into English. For others, see separate entries.

ENTRETIENS SUR LA POLITIQUE.

See 49/175

49/181

NOURRITURES ⟨Foods⟩, followed by excerpts from LA NAUSÉE ⟨Nausea⟩.

-- Jacques Damase, [1949]. Illustrated with dry-point etchings by Wols. 57 pages. Printing date: September 30, 1949. 450 copies on wood-free Johannot finish, 26 of which are lettered from A to Z and 424 of which are numbered from 27 to 450.

The piece, *Foods*, is on pages 13-19.

This volume is very rare and is not in the Bibliothèque Nationale.

See item 38/20.

49/182

"Jean-Paul Sartre reproche à Georges Lukács de ne pas être marxiste" ⟨Jean-Paul Sartre Criticizes George Lukács for Not Being a Marxist⟩, interview by François Erval.

-- *Combat*, January 20, 1949.

On the occasion of the French publication of his book *Existentialism or Marxism?*, Georges Lukács gave a series of lectures in Paris and made some statements to the press in which he sharply attacked Sartre and existentialism. In particular, the January 13, 1949, *Combat* published an interview of Lukács by François Erval entitled "L'existentialisme fait une apologie indirecte du capitalisme" ⟨Existentialism Indirectly Justifies Capitalism⟩. In his statements to the press, Lukács justified his having renounced his first works by claiming that their Hegelianism was outmoded. He also claimed that Sartre had not succeeded in bridging the gap between the Heideggerianism of BEING AND NOTHINGNESS and the Kantianism of EXISTENTIALISM IS A HUMANISM.

In this interview, Sartre replies that he does not like philosophical polemics in newspapers, but that Lukács' attacks cannot be left unanswered, even though *they have no real foundation.* After having characterized *Existentialism or Marxism?* in passing as *philosophical journalism*, he says that Lukács, who has disavowed his first works, is in an especially poor position to complain that he has changed his philosophy: *Lukács condemns me for having changed, but I haven't changed at all. Yet I claim the right to do so if the development of my thinking requires it. Each philosopher has developed during his career, without, however, making the hairpin turns characteristic of thinking subject to a predetermined line. A real philosopher feels no need whatsoever to renounce his earlier works as his thinking develops; Marx changed his doctrine too, but without pronouncing this* mea culpa *which Lukács claims is a proof of his sincerity. Furthermore, the term "renounce" alone suffices to show that we are in the midst of a way of thinking which is not free; it comes from a medieval and religious attitude and is conceivable only in a scholastic philosophy.* Sartre formally denies that he has changed between BEING AND NOTHINGNESS and EXISTENTIALISM IS A HUMANISM: everything new Lukács thinks he has discovered was already contained in BEING AND NOTHINGNESS. As for EXISTENTIALISM IS A HUMANISM, it is only an *oeuvre de passage*--Lukács criticizes Sartre's conception of freedom. Now he gives a definition of freedom which Sartre completely agrees with, even though his own is better. Lukács is in fact a *crypto-existentialist*. And since Lukács' Marxism is closer to the statistical method--which is antidialectical--than it is to Marxism, it is thus *crypto-Marxist* as well.

Since he pronounced his renunciation of his own past, Lukács has spent less and less time with philosophy in order to devote himself to a sort of sociology of philosophy which is highly debatable. When, for example, he speaks of the social content of the Cartesian "cogito," he practices very poor sociology. Of course this "cogito" will reflect a

49/182

certain protest by the rising bourgeois world, but what it demands is precisely the freedom of subjectivity. Descartes does not try to get involved in the political and social events of his time; in this sense one could say that he is the very type of the noncommitted, and thus anti-Marxist, thinker. And if we want to take a closer look at the content of his "cogito," which according to Lukács is allegedly more social than the existentialist "cogito," we must recognize that the latter is richer in social content than Descartes's because it implies the existence of others.

To conclude, Sartre relates his thinking to the acting of the R.D.R. ⟨Revolutionary Peoples' Assembly⟩: *It's beginning right now that we want to deal with men as free beings.*

49/183

"Pour Lukács la terre ne tourne pas" ⟨The Earth Does Not Turn for Lukács⟩, interview by François Erval.

-- *Combat*, February 3, 1949.

The polemic becomes more bitter. In this same issue, under the title "Sartre Is Sinning against Intellectual Integrity," Georges Lukács refuses his adversary the moral right to give his opinion on Marxism and characterizes him as a "mediocre academic."

In his reply, which was published in relation to the interview with Lukács, Sartre adopts an acidly polemic tone: *In speaking of a mediocre academic, Lukács has given us a perfect definition of himself.* He is astonished that in his book Lukács spoke of him as an "authentic thinker of high quality," whereas now he calls him "grotesque" and "mediocre." Yet his reasons are clear: they are political, and also have a psychological basis. *Lukács isn't used to being challenged any more, in his country he decrees with no risk of opposition. His arguments are null and void: he has not read* BEING AND NOTHINGNESS.

Sartre nevertheless tries patiently to refute certain objections Lukács has made about the problem of freedom:

If I take the freedom of the other as my objective goal, I do him violence. But if I take my own freedom as my goal, it involves requiring all the others to be free. In the choice I make of my freedom, the freedom of the others is demanded; but when I move to the level of action, I have to take the other person as a means and not as an end. Here we are obviously confronted with an antinomy, but it is precisely this antinomy which constitutes the problem of ethics. I shall examine this antinomy in my "Ethics," but I must point out right now that thinking which claims to be Marxist and is astonished by contradictions is already rotten.

Sartre further criticizes Lukács for not having had the courage to utter Galileo's "but it does turn" when he too had to abjure his convictions. But the reason probably is that for Lukács, *the earth doesn't turn any more*. He concludes by saying that he would be glad to have the same freedom of expression in Budapest that Lukács has in Paris.

Let us point out that *Les Temps modernes*, no. 50 (December, 1949), pp. 1119-21, published a short "Commentaire" ⟨Commentary⟩ in which Maurice Merleau-Ponty backed up Sartre: "In 1946 Lukács claimed for the writer the right to go beyond his past; in 1949 he must disqualify his works as a critic and an aesthetician, as if the high esteem in which he held Tolstoy had been only thoughtlessness and precipitancy. Thus communism goes from historical responsibility to naked discipline, from autocriticism to repudiation, from Marxism to superstition." (Reprinted in *Signes* [Gallimard, 1960], pp. 328-30 ⟨*Signs* [Evanston: Northwestern University Press, 1964], pp. 261-62⟩.)

49/183 A

"Sartre Enters 'a New Phase,'" interview-article by Joseph A. Barry.

a) New York Times Magazine, January 30, 1949.

b) Modified version, "Jean-Paul Sartre, Adventurous Pedagogue." In Joseph A. Barry. *Left Bank Right Bank: Paris and Parisians*. New York: W. W. Norton, [1951]. Pp. 99-109.

After having painted a vivid picture of Sartre, Joseph A. Barry relates many of Sartre's comments on DIRTY HANDS and on the American adaptation of the play.

I wrote the play so that at the end you could choose between Hugo and Hoederer. But I understand that Boyer's acting is so overpowering and that the performance, or the character, of Hugo so weakened, that the only strong one left is Hoederer. . . . Frankly, I am more sympathetic with Hoederer. You must have Hoederers in politics, but I think you also must have Hugos to kill the Hoederers from time to time. . . . For you, a Communist is someone across the Atlantic; but if I am walking down the street and slip on a banana peel, one out of three persons I bump is a Communist. You cannot know what the issue of communism means to us. And that may be why DIRTY HANDS *will be misunderstood in America.*

49/184

Réponse à François Mauriac ⟨Reply to François Mauriac⟩.

-- *Le Figaro littéraire*, May 7, 1949.

In an article entitled "La Politique de M. Sartre" ⟨M. Sartre's Politics⟩, which was published in the April 25, 1949, *Figaro*, Mauriac had attacked Sartre in relation to DISCUSSIONS OF POLITICS, concluding: "Our philosopher will just have to make the best of a bad job: Give up politics, Zanetto, and *studia la matematica.*"

Sartre's reply begins with these words: *The less a man knows what he's talking about, the more zestful he becomes: This is what happens to M. Mauriac when he tries to talk politics.* Since Mauriac had called him a "noble soul," Sartre says: *David Rousset, Rosenthal, and I are noble souls because we do not think that it is "necessary" under any circumstances to have the troops attack the workers. And if it were true that you were so bloodthirsty, I would take the liberty of writing, with your pen, that when a man does not believe in the soul it is a pleasant surprise for him to learn he has one--and a noble one to boot--but a man is really ill-favored by fortune when he believes his soul is immortal and it is eternally ugly.* Since Mauriac had said that he would back his candidacy for the French Academy, Sartre replies: *It's nice to be able to count on your vote on the day I decide to canvass for a seat in the academy. But I must decline your offer: I find in certain members of the academy so much bitterness, so much arrogance and, beneath a forced humility, such a consciousness of being superior to everyone else that it is definitely not the place I'll go to to learn about equality.*

Mauriac, in his published retort to Sartre's reply, deplores the latter's tone and complains, in substance, that he has been treated like an old man. He concludes: "I am surprised that a philosopher in his forties does not see advancing toward him from the mirror while he is shaving in the morning the redoubtable old man he already is."

NOTE: "M. Sartre's Politics" and three other articles Mauriac wrote about Sartre ("The Tribulations of a Slimy Rat," August, 1952; "J.-P. Sartre and the Jewish Question," March, 1953; "Sartre's Second Letter," December, 1952) are reprinted in François Mauriac, *Mémoires politiques* (Grasset, 1967).

49/185

Naissance d'Israël ⟨The Birth of Israel⟩.

-- *Hillel*, 2d ser., no. 7 (June, 1949), p. 6.

We reprint this text *in extenso*:

I have always hoped, and I still hope, that the Jewish problem will be solved within the context of a human community unrestricted by national boundaries, but since no developing society can skip the stage of national independence, we must be glad that an Israeli state has come to justify the hopes and battles of Jews all over the world. And since the Jewish problem is a particularly agonizing expression of the contradictions which are tearing contemporary society apart, the founding of the Palestinian state must be considered one of the most important events of our times, one of the few these days which let us keep on hoping. For the Jews it is the crowning of their sufferings and their heroic struggle; for all of us, it marks a concrete step toward a human community in which man will be the future of man.

49/186

Défense de la culture française par la culture européenne ⟨Defending French Culture by Defending European Culture⟩.

-- *Politique étrangère*, 14th Year, no. 3 (June, 1949), pp. 233-48.

This is the little-known text of a brilliant lecture given April 24, 1949, at the Centre d'Etudes de Politique étrangère. There is also a typed copy of the lecture, as well as an abridged translation by B. Frechtman, entitled *European Declaration of Independence*, in *Commentary*, IX (May, 1950), 407-14. A note indicates, however, that the source of this translation is not *Politique étrangère*: "This article is the condensed version of a speech given to the French League against Antisemitism."

In answer to the question, *Is our culture imperiled? Can we save it, and how?* Sartre develops his ideas along the following broad lines:

Every cultural object is both a fact from the past and a demand turned toward the future. *We shall say that a culture is living when the present community includes it and goes beyond it toward the future, when beyond each individual who is born there is still a totality of possibilities for development which correspond to what he is going to look for. In other words, the future of a community or a period is characterized on the cultural level by its going beyond its culture* (p. 236).

After having compared the situation of woman, who

lives in a masculine universe she is not responsible for--which prevents her from producing great works--with the situation of economically dependent countries, Sartre states that *there is a culture and the production of a culture when the totality of individuals who contribute to that culture are free and responsible for the society's values within a community which is itself relatively autonomous. . . . Communities which are inferior in terms of force question the ideology and culture of the stronger country as if it were their destiny. . . . Thus cultural ideas have a potential for diffusion which is wholly independent of their intrinsic value and depends on the economic or military importance of the country in question* (p. 238). A less powerful country which formerly had a living culture consequently has two different and opposed cultures: *one of which will be a sort of dream of destiny--the culture which comes from abroad, the other an outmoded dream of the past--its own culture in a half-dead state, forgotten and replaced. The result of this is that the relations between cultures is determined to a certain extent by power relations* (p. 239).

Thus France ought to establish cultural relations only with countries whose potential is the same as its own and to abstain from all commerce with countries whose potential is greater. But she is in no position to choose. *A country's political, economic, demographic, and military hegemony imposes nonreciprocal cultural exchanges* (p. 240). At this point it is a matter of considering *the present relation between the cultural elements which come to us from America and French culture properly speaking.* The latter *persists as a result of a misunderstanding: for though in France we find certain forms of culture and certain conceptions of intellectual life and work which we do not find elsewhere, these are tied to inadequate industrial equipment, to a society based on injustice, and to an inadequate birth rate. . . . It is precisely because we have not reached this degree of industrialization and social reconstruction or construction that we still present values which for us are futures but for many foreigners have the charm of the past* (p. 241).

The misunderstanding goes back to 1918, when France emerged victorious from a war which had ruined her demographically; but World War II confronted her with the real problem: *To recreate a milieu in which our ideas can still have potential and value, not as past but as a future for other countries, we must retool and industrialize. But in order to find this place . . . we are turning toward America, and from this moment forward American ideology and culture will necessarily come to us with screws, manufactured goods, and canned fruit juices* (p. 242).

What characterizes European culture in relation to American culture is an age-old struggle against evil. . . . *The evil in the world is inexpiable, and European culture is certainly a reflection on the problem of evil, on the thought, What can a man do, what can he be, what can he succeed at if we grant that evil is inherent in the world? Now generally speaking, evil is not an American concept. Americans are not pessimistic about human nature and social organization. If I were to compare French rationalism to American rationalism, I would say that American rationalism is white, in the sense of white magic, and that French rationalism is a black rationalism: . . . French rationalism is, as a matter of fact, always pessimistic. . . . Reason is that struggle against a universal which escapes us everywhere and which we keep trying to overtake; it's a sort of limited confidence in human freedom seen as being in a more or less desperate situation.* American rationalism, on the contrary, is optimistic; for *American reason is above all technical, practical, and scientific* (pp. 242-43).

In America, the intellectual and the writer are separate. *But in our country the intellectual and the writer are one and the same; and since for the moment and in the present state of our society there is no possibility of our seeing writers emerging from different layers of the proletariat and perpetually bringing us a breath of fresh air, if the American influence were to lead us writers to think that our social influence is limited and thereby lead us to estheticism, we would sink into scholasticism* (p. 244).

. . . *Can one defend French culture as such? My answer to that question is very simple: no. The situation seems inescapable: France, left to her own devices, has no other way out on the level of the bourgeoisie than to turn to America, ask for her aid, and consequently adopt her ideology; on the level of the social struggle, on the contrary, France's only way out is to turn to the ideology which comes to us from the countries of the East, and consequently to find common but conflicting elements and thus also lose her ideology. . . .*

So do we have another means of saving the essential elements of our culture? Yes. But only if we look at the problem in a completely different way and understand that today there can no longer be any more question of a French culture than there can be of a Dutch or Swiss or German one. If we want French culture to endure, it must be integrated into the framework of a great European culture (p. 245).

. . . *It's by shooting for a unity of European culture that we'll save French culture; but this cultural unity will make no sense and be a thing of words alone unless it's set within the context of a much more profound effort to achieve the political*

49/186

and economic unity of Europe. But this cultural politics does not have a chance unless it is a part of a politics which seeks to defend not only the cultural but the political and economic autonomy of Europe against America and the U.S.S.R., with the aim of making Europe a power existing in its own right between the two blocs. And not as a third bloc but as an autonomous power which will not let itself be torn between American optimism and Russian scientism. The cultural problem today is only one aspect of a much greater problem, the problem of the whole destiny of Europe. And if we once convince ourselves that we are powerless to act between the two blocs, that our Europe split up into two spheres of influence has to be a battlefield, then assuredly our European culture will be lost.

If we think that we shall save it through a sort of monkishness on the part of our writers, who would speak of birds within the convents while the battle raged outside the walls, then in any case, it will be lost and lost forever. But if, on the contrary, we assume that it is possible to build a unified and socialist European society in which economic problems are dealt with on a European rather than a national scale; and if this Europe tries to reestablish her autonomy by playing on the United States' hostility to the U.S.S.R. and the U.S.S.R.'s hostility to the United States instead of being buffeted from one to the other; then European culture can be saved. In other words, since culture is only one part of the total fact that is history, we are dealing with a problem that is total and calls for total solutions (pp. 247-48).

49/187

Le Noir et le Blanc aux Etats-Unis 〈Black and White in the United States〉 (excerpt from the "Ethics").

-- *Combat*, June 16, 1949.

As we know, the final lines of BEING AND NOTHINGNESS promised a work on ethics which has never seen the light of day, although it was announced long ago under the title "Man"[2] on the back cover of the Bibliothèque de Philosophie series edited for Gallimard by Sartre and Maurice Merleau-Ponty. Once BEING AND NOTHINGNESS was under way, however, Sartre drafted about two thousand pages on ethics. He gave this work up when, coming up against the contradictions of a historical development he had been unable to foresee at the time he began his work, he realized he was forging a purely idealistic ethics or, as he sometimes called it, a "writer's

2. This vague, attractive title was chosen as a joke by Merleau-Ponty.

ethics." (See also 49/192.) In the early fifties he continued to write pages on the ethical problem from time to time, but even though he pursued his reflections on it throughout his subsequent work, and even though it constitutes their basic concern, it was only recently (in 1964-65) that Sartre took up again the drafting of a completely new work which he had temporarily abandoned yet another time in order to complete his "Flaubert."

Although the pages *Combat* published are not of very high quality, they have the noteworthy interest of apparently being the only ones from the first manuscript to have been offered to the public. A note says, "We thank Jean-Paul Sartre for having been kind enough to let us have the pages below, which are excerpts from the "Ethics" he is presently writing. They are part of a chapter entitled "Revolutionary Violence."

In this part Sartre analyzes the relationship of oppressors to the oppressed, taking as an example racism in the United States. *Oppression does not become visible at first to the oppressor. It is hidden. He does not view it cynically as a de facto matter; de facto and de jure are inextricably mixed. Oppression is "in the nature of things," since the inferiority of Blacks to Whites is a natural fact. It is "by divine right," since nature in a world which has been created is ordered in accordance with the will of God.*

Sartre goes on to describe the spontaneously conservative attitude: *Concepts and values form an unchanging hierarchical series in which objects, and men too, participate, as Aristotelian matter participated in substantial forms. It is clear that conservative thought, when it is not realistic and cynical--which can never be the case for more than a small number of enlightened individuals--must be conceptualist, participationist, and finalist. And in order for the oppressor to get a clear view of an unjustifiable situation, it is not enough for him to look at it honestly; he must also change the structure of his eyes. As long as he looks at it with his conceptualist framework, he will judge it to be right and just. Now he has breathed in his conceptualism with the air of the time, for conceptualism is the philosophy of observation. If I observe that the balloon rises, I say it rises because it is light. If as a child I observe that the Blacks don't act the way we act, I say it is because they're black. I have to reverse my point of view to understand that the air pushes the balloon up and that we oblige the Blacks to act the way they do, because in both cases the determining factor is hidden.*

NOTE: We recently found a manuscript of around eight

49/187

hundred typed pages which Sartre says represents a tenth of what he has written on his "Ethics."

49/188

Jean-Paul Sartre ouvre un dialogue ⟨Jean-Paul Sartre Opens a Dialogue⟩.

-- *Peuple du Monde*, no. 11 (June 18-19, 1949). This monthly of the World Citizens came out as a supplement to *Combat*.

In 1949 the World Citizens' Movement, founded by the American Gary Davis, aroused great interest among European youth. Albert Camus especially gave it his public support. Questioned about it, Sartre replied in an article in which he revealed in a friendly way his objections to the World Citizens' somewhat naive ideology. He criticizes the utopian idealism of the project to form a world government but grants that this propagandistic theme may become *a myth in the Christian sense of the term.* He politely attacks their misunderstanding of economic, social, and political factors as well as short-range goals, and then points out that their refusal to make concrete and immediate commitments can only win them the ear of *certain upright, uneasy, mobile, and idealistic circles of the petty bourgeoisie and the middle classes who have no political experience.* He makes a definitive criticism of their moralizing attitude: *Doesn't your peace resemble the Kantians' categorial imperative, which is so pure and uncompromising that, as Kant himself recognized, no one on earth has ever followed it?*

On the other hand, this text seems to be the last one in which Sartre still appeals to the R.D.R. ⟨Revolutionary Peoples' Assembly⟩.

49/189

Introduction to *Journal du voleur* ⟨The Thief's Journal⟩, by Jean Genet.

a) Bulletin de la N.R.F., July, 1949, pp. 7-8.

b) Bulletin N.R.F., no. 213 (June-July, 1966), pp. 11-12.

This introduction is, in a way, expurgated: it lacks fifteen lines which stress the "scandalous" side of Genet and which are found in the English translations.

A Note on Jean Genet, translated by Bernard Frechtman.

t1) Merlin (Paris), II, no. 1 (spring-summer, 1953), 4-5.

t2) Used as Foreword. In Jean Genet. *The Thief's Journal*, translated by Bernard Frechtman. Paris: The Olympia Press, 1954. Pp. 7-8.

The same volume was reprinted in 1959 and has been reissued by Grove Press (1964), Bantam Books (1965), and Penguin Books (1968).

> It is hard to tell where this second thing Sartre wrote about Genet comes from. No doubt it is a letter addressed to some possible editor recommending a book that Sartre liked very much and that would moreover be dedicated to him (and to Castor ⟨Simone de Beauvoir⟩).
>
> It was at the Flore in May, 1944, that Sartre and Simone de Beauvoir first met Genet, who subsequently became one of their closest friends. In *The Prime of Life* (p. 459), Simone de Beauvoir says, "[Genet was] a completely free spirit. His understanding with Sartre was based on their common feeling for a freedom nothing could intimidate, and their common abhorrence of whatever hobbled it: nobility of soul, timeless moral laws, universal justice, big words and lofty principles, and idealistic systems." In 1947, Sartre was to dedicate his BAUDELAIRE to Genet and be responsible for his getting the Pléiade prize for *Les Bonnes*.
>
> On Genet see 46/104, 48/165, 50/202 and 52/215.
>
> NOTE: Refer to Richard N. Coe's *The Vision of Jean Genet* (London: Peter Owen, 1968) for a detailed study of the relationship between Sartre and Genet, and for a good bibliography (reviewed and corrected by the author in *Australian Journal of French Studies*, VI, no. 2 [January-April, 1969], 113-30).

49/190

I. "J'ai vu à Haïti un peuple noir fier de sa tradition de liberté" ⟨In Haiti I Saw a Black People Proud of Its Tradition of Freedom⟩, narrative recorded by Georges Altman.

-- *Franc-Tireur*, October 21, 1949.

II. "Haïti se jette avec passion sur tout ce qui évoque la culture française . . . et parmi les riches Antilles, cette république noire est la seule à crever de faim" ⟨Haiti Flings Itself Passionately On Everything Which Evokes French Culture . . . and This Black Republic Is the Only One of the Rich Antilles Which Is Dying of Hunger⟩.

49/190

-- *Franc-Tireur*, October 22-23, 1949.

III. "Haïti vu par Jean-Paul Sartre" ⟨Haiti As Jean-Paul Sartre Sees It⟩.

-- *Franc-Tireur*, October 24, 1949.

Upon his return from a long trip to Mexico, Central America, and the Antilles, Sartre granted Georges Altman, the editor of *Franc-Tireur*, a long interview during which he gave a detailed account of his stay in Haiti, where he had in particular been greatly impressed by the gatherings of the voodoo cult. Georges Altman has to be held responsible for the rather stupid tone of the remarks reported here. Sartre, in pointing out this little-known interview to us, recalled that they had "made him say stupid things."

49/191

Drôle d'Amitié ⟨Strange Friendship⟩, excerpts from Volume IV of *Les Chemins de la liberté* ⟨Roads to Freedom⟩.

-- *Les Temps modernes*, no. 49 (November, 1949), pp. 769-806; no. 50 (December, 1949), pp. 1009-39.

Drôle d'Amitié, which was written in 1949, was to be part of the volume "The Last Chance" which, although announced for publication many times, was finally given up for good by Sartre and never saw the light of day.

Let us reprint the summary Simone de Beauvoir gives in *Force of Circumstance* (p. 194): "A newly arrived prisoner at the Stalag, Chalais, a Communist, recognized Schneider as the journalist Vicarios who had left the party at the time of the Russo-German pact; the Communist Party had circulated a warning about him because they supposed him to be an informer. Chalais expressed his conviction that the U.S.S.R. would never enter the war and that *Humanité* was taking collaboration as the order of the day. Uneasy, indignant, distressed, when Brunet discovered from Vicarios that he was going to escape in order to confront his slanderers, he decided to go with him. This shared escape sealed the friendship which Brunet still felt for Vicarios despite the feelings of the others. Vicarios was killed, Brunet recaptured."

Primarily, *Strange Friendship* shows the sequels to the Nazi-Soviet Pact and stresses the disarray it caused among Communist militants, particularly after *L'Humanité* came out again in Paris in July, 1940. The reversal of the situations of Brunet and Vicarios foreshadows a technique which will be used in THE DEVIL AND THE GOOD LORD, whereas the discussions between Chalais and Brunet take up a theme already found in DIRTY HANDS.

Up to a certain point Vicarios may be identified with Nizan.

49/192

"La Dernière Chance" ⟨The Last Chance⟩, unpublished, unfinished.

There is a signed manuscript 223 pages long for the part of "The Last Chance" which was not published in *Les Temps modernes*. The catalogue of the Gérard de Berny Library (May 12, 1959, sale at l'Hôtel Drouot--Part II, p. 61, art. 164) indicates this manuscript and reproduces a facsimile of a page which presents us with Mathieu, Pinette, Garnier, etc., in a prison camp.

Another manuscript is now in the hands of an American professor, and we hope to be able to publish it in the near future.

Simone de Beauvoir, in *Force of Circumstance* (pp. 194-95), gives the following summary of this unpublished part:

"Brunet decided to make another [escape] try. They'd told him about a prisoner who was the leader of an underground railroad, and he looked for him. Just when he was finding him, Mathieu was taking part in the execution of a 'stool pigeon'. Having escaped, Mathieu, tired of being free 'for nothing' all his life, finally and happily decided in favor of action. Thanks to his help, Brunet escaped and reached Paris; there he discovered, with stupefaction, that--with a change of policy analogous to the one that forces Hugo to suicide at the end of DIRTY HANDS--the U.S.S.R. had entered the war, and that the Communist Party had condemned collaboration. Having succeeded in rehabilitating Schneider, he resumed his role as a militant member of the Resistance; but the doubt, the scandal and the solitude he experienced had revealed his subjectivity to him: in the depths of his commitment he had rediscovered his freedom. At the same time Mathieu was moving in the opposite direction. Daniel, who was collaborating, had managed to have him recalled to Paris as the editor of a newspaper controlled by the Germans. Mathieu avoided the post and went into hiding. In the Stalag, his activities had still been those of an individualistic adventurer; now, by submitting himself to a collective discipline, he arrived at genuine commitment: starting in one case from alienation from the Cause and in the other from abstract liberty, Brunet and Mathieu were the embodiments of the authentic man of action as Sartre conceived him. Mathieu and Odette returned each other's love; she left Jacques and she experienced the fullness of a freely shared passion. Then Mathieu was arrested and died under torture, a hero not in essence, but because he had *made himself* a hero. Philippe too joined the Resistance, to prove to himself that he was not a coward, and also as a revenge against Daniel. He was shot down during a raid on a cafe in the Latin Quarter. Mad with grief and rage, Daniel hid in his briefcase one of the grenades Philippe used to keep hidden in the apartment; he attended a meeting of German officials and blew up both them and himself. Sarah, having fled to Marseilles, threw herself out of a window with her child when the Germans came to arrest her. Boris was parachuted into the *maquis*. Everyone, or almost everyone, being dead, there was no one left to become involved in the problems that arose after the war."

Such as we know it, this fourth volume of *Roads to Freedom* is the most rigid and aesthetically the least successful of the series. This failure--which has been much caviled at--seems to correspond to the failure of the "Ethics" Sartre had projected since 1940, and marks the end of his ethical period.

Once again it is Simone de Beauvoir who indicates the reasons why Sartre could not give any conclusion to *Roads to Freedom* (see *Force of Circumstance*, pp. 195-96):

"But [it was] precisely the problems [that arose after the war] that at this time interested Sartre; he had nothing to say about the Resistance because he conceived the novel as a form that poses questions, and under the Occupation one knew exactly what to do: there could be no perplexity, no ambiguity about how to behave. For his heroes at the end of *Drôle d'Amitié*, the die was cast. . . . Without having abandoned the idea of a fourth volume, he always found work that needed his attention more. To skip ten years and hurl his characters into the anxieties of the present would have been meaningless; the last volume would then have disappointed all the expectations raised by the one before it. The last volume was too imperiously predetermined for Sartre either to change his original intentions or to conquer the distaste which the idea of conforming to them aroused in him."

Sartre himself, during a conversation in 1959 (see 59/318), gave his own explanation of this matter in answering a question about his reasons for coming back to the theater with THE CONDEMNED OF ALTONA: *First of all because I'm having a hard time finishing my novel. The fourth volume was supposed to deal with the Resistance. The choice then was easy--even though it took a lot of strength and courage to stick to it. You were either for or against the Germans. It was black or white. Today--and since forty-five--the situation has become more complicated. It takes less courage, perhaps, to choose, but the choices are much more difficult. I cannot express the ambiguities of our time in a novel situated in forty-three. And on the other hand this unfinished work weighs on me: it's hard for me to start another one before I've finished this one.*

1950

50/193

Faux savants ou faux lièvres? ⟨Which Are False, the Wise Men or the Elephants?⟩, preface.

a) In Louis Dalmas. *Le Communisme yougoslave depuis la rupture avec Moscou* ⟨Yugoslavian Communism since the Break with Moscow⟩. Terre des Hommes collection, Documents series. Sulliver, [1950].

Printing date: July 30, 1950. Sartre's text, pp. IX-XLIII.

b) Reprinted under the same title (without the question mark) in SITUATIONS, VI.

Louis Dalmas's book is both a documented eyewitness account of Communist Yugoslavia and a stand in favor of Tito, who at the time was being harshly attacked by the U.S.S.R. and the French Communists. In his preface, Sartre does not conceal his sympathies for the Titoist dissidence, but he is much more interested in its underlying causes and consequences than in its purely political aspects. He refers explicitly to Maurice Merleau-Ponty's *Humanism and Terror* in order to situate his thinking from the outset as the extension of what that work undertook. *Which Are False, the Wise Men or the Elephants?* marks a turning point in Sartre's political thought and constitutes a second and important step in the theoretical discussion he had been carrying on with Marxism since *Materialism and Revolution* (see 46/108).

Here he inquires into the reciprocal relationship of objectivity and subjectivity. After having stressed Marx's ambiguity about the subject, he shows that the dogmatic Marxism of the Stalinist bureaucrats has, by eliminating subjectivity or equating it with failure, error, or treason, made itself incapable of understanding the historical fact of a successful opposition. *The reason Titoism is exceptionally important to us is that it develops into a subjectivity which does not reappear as a formal ideal but is produced as an effective reality on the basis of objectivism and through the very movement of history. If they are absolute conquerors, the opposition determine objectivity; if they are conquered, they are crushed by the conqueror's objectivity. Tito's half-victory reintegrates subjectivity into the Yugoslav leadership and at the same time introduces it into the Soviet leadership.*

At the close of his preface, Sartre bets that Titoism will succeed and indicates what his own task will be beginning with the fifties: *We have to rethink Marxism; we have to rethink man.*

In spite of its implied theoretical rapprochement with Marxism, this piece was very badly received by the Communists and only gave them a new complaint about Sartre.

On the other hand, Sartre's stand won him the sympathy of Yugoslavia, which was the first socialist country in which his works were translated. His main books, except for his two major philosophical works, are widespread in Yugoslavia today and evoke much interest there. They are a source of inspiration for a good number of Yugoslav intellectuals. As for the general public, they are moved above all by the plays, which are frequently performed in even the small towns.

50/194

Preface to *La Fin de l'espoir* ⟨The End of Hope⟩, by Juan Hermanos.

a) Testimony translated from the Spanish. Les Temps modernes series, no. 1. Julliard, [1950]. Pp. 5-10. Printing date: April 25, 1950.

This volume inaugurated the Temps modernes series, which was edited at the outset by Sartre and Maurice Merleau-Ponty.

b) Reprinted as *La Fin de l'espoir*. *L'Observateur*, no. 3 (April 27, 1950).

c) Reprinted under the same title in SITUATIONS, VI.

This preface constitutes one of many stands Sartre took against the Franco regime. *The End of Hope* had been written in Madrid in January, 1946, by a Spaniard who used the name Juan Hermanos. *The author,*

50/194

Sartre tells us, *chose his pseudonym well: these Spaniards are our brothers.* Hermanos' pessimistic message undoubtedly had a profound effect upon Sartre in a time when he felt affected by his powerlessness in political matters.

50/195

Preface to *L'Artiste et sa conscience: Esquisse d'une dialectique de la conscience artistique* ⟨The Artist and His Conscience: Sketch for a Dialectic of the Artistic Consciousness⟩, by René Leibowitz.

a) L'Arche, [1950]. Pp. 9-38.

b) Reprinted in a modified version as *L'Artiste et sa conscience.* In SITUATIONS,IV.

The Artist and His Conscience, translated by Benita Eisler.

-- In SITUATIONS (1965).

No, we don't want painting, sculpture, and music to be committed too, or at least not in the same way, Sartre stated in *What Is Literature?*, without, however, specifying how we might conceive of the commitment of the painter, the sculptor, and the musician. The preface he wrote for the book by his friend René Leibowitz, the composer, allows him to pursue his reflections about commitment in the "non-signifying" arts; consequently it may also be considered a complement to the essay on literature. Leibowitz' book, which was presented as "Sketch for a Dialectic of the Artistic Consciousness" but does very little to fulfill the promise of this subtitle, tries to examine, in a Sartrian perspective, the problems raised by committing music. It challenges especially the Jdanovian Prague Manifesto which demanded that music be made to serve the masses and their socialist aspirations. For Leibowitz, the socially conscious composer's commitment consists as much in the radical innovations he brings to musical structures as it does in his choice of musical subjects. He cites as an example of a work which is committed in this dual sense Arnold Schoenberg's "The Survivor of Warsaw."

In his preface, which is undoubtedly not one of his best pieces, Sartre raises the level of the debate, presents the problem of the audience for a modern music which has become more and more complex, reminds us that music in itself has no ideological content because (in his language) it produces *sense* rather than *signification*, and suggests without reaching a conclusion that the musician's commitment in respect to the requirements peculiar to his art coincides with his overall involvement in the contradictions of his time.

Let us point out that the volume includes in its third part (pp. 131-59), a "Réponse à Jean-Paul Sartre" ⟨Reply to Jean-Paul Sartre⟩ which was written as a sequel to the preface. A piece from Leibowitz' book was published under the title *Le musicien engagé* ⟨The Committed Musician⟩ in *Les Temps modernes*, no. 40 (February, 1949), pp. 322-39.

50/196

Study of *Portrait de l'aventurier: T. E. Lawrence, Malraux, Von Salomon,* [L. N. Rossel] ⟨*Portrait of the Adventurer:* T. E. Lawrence, Malraux, Von Salomon⟩, [L. N. Rossel], by Roger Stéphane.

a) Le Sagittaire, [1950]. Pp. 9-29. Printing date: August 20, 1950.

b) New edition. Grasset, 1965.

c) Pocketbook edition: 10/18 series. Union Générale d'Edition, [1972].

d) Reprinted under the title *Portrait de l'aventurier.* In SITUATIONS, VI.

Here Sartre takes up again the criticism of the adventurer which he had already broached in NAUSEA, but refuses, after having compared them, to oppose the militant and the adventurer: *Adventurer or militant: I don't believe in this dilemma. I am too well aware that an act has two sides: negativity, which is adventuresome, and constructiveness, which is discipline.*

For many years Sartre and Roger Stéphane had rather close political ties (see 51/212).

50/197

Letter to Georges Courteline, 1912.

a) Reprinted in facsimile in "Les débuts de Jean-Paul Sartre dans la vie littéraire" ⟨Jean-Paul Sartre's Debut in the Literary Life⟩. *Le Figaro littéraire*, January 7, 1950.

b) The text also appeared in an article by Marcel Lapierre in *Presse-Magazine*, May 24, 1955.

This letter, which was posted January 26, 1912, when Sartre was six and a half, had been written at the instigation of Charles Schweitzer. It is addressed

50/197

to *Monsieur Courteline, Homme de lettres*, and reads as follows:

Dear Monsieur Courteline,

Grandfather told me they gave you a big medal this makes me very happy four I really laff when I read Théodore and Phanthéon Courcelle going buy in front of our house. I also tryed to translate Théodore with my German maid but my poor Nanny dint get the poynt of the joke

Your future friend (Happy New Year),

Jean-Paul Sartre age 6 1/2

Sartre was rather irritated that this letter should be reprinted in the newspapers (see THE WORDS, p. 53).

50/198

"Sartre de retour d'Afrique" ⟨Sartre Back from Africa⟩, interview-article by Yves Salgues.

-- *Paris-Match*, May 20, 1950.

An article intended for the general public which describes Sartre upon his return from Black Africa (see concerning this trip *Force of Circumstance*, pp. 204-23). Yves Salgues mixes into his report, which is generously illustrated with photographs, some of the remarks which Sartre made to him and which he seems to have reported without being overly concerned with accuracy.

There is nevertheless an interesting bit of information for the bibliographer to be noted: Sartre speaks of a letter he has just received from a gynecologist in the Jura Mountains who is caring for a sick man [*sic*] who has three of the "War Journals" Sartre lost in 1940 (see 42/33).

50/199

* *Le Cinéma n'est pas une mauvaise école* ⟨The Movies Are Not a Bad School⟩.

See 31/7.

50/200

Reply to a questionnaire: "Is Neutrality Possible?"

-- *L'Observateur*, no. 9 (June 9, 1950), p. 31.

L'Observateur had asked its readers and a certain number of political figures to reply to a questionnaire about the chances of France eventually becoming neutral.

Sartre takes a stand against the Atlantic Pact. His argumentation is as follows: *By means of the Atlantic Pact the American government wants to show that any war would be a war for the defense of Western Europe. The Atlantic Pact provides the Americans with endless pretexts for intervention: from now on Pearl Harbor is everywhere in Europe.* Moreover, the pact is a deeply divisive factor in France. By adopting a policy of neutrality, France would remove the justification for an American-Russian war undertaken in the name of the defense of Free Europe. Class conflicts would continue but neutrality would have the advantage of not creating new elements of discord. Although he doubts that a policy of neutrality can keep France out of the fighting in the case of a war, Sartre reminds us that such a policy is designed precisely to avoid war.

50/201

A propos du Mal ⟨Concerning Evil⟩.

-- *Biblio*, 1st Year, no. 5 (May-June, 1950), pp. 3-5.

A text unpublished at the time which corresponds broadly to pages 33-35 (Gallimard edition) of SAINT GENET. This issue of *Biblio* is mostly devoted to Sartre: it includes an article by Francis Jeanson, "L'Oeuvre philosophique de Sartre" ⟨Sartre's Philosophical Works⟩ as well as a rather substantial bibliography for the time.

50/202

Jean Genet, ou le Bal des Voleurs ⟨Jean Genet, or The Thieves' Ball⟩.

-- Series of six articles published in *Les Temps modernes*:

No. 57 (July, 1950), pp. 12-47.

No. 58 (August, 1950), pp. 193-233. Starting with this issue, the title changes to "Jean Genet, fragments" ⟨Jean Genet, selections⟩.

No. 59 (September, 1950), pp. 402-43.

50/202

No. 60 (October, 1950), pp. 668-703.

No. 61 (November, 1950), pp. 848-95.

No. 62 (December, 1950), pp. 1038-70.

This study had first been announced for publication in the March, 1950, *Temps modernes* under the title "Le langage et Jean Genet" ⟨Language and Jean Genet⟩.

The six articles correspond more or less to pages 49-220 (Gallimard edition) of SAINT GENET but include numerous changes. Evidently Sartre was not wholly satisfied with his first version and reworked it considerably for publication in book form. See 52/215.

50/203

* *De la vocation d'écrivain* ⟨On Being a Writer⟩.

-- *Neuf*, Journal of the Medical Association (edited by Robert Delpire), no. 2 (Christmas, 1950), pp. 35-36.

A photograph of Sartre by Brassaï accompanies these excellent pages which were excerpted from the manuscript of SAINT GENET and not included in the final volume.

50/203 A

A statement Sartre made in response to a survey Claudine Chonez was conducting, "What Is Humor?"

-- *Les Nouvelles littéraires*, December 28, 1950, p. 1.

The text *in extenso*:

The first thing to do is to distinguish humor and irony, Sartre told me. *One can scarcely be more than ironic about war's too serious, too crude aspects. Humor, on the other hand, presupposes that one has been able, to begin with, to obliterate the meaning of things. For example, a cartoon will show some bloated fat men, sweaty and poofed out, dressed in shorts and hacking around on a soccer field. The humor comes from the fact that there's really no question of sport or competition any more--that the meaning of the whole thing has been taken away. But what I am looking for in everything is precisely its meaning.*

Let's take the famous reflection on kings: "Even though they're seated on the world's most lofty throne, aren't they still sitting on their ass?" (Wasn't it Montaigne who said this?) What separates me from humor is precisely the fact that I myself think that a king's ass is not at all the same as any other man's. Let me say once more that I am always trying to find meanings, whereas humor tries to destroy them. That is why its role for me is much less important than the role of irony. I'll say too that humor is essentially analysis, and I have always tended toward synthesis."

The other statements in this survey, which was announced "to be continued," are by Marcel Achard, Jean Paulhan, Blaise Cendrars, the actor O'Brady, and Jean Effel.

50/204

The Chances of Peace, excerpts from a long letter-article addressed to the American people.

-- *The Nation*, December 30, 1950, pp. 696-700.

This letter, which was written especially for the eighty-fifth anniversary of *The Nation* but which arrived there too late to be incorporated in the commemorative issue of December 16, 1950, is in answer to the question, "Is it possible to negotiate an agreement with Russia without sacrificing the democratic principle?"

This very important text defines Sartre's political position in 1950 and his attitude toward the United States and the U.S.S.R. after the beginning of the Korean War. Sartre's argumentation is no longer quite the same as it was during his R.D.R. ⟨Revolutionary Peoples' Assembly⟩ period: it shows his pessimism and confusion, and allows us to foresee, to a certain extent, the new direction he will take by going to the Congress of Vienna in December, 1952. We have been able to procure the entire manuscript, in French, of the letter published in *The Nation*. Here are some excerpts from it:

Here in Europe we are simultaneously *in the Soviet sphere of influence (it's your Burnham who says so) and in the American sphere of influence (it's Ehrenburg who claims it). That gives us a sort of mournful freedom: we hear the two bells toll; we know the two sets of arguments. Does the United States want peace? And does the U.S.S.R.? Don't think these questions bring forth rapid answers from Europeans. . . .*

Your ethic is generous and Puritanical, and you are carrying out a policy which contradicts your ethic. You do so with a bad conscience, with the feeling that a curse is weighing on you, but it's not so much a question of that. The thing is that the Soviets' shrewdness leaves you everywhere with no support except from oppressive minorities. The Communists' orders are to defend the cause of the oppressed and the exploited everywhere on earth, remaining free to abandon them if Russian interests require it. They will always be on the side of the angels. . . .

So you are drawn into the infernal cycle which leads you to fight in Korea against the North Koreans among a population whose feelings for its defenders are at least doubtful, simply because when you were all-powerful you were unable to free the Southerners from their conditions of life through agrarian reforms, and because you have not subsequently tackled the problem of Korean unity honestly for fear that the Communists in the north would win the whole country.

. . . The Stockholm Appeal is a trap; but because there have been people in your country talking about the atomic bomb ever since your troops went into Korea, if only to announce that for the moment it would not be used, you are the ones who are giving the Appeal signatories.

. . . Western Europe cannot serve as a buffer zone between America and the U.S.S.R. unless she does not belong to either one. If both are in good faith, they can get together to support the rebirth of an independent Europe on a broadly social basis. . . . From the moment you stop seeing us as soldiers, you will find we are your friends again. As neutrals determined to resist all *aggression, we would be more useful to the cause of peace than, as belligerents without the means, we are at present to your war. . . .*

You and the Russians give the world the choice of being cynics or madmen. There is still a powerful minority in your country which thinks the democratic ideology is not exhausted, that it will find its old expansive force again if it is able to adapt to new conditions. If this minority could grow to the advantage of present circumstances, if it were possible that it might some day become the majority, the whole world would regain confidence in you, and your government at last could really try a policy of "calculated risk": risking not war but peace.

50/NOTE 1.

It was Maurice Merleau-Ponty and not Sartre who drafted the introduction to the Temps modernes series inaugurated in 1950 by Julliard. This introduction is found in most issues of *Les Temps modernes* beginning in May, 1950, as well as in the work of Frédéric Bon and Michel-Antoine Burnier, *Les Nouveaux Intellectuels* ⟨The New Intellectuals⟩ ([Cujas, 1966], p. 362).

50/NOTE 2.

An important article entitled "Les Jours de notre vie" ⟨The Days of Our Life⟩, which protests the existence of Soviet concentration camps, came out under the double signature of Maurice Merleau-Ponty and Sartre in the January, 1950, *Temps modernes* (no. 51, pp. 1153-68). This article was drafted by Merleau-Ponty alone (concerning the circumstances of its publication, see SITUATIONS, IV, pp. 225-27); it appears moreover in *Signs* ([Evanston, Ill.: Northwestern University Press, 1964], pp. 263-73) under the title "The U.S.S.R. and the Camps."

It was probably Merleau-Ponty too who drafted the editorial, "L'Adversaire est complice" ⟨The Adversary Is An Accomplice⟩, which was signed "T. M." and published in the July, 1950, *Temps modernes*, and which constituted an answer to an open letter J.-D. Martinet had written to Sartre and Merleau-Ponty in the May, 1950, *Révolution prolétarienne.*

50/NOTE 3.

During a tribute to Charles Dullin held at the Théâtre de l'Atelier on February 11, 1950, a message from Sartre was read by Madeleine Renaud and a scene from THE FLIES was performed by Olga Dominique and Jean Lanier.

50/NOTE 4.

According to the journal *Documents* (July, 1950, p. 768), there was allegedly an interview by Sartre in the newspaper *Frankfurter Neuen Presse.*

50/NOTE 5.

In 1950, Sartre appeared in a movie produced by Nicole Védrès, *La Vie commence demain* ⟨Life Begins Tomorrow⟩. For text and details, see Volume II.

1951

51/205

LE DIABLE ET LE BON DIEU ⟨The Devil and the Good Lord⟩, play in three acts and eleven tableaux.

a) Les Temps modernes, no. 68 (June, 1951), pp. 2113-68; no. 69 (July, 1951), pp. 94-125; no. 70 (August, 1951), pp. 261-99. Complete version with a certain number of variations no one of which is major, with the possible exception of the end of the first tableau, which has been eliminated from the final edition. Many scenes are numbered differently than they are in the book version.

b) Book. Gallimard,[1951]. 283 pages. Printing date: October, 1951.

c) Le Livre de poche series, no. 367. Gallimard,[1958].

d) Reprinted in THÉÂTRE (1962).

e) Reprinted in *L'Avant-Scène Théâtre*, "Spécial Sartre," nos. 402-3 (May 1-15, 1968), pp. 37-87.

f) Théâtre National Populaire series. Gallimard, November, 1968. 187 pages.

g) British textbook edition, presented and annotated by D. J. Conlon. London: Methuen, 1971.

h) Folio series, no. 52. Gallimard, [1972].

THE DEVIL AND THE GOOD LORD or LUCIFER AND THE LORD, translated by Kitty Black.

t1) LUCIFER AND THE LORD, a play in eleven scenes. London: Hamish Hamilton, 1953.

t2) THE DEVIL AND THE GOOD LORD, *and Two Other Plays* (KEAN and NEKRASSOV, translated by S. Leeson and G. Leeson). New York: Alfred A. Knopf, 1960.

t3) Ibid. in paperback. New York: Vintage Books, [1960].

t4) LUCIFER AND THE LORD *and* THE RESPECTABLE PROSTITUTE. Penguin Books, [1965]. With an introduction by Geoffrey Brereton.

Short excerpts of the play were presented by Paul Arnold and Edith Samuel in *Theatre Arts*, October, 1951, pp. 24-25, 87.

Sartre got his inspiration for THE DEVIL AND THE GOOD LORD from a play by Cervantes, *The Lucky Rascal*, that Jean-Louis Barrault had told to him in 1943, when they were both teaching at Charles Dullin's school. Barrault would have liked Sartre to adapt the play for him. Translated into French as *Le Rufian bienheureux* ⟨The Happy Ruffian⟩ or *Le Truand béatifié* ⟨The Blessed Vagabond⟩, Cervantes' play belongs to the genre of "comedia de santos" illustrated by Lope de Vega and Calderón. It tells the true story of Cristobal de Lugo, a brutal thug and rotten citizen who was nevertheless pure in spirit and decided to become a monk after he had won at cards because he had sworn that if he lost he would become a highway robber. The first act shows the prowess of the ruffian as he rules the lower depths of Seville; in the second, which takes place in Mexico, we see him take upon himself the wrongdoings of an impenitent, sinful woman; in the third act, finally, the monk suffers the worst evils before dying in a saintly way. The main thing Sartre retained from this play was the episode in which the swashbuckler decides to convert himself to doing good according to the luck of the game.[1] But he changes it by having his hero, Goetz, trick to lose and thus *choose* to commit himself to doing good.

Simone de Beauvoir tells us (see *Force of Circumstance*, pp. 237-38) that the play, which was started at the beginning of 1951, included in an early version of act 1 a character named Dosia who embodied nobility and whom Sartre later abandoned. Simone Berriau, who directed THE DEVIL AND THE GOOD LORD for the Théâtre

---

1. The way that Sartre sums up this episode in several interviews shows clearly that his basis was Jean-Louis Barrault's telling of the play, which must not have corresponded exactly to the plot of *The Lucky Rascal*.

Antoine, was determined that Louis Jouvet should produce it (see the article by Jacques Forestier, "Jouvet attend Sartre" ⟨Jouvet Is Waiting for Sartre⟩, *Opéra*, February 7, 1951). The play began rehearsals before it was completely finished, and it was already longer than a normal play. Frantic, Simone Berriau put pressure on Sartre to agree to cuts while he was still rewriting the final tableaux. ("Sartre claimed that when she wandered through the theater, her fingers automatically began to clack like scissors"--*Force of Circumstance*, p. 240). The press loudly echoed the "battle of the cuts" and the serious disagreements between Sartre and Jouvet; but it seems that the relations between the two men were, although sometimes strained, never as bad as people claimed. The ostentation of the means employed to stage the play (the program proudly mentioned the 19,400 hours of work required to effect the decors and the costumes); the anxieties of the directress; the incredible personality of Pierre Brasseur, who created the difficult part of Goetz; Sartre's delays; and perhaps even Jouvet's lack of interest in a play which went against his own convictions (see *ibid.*) suffice to explain the agitated atmosphere of the rehearsals. Jouvet, who was producing his final play, was already gravely ill with a heart ailment, and was to die a few months later on August 16, 1951.

THE DEVIL AND THE GOOD LORD opened at the Théâtre Antoine on June 7, 1951, (dress rehearsal, June 6), with settings by Félix Labisse and the following cast of characters for the main parts:

GOETZ	Pierre Brasseur
HEINRICH	Jean Vilar
HILDA	Maria Casarès
CATHERINE	Marie-Olivier
NASTY	Henri Nassiet
KARL	R.-J. Chauffard

The opening was the event of the theatrical season, and the play, which caused a scandal in Catholic circles, was a very big hit: it played continuously until March, 1952, and was revived in September of the same year for a special series of thirty performances.

The reception reserved for it by the chroniclers of Paris would lend itself to an interesting study in the "sociology of criticism." With very rare exceptions, the play gave rise to crude misunderstandings and was usually taken to be a "war machine against God." In this connection you may consult as a curiosity the article by Henri Daniel-Rops, who had managed to attend a rehearsal in secret so that he would have time to think about a firm warning for his flock (see "Le Blasphème dérisoire" ⟨Laughable Blasphemy⟩, *L'Aurore*, June 9-10, 1951). Daniel-Rops spoke especially of the only person who interrupted on opening night--who had blown repeatedly into a whirling whistle--as a sympathetic young Polyeuctes. As for François Mauriac, he chose as a title for his article an expression which was to become famous: "Sartre, l'athée providentiel" ⟨Sartre, the Providential Atheist⟩ (*Le Figaro*, June 26, 1951). The two articles most characteristic of the enlightened bourgeoisie are Thierry Maulnier's unfavorable one ("Y a pas de Bon Dieu" ⟨Ain't No God⟩, *Combat*, June 28 and 29, 1951) and Robert Kemp's favorable-but-with-qualifications one (*Le Monde*, June 13, 1951). A great number of critics compared THE DEVIL AND THE GOOD LORD to *Satin Slipper*, often stating that Sartre's play, in contrast to Paul Claudel's, lacked "flesh"--that it was intellectual, demonstrative, wordy, and condemned in advance by its vain "wish to prove the nonexistence of God." Even in the articles favorable to the play, one finds a frequent misinterpretation of the meaning of the murder Goetz commits at the end, which was generally interpreted as a return to Evil. On the Communist side, we must take note of the opinion of Elsa Triolet (*Les Lettres françaises*, June 14, 1951), whose main criticism was that the play lacked history and actuality, and who took as an illustration the peasants' being stirred up so by Nasty's lies that they revolted before the time was ripe for it, whereas the proletariat today is revolutionary and does not have to be lied to.

Speaking of the errors that the critics made at the time of the opening, Simone de Beauvoir writes the following lines, in which she quotes some unpublished notes of Sartre:

"In fact, Sartre was once more confronting the vanity of morality with the efficacy of *praxis*. This confrontation goes much further than it had in his previous plays; THE DEVIL AND THE GOOD LORD is the mirror of Sartre's entire ideological evolution. The contrast between Orestes' departure at the end of THE FLIES and Goetz's final stance illustrates the distance Sartre had covered between his original anarchistic attitude and his present commitment. He himself has made the following note: *The sentence, We have never been freer than we were during the Occupation, directly contradicts the character of Heinrich, an objective traitor who becomes a subjective traitor, then a madman. Between the two lie seven years and the divorce of The Resistance.* In 1944, Sartre thought that any situation could be transcended by subjective effort; in 1951, he knew that circumstances can sometimes steal our transcendence from us; in that case, no individual salvation is possible, only a collective struggle. However, this play differed from its predecessors in that the militant, Nasty, did not triumph over the adventurer; it is the latter who produces the synthesis Sartre had projected in his preface to Roger Stéphane's book (see 50/196): he accepts the discipline of the Peasant War without denying his own subjectivity, within the enterprise he preserves the negative moment; he is the perfect embodiment of the man of action as Sartre conceived him.

I made Goetz do what I was unable to do. Goetz transcended a contradiction Sartre had been feeling very sharply since the failure of the R.D.R. ⟨Revolutionary Peoples' Assembly⟩ and even more so since the war in Korea, without managing to surmount it: *The contradiction was not one of ideas. It was in my own being. For my liberty implied also the liberty of all men. And all men were not free. I could not submit to the discipline of solidarity with all men without breaking beneath the strain. And I could not be free alone*" (*Force of Circumstance*, pp. 242-43).

It seems that the interpretation of the part by Pierre Brasseur, who played the second half of the play--in which Goetz commits himself to Good--as a hypocritical ham actor, had a lot to do with leading the critics astray. The second half was, by the way, generally thought to be weaker than the first; yet Simone de Beauvoir rightly notes that when the Bochum Schauspielhaus staged the play at the Théâtre des Nations in 1956, with Hans Messemer in the leading role, the critics reversed their judgment. (*Ibid.*, p. 242.)

THE DEVIL AND THE GOOD LORD was revived in November, 1968, at the T.N.P. with François Périer in the role of Goetz. The sober, effective production by Georges Wilson, which was very different from that of the first, and the remarkable performance by François Périer, whose Goetz was more "internal" than Brasseur's, brought the most out of a work which, as most writers have stressed, could well be Sartre's best play. This is not always the view of academic criticism, which seems to us to have not yet done this play complete justice. Yet from a strictly theatrical point of view it is to us the most successful, the most responsive in any case to the requirements of a modern theater which has not denied the power of the spoken word, which in this play, by both its vigor and (in spite of what people have said) its emotional force, wins support which is far from being simply intellectual.

THE DEVIL AND THE GOOD LORD, whose meanings are much more immediately "legible" than those of THE CONDEMNED OF ALTONA, has many points in common with SAINT GENET, which is the best philosophical commentary on it. The play was very well analyzed by Francis Jeanson in *Sartre par lui-même* ⟨Sartre by Himself⟩ ([Seuil, 1955], pp. 52-71; pp. 48-67 of the new edition redone in 1967). Centering on the ethical problem and not, as has often been thought, on the metaphysical problem of God's existence or nonexistence, it illustrates the progress Sartre made in political consciousness between 1945 and 1950, during the time he was writing his "Ethics," whose conclusion he formulates in SAINT GENET as follows:

Either morality is stuff-and-nonsense or it is a concrete totality which achieves a synthesis of Good and Evil. For Good without Evil is Parmenidean Being, that is, Death, and Evil without Good is pure Nonbeing. To this objective synthesis there corresponds, as a subjective synthesis, the recovery of negative freedom and its integration into absolute freedom or freedom properly so-called. The reader will understand, I hope, that what is involved here is not a Nietzschean "beyond" Good and Evil, but rather a Hegelian "Aufhebung." *The abstract separation of these two concepts simply expresses man's alienation. The fact remains that, in the present historical situation, this synthesis cannot be achieved. Thus any Ethics which does not say explicitly that it is* presently impossible *contributes to men's mystification and alienation. The ethical "problem" stems from the fact that* for us *Ethics is both inevitable and impossible. It is in this perspective that, for example, we ought to view the problem of violence or that of the relationship between means and ends. To a conscience wracked by such an agony and at the same time forced to will and choose, all high-minded rebellion, all cries of protest, and all righteous indignation would seem old-fashioned rhetoric* (p. 177).

It is in the light of this passage that we have to understand the meaning of the murder which Goetz decides at the end of the play to commit, and through which he begins his practical moralization of a world in which violence and class struggle rule: *There's this war to be fought and I'll fight it.*

On the back of the cover of the Gallimard clean copy there is an introduction by Sartre which is excerpted from the interview 51/210 and reads as follows:

This play can be considered a complement or sequel to DIRTY HANDS, *even though the action takes place four hundred years earlier. I am trying to show a character who is just as alien to the masses of his time as Hugo, the young bourgeois hero of* DIRTY HANDS *was, and just as torn by contradictions. My hero Goetz, embodied by Pierre Brasseur, is torn because, as the bastard son of a noble and a peasant, he is equally rejected by both sides. The problem is to know how he will cut loose from his right-wing anarchism so that he can go fight in the peasant war. . . .*

I wanted to show that my hero Goetz, who's a sort of franc-tireur *and anarchist of evil, is not destroying anything when he thinks he is destroying a lot. He*

51/205

destroys human lives but neither society nor its foundations, and everything he does ends up working to the advantage of the prince, which profoundly disturbs him. When in the second part he tries to do absolutely unqualified good, this means nothing either. He gives lands to the peasants, but these lands are repossessed after a general war which has in fact broken out concerning his gift. Thus in wanting to do something absolute--good and evil--he only succeeds in destroying human lives. . . .

The play deals entirely with man's relations to God or, if you prefer, to the absolute.

INTERVIEWS ABOUT "THE DEVIL AND THE GOOD LORD"

51/206

"Jean-Paul Sartre nous présente *Le Diable et le Bon Dieu,*" ⟨Jean-Paul Sartre Presents THE DEVIL AND THE GOOD LORD⟩, interview by Christine de Rivoyre.

-- *Le Monde*, May 31, 1951.

My play is above all a play of crowds. The main characters are justifiable and comprehensible only thanks to the crowds they stir.

51/207

"'Si Dieu existe,' nous dit Sartre à propos de sa pièce, 'le Bien et le Mal sont identiques'" ⟨"If God Exists," Sartre Says Concerning His Play, "Good and Evil Are the Same"⟩, interview by Claudine Chonez.

-- *L'Observateur*, May 31, 1951.

Here Sartre praises the respect Louis Jouvet has had for the script in his production. Concerning Goethe's *Goetz von Berlichingen* he says, *There's no connection. As a matter of fact my Goetz is called that only because I did not want to pretend not to know the character.* Concerning the meaning of the play, let us select this remark: *Goetz . . . becomes aware of the total indifference of God, who lets him act without ever revealing Himself. Also when Heinrich, who has lost his faith, tells Goetz about it, he has to conclude that God does not exist. Then he understands, and turns toward men. Any ethics based on God cannot help becoming an anti-humanism. But Goetz, in the final tableau, accepts the relative and limited ethics which is proper to human destiny: he puts history in place of the absolute.*

51/208

"'Le Diable et le Bon Dieu,' nous dit Sartre, 'c'est la même chose . . . moi je choisis l'homme'" ("The Devil and the Good Lord," Sartre Says, "Are the Same . . . I Choose Man Myself"), interview by Marcel Péju.

-- *Samedi-Soir*, June 2-8, 1951.

Very good interview. Sartre says particularly, *Man is but a paltry thing when one believes in God: God must be lost that man may arise from His ruins.* The play's conclusion is described as a *conversion to man.* Then Péju asks if this is a sketch of the promised "Ethics," and Sartre replies, *For the first time, in fact, the solution has been thought out, decided upon, made possible.* THE DEVIL AND THE GOOD LORD *is in its way a sequel to* DIRTY HANDS *with Hugo getting converted.*

Explaining the play's anti-religious appearance, Sartre then says: *In order to respect the particular conditions of the sixteenth century, all the characters move in a religious atmosphere. . . . The road Goetz follows is a road to freedom. . . . Nasty is the revolutionary. But since he lives in the sixteenth century, he has a religious dimension. . . . What struck me when I studied the Reformation was that there is no religious heresy whose definitive key is not some social unrest, as expressed through the ideologies of the time. . . .*

Goetz is an adventurer whom failure will never turn into a militant but who will fight till death at the militant's side. . . . Goetz's failure is in a way the failure of anarchism--and also of paternalism, which is the anarchism of masters. . . . Through Goetz, the play is more or less optimistic. Through Henrich, we see its dark side . . . ; his problem is absolutely insoluble because he's mystified right down to the marrow of his bones.

51/209

"Avec *Le Diable et le Bon Dieu* c'est une chronique dramatique que veut nous offrir Jean-Paul Sartre" (With THE DEVIL AND THE GOOD LORD Jean-Paul Sartre Is Trying to Offer Us a Chronicle Play), interview by J.-B. Jeener.

-- *Le Figaro*, June 2-3, 1951.

I found myself facing a new problem for me, that is, the need to choose a technique in the tradition of the English, the Spanish, or our medieval mysteries.

51/210

"Dès que deux personnes s'aiment, elles s'aiment contre Dieu" ⟨As Soon As Two People Love Each Other, They Love Each Other in Opposition to God⟩, conversation with Louis Martin-Chauffier, Marcel Haedrich, Georges Sinclair, Roger Grenier, and Pierre Berger.

-- *Paris-Presse-L'Intransigeant*, June 7, 1951.

Conversation dealing with THE DEVIL AND THE GOOD LORD to start and then with general subjects. Sartre's declarations about the play are the one's reproduced on the back of the cover of the Gallimard clean copy which we have reprinted at the end of item 51/205. He adds further: *Broadly speaking this is what I mean. First, every love is in opposition to God. As soon as two people love each other, they love each other in opposition to God. Every love is in opposition to the absolute because it is itself absolute. Next: If God exists, man does not exist; and if man exists, God does not exist.*

Concerning the immense and pernicious influence he is said to have on the young, Sartre says: *In reality, there is always at a given moment in every age a certain convergence between the young and certain literary forms. . . . It's the moment when paternal values are being liquidated. As the young are not yet capable of creating new ones, they borrow from people whose age is the same as their fathers' but whose thought is opposed. . . . We are attacked as corruptors--Simone de Beauvoir, Camus, and I--because we are offering an ethic. The people who simply present a slightly drab image of the pleasures or the vices of an age are never attacked.*

Next he explains why he is involved in politics *(Since Marx, philosophy has been a social act, a concrete act, a commitment. There ought to be a relationship between a philosopher's ideas and his attitude as a citizen)*, and why the Communists are perhaps his most virulent critics: *Their ethic has become conformist. It's a petty-bourgeois ethic. The real enemy is always the one who's closest to you. To the extent that I am inspired by a rather broad Marxism, I am an enemy for Stalinist Communists.* But he immediately adds: *Until the new order the party will represent the proletariat for me, and I do not see how this situation could possibly change for some time. . . . It is impossible to take an anti-Communist position without being against the proletariat.* And that is why he intends to disassociate himself publicly from the uses that the movie DIRTY HANDS (see Appendix) risks being put to. Sartre also says he has not signed the Stockholm Appeal because certain signatures *indicate a political maneuver*, and he concludes by declaring apropos of David Rousset: *Politically, I cannot sign anything he signs.*

51/210 A

Interview.

-- *Le Matin* (Antwerp), June 7, 1951.

Sartre thinks that the play's eleven scenes let him *make it long enough and at the same time replace individual conflict with zones of tension like those we find in chapters of a novel.*

51/211

"Jean-Paul Sartre répond à la critique dramatique et offre un guide au spectateur pour suivre *Le Diable et le Bon Dieu*" ⟨Jean-Paul Sartre Answers the Critics and Offers the Spectator a Guide for THE DEVIL AND THE GOOD LORD⟩, remarks gathered by Jean Duché.

-- *Le Figaro littéraire*, June 30, 1951.

Excellent interview in which Sartre tries to clear up a certain number of misunderstandings which had arisen since the opening.

It has been said that I wanted to demonstrate that God does not exist, and I failed. But like every writer I am capable of writing in many forms: to prove that God does not exist I have the essay at my disposition. . . . I didn't want to prove anything. . . . I wanted to deal with the problem of man without God, which is important not certainly because of some sort of nostalgia for God, but because it is hard to conceive of man in our time existing between the U.S.S.R. and the United States and in what ought to be a socialist society. This is the contemporary problem, but the men of the twentieth century worry over it in an inarticulate way without thinking about it. You find analogous problems in the sixteenth century, embodied in men who thought about God. I wanted to transpose this problem into a personal adventure. THE DEVIL AND THE GOOD LORD *is the story of an individual.*

Was Sartre trying to write an anti-*Satin Slipper*? Jean Duché asks. *Writing anti-something or other is not a part of our literary traditions. But since you mention it,* Satin Slipper *is much more insulting to an atheist--to the Radical-Socialist of the time whom Claudel had in mind--than* THE DEVIL AND THE GOOD LORD *is to a Catholic. Now the Radical-Socialist didn't raise a big hue and cry. The Catholic did.*

Sartre then indicates that the lines which caused the greatest scandal all came from Christian authors: Nasty's phrase, *The Church is a whore*, comes from Savonarola; Goetz's answer to the man who says he is a bastard, *Sure; like Jesus Christ*, is from Clement VII; Goetz's monologue (scene 2, tableau 8) is directly inspired by Saint John of the Cross; Goetz's line to Hilda, *Give me the eyes of the Boetian lynx, that my gaze may pierce that flesh. . . . How can I, who am repelled at touching cow manure with my finger tip, be filled with the desire to hold the bag of excrement itself in my arms*, is from Odilon of Cluny, as reproduced in Huizinga, *The Waning of the Middle Ages*.

To the question, Are you sure that God does not exist? Sartre answers, *I'm convinced of it.* --Convinced or certain? --*Certain. I was born into a half-Protestant, half-Catholic family. In the face of the disputes, I had formed my convictions by the age of eleven. And on these were embroidered the reflections which made me certain.*

Jean Duché wonders whether Sartre is not responsible for the play's ambiguity, since the conflict is not in fact between the Devil and the Good Lord but between Good and Evil. *That's true. The problem is the same whether God exists or not. In any case it's not a matter of establishing an ethics in order to please Him but on a self-sufficient basis, and if God did exist, man would please Him by being himself, by accepting himself and accepting the others in their finitude. That phrase of Odilon of Cluny's which Goetz speaks means that God's love forbids him to love woman in her finitude. Hilda answers, "You don't love anything if you don't love everything." Goetz does not love men. But Jouhandeau said quite rightly that he could not love men if he did not love them in opposition to God, love them even in their abjectness which is in opposition to God. And Malraux, in* Man's Fate, *has Kyo say, "Men are not my fellows; men are those who look at me and judge me: my fellow men are those who love me and do not look at me, who love me in spite of everything--my fall from grace, my baseness, my betrayal--me and not what I have done or shall do, who would love me as much as I would love myself." This is what Goetz comes to understand. So it is absurd to say that Goetz returns to Evil. He discovers the way of a human truth.*

There's a Catholic criticism which seems to me to be the truest: that the kingdom of man begins with violence. I am well aware of this. But history shows well enough that violence also accompanies the Kingdom of God.

51/211 A

"Jean-Paul Sartre nous parle du Diable, du Bon Dieu et de l'Homme" ⟨Jean-Paul Sartre Talks about the Devil, God and Man⟩, interview by J.-F. Bergery.

-- *Liberation*, June 30, 1951.

Interview concerning the philosophical intentions of the work:

In this way [Goetz] *discovers his moral law: separation is real and absolute unity is necessary. Here again we meet the express fact that the individual is the goal of the collectivity and at the same time the collectivity is the goal of the individual.*

51/212

L'Affaire Thorez ⟨The Thorez Affair⟩.

-- *Les Temps modernes*, no. 63 (January, 1951), pp. 1343-44. Text signed J.-P. S. and R. S. [Roger Stéphane].

Little dialogue about Maurice Thorez' departure for the U.S.S.R. and the reactions of the French press (which found it scandalous that the secretary of the Communist Party should prefer to be operated on by Soviet doctors).

51/213

"Rencontre avec Jean-Paul Sartre" ⟨Meeting with Jean-Paul Sartre⟩, interview by Gabriel d'Aubarède.

-- *Les Nouvelles littéraires*, February 1, 1951.

Good interview, in which for one time (but one time does not make a rule) Sartre's remarks seem to be reported accurately. Gabriel d'Aubarède begins by painting a sympathetic portrait of Sartre and concludes with this sentence transfixed by a significantly astonished point: "There is nothing 'Sartrian,' in short, in Jean-Paul Sartre's appearance and conversation."

Sartre is questioned about the following subjects:

-- his childhood;

-- the writers who have influenced him: Marcel Proust, Paul Valéry, Alain (indirectly), André Gide (not at all);

-- his friendship with Paul Nizan;

-- commitment and literature;

-- his power to work: *One can be fruitful without working a whole lot. Three hours every morning, three hours every night. There's my only rule. Even on a trip. I carry out bit by bit a very consciously elaborated work plan. Novel, play, essay, each of my works is a facet of a whole whose meaning cannot really be appreciated until the day I have completed it;*

-- glory: *I spent almost two completely unsettled years! Success is a very heavy burden;*

-- his influence on the young: *The people who condemn me for perverting the young have an interest in concealing the fact that the causes of the corruption are social. Blinded by a personalist bourgeois culture, they look for the individual when the causes are general and, wishing to remain ignorant of collective factors, they take a writer for their scapegoat;*

-- the suicides which he allegedly provoked: *I would be happy if I could believe that a writer can provoke a suicide, because that would mean that he could stop one too. But I can't believe either. A book could not possibly act so directly in our society, at least not in our present society. The writer can have only a long-run, and very watered-down, influence in it . . . ;*

-- his interest in Genet;

-- the existentialists' stress on the basest functions: *The reason why we speak of even the most humble functions of the body is that we must not pretend to have forgotten that the spirit descends into the body, or in other words the psychological into the physiological. . . . I don't speak about these things for my amusement but because in my view a writer ought to grasp man whole. . . . There is an interaction between sex and thought, as we have been taught by psychoanalysis, to which we owe a considerable enhancement of psychology, and which is not yet sufficiently known.*

To conclude, Sartre explains why he often speaks in his writings of the sky and its clouds: *In my books the sky represents an escapist element. I learned to look at it when I was a prisoner. Those who feel wedged into the earth look up.*

This is an entirely fortuitous opportunity to quote a little-known text by Boris Vian, "Sartre et la . . ." ⟨Sartre and the . . . ⟩ (*La Rue*, no. 6 [July 12, 1946]), in which Sartre is effectively defended against the charge of scatophilia: "It seems to us the superficial exegetes commit a glaring error in attributing to him, by an unwarranted extension, exclusively latrinary preferences. They never have condemned him for loving the blue sky. Yet Sartre talks about it too sometimes. . . . One can only approve of Sartre's localizing 'it' on paper instead of flinging it to the four winds as careless writers (Claudel, Péguy, Romain Rolland) do."

51/214

Gide vivant ⟨The Living Gide⟩.

a) Les Temps modernes, no. 65 (March, 1951), pp. 1537-41.

b) Reprinted in SITUATIONS, IV.

The Living Gide

t1) Anonymous translation. In *The Spectator* (April 6, 1951), pp. 435-36.

t2) Ibid. In *Spectator Harvest*. London: British Book Center, 1953. Pp. 46-50.

t3) Translated by Benita Eisler. In SITUATIONS (1965).

Tribute to André Gide, written after his death in February, 1951.

Sartre had first met Gide in 1939. Two years later, having founded a group of resistance intellectuals after he returned from captivity (see 41/31), Sartre went to find Gide in the south of France in an effort to establish contacts with writers living in the Free Zone. After the war, the two men saw each other again three or four times, always, according to Sartre, with pleasure. Sartre felt a real friendship for Gide, and particularly enjoyed the playful cynicism he was capable of in private. Gide, on the other hand, particularly enjoyed THE RESPECTFUL PROSTITUTE, which he considered "a kind of masterpiece." Sartre was clearly responsive to this judgment, and on December 24, 1946, wrote Gide: *I want you to know that your praises are especially dear to me, both for all that draws me near to and for all that separates me from you* (see *Catalogue de l'exposition André Gide* ⟨Catalogue of the André Gide Collection⟩, Bibliothèque Nationale, 1970, p. 198).

In the summer of 1950, taking advantage of a call Sartre made, Marc Allégret, who was filming his movie, *Avec André Gide* ⟨With André Gide⟩, shot the two writers conversing in the garden of Gide's house in Cabris.

51/214

The sequence, which was technically imperfect, was not retained in the final version of the film (released in 1951).

51/NOTE.

In June, 1951, Sartre backed the candidacy of Paul Rivet, former director of the Musée de l'Homme who had been elected as a Socialist in 1946 but had changed labels to join the Progressive and Socialist Union. Sartre took part in an election meeting, at which he attacked the Atlantic Pact and said in particular that *neutralism is just the opposite of defeatism.* See *Paris-Presse*, June 14, 1951.

1952

52/215

SAINT GENET, COMÉDIEN ET MARTYR ⟨Saint Genet, Actor and Martyr⟩.

a) For the bits of the first version which were published prior to the original in *Biblio, Les Temps modernes,* and *Neuf*, see 50/201, 50/202, 50/203.

b) Book. Gallimard, [1952]. 578 pages.

Constitutes the first volume of the *Oeuvres complètes de Jean Genet* ⟨Complete Works of Jean Genet⟩. Printing date: June 28, 1952. The original edition consists of 198 copies numbered from 1 to 180 and from A to R. Reprinted in the Soleil series in 1969.

SAINT GENET, ACTOR AND MARTYR.

t1) Excerpts. "On Good and Evil," translated and with a commentary by Robert Champigny. *Journal of Philosophy*, LIV (May, 1957), 314-35.

Other excerpts from the book have been used as introductions to various translations of Genet.

t2) Excerpt, translated by Bernard Frechtman. In *Tulane Drama Review*, VII, no. 3 (spring, 1963), 19-36.

t3) Translated by Bernard Frechtman. New York: George Braziller, 1963; London: W. H. Allen, 1964.

t4) Same translation. Paperbacks. New York: Mentor Books, [1964]; New York: Plume Books, [1971].

Announced for publication in the fall of 1950 and finally published during the summer of 1952, SAINT GENET (whose title is that of the excellent baroque play by Jean de Rotrou published in 1646) was originally projected as a preface. When it came out, the book was received with astonishment and a little like a monster: it does in fact escape traditional categories, since it may be considered simultaneously a work of philosophy, a critical literary study, a treatise on ethics, a psychoanalytic biography, etc. In any case it is a major work, whose reading is as indispensable to a knowledge of Sartre as to one of Genet.

As a philosophical essay, SAINT GENET is situated halfway between BEING AND NOTHINGNESS and CRITIQUE OF DIALECTICAL REASON, and marks an important step in Sartre's thinking to the extent it alternately brings existential psychoanalysis and the Marxist method to bear. As a critical literary essay, it must undoubtedly be placed between the BAUDELAIRE and the "Flaubert" to come. The shortcomings of the first are remedied here, for this time SAINT GENET envisages the man and the work as an indissoluble totality within which, through a ceaseless dialectic which is patiently described, the *oeuvre* produces the man as much as it is produced by him. In this respect the work is beginning to be recognized today as an exceptionally successful piece of criticism (see especially Serge Doubrovsky in *The Reason for the New Criticism*).

Whereas he judged Baudelaire harshly, Sartre does not hide his sympathy for Genet, and admits his profound admiration for his moral and aesthetic extremism. For Sartre, Genet--although a sophist, a pederast, a thief, etc.--is *one of the heroes of our time* (p. 549); he is the individual who in spite of the most unfavorable circumstances has succeeded in making something out of what other people have made of him. Sartre's essay concludes with a "Please Use Jean Genet Properly" which advantageously replaces the customary "Please Insert" and whose beginning makes clear the author's intentions:

To show that psychoanalytic interpretation and Marxist explanation have their limits, and that freedom alone can account for a person in his totality; to reveal this freedom at grips with destiny, at first crushed by its inevitabilities and then turning back upon them to slowly digest them; to prove that genius is no gift but the way out one invents in desperate cases, to find the choice a writer makes of himself, his life, and the meaning of the universe, right down to the formal characteristics of his style and composition, the structure of his images, and the particularities of his tastes; and to retrace in detail the history of a liberation: that is what I sought to do (p. 536).

The dramatic illustration of the book is the play THE DEVIL AND THE GOOD LORD; there are in fact a number of resemblances between Goetz and the Genet Sartre describes: bastardy, looking for an absolute in

Evil, playing loser wins, trying to rid oneself of alienation, etc. In Genet, self-conquest detours through the literary work and, as André Gorz clearly perceived, "One of the conclusions of the work is that the most radical and strenuous work of liberation may only be able to be carried out in imagination because it cannot suppress the original condition of total alienation" (*Le Socialisme difficile* ⟨Difficult Socialism⟩ [Seuil, p. 209]).

The essay is followed by three appendixes, the last of which (Gallimard edition, pp. 562-73) is a study of *The Maids*. This study has been reprinted in English as the Introduction to *The Maids and Deathwatch: Two Plays by Jean Genet*. With an introduction by Jean-Paul Sartre. Translated by Bernard Frechtman. New York: Grove Press, 1964. Pp. 7-31.

The text corresponds to that of the Gallimard edition, but includes two paragraphs at the beginning which are not in the Gallimard edition and which explain the demonstrative, "*these* turnabouts."

Concerning Genet, see also 46/104, 48/165, 49/189.

52/216

Preface to the Guides Nagel.

-- This three-page preface has been reprinted since 1952 in the following volumes, all published by Nagel: *Les Pays nordiques* ⟨The Scandinavian Countries⟩, *Danemark, Finlande, Islande, Norvège, Suède*.

Sartre has made many trips to the Scandinavian countries, in particular in 1935 with his parents and in 1947 and 1951 with Simone de Beauvoir.

In this piece, Sartre reflects on the tourist's situation and points out what a modern guide should be: *I think this phrase of Camus's sums up our present curiosities quite well: "A convenient way of getting to know a city is to look for how one works there, how one loves there, and how one dies there." What interests us is our time and the past in our time. . . . We live with "Guides" which correspond to what our fathers wanted, but we don't have a single one which answers to what we want.*

For him, there are two original things about Scandinavia: it's there that the harsh climate has for centuries presented the inhabitants with a *singular challenge*, and it is also there that *socialist or socialist-like reforms have been advanced the farthest.*

52/217

"Il n'y a plus de doctrine antisémite" ⟨There Isn't Any More Antisemitic Doctrine⟩, interview.

-- *Evidences*, no. 23 (January, 1952), pp. 7-8.

The review *Evidences*, which was published in Paris under the aegis of the American Jewish Committee, had asked Albert Camus, Sartre, and the sociologist Michel Collinet to analyze in this issue the phenomenon of the resurgence in France of an openly antisemitic press. Quoting *Aspects de la France*, *Ecrits de Paris*, and *Rivarol*, Sartre declares that given the limited circulation of these periodicals, the problem has little importance. He says that the Right no longer makes a doctrine of antisemitism: *Drumont is no longer possible.*

France has ceased to be independent--economically, financially, militarily. . . . I would say that it is because France no longer has an army that Gaullism will never be any more than an incipient fascism. No more national grandeur, no more "France alone": the Right has lost its myths. . . . The antisemitic minority crystallizes projective tendencies or bad humor provoked by economic or social failure. It is nonetheless true that antisemitic collective representations or myths are disappearing.

52/218

"Il faut rétablir la justice" ⟨Justice Must Be Reestablished⟩, interview about the Henri Martin Affair by Georges A. Astre.

-- *Action*, January 24, 1952.

Interview done shortly after Sartre had been received by President Vincent Auriol, to whom he presented a request in favor of Henri Martin. Sartre shows the respects in which the case of Henri Martin is exemplary: *He reflects the plight of an entire younger generation, in a society it no longer approves of, when it has come to grips with principles and aspirations which bear it in directions very different from the ones people want to impose on it. . . . He is a manifestation of that strange situation in which politics takes priority over every other value. Here the division of the world takes primacy over justice. The Henri Martin Affair becomes Truman against Stalin!* (see 53/233).

52/219

Sommes-nous en démocratie? ⟨Are We in a Democracy?⟩.

a) Les Temps modernes, no. 78 (April, 1952), pp. 1729-33.

b) Reprinted in SITUATIONS, VI.

Article written for a special issue of *Les Temps modernes* about the French press, which was supposed to be the first part of an investigation of *the way French democracy* really *functions*.

52/220

Les Communistes et la Paix ⟨The Communists and Peace⟩ (I and II).

a) Les Temps modernes, no. 81 (July, 1952), pp. 1-50; nos. 84-85 (October-November, 1952), pp. 695-763.

b) Reprinted in SITUATIONS, VI.

c) Reprinted in IL FILOSOFO E LA POLITICA ⟨The Philosopher and Politics⟩ (1964).

The Communists and Peace.

t1) Translated by Martha H. Fletcher. In THE COMMUNISTS AND PEACE, *with a Reply to Claude Lefort*. New York: George Braziller, [1968].

t2) Translated by Irene Clephane. In THE COMMUNISTS AND PEACE, *with an Answer to Claude Lefort*. London: Hamish Hamilton, [1969].

Nineteen fifty-two marks an important turning-point in Sartre's political thinking. Since the end of 1949, the date of the final failure of the R.D.R. ⟨Revolutionary Peoples' Assembly⟩ experiment, Sartre, without abandoning any of his principles or objectives, had undertaken to broaden his philosophy in the direction of Marxism. On the political level, a rapprochement with the Communist Party is effected at the beginning of 1952 in connection with the Henri Martin Affair (see 52/218). Sartre was in Italy when he learned about Jacques Duclos's being arrested after the May 28, 1952, manifestation protesting General Ridgway's arrival in Paris to take Eisenhower's place at the head of S.H.A.P.E. He was "overwhelmed with anger" (*Force of Circumstance*, p. 261) by the triumphant reaction of the Right, which was quick to take the failure of the protest strike the P.C. ⟨Communist Party⟩ had called on June 4 to be a clear rejection of the P.C. by the working class as a whole. *When I came back hurriedly to Paris, I had to write or I would suffocate. I wrote, day and night, the first part of* The Communists and Peace (SITUATIONS, IV, p. 249).

We refer once again to Michel-Antoine Burnier's indispensable study, *Choice of Action* (pp. 78-95),

52/220

which provides an analysis of these articles and recalls in detail the context in which they appeared.

The first article, full of polemical verve, replies to different accusations brought against the P.C. by the Right and the non-Communist Left. Sartre's goal here is to find out *the extent to which the P.C. is the* necessary *expression of the working class and the extent to which it is the* exact *expression of it.*

The second article shows that the failure of the June 4 strike is explained by the workers' discouragement. Here Sartre makes a basic distinction between the *masses*, an agglomeration of isolated and powerless individuals, and the *working class*, united by a revolutionary *praxis* of which the P.C. is the necessary mediator.

The third article was not written until a year and one-half later (see 54/254), but in between time Sartre developed the reasoning of the first two in his *Reply to Claude Lefort* (53/238). Let us point out to begin with that Sartre's stand (*the purpose of this article is to state my agreement with the Communists on precise and limited subjects, reasoning on the basis of* my *principles and not* theirs--SITUATIONS, VI, p. 168) had sizable repercussions within the confines of the intellectual Left. Within the *Temps modernes* staff itself it provoked two resignations, that of Maurice Merleau-Ponty (who did not publicly express his disagreement with Sartre until after the third article had appeared) and that of René Etiemble (see his "Lettre ouverte à Jean-Paul Sartre sur l'unité de mauvaise action" ⟨An Open Letter to Jean-Paul Sartre about the Unity of Bad Action⟩ in *Arts*, July 24-30, 1953, reprinted in Etiemble, *Hygiène des lettres (II): Littérature dégagée (1942-1953)* ⟨Literary Hygiene (II): Disengaged Literature (1942-1953)⟩ [Gallimard, 1955]). Simone de Beauvoir says specifically that "despite the difficulty of his position, Sartre still knew that he had been right to take it" (*Force of Circumstance,* p. 262).

52/221

"Besuch bei Jean-Paul Sartre" ⟨A Visit with Jean-Paul Sartre⟩, interview by S. F.

-- *Die Presse* (Vienna), no. 28 (July 12, 1952), p. 6.

Datelined "Menton, July," this article relates Sartre's comments about his work habits. He says a sort of inner dictatorship forces him to carry out his many projects. After a brief correction concerning existentialism, Sartre announces the approaching (October) publication of "The Last Chance," the book he is presently working on and expects much of:

"The Last Chance" has little to do with existentialism; the novel has an almost Kantian starting point (if I may dare to put myself in the shadow of the greatest of the greats) . . . I would almost want to say that this book seems to me to constitute an important new departure in my work. But let's not make any predictions. Finally Sartre points out that his work on Jean Genet will be published any day now.

52/222

Un Parterre de capucines ⟨A Garden of Capucines⟩.

a) L'Observateur, July 24, 1952, pp. 16-17.

A note specifies: "Back from a long stay in Italy, M. Jean-Paul Sartre has been kind enough to excerpt for *L'Observateur* the following bit from a book to be published."

b) Reprinted in SITUATIONS, IV.

Venice from My Window (see 53/235) and *A Garden of Capucines* are the only published fragments of a book abandoned after 500 pages and devoted to Italy. This book was to be entitled "Queen Albemarle and the Last Tourist," the "last tourist" being the narrator (that is, Sartre himself). He was the only one to escape the myths of tourism and the traps set for him by his faithless guide, a half-historical, half-allegorical character, Queen Albemarle.

Simone de Beauvoir specifies concerning this work: "In it [Sartre] gave a capricious description of Italy, its present structure, its history and its countryside, and also meditated on what it means to be a tourist" (*Force of Circumstance*, p. 199).

52/223

Rêponse à Albert Camus ⟨Reply to Albert Camus⟩.

a) Les Temps modernes, no. 82 (August, 1952), pp. 334-53.

b) Reprinted in SITUATIONS, IV.

Reply to Albert Camus, translated by Benita Eisler.

-- In SITUATIONS (1965).

Sartre and Camus, who had devoted laudatory articles to one another (on NAUSEA and THE WALL--see 39/21--and *The Stranger*--see 43/39), met for the first time in June, 1943, at the dress rehearsal of THE FLIES.

Shortly afterward, Sartre offered him the chance to create the part of Garcin in NO EXIT and to produce the play, which Marc Barbezat suggested be sent on tour in the provinces. The project fell through, but it provided the occasion for the two men to forge bonds of friendship which were strengthened by their common involvement in the Resistance, where Camus, however, had much greater practical responsibilities than Sartre, since he was in charge of publishing the underground *Combat*. During the final months of the Occupation and the war, they saw each other frequently, on an intimate basis, within a group of friends which included among others Michel Leiris and Raymond Queneau. For the "Encyclopedia" which Gallimard planned to publish, Camus, Maurice Merleau-Ponty, Sartre, and Simone de Beauvoir were to write the part devoted to ethics, and they wanted to make it a "joint manifesto" (*The Prime of Life*, p. 445). Camus was also to take part in the editing of the magazine Sartre was projecting. At the Liberation, Camus, who edited the newspaper *Combat*, which had finally come out from underground, asked Sartre to do a report on these historic days (see 44/51), and several months later offered him the chance to represent *Combat* in the United States (see 45/65). Too busy with his newspaper work, Camus did not join the editorial committee of *Les Temps modernes*. By the end of 1945, with Camus increasingly giving in to anti-Communism, serious political dissensions between the two writers came to light, without the cordiality of their personal relationships being yet, however, affected by them. Shortly afterward, a first estrangement, due as always to a political disagreement aggravated by the scarcely conciliatory character of Camus, separated them until March, 1947 (see *Force of Circumstance*, p. 111). They were reconciled at the time *The Plague* was published, but this did not stop the divergences of their thinking from becoming sharper. Politically, there were the beginnings of an ephemeral rapprochement, on the grounds of their common hostility to Gaullism, at the time of the "First Call to International Opinion" (see 48/167), which both Camus and Sartre signed. On the other hand, Camus did not sign the call to create the R.D.R. ⟨Revolutionary Peoples' Assembly⟩ or join the movement; although he did support a few months later the World Citizens' Movement which Sartre judged to be naive and ineffectual (see 49/188).

The publication of *L'Homme révolté* ⟨The Rebel⟩ (Gallimard, 1951), in which Camus expressed philosophical, ethical, and political positions very opposed to Sartre's, was to precipitate a break which friendship henceforth could not help avoid. The book came out during the fall of 1951 and plunged the whole *Temps modernes* staff into deep perplexity, as Simone de Beauvoir amusingly recalls: "In November, Sartre asked for a volunteer to review . . . *The Rebel*. He wouldn't let anyone say anything bad about it because of their friendship; unfortunately none of us could think of anything good. We wondered how we were going to get out of the dilemma" (*Force of Circumstance*, p. 252). The embarrassment of *Les Temps modernes* was expressed by more than six months of silence, but finally Francis Jeanson made up his mind to turn the knife in the wound, and did it more brusquely than Sartre would no doubt have wished.[1] His article, entitled "Albert Camus ou l'âme révoltée" 〈Albert Camus, or The Soul Rebel〉 (*Les Temps modernes*, no. 79 [May, 1952], pp. 2077-90), condemned Camus, in sometimes biting terms, for his "rejection of history," the moralizing, ineffectual attitude of the noble soul. Camus retorted as Sartre had previously invited him to. But instead of replying to Jeanson, he pretended not to know him and, going over his head, addressed himself to Sartre as "M. le Directeur" (see "Lettre au directeur des *Temps modernes*" 〈Letter to the Editor of *Les Temps modernes*〉 [dated June 30, 1952], *Les Temps modernes*, no. 82 [August, 1952], pp. 317-33; reprinted in *Actuelles II* under the title "Révolte et servitude" 〈Rebellion and Slavery〉, and then in the Pléiade volume, *Essais*, pp. 754-74). The tone of Camus's reply was haughty and curt; he said particularly that he was tired of getting "lessons in effectiveness from professional critics who never put any more than their armchairs on the line of history." From this point on, Sartre felt called upon to defend Jeanson by clearly expressing his own still harsher view of Camus's attitude. He did it, in his own words, *without any anger but, for the first time, . . . without mincing any words*. And Jeanson then went him one better in a letter whose intention was well summed up by its title, "Pour tout vous dire . . ." 〈 To Tell You the Whole Truth 〉 (*Les Temps modernes*, no. 82 [August, 1952], pp. 354-83). The whole business was given a publicity Sartre deplored, he who had hesitated to get involved in this polemic for fear of the use their common adversaries might put it to. *Combat* especially (September 18, 1952) published in a two-page spread and without his authorization long excerpts from his reply as well as excerpts from the texts by Camus and Jeanson.

Those are the public vicissitudes of a break which was to be final: the two writers never met again. Yet when Camus died, Sartre devoted a moving article to him (see 60/344); for even though he thought he was weak as a thinker and sometimes to be condemned for his political abstentions, he had kept his sympathetic feeling for the man and his esteem for the writer.

In re-reading the four texts of this polemic now, one is struck to begin with by their high level. It goes far beyond a simple authors' quarrel, for it begins a political and moral debate which in many respects is still urgent and open. Whether one supports

---

1. It is intriguing to note that the same sort of difficulty seems to have been generated several years later at the *Temps modernes* precisely by a book of Francis Jeanson's, *Lettre aux femmes* 〈A Letter to Women〉 (Seuil, 1965).

55/223

the positions of Sartre and Jeanson or prefers Camus's or rejects both, one cannot but admire the quality (of thought as well as of expression) of a controversy which undoubtedly constitutes one of the great moments of postwar French intellectual life.

Sartre's reply is indispensable to the knowledge of his thinking as it developed at the outset of the fifties, especially concerning the ethical problem. We must point out, finally, that this text was written between the two first parts of *The Communists and Peace*. As Simone de Beauvoir remarks, "These two pieces of writing had the same meaning: the postwar period was over" (*Force of Circumstance*, p. 262).

52/224

"M. Pinay prépare le chemin d'une dictature" ⟨M. Pinay Is Preparing the Way for a Dictatorship⟩.

-- *Libération*, October 16, 1952.

Short declaration protesting the arrest of Alain Le Léap, secretary general of the C.G.T. ⟨General Confederation of Labor⟩, charged with "demoralizing the nation" by having opposed the war in Indochina. *The fact that the war in Indochina is immoral is not a strictly Communist opinion. Yet that's what the government wants to make us believe by arresting people or trying to remove the parliamentary immunity of some Communists.*

55/225

"Ces actes semblent indiquer chez le gouvernement l'intention d'utiliser l'anticommunisme à l'américaine" ⟨These Acts Seem to Indicate the Government's Intention to Use Anti-Communism American-Style⟩, statement concerning the arrest of the C.G.T. ⟨General Confederation of Labor⟩ leader, Alain Le Léap.

-- *Ce Soir* and *L'Humanité*, October 17, 1952.

TEXTS RELATING TO THE CONGRESS OF VIENNA

Sartre began to get interested in the Peace Movement's activities during the summer of 1952. He took part, as an individual, in the Peoples' Peace Congress, organized in Vienna from December 12 to 19, 1952, by the World Council for Peace. We have been able to count the following texts resulting from that participation.

52/226

Interview by Paule Boussinot.

-- *Défense de la Paix*, special issue (December, 1952), pp. 12-14.

Before leaving for Vienna, Sartre sets forth his reasons for participating in the Congress, to which he accords the greatest importance. The positions he will defend are these: peaceful coexistence based on East-West exchanges, reunification of Germany without changing the economic regime of the two zones, peace in Indochina, and admission of China to the U.N.

52/227

Intervention de M. Jean-Paul Sartre ⟨Remarks by M. Jean-Paul Sartre⟩, at the opening session on December 12, 1952.

a) Complete text. *Congrès des Peuples pour la Paix* ⟨Peoples' Peace Congress⟩, News Service, Vienna, no. 2 (December 13, 1952), p. 7. B.N. call no.: Gr. Fol. G. 67.

b) Reprinted in *Congrès des Peuples pour la Paix, Vienne, 12-19 décembre 1952*. Paris, 1953. Pp. 48-54.

c) Excerpts of main parts. *On ne construit rien dans l'abstrait* ⟨Nothing Is Ever Built in the Abstract⟩. *Défense de la Paix*, January, 1953, pp. 24-29.

> . . . *Today's thought and politics are leading us to the slaughter because they are abstract. The world has been chopped in two and each half is afraid of the other. From that point on each man acts without knowing the will and decision of his next-door neighbor; we make conjectures, we don't believe what is said, we interpret and adapt our behavior to what we think the adversary will do. On this basis there is only one possible position, which is summed up by an age-old bit of foolishness: if you want peace, get ready for war. A victory for abstraction. In this perspective men themselves become abstract. Each man is* the Other, *the possible enemy; we* mistrust *him. It is rare to meet men in France, my country: you meet labels above all, and names. What is new and admirable about this Peace Congress is that it is bringing* men *together.*
>
> . . . *We have made our minds up not to take the place of our governments but to communicate with one another without them. . . . Since sovereignty comes from the people, we are gathering, we the governed, to agree upon our needs, and when we have returned to our homes, we shall show forth--within a* national framework--*a will which will be both that of each people and that of all. . . .*
>
> *If there are still people in the U.N. who think*

52/227

that World War III will be the struggle of Good against Evil, we are telling them that they are wrong: the people have seen each other, they have spoken to each other, they have touched each other, and they are united in saying that, in any case, *the Peace that they want to make and that they shall make is a Good. They won't pull that crusade bit on us again.*

. . . We know that we cannot condemn war in general or praise Peace in the abstract. The pacifist is in a very bad position to answer the warrior. Since he wants Peace at any price, why not accept a Peace imposed by arms? . . . We don't want just any peace. And above all, we don't want peace through terror. . . . Unlike Gary Davis, we know that we have *to get involved in politics, and that Peace is not a stable state we get one day like a good conduct medal but a long and exacting labor of construction which has to be carried out on a worldwide scale and which requires the collaboration of all the world's peoples. . . .*

War between the capitalist and socialist states would be inevitable if it could be proved that their coexistence is economically *impossible; that is, if it turned out that the peoples living under one of the regimes needed to destroy the other in order to work and eat their fill. Now nobody is claiming that. . . .*

When people talk about the coexistence of two economic systems, I don't think they mean to talk of the coexistence of two blocs. Coexistence doesn't mean juxtaposition. That involves mistrust and ends by leading from the cold war to the hot war. . . .

This Congress ought to be our conscious will, and it is in the name of this will that we shall find ourselves once more in our countries with new obligations and new tasks. . . .

Personally, I know many good people who ought to be here with us and aren't. Why? Well, out of pessimism, resignation, and then they've been made to fear that the Congress is a cooptation. . . . They have to say to themselves: we wanted peace, sincere men gathered to try to make it, and we weren't there. The day that their regrets make their mistrust and fear melt a little, that no man's land, anti-Communism, will have retreated, and we shall be able to say that before helping bring about international pacification, we have helped bring about reconciliation at home.

52/228

"Le Dialogue est engagé, c'est là le fait le plus chargé de promesses" ⟨The Dialogue Has Begun; That Is the Most

Promising Fact〉, short statement made in Vienna on December 16, 1952.

-- *Ce Soir*, December 17, 1952.

52/229

"C'est la première fois que je vois un espoir se dessiner parmi les hommes" 〈This Is the First Time I Have Seen the Outlines of a Hope for Men〉, interview by Jean Bedel.

a) Libération, December 18, 1952.

b) Russian translation. *Vetchernaia Moskva*, [December] 19, and *Izvestia*, [December] 20, 1952.

Interview of no great interest. Sartre stresses the fact that freedom of expression at the congress was complete, and says he is persuaded that the congress will have a considerable impact, even though it is inevitable that its achievements will be slandered or ignored.

52/NOTE.

To the question that *Le Figaro* asked a good number of Parisian notables--"Would you send a telegram to President Gottwald to save those condemned in Prague?"--Sartre answered laconically: *Refuse systematically to make any statement in* Figaro. See *Le Figaro*, November 29, 1952.

1953

53/230

"Ce que j'ai vu à Vienne, c'est la Paix" ⟨What I Saw in Vienna Was Peace⟩.

-- *Les Lettres françaises*, January 1-8, 1953.

Complete text of Sartre's speech at the December 23, 1952, meeting in the Vélodrome d'Hiver, where the big names who had taken part in the Congress of Vienna reported on it. For additional details about this meeting, see *Force of Circumstance*, p. 288, and the reports in *Libération* (December 24, 1952) and *Ce Soir* (December 25, 1952).

Having gone to Vienna without the mandate of any group, Sartre wants to bear witness as a writer. He shows how the press mystified people and provoked their mistrust by presenting the Congress as Communist-inspired. He himself had been subjected, before he left, to friendly pressures from people who were afraid he was being used. He gives precise examples of certain lies by the press, and tells about several episodes at the congress which were deliberately misinterpreted by the correspondents for bourgeois papers.

Sartre states that the congress was an extraordinary experience for him: *There have been three of them for me since I became a man, three which suddenly gave me hope again: the Popular Front of thirty-six, the Liberation, and the Congress of Vienna.*

Replying to the arguments which sought to minimize the importance of what had been accomplished in Vienna, Sartre says that what counts is not so much the final resolutions made as the contacts, discussions, and brotherhood among men who are very different. *So I testify that the Congress of Vienna is and, in spite of all the slander, will remain a historic event.*

Les Lettres françaises for January 8-15, 1953, reprints "Appel des écrivains réunis à Vienne" ⟨Appeal of Writers Gathered in Vienna⟩, which is signed by one hundred three writers, including Sartre (who may have drawn it up), and which reads as follows:

"We who believe in the power of the written word and whose job is to bear witness for ourselves and others who are like us have decided to harmonize our works and our will to peace, and we say that we shall fight against war through our writings. How, and to what extent, each one of us will decide for himself. But above and beyond our religious, philosophical, political, and literary differences, we agree in denouncing--in all of its disguises, including the disguise of literature--the war that people are preparing for us, in bearing witness in the name of all of those who suffer from this preparation, in showing the road to peace, and in affirming our confidence in man. . . ."

It must be recalled in this connection that in an interview in *L'Humanité* (see 55/271), Sartre said in speaking of NEKRASSOV: *I want to make a writer's contribution to the struggle for peace. We made commitments in Vienna; we must uphold them.*

53/231

Le Congrès de Vienne ⟨The Congress of Vienna⟩.

-- *Le Monde*, January 1, 1953.

Text appearing in the "Libres opinions" column. We reprint it *in extenso* below:

The papers had told us that by simply being there we would serve as hostages, be prevented from speaking, and act as a cover for hidden maneuvers. We are back; what are they waiting for to deny what they said? The press have had to tone down their attacks, but they are only changing their tactics. They had to show that the Congress of Vienna was, in spite of superficial differences, simply a repetition of the one in Warsaw: so they underhandedly equate it with a diplomatic conference and demand--or pretend to demand--that it produce results that not even the U.N. could produce, so that they can say that they are disappointed and that it has not produced anything new. They have simply ignored its true nature: it is a peoples' *congress. Even agreeing to discuss it on the level of diplomatic results, it would be easy to show the progress made--and especially the passage in the Appeal to the peoples of the world which concerns neutral states and the guarantees which ought to be accorded them--but I think it more important to stress this* popular *aspect of the congress, just because they're trying to conceal it.*

Yes. Of course there were Communist delegates. One hundred percent, I imagine, of the delegations from the peoples' democracies--but weren't they the ones we came to meet?--and a small minority of the Western delegations. But today the press can no longer conceal the fact that the Western delegations included men of all walks of life and very different opinions. Now only twenty or so abstentions kept the final motions from being unanimously approved. So there were liberals in Italy and radicals in France who, without denouncing the principle of colonization, voted for the same motion as the Vietnamese.

Naturally the anti-Communists have a ready answer: these poor guys are suckers or accomplices; in any case they don't belong to the political parties or religious groups they claim to; you should look at them instead as those unassimilated elements found on the lunatic fringe of every community; they have no more than a name in common with the Christian Democrats, the Socialists, or the M.R.P. ⟨Peoples' Republican Movement⟩. I don't know whether such explanations are convincing seen from here; but when we read them out there, they made us laugh. At first we had not known the opinions or beliefs of our non-Communist comrades, but before we "situated" them politically, each of us was able to see that the others were alert, determined men composed of equal measures of mistrust and hope, and that they were prepared to fight if need be to express their point of view; and then we each of us gradually relaxed, gained confidence, and ended up voting enthusiastically.

As for those who belonged to a political group, we know today that they were closely tied to the parties whose label they bore and whose principles they shared. Whether you like it or not, those really were radicals, members of the M.R.P., and socialists, and they were "of sound mind and body" when they voted for the appeal to the peoples of the world. That is exactly the importance of the congress: all these men were the image of millions of non-Communist Frenchmen who had like them come to an agreement with the Communists in order to preserve peace. And yet these millions of Frenchmen did not get themselves represented in Vienna: they wanted a détente between the East and West, but people persuaded them that they would be dupes if they joined the delegates of the East in looking for means to achieve it. The ruinous policy of rearmament, the threat a new Reichswehr would constitute, the hysteria of anti-Communism, all this disturbs them; the absurdity of the old adage Si vis pacem, para bellum is as plain to them as the nose on their face; but they're afraid: they would like to find concord without losing the "margin of security" that the atom bombs give them. And then, above all, propaganda has done its work well; it has created between the inhabitants of the same country an invisible no man's land which is more *uncrossable than a wall of fire. A Communist is a devil; you don't judge by what he says but by what he is. To vote with the Communists for a resolution favoring peace is to make a deal with Satan. It is not impossible that Satan will give us peace, but it will be a bad peace--and in any case we will be damned.*

The Frenchmen who went to Vienna differ from their fellow citizens in only one respect: they wanted their desire for peace to be transformed into action; they wanted to reject Manicheism and prove that systematically interpreting Soviet behavior as Machiavellian is a sign of interpretive madness rather than of political wisdom. They refused to take the motions of the congress a priori as verbal weapons of the cold war. Instead of condemning a text for the signatures on it, they preferred to judge it by its content.

I don't know whether maxims such as "Accept a motion for peace simply on the basis of the ideas in it" and "Think it probable that those who vote for it are friends of peace" are very naive or very daring. In any case they're very old and very new: it has been more than twelve years since we've applied them. Perhaps the day that we arrived we ourselves were still separated by our misgivings and that unending propaganda which divides the world up into two hostile blocs; but through our very act of coming to Vienna and speaking together, the cards were dealt and men were grouped in a different way. For a few hours those from the West and those from the East confronted one another; and then, immediately afterward, there were those who wanted peace and put their trust in it--and we, their representatives--and those who dreamed of peace, who wanted it in all sincerity, but who remained mistrustful.

Then I had an inkling that the congress could be an example, and that it would perhaps let us in turn remove the no man's land *which is dividing us. Out there peace was our only concern; we were friends--beyond our differences--through our common will. Perhaps it will be possible, if we can speak of what we saw, to bring together all those who, regardless of their party, believe in peace, and to reserve the other side of* no man's land *for those who no longer believe in anything but war.*

When we came home the Machiavellis of the press were waiting for us with a staggering objection. "Your congress wasn't homogeneous. The West had irresponsible delegates or, at best, the proxies of a tiny political or professional group; the East had veritable plenipotentiaries. The game wasn't fair. In short, you had *to line up with the Soviets." But to begin with, although it's true we did not know the precise form the congress would give to its final motions, we knew the Peace Movement's principles and general themes. The reason we went to Vienna was that we already supported a "cease fire" in Korea, and were convinced that in one form or another the coexistence of the two blocs was not impossible.*

But above all people claim not to see that the congress is one step in a long development. The dialogue between the East and West is very slow; not all the questions which were raised found immediate answers. But it's just that time is needed to transmit them to the competent authorities. In fact, these contacts have an importance which outstrips simply the immediate dialogue: they are the only chance that we citizens--who have no power, no protection against the lies of the press, and no qualified representatives of our interests and hopes--have to meet and know the representatives of the Soviet Union; and they are for the Soviet delegation their only chance to become familiar with that important fraction of French opinion which, without being Communist, condemns both anti-Communism and the arms race. Believe me, the Soviet delegates know how to take it into consideration: we saw a sort of progressive "correction" of the Soviet remarks, which adapted themselves to the Western currents of opinion. Ehrenburg's statement on neutralism and guarantees of nonaggression has been much discussed here, but the fact that it responded explicitly *to questions asked at the Warsaw Congress has not been generally known. I sometimes hear anti-Communists regretting that the U.S.S.R. has nothing but a mistaken image of France. It's certainly possible; but if so, there was one place on earth in December, and only one, where its representatives could become enlightened--Vienna. Only in Vienna could they converse in a friendly way with pastors and curés, with radicals and members of the M.R.P., about the daily life of Frenchmen--their fears, their hopes, their interests--about Soviet or French culture. Only in Vienna could we tell them, and did we tell them, what our desire for national independence meant. Even if we had ended with no more than this tranquil confrontation, it still would seem to me that the Congress of Vienna had served the cause of peace.*

Everyone felt it just as I did. I can easily understand why certain papers either said nothing about or ridiculed that final day's enthusiasm; *all's fair in love and* war. *But that enthusiasm meant something. It was slowly, timidly born during the first days; it grew progressively and finally burst forth. It was neither an ephemeral complaint nor a collective hysteria: each one of us had lots of time to test it, to compare it to what happened at the congress, to check it out. For me it was indistinguishable from a sort of certainty which each day was strengthened: "There's a* real force *and a* real will for peace *here--and that force is ours and that of the men and women who sent us here.* We *are the congress; it will be what we make of it; it* is *what we are making of it." The upshot of this certainty was that in the great hall of the Konzerthaus, where we were more or less the guests to start with, each of us felt at home, each one, together with his people, saw his own will in the final motions.*

You may smile at this conviction based on feeling. Yet I do not think that it would be in the interests of our realists, even if they were Machiavellians, to underestimate emotions: they would be risking making the mistake which damned their elders, the realists of 1943.

53/232

"Jean-Paul Sartre retour du congrès de Vienne: Nous avons, l'écrivain soviétique Korneitchouk et moi-même, décidé de poursuivre un dialogue fécond" ⟨Jean-Paul Sartre Back from the Congress of Vienna: The Soviet Writer Kornetshuk and I Decided to Carry On a Fruitful Dialogue⟩, interview by Régis Bergeron.

-- *France-U.R.S.S.*, no. 90 (February, 1953), pp. 7-8.

Here Sartre talks about the conversations he had with Soviet writers at the Congress of Vienna, and wonders what sort of literature is possible in the U.S.S.R. and Western Europe, respectively. It seems to him the only sort worthwhile is *a literature of conflict, even though conflicts--class conflicts, for example--have been done away with in the U.S.S.R.* Let us point out also the following statement: *I know Soviet literature very well--up to 1934-1935.*

53/233

L'AFFAIRE HENRI MARTIN ⟨The Henri Martin Affair⟩.

Commentary by Jean-Paul Sartre. Writings by Hervé Bazin, Marc Beigbeder, Jean-Marie Domenach, Francis Jeanson, Michel Leiris, Jacques Madaule, Marcel Ner, Jean Painlevé, Roger Pinto, Jacques Prévert, Roland de Pury, Jean-Henri Roy, Vercors, Louis de Villefosse.

-- Gallimard, [1953]. 289 pages.

Printing date: October 20, 1953.

Having joined the F.T.P. ⟨Partisan Snipers⟩ at the age of seventeen, Henri Martin had enlisted in the navy in 1945. At the end of that year, he volunteered for the campaign against Japan and was sent to Indochina, where he thought he was to fight the Japanese who had not laid down their arms. The truth, as is known, is quite different: instead of unyielding Japanese, he found a people fighting for independence. Three times he asked that his tour be ended. Having never received any response, he fulfills his duties as a soldier irreproachably but with an increasing sense of taking part in a terrible injustice. Back in France at the end of 1947, he is assigned the following year to the Arsenal in Toulon. Beginning in July, 1949, he starts to write and pin up tracts protesting the war in Indochina. He is arrested in May, 1950, and brought to trial in October by the Navy Courts Martial of Toulon, which condemns him to five years in prison. One year later, both the verdict and the sentence are upheld by the Navy Courts Martial of Brest.

During 1951, the Communist Party had begun a campaign for the liberation of Henri Martin. In December, some party intellectuals asked Sartre to take part in it. He agreed and, along with a group of non-Communist big names, signed a demand for pardon addressed to the president of the Republic. This is how it was that he was received in January, 1952, by Vincent Auriol (see 52/218), who told him that he realized that the punishment inflicted on Henri Martin was too severe, but added that he could never consider pardoning him as long as the Communist campaign continued. The P.C. ⟨Communist Party⟩ did not give in to this blackmail, and it was through popular pressure that Henri Martin was finally freed on good behavior in August, 1953.

Sartre had committed himself at the beginning of 1952 to collaborate in the editing of a book which was to give a detailed account of the whole business. This book was supposed to back up the demand for pardon. In the end, Sartre drafted all by himself a long commentary (which is printed in italics in the book and takes up about one hundred pages) on the collected documents and testimonies; but the work did not come off the press until October, 1953, that is, after Henri Martin had been freed. In his foreword, Sartre explains that now the book's aim is to reopen the trial.

An occasional piece, the work of a militant intellectual, and similar to the writings Voltaire devoted to the Calas Affair, THE HENRI MARTIN AFFAIR is far from having lost all interest in losing its currency. Sartre's is a model text of a kind which numbers few successes--the polemical commentary on present history. A model of style in the first place, swift and effective; incomparable too in its lively or sarcastic irony; but a model also of the strict honesty of a defender trying to convince and never overwhelm. We find in it, in a compact and hammering form, ideas developed at greater length in writings from the same period, especially in *The Communists and Peace* (relationships between the individual and his class) and SAINT GENET (the ethical Manicheism of the bourgeoisie). For this reason alone THE HENRI MARTIN AFFAIR, which is without a doubt the most neglected of all Sartre's volumes, is worth at least a reading.

53/234

Mallarmé 1842-1898, critical article.

a) In *Les Ecrivains célèbres*, Vol. III, edited by Raymond Queneau. Lucien Mazenod, 1953. Pp. 148-51. This luxurious work consists of a series of articles about the great authors written by the best contemporary writers: Herman Melville is done by Albert Camus, Edgar Allan Poe by Julien Gracq, etc.

Printing date: November 15, 1952.

b) Reprinted without change as the preface to Stéphane Mallarmé. *Poésies*. Poésie series. Gallimard, [1966]. Pp. 5-15.

c) Reprinted in SITUATIONS, IX.

Toward 1948-49, Sartre wrote almost five hundred pages on Mallarmé which he later lost, although a few unpublished bits still remain. Sartre was asked by Raymond Queneau to do the study Mazenod published, and he wrote it in 1952.

Subsequently Sartre came back often to Mallarmé and even projected writing a book about him.

It is beginning with the texts on Mallarmé and Jean Genet that we see Sartre's reflections on the proper function of literary *praxis* deepening. The radicalism of Mallarmé's literary project--what Sartre calls his *well-mannered terrorism*--gives his works, in spite of their apparent "disengagement," a revolutionary bearing. In an interview he gave to Madeleine Chapsal in 1960, Sartre says more specifically:

Mallarmé and Genet . . . I go to with complete sympathy: both of them consciously committed themselves. Mallarmé must be very different from the image people have created of him. He's our greatest poet. A passionate, furious man. And master of himself to the point of being able to kill himself simply by moving his glottis. . . . His commitment seems to me to be as total as is possible--socially as well as poetically.

53/235

Venise, de ma fenêtre ⟨Venice from My Window⟩.

a) Verve, III, nos. 27-28 (1953), 89-90.

Printing date: January 15, 1953.

A note indicates: "Part of a work to be published. Copyright Gallimard."

53/235

b) Reprinted in SITUATIONS, IV.

Part of an abandoned work: "Queen Albemarle and the Last Tourist." See 52/222.

53/235 A

"Le Problème colonial et celui de la démocratie sociale en France sont indissolublement liés" ⟨The Colonial Problem and the Problem of Social Democracy in France Are Inextricably Connected⟩, interview.

-- *La République algérienne*, January 16, 1953.

This short interview consists of three written answers. In it Sartre states that the function of the intellectual is to *ceaselessly show that the colonial regime is wicked, and that it has become harmful to the French national interest.*

53/236

Message (in support of André Kedros).

-- *Les Lettres françaises*, January 29-February 5, 1953.

Sartre was unable to attend an evening of tribute organized January 26, 1953, at the Mutualité to protest the threat of expulsion weighing over André Kedros, a Greek national writing in French. He sent a message the beginning of which reads as follows:

In 1945 André Kedros receives a grant from the French government; in 1952, without a word of explanation, they want to kick him out. Is it he who has changed? Is it France? No, it's neither. What has changed is the French government. In 1945 our representatives and ministers were free and wanted freedom for all. In 1952 they're slaves and won't allow anyone but slaves. In 1945 "collaboration" had just ended; today it is starting again.

53/237

Réponse à M. Mauriac ⟨Reply to M. Mauriac⟩.

-- *L'Observateur*, March 19, 1953.

New episode in the Sartre-Mauriac dispute. This time, Mauriac had condemned Sartre in the March 17, 1953, *Figaro* for his silence about antisemitism in the U.S.S.R. Sartre replies, without too much zest for it, that *Les Temps modernes* is getting ready to tackle the problem in an article on the Slansky Affair and also in the next part of *The Communists and Peace. M. Mauriac is disturbed by my silence. Let him rest assured; the monthlies seem silent only because the dailies are too talkative.* Sartre assures his readers that, contrary to what Mauriac thinks, he has no intention of justifying Russian antisemitism dialectically, and that he still thinks the final sentence of ANTI-SEMITE AND JEW is true. He says that he will not speak about this problem in order to win *Le Figaro*'s esteem, but will address himself to his *friends on the Left, whether they be Communists or not, Jews or not, because the problem concerns them first of all, and for them alone takes the form of a drama. They alone, and not M. Mauriac, have the right to ask me what I think, and they're the only ones I want to ask about their thoughts.*

Sartre continues: *In order to tempt me, M. Mauriac lets me glimpse the possibility that in the near future I might be able to "become what I am." In short, he invites me to adopt an attitude which will determine my form "forever." But I'm not concerned about my form. I've always thought that the important thing is not what a man is but what he does.*

53/238

Réponse à Claude Lefort ⟨Reply to Claude Lefort⟩.

a) Les Temps modernes, no. 89 (April, 1953), pp. 1571-629. A sequel to Claude Lefort's article, "Le marxisme et Sartre" ⟨Sartre and Marxism⟩, pp. 1541-70.

b) Reprinted in SITUATIONS, VII.

A Reply [or *An Answer*] *to Claude Lefort.*

t1) Translated by Philip Berk. In THE COMMUNISTS AND PEACE, *with a Reply to Claude Lefort.* New York: George Braziller, [1968].

t2) Translated by Irene Clephane. In THE COMMUNISTS AND PEACE, *with an Answer to Claude Lefort.* London: Hamish Hamilton, [1969].

Claude Lefort, friend of Maurice Merleau-Ponty, intellectual with a Trotskyite background, and regular collaborator of *Les Temps modernes*, had hot discussions with Sartre about the positions he had adopted in *The Communists and Peace.* Sartre suggested that he formulate his criticisms in the magazine. He did so in a rather ill-tempered way, and Sartre, angered, replied in the

53/238

same vein, having recourse in the process to personal attacks which upset Merleau-Ponty so much that he threatened to resign. Sartre agreed to withdraw a *needlessly violent* paragraph (see SITUATIONS, IV, p. 257).

Lefort's criticisms bear essentially on Sartre's way of conceiving of the revolutionary *praxis* of the working class and of the role of the party. In his reply, which is much more elaborate than Lefort's article, Sartre takes up these questions at length and thereby provides an indispensable complement to the first two parts of *The Communists and Peace* (see 52/220), whose theses, moreover, it simply confirms.

To situate rapidly the problems raised in this polemic, we may say that the Lefort-Sartre controversy occurs as part of the continuing debate within the international labor movement between those who hold to "spontaneism" and those who hold to "democratic centralism." In this period, Sartre supported the Bolshevik theses as Lenin in particular had set them forth in *What Is to Be Done?*

Lefort replied in a letter dated June, 1953, and entitled "De la réponse à la question" ⟨From the Answer to the Question⟩ (*Les Temps modernes*, no. 104 [July, 1954], pp. 157-84), which Sartre follows with these few words: *This letter adds nothing new concerning the precise problems I analyzed in my reply to Lefort. As for the additional questions it raises and the misgivings it expresses, the last part of* The Communists and Peace *will respond to them.*

53/239

"La Machine infernale" ⟨The Infernal Machine⟩, excerpts from a speech recorded during a debate at the Mutualité on May 5, 1953.

-- *Défense de la Paix*, June, 1953, pp. 15-21.

The infernal machine in question in this analysis of the situation of France in the spring of 1953 is the one which government policy since 1947 has succeeded in building. Sartre tries to show that the government's intention of internationalizing the war in Indochina at the moment negotiations have begun to put an end to the Korean conflict makes French policy *one of the principal causes of international tension*, and risks unleashing a worldwide conflict.

53/240

* *Les Animaux malades de la rage* ⟨Mad Beasts⟩.

a) Libération, June 22, 1953.

b) Reprinted in *Le Chant interrompu: Histoire des Rosenberg*. Texts assembled and presented by Catherine Varlin and René Guyonnet. Gallimard, [1955]. Pp. 224-28.

Sartre learned during a long stay in Venice of the execution of the Rosenbergs, several manifestoes in support of whom he had signed. His wrath brought forth one of the strongest things he ever wrote.

Les Temps modernes (no. 92 [July, 1953], pp. 1-5) also published an editorial about the Rosenberg Affair called "American Way of Death."

See also 54/252.

53/241

"Le Devoir d'un intellectuel est de dénoncer l'injustice partout" ⟨An Intellectual's Duty Is to Denounce Injustice Wherever It Occurs⟩, interview by Serge Montigny.

-- *Combat*, October 31-November 1, 1953.

Interview given on the occasion of the publication of THE HENRI MARTIN AFFAIR. Sartre explains in detail the reasons why the book was written and the meaning it assumes after the administrative step liberating Henri Martin in August, 1953 (see 53/233).

The second part of the interview bears on the role of intellectuals in the context of the cold war. Sartre says especially that the petitions and protests by Western intellectuals which are directed against the injustices committed in Communist countries have no effect on the governments of these countries and are consequently *purely ceremonious* acts which inevitably turn, in the present climate, into *acts of war*. He adds: *This in no way alters the intellectual's duty to denounce injustice wherever it occurs. But cut off as he is in the present situation from half the world, his only recourse in the matter of events which occur in this half is to publish articles or books which comment on and denounce them with complete objectivity.* This is the goal *Les Temps modernes* sets itself in its articles on the Slansky Affair.

The interviewer then asks Sartre if he would rewrite DIRTY HANDS today: *No; I wouldn't rewrite it, but do you think I would rewrite any of my other works?*

53/241

That doesn't mean I disown them. I don't disown DIRTY HANDS *and I am far from being sorry about the play. It expressed a position which was perfectly legitimate in 1948.*

Sartre says in conclusion that he is working presently on his "Ethics" and his autobiography. This confirms that although he had abandoned his treatise on ethics in 1949 (see 49/187), he had subsequently continued to write intermittently about the subject.

53/NOTE.

The script "Typhus," which was written by Sartre in 1943-44, was used for Yves Allégret's movie *The Beautiful and the Damned*, which came out in 1953 (see Appendix). There is a typed version of 112 pages covering 32 scenes and prepared for eventual publication in book form. The project was not carried out.

1954

54/242

KEAN, adaptation in five acts of *Kean ou Désordre et génie* ⟨Kean, or Disorder and Genius⟩, comedy by Alexandre Dumas, senior.

a) Alexandre Dumas. *Kean.* Adaptation by Jean-Paul Sartre. Gallimard, [1954]. 309 pages.

Printing date: February 15, 1954.

56 copies on vergé de Hollande, 170 on vellum and 750 bound on esparto grass.

The second part of the volume also gives the complete text of Dumas's play.

b) Adaptation alone reprinted in THÉÂTRE (1962).

c) English textbook edition. With introduction and notes by David Brady. Clarendon French Series. London: Oxford University Press, 1972. Includes the play by Alexandre Dumas.

KEAN, *or Disorder and Genius*, based on the play by Alexandre Dumas.

t1) Translated by Kitty Black. London: Hamish Hamilton, 1954. (Same translation in *t2-t4*).

t2) THE DEVIL AND THE GOOD LORD, *and Two Other Plays* [KEAN, NEKRASSOV]. New York: Alfred A. Knopf, 1960.

t3) *Ibid.* in paperback. New York: Vintage Books, [1960].

t4) In KEAN; NEKRASSOV; THE TROJAN WOMEN, in paperback. Penguin Books, [1969].

54/242

t5) Translated by Frank Hauser. Playscripts series. London: David Poynter, 1971.

KEAN was performed for the first time at the Théâtre Sarah-Bernhardt on November 14, 1953, in a production by Pierre Brasseur and with settings by Alexandre Trauner. Main parts:

KEAN	Pierre Brasseur
ANNA DAMBY	Marie-Olivier
ELENA, comtesse de Koefeld	Claude Gensac
Etc.	

To situate his adaptation, Sartre wrote the following text (which we reproduce in its entirety):

53/243

A propos de Kean ⟨Concerning KEAN⟩, text dated November 8, 1953.

-- Program for KEAN, Théâtre Sarah-Bernhardt. 1953-54 season.

While the celebrated Kean, passing through Paris, was playing Shakespeare in English on the Odéon stage, Frédérick Lemaître took him for a tour around the cabarets. Kean drank and told him the story of his life; Lemaître drank and listened, thinking, "There are only two actors in this world, he and I." Kean went back to England and soon after died. Frédérick Lemaître thought, "Now there's only one actor in this world," and to better persuade the public of it he developed the crazy urge to identify himself with the dead man. So M. de Courcy, the renowned polygraph, received the command to do a play about Kean in which Lemaître would play the leading role. And Alexandre Dumas? What does he have to do with all this? I guess we'll never know; but one thing sure is that he signed the play and got paid for it, and today it's listed among his complete works with his signature alone. Success went so much to the French actor's head that he ended by identifying himself completely with his English counterpart: toward the end of his life he made the painful discovery that Kean *was being revived--at the Odéon, I believe--but with an Italian actor; and in his rage he covered Paris with notices bearing these words, "I am the real Kean." Later, the role fascinated other actors, especially Lucien Guitry. After World War I, Ivan Mosjukine played Kean in the movies. The explanation for the play's continuing success is that it's always up-to-date: every twenty-five years it lets a famous actor "take his bearings." Lemaître, Guitry, Mosjukine came in turn to speak to the public about their craft, their private life, their troubles and misfortunes, but according to the rules of their profession: discreetly, modestly, that is to say, by slipping into someone else's skin. All these famous dead who successively played the part enriched it with their memory. Today Kean, with his disorders, genius, and misfortunes, has ceased to be a historical character and has risen to the level of a myth: he is the patron saint of actors. Tonight, if Pierre Brasseur has the good luck I wish him, the miracle which for one hundred years has made the play's fortune will take place again: you will no longer know whether you are seeing Brasseur playing Kean or Kean playing Brasseur. The adapter's task was modest: it was only necessary to remove the rust and a few bits of mould, in short clean up, trim up, to let the public give its full attention to this exceptional spectacle--that of an actor whose role is to embody his own character.*

This introduction gives most of the historical information needed. Let us add that the English actor Kean lived from 1787 to 1833 and that the Dumas-Courcy play was written specially for Frédérick Lemaître in 1836.

Sartre had already mentioned his interest in *Kean* during the rehearsals of THE DEVIL AND THE GOOD LORD. When a little later Pierre Brasseur suggested he adapt the play, Sartre, "who adores melodramas, didn't say no" (*Force of Circumstance*, pp. 286-87). He put the adaptation together "in a few weeks, having lots of fun" (*ibid.*, p. 297). The manuscript is dated Rome, July, 1953.

The rehearsals of KEAN do not seem to have presented any problems, and the play, achieving great success, was performed from November 14, 1953, to June 5, 1954, with one three-week interruption due to Brasseur's illness.

Francis Jeanson, in his *Sartre by Himself* (Seuil edition, pp. 78 ff.), shows in an excellent way what links Kean to the other bastards in Sartre's works--Genet, Goetz, Hugo, Orestes, etc.--and finds in the play not only a marginal expression but a tension which is "the most personal, the most intimately *Sartrian*" (p. 29).

A comparative study of the plays of Dumas and Sartre may be found in the communication from Annie Ubersfeld, "Structures du théâtre d'Alexandre Dumas père" 〈The Structures of the Plays of Alexandre Dumas the Elder〉, published in *Linguistique et littérature:* Colloque de Cluny (special edition of *La Nouvelle Critique*, 1968).

INTERVIEWS ABOUT "KEAN"

53/244

"Pourquoi j'ai modernisé Dumas" ⟨Why I Modernized Dumas⟩.

-- *Le Figaro*, November 4, 1953.

Short statement of no great interest.

53/245

"Jean-Paul Sartre a coupé *Kean* (la pièce d'Alexandre Dumas) aux mesures de Pierre Brasseur" ⟨J.-P. Sartre Has Tailored KEAN (the Alexander Dumas Play) to Fit Pierre Brasseur⟩, interview-article by Paul Morelle.

-- *Libération*, November 4, 1953.

This interview tells about the tumultuous life of the real Kean. Asked about his projects, Sartre talks about his autobiography: *Through my own history, I want to record the history of my time.*

53/246

"Mon adaptation d'Alexandre Dumas ne sera pas une pièce de Jean-Paul Sartre" ⟨My Adaptation of Alexander Dumas Will Not Be a Play by Jean-Paul Sartre⟩, interview by Jean Carlier.

-- *Combat*, November 5, 1953.

Sartre says he has tried *to bring the melodrama up to date without at any time intending to make a parody of it*, and he points out that the adaptation led him to a general reflection about actors: *The actor is the opposite of the player, who, when he has finished work, goes back to being just another man again, whereas the actor "acts himself" every second. This is both a wondrous gift and a curse: he is in the proper sense the victim of it, never knowing who he really is, whether he is acting or not.*

53/247

"Quand Sartre 'rewrite' Dumas pour s'amuser et exaucer Brasseur" ⟨When Sartre "Rewrites" Dumas to Have Some Fun and Satisfy Brasseur⟩, interview-article by Jean Duché.

-- *Le Figaro littéraire*, November 7, 1953.

This is an intelligent, well-documented article, the beginning of which relates some remarks by Sartre mixed with ample commentary.

53/248

"La Véritable Figure de Kean" ⟨The True Face of Kean⟩, interview by Renée Saurel.

-- *Les Lettres françaises*, November 12-19, 1953.

Sartre gives numerous historical details about the personality and career of Kean, *that man who became an actor to escape his resentment against society, and who brought a sort of revolutionary force along with him.* To him, Kean is also *the Myth of the Actor itself. The actor who never stops acting, who acts his life itself, who does not recognize himself, who no longer knows who he is. And who, in the last analysis, is nobody.* Before saying he is fascinated by the *Kean-Lemaître-Brasseur trinity*, Sartre continues: *All the characters in* KEAN *are more or less this way: great men who are locked in struggle with shadows which are their own characters. There is only one character which is more or less authentic--that of Anna Damby.*

The interview ends with these words: *There's something of* Hernani *in* Kean, *and I like* Hernani *very much.*

54/248 A

"Une Interview de Jean-Paul Sartre" ⟨An Interview by Jean-Paul Sartre⟩, on KEAN:

-- File R. Supp. 3912 in the Fonds Rondel at the Bibliothèque de l'Arsenal includes a newspaper clipping with no source indicated which records some comments by Sartre on KEAN:

> *An existentialist Dumas? You're joking! I got this idea of the actor sometimes acting to himself from conversations with certain great actors, like Pierre Brasseur especially. For them, it's a problem. Dumas had already touched on it, by the way; I just finished things up. But you must definitely not conclude from the play that everyone is just acting, and above all you mustn't build a theory on it.*

54/249

"KEAN, c'est tout le drame de l'acteur de génie" ⟨KEAN Is the Whole Drama of the Actor of Genius⟩, interview.

-- *Ciné-Club*, special issue, April, 1954.

Sartre talks about the Soviet film, KEAN, by Volkov, which was made in 1924 with Mosjukine in the leading role. He saw this movie almost thirty years ago and then again after he had written his adaptation; he notes that Volkov too changes the last act of Dumas's play, and he wonders what problems a movie adaptation of Kean's real life would present in 1954.

Sartre had in fact planned for a while to write a film script for Pierre Brasseur which would have had to do with the last years of Kean's life. This movie was to be made by Alexandre Astruc, but the project did not pan out. The Dumas-Sartre play, on the other hand, was brought to the screen in Italy by Vittorio Gassman (see Appendix).

54/250

Preface to *D'une Chine à l'autre* ⟨From One China to the Other⟩, by Henri Cartier-Bresson and Jean-Paul Sartre.

a) Neuf series, no. 14. Delpire, [1954].

Printing date: November 30, 1954. Copyright: beginning of 1955. The volume consists of 144 photographs by Cartier-Bresson (taken in 1948-49 and inscribed by the photographer) and Sartre's text (which covers 9 pages).

b) Two parts reprinted as "Le Journal de voyage de H. Cartier-Bresson" ⟨The Travel Diary of H. Cartier-Bresson⟩. *Les Lettres françaises*, December 30, 1954-January 6, 1955.

c) Important part entitled "Jean-Paul Sartre et Henri Cartier-Bresson racontent: La Chine sans lotus ni Loti" ⟨Jean-Paul Sartre and Henri Cartier-Bresson Show Us China with No Lotus or Loti⟩. *Horizons*, no. 45 (February, 1955), pp. 11-19.

d) Complete text under the title *D'une Chine à l'autre*. In SITUATIONS, V.

Preface to *China in Transition: A Moment in History*, translated by Edward Hyams.

-- London: Thames and Hudson, 1956.

In the American edition of the book, entitled *From One China to the Other* (New York: Universe Books, 1956), Sartre's preface is replaced by a text by Han Suyin.

This engaging piece was written during Sartre's stay in Russia in June, 1954, that is to say, well before his trip to China in the fall of 1955 (see concerning this subject 55/281). Commenting on Cartier-Bresson's photographs, Sartre shows how his authentic and generously humanistic gaze is in contrast with the mythico-touristic vision of China.

The piece includes an excellent autobiographical section (see SITUATIONS, V, p. 8).

In *La Longue Marche* ⟨The Long March⟩ (Gallimard, 1957), Simone de Beauvoir points out the following fact: "*Le Figaro* reprinted certain photos (dated, by the way) which were in *D'une Chine à l'autre* and attributed them to the Communist regime, whereas they had been taken before the liberation of Shanghai" (p. 441).

Let us recall that Cartier-Bresson is the man who took what might be called *the* classical photo of Sartre.

54/251

"Una entrevista con Jean-Paul Sartre" ⟨An Interview with Jean-Paul Sartre⟩, interview in Spanish by Marcel Saporta.

-- *Cuadernos Americanos*, 13th Year, LXIII, no. 1 (January-February, 1954), 57-64.

In this interview he granted in the fall of 1953, Sartre speaks almost exclusively of politics. On a general scale, he protests the "Marshallization" of Europe and advocates an independent European politics. On a national scale, he maintains that French politics has ossified as a result of economic Malthusianism and the war in Indochina (which binds France to the U.S.A.), and he says that a new Popular Front is needed.

Next he gives his interpretation of DIRTY HANDS by contrasting Hoederer and Hugo: the former, with his synthesizing turn of mind, represents the Popular Front and an effective social policy, whereas the latter is simply a young bourgeois at grips with the contradictions inherent in his social class, contradictions he cannot resolve except by dying. Goetz's development in THE DEVIL AND THE GOOD LORD shows how one may escape the idealism-opportunism dilemma, and we see in the last tableau what Hugo could have done if he had been able to dominate his contradictions.

To conclude, Sartre says that he is not responsible for intellectual anti-Communism, that he has always wanted to act in concert with the Communists, and that

54/251

it is the role of *Les Temps modernes* to favor this unity of action and to allow a Popular Front ideology to be reconstituted.

For another interview by Saporta, see 48/166.

54/252

Les Enfants Rosenberg ⟨The Rosenberg Children⟩.

-- *Libération*, February 22, 1954.

Libération had announced for publication an article by Sartre on the fate of the Rosenberg children, which had aroused great concern. Since less alarming news had been received in Europe, he stopped writing the article and gave his reasons for doing so in a short piece in which he nevertheless called for vigilance.

54/253

Opération "Kanapa" ⟨Operation "Kanapa"⟩.

a) Les Temps modernes, no. 100 (March, 1954), pp. 1723-28.

b) Excerpts. "Jean-Paul Sartre exécute Kanapa" ⟨Jean-Paul Sartre Executes Kanapa⟩. *L'Observateur*, March 11, 1954.

These excerpts were published without the authorization of *Les Temps modernes* (see Marcel Péju's letter in *L'Observateur*, March 18, 1954).

c) Reprinted in SITUATIONS, VII.

The manuscript is dated February 28, 1954.

Jean Kanapa, Communist newspaperman and former student of Sartre, had attacked the latter frequently from 1946 to 1950 (see especially *Comme si la lutte entière. . .* ⟨As If the Whole Struggle . . . ⟩, [Nagel, 1946], in which Sartre is represented in the features of Labzac, and *L'Existentialisme n'est pas un humanisme* ⟨Existentialism Is Not a Humanism⟩ [Editions sociales, 1947]), but had made up with him in 1952.

On February 22, 1954, Kanapa published an article in *L'Humanité* entitled "Un 'nouveau' révisionnisme à l'usage des intellectuels" ⟨A "New" Revisionism for Intellectuals to Use⟩ which was meant to stigmatize the book, *Communism*, by the "renegade" Dyonis Mascolo and to condemn Colette Audry for having given a favorable account of it in *Les Temps modernes*. Sartre, who had supported the politics of the Communist Party since 1952, felt directly attacked and energetically defended his magazine: *It takes more than one swallow to make a spring, and more than one Kanapa to dishonor a party.*

Later Kanapa published a letter in *L'Humanité* (March 24, 1954) stating that there had been a misunderstanding and that he had not intended to hit at Sartre.

In *(a)*, *(b)* and *(c)*, Kanapa's first article precedes Sartre's piece.

54/253 A

"In gesprek met Jean-Paul Sartre" ⟨Talk with Jean-Paul Sartre⟩, interview-article in Dutch by C. A. Van Peursen.

-- *Wending* (The Hague), IX (March, 1954), 15-24.

Text bearing on Sartre's philosophical works and reporting his comments on them in an indirect but apparently accurate way.

Sartre thinks that for the time being he is through writing about ontological problems as he formulated them in BEING AND NOTHINGNESS. His thought is at present moving in the direction of a philosophical ethics. He had originally thought of this ethics as a general whole constructed parallel to his ontological work, but now he wants to set out from concrete social problems and avoid abstract exposition. In this way the problem of freedom is set within the framework of society, and social and political commitment is given priority. The past is built in freedom, but for the present it is an established given which determines individual life; and the job of a philosopher oriented toward action is to show how this "given" can be assumed in collective freedom. In the Communist world, philosophy is very important because it is not just a theory but a force acting amidst the realities of everyday life. Sartre himself wants to move toward a theory which will be at the same time a *praxis* and which will reintegrate the elements Marxism has neglected or rejected into the framework of freedom.

54/254

Les Communistes et la Paix ⟨The Communists and Peace⟩ *(III)*.

a) Les Temps modernes, no. 101 (April, 1954), pp. 1731-819.

This article bears the note "To Be Continued," and the final part of *The Communists and Peace* is announced for publication up through February, 1956. In May, 1956, a note points out: "As a conclusion to "The Communists and Peace," we shall publish in one of our upcoming issues an article by Jean-Paul Sartre, *Réponse à Pierre Hervé et à quelques autres*" ⟨Reply to Pierre Hervé and to Several Others⟩. This last title is again announced for publication in September-October, 1956, and then seems to have given way to *The Ghost of Stalin* (see 57/291).

b) Reprinted in SITUATIONS, VI with a supplementary note (p. 384).

c) Reprinted in IL FILOSOFO E LA POLITICA ⟨The Philosopher and Politics⟩ (1964).

For parts I and II, and the translations, see 52/220.

In this part Sartre seeks the causes of the workers' discouragement which was revealed by the events which had evoked his first two articles. He refers to nineteenth-century history--as studied by Henri Guillemin, in particular--to show that the massacres of June, 1848, and 1871 are the source of the climate of fear, hatred, violence, and civil war in which the class struggle was established in France. *For all the world's workers, the bourgeois is the product of capital; for ours he is also the son of his works, a killer--and he's going to keep on being so for a long time.* The bourgeoisie, confronted with the constant threat to its power constituted by the working class, resorted to economic Malthusianism to assure social stability. The French proletariat is the victim and the product of Malthusianism, *its struggle itself is conditioned by the evil it should struggle against . . . the proletariat's discouragement is a product of industrial underproduction; it is the subjective expression of the objective limits which the economic structure imposes on the* praxis. Sartre then describes the division of the working class into skilled laborers, whose interests were expressed in revolutionary syndicalism, and O.S. (*ouvriers spécialisés* ⟨unskilled laborers⟩), who appeared with automation. The O.S., who are subjected to the most radical oppression, have the only true perspective on society, that of the least favored. It is on the O.S., in other words, on the masses, that a *humanism of need* is based. But the masses, in order to go beyond their status as the masses, can act on society only through the one party which represents them, the Communist Party.

Such is, very schematically summarized, the line of argument developed in the third article, which is the most important of the three. For today's reader, who gains knowledge of it in SITUATIONS, VI, *The Communists and Peace* is limited by the fact that it is both an ad hoc polemical piece and a theoretical analysis in which Sartre ran into, especially in respect to the Malthusianism of the propertied bourgeoisie, problems he did not solve until CRITIQUE OF DIALECTICAL REASON. At the end of that work, Sartre does as a matter of fact refer explicitly to his preceding analysis: *I tried elsewhere to show how French management's Malthusianism was--even considered only in a national context--a truly repressive practice which originated in the bloody repressions of the nineteenth century. Readers have often asked me concerning this subject how this Malthusianism could have any meaning as* praxis *and class process since I rejected both the idea of an individual-to-individual understanding--which would make the class a group in action--and the idea of a hyperorganism whose individual acts would reflect hyperindividual decisions* (p. 704). In the pages which follow, Sartre uses two concepts he lacked at the time of *The Communists and Peace*, those of the *practico-inert* and *serial otherness*, to show how we can account for the contradiction between management's Malthusian practices and its search for profits through expansion, which is precisely what defines the capitalist: *Here again everything is perfectly understandable: it is just a matter of putting into practice what is already inscribed in the practico-inert. . . . There is no conspiracy, no deliberation, no communication, no common regrouping, except in the case of the powerful groups who have invented and inaugurated the practice. Everything has taken place serially, and* Malthusianism *as an economic process is seriality* (p. 729).

Moreover, the quality of the three articles from 1952 to 1954 suffers from the haste in which they were written. Like many pieces in which Sartre has not had time to be brief, these are repetitious; a certain disorder in the sequence of ideas also mars at times their expository clarity.

It must be noted that although Sartre never renounced these articles, he subsequently recognized their inadequacies. Michel-Antoine Burnier relates that Sartre told him in 1963, in speaking of his explanation of the postwar French social situation in terms of Malthusianism, that *his article was becoming dated while he was writing it (Choice of Action* [Gallimard edition, p. 93]). In 1965 Sartre made this additional interesting comment to Burnier concerning the theoretical gaps in *The Communists and Peace* (pp. 85-86): *In a period when the party is nothing but what keeps the group from becoming serialized . . . , the party represents itself alone. Which raises the following problem: Is democracy within the party conceivable except in a revolutionary period? The party in a nonrevolutionary period is a party in waiting. It must simultaneously mobilize its supporters and demobilize them (to make them wait). Its problem is comparable to that of the church when it became evident that the Kingdom of God was not at hand. Thus the party*

54/254

in waiting can only be judged by its actions; it is not inherently legitimate. It is only legitimate if it acts the way it ought to act. That is why one cannot conceive of actual *representatives of the proletariat in a period of waiting or in a Stalinist dictatorship. And this reflection on the concept of legitimacy is what* The Communists and Peace *lacks. . . . In France at the present time, the party itself has become serial.*

Maurice Merleau-Ponty had been separating himself politically from Sartre since 1950. He waited until 1955 to state publicly his disagreement with the positions taken in *The Communists and Peace*. In "Sartre and Ultra-Bolshevism," chapter 5 of *Les Aventures de la dialectique* ⟨Adventures of the Dialectic⟩ (Gallimard, 1955; Evanston, Ill.: Northwestern University Press, 1973), he explains these positions in terms of what he considers the basic weaknesses of Sartre's thinking, its antidialectical subject-object dualism, its "Cogito madness," and its voluntarism. Sartre refrained from replying to these attacks, but Simone de Beauvoir, in an article entitled "Merleau-Ponty et le pseudo-sartrisme" ⟨Merleau-Ponty and Pseudo-Sartrianism⟩ (*Les Temps modernes*, no. 114-15 [June-July, 1955]; reprinted in *Privilèges*), rose to his defense with vigor and in a more polemical tone than Merleau-Ponty himself had taken.

54/255

A nos lecteurs ⟨To Our Readers⟩.

-- *Les Temps modernes*, no. 102 (May, 1954), pp. 1923-24.

The previous issue of *Les Temps modernes* (no. 101 [April, 1954]) originally included an editorial entitled "We Will Not Go Off on the Crusade" which had been drawn up by Marcel Péju but signed T. M. When Sartre found out about it by reading it in the already bound issue, he decided to cut it out, and the pages it was on were removed from all copies prior to distribution. Nevertheless *L'Unità* (April 29, 1954) reprinted part of the editorial (without having asked Sartre for his authorization), and a passage was then retranslated from the Italian newspaper in an article by Pierre Simier, "Quand Sartre se tait . . . l'écho communiste répète . . ." ⟨When Sartre Holds His Tongue . . . the Communist Echo Repeats What He Says⟩ (*Le Populaire*, May 28, 1954): "And let us especially admire all these little men who, on foot in jungles and in mountains, sprouting from the earth like grain, carrying their rice rations and shells on their backs, fling themselves beneath a napalm sky against the barbed wire which is making their country a prison. It must be said: we are on their side. These soldiers are fighting for us and with us against all the men in the world who are denying men the right of being men."

This was precisely the passage which had led Sartre to make his decision: as a matter of fact, the phrase originally printed had even spoken of "these little yellow men," and Sartre rightly thought this was a tactless way of putting things. But out of consideration for the editor's feelings, he said publicly that the reason for this self-censorship was the risk of confiscation the magazine would run if it took a stand in favor of the Vietnamese nationalists. The May 2, 1954, *Express* pointed out, however, that the accused editorial had been cut out because it was too badly written.

It is understandable that Sartre should, out of editorial solidarity, give a somewhat different explanation here of the omission of the editorial. Correcting what he said gave him a chance to define the objectives of *Les Temps modernes* more precisely: *What the public wants our magazine to do is not* to agitate *but to expose events, analyze situations, clarify their meaning if it can, in short, to comment on and convince. We shall not retreat before the risk of confiscation when it is a matter of providing documents or news for our readers: when we talked about the atrocities of the war in Indochina, the government didn't dare to go after us because it knew that we could prove what we said. But we shall not try deliberately to have our magazines confiscated: we want to bear witness; that is our role. All our readers know that we consider the government's policy baneful and the men behind it contemptible: but our job is to constantly show it. It's only by* showing *that we can hope to be of service. We shall go on doing it: if it is forbidden to call Bidault a criminal, we shall say that he is a major culprit; if we are denied the right to speak of the blood on his hands, we shall speak of the scales on his eyes. It's just a matter of terminology.*

54/256

Les Boucs émissaires ⟨The Scapegoats⟩.

a) Libération, May 17, 1954.

b) Excerpts in *L'Humanité*, May 18, 1954.

c) Russian translation in *Literaturnaia Gazeta*, [June] 5, 1954.

Following the defeat at Dien Bien Phu, the Laniel government had banned the performances of the Russian ballet in Paris. Alluding to a comic incident of which the president had been the victim, Sartre speaks of the *providential kick* [which let] *M. Laniel rise for*

54/256

the first time in his life above the level of the commonplace, and then he brings out very well the meaning of this governmental reflex: when one has lost a war through one's own fault alone, one must, in order to prevent public opinion from turning against one, hold someone else responsible, and there is no better way of doing so than to hit out at them: so the Russian ballet is banned, and public opinion, mystified, says to itself: *To make the government ban the ballet, to threaten it with burning the Opéra, I must have really been angry. And I do feel indignant. So was I angry* at the Communists? But the tactic will fail, because everybody knows that it was the Bidault, Laniel, and Pleven government who wanted this war and who lost it. The Russian ballet will come back again: *For next year, Monsieur Laniel, Ulanova will still be dancing. But you won't be president.*

54/257

Les Peintures de Giacometti ⟨The Paintings of Giacometti⟩.

a) Derrière le miroir (Maeght Gallery Review), no. 65 (May, 1954).

Piece written for a show at the Maeght Gallery (May 14-June 15, 1954).

b) Les Temps modernes, no. 103 (June, 1954), pp. 2221-32.

c) Reprinted in SITUATIONS, IV.

Giacometti in Search of Space, or *The Paintings of Giacometti.*

t1) Giacometti in Search of Space, translated by Lionel Abel. *Art News*, September, 1955, pp. 26-29, 63-65.

t2) The Paintings of Giacometti, translated by Warren Ramsey. In *Art and Artist*. Berkeley and Los Angeles: University of California Press, 1954. Pp. 179-94.

t3) Ibid., translated by Wade Baskin. In ESSAYS IN AESTHETICS (1963).

t4) Ibid., translated by Benita Eisler. In SITUATIONS (1965).

For Sartre, Giacometti is the man who has succeeded in *painting the void*. Concerning Giacometti, see 48/162.

On the second page of the article, Sartre describes at length the crisis of agoraphobia he suffered from in April, 1941, when he returned from captivity.

54/258

* *Julius Fucik*

-- *Les Lettres françaises*, June 17-24, 1954.

Sartre read this piece before an audience of workers during a meeting organized by the C.N.E. ⟨National Writers' Committee⟩ in a big factory in the suburbs of Paris.

Commenting on the book *Written in the Shadow of the Gallows* by the Czech writer Julius Fucik, Sartre devotes himself to a very moving ethical reflection on torture and that question many have asked themselves: "And what about us; would we have resisted if we were tortured?"

54/259

La Bombe H, une arme contre l'Histoire ⟨The H-Bomb, an Anti-Historical Weapon⟩.

a) Summary in *Pravda*, May 27. Complete translation in *Literaturnaia Gazeta*, May 29, 1954.

b) Défense de la Paix, no. 38 (July, 1954), pp. 18-22.

Speech given during a special session of the World Council for Peace in May, 1954, in Berlin.

Sartre develops this idea: *To stop the world from going on, people are threatening to eliminate History by liquidating the historical agent. . . . The bomb is in itself the basis and the sum of a policy which is completely hostile to the true development of mankind, and which wishes to impose this alternative: the status quo or radical destruction.*

54/259 A

Message broadcast by Tass.

a) Pravda and *Literaturnaia Gazeta*, June 24, 1954.

b) Libération, June 25, 1954.

This broadcast summarized a press conference Sartre held in Moscow on June 23, 1954, as he was leaving the U.S.S.R.: *I leave having seen men who want to build a better world for themselves and their children, men you can't help being friends with.*

NOTE: During his trip to the U.S.S.R., Sartre made two statements on Radio Moscow, one broadcast on June 4

54/259 A

in which he thanks the Soviet Writers' Union for having invited him, the other made at Tashkent on June 16 in which he says he is struck by *the indissoluble tie between the popular art of the past and the culture created by the Uzbek people during these past years.*

54/260

"LES IMPRESSIONS DE JEAN-PAUL SARTRE SUR SON VOYAGE EN U.R.S.S." ⟨Jean-Paul Sartre's Impressions on His Trip to the U.S.S.R.⟩, comments gathered by Jean Bedel in 5 articles.

I. "La Liberté de critique est totale en U.R.S.S. et le citoyen soviétique améliore sans cesse sa condition au sein d'une société en progression continuelle" ⟨There Is Complete Freedom to Criticize in the U.S.S.R., and the Soviet Citizen Is Constantly Improving His Lot in a Constantly Progressing Society⟩.

-- *Libération*, July 15, 1954.

II. "De Dostoïevski à la littérature contemporaine, un grand débat est ouvert entre les écrivains: Pour ou contre le roman héroïque" ⟨From Dostoievsky to Contemporary Literature, Writers Have Begun a Great Debate: For or Against the Heroic Novel?⟩.

-- *Libération*, July 16, 1954.

III. "Ce n'est pas une sinécure d'appartenir à l'élite car elle est soumise à une critique permanente de tous les citoyens" ⟨It Is No Special Privilege to Belong to the Elite because It Is Always Being Criticized by All Citizens⟩.

-- *Libération*, July 17-18, 1954.

IV. "Les Philosophes soviétiques sont des bâtisseurs . . . le marxisme est pour eux ce que sont pour nous les principes de 89" ⟨The Soviet Philosophers Are Builders . . . Marxism for Them Is What the Principles of Eighty-Nine Are for Us⟩.

-- *Libération*, July 19, 1954.

V. "La Paix par la paix. L'Union soviétique poursuit sa marche vers l'avenir" ⟨Peace through Peace: The Soviet Union Continues Its March toward the Future⟩.

-- *Libération*, July 20, 1954.

This piece was also published in *L'Unità* beginning July 15, 1954, and translated in *Oktiabr* (Moscow), no. 10 (October, 1954), pp. 130-41.

Libération made a separate printing of this interview and distributed it in tabloid form. This version was translated into German as *Meine Reise in die Sowjet-Union* (Düsseldorf: L. Zimmerer, 1954).

The titles, which Sartre had nothing to do with, give an idea of the low level of this interview, which shows unchecked enthusiasm. Remember that Sartre became ill in the U.S.S.R., and that his state of exhaustion upon his return must have blurred his customary critical sense a bit. Simone de Beauvoir adds concerning this interview: "[Sartre] rushed through it and when they offered to let him read what they had taken down, he begged off" (*Force of Circumstance*, p. 308). A few pages later, she tells us that even Ehrenburg "rebuked Sartre, in a friendly and almost grandfatherly tone, for certain details in the interview he had given to *Libération* (pp. 324-25).

54/261

Réponse de Sartre à une lettre de Hélène et Pierre Lazareff ⟨Sartre's Reply to a Letter from Hélène and Pierre Lazareff⟩.

-- *Libération*, July 22, 1954.

The Lazareffs, who had traveled in the U.S.S.R. at about the same time Sartre had, published a report in *France-Soir* which was rather hostile to the U.S.S.R. Sartre attacked them about this in his *Libération* interview, and the Lazareffs wrote a threatening letter to this magazine's editors, which Sartre, who was in Italy by then, replied to in a tone which was more playful than polemical.

54/262

"La coscienza dei francesi" ⟨The French Conscience⟩, interview.

-- *Il Contemporaneo* (Rome), July 31, 1954.

Interview dealing above all with the political situation in France after the armistice in Indochina.

54/263

"Une Interview de Jean-Paul Sartre" ⟨An Interview with Jean-Paul Sartre⟩, by Albert-Paul Lentin.

-- *France-U.R.S.S.*, no. 107 (August, 1954), p. 5; no. 108 (September, 1954), p. 4.

Reprints the gist of the remarks made to *Libération* (see 54/260).

55/264

L'Amitié, seule politique possible ⟨Friendship, the Only Possible Policy⟩, message addressed to the France-U.S.S.R. Congress in December, 1954.

-- *France-U.R.S.S.*, no. 112 (January, 1955), p. 15.

Sartre had not been personally able to attend this France-U.S.S.R. Congress, during which he was made vice-president of the association. In his message he affirms the need for Franco-Soviet friendship and states: *When I left for the U.S.S.R., I had been won over forever to the cause of peace: but since I have returned, I do not hesitate to denounce as perfectly criminal any policy which would risk taking the life of any one of these men and women whose work and immense hope moved me so deeply.*

1955

55/265

NEKRASSOV, play in eight tableaux.

a) Les Temps modernes, nos. 114-15 (June-July, 1955), pp. 2017-71; no. 116 (August, 1955), pp. 85-125; no. 117 (September, 1955), pp. 277-323.

Complete text of the play. The fifth tableau (*Les Temps modernes*, no. 116) has a mistake in the numbering: the last scene is marked 9 instead of 8.

b) Book. Gallimard, [1956].

There are only minor changes: the cast on pp. 6-10 has been added, and the mistaken numbering of the fifth tableau has been corrected.

c) Scenes 3 and 4 of the fourth tableau were first published in *Libération*, June 20, 1955.

NEKRASSOV, a farce in eight tableaux, translated by Sylvia Leeson and George Leeson.

t1) London: Hamish Hamilton, 1956.

t2) In THE DEVIL AND THE GOOD LORD, *and Two Other Plays* [KEAN, NEKRASSOV]. New York: Alfred A. Knopf, 1960.

t3) Ibid., in paperback. New York: Vintage Books, [1960].

t4) In KEAN; NEKRASSOV; THE TROJAN WOMEN. Penguin Books, [1969].

55/266

55/266

* *Tableau inédit de "Nekrassov": Le Bal des Futurs Fusillés* ⟨Unpublished Act from NEKRASSOV: The Future Victims' Ball⟩.

-- *Les Lettres françaises*, June 16-23, 1955.

This act, although one of the play's most successful, was cut out at the urging of Simone Berriau and Jean Meyer (see *Force of Circumstance*, p. 320). In it Sartre speaks in a scarcely concealed fashion of a number of well-known people: the newspaperman Champenois is very much like Georges Altman, and the writer Cocardeau like André Malraux.

NEKRASSOV was performed for the first time on June 8, 1955, at the Théâtre Antoine (under the direction of Simone Berriau) in a production by Jean Meyer with settings by Jean-Denis Malclès. Leading roles:

GEORGES DE VALERA	Michel Vitold
INSPECTEUR GOBLET	R.-J. Chauffard
JULES PALOTIN	Armontel
SIBILOT	Jean Parédès
VÉRONIQUE	Marie-Olivier

Like most of Sartre's plays, NEKRASSOV had rather tumultuous rehearsals: the opening had to be delayed several times as a result of the defection of several actors (including René Lefèvre), the apprehensions of Simone Berriau, and the problem of the length of the original manuscript. This manuscript, which included eleven tableaux in April, 1955, was reduced to eight and then in turn to seven. The printed version, such as we know it, was noticeably shortened during the performance.

On opening night, a tract handed out by the "Free Center for Russian States" condemned the play as "the mystification of a lounge lizard who never fought anywhere and whose hands have been dirty ever since he shook those of the executioners of the Russian people."

Labeled a "crypto-Communist" work, NEKRASSOV was of course ripped to shreds by the anti-Communist critics and lasted only sixty performances. On the other hand, the play was defended by Jean Cocteau in a letter published in *Libération* (June 20, 1955): "Sartre's play is something new. It shakes up all the comfortable little commitments everyone had settled into by giving Sartre as a reference. In NEKRASSOV he graciously makes fun of the people who didn't listen to and hear him properly. One could not possibly imagine any more grace, any more ease, any more malice without a shadow of spitefulness than there is in this *opéra-bouffe*, this end-of-the-century review. I imagine that *The Marriage of Figaro* was the same sort of escapade."

Revived in the fall of 1955, NEKRASSOV had its one hundredth performance in October and was even staged for the personnel at the Renault plant. The play was a great success beginning in November, 1955, at the Theater of Satire in Moscow under the title *Georges de Valera* (since Nekrassov was the name of a classical Russian writer). It was immediately translated as "Tol'ko pravda" ⟨It Is Nothing But the Truth⟩ by O. Savitch and Ilya Ehrenburg in the journal *Znamia* (no. 8 [1955], pp. 114-71) and was subsequently published in book form with an introduction by Ehrenburg (Moscow: Iskusstvo, 1956; 10,000 copies printed). There is also a Ukrainian translation (*Nekrassov* [Kiev, 1956]) and a Hungarian translation (*Föbelovendök Klubja* ⟨The Firing-Squad Victims' Club⟩ [Budapest, 1955]).

Sartre seems to have had the idea for NEKRASSOV since 1952, when he was writing the first part of *The Communists and Peace*. A bit of gossip published in the June 24, 1952, *Paris-Presse-L'Intransigeant* points out: "The subject . . . of Sartre's next play will be war and peace. It is to be a work which is still a little philosophical [reference to THE DEVIL AND THE GOOD LORD] but is meant to be a burlesque." Subsequently, this idea became more precise and turned into a projected play about McCarthyism and psychoanalysis. The work will be announced untitled by the press at the beginning of 1955 and described in May, 1955, as a "farce in eight tableaux."

In an interview given in 1960 (see 60/346), Sartre says: [NEKRASSOV is] *only a half successful play. I should have focused on the paper rather than the theft, which has no intrinsic interest. It would have been better to show it as a part of running the paper. But that isn't the only reason the critics thought the play was bad. I attacked the press; the press counterattacked.*

We are sorry that NEKRASSOV has not been performed on a Parisian stage since 1955, because it reads like one of the best Sartre has ever written. Furthermore, it has been recently revived by Hubert Gignoux at the National Theater in Strasbourg with great success. One may consult with profit the *Cahier de documentation*, no. 31, on NEKRASSOV, published on that occasion by the theater.

Excerpts from the play have been recorded by Pierre Brasseur for Pathé-Marconi, on record no. DTX 148, 1955.

INTERVIEWS ABOUT "NEKRASSOV"

55/267

"Avant la création de *Nekrassov* au Théâtre Antoine, Sartre nous dit . . ." ⟨On the Eve of the Opening of NEKRASSOV at the Antoine Theater, Sartre Says . . . ⟩.

-- *Le Monde*, June 1, 1955.

" . . . Said Jean-Paul Sartre," translated by Rima Rell Dreck.

-- *Yale French Studies*, no. 16 (winter, 1955-56), pp. 3, 7.

Very important interview which gives some details about NEKRASSOV (a play which *barely alters contemporary reality* and is *in the tradition of Aristophanes*) and then tackles more general topics.

Sartre deplores the ostracism which seems to have been decreed for NEKRASSOV: *Some newspapers are refusing to accept publicity notices--which are paid, of course--for my play.* Then he speaks at length of his autobiography (see 63/383), of his projected essay on existentialism and Marxism, of the R.D.R. ⟨Revolutionary Peoples' Assembly⟩ (see 48/168-48/178), of the character Dubreuilh in Simone de Beauvoir's *The Mandarins*:

In a sense, Dubreuilh is not like me at all. He holds a political position, he assumes political responsibilities: he has gone a lot farther than I have. All I want to do myself is prove that it is possible for left-wing writers to keep on acting as writers.

At the same time he shows how he conceives of his political role:

On the level of technical political action, I am incompetent. My own involvement in politics is limited to voting. If the sufferings of our time and the way out of them I glimpse are reflected in what I write, it's as a writer that I am aware of this and happy about it: in this sense there is bad faith in condemning me for not being any more of a man of action than Mauriac and Montherlant.

To conclude, Sartre defines his relations with the Communist Party.

If I were convinced of the truth of new facts, I would reveal them even though doing so might by chance embarrass the P.C. ⟨Communist Party⟩ . . .

But I insist on saying that in order to have the right to make any valid criticism of the Communist movement, a man has to work with it. Ninety percent of the criticisms made of it are based upon a major failure to understand its definition and vocation.

55/268

"Il n'y a pas de méchants dans *Nekrassov*" ⟨There Are No Bad Guys in NEKRASSOV⟩, interview by Raphaël Valensi.

-- *L'Aurore*, June 7, 1955.

The only things of interest in this interview are Valensi's perfidious comments. On June 6, 1955, all the journalistic hacks of Paris were called on to appear at Louis Jouvet's loge at the Théâtre Antoine to be received one at a time by Sartre. Valensi finds this a rather cavalier way of managing things.

There are probably other interviews besides the ones we cite below.

55/269

"Au train où vont les réactions je ne suis pas sûr que ma pièce trouve un public" ⟨At the Rate Things Are Going, I Am Not Sure My Play Will Have an Audience⟩, interview by Serge Montigny.

-- *Combat*, June 7, 1955.

I meant NEKRASSOV *to be a satire. In the first place because that's the only way one can talk about today's society, and then because we've had a sort of latent censorship in France which has been suffocating this kind of theater. . . .*

A certain kind of newspaper is already protesting without knowing what my play is about and without having been hurt by it.

55/270

"*Nekrassov* n'est pas une pièce à clef" ⟨NEKRASSOV Is Not a *Piece à Clef*⟩, interview by Paul Morelle.

-- *Libération*, June 7, 1955.

My play is an undisguised satire on the machinations of anti-Communist propaganda.

55/270

Sartre also says that he did not mean to attack any Parisian newspaperman directly, and he cites as an example the character of Palotin: this part was originally supposed to be played by Louis de Funès, whose short stature would have made the audience think of Pierre Lazareff, but he was replaced by Armontel who, at six feet five, made those who insisted on finding real people in the play think not of Lazareff but Pierre Brisson.

55/271

"En dénonçant dans ma nouvelle pièce les procédés de la presse anticommuniste . . . je veux apporter une contribution d'écrivain à la lutte pour la paix" ⟨By Denouncing the Tactics of the Anti-Communist Press in My New Play . . . I Wanted to Make a Writer's Contribution to the Struggle for Peace⟩, interview by Guy Leclerc.

-- *L'Humanité*, June 8, 1955.

I want to make a writer's contribution to the struggle for peace. We made commitments in Vienna; we must uphold them. . . . This play shows my intention to deal with social reality without myths. I want to be completely clear. But it must be said, and said clearly, that there is a gap between the subjects I want to deal with and contemporary Parisian audiences. Under such conditions, there is a basic paradox in having a play performed at all.

55/271 A

"Quand Jean-Paul Sartre présente *Nekrassov*" ⟨When Jean-Paul Sartre Presents NEKRASSOV⟩, interview by A. L.

-- *Le Parisien libéré*, June 8, 1955.

55/272

"Avec Jean-Paul Sartre à la veille de *Nekrassov*" ⟨With Jean-Paul Sartre before the Opening of NEKRASSOV⟩, interview by Claudine Chonez.

-- *France-Observateur*, June 9, 1955.

55/272 A

"*Nekrassov*: Nous avons posé, avant la générale, des questions à J.-P. Sartre. Voici ses réponses" ⟨NEKRASSOV: Before the Dress Rehearsal We Asked J.-P. Sartre Some Questions. Here Are His Answers⟩, interview.

-- *Aux Ecoutes*, June 10, 1955.

This play is meant to deal with reality without myths . . . NEKRASSOV *takes place in 1952. . . . When readers can only choose between a skimpy left-wing press and an immense right-wing press maneuvered by the monied interests, there isn't a free press.*

Sartre also points out that his play was inspired by Gogol's *Revizor*.

55/273

"La Pièce vise les institutions et non des individus" ⟨The Play Aims at Institutions, Not Individuals⟩, interview-article by J.-F. Rolland.

-- *L'Humanité-Dimanche*, June 19, 1955.

I didn't want . . . my characters to be simply black or white: Sibilot is not just a newspaperman who has sold out. He is also mystified, a victim of the ideology his paper upholds. . . . A left-wing satire ought to satirize institutions rather than individuals.

After having commented on the newspapers' responses and on the criticisms of his play, Sartre announces the interview he is going to give to *Théâtre populaire* (see 55/276) and talks about the contradictions and the crisis of bourgeois theater.

55/273 A

Short statement to René Gordon.

-- *Les Dernières Nouvelles d'Alsace*, June 20, 1955.

I wanted to give my play the tone of a farce by enlarging the truth.

55/274

Speech given in Helsinki on June 26, 1955, to the World Peace Assembly.

a) Complete text in *Assemblée mondiale de la Paix, Helsinki, 22-29 Juin 1955* ⟨World Peace Assembly, Helsinki,

June 22-29, 1955⟩. Published by the Secretariat of the World Peace Council. Pp. 220-27. B.N. listing: 8° R. 60722.

b) Excerpts. *La Paix que nous voulons ne doit pas ressembler à ce qu'on a nommé "l'entre-deux guerres"* ⟨The Peace We Want Must Not Be Like the So-called "Time between the Wars"⟩. *L'Humanité*, June 27, 1955.

Cold War and Anti-Communism.

-- *Masses and Mainstream*, VIII, no. 8 (August, 1955), 26-30.

Sartre means to show what brings men of very different outlooks together in Helsinki in spite of their differences: the desire for peace, of course, but not just any peace. According to Sartre, the desire for peace is strongest in the masses today. This desire is perhaps a result of the H-Bomb:

The H-Bomb has a sort of negative universality: it can have an effect on anyone no matter how far away. This negative universality has led directly to a movement of positive universalization; permanent and universal danger has given a concrete, precise meaning to that formerly vague term, the human species. The human species is no longer a biological but a historical, social, political term; it is made up of those hundreds of thousands of men who, although still separated by very different interests and beliefs, are united by a common danger and a common will to escape catastrophe at any cost . . . Either this peace will never come about, or the people will impose it on their governments.

It is not a question of maintaining the status quo--coalition politics and the cold war--but of the people's breaking up the coalitions. *It is not just a question of demanding certain negative measures such as banning atomic weapons; wanting to change the world and wanting peace are one and the same.* [The cold war] *is a structure of international relations which has had repercussions even in the internal structure of nations.* Sartre attributes the cold war implicitly to Stalinism and explicitly to McCarthyism, which has engendered internal rigidity and terror. Peace must be a new regime, *an indissoluble whole, an indestructible bond between a certain kind of international relations and a certain kind of political and social relations within nations. . . . Beyond the great division among social regimes, a new economic fact must appear: peace and peaceful coexistence are tied to economic stability, and economic stability, in a period of reconversion* [i.e., of war industries], *is tied to a sort of giveaway economy* [i.e., for underdeveloped nations]. Aid should be given simultaneously by the two great powers without any intention to enslave. Coexistence is not the mere contiguity but the cooperation of the U.S.S.R. and the U.S.A. *This cooperation alone can break up the coalition system.*

Sartre then comes out in favor of the independence and sovereignty of nations rather than their neutrality, which has meaning only after war has already broken out. He takes a stand in favor of German reunification.

Then he attacks the colonial problem, and says that the colonial period is ending: *The increasing consciousness of African and Asiatic nations should be a factor for peace.* France ought to concede to the Algerian, Tunisian, and Moroccan claims through peaceful negotiation.

Sartre concludes that to want peace and to want freedom are one and the same: *Since peace . . . requires that each nation--whether in the West, or in the East--return to independence, mutual respect and coexistence in equality, our peace can mean only one thing: the possibility for nations and for men to be the masters of their own fate, in a word, freedom. This, it seems to me, is the common sense of our undertaking: we want to build peace through freedom and bring freedom to the peoples of the world through peace.*

55/275

La Leçon de Stalingrad ⟨The Lesson of Stalingrad⟩.

-- *France-U.R.S.S.*, no. 115 (April, 1955), pp. 4-5.

Text of a short speech given on February 20, 1955, at the Salle Pleyel, during a commemorative meeting organized by the France-U.S.S.R. Association.

In this speech, which marks without a doubt the height of his pro-Soviet position, and whose emphatic nature is partly explained by the fact that it was a speech given at a meeting, Sartre begins by recalling the historic importance of the battle:

Our fate was not decided in Normandy or in Belgium but in the U.S.S.R. beside the Volga. It was Stalingrad that made the Normandy landing possible; I'd even say necessary. If the English and Americans wanted to take part in the final victory, they had to, willy nilly, take part in the assault. So what the repeated requests of the Russian command had failed in the dark hours to obtain was hastily agreed upon after Stalingrad. That's not the first time someone has rushed reinforcements to a victory.

Sartre sees two lessons to be drawn from this victory:

The first is that it would be dangerous to make a distinction between the Russian people and their leaders. The courage and will with which the Soviet soldiers fought prove that the regime has popular support. *It has been claimed they fought for patriotic motives. And this is certainly not false. But a homeland is not a climate or a soil or even a language. It's a collective undertaking, a struggle against the past, a patient building of the future. These men agreed to die for Russia. But it was not for the Russia of the czars they gave their lives, nor for eternal Russia. It was for* their *Russia, for the Socialist Russia which had freed them from oppression and was building their sons' future. . . . The people have made their regime and it is inseparable from them. . . . The second lesson we should draw, since 1943, from Stalingrad, is that--all recognition and social considerations set aside--our political interest is to draw closer to the U.S.S.R. . . . On the occasion of this new anniversary of Stalingrad, we must reveal the absurdity of those of our leaders who are making the unforgivable mistake of misunderstanding the most elementary necessities by reversing alliances and arming the Germans, our age-old enemies, against Russia, our ally in 1914 and 1940.*

Before a people who have shed their blood to save their future--and the future of the universe--and who have proved by their sacrifices that they meant to make *history, not submit to it; before a people who were for half a century, each time Germany threatened the peace, always there at our side, only one attitude is possible--gratitude and friendship.*

Let us recall that Sartre was a member of the France-U.S.S.R. Association until November, 1956.

55/275 A

Otrazhat' nastoiachtcheie skvoz' prizmu buduchtchego ⟨Reflect the Present through the Prism of the Future⟩.

-- *Inostranaia Literatura*, no. 5 ([May], 1955), pp. 252-54.

In this article, written especially for Russian readers on the occasion of a special issue of *Inostranaia Literatura* on the October Revolution, Sartre defines the writer's role and shows what he can contribute to the ideological battle and the struggle for peace.

55/276

"Jean-Paul Sartre nous parle de théâtre" ⟨Jean-Paul Sartre Talks about the Theater⟩, talk with Bernard Dort.

a) Théâtre populaire, no. 15 (September-October, 1955), pp. 1-9.

b) Excerpts. *Controverse J.-P. Sartre-Jean Vilar* ⟨The J.-P. Sartre-Jean Vilar Controversy⟩. *L'Express* (daily), November 24, 1955.

Jean Vilar replies to Sartre's claim *The T.N.P.* ⟨Théâtre National Populaire⟩ *has no popular audience.*

In this important interview, Sartre begins by contrasting the bourgeois theater and the people's theater, and then situates the contemporary playwrights.

People's theater. . . . To me this expression means all the theater. . . . The first thing to show a popular audience is plays meant for it--written for it and talking about it. . . . In France, the only example of popular theater I know of was the tour Claude Martin made in the factories with a play about Henri Martin. . . . Only bourgeois theater has not been a people's theater. The whole theatrical tradition was popular till the advent of the bourgeoisie.

Sartre sees a break between Corneille and Racine, however, and a break in the tradition of people's theater between 1660 and 1730. He continues:

Personally, I no longer have anything to say to the bourgeois.

But the real problem is undoubtedly not that of the structures of the people's theater, or even of its themes, but of its technique. . . .

Yes, for me that's the real problem: to organize act and spoken word in such a way that the spoken word, instead of seeming merely superfluous, retains a power surpassing simple eloquence. . . .

I liked Waiting for Godot *very much. I'd even say that it's the best thing which has been done in the theater for thirty years. But all the themes in* Godot *are bourgeois: the themes of loneliness, despair, the commonplace, the inability to communicate. They are all inner products of bourgeois loneliness. And what Godot stands for--God or the Revolution--is not what matters. . . . What matters is that Godot does not come because the heroes are weak men, and that because of this "sin"--because men are this way--he cannot come.*

55/276

.. All Ionesco's work shows us a proverbial society: the unity of man seen inside out. . . . The problem for these writers is integration, . . . any kind of integration, their integration into any kind of society: in this sense, in being apolitical they are also reactionary.

Adamov's case is a little different. In fact, he's the only one we can expect something of in the realm of people's theater.

Before concluding with a discussion of *The Salem Witches* (see 56/287), Sartre alludes to a show, *a peace festival*, he planned to put on at the Vél d'Hiv' around 1953 with Fernand Léger, and then points out what separates him from Bertolt Brecht: *I deeply believe myself that all that mystification should be in a sense mystifying. Or rather that when you're dealing with a partly mystified crowd you can't rely solely on the crowd's critical responses. You have to give it a counter-mystification. Just the way it was done during the Counter-Reformation by the Jesuits--those Jesuits who were the teachers of our friends the Communists.*

55/277

Ces gens-là nous aiment . . . ⟨Those People Love Us⟩.

-- *France-U.R.S.S.*, no. 121 (October, 1955), pp. 3-4.

On the eve of MM. Edgar Faure and Antoine Pinay's trip to Moscow, Sartre, referring to the enthusiastic welcome Leningrad gave to the French voyagers on the liner *Batory*, hopes for a political rapprochement between the U.S.S.R. and France and exhorts the French ministers to keep in mind the friendship which is growing up between the two peoples.

55/278

"Une Soirée à Pékin avec Jean-Paul Sartre et Simone de Beauvoir" ⟨An Evening in Peking with Jean-Paul Sartre and Simone de Beauvoir⟩, interview-article by Paul Tillard.

-- *L'Humanité-Dimanche*, October 23, 1955.

Tillard, who spent an evening with the two writers at a Peking little theater and then a restaurant, reports their comments, which express an unreserved enthusiasm for China.

55/279

"Tout dans ce pays est émouvant" ⟨Everything in This Country Moves You⟩, interview by Pierre Hentges.

-- *L'Humanité*, November 1, 1955.

Interview made in Moscow upon Sartre's return from China and giving his impressions of the U.S.S.R., which he is visiting for the second time.

To the question, "What do they think of the Russians in China?" Sartre replies: *I'll only say this: every time I walked around the streets there, they took me for a Russian (for the Chinese, a white man is a Russian) and they welcomed me with open arms. . . . To think there could be any reason for a break between these two peoples is sheer madness.*

Sartre says of the U.S.S.R.: *This country is far more moving, more touching than anything I'd been able to imagine.*

55/280

Mes impressions sur la Chine nouvelle ⟨My Impressions of the New China⟩, article translated into Chinese.

-- *Jen Minh Jen Pao* ⟨The People's Daily⟩ (Peking), November 2, 1955.

This article is cited by David Rousset, who attacks it very violently in *Demain* (January 5-11, 1955). We were unable to consult it. Sartre says that he said more or less the same thing he said in his article for *France-Observateur* (see 55/281). Concerning the attack by Rousset, who in his article had written "Sartre is a traitor," the latter had this to say: *I let him talk: you don't answer Rousset; you let him earn his daily bread the best he can* (SITUATIONS, VII, p. 135).

55/281

La Chine que j'ai vue ⟨The China I Saw⟩.

-- *France-Observateur*, December 1, 1955; December 8, 1955.

A preliminary note specifies: "This article is excerpted from a long study which Jean-Paul Sartre is presently writing about his recent trip to China."

Sartre never completed this project. It was Simone de Beauvoir who took it up with her book, *La Longue Marche* ⟨The Long March⟩ (Gallimard, 1957). *Les Temps modernes* also published a special issue (nos. 127-28 [September-October, 1956]) entitled "Chine d'hier et d'aujourd'hui" ⟨China Yesterday and Today⟩ (see also 54/250).

The article begins by comparing the Russian Revolution, which sprang from defeat, and the Chinese Revolution, which was born of victory. What is striking from the outset in China is that the country is in order: *Paradoxically, the Chinese Revolution began by banishing inflation, destitution, price rises, insecurity, anarchy, and local despotisms--in short, the train of abuses which conservatives think must accompany revolutions. . . . All the terrors of the revolution were caused by the weakness of the central authority: the reason why terror is an unknown word in China, why Mao Tse-tung's government has been able to show the admirable moderation I saw so many signs of, is that his victorious army, by putting down roots among the people, gave him from the start what no other revolutionary government ever had--the calm of omnipotence.*

Sartre continues with a description of the original characteristics of the Chinese Revolution. He stresses especially the example of the "happy capitalist" whom the state maintains because he knows his job: *Yes, that's what you can see in China: a capitalist who is artificially maintained by the very process which ought to "eliminate" him, a capitalist who by his unfailing pursuit of his capitalist activities, voluntarily contributes to the construction of the regime which will destroy him.*

Speaking of the construction of Chinese socialism, Sartre notes: *Everything leads us to a singular discovery: the present reality of China is her future. . . . In fifty years, Mao Tse-tung promises that a new civilization will flower. . . . Sometimes this projected half-century set down on the great plains upset us personally: it created a complicity among the Chinese welcoming us which left us out. One of us said, "In China, you feel already dead." That's often true; for the most tangible reality is a future the young will see and we most certainly will not. A hospital--brand new, well painted, very modern, but still waiting for some of its equipment and all of its patients--a factory as big as a town but still empty, all these ruins of the future lead you far more than the Colosseum does to meditate on death.*

55/282

"Sartre Views the New China," interview by K. S. Karol.

-- *New Statesman and Nation*, December 3, 1955.

After having noted that Sartre is very hard to interview because he talks so much, leads the discussion himself, and changes the subject very quickly, Karol summarizes the comments which Sartre made on his return from China and which are exactly the same as those in the *France-Observateur* article.

NOTE: On February 2, 1956, Sartre presided over a press conference on China which was organized at the Palais d'Orsay by the Friends of France and China. He especially protested certain articles by Robert Guillain and said in particular that he had had complete freedom of movement during his trip to China. See *L'Humanité* for February 3 and some excerpts from Sartre's remarks in the February 18, 1956, *Femmes françaises*.

55/NOTE 1.

In his book, *Sartre par lui-même* ⟨Sartre by Himself⟩ (Seuil, 1955) Francis Jeanson quotes many scraps from conversations he had with Sartre. Let us point out that this excellent study, which we have mentioned many times already, is at the present date the biggest success in the Ecrivains de toujours series, with 150,000 copies printed up to 1968.

55/NOTE 2.

In the "Connaissance de Sartre" ⟨Understanding Sartre⟩ issue of the *Cahiers de la Compagnie Madeleine Renaud--Jean-Louis Barrault* ⟨Notebooks of the Madeleine Renaud--Jean-Louis Barrault Company⟩ (Cahier XIII [October, 1955]), Colette Audry reports on pp. 54-55 the subject of a play Sartre was planning to write and told to her. This subject, in which we find elements of BARIONA, THE CHIPS ARE DOWN, and THE FLIES, is entitled "Le Pari" ⟨The Wager, as in Pascal's famous "Le Pari"⟩. We reprint the passage *in extenso* below:

"The curtain rises on a destitute couple of displaced persons who are at the depths of their despair, all the more so since the woman has discovered she is expecting. The woman and the man are talking. The husband wants the wife to have an abortion; the wife instinctively rebels. The husband argues, tells her that if it's to have a kid who'll have a life like theirs, it really isn't worth it to bring another wretch into this world. The wife answers, 'But, who says he'll be wretched?' Discussion between husband and wife, who do not agree about what will come out of this pregnancy. Suddenly, a thunderclap; fantastic effect in the style of the medieval theater.

"Appearance of a supernatural, let's say more-or-less diabolical character.

"This character takes an interest in the couple and says, 'My friends, I see you are uncertain about your child's lot. I'm going to give you a big present. I'm going to show you the life which awaits him, and then by contemplating it you shall decide whether you ought to keep it or get rid of it. You understand of course that his life is irrevocably traced out on the level of episode, plot, and action: nothing in it can be altered. Everyone is ready behind that curtain; one person only is missing--your child. Do you wish to see his life?' The couple acquiesces. Thunder-clap.

"The curtain parts and reveals a stage filled with different mansions, as in the Middle Ages. All the characters who are to meet the child and then the man are there, each one in a square.

"With the help of the characters in the different squares, the supernatural character gives a lively description of the existence of this human being who is to be born. It is an atrocious existence: troubles, poverty, and finally death at the stake.

"It grows dark, the curtain falls and the supernatural character now says to the couple, 'Now that you know the life your child will have, all you have to do is decide. Good-by, my friends.' And he disappears.

"The husband gloats and says to his wife, 'Well now you know what you have to do; if you feel like giving birth to a wretch, go ahead, but you know for sure his life will be a martyrdom.' And the wife stubbornly replies, 'Personally, I'll bet he'll pull through all right.'

"--But you idiot, how can he, since nothing in his life can be changed?--Maybe he won't change his life, but I'll bet he'll transform it."

"Faced with a dimwit like this, the husband is discouraged, and the couple disappears after having decided that the wife will have her kid. This is the end of the first part.

"When the second part begins, the curtain rises on the same squares with the same characters as before, only this time there is one extra character--the young man who is the son of the couple of displaced persons.

"Thus the audience knows what his life will be and he is the only one who does not know what is going to happen.

"As a matter of fact he makes no material changes in

his existence, and his life ends as agreed at the stake. But thanks to his personal contribution, his choice, and his sense of freedom, he transforms this atrocious life into a sublime life.

"I think that this is a subject which gives us an almost physical understanding of what Sartre means by the word *freedom*."

55/NOTE 3.

In an article entitled "Jean-Paul Sartre: A Portrait" (*Dalhousie Review*, XLV, no. 1 [spring, 1967], 78-89), Peter H. Thomas describes a lecture on time Sartre gave at the Amphithéâtre Richelieu of the Sorbonne in the fall of 1955.

1956

NEKRASSOV, play in eight tableaux.

See 55/265.

56/282 A

"Jean-Paul Sartre," interview in Russian.

-- *Teatr* (Moscow), no. 1 ([January], 1956), pp. 156-59.

Excellent interview Sartre gave in Moscow on his return from China about contemporary French theater. Criticizing the conditions under which French theater operates (bourgeois public limited to two to three hundred thousand people, excessive centralization in Paris, influence of the right-wing press), Sartre advocates a new theatrical policy which would give the true calling of the theater, that of reaching the masses, back to it. He takes a dig in passing at Jean Anouilh (who *for thirty years has done nothing but elaborate one sole and solitary idea: purity can only be attained in death; life is a compromise*), and defends, in spite of certain reservations, the Théâtre National Populaire, which he would like to see perform in Moscow. He judges, to conclude, that the predominant foreign influence is that of Bertolt Brecht and that the success of Anton Chekhov's plays in France is due to their lack of action and their atmosphere of impotence and suffocation.

56/282 B

Slovo k sovietskim druziam ⟨Message to Our Soviet Friends⟩.

-- *Pravda*, [January] 2, 1956, p. 2.

A brief New Year's message in which Sartre expresses satisfaction that 1955 has brought an increased number of contacts between France and the U.S.S.R.; he hopes that in the interest of peace there will be more in 1956.

56/283

Le Réformisme et les fétiches ⟨Reformism and Fetishes⟩.

a) Les Temps modernes, no. 122 (February, 1956), pp. 1153-64.

b) Reprinted in SITUATIONS, VII.

Pierre Hervé, a Communist intellectual who performed important functions in the P.C. ⟨Communist Party⟩ had published in January, 1956, a little work entitled *La Révolution et les fétiches* ⟨Revolution and Fetishes⟩ (published by La Table Ronde) in which he criticized in a guarded way the absence of democratic discussion and the dogmatism of his party. The book had some repercussions and was violently attacked by the Communist press, especially by Guy Besse in the January 25, 1956, *Humanité*. On February 14, Hervé was expelled from the party by decision of the Political Bureau.

The article Sartre devoted to the affair is dated February 10, 1956, that is, four days before Hervé's expulsion. It is striking in the moderation of its tone, even though it judges Communist intellectuals very harshly. Wanting to maintain the good relations with the P.C. he enjoyed at the time, Sartre pointed out the inadequacies of Hervé's book but at the same time deplored the methods Guy Besse used to criticize him. He added: *Borne by history, the P.C. shows extraordinary objective intelligence--it is rarely wrong and does what is needed--but this intelligence, which is one with* praxis,*is not often embodied in its intellectuals*. As a matter of fact, although [Marxism] *has been, since the death of bourgeois thought, our only Culture, since it alone enables us to understand men, works, and events*,the Communist intellectuals' resignation has left it to non-Marxists to carry out investigations for which Marxist methods would have been more fruitful. (Among the books which *have advanced knowledge* and which he emphasized *have* never *included Communists as their authors*, Sartre cites in particular the works of Guillemin and Lévi-Strauss.) His conclusion is decisive: *Marxism in France has come to a halt*. Sartre will subsequently analyze the causes of this halt in *Search for a Method* (see also 56/284).

56/283

Hervé replied in *Lettre à Sartre et à quelques autres par la même occasion* ⟨A Letter to Sartre and Some Others Concerning the Same Subject⟩ (La Table Ronde, April, 1956). In their May, 1956, issue, *Les Temps modernes* announced for publication an article by Sartre entitled "Réponse à Pierre Hervé et à quelques autres" ⟨Reply to Pierre Hervé and to Several Others⟩. It was to serve as a conclusion to *The Communists and Peace* but was never written, having given way to *The Ghost of Stalin.*

56/283 A

Interview given to a Slovak paper.

a) Pravda [?], beginning of 1956. Unconsulted text whose date is difficult to determine.

b) Excerpts translated into Russian in *Literaturnaia Gazeta* ([March] 15, 1956), p. 4.

This interview, given in Paris, bears on literature and on Sartre's projects:

Literature is worthless if politics is unknown to it and it has no connection with real life. By real life I mean life in all its complexity, richness and diversity. . . . The writer must show not only the destiny of heroes but also the social conditions which determine that destiny. . . . I think so-called "psychological novels"--those whose authors stress only the passions of their characters--are doomed to failure.

Concerning his autobiography, Sartre says: *I would like many fifty-year-olds to recognize themselves in the hero of this book* ⟨from French translation by Rybalka and Contat⟩.

56/284

Réponse à Pierre Naville ⟨Reply to Pierre Naville⟩.

a) Les Temps modernes, no. 123 (March-April, 1956), pp. 1510-25.

b) Reprinted in SITUATIONS, VII.

Reply, dated March 23, 1956, to an article by Pierre Naville entitled "Les mésaventures de Nekrassov" ⟨The Misadventures of Nekrassov⟩ (*France-Observateur*, March 8, 1956). This article attacked the one Sartre wrote about Hervé (see 56/283). Naville, in substance, wrote that it is false to claim that Marxism has come to a halt unless one equates Marxism, as Naville said

Sartre had, with the Communist Party. Sartre denounces Naville's mistaken interpretation of his article. His reply gives him a chance to say more precisely what he thinks about the claim Naville contested, to state briefly his idea of the meaning of the de-Stalinization announced by the Twentieth Congress, and to ask that there be, among leftists, *even in the liveliest discussions, a tone of courtesy and camaraderie*. You will note that this is the last article, prior to the break following the Hungarian business, in which Sartre defends the P.C. ⟨Communist Party⟩ *(I am far from claiming that the party has never been wrong. I am only saying that on the whole, its stands have been correct)*.

Naville replied with "Les nouvelles mésaventures de Nekrassov" ⟨The New Misadventures of Nekrassov⟩ (*France-Observateur*, April 19, 1956). His two articles are reprinted in the book *L'Intellectuel Communiste* ⟨The Communist Intellectual⟩ (Rivière, 1956, pp. 57-60 and 60-64). Let us recall, if need be, that Pierre Naville had been since 1927 a Marxist oppositional intellectual of Trotskyist tendencies, and the author of numerous works which Sartre in this article judges very harshly.

56/285

Le Colonialisme est un système ⟨Colonialism Is a System⟩.

a) In *Colonialisme et guerre d'Algérie* ⟨Colonialism and the Algerian War⟩. Brochure. Centre des Intellectuels, 1956. Includes, among others, pieces by Jean-Jacques Mayoux, Dyonis Mascolo, Robert Barrat, Daniel Guérin, Michel Leiris, and Jean Rous.

b) Les Temps modernes, no. 123 (March-April, 1956), pp. 1371-86.

c) Reprinted in SITUATIONS, V.

Text of remarks made at a meeting for peace in Algeria held on January 27, 1956, at the Salle Wagram under the aegis of the Action Committee of Intellectuals Against Continuing the War in North Africa. Sartre's remarks of this meeting are preceded in the same issue of *Les Temps modernes* (pp. 1366-70) by Aimé Césaire's.

Sartre warns against *neocolonialist mystification* and in doing so undertakes an analysis of the economic mechanisms of colonial exploitation from the nineteenth century to the present. His argumentation, which is thoroughly documented, scarcely seems contestable. He arrives at the following conclusion: *The only thing we can and should try to do--but today it is the main thing that needs to be done--is to struggle*

56/285

[at the] *side* [of the Algerian people] *to free the Algerians and the French together from colonial tyranny.*

56/286

Interview by M. N. in Serbian.

-- *Politika* (Belgrade), [July] 25, 1956, p. 7.

Interview given during a trip to Yugoslavia and dealing chiefly with the theater (Samuel Beckett, Arthur Adamov, Eugène Ionesco).

Sartre will subsequently give several interviews and articles to *Politika.*

56/287

Les Sorcières de Salem ⟨The Salem Witches⟩, film script drawn from Arthur Miller's play, *The Crucible.*

a) "*Les Sorcières de Salem* à l'écran: Dans la prison de Salem. Dialogue de Jean-Paul Sartre" ⟨The Salem Witches on the Screen: In the Salem Jail. Dialogue by Jean-Paul Sartre"⟩. *Les Lettres françaises*, August 2-8, 1956.

Only published excerpt of Sartre's adaptation: one of the final scenes between John Proctor and his wife, Elizabeth. Proctor is going to be hanged if he does not sign a confession that he is a witch. His wife comes to beg him to live. He refuses. She finally approves of his choice.

This Cornelian situation (cf. *Polyeucte*) is rendered in an eminently Sartrian dialogue. Example: *You thought I was your judge and I was only your executioner.*

b) Unpublished script. There are several manuscripts of this, one of which is dated "November '55-February '56," and then, for the last part, "April-May, '56," and another of which is a typed version 286 pages long (with notes added to the beginning and the end) covering 669 shots.

Sartre had once thought about publishing the text of *The Salem Witches* and of "Typhus" in a single volume (see 53/NOTE).

The story of this script is rather easy to determine. Sartre had judged very harshly the adaptation by Marcel Aymé staged with great success at the Théâtre Sarah-Bernhardt in 1955, and he had spoken at length about the play in an interview given to *Théâtre populaire* (see 55/276) shortly after NEKRASSOV:

[I like] *many things about Rouleau's production. As for the play, what bothers me is the ambiguity of its conclusion. Out of a specifically American phenomenon they've made something which is universal and which, at the same time, no longer says anything, except perhaps that intolerance is everywhere and that everything always comes down to the same thing.*

The mistake was no doubt to have let Marcel Aymé adapt the play. Thereby the whole violent, passionate side of it disappeared. The "witches" are no longer stressed; the social dimension of the business has been completely blurred out.

As a matter of fact, the play concerns a struggle between old-stock immigrants and new, between rich and poor, for land ownership. We no longer see this in Aymé's adaptation. We see a man being pursued for no clear reason, and the entire conclusion of The Salem Witches *springs from a disturbing idealism. Montand's death, and the fact that he accepts it, would have made sense if this had been presented as a rebellious act at the heart of a social struggle. But in the performance at the Théâtre Sarah-Bernhardt, this social struggle has become incomprehensible, and Montand's death seems to be a purely ethical attitude, not a free act he performs in order to spread scandal abroad and effectively reject his situation, the only act he can still perform.*

Watered down and castrated this way, Miller's play seems to me to be in a very precise sense a mystifying play. . . . And this because we never get a clear view of the real political and social aspects of the witch-hunt phenomenon.

What led Sartre to adapt *The Salem Witches* to the screen was his need, after NEKRASSOV, to write another piece against McCarthyism. The script was written between November, 1955, and May, 1956. The movie, which was produced by Raymond Rouleau and starred Yves Montand, Simone Signoret, and Mylène Demongeot in the leading roles, came out in 1957 (see Appendix).

56/288

Remarks at a colloquium organized in Venice from March 25 to March 31, 1956, by the European Culture Society.

a) Complete text of the debates. "Discordia Concors: Rencontre Est-Ouest à Venise" ⟨*Discordia Concors*: The East-West Meeting in Venice⟩. *Comprendre* (Venice), no. 16, September, 1956, pp. 201-301. An index allows one to refer rapidly to Sartre's remarks.

b) Excerpts. "Entre Merleau-Ponty, Sartre, Silone et les écrivains soviétiques, premier dialogue Est-Ouest à

56/288

Venise" ⟨The First East-West Dialogue in Venice between Merleau-Ponty, Sartre, Silone and the Soviet Writers⟩. *L'Express*, October 19, 1956.

The European Culture Society is an organization which was founded in 1950 and which brings together scientists, artists, writers, and intellectuals from most Eastern and Western European countries. At the Venice meeting the following big names took part: Mikhaïl Alpatov, Karl Barth, J. D. Bernal, Umberto Campagnolo, Konstantin Fedine, Jacques Havet, Jaroslaw Iwaszkiewicz,Carlo Levi, Maurice Merleau-Ponty, Guido Piovene, Boris Polevoi-Kampov, Alan Pryce-Jones, Marko Ristić, Sartre, Ignazio Silone, Stephen Spender, Giuseppe Ungaretti, Vercors, and Victor Volodine.

The complete text of the debates is rather dull reading, but as a document it has a certain interest--especially if one considers its date. The Twentieth Congress of the C.P. ⟨Communist Party⟩ of the Soviet Union had just taken place, and had speeded up the thaw in East-West relations. A few months later the Hungarian business was going for a time to put a brutal stop to these developments, and the "board conference" decided on for the coming year at the end of the meeting could not be held.

The debate begins with the concept of commitment and continues, with many detours, with an exploration of the possibilities of exchanges between cultured men in the East and West.

For us the chief interest of this text is that it is the only one recording a discussion between Sartre and Merleau-Ponty--(concerning the circumstances in which the two men come together again at this meeting in Venice after nearly three years of separation, see SITUATIONS, IV, p. 280). We reprint below the essential parts of this discussion, which took place during the second session on March 26. Merleau-Ponty had intervened to demand that the debates be brought to bear on the philosophical problems raised by the "thaw"; he asked whether the new Soviet line implied that they were abandoning the "intellectual line of the cold war, according to which the intellectual life is not a dialogue but a struggle," and whether the thaw was going to provide the basis for a "new universalism." And he added, "In my opinion this is possible only at the price of a very deep and consubstantial change in the Soviet regime."

SARTRE: *I'd like to reply to a point Merleau-Ponty raised about the thaw and the situation it puts us in. It seems to me there's one question Merleau-Ponty forgot to ask, because he evidently considers the thaw--he said so himself--to be the thaw of that half of mankind which is Communist. But when it's so cold that half of mankind is frozen, it's only reasonable to see if the other half isn't frozen too. So what*

I wished someone had asked is not simply what we ought to do in the face of the Russian thaw, but how we too ought to thaw ourselves out, and do so in relation to the Russians. It seemed to me that Merleau-Ponty's way of putting the problem didn't get us any farther along; because as Silone said, it had been put the same way earlier. I noticed a turning point in Merleau-Ponty's remarks. I was completely in agreement with him up through his demonstration, in terms of texts of Engels and Marx, that mankind's masterpieces have no immediately determinable relationship to socioeconomic conditions, and that consequently we could legitimately ask the Russians and the Peoples' Democracies to appreciate works created in different conditions without trying to relate them immediately to socioeconomic criteria. And then immediately after this he said he was putting the question this way to the Russians: Do you grant that, not only in the realm of works of art but in that of American sociology and psychology, there can be truths which outstrip the level of research in the Eastern countries? Now it seems to me that this way of putting the question involves a leap. Because in this case it has to be made quite clear that a sociology has aims, forms part of an ideology, and has methods which are not a dialectical method, that it has goals, even social goals; and although truths may be effectively discovered by these methods, a Marxist can never consider them in isolation.

MERLEAU-PONTY: I stated very clearly that there is no question of using these methods to justify American sociology. I only asked whether they admit, with their new perspective, that truths can be discovered in a socially inferior regime.

SARTRE: *O.K. Only what has to be added is, on condition that these truths be recognized from the Marxist point of view, on condition that the Marxists want to integrate them into their system. I do not think that--thaw or not--people with a cultural ideology like Marxism can be asked to accept a truth which is part of another ideological system without trying first to determine the conditions under which it might be integrated into Marxism. I am raising the question precisely because in the many conversations I've had today with Communist intellectuals I've found that this is their position.*

Here we're getting at the basis of the cultural problem, which is that cultures are also ideologies. We're not recognizing this here, and I consider our failure to do so one of the proofs that we in the West are not thawed out ourselves. We are not recognizing that we live in an age of bourgeois ideology in exactly the same way as the Russians' ideas are conditioned by the Russian ideology. This conditioning is direct and systematic. In our part of the world, what is proper to the bourgeois ideology is diversity. But it wouldn't be hard to point out, in most of the things I've heard this morning, what constitutes bourgeois idealism, to show what level it belongs to, and to prove that we haven't done such a good job of making the problem clear because it is not just a matter of finding the universal by trying to put the question properly; we are dealing with a culture contact between two ideological types. So for me the real problem is not to look for a universal in the sense of ideas valid in both systems, but rather to ask the Communists to discuss ideas from the Marxist point of view, seeing what they can accept, in the same way that we ourselves should understand the ideas from our ideological point of view, on our basis. Thus it would not be a matter of an unopposed universality, but on the contrary, of a universality through opposition, a progressive universality. I think we should begin a movement toward rapprochement through discussion, but not hope to find a common content for any given idea.

In these discussions, we ought to try to change our point of view too. It seems to me that till now we have been mainly asking the Russians questions, and it seems quite natural to me that we should: "What do you want to do? What will you accept? What cultural changes are contemporary events producing in the U.S.S.R.?" These questions should be asked; and in my view the Russians would be right to ask us the same sorts of questions.

MERLEAU-PONTY: I didn't try to establish a common content by suppressing what separates us, which is what the Marxists condemn us for doing. I have no objections to the idea that we ought to try to understand the socioeconomic origin of our biases and ideologies, while the Russians would try to integrate things from outside into their way of thinking. I don't think I said anything which would deny this.

SARTRE: *Just the same you were concerned with universality, weren't you?*

MERLEAU-PONTY: I used the word *universality* because there is after all a question of universality. And Sartre is talking universality too when he talks this way. Because he's thinking in terms of ideology, and what does our meeting here represent from an ideological point of view? It is obviously a superstructure of the Western bourgeoisie. But does this fact negate everything we'll do here?

SARTRE: *No, because we also have representatives of the other side in our midst.*

MERLEAU-PONTY: But up till now they haven't spoken. And even if they don't, I think the time will not be wasted, because as soon as you begin to discuss in the way we are discussing, you necessarily go beyond the concept of ideology. Ideology, when I use it in speaking to someone, consists in telling him that I cannot consider anything he says intrinsically, because he is part of a particular social structure, and that anything I say has no truth value, because I too am only the expression of a different social class. As soon as we speak the way we're speaking now, we go beyond the conception of ideologies.

SARTRE: *I don't think we do; because then you're considering ideology in an extreme form the way Hervé does in the preface to his book. Ideas can have value, even great value, within an ideology; but their value springs from two inseparable critical estimates. Because I reject the "either internal criticism or socioeconomic criticism" alternative. I think both criticisms are necessary, and both are interrelated.*

For some time now I've been insisting on what I call, in unfortunate terminology, a totalitarian criticism, that is an internal and a socioeconomic criticism combined. I don't think this means giving up the ideological point of view, but simply giving up the sectarian ideology which consists in saying that everything which comes from here is false because it's ideologically false, and that everything which comes from there is good because it's ideologically good.

MERLEAU-PONTY: I tried to put myself in a Marxist's shoes by repeatedly emphasizing that what I was saying went beyond its Marxist content, but that it could after all be integrated into Marxism on condition that it be looked at in such and such a way. Sartre was saying that you can't ask a Marxist to grant a truth which comes from outside his way of thinking unless it can be integrated into it. But what is Marxism anyhow? . . .

SARTRE: *It's a position which cannot acknowledge an organized body of American investigations and inductions unless they are taken up again in a Marxist context, that is, unless at bottom there is a study of the economic structure and so on which will allow us to situate a superstructure. I am so convinced of this that I recently told a Communist that the whole of psychoanalysis can be integrated into Marxism, but I will never ask a Marxist to accept psychoanalysis as an isolated discipline. I'll ask him to reintegrate it, by having him notice, for example, that after all, the life history of an uncouth individual simply repeats his family history, that is, the history of the society, and that consequently one may very well, to a certain extent and even normally, reinstate psychoanalysis as a discipline forming part of socioeconomic inquiry. But I will never ask him to take psychoanalysis as a truth which goes beyond Marxism.*

MERLEAU-PONTY: In order for the Marxist to integrate it into Marxism, he'd have to begin by taking it seriously. And he couldn't strip it of all value by simply saying it's a bourgeois ideology.

56/288

SARTRE: *It's true that it's a bourgeois ideology, but it won't be any longer if it is liberated from the other side. It's bourgeois in its limitations and negations, but it doesn't have to be if it is taken up again within a whole.*

MERLEAU-PONTY: That is a transubstantiation. We still have to begin by recognizing that this bourgeois problem has hit on something, and that to this extent, consequently, the theory of ideologies is inadequate.

SARTRE: *You can always say that a particular truth can be found in any ideology; but if you transport it into a different ideology, it has to be viewed, reviewed, and integrated. And I don't think you'll find any disagreement about this today, at least not among the French Marxist intellectuals I've spoken to. They can see the possibility of adopting any particular truth whatsoever, as long as it is integrated into Marxism.*

MERLEAU-PONTY: My question grants that all this is possible in conversation. We've been doing it for years in our conversations with our Communist compatriots, who are nice and intelligent in conversation. But in practice, it's something else.

SARTRE: *All I'm asking is that instead of arriving at the coexistence of an idea here and an idea there, as Merleau-Ponty seems to want us to, we grant that coexistence can only be a dynamic movement of integration.*

The two philosophers' disagreements come out clearly in this discussion. We must point out that they defended the same positions during the debate on the final statement, and that Merleau-Ponty granted during a subsequent session that Sartre's points about the need for a "thaw" in the West were well taken.

56/289

"Après Budapest, Sartre parle" 〈After Budapest, Sartre Speaks〉, interview.

-- *L'Express*, supplement to no. 281 (November 9, 1956). This interview was widely disseminated in other countries.

"After Budapest," anonymous translation.

-- *Evergreen Review*, I, no. 1 (1957), 5-23.

Sartre was in Rome when the Hungarian uprising broke out. The Soviet repression of it filled him with anguish and rebelliousness: he did not hesitate an instant in denouncing it, although he did not want to deny completely the efforts he had made since 1952 to establish a rapprochement with the P.C. 〈Communist Party〉 by struggling with all his might against anti-Communism (see *Force of Circumstance*, pp. 357-64).

Once back in Paris he lost no time, after the second Soviet intervention (November 4), in making known his outraged condemnation. Sartre's relations with *France-Observateur* were strained at this time (see SITUATIONS, VII, pp. 135 ff.); this accounts for his having given *L'Express* the interview. Moreover, he had the weekly explain that the reason why he chose it in spite of their many political disagreements had been "to state his position as soon and as fully as possible."

That position is perfectly clear: although Sartre explains the intervention in terms of the threat of a *complete liquidation of what are called the socialist bases of the regime,* he immediately adds: *But to explain is not to excuse: no matter what the cause, the intervention was a crime. . . . And the crime, in my eyes, does not consist in the armored attack on Budapest* alone, *but in the fact that the attack was made possible and perhaps necessary (from the Russian point of view, obviously) by twelve years of imbecility and terror. . . . What the Hungarian people are showing us with their blood is the complete bankruptcy of socialism as imported Russian merchandise.* Without trying to diminish the Russian responsibility, he also points out the role that American policy played in the process whose upshot was the Hungarian business: *The Marshall Plan, to begin with. Its avowed aim was to prevent the construction of socialism in the "satellites." America's responsibility in the present events is undeniable.* But the brutal revelation of Khrushchev's secret report to the Twentieth Congress of the Communist Party of the Soviet Union seemed to him to be a serious blunder: *They should have known what they wanted and how far they were willing to go, and undertaken reforms without shouting it beforehand from the rooftops, but doing it progressively. From this point of view, their most grievous error was probably the Khrushchev report; for in my opinion it is crazy to make a public, official denunciation of a sacred character who has long represented the regime, and to set forth all his crimes in detail, unless the populace have been previously prepared for such frankness by a sizable increase in their standard of living.*

Sartre sums up his own position in the following terms: *I condemn the Russian aggression completely and unreservedly. Without holding the Russian people responsible for it, I repeat that their present government has committed a crime, and that a factional struggle within the ruling circles has given to one group (military "hardliners," old Stalinists?) a power greater than that of the Stalinism it denounced.*

All history's crimes are forgotten; we have forgotten ours and gradually other nations will forget them. The day may come when this crime of the U.S.S.R. will be forgotten, if its government changes and those who replace it try to really apply the principle of equality in their relations to socialist and nonsocialist nations alike. For the time being there is nothing else to do but condemn. Regretfully, but completely, I am breaking my ties with my friends among Russian writers who are not denouncing (or cannot denounce) the Hungarian massacre. It is no longer possible to be friendly toward the ruling faction of the Soviet bureaucracy: horror is in power.

Sartre condemns just as firmly the leadership of the P.C.F. ⟨French Communist Party⟩, which approved the Russian Army's bloody intervention: *As much as I say that after years of uneasiness, rancor, and bitterness it may be possible to reestablish relations with the Soviet Union--all it would take would be a clear change in its political tendencies--just as much do I say that it is not and never will be possible to reestablish relations with the men who are presently leading the French Communist Party. Each one of their phrases, each one of their gestures, is the end result of thirty years of lying and sclerosis. Their reactions are without qualification the reactions of irresponsible men.*

Speaking finally of the repercussions the Hungarian business is having for the situation of the Left in France, Sartre says that his hope rests ultimately in *a new kind of Popular Front whose mediating element could be the "New Left." The Christian Left, which really does exist and which is really on the Left, and the dynamic elements of radicalism itself, the unorganized, could join this broad stream. But if this development does not take place, we must say frankly that the Left is lost.* And he concludes: *No matter how much I dislike breaking with the Communist Party, I can do it because I denounced the Algerian War in time. I am not in contradiction with all the sincere, honest men on the Left, even those who are still in the ranks of the P.C. I am still in solidarity with them, even if they reject me tomorrow.*

In *The Ghost of Stalin* (see 57/291), Sartre developed the reasons for his condemnation at length.

It must be recalled once again that on November 7, Sartre, along with the other members of the board of directors of the C.N.E. ⟨National Writers' Committee⟩ (which he belonged to at the time), signed a letter (published under the title "Contre l'intervention soviétique" ⟨Against the Soviet Intervention⟩, *France-Observateur*, November 8, 1956, and translated in *Dissent*, IV [winter, 1957], 2, 95), which was concerned in particular with asking Janos Kadar to "protect the physical and moral interests of Hungarian writers." Thirty-five Russian writers signed an Open Letter to French Writers (*Literaturnaia Gazeta*, November 21, 1956) in which they disapproved of the stand that Sartre and his fellow writers had taken. The reply, which included Sartre as one of its signers, is entitled "Réponse collective aux écrivains soviétiques" ⟨A Joint Reply to Soviet Writers⟩ and was published in *France-Observateur* (November 29, 1956). Let us point out in this connection that *Les Temps modernes* (nos. 129-31 [January, 1957], p. 1061) reprints a passage from an interview Claude Roy gave to *Nowa Kultura*: "--What do you think of Jean-Paul Sartre's attitude?--That it's an emotional reaction, which Sartre luckily reconsidered, since he signed a letter to Soviet writers and thus revived a discussion with them which is more needed now than ever." This quotation is followed by a note by the editorial staff: "This is Claude Roy's own personal opinion." Finally, Michel-Antoine Burnier provides this information: "December 1 and 2, in the presence of Laurent Casanova, Sartre, and other non-Communists succeeded in getting the National Council of the Peace Movement to adopt a resolution demanding that the Russian troops be withdrawn" (*Choice of Action* [Gallimard edition, p. 115]). Although Sartre had resigned from the France-U.S.S.R. Association in protest against the Russian intervention, he remained a member of the Peace Movement.

56/290

Prefacing letter to *La Tragédie hongroise ou Une Révolution socialiste antisoviétique* ⟨The Hungarian Tragedy, or An Anti-Soviet Socialist Revolution⟩, by François Fejtö.

-- Editions de Flore, 1956. Sartre's letter is on pp. 13-15.

Foreword to *Behind the Rape of Hungary*, translated by Norbert Guterman.

-- New York: David McKay, 1957. Pp. V-VI.

In this very laudatory prefacing letter, Sartre begins by saying that the same author's *History of the People's Democracies* is the sole work capable of informing the public *about these countries which are so near and yet, for the past ten years, so mysterious to us.* He praises Fejtö's objectivity, his complete impartiality, and the quality of his articles, which foreshadow the book being presented. *In this troubled age of lies and violence, what we need above all is what you give us concerning Hungary: the truth.*

1957

57/291

Le Fantôme de Staline ⟨The Ghost of Stalin⟩.

a) Les Temps modernes, nos. 129-31 (November-December, 1956-January, 1957), pp. 577-697.

Published toward mid-January, 1957.

b) Reprinted in SITUATIONS, VII.

c) Reprinted in IL FILOSOFO E LA POLITICA ⟨The Philosopher and Politics⟩ (1964).

The Ghost [or *The Spectre*] *of Stalin.*

t1) Final section translated in a slightly abbreviated form by Michael Segal. *Is This the Time? New Reasoner* (London), no. 1 (summer, 1957), pp. 87-97.

t2) THE GHOST OF STALIN, translated by Martha E. Fletcher. New York: George Braziller, [1968].

Included in a "Glossary and Index" of names, organizations, and events.

t3) THE SPECTRE OF STALIN, translated by Irene Clephane. London: Hamish Hamilton, [1969].

The triple issue of *Les Temps modernes* entitled "La Révolte de la Hongrie" ⟨The Hungarian Revolt⟩ had been almost completely made up by François Fejtö, Ladislas Gara, and Gérard Spitzer before the insurrection broke out. Sartre wrote *The Ghost of Stalin* to set forth more precisely his motives for condemning the Russian repression. The article, which was intended in the first place to reply to the objections raised by the stand he took in *L'Express*, takes up one by one the arguments he used there and develops them further. They are set forth here by means of a detailed examination of the events, an analysis of the contradictions springing from the Communist takeover in Hungary, and an explanation of Stalinism and of the causes and modes of de-Stalinization. (You will find in particular, on pp. 229-33 of SITUATIONS, VII, enlightening ideas about the social significance of the cult of personality in the U.S.S.R.) Sartre conclusively attributes the Russian repression to a provisional victory of the non-de-Stalinized faction of the ruling bureaucracy in the U.S.S.R.

Given the pro-Communist stands Sartre had previously taken, *The Ghost of Stalin* made quite a stir (the January 18, 1957, *France-Soir*, for example, reprinted long excerpts from it). The article may be considered the conclusion of the unfinished series *The Communists and Peace*. The part of this conclusion which pertains to Sartre's relationships with the P.C. ⟨Communist Party⟩ is formulated as follows: *For our part, it has been twelve years now that we have been discussing issues with the Communists. Violently at first, then later in friendship. But our aim was always the same: to contribute with our weak strength to the realization of that union of the Left which is the* only *thing which can still save our country. Now we are going over to the opposition again for the simple reason that there is no other choice; alliance with the P.C. as it is and intends to remain can only compromise the last chances for a United Front. Our program is clear: through a hundred contradictions, inner struggles, and massacres, de-Stalinization is going forward; it is the only effective policy at present which can serve socialism, peace, and the rapprochement of the workers' parties; so with the resources we have as intellectuals, and with our intellectual readership, we shall try to help de-Stalinize the French Party.*

57/292

* *Brecht et les classiques* ⟨Brecht and the Classical Dramatists⟩.

a) Program of the *Théâtre des Nations*. "Hommage international à Bertolt Brecht ⟨An International Tribute to Bertolt Brecht⟩, April 4-21, 1957. B.N. listing: 4° Wz. 672.

b) Reprinted with an English translation ("Brecht as a Classic") in *World Theater/Théâtre dans le Monde*, VII, no. 1 (1958), 11-12, 16-19.

In this piece written on the occasion of the Berliner Ensemble's first performances in France at the Théâtre des Nations, Sartre shows how Brecht ties in with the classical tradition and stresses the kinship between Brechtian "alienation" and the cathartic effect sought by ancient and classical tragedy. *Today "catharsis" has a different name*--prise de conscience.

57/293

"Vous êtes formidables" ⟨You Are Really Something⟩.

a) Les Temps modernes, no. 135 (May, 1957), pp. 1641-47.

b) Reprinted in SITUATIONS, V.

c) Reprinted in IL FILOSOFO E LA POLITICA ⟨The Philosopher and Politics⟩ (1964).

The newspaper *Le Monde* had asked Sartre to comment on the pamphlet *Des rappelés témoignent* ⟨Reservists Testify⟩, in which young soldiers described the tortures they had witnessed in Algeria. From the seventh to the sixteenth of April, Sartre wrote a piece called "Une Entreprise de démoralisation" ⟨An Effort to Demoralize⟩ which *Le Monde* found too violent. So Sartre decided to publish a slightly modified version in *Les Temps modernes*, giving it the title of a radio program by Jean Nohain which was very popular at the time.

A third version of *You Are Really Something* was used by Sartre for a speech at a Peace Movement meeting on June 1, 1957.

57/294

"Jean-Paul Sartre on His Autobiography," interview by Olivier Todd.

-- *The Listener*, June 6, 1957, pp. 915-16.

English translation of a B.B.C. interview.

An important interview, especially considering its date of publication. In it Sartre discusses the autobiography he is writing, the nature of his Marxism, the way he sees BEING AND NOTHINGNESS now, and his own conception of psychology--which he illustrates by analyzing the case of Flaubert at length. So this interview announces the main works to come, from CRITIQUE OF DIALECTICAL REASON through THE WORDS to "Flaubert."

57/295

Marksizm i Egzystencjalizm ⟨Marxism and Existentialism⟩, translated from the French by Jerzy Lisowski.

a) Twórczość (Cracow), XIII, no. 4 (special issue on France) (April, 1957), 33-79.

b) Excerpts retranslated from Polish. "Il faut savoir

le polonais pour savoir où en est Sartre" ⟨You Have to Know Polish to Know Where Sartre Is At⟩. *L'Express*, June 21, 1957.

Sartre had been thinking for several years about writing a study of the relationships between existentialism and Marxism. He got the opportunity when one of the people in charge of *Twórczość* asked him during a trip to Poland to write about the subject "Where Existentialism Stands in 1957" for the special issue on French culture the journal was making up. Later, Sartre rewrote this piece and changed it considerably *to adapt it to the requirements of French readers* (CRITIQUE OF DIALECTICAL REASON, Preface, p. 9). It was then published in *Les Temps modernes* as *Questions de méthode* ⟨Search for a Method⟩ (see 57/296).

Les Temps modernes (nos. 173-74 [August-September, 1960], pp. 394-417) published an article by Adam Schaff translated from Polish, "On Marxism and Existentialism," which analyzes Sartre's essay in *Twórczość*.

NOTE: It was in 1957 that a one-volume edition of the Polish translation of NO EXIT, THE RESPECTFUL PROSTITUTE and NEKRASSOV by Jan Kott and of THE FLIES by Jerzy Lisowski was published.

The reception of Sartre's works in Poland has been studied in an article by Aleksandra Hoffmann-Liponska, "Jean-Paul Sartre w polskie; prasie kulturalnej" ⟨Jean-Paul Sartre in Poland: Toward a Cultural Praxis⟩, *Kwartalnik neofilologiczny*, XV, no. 3 (1968), 319-29.

57/296

Questions de méthode ⟨Search for a Method⟩.

a) *Les Temps modernes*, no. 139 (September, 1957), pp. 338-417; no. 140 (October, 1957), pp. 658-98.

b) Reprinted without any major changes but with a conclusion added. In CRITIQUE DE LA RAISON DIALECTIQUE, preceded by *Question de méthode*. Gallimard, [1960]. Pp. 13-111 (see 60/332). The recent editions have restored *Questions de méthode* (the plural).

c) Text *(b)* reprinted as a separate volume. QUESTIONS DE MÉTHODE. Idées series. Gallimard, [1967] (see 67/451).

SEARCH FOR A METHOD or PROBLEM OF METHOD, translated and with an introduction by Hazel E. Barnes.

t1) SEARCH FOR A METHOD. New York: Alfred A. Knopf, 1963.

t2) Ibid. in paperback. New York: Vintage Books, [1968].

t3) PROBLEM OF METHOD. London: Methuen, [1964].

In his preface to CRITIQUE OF DIALECTICAL REASON, Sartre gives an account of the origin of this very important essay (see also 57/295): Search for a Method *was written for a particular occasion, and this accounts for its slightly hybrid character. For this reason, too, the problems it raises seem always to be approached indirectly. . . . The essay, which was originally called* Existentialism and Marxism, *is now called* Search for a Method. *Because in the last analysis there is one and only one question I am asking: Do we have the means today of constituting a structural, historical anthropology?*

The essay is divided into three parts. In the first part Sartre begins by situating existentialism in relation to Marxism. The latter *remains the philosophy of our time. We cannot go beyond it because we have not gone beyond the circumstances which engendered it.* It alone is capable of providing knowledge in the strict sense. But this knowledge, for contingent historical reasons, has stopped developing and has been transformed into a rigid dogma which has proved to be incapable of accounting for the lived dimension of the human phenomena it claims to *explain*, even though it does not *understand* them. It is this failure of twentieth-century Marxism which has given birth to existentialism, an ideology which lives on the edge of knowledge and tries to integrate itself into it in order to give it new life from within. Existentialism is thus a provisional enclave in Marxist philosophy. And Sartre says specifically: *Just as soon as* everyone *has a margin of real* freedom *beyond the production of life, Marxism will have seen its day; it will be replaced by a philosophy of freedom. But we ourselves do not have any means, any intellectual instrument, any concrete experience which allows us to conceive of this freedom or this philosophy.*

The second and third parts of the essay are chiefly devoted to a criticism of the "lazy" Marxism which seeks to erect a certain number of a priori claims into an established body of knowledge. Existentialism, on the contrary, seeks to be no more than a *heuristic method* which borrows its principles from Marxism and takes them as *regulative ideas* or *indicators of tasks* rather than as concrete truths. And Sartre insists especially that *only the project, as the mediation between two objective phases, can account for history, that is for human* creativity. Primarily on the basis of examples from the French Revolution and the case of Flaubert, Sartre shows on the one hand that Marxism must make use of the contributions of American sociology in its understanding of history, and on the other hand that it must integrate psychoanalysis in order to comprehend the individual as a whole.

The approach to problems defined in *Search for a Method* is taken up again and given a philosophical foundation in CRITIQUE OF DIALECTICAL REASON (see 60/332).

According to the catalogue of the Gérard de Berny Library (Part II, p. 61, art. 165--May 12, 1959, sale at the Hôtel Drouot), there is an unbound signed manuscript of 181 pages which is described as follows: "Questions de Méthode, I. Marxisme et existentialisme--II. Le Problème des Médiations et des Disciplines auxiliaires" ⟨The Problem of Mediations and the Special Sciences⟩.

This manuscript is alleged to show "a great number of differences (changes, eliminations, additions)" in respect to the text published in *Les Temps modernes*.

57/297

Reply to Daniel Guérin.

-- *Les Temps modernes*, no. 142 (December, 1957), p. 1137.

In *Search for a Method*, Sartre takes examples from the French Revolution of Marxist historical method. He makes use of a book by Daniel Guérin, *La Lutte des classes sous la première République* ⟨The Class Struggle under the First Republic⟩ (Gallimard, 1946), which he calls *open to question but fascinating and rich in new insight, . . . one of the few* enriching *contributions that contemporary Marxists have made to the study of history* (CRITIQUE OF DIALECTICAL REASON, Gallimard edition, p. 34 [*Search for a Method*, p. 37, n. 2]). Sartre nevertheless makes a number of criticisms bearing on Guérin's *wish to force history*. In a letter published by *Les Temps modernes* (same issue, pp. 1132-37) under the title, "Sartre, Lukács et . . . la Gironde" ⟨Sartre, Lukács, and the Girondist Party⟩, Guérin challenges the justification of these criticisms. Sartre comments: *Guérin's reply not only proves that he has not understood a word of what I said; it shows--and this is more serious--that he doesn't understand anything in his own book. So I'll restrict myself to assuring him that it's an excellent book. His best by far.*

57/298

Preface to *"Portrait du colonisé," precédé du "Portrait du colonisateur," par Albert Memmi (éd. Corrêa)* ⟨*A Portrait of the Colonized,* Preceded by *A Portrait of the Colonizer*, by Albert Memmi (Corrêa publ.)⟩.

a) Les Temps modernes, nos. 137-38 (July-August, 1957), pp. 289-93.

b) Reprinted in SITUATIONS, V.

c) Reprinted as preface. In Albert Memmi. *Portrait du colonisé*, preceded by *Portrait du colonisateur.* Libertés series. J.-J. Pauvert, 1966.

Translated by Lawrence Hoey.

t1) Included as Introduction in Albert Memmi. *The Colonizer and the Colonized.* New York: The Orion Press, 1965.

t2) Freedom from Exploitation: The Colonizer and the Colonized. In Jean-Paul Sartre. *Of Human Freedom*, edited by Wade Baskin. New York: Philosophical Library, 1966. Pp. 137-43.

> *No one can treat a man "like a dog" unless he first considers him a man. The impossible dehumanization of the oppressed turns back and becomes the alienation of the oppressor: it is he himself who by his slightest gesture revives the humanity he seeks to destroy.*

57/299

"Gespräch mit Jean-Paul Sartre" ⟨Conversation with Jean-Paul Sartre⟩, interview by Ingeborg Brandt.

-- *Welt am Sonntag* (Hamburg), October 6, 1957.

> Interview of no great interest which took place during a trip Sartre made to Capri. Sartre speaks briefly of the projects he is working on: the study of Tintoretto and the one on existentialism and Marxism, his book on Flaubert, and finally his autobiography (whose first volume he says will go up to the age of twenty). Concerning the "Tintoretto" (see 57/300 and 66/448), he says more specifically: *My Paris editor Gallimard wanted a piece on painting, something easy to illustrate. I myself had very different things in mind at first. Since 1947 I have been coming to Italy almost every year. I have a weakness for this country and I wanted to devote a big monograph to it, with historical background, social problems, political configurations, antiquity, the church, tourism--the*

whole works. Then I saw the subject was much too broad, too big. Then the Tintoretto solution seemed to me to be a convenient way of putting my Italian experience together ⟨from French translation by Rybalka and Contat⟩. Let us recall that the work Sartre alludes to here was to be called "Queen Albemarle and the Last Tourist" (see 52/222 and 53/235).

57/300

Le Séquestré de Venise ⟨The Prisoner of Venice⟩.

a) Les Temps modernes, no. 141 (November, 1957), pp. 761-800. A note specifies: "Part of a study of Tintoretto which will be published by Gallimard."

b) Reprinted with minor changes in SITUATIONS, IV.

From a Study on Tintoretto, The Venetian Pariah, or *The Prisoner of Venice.*

t1) From a Study on Tintoretto, translated by Richard Howard. In Georges Borchardt, ed. *New French Writing*. New York: Criterion Books, 1961; Evergreen Books (paperback), 1961. Pp. 9-54.

t2) The Venetian Pariah, translated by Wade Baskin. In ESSAYS IN AESTHETICS (1963).

t3) The Prisoner of Venice, translated by Benita Eisler. In SITUATIONS (1965).

This is part of a book Sartre had almost finished but gave up because he did not like its style. Another part was published in 1966 under the title *Saint George and the Dragon* (see 66/448).

Simone de Beauvoir says in *Force of Circumstance* (p. 372): "A publisher asked him for a study of a painter to be published as one of a series of art books. Sartre had always loved Tintoretto: even before the war, and especially since '46, he had been interested in his way of conceiving of space and time."

Sartre had as a matter of fact discovered Tintoretto during a trip to Venice in 1933. He subsequently referred to the Venetian painter many times in his works, especially in SITUATIONS, II (p. 61). In May, 1954, *Les Temps modernes* (no. 102, pp. 1965-2006) published an article by Jules Vuillemin, "La Personnalité esthétique du Tintoret" ⟨Tintoretto's Aesthetic Personality⟩, in which Sartre saw the confirmation of some of his ideas. Vuillemin's name is cited in a note to this article, but the exact information about his article is omitted.

57/300

Sartre's analysis of Tintoretto is both sociological and existential: it shows the dialectical relation between the history of a city and the passion of a man. The text, moreover, clarifies certain aspects of THE CONDEMNED OF ALTONA, especially the theme of Puritanism.

Bernard Pingaud gives an excellent summary of *The Prisoner of Venice* in *L'Arc* (no. 30 [1966], p. 35).

57/301

Quand la police frappe les trois coups . . . ⟨When the Police Give the Three Raps⟩.

a) *France-Observateur*, December 5, 1957.

b) Reprinted in SITUATIONS, VII.

Sartre parallels *The Queen of Cesarea*, the play by Robert Brasillach which provoked former resistants to demonstrations which were violently attacked by the right-wing press, to Jean Genet's *The Balcony* in order to analyze the political conditions under which the Parisian theater has to function.

57/NOTE.

In a report of the Ben Sadok trial, *Le Monde* (December 12, 1957, p. 2) points out that Sartre testified in favor of the accused on December 10, and that he even compared him to Charlotte Corday.

Concerning the trial, see the many details in *Force of Circumstance*, pp. 402-5.

1958

58/302

Une Victoire ⟨A Victory⟩.

This piece--which, although not technically a preface, was written about *The Question*, the work by Henri Alleg published February 17, 1958, by Minuit and dealing with the problem of torture in Algeria--had an eventful publication history and caused quite a political stir.

Henri Alleg, a member of the Algerian Communist Party, had been the editor of the newspaper *Alger rêpublicain* from 1950 until it was banned in September, 1955. In November, 1956, he went underground. Arrested in June, 1957, by the parachutists of the 10th Airborne Division, he was placed in solitary for a month at El-Biar. This detention is what he tells about in *The Question*.

a) First published in *L'Express*, March 6, 1958.

This issue of *L'Express* was confiscated by the authorities because of Sartre's article. Some time later, on March 27, the government, taking a step which had had no precedent in France since the eighteenth century, decided to confiscate *The Question* too for "being part of an attempt to demoralize the army with the aim of damaging the national defense."

Following the confiscation of *L'Express*, excerpts from *A Victory* were reprinted by the foreign press (see especially *The Observer*, March 9, 1958, "Almost as Mute as during the Occupation") and the text was reprinted in:

b) A booklet [March, 1958], which was immediately confiscated and destroyed.

c) Le Canard enchaîné, March 12, 1958.

Put out in scroll form, Sartre's article was printed in tiny characters but could still be read with a magnifying glass.

d) A volume printed in Switzerland which included both Alleg's and Sartre's texts: Henri Alleg, *La Question*; Jean-Paul Sartre, *Une Victoire*. Lausanne: La Cité, 1958. Printed April 11, 1958.

Sartre's article is on pp. 95-125.

e) *Témoignages et Documents*, no. 2 [March or April, 1958].

f) *Témoignages et Documents*, no. 3 [April, 1958].

This periodical reprinted the complete text of *A Victory* twice, but preceding *The Question* in the second printing.

g) Reprinted in SITUATIONS, V.

h) A new edition whose content is the same as *(d)*. *La Question*, followed by *Une Victoire*. Libertés series. J.-J. Pauvert, 1966.

A Victory, translated by John Calder as an introduction to *The Question*, by Henri Alleg.

t1) London: Calder, 1958.

t2) New York: George Braziller, 1958. Pp. 13-36.

Les Temps modernes (no. 145 [March, 1958], pp. 1529-30) published an editorial signed T. M. and entitled, "La réponse d'Henri Alleg" ⟨Henri Alleg's Reply⟩.

In writing *A Victory*, Sartre not only denounces torture, but deepens a reflection on the dialectic of the torturer and his victim which had persistently preoccupied him since the Occupation and THE VICTORS.

Twentieth-century ethical thought cannot evade the problem of torture, and Sartre gives us a basic text about it.

NOTE: Concerning *The Question*, André Malraux, Roger Martin du Gard, François Mauriac, and Sartre sent an "Official Message" to the president of the Republic protesting the attacks on freedom of speech and the confiscation of Henri Alleg's work, demanding that an explanation of the facts he reported be given, and calling on the government to condemn unequivocally the use of torture.

58/303

Des Rats et des hommes ⟨Of Rats and Men⟩, preface to *Le Traître* ⟨The Traitor⟩, by André Gorz.

a) Seuil, [1958]. Pp. 11-47. Second edition, 1973.

b) Excerpt. *Portrait de l'indifférent* ⟨Portrait of the Indifferent Man⟩. *L'Express*, April 3, 1958.

c) Reprinted in SITUATIONS, IV.

Rats and Men or *Of Rats and Men.*

t1) Rats and Men, translated by Richard Howard. In André Gorz. *The Traitor*. New York: Simon and Schuster; London: Calder, 1960. Pp. 1-36.

t2) Of Rats and Men, translated by Benita Eisler. In SITUATIONS (1965).

This admirable preface, which is without a doubt among the best of Sartre's writings, introduces one of the most outstanding books in recent times. The Traitor *is less and more than a work of literature. . . . Since what the work of art broadcasts to the four winds is the name of its author, that great dead man who put it all together,* The Traitor *is not a work of art. It is an event, a sudden precipitation, a confusion of words making sense. You hold between your hands this surprising object,* a work *creating* its *author*.

The work represents an intellectual's radical effort to discover his truth in creating it, and to understand, by means of a method which owes more to Sartre than to Marx and Freud, and on the basis of his life history, the source of his choices, his singularity, and the movement of his thought. Sartre, who plays an important role in the book, is depicted in it under the name of Morel (see 46/NOTE 1).

André Gorz, whom Sartre had met in Lausanne in 1946, has been a managing editor of *Les Temps modernes* since the magazine was reorganized in February, 1961. His special responsibility, like Jean Pouillon's, is political questions; he has written many editorials and taken charge of quite a few special issues on "Problems of the Labor Movement." Thus he is the one who to a certain extent has taken over the role Maurice Merleau-Ponty played on the magazine from 1945 to 1950, and who has helped give *Les Temps modernes* its present political orientation. Gorz, who makes his living as a newspaperman specializing in economics, is a political theorist of the first order (*Stratégie ouvrière et néo-capitalisme* [Seuil, 1964] ⟨Strategy for Labor, translated by Martin A. Nicolau and Victoria Ortis [Boston: Beacon Press, 1967]⟩; *Le Socialisme difficile* ⟨Difficult Socialism⟩ [Seuil, 1967]) and is the best commentator

58/303

on Sartre's philosophical thought in contemporary France (see especially "Sartre et le marxisme" ⟨Sartre and Marxism⟩, in *Le Socialisme difficile*, pp. 215-44).

Excerpts from *The Traitor* had appeared prior to publication in the October, 1957, and March, 1958, *Temps modernes*. Gorz presented a sequel to this work called "Le Vieillissement" ⟨Growing Old⟩ (*Le Temps modernes*, no. 187 [December, 1961], pp. 638-65; no. 188 [January, 1962], pp. 829-52) whose pages certainly constitute his greatest literary success up till now.

Sartre's preface was written in Rome during the summer of 1957. It is above all an impassioned reflection on those troublesome beings called intellectuals: *Intelligence is neither a gift nor a taint; it's a drama. Or if you like, it is a temporary solution which is most commonly transmuted into a life sentence. Someone said to this traitor of ours, "You stink of intelligence the way someone's armpits stink." And it's true. Intelligence stinks. But not any more than stupidity. There are smells for every taste. Stupidity smells like wild beasts; intelligence smells like men.* The piece ranges from personal souvenirs to allusive portraits (Vercors, pp. 49-50 of SITUATIONS, IV; Arthur Koestler, *ibid.*, pp. 50-52; Jean Cocteau, *ibid.*, pp. 62-63) to general comments on our situation as *rats who are a prey to men* to a patient description of the liberating undertaking which makes Gorz's book an "Invitation to live." The title, *Of Rats and Men*, refers to a short story by Frank M. Robinson called "The Labyrinth" which Boris Vian translated for the October, 1951, *Temps modernes*. This science fiction tale shows astronauts landing on Venus and, without being aware of it, serving as guinea pigs for the invisible inhabitants of the planet they think they are conquering. *This is what our common situation seems to me to be, the only difference being that we are our own Venusians and guinea pigs. Open* The Traitor, *and you become colonists; shaking your head in disbelief, you contemplate a strange animal--a native, perhaps--who runs around madly on the surface of Venus. But I won't give you even two minutes to discover that the native is a rat and the rat is no one else but you.* This image runs throughout the piece to illustrate the theme of otherness, which finds its most gripping expression in this preface.

58/304

"Le Théâtre peut-il aborder l'actualité politique? Une 'table ronde' avec Sartre, Butor, Vailland, Adamov" ⟨Can the Theater Deal with Contemporary Political Reality? A Round-Table Discussion with Sartre, Butor, Vailland, Adamov⟩.

a) France-Observateur, February 13, 1958.

b) Book. Arthur Adamov. *Ici et maintenant* ⟨Here and Now⟩. Pratique du Théâtre series. Gallimard, [1964]. Pp. 65-73.

> Gilles Martinet and Morvan Lebesque also take part in a discussion which centers on Adamov's play *Paolo Paoli* and bears on the problems of the theater and contemporary reality, censorship, and technique.
>
> Taking *The Red and the Black* as an illustration, Sartre states: *Someone who wanted to rewrite this book today would have to make Julien* [Sorel] *a feminine character. For that's the way our society has developed: woman's liberation has created a reality. . . .* And later he goes on: *I should like to defend plays dealing with contemporary realities by saying that they are the only plays today which give us a chance to give new life to the theater. These plays don't necessarily have to be boring. They can be treated like Broadway plays, but with a different technique. What has to be fought against above all is the idea that the play that talks about the world the way it is has to be a play like* The Little Hut. *When the spectators go to see* The Little Hut, *they go to see the eternal feminine. Some day they ought to be shown a woman of today, that woman à la Julien Sorel I was talking about a while ago, and they would make the necessary adjustments.*
>
> Sartre puts forth an idea here which he will develop more seriously in 1961-62 in projecting a play about Alcestis, the wife who agrees to be sacrificed in her husband's place (see interview 61/363). He is clearly thinking of writing what will later become THE CONDEMNED OF ALTONA; he speaks in fact of *a play about the way in which a family can fall apart as a consequence of a reservist remaining silent when he comes back from Algeria.*

58/305

Nous sommes tous des assassins ⟨We Are All Assassins⟩.

a) Les Temps modernes, no. 145 (March, 1958), pp. 1574-76.

b) Reprinted in SITUATIONS, V.

c) Reprinted in IL FILOSOFO E LA POLITICA ⟨The Philosopher and Politics⟩ (1964).

> In reference to the sentencing to death of the Guerroudj couple as accomplices to an act of sabotage connected with the Algerian War, Sartre opportunely reminds the French of their guilt in the bombardment of Sakiet.

58/305

Simone de Beauvoir had been a character witness for Jacqueline Guerroudj, one of her former students (see *Force of Circumstance*, p. 382). The same issue of *Les Temps modernes* has an article about the affair by Michel Brugier, the Guerroudj's lawyer, as well as Abdelkader Guerroudj's statements at the trial. Let us recall that the campaign waged by the Left won a pardon for the condemned couple.

58/305 A

"Poseta Sartru" ⟨A Call on Sartre⟩, interview-article by Leon Lavitcho.

-- *Politika* (Belgrade), May, 1958, p. 18.

Lavitcho tells about a talk he had with Sartre at 42, rue Napoléon (*sic*). Sartre talks about Yugoslavia, says he is impressed by the level of theoretical discussions in that country and then comes to the Algerian problem and Henri Alleg's *The Question*.

58/306

Le Prêtendant ⟨The Pretender⟩.

a) *L'Express*, May 22, 1958.

b) Reprinted in SITUATIONS, V.

c) Reprinted in IL FILOSOFO E LA POLITICA ⟨The Philosopher and Politics⟩ (1964).

A first stand taken against Charles de Gaulle in which Sartre, right after the May 13 coup and the famous press conference at which de Gaulle announced that he was "ready to assume the powers of the Republic," analyzes the domestic situation in France and concludes: *The solitude of this man walled up in his own grandeur will not allow him, under any circumstances whatsoever, to become the head of a republican government. Or what comes down to the same thing, will not allow any government he is the head of to remain a republic.*

58/307

May 30, 1958, press conference on violations of human rights in Algeria.

-- *Témoignages et documents sur la guerre d'Algérie*, no. 5, special issue (June, 1958).

Laurent Schwartz, François Mauriac, Daniel Mayer, the head of the French Bar, René Thorp, and General Billotte all took part in this press conference.

Sartre speaks of the problem of torture in Algeria and of the task of providing information which falls to intellectuals and newspapermen.

58/308

Introduction à une critique de la raison dialectique ⟨Introduction to a Critique of Dialectical Reason⟩.

-- *Voies nouvelles*, no. 3 (June-July, 1958), pp. 4-9.

First published part of the then unpublished CRITIQUE OF DIALECTICAL REASON. It corresponds to pages 118, line 10, through 130, line 21 (plus the note on page 130) of the Gallimard edition.

58/309

La Constitution du mépris ⟨The Constitution of Contempt⟩.

a) L'Express, September 11, 1958.

b) Reprinted in *Témoignages et documents*, no. 7 (September, 1958).

c) Reprinted in SITUATIONS, V.

d) Reprinted in IL FILOSOFO E LA POLITICA ⟨The Philosopher and Politics (1964).

58/310

Les Grenouilles qui demandent un roi ⟨The Frogs Who Wanted a King⟩.

a) L'Express, September 25, 1958.

b) Reprinted in SITUATIONS, V.

c) Reprinted in IL FILOSOFO E LA POLITICA ⟨The Philosopher and Politics⟩ (1964).

According to *Force of Circumstance* (p. 436), Sartre made an agreement with Jean-Jacques Servan-Schreiber in Rome to write three articles in the September 11, 18, and 25 *Express* against the referendum on the Gaullist constitution. In the end he wrote only two. The first was drafted in Rome. In spite of the cuts Simone de Beauvoir and Servan-Schreiber undertook to make in it, Sartre was

58/310

not satisfied with it. It seemed dull to him. When he returned to Paris, he forced himself in spite of great weariness to work at giving more life to the second article, spending twenty-eight straight hours writing it. Simone de Beauvoir once again took it upon herself to make the cuts, and she concludes in her journal: "The article is really excellent, and the patch-ups don't show too much" (*Force of Circumstance*, p. 444).

La Constitution du mépris ⟨The Constitution of Contempt⟩ denounces the blackmail the referendum is based on, and calls for a no vote to the question it puts.

In *The Frogs Who Wanted a King*, which is actually far superior, Sartre tries to show by a relevant analysis why the Fourth Republic, which came out of the Liberation, went bankrupt. Addressing himself to the level of good technicians much taken with efficiency from which the *Express* readers come, he tries to show that Charles de Gaulle is simply perpetuating the system which has been so rightly decried, and he sketches the broad outlines of a really innovative program.

Referring especially to these articles, Sartre will say in a 1964 interview (see 64/412): *Personally, I reproach myself for having been far too respectful toward de Gaulle in my articles. I ought not to have taken account of the fact that he was respected by a great number of Frenchmen and shown respect for this respect. I ought to have attacked him openly as a harmful person.*

58/NOTE.

During the ceremony for the "Granting of the Lenin Prize for Consolidating Peace among Peoples to M. Emmanuel d'Astier," which was held at the Hôtel Lutétia in Paris on February 21, 1958, Mme Yves Farge read the gathering a message from Sartre. In his warm tribute, Sartre stressed in particular the role Emmanuel d'Astier played in the Peace Movement at a time when it was suffering from serious internal discord after the Hungarian affair: *Your greatest merit, in that year of 1956, was to keep peace within the Peace Movement itself. . . . Neither you nor I believe that individual action is effective, and you would laugh if I said that you alone kept our movement together. But what seems undeniable to me is that it was your fight and that of the men who supported you--whatever circles, whatever party, whatever country they may have come from--yes, it was your fight which enabled us to go beyond our contradictions toward a new unity. In this sense you were really a man of peace, for it is our movement--which is truly and authentically a movement of the peoples of the world, and whose tasks are more urgent than ever today--which must be protected from every threat to it.* In another connection, Sartre expressed regret that the Ceylon Congress had not deemed it necessary to adopt Astier's proposal aiming to eliminate the death penalty in political cases, but he said he was convinced that the idea would eventually be adopted. In conclusion, he calls on the Peace Movement to campaign for Algerian independence.

This text was not published, but it appears in the typed record of the meeting, of which there are mimeographed copies.

1959

59/311

LES SÉQUESTRÉS D'ALTONA ⟨The Condemned of Altona⟩, play in five acts.

a) Excerpts in *France-Observateur*, September 24, 1959.

b) *Les Temps modernes*, no. 164 (October, 1959), pp. 584-656; no. 165 (November, 1959), pp. 813-74.

Complete text of the play. It has two mistaken numberings of scenes from acts 1 and 4.

c) Book. Gallimard, [1960]. 227 pages. Printing date: February, 1960.

Published also in the Soleil series.

The volume includes a preliminary note in which Sartre begs the pardon of the friends and next of kin of Hellmuth von Gerlach, one of *the most courageous and notable adversaries of national socialism*, for having unknowingly borrowed his name.

d) Reprinted in THÉÂTRE. Gallimard, [1962].

e) Le Livre de poche series, nos. 1418-49. Gallimard, [1965].

f) Edited and with an introduction by Philip Thody. Textes français classiques et modernes series. London: University of London Press, [1965].

This very carefully prepared edition includes especially an introduction which provides a detailed study of the play.

g) Folio series, no. 40. Gallimard, [1972].

LOSER WINS, THE CONDEMNED OF ALTONA, or ALTONA, translated by Sylvia Leeson and George Leeson.

t1) LOSER WINS. London: Hamish Hamilton, 1960.

t2) THE CONDEMNED OF ALTONA. With a preface by Henri Peyre. New York: Alfred A. Knopf, 1961.

t3) Ibid. in paperback. New York: Vintage Books, [1963].

t4) Paperback. ALTONA; MEN WITHOUT SHADOWS; THE FLIES. Penguin Books, [1962].

During a round-table discussion of the theater and contemporary political reality which took place in February, 1958 (see 58/304), Sartre had brought up (without presenting it as a project) the subject of a play about torture and *the way in which a family can fall apart as a consequence of a reservist remaining silent when he comes back from Algeria.* Judging by what was said on this occasion, it seems that Sartre originally wanted to set the play he was thinking about in France, and that the risk of having the subject which was to become THE CONDEMNED OF ALTONA banned by the censor in part persuaded him to set it in Germany instead. The play, which was sometimes announced incorrectly under the title "Love," was promised to Simone Berriau, director of the Théâtre Antoine, for the 1958 season. Interrupting the writing of CRITIQUE OF DIALECTICAL REASON, Sartre began to write at the beginning of July in Rome, thinking he could finish the play in short order. After the near-fatal attack he suffered as a result of having imposed an intense mental and emotional strain on himself (see *Force of Circumstance*, pp. 451-53), the play was put off till the following fall. Simone de Beauvoir, who had made harsh judgments about the first stages of this frequently revised play, tells us that Sartre, "possibly because of the circumstances in the midst of which he began work on it, never felt any great liking for this play" (*ibid.*, p. 472). Of all his theatrical works, this one cost him the most effort. Except for Frantz's final monologue, which did not take on its final version until rehearsals, the play was finished in the summer of 1959 and, after a certain number of cuts, had its premiere at the Théâtre de la Renaissance on September 23, 1959, under the direction of Véra Korène, in a production by François Darbon, and with the following cast for the leading roles:

FRANTZ	Serge Reggiani
LE PERE	Fernand Ledoux
JOHANNA	Evelyne Rey
LENI	Marie-Olivier
WERNER	Robert Moncade

59/311

THE CONDEMNED OF ALTONA was on the whole favorably received by the critics, most of whom were united in praising the play as one of Sartre's most important, if not the best. It was a great public success and ran the whole 1959-60 season. Serge Reggiani's remarkable interpretation won almost unanimous approval, but the production and settings were sharply criticized. The play was once again a success when it was revived in 1965 at the Théâtre de l'Athénée in a production by François Périer. It was also put on in 1963 in a movie version which Sartre said he was not satisfied with (see Appendix).

A massive and complicated work, imposing in the breadth of its ambitions, sometimes tiresome in its heavy passages or confusing in its obscure ones, and sometimes annoying too in its popular theatrical gimmicks, THE CONDEMNED OF ALTONA is certainly not Sartre's most successful play. But in spite of its flaws--which come mainly in acts 1 and 3--it has a richness of meaning, a strictness of construction, and a tautness of dialogue which class it, along with NO EXIT and THE DEVIL AND THE GOOD LORD, as one of his three major plays.

As far as its meaning is concerned, it presents interpretive problems which the CRITIQUE OF DIALECTICAL REASON throws the most revealing light on. For just as NO EXIT gets its commentary from the phenomenology of "bad faith" constituted by BEING AND NOTHINGNESS, and just as THE DEVIL AND THE GOOD LORD is arranged according to the dialectic of Good and Evil described in SAINT GENET, THE CONDEMNED OF ALTONA can be understood exactly only in terms of the concept of *serial otherness* set forth in the CRITIQUE. Deliberately ambiguous, the play stages totally impotent characters who are the willing victims of a process they have no grip on and yet remain completely responsible for, even though it condemns them irremediably to failure and solitariness, that is, to solitary confinement. In this respect it constitutes the darkest, most pessimistic moment in all of Sartre's works.

INTERVIEWS ABOUT "THE CONDEMNED OF ALTONA"

59/312

"Entretien avec Sartre" ⟨Conversation with Sartre⟩, by Madeleine Chapsal.

-- *L'Express*, September 10, 1959.

Interview made during rehearsals. In it, Sartre makes an interesting comparison of the dramatic structure of THE CONDEMNED to that of NO EXIT: *In* NO EXIT *there were three characters to set in motion--there are five in this one--and no events. Everything depended upon the movement the characters produced by acting on one another. It's the same in this one, but instead of three there are five characters to develop, five characters who are held and commanded by each other. So there are more difficulties. Two of these characters, the father and the son, communicate at a distance without seeing one another. I see this movement--which could be different, sinusoidal, helicoidal, in each play--as spiral. This was not easy to get just right. Furthermore, I wanted to get a dimension into* THE CONDEMNED *which wasn't in* NO EXIT*--the past. The past was discussed in* NO EXIT*, but it did not intervene to change the present. In this one the characters are constantly commanded and held by the past as they are by each other. It is because of the past--their own and everybody's past--that they act the way they do. As in real life.*

59/313

"Entretien avec Sartre" ⟨Conversation with Sartre⟩, by Maria Craipeau.

-- *France-Observateur*, September 10, 1959.

Nothing memorable.

59/314

"Voici l'histoire des *Séquestrés d'Altona*" ⟨Here Is the Story of THE CONDEMNED OF ALTONA⟩, interview.

-- *Le Figaro*, September 11, 1959.

The whole play centers on the problem of filial and paternal love.

59/315

"Jean-Paul Sartre fait sa rentrée après quatre ans de retraite" ⟨Jean-Paul Sartre Makes His Comeback after Four Years of Retirement⟩, interview by Pierre Berger.

-- *Paris-Journal*, September 12, 1959.

Interview without much of interest about the play. Sartre defends himself against the rumor that

59/315

> he has been silent for several years and cites his recent works. *There wasn't any silence. As far as the theater is concerned, I ordinarily write a play every three or four years. Furthermore, I'm not a dramatic writer but a writer who thinks he ought to write for the theater, and who likes to.*

59/316

"Sartre fait sa rentrée au théâtre (de la Renaissance) avec une pièce sur les séquelles de la défaite allemande" ⟨Sartre Makes His Comeback in the Théâtre (de la Renaissance) with a Play about the Sequels to the German Defeat⟩, interview by Jacqueline Fabre.

-- *Libération*, September 14, 1959.

59/317

". . . On ne peut émouvoir qu'avec de vrais problèmes . . ." ⟨You Can Only Move People with Real Problems⟩, interview by Georges Léon.

-- *L'Humanité*, September 16, 1959.

> *I tried to show the past swelling the present. I took a world heading toward death, which could only go toward death. I only wanted to draw up a death warrant, to confirm the liquidation of one world and to indicate the beginning of another. This, in my judgment, is the law of modern theater.*

59/318

"Deux heures avec Sartre" ⟨Two Hours with Sartre⟩, talk with Robert Kanters, Françoise Giroud, etc.

-- *L'Express*, September 17, 1959.

Translated into Italian as "La parte del diavolo." *L'Illustrazione*, October, 1959, pp. 27-30.

"The Theater," translated by Richard Seaver.

-- *Evergreen Review*, IV, no. 11 (January-February, 1960), 143-52.

> Important conversation. In it Sartre first gives his reasons for not having finished "The Last Chance" (see 49/191 and 49/192). Then, speaking of possible themes for the theater, he says: *We all know that*

the world changes, that it changes man, and that man changes the world. And if this isn't what the underlying subject of every play should be, then the theater no longer has a subject.

A major part of the conversation is then devoted to Bertolt Brecht, whom Sartre says he agrees with in his rejection of a bourgeois theater based on emotional participation in and identification with the characters. *The ideal in Brecht's theater would be to have an audience like a group of ethnographers suddenly encountering a savage tribe. Coming up to have a look and suddenly saying to each other, these savages are us. It is at this moment that the audience itself becomes coauthor of the play. By recognizing itself, but as strange, as if it were another, it* makes itself exist *before itself as an* object, *and it sees itself without being* embodied, *and thus sees itself in understanding itself.* For Sartre, the ideal in his own dramaturgy would be to *show and move simultaneously.* He tried to in THE CONDEMNED by introducing the viewpoint and judgment of the future: *I'd like the audience to see that strange thing, our century, from the outside, as a witness. And at the same time I'd like it to take part in it, because it is creating this century. Besides, there's something special about our era: we know we'll be judged.*

59/319

"Entretien avec Jean-Paul Sartre" ⟨Conversation with Jean-Paul Sartre⟩, by Charles Haroche.

-- *France nouvelle*, September 17, 1959.

Sartre gives an interesting summary of the play, stressing the historical contradictions the characters are trapped in. *I did not want just to create the characters but to suggest that objective circumstances condition the shaping and behavior of a given individual at a given moment: I had thought of giving my play a different title--"Loser Wins," for example--but that would have lacked the other side of the coin, which seems equally important to me, "Winner Loses."* [Let us recall that the play was performed in England as *Loser Wins.*] *I wanted . . . to establish a world's death warrant. . . .*

When I speak of the ambiguity of our time, I mean that man has never been as ready as he is today to win his freedom, and that at the same time he is caught up in the most serious of battles. . . . Up till now I have created plays with heroes and conclusions which in one way or another overcame the contradictions. This is so of THE DEVIL AND THE GOOD

59/319

LORD. *But in the bourgeois society we live in, it is very hard for an author like me to do anything but critical realism. If a hero is reconciled with himself in the end, then the audience which sees him do it in the play risks being reconciled with its interrogations, its unresolved questions.*

59/320

". . . Il ne s'agit ni d'une pièce politique . . . ni d'une pièce à thèse" ⟨It Is Neither a Political Play . . . Nor a Problem Play⟩, interview by Claude Sarraute.

-- *Le Monde*, September 17, 1959.

In this interview Sartre denies having transposed to a German setting the case of a reservist who tortured people in Algeria: *I don't think a one-to-one comparison between our present situation and our neighbors' former one can be made. The two are radically different. So what is left is a general question of the responsibilities of a soldier who has been led by circumstances to go too far, a question of conscience which will come up always and everywhere. To set it spatially and temporally in today's France involved too much risk. Not the least of which was to fall into socialist realism, the very negation of theater. Note that it is not a question of a political play but of a contemporary subject concerning which I meant to keep my distance in order to transcend it and thereby leave room for the mythological dimension. In* NEKRASSOV, *the only play of mine whose action unfolds in our country and in our time, I think it was the comedy, the grotesqueness of the situation, which gave me the distance I wanted. All my other plays, with the exception of* THE VICTORS, *show this same desire for distance.*

Let us point out further in passing a flattering statement about Françoise Sagan: *Her success is entirely warranted. Setting out from a personal experience, she brought us . . . something new.*

In reply to a barbed question, Sartre recognizes willingly that he gave up writing novels partly because he lacked personal experience. The conversation ends with a quick commentary on the autobiography he has started.

59/321

"Jean-Paul Sartre: 'Frantz non plus n'était pas nazi'" ⟨Jean-Paul Sartre: "Frantz Wasn't a Nazi Either"⟩, interview by Jacqueline Autrusseau.

-- *Les Lettres françaises*, September 17-23, 1959.

I wanted to show only the negative. Those people cannot renew themselves. It's total collapse, the "twilight of the gods."

59/322

"A la veille de la première des *Séquestrés d'Altona*, Jean-Paul Sartre fait le point" ⟨Just Before THE CONDEMNED OF ALTONA Opens, Jean-Paul Sartre Takes His Bearings⟩, interview by Claudine Chonez.

-- *Libération*, September 21, 1959.

Interview bearing chiefly on politics. Note the following statement about the title "Love," which was attributed to THE CONDEMNED for a time: *I'll never write a play about love; I'm not interested in it.*

Sartre also says he cannot explain the attacks André Malraux made on him during an official trip to Brazil. Let us recall that Malraux had given a Brazilian audience to understand that Sartre had collaborated by having THE FLIES performed during the Occupation with the blessings of the German censor. Sartre says here that the play was staged with the consent of the C.N.E. ⟨National Writers' Committee⟩.

59/323

"*Les Séquestrés d'Altona* nous concernent tous" ⟨THE CONDEMNED OF ALTONA Concerns Us All⟩, conversation with Bernard Dort.

-- *Théâtre populaire*, no. 36 (4th trimester, 1959), pp. 1-13.

The most interesting of all the discussions of the play. In answering the objections Bernard Dort makes in terms of a Brechtian conception of the theater, Sartre is led to state more precisely than he had before just what he was trying to do.

To justify performing the play in a bourgeois theater, Sartre begins by explaining its relationship to the Algerian War situation, and shows that the work is chiefly concerned with the contradictions of the bourgeoisie. *But I don't mean that I wrote* THE CONDEMNED OF ALTONA *for an exclusively bourgeois audience. . . . In this play I tried to demystify (military) heroism by showing its relation to unconditional violence. This concerns us all. . . . Although we are not the Germans, although our problems*

59/323

are not the same as the ones they had in the Nazi period, there are some very special connections between us and the Germans. We were in exactly the same situation in relation to them that the Algerians are in relation to us today. . . . What I am arguing in THE CONDEMNED *is that no one in a historical society which becomes a repressive society is free of the risk of torturing someone.*

Sartre then defends himself against the charge of having chosen characters who are too unusual: *With characters like the Gerlachs, I immediately had a fundamental contradiction at my disposition, the contradiction between the industrial might, the hereditary title, the past, the culture of these people, and their collaboration with the Nazis they scorn. They think against and act for. So I could present clearly the problem of* collusion, *which is essential if you want to understand men.* He also explains that the subject he had chosen forced him to adopt the tragic mode: *My subject is a young man who comes back from Algeria, who has seen certain things down there, who maybe has taken part in them, and who doesn't talk. It's impossible for us to scorn him, to put him at a distance from us by treating him comically--impossible theatrically and even politically. For after all, the French situation also requires us to get such men back, in spite of the dirty things they may have done. . . . We have to show people the way they are* afterward. *They were torturers, they agreed to be, how are they going to work it out or not work it out? My ideal subject would have been to show not only the man who comes back and has made himself the way he is but his family around him--around his silence. He is there like a ferment making contradictions multiply, and he himself is nothing but a knot of contradictions. . . . On this basis you could sketch out, theatrically, a real social study. In* THE CONDEMNED *I blew this subject up into a myth.*

The conversation goes on to discuss questions of production and setting in relation to the Brechtian stagecraft Dort refers to in his criticism of the way the play was staged.

60/324

"Entretiens avec Jean-Paul Sartre" ⟨Conversations with Jean-Paul Sartre⟩, by Alain Koehler.

-- *Perspectives du Théâtre*, no. 3 (March, 1960), pp. 18-23; no. 4 (April, 1960), pp. 5-9.

In this long and rather jumbled conversation, Sartre repeats most of the ideas he set forth in other interviews about THE CONDEMNED. To begin with, he analyzes the two female characters and their relationship to Frantz (*At bottom, Frantz's only human relation is to his father*). The Gerlach family's Protestantism, on which he puts great stress, gives him a chance to make some general comments about Protestants as well as this personal specification: *Generally speaking, I have certainly gotten on rather better with Protestants or Protestant readers in the literary world than I have with Catholic readers. With obvious reservations stemming from their beliefs, these Protestants were much closer to accepting ideas such as the idea of man's loneliness and forlornness. We found ourselves in complete agreement concerning the solitary man.*

The second part of the conversation bears more particularly on the relationships between philosophy and the theater. *In my opinion, what philosophy always misses is the singular as such, that is, what happens to an individual.* Although the novel or the movies can reach the individual in his singularity (Sartre cites Proust and *Citizen Kane*), the function of the theater is to present the individual in the form of myth: *It's a matter . . . of finding a character who embodies, in a more or less condensed way, the problems confronting us at a given moment.*

60/325

"Wir alle sind Luthers Opfer" ⟨We Are All of Us the Work of Luther⟩, interview by Walter Busse and Günther Steffen.

a) Der Spiegel (Hamburg), no. 20 (May 11, 1960), pp. 70-79.

b) Excerpts translated in *L'Express*, May 26, 1960.

During this talk, which was aimed at the German public, Sartre concentrates on making it clear that he has not tried to deal with the specific problems of contemporary Germany. Then he makes a long and interesting analysis of the universalist ethics of Protestants (*aristocrats of the Universal*) and compares their attitude to that of the Catholics. The talk goes on to consider the idea of collective guilt (concerning which Sartre says he is to a certain extent inspired by Karl Jaspers' ideas) and of individual responsibility. He stresses the fact that Frantz did not commit suicide out of remorse but because he had become aware of his complete uselessness (*it's his impotence that kills him*). According to Sartre, the play offers a description, not an ethic. To conclude, Sartre says he would have liked to develop Werner's

60/325

character in a more positive direction if the play had not been too long already.

65/326

La Question ⟨The Question⟩.

a) Program notes for the revival of THE CONDEMNED OF ALTONA at the Théâtre de l'Athénée. *Théâtre vivant*, cahier no. 9 (September, 1965), 1965-66 season.

b) Reprinted, minus the first few lines at the beginning. In Michel Contat. *Explication des* SÉQUESTRÉS D'ALTONA *de Jean-Paul Sartre* ⟨An Analysis of THE CONDEMNED OF ALTONA by Jean-Paul Sartre⟩. Archives des Lettres modernes series, no. 89. Minard, 1968. Pp. 72-73.

> *Not too long ago* THE CONDEMNED OF ALTONA *condemned an intolerable practice. Today, now that we have peace again, this practice has disappeared in France. The reason why the play is being revived today, the reason why it is still in some respects, I hope, of interest now, is that without making any judgment or reaching any conclusion, and almost in spite of my own efforts, it confronted the audiences of that time, and still confronts today's audiences, with* the *main question: What have you done with your life?*

See also 65/428 A.

65/327

Lettre de Sartre ⟨Letter from Sartre⟩, dated November 6, 1965, to the director of K.N.S. Nederlands Toneel, Dre Poppe, on the occasion of the performance of *De Gevangenen van Altona* from November 20 to 29, 1965. Followed in the program by the Dutch translation of *The Question*.

NOTES:

Sartre gave an interview on the *Europe no. 1* station when the play was first staged in September, 1959.

On April 27, 1966, Sartre attended a trial of Frantz which took place during a "Conférence Berryer" (a speaking contest for young lawyers). Frantz was condemned to be scorned and forgotten. Sartre had this to say about the decision: *I agree with this verdict: What he deserves is to be forgotten. On condition that he kill himself, as he does in my play. Torture is a radical act which can only be wiped out by the torturer's suicide.* (See Jean-Paul Lacroix's article, "LE SÉQUESTRÉ D'ALTONA condamné à un deuxième suicide" ⟨THE CONDEMNED OF ALTONA Is Condemned To a Second Suicide⟩, *Paris-Presse*, April 29, 1966.

59/328

Marxisme et philosophie de l'existence ⟨Marxism and Philosophy of Existence⟩.

-- Letter. In Roger Garaudy. *Perspectives de l'homme: existentialisme, pensée catholique, marxisme* ⟨Perspectives for Man: Existentialism, Catholic Thought, Marxism⟩. P.U.F., 1959. Pp. 111-14. 3d ed. (1961), pp. 110-13.

Roger Garaudy's work, the purpose of which is to examine the main currents of contemporary thought, has a chapter on existentialism, the first part of which is devoted to Sartre. It is a survey which skims rather lightly over the development of Sartre's thought, giving a rapid presentation of the chief Marxist criticisms of it. Garaudy's conclusion is that existentialism must choose between irrational faith and integration into Marxism, which it can accomplish only by abandoning its present premises.

Garaudy had submitted the manuscript of this part of his work to Sartre and asked him to comment on it. Sartre's very well expressed letter was apparently written in 1959. It says nothing *Search for a Method* (see 57/296) did not say, but it has the interest of setting forth in a few pages and with greater clarity his position in respect to Marxism.

As far as I'm concerned--since you have consented to talk about me--you have been accusing me for a long, long time now of irrationalism, whereas in contrast to Kierkegaard I base Reason on the difference between Knowing and Being. So you can easily show how Marxism gradually won me over to rigorous dialectical thinking, whereas twenty years earlier I was still wandering around in the darkness of ignorance. But the fact is that I have always thought that the methods of phenomenology and the comprehension of existential projects are excellent tools to use in attacking the basic question of the praxis. . . . *It's for reasons of its own that existential thinking (mine at least) is rejoining Marxism and trying to integrate itself into it, and not because of the excellence of contemporary Marxist thought. . . . Atheistic existentialism endures because today there is no* concrete *Marxism, or better because this immense doctrine which ought to be a* Culture *is only a voluntaristic idealism, that is, a few statements about the* idea *of matter and the dialectical* idea *which are backed up by force. . . . Marxism is still* to be created. . . . *Between the special sciences without a philosophical foundation which characterize bourgeois thought and the foundation unrelated to the special sciences which historical materialism has continued to be, our century is still--the sciences excluded--the unknowing century. . . . It would seem to me a bit presumptuous*

59/328

for you, my dear Garaudy, situated as you are in the no man's land which contemporary Marxism is, to wait expectantly for us, your head full of knowledge and your arms full of flowers, as if we were your prodigal children. . . . I am convinced personally that only concrete investigations will allow the philosophy we all think in terms of to enrich itself and reveal dialectically what its real problems are. It seems to me, furthermore, that we have taken the lead in this respect: we are concerned with men and you, I'm afraid, have forgotten them a little.

See also 62/369.

59/329

* "Interview de Sartre" ⟨Interview of Sartre⟩, by Francis Jeanson.

a) Vérités pour. . . (underground monthly), no. 9 (June 2, 1959), pp. 14-17.

b) Reprinted as "L'Interview de Sartre." *Essais* (Bordeaux), nos. 2-3 (spring, 1968), pp. 76-83.

Francis Jeanson was long one of Sartre's closest collaborators: from January, 1951, to November, 1956, he managed *Les Temps modernes*. When Jeanson refused to follow Sartre in his harsh condemnation of the Russian intervention in Hungary during the 1956 uprising, the two men stopped seeing each other until their common--and radical--opposition to the Algerian War brought them together again in May, 1959 (see in this connection the postscript, *A Certain Man Named Sartre*, Jeanson wrote for the 1965 edition of his book, *Sartre's Thinking and the Moral Question*, Seuil edition, pp. 298-300 [see 47/122]). In the interim, Jeanson, who had already in 1955 published, in his *L'Algérie hors la loi* ⟨*Outlaw Algeria*⟩ (Seuil), a vigorous defense of the Algerian revolution, had gone into underground activity by participating in the organizing of a network supporting deserters and the F.L.N. ⟨National Liberation Front⟩. Following a suit brought against several members of the network in September, 1960, the network was named after its leading spirit, and henceforth the press spoke of the "Jeanson network." From the beginning of 1958 the network disseminated clandestinely a mimeographed newsletter called *Vérités pour . . .* ⟨Truths for . . . ⟩.

In *A Certain Man Named Sartre,* Jeanson tells us that the present interview comes from that first meeting after two years of separation: "When [Sartre] left two hours later, I had an interview with him for our underground paper, as well as some addresses which were to become invaluable to us." In agreeing to have his comments reported in his name, Sartre knowingly laid himself open to possible prosecution. Testifying by letter one year later in behalf of the members of the support network (see 60/352), Sartre would, moreover, say specifically, *I suppose* [that one of the questions the military tribunal could have asked me] *could have been about the interview I granted Francis Jeanson for his newsletter,* Vérités pour . . . *and I shall give a straightforward answer. I no longer remember the exact date or the precise terms of this talk. But you can find them out easily enough if this article is part of the evidence. What I do know is that Jeanson sought me out in his role as leading spirit of the "support network" and the underground newsletter which was its organ, and that I met him with full knowledge of the situation.*

59/330

"Jean-Paul Sartre spiega la crisi della gioventu di oggi" ⟨Jean-Paul Sartre Explains the Crisis of Today's Youth⟩, interview-article by Costanzo Costantini.

-- *Il Messagero di Roma*, August 25, 1959.

Sartre speaks here of the crisis of youth (bikies, etc.) and the bankruptcy of preceding generations. The youth rebellion is tied to the cold war as well as the progressive rigidity and drowsiness of contemporary society. Sartre includes the U.S.S.R. in his criticism and says in passing, *Joining the Communist Party today means joining a party which is practically conservative.*

This seems to be the first time that Sartre emphasizes bikies and rebellious youth.

59/331

Introduction to the Francine Galliard-Risler exhibition.

-- Introduction to the exhibition catalogue. Sets and costumes by Francine Galliard-Risler, Chez Dominique, November, 1959.

Excerpt:

The stage designer frequently lives in exile: he is asked to represent the earth, stones, selected vegetables, and, if need be, certain industrial products; but not the human face . . . Francine Galliard-Risler avoids this curse.

59/331

Galliard-Risler designed the costumes for THE DEVIL AND THE GOOD LORD in 1951.

59/NOTE 1.

In April, 1959, *L'Express* had given its readers a questionnaire, "Do You Believe in Democracy?" and had subsequently asked Colette Audry to write an analysis of it. The analysis appeared in the August 27, 1959, issue under the title "La Démocratie et nous" ⟨Democracy and Us⟩. It includes two short statements Sartre made during a discussion of the questionnaire. We reprint them below:

Our society aims to produce exceptional people and at the same time excludes them. It produces talented people and puts idiots in charge. Because it's purely a matter of chance when a man ends up doing what he's prepared to do. I don't like the word "elite." A man of the elite is just the opposite of a complete man. He's a sick man with a specialty.

It is certain that one is not a complete man if one does not take one's political lot in hand along with one's other responsibilities. It is certain too that this integration into social life should not prevent the individual from assuming his responsibility for his individual life. And let's be quite clear about this: there is a real contradiction between the demands of society and the destiny of the individual; and it is by no means certain that the two can be reconciled.

59/NOTE 2.

The July 8, 1959, *Komsomolskaia Pravda* (Moscow) published a short message from Sartre ("Youth is Our Future") hailing the Seventh World Youth Festival being held at that time in Budapest.

1960

60/332

CRITIQUE DE LA RAISON DIALECTIQUE ⟨Critique of Dialectical Reason⟩, preceded by *Questions de méthode* ⟨Search for a Method⟩. (The first impressions, by mistake, bear the title *Question de méthode* in the singular.) Vol. I, *Théorie des ensembles pratiques* ⟨Theory of Practical Wholes⟩.

a) For *Search for a Method*, see 57/296.

b) Excerpt in *Voies nouvelles* (see 58/308).

c) Book. Bibliothèque des idées series. Gallimard, [1960].757 pages. Dedicated "Au Castor" ⟨To the Beaver⟩ [Simone de Beauvoir].

Printing date: April 6, 1960. The original edition includes 105 copies numbered from 1 to 95 and from A to J. Part of the current edition has been rebound.

CRITIQUE OF DIALECTICAL REASON has led to many comments and articles, but no complete translation of the volume is yet available in English.

t1) For a translation of *Search for a Method*, see 57/296.

t2) Large excerpts translated by Starr and James B. Atkinson. In *The Philosophy of Jean-Paul Sartre*, edited by Robert Denoon Cumming. New York: Random House, 1965. Pp. 421-83. London: Methuen, 1968.

For a critical summary of the book by R. D. Laing, see part 3 of R. D. Laing and D. G. Cooper. *Reason and Violence*. London: Tavistock Publications, [1964].

Just as BEING AND NOTHINGNESS had been underway since 1933 even though it was not drafted until

1941-43, Sartre's second major philosophical work is the result of sustained thinking which began in the fifties, that is, at the same time he was drawing closer to the communists politically. Beginning then, Sartre set to re-reading Marx and the chief Marxist writings, and from then on he never stopped asking himself how existentialism and Marxism were related. In other words, he never stopped looking for a way to synthesize his own approach, whose starting point is subjectivity, and the objective method of dialectical materialism. His different writings during this period, although in no way rejecting his original stand, show a constant progression toward Marxism; and Simone de Beauvoir is able to note that in 1956, Sartre, "converted to the dialectical method, . . . was attempting to reconcile it with his basic existentialism" (*Force of Circumstance*, p. 346). He and Roger Garaudy decided at that time to establish the comparative effectiveness of the existentialist and Marxist methods by writing parallel studies of Flaubert. This comparison did not lead immediately to a publication, but it got Sartre ready for the essay which the Polish journal *Twórczość* asked him to write (see 57/295 and 57/296). It was when this essay was published that he undertook the writing of CRITIQUE OF DIALECTICAL REASON: "He had been pondering the subject for years, but had felt that his ideas were not yet ripe; he had needed some external stimulus before being able to take the plunge" (*Force of Circumstance*, p. 372).

The complete work was written, with interruptions and at the cost of an exhausting effort, between the end of 1957 and the start of 1960. Simone de Beauvoir, who gives a detailed depiction of the sinister climate with which the Algerian War surrounded Sartre's work, describes his work for us in this way: "He did not work as he usually did, pausing to think and make corrections, tearing up pages and starting them over again. For hours on end he rushed on from page to page without re-reading what he'd written, as if he had been swept up by the ideas that his pen, even at that speed, could not catch up with. I could hear him, in his effort to keep up this pace, crunching the corydrane pills he gobbled a bottle of per day" (*ibid.*, p. 289).

When in the fall of 1958 the emotional strain due to the lamentable defeat of the Left by Gaullism was added to this effort which had stretched him to the limit of his strength, Sartre just missed becoming the victim of a serious attack and had to cease his labors momentarily. He subsequently went on with his work at a slower pace, at the same time completing THE CONDEMNED OF ALTONA.

CRITIQUE OF DIALECTICAL REASON, which is a good one-third longer than BEING AND NOTHINGNESS (390,000 words compared to 250,000 words for an evidently equal number of pages, as Anthony Manser notes with some awe in his *Sartre, A Philosophical Study*), clearly smacks of the frenzied haste in which Sartre wrote it. He could say of himself what Marx said of *Capital*, "I didn't have the time to make it short." In his talk with Pierre Verstraeten (see 65/430), Sartre replied as follows to a complaint that the work is hard to read: *These are anecdotal questions, but I certainly could have written the* CRITIQUE OF DIALECTICAL REASON *better. By this I mean that if I'd read it one more time, cutting and trimming it, it might not have seemed so dense. So from this point of view we do have to take the anecdotal and individual dimension of the work into consideration. But except for this bit of self-criticism, the work would have been very much the way it is; because at bottom the reason why each sentence is so long and so full of parentheses, quotes, expressions like "insofar as," etc., is that each sentence represents the unity of a dialectical movement.*

Do we have today the means to constitute a structural and historical anthropology? The first volume of CRITIQUE OF DIALECTICAL REASON is devoted to answering this question. The Kantian title of this volume, as well as the parodying subtitle, "Prolegomena to Any Future Anthropology," which Sartre gave it on the spur of the moment (Gallimard edition, p. 153), indicates clearly the nature, aspirations, and limits of a work which aims, as a first step, to establish the critical foundations of Marxist historical materialism by examining the *formal* conditions of possibility and intelligibility of the dialectic of History, and not the concrete development of actual history. The project is thus a purely philosophical one which aims to give the truth of Marxism an ontological foundation, so that Marxism can account for itself--that is, can understand its own presuppositions.

To make a very schematic connection between BEING AND NOTHINGNESS and CRITIQUE OF DIALECTICAL REASON, we could say the problem Sartre is trying to solve in the second work is the following: how can we understand the fact that History, which is produced by free human *praxis*, turns back upon its agent and turns into an inhuman necessity which makes man the object of the historical process? The essentially psychological perspective of BEING AND NOTHINGNESS thus is broadened in CRITIQUE OF DIALECTICAL REASON into a historical and sociological perspective which should enable us to account for the existence of *alienated* freedom.

The transition from BEING AND NOTHINGNESS to CRITIQUE OF DIALECTICAL REASON raises serious philosophical problems which up till now do not seem to have been studied in a thorough, rigorous way. Sometimes the commentators have said that CRITIQUE

OF DIALECTICAL REASON showed Sartre's pure and simple abandonment of his initial positions (see Serge Doubrovsky in *Nouvelle Revue française*, September-November, 1961); sometimes, on the contrary, the emphasis has been put on the absolute continuity between the two works, whether in order to claim that both have the same basic flaws (see Roger Garaudy in *Perspectives de l'homme* ⟨Perspectives for Man⟩, new enlarged edition [P.U.F., 1969]) or to attest that they are perfectly compatible (see Colette Audry in *Sartre et la réalité humaine* ⟨Sartre and Human Reality⟩ [Seghers, 1966]). The chief difficulty which seems to us today to need removing is that of knowing whether there is or is not an "epistemological break" between BEING AND NOTHINGNESS and CRITIQUE OF DIALECTICAL REASON.

Generally speaking, there is no denying that the major work of the "second Sartre" has been, especially in France, very inadequately studied and, what is even more regrettable, that up till now it has inspired only a very few original works. Among these works, those of André Gorz and Nicos Poulantzas are noteworthy. Whereas there is a great number of books and articles introducing and summarizing BEING AND NOTHINGNESS, to our knowledge, only the useful little work of popularization by Colette Audry which we cited above partially serves this function for CRITIQUE OF DIALECTICAL REASON, which, however, offers far greater difficulties for the nonspecialized reader. It must be pointed out, however, that in England and the United States, the invaluable books by Ronald D. Laing and David G. Cooper, *Reason and Violence: A Decade of Sartre's Philosophy 1950-1960* (London: Tavistock, 1964), and by Wilfrid Desan, *The Marxism of Jean-Paul Sartre* (New York: Doubleday, 1965), enable English-speaking readers to acquaint themselves with faithful presentations of an as yet untranslated work.

The reception of CRITIQUE OF DIALECTICAL REASON could give rise to a complete study itself. We can do no more here than note in passing that although the work was generally favorably received by philosophers (see, for example, Mikel Dufrenne in *Esprit* [April, 1961], and Pierre Javet in *Revue de Théologie et de Philosophie* [1961]), it brought forth basic objections from specialists in the human sciences (see especially the chapter "History and Dialectic" in Claude Lévi-Strauss's *The Savage Mind*; in 1961, Lévi-Strauss devoted a whole semester of his seminars at the Ecole Pratique des Hautes Etudes to an examination of the CRITIQUE; these seminars were inspired by Jean Pouillon. It is to be hoped that the work done in all of them will soon be published).

Many commentators said they wanted to wait until the publication of the second volume announced by Sartre in his preface, so that they could make an overall judgment of the work. This second volume will probably never appear (see 69/511). At the present time only two chapters are complete. Sartre wrote them right after the first volume was published. One of them is a description of a boxing match, the other is devoted to Stalin. Sartre stopped writing when he realized that elaborating the second volume--which, let us recall, was to reach the level of concrete history--would require a series of readings and historical investigations which would represent a life's work for a single philosopher or, for a research team, many years' work. Let us point out further that in Sartre's mind, the elaboration of this second volume and of the "Ethics" have always constituted two distinct projects, and that although he has given up the first, the second should be completed in the relatively near future.

60/333

Foreword to *Aden Arabie*, by Paul Nizan.

a) New edition with an introduction by J.-P. Sartre. Cahiers libres series, no. 8. Maspero, 1960. Pp. 9-62.

Sartre's text is dated March, 1960.

The book was one of Maspero's best sellers, and was reprinted in 1967 in the series Petite Collection Maspero.

b) Reprinted under the title *Paul Nizan.* In SITUATIONS, IV.

Paul Nizan.

t1) Translated by Benita Eisler. In SITUATIONS (1965).

t2) Translated by Joan Pinkham as foreword to Paul Nizan. *Aden Arabie.* New York and London: Monthly Review Press, 1968. Pp. 7-56.

t3) Ibid. in paperback. Boston: Beacon Press, 1970.

This foreword, which was written under rather difficult conditions (see *Force of Circumstance*, pp. 489, 498) and finished in March, 1960, while Sartre was on a trip to Cuba, may be considered one of his major writings. It is not only a penetrating study of Nizan but an engaging autobiography in which Sartre indicts his whole era and brings himself unsparingly to judgment. (Maurice Merleau-Ponty, in the preface to his *Signs* [Evanston: Northwestern University Press, 1964], comments on this piece at length, and to a degree defends Sartre against his own self-criticism.)

The relations between Sartre and Nizan are analyzed in detail in Jacqueline Leiner's doctoral thesis

(Klincksieck, 1970) on the author of *Aden Arabie*. We shall be content here to recall a few facts in passing. The same age as Sartre, Paul Nizan was his closest friend since their beginning years at the Lycée Henri IV (1916). Both took the same courses (final courses at this same Lycée Henri IV, prep courses at the Lycée Louis-le-Grand for the entrance exams to the Ecole normale supérieure; they both passed the exams in 1924, undertook philosophical studies at the rue d'Ulm, and then the *agrégation* in philosophy in 1929) and took part in the same activities (contributed to *La Revue sans titre*, proofread the translation of Jaspers' *General Psychopathology*, etc.). They were so often seen together that they were sometimes mistaken for one another and, at the Ecole normale, called "Nitre and Sarzan." Sartre himself writes: *From 1920 to 1930, especially, first as schoolboys and then as students, we were indistinguishable.* In the thirties, their relationship took a different turn and became more distant, chiefly as a result of Nizan's militancy and Sartre's apolitical attitude. But they continued to be friends up till Nizan's death in May, 1940. The nature and significance of this friendship can be better determined by reference to the extensive information to be found in our subsequent items and in the memoirs of Simone de Beauvoir.

Sartre's foreword also has the autobiographical interest of making the first public reference to his relations with his stepfather (*I lived ten years of my life under the thumb of a* polytechnicien . . . , [SITUATIONS, IV, pp. 160-61]). It also seems to be the first time that Sartre, in speaking to young people, paints such a somber picture of the French situation since 1945 and makes such an indictment of his own generation (*We have nothing more to say to young people: fifty years of living in this backward province France has now become is degrading*). The *radical impotence* of the Left is stressed in what today could be called "Leftist" terms: *Do people really think the Left, this great cadaver fallen on its back and thick with worms, can attract our sons? It stinks, this rotting corpse.*

Sartre was not mistaken in sensing that Nizan had something to say to young people in 1960: accompanied by his explosive preface, the new edition of *Aden Arabie* raised quite a stir and was the beginning of a renewed interest in a work which, although in some respects dated, is nonetheless one of the most significant works of our time.

On the "Nizan affair," see 47/128.

60/334

"Jean-Paul Sartre," interview by Madeleine Chapsal.

a) Madeleine Chapsal. *Les Ecrivains en personne* ⟨Writers in Person⟩. Julliard, [1960]. Pp. 203-33. New edition, 10/18 series, 1973.

b) Reprinted as "Les Ecrivains en personne." In SITUATIONS, IX.

"To Show, to Demonstrate . . . ," anonymous translation.

-- *Yale French Studies*, no. 30 (winter, 1962-63), pp. 30-44. About two-thirds of the French text.

This talk, which was given shortly before the publication of CRITIQUE OF DIALECTICAL REASON and before the trip to Cuba, is essential to an understanding of Sartre: it enables him to take his bearings on his past and present work, on himself, and on the role that literature should play in 1960. The whole talk definitely revolves, in fact, acround the idea of commitment. Let us repeat in this connection the following passages:

If literature is not everything, *it isn't worth one hour of trouble. . . . If you reduce it to innocence, to lyrics, it withers away. If every written phrase does not resound to all the levels of man and society, it does not mean a thing* (p. 211).

The true labor of the committed writer . . . : to show, demonstrate, demystify, and dissolve myths and fetishes in a little bath of critical acid (p. 230).

Sartre also deals with the relationship of philosophy to literature and the theater, talks about Stéphane Mallarmé and Gustave Flaubert, and gives his opinion of many contemporary writers: Nathalie Sarraute (in her books, *the whole shines forth by its absence*), Alain Robbe-Grillet (a two-page analysis with rather moderate conclusions), Samuel Beckett, and above all Michel Butor (*There is only one person in France who has clearly formulated the problem and responded to the demands of the* whole--*Butor*).

Throughout the talk Sartre gives numerous autobiographical details and foreshadows already many themes he will develop in THE WORDS.

WRITINGS CONNECTED WITH SARTRE'S TRIP TO CUBA IN 1960

Sartre had not gone back to Cuba since his first visit in 1949 during his trip to Central America and the Caribbean.

In 1959, absorbed as he was in writing CRITIQUE OF DIALECTICAL REASON, he did not express his sympathy for the Castroite revolution publicly. Toward the end of the year, he was invited by Carlos Franqui, editor of the Cuban magazine *Revolución*, to come with Simone de Beauvoir and observe for himself the progress of a revolution in the making. The trip Sartre and Simone de Beauvoir made was to last about a month (from February 22 till March 20, 1960). It took on the air of an official visit and consequently created a big stir. Sartre met Che Guevara in particular, toured the island with Fidel Castro, had many talks, and even appeared at length on Cuban television.

This trip had two aims, one personal and the other political. On the one hand, Sartre, who had been sickened by the French domestic situation and by the Algerian War, wanted to keep from "shriveling up in the French misery" (as Simone de Beauvoir put it) and wanted to find a hope in the Cuban Revolution. On the other hand, he thought he might be useful to the revolution at a moment when its significance was poorly understood overseas and it was beginning to suffer from American hostility. Sartre reached Havana in the midst of the euphoria of the "Cuban festival" and what has since been called "the honeymoon of the revolution." Increasing his contacts, visiting the island from one end to the other, informing himself in minute detail, he lived through that privileged moment of every social upheaval which he had just described in CRITIQUE OF DIALECTICAL REASON: the moment of "fusion" and revolutionary spontaneity, in which each is linked to all at the heart of a collective undertaking. His hopes were fulfilled beyond all expectation: for the first time Sartre had found a revolution he could wholeheartedly support (see also *Force of Circumstance*, pp. 488-91). The deep friendship he developed with Fidel Castro added the sense of a personal link to the Cuban Revolution to his ideological approval of it, and upon his return to Europe he spoke of it with unqualified enthusiasm.

At the end of the year, when he went back through Cuba after his trip to Brazil, Sartre saw that the regime had gotten tougher in response to the threat from abroad (the first clear sign of which he had seen nine months earlier in the explosion of *La Coubre*). The "honeymoon of the revolution" was over (see *Force of Circumstance*, p. 569).

Sartre's stay in Cuba coincided with the National Theater's performances of THE RESPECTFUL PROSTITUTE. Sartre had scarcely arrived before he was the target of sharp attacks by the far-right newspaper *Diario de la Marina*, which protested the presence in Cuba of the author of THE RESPECTFUL PROSTITUTE, an "immoral and heretical work." In an article entitled "Bienvenido Jean-Paul Sartre" ⟨"Welcome Jean-Paul Sartre"⟩, the February 26, 1960, *Revolución* came forcefully to Sartre's defense. Sartre, accompanied by Fidel Castro, attended a performance of his play. His comments on the production--which he found to be excellent--and the acting--which he had reservations about, especially in respect to the role of the senator--are quoted in an article by Humberto Arenal published in the March 19, 1960, *Revolución*, which also reprints a facsimile of a short statement Sartre wrote in the National Theater guest book.

60/335

"Sartre y Beauvoir por la Provincia d'Oriente" ⟨Sartre and de Beauvoir in favor of Oriente Province⟩, interview-article by Lisandro Otero.

-- *Revolución*, February 27, 1960.

Otero reports at length the comments Sartre and Simone de Beauvoir made during their visit to Oriente Province. Sartre also gives his impressions of Fidel Castro: what he likes most of all about him is his shyness. The piece is illustrated with many photographs by Korda.

60/336

An interview about Cuba that Sartre gave on March 11, 1960.

-- Interview broadcast by the Cuban news agency Prensa Latina, which we only got to see a mimeographed copy of in the *Express* archives.

60/337

"Cuba es una democracia directa" ⟨Cuba Is a Direct Democracy⟩, televised press conference by Sartre and Simone de Beauvoir at the Hotel Nacional of Havana (complete text).

-- *Revolución*, March 11, 1960.

Sartre puts particular emphasis on two aspects of the Cuban Revolution: its pedagogical character and the fact that since it has no preconceived ideology it is not in any way dogmatic. The Cuban Revolution is distinguished from traditional Communist revolutions by the fact that it comes from the countryside and out of a war of liberation. This press conference, which was broadcast throughout the island, made Sartre very popular in Cuba.

60/338

"Discussion avec les étudiants de l'Université de La

60/338

Havane" ⟨Discussion with the Students of the University of Havana⟩ (March 14, 1960).

-- *Revolución*, March 15, 1960.

In response to students' questions, Sartre says his philosophy was never pessimistic, criticizes bourgeois individualism, and points out some traits of the Cuban personality (gaiety, the peasants' sense of responsibility, the Blacks' dynamism). According to him, the Cuban Revolution is original in respect to the French and Russian revolutions in that it is creating its theory out of its practice. In conclusion, Sartre asks the students some questions himself.

60/339

Ideología y revolución ⟨Ideology and Revolution⟩ (in Spanish).

a) Lunes de Revolución, no. 51 (March 21, 1960).

This piece, a page of the manuscript of which is reprinted in facsimile, is part of a special issue entitled "Sartre visita a Cuba" ⟨Sartre Visits Cuba⟩, which includes also the conversation mentioned below.

b) Reprinted in SARTRE VISITA A CUBA. Havana: Editiones R., 1960.

A short excerpt is also reprinted under the title "Testimonio de Jean-Paul Sartre" ⟨The Testimony of Jean-Paul Sartre⟩. In *Cuba: transformación del hombre* ⟨Cuba: The Transformation of Man⟩. Havana: Casa de Las Americas, 1961. After p. 120.

Ideology and Revolution, anonymous translation.

t1) Studies on the Left, I, no. 3 (1960), 7-16.

t2) Published as a pamphlet by the Fair Play for Cuba Committee. New York, 1960.

t3) In SARTRE ON CUBA. New York: Ballantine Books, 1961. Pp. 146-60.

This article, which was written in Cuba, was apparently never published in French. In it Sartre answers a question which he had been asked during his discussion with the University of Havana students and which he says he dealt with too hurriedly: "Can there be a revolution without ideology?" The elaborations he gives here take up, without adding anything striking, his idea that the originality of the Cuban Revolution consists in the fact that it is forging its ideology in the revolutionary *praxis* and thus avoiding both empiricism and voluntarism. Sartre also shows how the process of permanent radicalization of the revolution is a consequence of the threat from abroad and a response to the concrete needs of the populace.

60/340

"Sartre conversa con los intellectuales cubanos en la casa de Lunes" ⟨Sartre Talks with the Cuban Intellectuals in the Casa de Lunes⟩.

-- *Lunes de Revolución*, no. 51 (March 21, 1960).

May be the interview reprinted in SARTRE VISITS CUBA.

60/341

Press conference held in New York by Sartre and Simone de Beauvoir on their return from Cuba.

-- Report in *France-Observateur*, March 24, 1960.

The regime produced by the Cuban Revolution is a direct democracy. . . . The Cuban Revolution is a real revolution.

60/342

Ouragan sur le sucre: Un Grand Reportage à Cuba de Jean-Paul Sartre sur Fidel Castro ⟨Storm Over Sugar: A Major Report on Fidel Castro from Cuba by Jean-Paul Sartre⟩, a series of sixteen articles published in *France-Soir* from June 28 to July 15, 1960.

Wanting to broadcast what he had seen in Cuba as widely as possible, Sartre suggested that *France-Soir* publish *Storm over Sugar*. *France-Soir* agreed and gave this report big publicity, at the same time saying in each issue that the newspaper did not agree with some of Sartre's ideas.

Simone de Beauvoir (*Force of Circumstance*, p. 498) provides the following details: "He had begun an enormous work on Cuba which was going to be far larger in scope than the reporting he had offered to do for *France-Soir*. Lanzmann helped him extract a series of articles from it. This way of doing things accounts for certain weaknesses which become apparent when one re-reads a report which was at the time particularly effective in bringing before the general public historical and economic information not ordinarily found in the 'leading dailies.'"

Contrary to our usual procedure, we are reprinting the main subtitles of the articles ⟨in English only⟩ in order to give a better idea of their content. These titles are by Claude Lanzmann.

Torrents of electric light streamed over Havana, lighting up boulevards, restaurants, night clubs. "It's foreign gold that's lighting it," I said to myself. For all these riches were not Cuban and the U.S. companies are the real owners of the island.

-- *France-Soir*, June 28, 1960.

The article is dated "Havana . . . June," no doubt to anchor it more firmly in the present.

They were eighty coming from Mexico, piled into an old tub. The police and the army were waiting for them on the beach and massacred them. Those who escaped took refuge in the mountains, and on that day (December 2, 1956) the revolution began.

-- *France-Soir*, June 29, 1960.

"What luck! The U.S.A. has decided to buy our sugar above the world market price." In 1902 the Cubans uttered cries of joy. But 25 years later they saw they had been sold out.

-- *France-Soir*, June 30, 1960.

Of 100 Cubans, 45 were illiterate when Castro seized power: half the teachers were on unlimited leave with no pensions.

-- *France-Soir*, July 1, 1960.

"This can't go on any more," groaned the sugar cane slaves. A young son of a country squire heard these plaintive cries one day and decided to save these poor people: it was Castro.

-- *France-Soir*, July 2, 1960.

Hidden in the mountains, the rebels sprang out suddenly like devils. Their tactics: harass the regular army with the help of the peasants they had gradually succeeded in winning over.

-- *France-Soir*, July 3-4, 1960.

"Seven times they came looking for me to execute me. In the morning they let me go. . . . The police, who were crazed with fear, increased the tortures and assassinations," says Franqui, one of the network leaders.

-- *France-Soir*, July 5, 1960.

"Put God back in the Constitution!" Fidel Castro shouts

furiously when he discovers, after he has won, that the new ministers wanted to wipe this august word out of the official texts.

-- *France-Soir*, July 6, 1960.

The sugar potentates will never again return to their empty palaces. Their lands have been redistributed--27 acres per five-person family--but the cultivation of sugar cane requires collective exploitation.

-- *France-Soir*, July 7, 1960.

The Cubans are anxious to have tomato fields and steel mills. They want a workers' democracy but are delaying their choice of institutions.

-- *France-Soir*, July 8, 1960.

No old people in power: the average age of the ministers is 29. On this island stripped of its technicians, the doctors, turned into Jacks-of-all-trades, work at finance as well as agronomy.

-- *France-Soir*, July 9, 1960.

"Come early: at midnight," the state bank director told me. The other visitors are received at 2 in the morning. Working without a break, the directors of the new regime trim their sleep as much as they can.

-- *France-Soir*, July 10-11, 1960.

A picture shows Simone de Beauvoir and Sartre talking to Che Guevara, at that time president of the Cuban national bank.

A beard and long hair are still the badge of the 3000 pioneers of the rebellion. What protects the Cuban Revolution today is that it is controlled by the rebellion.

-- *France-Soir*, July 12, 1960.

A picture shows a close-up of Sartre with Fidel Castro.

This giant lying in the dust and drawing the plans for a village: Castro. He oversees everything, inspects everything, and if someone fails to do his job: "Tell the men working for you that if they don't try to solve their problems they'll have problems with me."

-- *France-Soir*, July 13, 1960.

"Fidel, give me a million to do the job. If I lied, have me shot," the old priest begs, as he tells Castro there's oil under his parish.

-- *France-Soir*, July 14, 1960.

Another photo showing Sartre and Fidel Castro touring the Cuban countryside.

In this article, Sartre tells about a conversation with Castro which he considers very important because it had just confirmed one of his basic ideas:

I said:

-- Does everyone who asks for something have the right to get it, no matter what it is he's asking for . . . ?

. . . Fidel did not answer. I insisted:

-- Is that what you think?

He puffed on his cigar and said emphatically:

-- Yes!

-- Because in one way or another, asking expresses a need?

Without turning around, he answered:

-- A man's need is the most basic of all his rights.

-- And suppose someone asked you for the moon? I said, knowing what his answer would be.

He puffed on his cigar, saw it had gone out, put it down, and turned toward me.

-- If someone asked me for the moon, it would be because he needed it, he answered.

I have few friends, because friendship is very important to me. After that answer, I had the feeling he had just become one of them; but I didn't want to waste his time by telling him. I just said:

-- You call the Cuban Revolution a humanism. And why shouldn't you? But as far as I'm concerned, there's only one humanism; and it isn't based on labor or culture but above all on need.

-- There's no other kind, he said.

And turning toward Simone de Beauvoir:

-- Sometimes, I admit, they really awe me. Thanks to us they're daring to discover their needs, they have the courage to understand their sufferings and to insist that we put an end to them, in short, they are men now. And what are we giving them?

His thinking took a sudden turn, but I had no trouble following it. He said in a brusque voice:

-- We have to ask that everyone do all he can, but I shall never sacrifice this generation to the ones to come. That would be abstract.

Pretty girls followed the Mardi Gras floats and took up a collection to buy arms. The sabotage explosion of the munitions-laden cargo ship La Coubre *(200 dead)--coming as it did in the middle of the Mardi Gras festivities--had cast a sudden pall of anguish over the rejoicing crowd and turned the feast days into days of mourning.*

-- *France-Soir*, July 15, 1960.

Photo of Fidel Castro, Sartre, and Simone de Beauvoir.

Here is the conclusion of the report:

These men, hard at work without relaxing their vigilance for a moment, are struggling underneath the threat from abroad to safeguard their two most precious conquests: the freedom, hitherto unknown in Cuba, which they created and which justifies their reforms; and that new covenant of the revolution, the confidence and friendship which unites them. I do not think that any people can set any goal for itself today which is more pressing or more worthy of its efforts. The Cubans have to win or we'll lose everything, including hope.

This report may be divided into three main parts. In the first, Sartre recalls his trip to Cuba in 1949, shows what the situation was before Castro, and gives the history of the Castro revolution; in the second, he sets to describing the economic and social reality of Cuba in 1960; in the third, finally, he stresses human reality and tells about the personal contacts he was able to have with not only Fidel Castro and Che Guevara but also the Cuban peasants.

Aware of the limitations of the report, Sartre has always refused to have it published in book form in France. He has, however, authorized translations into Spanish, Portuguese, English, Italian, Polish, and Turkish. We have been able to discover the following works:

-- HURACÁN SOBRE EL AZUCAR 〈Storm Over Sugar〉. Buenos Aires: Editorial Uno, 1960; Lima: Editorial Prometeo, 1961; Havana: Ministerio de Relaciones Exteriores, Departamento de Asuntos Culturales, n.d.

-- SARTRE ON CUBA. New York: Ballantine Books, 1961.

60/342

This anonymous translation was undoubtedly made from Spanish. The last chapter of the book consists of "Ideology and Revolution" (see 60/339).

The report was also published in *Der Spiegel* and *Izvestia* (July 15, 19, 23, 30; August 4 and 6, 1960), as well as in SARTRE VISITS CUBA. It was the target of a refutation written by a former newspaperman and ardent supporter of Batista. (José Domingo Cabus. *Sartre, Castro y el azúcar* ⟨Sartre, Castro and Sugar⟩ [Mexico: Editores Mexicanos Unidos, 1965]).

Cabus analyzes Sartre's statements in minute detail, challenges most of the figures he gives, and maintains that everything was fine during Batista's rule.

The Portuguese translation is of special interest because it has an original preface by Sartre:

60/342 A

Ao leitor brasileiro ⟨To the Brazilian Reader⟩, preface.

-- Jean-Paul Sartre. FURACÃO SÔBRE CUBA ⟨Storm Over Cuba⟩. Rio de Janeiro: Editôra de Autor, [1960]. Pp. 7-10.

Written during Sartre's stay in Brazil and datelined Rio de Janeiro, September 12, 1960, this text stresses the importance of the Cuban Revolution for Latin America and notes that the United States must choose between losing everything in a violent way or changing her policy. *My only hope*, Sartre concludes, *is that this unpretentious book contributes to the examination of present problems without any dodges.*

This preface precedes Sartre's fifteen chapters of reporting as well as two pieces on Cuba by Rubem Braga and Fernando Sabino.

Storm over Sugar was also published by the Brazilian daily *Ultima Hora*.

60/343

SARTRE VISITA A CUBA ⟨Sartre Visits Cuba⟩.

-- Havana: Editiones R., 1960.

Bound volume dedicated "To the Cuban Revolution." Printing date: October 31, 1960. New paperback edition in 1961. Let us recall that the title was originally that of a special issue of *Lunes de Revolución*.

The work includes:

- -- Ideologia y revolución ⟨Ideology and Revolution⟩ pp. 1-17
- -- Una entrevista con los escritores cubanos ⟨An Interview with the Cuban Writers⟩ 19-54
- -- Huracán sobre el azúcar ⟨Storm over Sugar⟩ 57-244
- -- Testimonio gráfico ⟨Photographic Testimony⟩ 247 ff.

This final part contains a series of photographs of Sartre and Simone de Beauvoir taken during their stay in Cuba.

60/343 A

"Cuba, la révolution exemplaire" ⟨Cuba, the Model Revolution⟩, interview of Sartre and Simone de Beauvoir by Jean Ziegler.

-- *Dire* (monthly review published in Geneva), no. 4 (August, 1960), p. 13.

Good interview which takes up the themes already developed in the other pieces about Cuba. Jean Ziegler is a professor of sociology and journalist who is very well known in Switzerland.

Concerning Cuba, see also 61/361, 68/485 and 68/486.

60/344

Albert Camus.

a) France-Observateur, January 7, 1960.

b) Reprinted in SITUATIONS, IV.

Albert Camus or *Tribute to Albert Camus.*

t1) Anonymous translation. *Tribute to Albert Camus. The Reporter*, February 4, 1960, p. 34.

t2) Ibid. In *New Left Review*, no. 2 (March-April, 1960), p. 25.

t3) Albert Camus, translated by Benita Eisler. In SITUATIONS (1965).

Camus died in an automobile accident with Michel Gallimard on January 4, 1960.

60/344

Let us stress the following passage from this often quoted and translated text: *We quarreled, he and I; but a quarrel isn't anything--even if we are never to see one another again--it's just another way we have of living together and without losing sight of one another in the narrow little world we're given.*

Concerning Camus, see 43/39 and 52/223.

60/345

"Les Grands Contemporains à la recherche d'un absolu--no. 1--Jean-Paul Sartre et les jeunes" ⟨Our Famous Contemporaries in Search of an Absolute--No. 1--Jean-Paul Sartre and the Young⟩, interview by Patrice Cournot.

-- *Le Semeur*, nos. 7-8 (February, 1960), pp. [2-5].

Le Semeur was a newspaper for young people published by Patrice Cournot, nephew of the movie critic Michel Cournot (thanks to whom we were able to find this newspaper, which is not listed in any library).

The interview is dated January 14, 1960.

Sartre does his best to answer the questions put to him by a seventeen-year-old interviewer. He ducks several questions about Antoine de Saint-Exupéry and speaks in very vivid terms about his quarrel with Albert Camus *(Camus never played any "dirty tricks" on me, as far as I know, and I never played any on him)*; teaching, adolescence *(There are two important periods in a man's life: his early childhood [the first two years] . . . and the four or six years of adolescence)*; jazz *(I saw Parker here, shortly before he died, and you know where he wanted to play? At the Conservatoire de Paris!)*; and the Algerian War *(For the young man on the Far Left who's being sent to Algeria, there isn't a whole flock of options: either he deserts or he becomes a conscientious objector)*.

60/346

"Sartre 1960: Entretien avec Jean-Paul Sartre" ⟨Sartre 1960: Talk with Jean-Paul Sartre⟩, interview by Jacques-Alain Miller.

a) Les Cahiers libres de la jeunesse, no. 1 (February 15, 1960), pp. 2-4.

b) Excerpts. "Sartre répond aux jeunes" ⟨Sartre Answers the Young⟩. *L'Express*, March 3, 1960, pp. 29-30.

In this interview he granted to a young man, Sartre takes his bearings on his *oeuvre*: he speaks in turn of his plays (THE FLIES, THE VICTORS, DIRTY HANDS, THE DEVIL AND THE GOOD LORD, NEKRASSOV and, above all, THE CONDEMNED OF ALTONA), his conception of literature, and his ideas about justice, reason, the dialectic, communism, etc.

Let us point out the following passage:

I'm not sure that the concept of justice is essential to society. I suppose it's a concept which comes from some ancient theological layer. If you don't have any god, it doesn't make sense any more, except as a protection against a certain category of individuals. The concept of justice is really useless.

To the question, "In the name of what will you struggle, and for what precise objectives?" Sartre replies: *In the name of two complementary principles: Number one, no one can be free unless everyone is; number two, I shall struggle for the improvement of living standards and working conditions. Freedom--not metaphysical but practical freedom--is conditioned by proteins. Life will be human on the day that everyone can eat his fill and every man can work at a job under suitable working conditions. I shall struggle for not only a higher living standard but democratic living conditions for everyone, for the liberation of all who are exploited and oppressed.*

After having said that the impact of the writer *can never be more than keeping the worst from happening,* Sartre concludes: *If everyone in a society of exploitation and oppression seems to be putting up with it, there must be writers to bear witness to the lives of those who are not putting up with it: it's then that the worst is kept from happening.*

60/347

* *Jean-Paul Sartre vous présente "Soledad"* ⟨Jean-Paul Sartre Presents *Soledad*⟩.

-- Program notes to *Soledad*, three acts by Colette Audry, Théâtre de Poche (Comédie Caumartin), April, 1960.

This text was kindly sent to us by Colette Audry, who told us that Sartre's original manuscript, which unfortunately has been lost, had been abridged because there was not room for it all.

60/348

L'Artiste est un suspect . . . ⟨The Artist Is a Suspect⟩,

text for André Masson's *Vingt-deux dessins sur le thème du désir* ⟨Twenty-two Sketches on the Theme of Desire⟩.

a) Part of this text appeared in *L'Arc*, no. 10 (spring, 1960), pp. 19-22.

b) André Masson and J.-P. Sartre. *Vingt-deux dessins sur le thème du désir*. Fernand Mourlot, 1961. Pp. 15-43. Deluxe edition, 35 x 45 format, limited to 195 numbered copies.

c) Reprinted as *Masson*. In SITUATIONS, IV.

These twenty-two drawings date from 1947: four of them are reprinted in an article about André Masson, "Balance faussée" ⟨Rigged Scales⟩, which appeared in *Les Temps modernes*, no. 29 (February, 1948), pp. 1381-94. Sartre's text was written during the same period and thus could have been published before 1960.

In Masson's work, *"nature" and "culture" are indistinguishable*, and *the project to paint is not distinguished from the project to be a man.* His painting, *which is essentially mythological,* is characterized by an *explosive unity, the intrusion of an existential element.*

Masson is an old friend of Sartre; he is the one who painted the sets for THE VICTORS in 1946.

60/348 A

"Odavno se poseono interesujem za Yugoslaviju" ⟨I Have Long Been Interested in Yugoslavia⟩, interview by S. Glumatz.

-- *Borba* (Belgrade), [May] 11, 1960.

Invited by the Yugoslavian Writers Union, Sartre and Simone de Beauvoir made a stay of several days in Yugoslavia in May, 1960. This short interview was given on May 10 at Orly Airport, shortly before they left for Belgrade.

After a few words about Yugoslavia, Sartre talks about THE CONDEMNED OF ALTONA, the problem of translating the play, and the project he and Jules Dassin have to adapt it to the movies. He also says he is writing a book on Cuba which he plans to draw upon for some *France-Soir* articles.

This interview accompanies an article which tells about Sartre's arrival in Belgrade and reproduces a short statement by him. Subsequently, Sartre attended performances of THE CONDEMNED OF ALTONA and NO EXIT, had a discussion on May 12 with philosophy students, was received on May 13 by President Tito, and left on May 14 for Zagreb.

60/348 B

"Ravnoduchnost u svim oblastima frantsuske umetnosti" ⟨Apathy in All Areas in France⟩, interview by Olga Bozhitchković.

-- *Politika*, [May] 14, 1960.

This interview bears on three subjects: the Algerian War, which is demoralizing the young and leading to an atmosphere of indifference and noncommitment; his stay in Belgrade (factory visits and management problems); the performance of THE CONDEMNED OF ALTONA.

60/348 C

"Zapazio sam velike promene u vachoi zemlji" ⟨I Have Noticed Major Changes in Your Country⟩, interview broadcast by the Tanjug Agency.

-- *Borba*, [May] 15, 1960.

Short interview given as he was leaving Belgrade in which Sartre talks about French literature and Yugoslavian literature, and in which he notes that he had a long talk with local writers.

60/348 D

"Gospodja Bovari niie zhena . . ." ⟨Madame Bovary Is Not a Woman⟩, interview by Miodrag Bulatović.

-- *Nin* (Belgrade), [May] 22, 1960.

This interview has to do with the relationships between literature and politics, and with Gustave Flaubert, Samuel Beckett, and Eugène Ionesco (who has *a purely expressionist orientation*). Bulatović asks Sartre if he can conceive of a "Sartrian" analysis of his own work, and the discussion then turns toward the autobiography Sartre is writing. Toward the close, talking about his projects, Sartre notes that he would like to write a novel.

60/349

Un Texte inédit de Sartre ⟨An Unpublished Text by Sartre⟩, excerpts from a lecture on the theater.

a) Premières (World Premières/Premières mondiales), 11th Year, no. 9 (June, 1960), pp. 1-2, 8.

B.N. listing: Gr. fol. Jo. 8190.

b) Part of *a)* reprinted as "Notes sur le théâtre" ⟨Notes on the Theater⟩. *Paris-Théâtre*, no. 166 (December, 1960), pp. 2-5.

Beyond Bourgeois Theater, translated by Rima Rell Dreck.

t1) Tulane Drama Review, V, no. 3 (March, 1961), 3-11.

t2) In *Theatre in the Twentieth Century*, edited by Robert W. Corrigan, pp. 131-40. New York: Grove Press, 1963. Paperback edition, 1965.

Excerpts from a lecture given in Paris in the main amphitheater of the Sorbonne on March 29, 1960. Here is how a British spectator describes the lecture:

"He spoke simply, clearly, rapidly, yet doggedly and solidly, like an expert bricklayer building up a wall in front of your eyes. He went on and on, without pause, for two-and-a-quarter hours, so that by the end the audience, although still completely fascinated, was as collapsed and wilting as people are during the final stages of a long train journey. You felt that he might have gone on all night and had stopped only as a concession to frailer humanity.

"It was a wonderful performance--the sort of lecture that ploughs up the minds of the hearers as a tractor ploughs a field. I sat next to an American professor, who said enthusiastically as we came out across the courtyard: 'St. Thomas must have lectured like that'" (John Weightman, in *Encounter*, June, 1961, p. 42).

The text published in *Premières* comes from a shorthand version Sartre did not check. Complete text is now available in the volume *Un Théâtre de situations* ⟨A Theatre of Situations⟩ (Idées series, Gallimard, [1973]).

Here Sartre tries, with due allowances made, to do for the theater what he had done in *What Is Literature?* in 1947. He shows the social nature of the theater, criticizes the bourgeois theater (represented by, among others, Samuel Beckett and Eugène Ionesco), expresses his reservations about Bertolt Brecht's epic theater, and definitively extols a form of dramatic theater. The lecture ends with a call for unity:

It seems that all the forces which the young theater can bring to bear on the bourgeois plays we have now should be united, and that there is not, in short, any real antagonism between the dramatic and the epic form, except that one of them tends toward making its object, man, quasi-objective--and its mistake is to think it can present the spectator with a society-as-object--whereas the other, if it were corrected with the aim of making it objective, would tend too far toward sympathy, and thereby risk coming down on the side of the bourgeois.

60/350

"Jeunesse et guerre d'Algérie" ⟨Youth and the Algerian War⟩, interview with K. S. Karol.

-- *Vérité-Liberté*, no. 3 (July-August, 1960).

"Sartre on Violence" (excerpts), interview-article by K. S. Karol.

-- *New Statesman and Nation*, June 25, 1960.

Sartre was a member of the board of directors of *Vérité-Liberté*, which succeeded *Témoignages et documents* beginning in May, 1960.

The interview took place prior to the Manifesto of the 121. In it Sartre is asked about the problem of young people who prefer direct action and insubordination to the traditional forms of political action. According to him, the Left has devalued verbal action, and young people find no viable institution which allows them to act. The sole means remaining to them is to try to *cross a threshold of influence* by evoking a shock in public opinion which will recall *the truth which adults have completely forgotten: the violent character of the Left.* It is the Left's lack of determination in its opposition to the Algerian War which is forcing the young to take extreme measures: *The Left is tired. Its cadres have gotten old. Believe me, old age is a factor which Marxism didn't envisage but which exists, for it is easy to get old in our society. Young people are the only ones who have responded to mystification the way it ought to be responded to, that is by violence. . . . As far as I'm concerned the only real men of the Left in France today are found among the twenty-year-olds.*

The importance of this interview lies in the fact that in it Sartre expresses for the first time the idea which will be the basis of the Manifesto of the 121: *The French Left ought to be in solidarity with the F.L.N.* ⟨Algerian National Liberation Front⟩. *Their fates are actually bound up with one another. The F.L.N.'s victory will be the Left's victory.*

This interview is one of the texts indicted for "provoking military personnel to disobey and threaten

60/350

national security" which led to the confiscation of the issue and the shadowing of the main members of the *Vérité-Liberté* staff.

60/351

"M. Jean-Paul Sartre dresse un parallèle entre Cuba et l'Algérie" ⟨M. Jean-Paul Sartre Draws a Parallel between Cuba and Algeria⟩, dispatch of the A.F.P. (Agence France-Presse ⟨French News Service⟩) reporting a lecture given by Sartre on August 31, 1960, at the Brazilian Institute of Advanced Studies in Rio de Janeiro.

-- *Le Monde*, September 1, 1960.

Sartre establishes a parallel between the evolution of the Cuban and Algerian situations. He concludes by saying that it is the duty of world public opinion to take an active part in the struggle for decolonization: *That is why I, a Frenchman, am talking to you about a national blot we have no right to be silent about. If we old Europeans wish to remain friends with the young nationalisms, we must rediscover our tradition of internationalism, whereas the underdeveloped countries can only grow by affirming their own nationalism.*

60/352

Letter to the military tribunal during the "Jeanson Trial."

a) Le Monde, September 22, 1960.

Also reprinted by most of the French press.

b) Reprinted in Marcel Péju. *Le Procès du réseau Jeanson* ⟨The Trial of the Jeanson Network⟩. Cahiers libres series, no. 17-18. Maspero, 1961. Pp. 116-19.

c) Reprinted in *Le Droit à l'insoumission (Le Dossier des 121)* ⟨The Right of Insubordination (The Dossier of the 121)⟩. Cahiers libres series, no. 14. Maspero, 1961. Pp. 85-88.

d) Reprinted in Simone de Beauvoir. *Force of Circumstance*. Pp. 545-48.

This letter, dated September 16, 1960, and addressed to M. Roland Dumas, the defendants' lawyer, caused quite a stir. Simone de Beauvoir tells us in *Force of Circumstance* (p. 545) that it was actually drawn up by Claude Lanzmann and Marcel Péju, whom Sartre, who was in Brazil at the time, had told by telephone what he meant to say to the tribunal. The letter was read before the military tribunal at the hearing of Tuesday, September 20, 1960. It had been preceded by a telegram in which Sartre apologized for not being able to testify in person.

This text is too well known for us to quote it here. Let us recall, nevertheless, that the violence of its language is explained in part by the fact that Sartre was determined to get himself imprisoned for signing the Manifesto of the 121 (see 60/NOTE 3 and 59/329).

60/353

Press conference held by Sartre and Simone de Beauvoir in Paris on December 1, 1960.

a) Report under the title "La Gauche doit répondre 'non' au référendum" ⟨The Left Ought to Answer No to the Referendum⟩. *Libération*, December 2, 1960.

b) Report under the title "Voici le but à atteindre . . ." ⟨Here's the Goal We Have to Reach⟩. *L'Express*, December 8, 1960.

Press conference held by Sartre and Simone de Beauvoir upon their return from South America. A section of the press had announced that Sartre would be imprisoned as soon as he got back to France for having signed the Manifesto of the 121. Sartre, who was trying to get imprisoned, states here that he took part in writing the manifesto and in collecting signatures, and so he insists on assuming the same responsibilities as the thirty signers who were actually locked up. As far as insubordination is concerned, he says: *We are not saying that men have to be insubordinate. We are saying that we support those who are. . . . We are perfectly well aware that supporting those who are insubordinate is not the only way of getting peace.*

He then announces that he will campaign as a writer for a no to the referendum on self-determination: *If the question asked by the government were: "Are you for self-determination through a peace negotiated unconditionally with the F.L.N.* ⟨Algerian National Liberation Front⟩*?" I would vote yes, although I am totally opposed to this regime. But the Left ought to answer no to any question which would lead to a solution to the Algerian problem bestowed by the regime.*

60/354

Parts of letters and various writings.

-- Simone de Beauvoir. *La Force de l'âge*. Gallimard, [1960]. ⟨Simone de Beauvoir. *The Prime of Life*, translated by Peter Green. Cleveland: World Publishing, 1962. The following page references are to the English-language edition.⟩

We point out below the main parts given by Simone de Beauvoir:

	Page
-- Part of a poem.	41
-- Letter written in October, 1931 describing the tree which will have a big place in NAUSEA.	89
-- Part of a song.	159
-- Letter about Italy sent to Olga Kosakiewicz during the summer of 1936.	215-16
-- Letter about "Melancholia" and Sartre's seeing Jean Paulhan and Brice Parain at Gallimard.	236-39
-- Short "strophe" on Bost.	244
-- Letter about "Lucifer," summer, 1938.	261-62
-- Letter to Adrienne Monnier about army life.	340
-- Unposted letter to Brice Parain.	342-43

For *Force of Circumstance*, see 63/391.

60/NOTE 1.

Excerpts from the deposition Sartre made on June 17, 1960, at the trial of the writer and journalist Georges Arnaud have been published in Georges Arnaud. *Mon Procès* ⟨My Trial⟩. Illustrated by Siné. Minuit, [1961]. Pp. 79-82.

Defending Georges Arnaud, who was imprisoned for having reported an underground press conference by Francis Jeanson, who was himself being sought at the time by the police (see "Les Etranges Confidences du 'professeur Jeanson'" ⟨The Strange Secrets of "Professor Jeanson"⟩, *Paris-Presse*, April 20, 1960), Sartre denounces the Algerian War as well as the oppression in France accompanying it: *The only tribunes we have left are tribunals*. He also stresses the way in which the war has disturbed the young.

60/NOTE 2.

During a press conference held in Rio de Janeiro, Sartre said notably: *Of the two imperialisms, American and Russian, the former is more dangerous.* (See *Le Monde*, August 7, 1960.)

60/NOTE 3.

The Manifesto of the 121. Sartre was not one of the initiators of the "Déclaration sur le droit à l'insoumission dans la guerre d'Algérie" ⟨Declaration Concerning the Right of Insubordination in the Algerian War⟩. He was, on the other hand, one of the first to sign it. It was distributed as a tract by the middle of the summer of 1960. The August issue of *Les Temps modernes*, which reprinted it, was immediately confiscated. A second issue (*Les Temps modernes*, nos. 173-74, special issue after confiscation [August-September, 1960]) includes two blank pages--censored--beneath the title of the declaration (pp. 194-95); they are followed by the list of the 121 names of the original signers, among whom there is not a single Communist. The text of the manifesto and all the details of the political action it crystallized may be found in *Le Droit à l'insoumission (Le Dossier des 121)* ⟨The Right of Insubordination (Dossier of the 121)⟩ (Maspero, 1961). Let us recall that a more restrained manifesto included Maurice Merleau-Ponty among its signers.

1961

61/355

Preface to *Les Damnés de la terre* ⟨The Wretched of the Earth⟩, by Frantz Fanon.

a) Excerpts in *Jeune Afrique* (September 6-12, 1961).

b) Frantz Fanon. *Les Damnés de la terre*. Cahiers libres series, no. 27-28. Maspero, 1961. Pp. 9-26.

c) The book was reprinted in 1968 in the Petite Collection Maspero series without Sartre's preface but with a separate supplement entitled "Frantz Fanon, fils de violence" ⟨Frantz Fanon, Son of Violence⟩, which contained the complete preface. (It was Fanon's widow who insisted that the preface be taken out because she disapproved of the position Sartre took at the time of the Israeli-Arab conflict--see the interview of Josie Fanon in *El Moudjahid*, June 10, 1967).

d) Reprinted under the title *Les Damnés de la terre*. In SITUATIONS, V.

Preface to *The Wretched of the Earth*, translated by Constance Farrington.

t1) Negro Digest (July, 1965), pp. 80-96.

t2) Frantz Fanon. *The Wretched of the Earth*. New York: Grove Press; London: MacGibbon, 1965.

t3) Paperback. Grove Press, Black Cat, 1968.

"Fanon had asked Sartre to write a preface for *The Wretched of the Earth* and had sent him a manuscript via Lanzmann. While in Cuba, Sartre had recognized the truth of what Fanon was saying: it is only in violence that the oppressed can attain their human status. He was in agreement with Fanon's book--an extreme, total, incendiary, but at the same time complex and subtle manifesto of the Third World; he agreed gladly to do a preface for it" (*Force of Circumstance*, p. 591). Simone de Beauvoir, in the pages following this quotation, paints an engaging, rather fascinating portrait of Fanon, a Martinican doctor and member of the Algerian provisional government whom she and Sartre met in Rome in July, 1961, and whose strong personality struck them both. Attacked by leukemia, he was to die in a Washington hospital at the end of the year. Sartre had long talks in Rome with this now famous theoretician of colonial revolution. His preface, dated September, 1961, is one of the most violent pieces he has written. In it we find the most radical and literarily effective formulation of a position he had adopted beginning in 1959 (see 59/329), that of political and practical solidarity with the Algerian fighters. Here this position is generalized to include the overall struggle of underdeveloped countries, and it can be said that Sartre's preface and Fanon's book, by the great stir they caused, made an important contribution to creating the "third-worldism" of revolutionary young intellectuals.

61/356

Le Peintre sans privilèges <The Unprivileged Painter>.

a) Preface to the catalogue for the Lapoujade show: paintings on the theme of *Riots*, *Triptych on Torture*, *Hiroshima*. Pierre Domec Gallery, 33, rue Saint-Placide, Paris-VIe, March 10-April 15, 1961. Not paginated.

b) Excerpts in *France-Observateur*, March 9, 1961.

c) Reprinted entire in *Médiations*, no. 2 (2d trimester, 1961), pp. 29-44.

d) Reprinted in SITUATIONS, IV.

The Unprivileged Painter: Lapoujade, translated by Wade Baskin.

-- In ESSAYS IN AESTHETICS (1963).

This piece, which is probably more important than the works it comments on, is also one which probably lends itself most to a criticism of Sartre's esthetic ideas. In it one finds certain analyses from CRITIQUE OF DIALECTICAL REASON, especially the analysis of crowds, being used to think about pictorial art. The main interest of this piece stems from it being the only one in which Sartre makes an extended exploration of the problem of the subject in painting.

61/356

Paradoxically, when the human face is imitated, the demand for a just likeness comes from without; but when there is no longer any imitation, this demand comes from Art itself.

. . . Lapoujade is that strange contradiction: he is, along with a few others his age, the one who has reduced painting to the sumptuous austerity of its essence; yet amidst the human presences embodied in his canvas, he is the first to give himself no special privileges. He is a painter whose paintings rip away the artist's mask. All that remains are men and the artist, without prerogatives, one of us, the painter denying himself through the splendor of his works. . . . The most surprising yet the simplest truth is that choosing the abstract was to lead, in the name of art itself, to the reinstatement of man on the canvases of Lapoujade.

The other painters Sartre talks about here are Goya, Titian (his *bête noire* in painting), Picasso (concerning *Guernica: the luckiest artist took advantage of the most unexpected piece of good luck*), Guardi (vaunted to the disadvantage of Canaletto), and Van Gogh.

61/357

"Entrevista concedida ao Instituto Brasileiro de Filosofia Secçao do Ciará" ⟨Interview Granted to the Brazilian Institute of Philosophy, Secçao do Ciará [Fortaleza]⟩, interview in Portuguese.

-- *Revista Filosofica do Nordeste* (Fortaleza), no. 2 (1961), pp. 20-21.

A text we did not look at.

Since Sartre gave several interviews and lectures during his stay in Brazil from August to November, 1960, there is a certain number of texts in the Brazilian press during this time which we were not able to list.

See, concerning the trip to Brazil, Simone de Beauvoir's long account in *Force of Circumstance*, pp. 509-69.

61/358

"L'Analyse du référendum" ⟨Analysis of the Referendum⟩, interview.

a) L'Express, January 4, 1961.

b) Reprinted with a few minor changes in SITUATIONS, V.

c) Reprinted in IL FILOSOFO E LA POLITICA ⟨The Philosopher and Politics⟩ (1964).

Sartre explains why it is necessary to vote no to the Gaullist referendum on self-determination for Algeria: the question being asked ties self-determination to the establishment of provisional institutions in Algeria whose aim is to bring to power a hypothetical third force between the far-Right and the F.L.N. ⟨National Liberation Front⟩. To those in certain circles of the Left who feel repugnance at combining their votes with those of the far-Right and are recommending a blank vote, Sartre replies: *The best way to refuse to play the rigged game they're trying to get us to play is not to say "I'm not playing"--because if we don't play the others will play for us--but to say no, no to that man, no to Machiavellianism, no to the plan they're offering us. . . . To vote yes is to refuse to wake up, to cling to dreams. To vote no is to wake up. It means, We've had enough of being conned for two years by this guy.*

61/359

"Entretien avec Jean-Paul Sartre" ⟨Talk with Jean-Paul Sartre⟩, interview by Claude Deville, Claude Arrieux, and Labre.

-- *La Voie communiste*, n.s., no. 20 (February, 1961).

La Voie communiste is a Trotskyite journal which seems to have been the first to publish the complete text of the Manifesto of the 121 in its issue no. 16 (September, 1960), which was, by the way, immediately confiscated.

The interview Sartre granted to a group of militants bears exclusively on political questions. It begins with an analysis of the Gaullist referendum on Algerian self-determination and continues by examining the possibilities of negotiations with the F.L.N. ⟨Algerian National Liberation Front⟩. The objectives of the F.L.N. are authentically socialist and revolutionary.

Sartre then tackles in a more general way the problem of colonialism. He takes the example of the Philippines to show that a capitalist state cannot, according to the norms of capitalism itself, aid a totally independent country. He goes on to show the mechanism of colonial exploitation and stresses the fact that the working class of the European countries took part in that exploitation. The assimilation of the Muslims which the liberals are preaching is impossible for economic reasons: *Colonial status engenders revolution and cannot engender anything else.* The campaign for peace in Algeria must be waged on the basis of solidarity in the actions of the Algerian revolutionaries and the French working class. Concerning the Manifesto of the 121, Sartre says: *One of the reasons motivating me to sign was precisely that we need today a whole series of radical stands which, whether they're followed or not, make people express their solidarity.* He explains the French Left's lack of radical and effective support for the Algerian Revolution in terms of the slow disappearance of internationalism after the success of the Russian Revolution. As far as France is concerned, he foresees a big economic crisis which will jeopardize the future of Gaullism. To finish, Sartre talks about the Cuban Revolution and American fears that the Cuban example will be contagious.

61/359 A

"Una conversación con Jean-Paul Sartre" ⟨A Conversation with Jean-Paul Sartre⟩, portrait-interview by Alejo Carpentier.

-- *Revista de la Universidad de Mexico*, XV, no. 6 (February, 1961), 11-12.

After a short description of the trip Sartre and Simone de Beauvoir took to Cuba, Alejo Carpentier asks some questions about the novel and writing. Sartre answers that he would like very much to write a novel, but that he will never finish *Roads to Freedom*. Our time demands a new kind of novel; he is himself looking for another way of saying things, but he has not found it yet. Following the example of Proust, who was a faithful witness to his time yet fully aware of problems of form, today's writer should look for a perspective which will allow him to give an account of a totality.

61/360

"An Interview with Jean-Paul Sartre," by Oreste F. Pucciani.

-- *Tulane Drama Review*, V, no. 3 (March, 1961), 12-18.

This interview, which was made at the beginning of 1960 by Oreste F. Pucciani, professor at the University of California at Los Angeles and, let us stress, one of the most knowledgeable people in the U.S. about Sartre's thought, deals above all with the idea of commitment and with THE CONDEMNED OF ALTONA. Sartre believes that commitment is more difficult in America because there are no precise frameworks, and he repeats in concluding that the function of literature is to *keep the worst from happening*.

61/361

"L'Assaut contre Castro" ⟨The Assault against Castro⟩, interview.

a) L'Express, April 20, 1962.

b) Translated into Russian. "Naemniki protiv Kuby" ⟨Mercenaries against Cuba⟩. *Inostranaia Literatura*, no. 8 (August, 1961), pp. 234-41.

Long interview held the day following the attempted landing in the "Bay of Pigs," at a time when it was not certain it would fail.

Sartre begins by analyzing the American Cuban policy. *The reason why the United States cannot tolerate the existence, a short distance away from Florida, of a little sovereign state of six million inhabitants which is making its own reforms is that this state challenges the new meaning of the "Monroe Doctrine." The Monroe Doctrine used to be America for the Americans. Now it's South America for the North Americans.* The United States is not really, as its propaganda claims, hostile to Cuba because it constitutes a Communist threat at its gates, but because it is afraid that the Cuban example will spread to the South American countries it dominates economically. Sartre continues with a long restatement of the analysis of American exploitation in Cuba he made in his reporting for *France-Soir* (see 60/342), and he concludes: *Well then, how does this differ from colonialism? In one respect only: the Americans' hypocritical puritanism. . . . The fantastic thing is that the wildest sort of propaganda has been made against Castro in America without the American people ever having realized that it was propaganda.* A refutation of the main arguments American propaganda makes against Cuba follows: Sartre shows that the anti-Castroite refugees are for the most part *bourgeois conservatives who want a bourgeois regime.* He goes on: *I don't want to go into the details of each incident, but the violence Cuba has been criticized for has been in every instance counterviolence. The Americans said to themselves: "Since we can't reveal what's behind the whole business--that the Cuban Revolution is robbing us--we're going to present a different scenario: we're going to push these people into the arms of the U.S.S.R. and China." They didn't even succeed, because Cuba's sovereignty is dear to her. Cuba is the ally of the U.S.S.R. and China, but she isn't communist. The Americans really would have liked her to be.* Concerning Castro's personality itself, Sartre declares: *I don't have to defend Castro. Castro, to me, is an admirable man, one of the rare men for whom I have a feeling of respect. What we need to do is show the stupidity of the people who attack him.* He explains particularly why Castro's speeches are so long: it is because they are didactic.

Sartre talks next about the landing and shows that it has little chance of succeeding because the masses have been profoundly won over to the regime, and then ties the landing to American responsibility: *In any case, the Americans' responsibility in the operation now underway is total. The invasion could not have taken place without them and cannot continue without their help. I don't mean that Kennedy is personally responsible for all this. I don't know whether he is or not. But I don't have much confidence in the Kennedy administration. Its differences from the preceding one seem to me to be chiefly verbal.* Sartre is afraid that the Americans will defy the Russian warnings. *But crushing Castro will also have the effect of radicalizing the South American people and reinforcing their rejection of imperialism. . . . We have to understand what the defeat of Cuba would mean--to us, to begin with, but above all to all the underdeveloped countries, to what is called the Third World. . . . So the Cuban business is not just a matter of an injustice. It is one, of course, and an especially outrageous one at that: it is ignoble for a great power to bend all its efforts to overthrowing a little country which is struggling to rebuild its society after more than a half-century of domination. But that is not the problem. The reason we have to commit ourselves without reservation to Castro's side is that they are trying to crush left-wing politics along with him.* And finally, Sartre concludes: *The Cuban War is like the Algerian War. It is more underhanded, because the people going over to fight it are mercenaries they claim are "Cubans," but it's the same thing. And then at a certain point, if they want to win the war, since there aren't enough mercenaries America will have to intervene with all its power.*

This off-the-cuff interview obviously contains some claims which history has disconfirmed, but many points in Sartre's analysis have been subsequently confirmed.

61/362

"Comment faire face au terrorisme" ⟨How Can We Confront Terrorism?⟩, talk with Gilles Martinet.

-- *France-Observateur*, May 18, 1961.

After the Melun talks (the first official negotiations to end the Algerian War), the O.A.S. ⟨Secret Algerian Organization⟩ carried out a series of terroristic acts. One of these in particular had hit the *France-Observateur* offices. The signers of the Manifesto of the 121 were also threatened. This interview has to do with these events.

Sartre shows that the O.A.S. terrorism is being carried out by a small number of individuals, and that it is a *terrorism of the rich* which aims to break off the negotiations by making the threat of civil war in case of their success hover over France. But the O.A.S. is wrong in its thinking, because the popular response to these acts has been to want peace as soon as possible. In this sense, *the terrorism is helping the people of France come out of their lethargy.* The Left, to fight these acts, has to demand that the government, whenever possible, arrest those who are known to be even indirectly responsible. *The more there's terrorism, the more the Left will organize and the more the government can be led to take a step ahead* (i.e., in negotiations).

61/363

"Sartre Talks to Tynan," interview by Kenneth Tynan.

a) The Observer, June 18, 1961; June 25, 1961.

b) Reprinted in Kenneth Tynan. *Tynan Right and Left.* New York: Atheneum, 1967. Pp. 302-12.

c) Incomplete French version. In *Afrique Action*, July 10, 1961.

Also translated into German. In *Die Zeit*, nos. 28-29 ([July], 1961).

This important interview tackles the following subjects: Jean Genet (*The Screens* and *The Blacks*); theater and movies; THE CONDEMNED OF ALTONA; politics and literature; Bertolt Brecht, Samuel Beckett; the movie about Freud and psychoanalysis; THE RESPECTFUL PROSTITUTE in Moscow, etc.

In addition, Sartre mentions a project he describes in this way: *If I write another play, it will be about the relationship of a husband and a wife. In itself, that would be boring, and so I shall take the Greek myth of Alcestis. If you recall, Death comes to seek out King Admetus. This doesn't please Admetus at all; 'I have things to do,' he says, 'I have my kingdom to rule, I have a war to win!' And his wife Alcestis, who regards herself as utterly superfluous, offers to die in his place. Death accepts the bargain; and then, taking pity on her, sends her back to life. That is the plot. But my version would imply the whole story of female emancipation: the woman chooses the tragic course at a moment when her husband has refused to face death. And when she returns, she is the powerful one, because poor Admetus will always be the man of whom it is said: "He allowed his wife to die for him!"*

It was no doubt as a result of a misunderstanding about the name "Alcestis" that the November 20, 1962, *Figaro* announced that Sartre's next play would revolve around a "neomisanthrope," "a character whose traits will not be far from reminding you of Molière's Alcestis."

Let us also quote the following passages: *I don't think theatre can be directly derived from political events. For instance, I would never have written* ALTONA *if it was merely a simple question of a conflict between Left and Right. For me,* ALTONA *is tied up with the whole evolution of Europe since 1945, as much with the Soviet concentration camps as with the war in Algeria. The theatre must take all these problems and transmute them into mythic form. I don't think that a playwright's commitment consists simply in stating political ideas. That can be done through public meetings, newspapers, agitation, and propaganda. . . .*

Although Godot *is certainly not a right-wing play, it represents a sort of universal pessimism that appeals to right-wing people. . . .*

If our society can disengage itself from the cold war; if it can manage to shed its colonies in peace; and if there is an evolution of the West under the influence of the East, I see no reason why Soviet Communism need be exported to the West. What I hope is that something will happen akin to the Counterreformation that followed Protestantism--a movement in the other direction. Just as Catholicism has evolved its own kind of Protestantism, I look forward to a day when the West will become Socialist, without ever passing through Communism.

61/364

"Une Génération spontanée d'alexandrins" <A Spontaneous Generation of Alexandrines>, comments reported in an article entitled "Cinq écrivains racontent leur expérience de la drogue" <Five Writers Tell about Their Drug Experience>, apparently by Nicole Bonnet.

-- *Arts*, June 14-21, 1961.

This investigation contains the accounts that Sartre, Jean Cocteau, Aldous Huxley, Christiane Rochefort, and Romain Gary gave of their drug experiences. The title given to Sartre's account refers to a story he tells about Pierre Bost, who had written, under the influence of orthedrine, a scenario completely in alexandrines. Sartre admits that he uses corydrane when he has to write something he would not have written spontaneously. He recalls the "parahallucinations" he experienced during his experiment with mescaline (which he told about in PSYCHOLOGY OF THE IMAGINATION): perceptual disturbances without loss of his sense of reality. According to him, the main effect of drugs is to release inhibitions. *The writer . . . is a victim of multiple timidities--about his subject, his style, himself. These timidities block the road to "authenticity." . . . In any case there are no general rules. The effect of drugs varies with the user's temperament. The conclusions which a given artist draws from his experiences are in most cases valid for him alone.*

61/364 A

Short piece on the movies.

-- *L'Europa letteraria*, nos. 9-10 (June-August, 1961), pp. 268-69.

Statement of no great interest in part of a larger piece called "Contradditorio francese" <French Debate> and containing accounts of movies by Simone de Beauvoir, Roger Vailland, André Malraux, Claude Mauriac, André Bresson,etc.

61/365

Merleau-Ponty vivant <Merleau-Ponty Alive>.

a) Les Temps modernes, nos. 183-85 (October, 1961), pp. 304-76. This special issue about Maurice Merleau-Ponty was personally directed by Sartre.

b) Reprinted in SITUATIONS, IV.

c) Reprinted in IL FILOSOFO E LA POLITICA ⟨The Philosopher and Politics⟩ (1964).

NOTE: There is a German translation in an independent volume, *Freundschaft und Ereignis: Begegnung mit Merleau-Ponty* ⟨Friendship and Circumstance: Encounter with Merleau-Ponty⟩ (Frankfurt am Main: Insel-Verlag, 1962).

Merleau-Ponty, translated by Benita Eisler.

-- In SITUATIONS (1965).

As soon as Merleau-Ponty died on May 4, 1961, Sartre made up his mind to pay tribute to him with a special issue of *Les Temps modernes*. Here he makes a lengthy analysis, providing many autobiographical details, of his whole relationship to Merleau-Ponty, and in so doing also provides a valuable history of *Les Temps modernes*.

Let us briefly recall the relations between the two men. Three years younger than Sartre, Merleau-Ponty entered the Ecole Normale Supérieure in 1927. Their first meeting is described in this way in *Sense and Non-Sense* (Evanston: Northwestern University Press, p. 41): "I met him one day . . . when the Ecole normale unleashed its fury against one of my schoolmates and myself for having hissed the traditional songs, too vulgar to suit us. He slipped between us and our persecutors and contrived a way for us to get out of our heroic and ridiculous situation without concessions or damages."

Afterward, the two *normaliens* more or less lost sight of one another until 1941, although Merleau-Ponty wrote a favorable but not wholly approving review of IMAGINATION. When in 1941 he joined the "Socialism and Liberty" group Sartre had just founded, the two men began a collaboration which was to last until 1952-53, and whose principal field of action was *Les Temps modernes*. In the years following the Liberation, Merleau-Ponty was closer to the communists than Sartre and stayed away from the R.D.R. ⟨Revolutionary People's Assembly⟩. He wrote several laudatory articles about Sartre (see especially "A Scandalous Author" and "The Quarrel over Existentialism," which are reprinted in *Sense and Non-Sense*) and a good number of the editorials of the magazine they ran together. The editorial, "The Days of Our Life," which denounced the existence of the Russian concentration camps, was published in January, 1950, beneath the dual signature of Sartre and Merleau-Ponty, but was composed by the latter alone.

The break between the two came about imperceptibly from the time Sartre began his rapprochement with the Communists and Merleau-Ponty, inversely, accepted the Chair of Philosophy at the Collège de France. Merleau-Ponty dedicated one last article to Sartre, "Le Langage indirect et les voix du silence" ⟨Indirect Language and the Voices of Silence⟩ (*Les Temps modernes*, June-July, 1952), then left the magazine for good. In April, 1955, he brought out *Les Aventures de la dialectique* ⟨Adventures of the Dialectic⟩ (Gallimard), a work in which he sharply attacked the stands Sartre had taken in *The Communists and Peace*, and accused him of being an ultra-Bolshevik. Sartre himself did not reply, but Simone de Beauvoir came to his defense in an article entitled "Merleau-Ponty et le pseudo-sartrisme" ⟨Merleau-Ponty and the Pseudo-Sartrianism⟩ (*Les Temps modernes*, nos. 114-15 [June-July, 1955]; subsequently reprinted in *Privilèges*). *Adventures of the Dialectic* was also criticized by the Communists, especially Roger Garaudy, in the brochure, *Les Mésaventures de l'antimarxisme: les malheurs de M. Merleau-Ponty* ⟨The Misadventures of Anti-Marxism: The Misfortunes of M. Merleau-Ponty⟩ (Editions sociales, 1956).

Merleau-Ponty and Sartre met again in March, 1956, in Venice, at a meeting of the Société Européenne de Culture (see 56/288), and then during the summer of 1958 in Italy. Their relations were normalized but did not regain the degree of friendship they had before the break. In 1960, Merleau-Ponty took advantage of a preface (to *Signs*) and the piece Sartre had written about Paul Nizan to go back over their whole relationship.

The philosophical differences between Sartre and Merleau-Ponty would be worth an in depth study, but they have been very well summarized by Jean Hyppolite in an article accompanying *Merleau-Ponty Alive*:

"Sartre's philosophy remains a philosophy of the *cogito* at the heart of a *praxis*; Merleau-Ponty's rejects the dualism of the *en-soi* and the *pour-soi*, of total inertia and active project, . . . we are already situated in history, and we prolong a natural anonymous existence whose meaning is ambiguous and inseparable from its expression.

" . . . For Sartre the dialectic is a totalizing project and totalities are imaginary. . . . For Merleau-Ponty, these totalities exist."

Subsequently, structuralism will adopt--often in opposition to Sartre--a good number of Merleau-Ponty's positions.

NOTE: The study by Albert Rabil, Jr., *Merleau-Ponty: Existentialist of the Social World* (New York: Columbia

61/365

University Press, 1967), contains the best bibliography of Merleau-Ponty presently available and establishes his relations with Sartre.

61/366

"Una nuova generazione è apparsa rinasce con essa la fiducia nella libertà" ⟨A New Generation Is Here, and with It Faith in Freedom Is Reborn⟩, interview by Ugo d'Ascia.

a) *Avanti* (Rome), December 16, 1961.

b) Excerpts. "Pas de lutte efficace sans l'union avec les communistes" ⟨No Effective Struggle without Uniting with the Communists⟩. *L'Humanité*, December 21, 1961.

c) Quoted in *Le Monde*, December 22, 1961.

Sartre says in particular, *I am not a Communist, but I feel bound organically to the Communists.*

On December 13, 1961, Sartre gave a lecture, "French Democracy and the Algerian Problem," at the Palazzo Brancaccio in Rome (see report and summary in *L'Unità*, December 14, 1961).

During the same stay, Sartre took part in a debate at the Gramsci Institute, where he also delivered a lecture, entitled "Marxism and the Problem of Subjectivity" (see summary in *L'Unità*, December 16, 1961).

61/NOTE 1.

The text entitled "La Vie et l'oeuvre de Flaubert" ⟨The Life and Works of Flaubert⟩ published by *Les Amis de Flaubert* (no. 19 [1961], pp. 5-16) is an excerpt from CRITIQUE OF DIALECTICAL REASON, *Search for a Method.*

61/NOTE 2.

Sartre wrote a short message for a press conference organized on May 19, 1961, in Paris by the P.S.U. ⟨Unified Socialist Party⟩ to protest the banning of an anti-O.A.S. ⟨Secret Algerian Organization⟩ meeting. In it he said especially: *This government had a way of proving that there was at least no collusion at the summit: letting us speak. By banning this meeting, it seems to be demonstrating just the opposite: it is gagging the mouths that the terrorists claimed they would stop forever. . . . If we had the least bit of confidence in this rotten, flimsy and despotic hierarchy which claims to rule France, we should protest the banning of this meeting. But we're beyond that point; all we have to do is take note of it and let the nation know the truth: today we are no longer content to defend it badly; we want to take away its power to defend itself.* (This text was distributed in mimeographed form by the P.S.U. ⟨Unified Socialist Party⟩, Paris Federation.)

61/NOTE 3.

On November 1, 1961, Sartre took part in a silent protest at the Place Maubert against the repression of the Parisian Algerians' manifestation on October 17; and on this occasion he made a short statement which is reprinted in *Témoignages et Documents* (no. 32 [November, 1961]).

1962

62/367

THÉÂTRE ⟨Plays⟩, illustrated edition of all the plays by Sartre performed from 1943 to 1959.

-- THÉÂTRE: LES MOUCHES. HUIS CLOS. MORTS SANS SÉPULTURE. LA PUTAIN RESPECTUEUSE. LES MAINS SALES. LE DIABLE ET LE BON DIEU. KEAN. NEKRASSOV. LES SÉQUESTRÉS D'ALTONA. ⟨Plays: The Flies; No Exit; The Victors; The Respectful Prostitute; Dirty Hands; The Devil and the Good Lord; Kean; Nekrassov; The Condemned of Altona⟩. With twenty watercolors by H.-G. Adam, A. Masson, R. Chapelain-Midy, L. Coutaud, and F. Labisse. Gallimard, [1962]. 881 pages.

Cloth edition bound on vellum according to Paul Bonet's dummy with 10,250 copies printed on March 27, 1962.

The text is the same as that of THÉÂTRE, I, and the current Gallimard editions, except that the information about the casting for the plays, and about the time and place of the premieres, has been eliminated. The text of KEAN is reprinted by itself, without Alexandre Dumas's play.

62/368

* BARIONA, OU LE FILS DU TONNERRE ⟨Bariona, or The Son of Thunder⟩, play written in December, 1940.

a) First edition. BARIONA. Atelier Anjou-copies, [1962]. II + 112 pages. Reprinted from a typed stencil and limited to 500 numbered copies not for sale.

There is a letter from Sartre at the beginning of the book which is dated October 31, 1962, and authorizes its publication.

b) Second edition. BARIONA, edited by Elisabeth Marescot, [1967]. III + 115 pages. Printed by Atelier Anjou-copies from a typed stencil.

On page II there is an excerpt from Sartre's letter, and on page III an editor's note, dated December, 1967, which thanks Sartre for having authorized "completely free of charge," "a second and limited edition of his work," and which points out that this edition was suited to the needs of scholars.

Although not in principle for sale, this edition was placed on sale in 1968 in several Parisian bookstores at the high price of 30 or 35 francs.

Sartre kindly authorized us to reprint (see Vol. II) the complete text of BARIONA, OR THE SON OF THUNDER, which will be the first regular edition of the play.

BARIONA, *or The Son of Thunder,* translated by Mary Mayer and Bernard Seal.

-- *Adam International Review*, nos. 343-45 (1970), pp. 37-85.

At Stalag XIID in Treves, where he had been a prisoner since August, 1940, Sartre was on good terms with several priests, especially the abbé who, we are told, had won his affection by his charm and by "the rigorous way in which he made his conduct match his beliefs." This is the way Simone de Beauvoir describes the relationship between the two men (see *The Prime of Life*, pp. 404-5):

"[The abbé] had a keen sense of what freedom meant; in his eyes Fascism, by reducing men to bondage, was defying God's will: 'God,' he said, 'has so great a respect for liberty that He willed His creatures to be free rather than incapable of sin.' This conviction, coupled with his deep-seated humanism, endeared him to Sartre. During endless discussions, which Sartre became passionately interested in, he argued against the Jesuits in the camp that Christ had become fully man. Jesus had been born, like every child, in filth and suffering; the Virgin had not been granted a miraculous delivery. Sartre backed him up: the myth of the Incarnation lost its beauty if Christ did not take all the ills of our human condition upon him."

It was after these discussions and to arouse his fellow captives' spirit of resistance to the Germans that Sartre agreed to write a "mystery play" about the birth of Christ. Sartre had this to say about the subject in a recent interview (see 68/487):

Certain people, when they saw that I had written a mystery play, thought that I was going through a spiritual crisis. I was not! What bound me to the priest imprisoned in the camp with me was our common opposition to nazism. The Nativity seemed to me to be the subject which was capable of creating the broadest union of Christians and nonbelievers and it was agreed that I should say what I wanted.

The important thing for me in that experience was that I was going to be able to speak as a prisoner to other prisoners and bring up our common problems. The play was full of allusions to the situation we were in, and each one of us understood them perfectly well. In our minds, the Roman envoy to Jerusalem was the German. Our captors saw him as the Englishman in his colonies!

BARIONA was written rather quickly and performed on Christmas Day, 1940, before an audience of prisoners. Sartre was so excited about the undertaking that he took over the production himself and played the part of the Wise Man Balthazar (this is worth pointing out for the sake of an eventual interpretation of the play). The sets had been painted by a friend of Sartre who also played a part (Simone de Beauvoir, in *The Prime of Life*, p. 403, says he played the part of Pilate, which is not in the play, but which is undoubtedly that of the Roman bureaucrat Lelius). According to a report picked up by Rémy Roure in an article in the *Figaro littéraire* ("Jean-Paul Sartre a sauvé une âme" ⟨Jean-Paul Sartre Saved a Soul⟩, March 26, 1960), BARIONA was a great success with the prisoners and allegedly even led to the conversion of one of them who was especially overwhelmed by the acting of Balthazar-Sartre, which was "sincere, passionate, and inflamed with faith." At the end of *A Very Easy Death*, however, Simone de Beauvoir says that the story is false.

In a text published in English in *Theatre Arts* (see 46/107), Sartre says that this first experience of putting on a play was an especially successful one:

No doubt it was neither a good play nor well acted: the work of an amateur, the critics would say, a product of special circumstances. Nevertheless, on this occasion, as I addressed my comrades across the footlights, speaking to them of their state as prisoners, when I suddenly saw them so remarkably silent and attentive, I realized what theater ought to be--a great collective, religious phenomenon.

Sartre later lost the manuscript of BARIONA, but several copies of it had been kept by Catholic former fellow prisoners of Sartre, who repeatedly urged him to authorize its performance and publication. Sartre agreed to let the play be performed on condition that it be preceded by an announcement in which he could express certain reservations and explain the circumstances in which it had been written, and that is where the project remained. On the other hand, Sartre finally agreed, in a letter to Yves Frontier on October 31, 1962, that there could be a private printing of five hundred copies of BARIONA meant chiefly for his former fellow captives, and the text was mimeographed in December, 1962. For several years the only available copy was the one in the Bibliothèque Nationale, which was, moreover, subsequently mutilated. We have recently succeeded in finding the original manuscript of the play.

Sartre has never had a very high opinion of his play. In the interview we have already cited (68/487), he does not hesitate to say: *Why didn't I revive* BARIONA *later? Because it was a bad play. It gave too much place to long demonstrative speeches.* Certainly the work, which makes one think at first of one of these low-budget Italian superproductions, shows the effects of hurried writing, and to say that it has the quality of Sartre's subsequent plays would undoubtedly be an exaggeration. Nevertheless, it does have several very fine passages and a thematic development which we think give it a not negligible place among Sartre's theatrical works.

The only critical studies in any depth of BARIONA are Thure Stenström's ("Jean-Paul Sartre's First Play," *Orbis litterarum*, XXII [1967], 173-90) and Henning Krauss's in *Die Praxis der "littérature engagée" im Werk Jean-Paul Sartre 1938-1948* ⟨The Praxis of "littérature engagée" in the Works of Jean-Paul Sartre, 1938-1948⟩ (Heidelberg: Carl Winter-Universitätsverlag, 1970, pp. 84-96). The period Sartre spent at Stalag XIID is presently being studied by one of his former fellow captives, and BARIONA will shortly be subjected to a clarification by Michel Rybalka which will bring out a good number of new elements.

62/369

Participation in a debate about the dialectic.

-- Complete text in Jean-Paul Sartre, Roger Garaudy, Jean Hyppolite, Jean-Pierre Vigier, and Jean Orcel. *Marxisme et existentialisme: Controverse sur la dialectique* ⟨Marxism and Existentialism: A Controversy about the Dialectic⟩. Tribune libre series. Plon, 1962. Pp. 1-26, 81-83.

This work consists of the complete shorthand record of the opening session, on December 7, 1961, of the "Marxist Thought Week" organized at the Mutualité by the Center for Marxist Studies and Investigations headed by Roger Garaudy. The theme of the debate was, "Is the dialectic just a law of history

62/369

or is it a law of nature too?" The debate, which was speculative and abstract, was followed with rapt attention by an audience of more than six thousand, most of them young people.

The positions Sartre elaborates are those of CRITIQUE OF DIALECTICAL REASON. They can be summed up as follows: Marxists postulate the existence of a dialectic of nature by means of a reasoning by analogy which anthropomorphically projects the dialectical process of human development onto the movement of matter. It seems to Sartre that, given the present state of scientific knowledge, the hypothesis of a dialectic of nature, which has not been in any way confirmed, is a risky one and has something of the theological about it--unless it is explicitly reduced to nothing but a heuristic method whose theoretical validity it is the business of scientists to establish through their discoveries. Sartre says he shares the fear which Jean Hyppolite expressed during the debate when he wondered if the deeper meaning of saying that there is a dialectic of nature is not to historicize nature in order to naturalize history.

62/370

"An Interview with Jean-Paul Sartre," interview-article by Ryo Tanaka.

a) Text originally appeared in Japanese in *Sekai Magazine*, [March], 1962.

b) Orient/West (Today's Japan), VII, no. 5 (May, 1962), 63-69.

Ryo Tanaka tells about a talk he had with Sartre in Paris along with the Japanese writers Kenzaburo Ohye and Ken Kaiko. The problems dealt with are political: Sartre shows the contradictions of capitalism and neocapitalism, argues that the attitude of the U.S.S.R. is more positive than that of the U.S.A., and compares the individualism of the bourgeoisie with that of the young Russians. He concludes with this remark: *I don't think an antheap society will be established in the East.* The talk goes on to consider China and Japan, and ends with some remarks about literature: *I don't think there's any literature today which is as shocking as American literature used to be.*

Let us point out that Sartre repeatedly comes back to the idea of political polycentrism as expressed by the Italian Communist leader Palmiro Togliatti.

There is an interesting portrait of Sartre by the writer Kenzaburo Ohye which came out of the same interview in *Orient/West*, VII, no. 9 (September, 1962), 33-41.

62/371

"Entretien avec Jean-Paul Sartre" ⟨Conversation with Jean-Paul Sartre⟩, interview by Jean-Paul Naury (pseudonym of Michel-Antoine Burnier).

a) Tribune étudiante (organ of P.S.U. ⟨Unified Socialist Party⟩ students) nos. 5-6 (January-February, 1962), pp. 6-7.

b) Excerpts in *L'Express*, March 15, 1962.

Interesting talk devoted for the most part to politics: the relationship of capitalism to fascism, Gaullism and the Algerian War, the attitude of the Communist Party, Third World problems (*They don't have anything to offer the Third World but a pittance and, if it protests, the butt of a rifle*), and the European situation (*The mental and intellectual level of Europeans is getting constantly lower, as a result both of the depoliticizing and of the organizing of life. Apoliticism leads to our having to accept things a humanistic society could not swallow*). The end of the talk gives information about the book on Cuba, the study of Gustave Flaubert, the movie *Freud*, etc. Sartre says in particular that he thought about writing a new work of fiction.

62/372

"Repondre à la violence par la violence?" ⟨Answer Violence with Violence?⟩, debate among Jean-Paul Sartre, Laurent Schwartz, Serge Mallet, Gilles Martinet, etc.

-- *France-Observateur*, February 1, 1962.

This debate was held following the founding of the "League for an Anti-Fascist Assemblage" by Sartre, Laurent Schwartz, and Jean-Pierre Vigier.

Speaking for himself, since the league's stand on O.A.S. ⟨Secret Algerian Organization⟩ terrorism had not been established yet, Sartre says: *In my view the essential problem is to reject the theory according to which the Left owes it to itself not to respond to violence with violence. It is considered legitimate to denounce the people who give money to the O.A.S. or who state publicly that they are members of the O.A.S. But in my opinion--and I'm only stating my own view--this is not enough.* (Let us recall that

62/372

Sartre's apartment had been bombed for the second time on January 7, 1962.) In opposition to the other participants in the debate, who are bent on tying the individual acts of terror to mass violence, Sartre favors bombings made by shock groups in response to O.A.S. terroristic acts. Sartre's political analysis is as follows: the O.A.S., which the government is involved with, is threatening to prolong the war. *So it has to be made clear that fighting the O.A.S. means fighting the government too.*

62/373

Comments at a session of the League for Action on an Anti-Fascist Assemblage on February 11, 1962.

-- *Bulletin intérieur du F.A.C.* (F.A.C.U.I.R.A. ⟨Action and Coordination Front of University Members and Intellectuals for an Anti-Fascist Assemblage⟩), no. 1 (February-March, 1962).

Sartre insists on the need for a united organization to *crush fascism*, and says the government is using the O.A.S. ⟨Secret Algerian Organization⟩ against the people. *We won't be past the risk of fascism until personal rule has been overturned.* Alluding to the negotiations being readied between the F.L.N. ⟨Algerian National Liberation Front⟩ and the French government, Sartre says that *if a formal agreement were signed, the Algerian Revolution would still run a considerable risk for years*, and that the duty of the antifascist forces will be to see to it by what they do that the agreement is respected.

62/374

"*Quick* interviewt Sartre" ⟨*Quick* Interviews Sartre⟩.

-- *Quick* (Munich), March 31, 1962.

Long interview bearing on political subjects (Algeria, the O.A.S. ⟨Secret Algerian Organization⟩, the French internal situation, de Gaulle's successor) as well as more general ones: the atom bomb, women and politics, Germany, German philosophers, the French, the young.

62/375

Les Somnambules ⟨The Sleepwalkers⟩.

a) Les Temps modernes, no. 191 (April, 1962), pp. 1397-1401.

b) Reprinted in SITUATIONS, V.

c) Reprinted in IL FILOSOFO E LA POLITICA 〈The Philosopher and Politics〉 (1964).

Dated February 19, 1962, that is, the day following the cease-fire in Algeria, this bitter, disillusioned piece (. . . *in 1945, Parisians cried for joy because they were being liberated from their sufferings; today they feel a taciturn relief because they are being rid of their crimes*) nevertheless calls upon the Left to guard against an attempt by the army to sabotage the agreements and to struggle against the threat of fascism in France.

62/376

"Bilan et perspectives de la lutte antifasciste" 〈Balance and Perspectives in the Fight against Fascism〉, interview by Simon Blumenthal and Gérard Spitzer.

-- *La Voie communiste,* n.s., no. 29 (June-July, 1962).

Important interview because it shows Sartre's disillusionment after his action for peace in Algeria.

Sartre speaks chiefly of the action of the F.A.C. (see 62/373),an organization he had placed great hope in because of its united character. And yet serious differences with the Communists concerning the line and bearing of the struggle undertaken arose within the F.A.C. *Collaboration with the P.C.* 〈Communist Party〉 *is something both necessary and impossible. . . . The P.C. wants to shut fellow-traveling intellectuals up in a ghetto.* Sartre blames the depoliticization of the working class: *They make out all right on the social level, but they don't even talk about the political struggle any more.* Even the general strike is not adapted any more to present conditions, for which new means of struggle must be found.

The balance of the F.A.C. is clearly zero, because people feel demobilized by the return of peace in Algeria. And yet the risk of fascism in France is increasingly great: *It is not true that peace in Algeria means the end of fascism in France.* To conclude, Sartre once again justifies the action of draft dodging as *an extremely positive action and not some kind of romantic madness.*

62/377

Sartre's reply to a letter by Marcel Péju in "Letters."

-- *Les Temps modernes*, no. 194 (July, 1962), pp. 182-89.

Marcel Péju had been secretary general of *Les Temps modernes* since 1953. When the magazine was reorganized in 1960, he was on the newly created managing committee. In June, 1962, he was kicked off it. In case history should be concerned with the vicissitudes of the "Péju Affair," here are the relevant texts: In its June, 1962, issue (no. 194), *Les Temps modernes* announces, without saying why, that the managing committee has asked Péju to resign. Péju counterattacks in a letter in the June 17, 1962, *Le Monde* to which the managing committee of *Les Temps modernes* replies in the June 19, 1962, edition of the same paper. In the interim, Péju had called upon *Les Temps modernes* to publish in their July issue a clarification dated June 16. *Les Temps modernes* complied and published at the end of Péju's text a reply by Sartre dated "Paris, June 30."

Sartre's reply, which is admirably written--no doubt to teach a lesson to an ex-editor whose style had caused the magazine some trouble--sets forth in restrained yet harsh terms his point of view in an affair which scarcely has any interest today. Let us recall just the same that in substance Péju was condemning Sartre for having kicked him off because he maintained "too fraternal a relationship with the F.L.N. ⟨Algerian National Liberation Front⟩," and that Sartre answers: *According to him then, we are supposedly a little bit the brothers of the Algerian fighters, but just a little bit, for fear of becoming too much so. Foster brothers, maybe, or who knows, bastard brothers? Nothing in this curious monument of depressing self-satisfaction which he demands we publish seems more stupid to me than that "too fraternal." Or more nauseating.*

This text, aside from providing one more display of Sartre's redoubtable qualities as a polemicist, offers some interesting glimpses of the internal history of *Les Temps modernes* and completes the historical account of the magazine he wrote on the occasion of Maurice Merleau-Ponty's death (see 61/365). He concludes with these words: *After the ablation of Péju, the magazine is once again the way it always has been--free.*

62/377 A

"Demokratitcheskie sily dolzhny obiedinit'sia" ⟨The

Democratic Forces Should Unite⟩, interview-article by a Tass correspondent.

-- *Pravda* and *Literaturnaia Gazeta*, [June] 5, 1962, p. 3; *Sovietskaia Kultura*, [June] 5, 1962, p. 4.

Text written during a stay Sartre and Simone de Beauvoir made in Moscow. Sartre says he came to the U.S.S.R. to establish ties with Soviet intellectuals. He stresses the risks of fascism in France, judges that Moscow has changed for the better since he last visited in 1954, and finds that the Russian people look happier.

62/377 B

"Ia videl raztsvet kultury" ⟨I Have Seen a Cultural Flowering⟩, remarks.

-- *Pravda*, [June] 21, 1962, p. 4.

Comments made on June 20, 1962, during an interview of Sartre with Soviet writers at the Writers' Center. Speaking of his trip to the U.S.S.R., Sartre notes the Russian people's cultural development and deep interest in literature, especially poetry. He says he was struck by a reading of Voznesenski's poems, as well as by two films: *The Childhood of Ivan*, by Andrei Tarkovski, and *Bania,* by S. Iutkevitch.

62/377 C

"Seitchas v SSSR vce v raztsvete i dvizhenii" ⟨At This Moment in Russian History, Everything Is Flowering and On the Move⟩, comments.

a) Pravda, [June] 23, 1962, p. 4.

b) Sovietskaia Kultura, [June] 26, 1962, p. 4.

Comments made on June 22 in Moscow during a press conference with Simone de Beauvoir. Sartre notes the progress the U.S.S.R. has made since 1954 on the material as well as the cultural level, and announces he will be back for the World Peace Congress. Simone de Beauvoir promises to give her impressions in her memoirs. See the very vivid report she made of the whole trip in *Force of Circumstance*, pp. 652-70.

62/377 D

"Sartre o ZSRR" ⟨Sartre on the U.S.S.R.⟩, interview by Adam Perlowski.

a) Polityka (Warsaw), [June] 23, 1962.

b) Almost complete translation in Russian by S. Larin. In *Voprosy Literatury*, no. 10 ([October], 1962), pp. 160-63.

Interview done in Moscow shortly before the stay Sartre and Simone de Beauvoir were to make in Poland. Sartre speaks above all of Russian cultural life (poetry, movies, youth, etc.), but without any great originality in relation to the preceding texts. He stresses, in concluding, the aims of his trip to Poland and the many ties which bind him to this country and its intellectuals.

62/377 E

"Intelektualiści a świat współczesny" ⟨Intellectuals and the World Today⟩, talk with the *Polityka* staff.

a) Polityka (Warsaw), [July] 7, 1962, pp. 1, 7.

b) Translated in *Il Contemporaneo*, September, 1962.

In this talk held in Poland with Tadeusz Drewnowski, Jerzy Lisowski, Maria Rutkiewicz, and Marian Turski as questioners, Sartre talks about the situation of the French intellectual (André Gide and Romain Rolland especially), East-West relations, and problems of decolonization (Frantz Fanon).

62/378

"La Poésie pour la jeunesse russe c'est le contrepoids de la technique" ⟨For Russian Youth, Poetry Provides the Counterpoise to Technique⟩, interview by Paul Morelle.

-- *Libération*, July 11, 1962.

Interview of no great interest made on the return from a trip to the U.S.S.R., to which Sartre had been invited by the Union of Soviet Writers. It bears on the problems of culture in the U.S.S.R., especially the problems of architecture and the plastic arts in general, of literature, and in the realm of movies. Sartre sees artistic creation in the U.S.S.R. as still dominated by the principle of utility, but discerns an obvious improvement, chiefly in poetry. Speaking of poetry, he says: *What it is trying to express . . . --with the help of a highly metaphorical form which moves forward more by means of approaches, approximations, and equivalents than by affirmations--are the relationships of man to man in Russian society today, but always against the background of building the U.S.S.R.*

62/379

Interview by a Tass correspondent.

-- *Pravda*, [July] 12, 1962, p. 5.

62/379 A

"Jean-Paul Sartre: Khorocho!" ⟨Jean-Paul Sartre: Excellent!⟩ interview by N. Mar.

-- *Literaturnaia Gazeta*, [July] 12, 1962, p. 1.

These two interviews are almost identical. Arriving in Moscow on July 10 from Warsaw to take part in the World Peace Congress, Sartre almost immediately attended Nikita Khrushchev's inaugural speech. Here he comments favorably on it and tells what the aims and aspirations of the congress are.

62/379 B

La Dêmilitarisation de la culture ⟨The Demilitarization of Culture⟩.

a) Summary and quotations in *Literaturnaia Gazeta* and *Moskovskii Komsomoletz*, [July] 14, 1962.

b) Long excerpts in *France-Observateur*, July 17, 1962.

c) Excerpts in Italian. In *Rinascita* (Rome), July 21, 1962.

d) Complete text in Italian. "Coesistenza pacifica e cultura" ⟨Peaceful Coexistence and Culture⟩. In IL FILOSOFO E LA POLITICA ⟨The Philosopher and Politics⟩ (1964). Pp. 277-87 of the pocket edition [1965].

e) Reprinted in an incomplete form in SITUATIONS, VII. In addition to the cut indicated on p. 330, there is a page missing at the beginning, as well as a long passage preceding the first paragraph on p. 324.

62/379 B

f) Bad German translation. "Die Abrüstung der Kultur" ⟨The Disarmament of Culture⟩. *Sinn und Form*, 14th Year, V-VI (1962), 805-15.

Speech given in Moscow at the World Congress for General Disarmament and Peace (July 9-14, 1962).

Examining the problem of culture in the form it took in the context of the cold war, Sartre relies chiefly on the example of Franz Kafka to show how culture has been called into the service of partisan goals. *Culture does not need to be defended . . . we don't have to* protect *culture; the only service it expects it's up to us, the intellectuals, to provide: we have to demilitarize it.* Sartre tries to convince the Russian Marxists that they have everything to gain by integrating Western culture instead of rejecting it in a lump. Referring to Nikita Khrushchev's thesis of coexistence based on peaceful competition, he says: *I apply what he* [Khrushchev] *said to culture and conclude that it should be competitive, that its synthetic unity implies in every case a competition which in my opinion should work to the advantage of Marxism.*

62/379 C

"Interview tcherez chest' let" ⟨Six Years After⟩, on contemporary French theater.

-- *Teatr* (Moscow), no. 9 ([September], 1962), pp. 184-85.

This is the second interview granted to the review *Teatr* (see also 56/282 A). Sartre regrets the fact that theatrical conditions are such in France that the playwrights are compelled to deal with the Algerian War in an indirect way. He sees only a few political plays that are worth considering: Michel Vinaver's *The Koreans*, Jean Genet's *The Blacks*, and above all Kateb Yacine's *The Encircled Corpse*. He is nevertheless pleased that there has been no play in favor of the war or any pseudo-patriotic melodramas glorifying the paratroops.

To conclude, Sartre speaks of the influence of Bertolt Brecht and analyzes at some length the then unpublished play by Georges Michel, *Sunday Stroll* (see 66/442).

62/379 D

Discussion sur la critique à propos de "L'Enfance d'Ivan"

⟨Discussion of the Criticism of *The Childhood of Ivan*⟩.

a) First published as *Lettere di Sartre a "L'Unità"* ⟨Letter from Sartre to *L'Unità*⟩. *L'Unita*, October 9, 1962.

b) Reprinted in IL FILOSOFO E LA POLITICA ⟨The Philosopher and Politics⟩ (1964).

c) French version, translated from Italian. In *Les Lettres françaises*, December 26, 1963-January 1, 1964.

d) Text *(c)* reprinted in SITUATIONS, VII.

A note indicates: "This is a translation, the original having gotten lost in Italy."

> Sartre and Simone de Beauvoir had seen Andrei Tarkovski's movie during their stay in the U.S.S.R. in June-July, 1962 (see *Force of Circumstance*, p. 629). Shown the same year at the Venice Film Festival, *The Childhood of Ivan* shared the Lion d'Or with Valerio Zurlini's *Family Chronicle* but got a rather qualified reception in the Italian Communist press. Sartre, who was in Italy at the time, decided to come to the defense of the movie and wrote a letter to that effect to Mario Alicata which was published in *L'Unità*.
>
> Sartre says that *The Childhood of Ivan* is *one of the finest films* [he] *has had the opportunity of seeing during the past few years* and compares it with Truffaut's *The Four Hundred Blows: a child all broken up by his parents--here's the bourgeois tragi-comedy. Thousands of children destroyed alive by the war--there's one of the Russian tragedies.*

62/380

La guerra fredda e l'unità della cultura ⟨The Cold War and the Unity of Culture⟩.

a) Rinascita (Rome), no. 23 (October 13, 1962).

b) Reprinted in IL FILOSOFO E LA POLITICA ⟨The Philosopher and Politics⟩, pp. 257-67 (pp. 297-308 of the pocket edition). See 64/398.

c) Translated into Russian, with two cuts toward the end. In *Inostranaia Literatura*, no. 1 ([January], 1963), pp. 222-29.

A short introduction warns the reader of certain "inexactitudes and debatable claims" by Sartre; the two cuts have to do with the Marxist crisis in the West and cultural renewal in the U.S.S.R.

62/380

This text, which is not published in French, takes up again for Western readers, and in a more developed and precise form, the ideas Sartre expressed in Moscow at the World Congress for Disarmament and Peace (see 62/379 B). Sartre uses the example of Franz Kafka again to show that the cold war led not only to the militarization of science but to the breaking off of East-West cultural contacts. He says that he is convinced that the contacts made in Moscow between Russian intellectuals and those from the West and the Third World will contribute to renewing these contacts, and that contemporary historical developments have made a truly universal culture not only possible but necessary.

62/381

"Deux heures avec Jean-Paul Sartre" ⟨Two Hours with Jean-Paul Sartre⟩, interview-article by L. Gendlin and S. Razgonov.

-- *La Culture et la Vie* (French language monthly in Moscow), no. 19 ([September], 1962), pp. 35-36.

"Two Hours with Jean-Paul Sartre."

-- *Culture and Life* (Moscow), no. 9 ([September], 1962).

Excerpts from a talk given in July, 1962, at the Writers' Center, with a picture of Sartre and Simone de Beauvoir visiting Konstantin Fedine's house. Sartre talks about the cities he has just visited (Kiev, Leningrad), the progress he has observed since his 1954 trip, the impressions he felt at a public poetry reading by Andrei Voznesenski, and the plays and movies he has seen (especially Andrei Tarkovski's *The Childhood of Ivan*). The talk ends with a discussion of literature in France and the situation created by the Algerian War. Sartre also says: *I class myself among the realist writers because I don't think there can be a literature without realism.*

This talk was reprinted in other foreign-language editions of the same periodical.

62/382

"Encounter with Jean-Paul Sartre," interview-article by László Róbert.

-- *The New Hungarian Quarterly* (Budapest), III, no. 8 (October-December, 1962), 246-48.

Without affectation and with a good number of quotations, Lászlő Róbert tells about the two talks he had with Sartre during the World Congress for General Disarmament and Peace held in Moscow in July, 1962 (see 62/379 B).

During a brief first exchange, Sartre expresses his satisfaction at Franz Kafka's being published in Hungary and stresses the chief contradiction the participants have to confront during the congress: they must on the one hand work for a universal culture and for peace, and on the other hand continue their ideological warfare.

The second conversation takes place at breakfast in the presence of a young Cuban poet. After having lamented the poor quality of the coffee sold in Russian restaurants, the three men talk about the literary life in Cuba, Hungary, and the U.S.S.R. Sartre expresses some reservations about the situation in Cuba: *I have the impression that at the present time in Cuba they are hobbling the development of different literary tendencies. . . . I realize that Fidel can't pay attention to everything . . .* ⟨from French translation by Rybalka and Contat⟩. He does not completely share his Cuban interlocutor's view of self-condemnation by the writer and suggests that he study Hungarian intellectual life--and *not simply in order to avoid the mistakes that were made in Hungary*.

The second part of the conversation is more official: Sartre talks about the aims the Moscow Congress is trying to achieve and about problems of peace.

62/382 A

Idealy vysokogo gumanizma" ⟨The Ideals of an Exalted Humanism⟩, interview.

-- *Moskva*, no. 11 ([November], 1962), pp. 175-77.

This interview, written in a very sentimental tone, is in many respects identical to the one given to *Libération* (see 62/378). In it Sartre talks about his trips to Leningrad, Kiev, Rostov-Iaroslavskii, and Moscow, compares cultural life in France and in the U.S.S.R. (above all in respect to poetry), and expresses his pleasure at having attended the four hundredth performance of *Lizzie Mackay* (Russian title of THE RESPECTFUL PROSTITUTE).

62/NOTE 1.

Excerpts from Sartre's works are reprinted in the

62/NOTE 1.

following textbook: Jean-Paul Sartre. *Choix de textes* ⟨Selected Writings⟩, Introduction by J. Sébille. Problèmes series, no. 2. Brussels: Editions Labor, and Paris: Nathan, 1962.

62/NOTE 2.

Since 1958, Sartre had worked on a script about the life of Freud for John Huston. The manuscript was almost eight hundred pages long. When the final version of the film was ready to come out in 1962, Sartre decided that his script had been too mutilated, and had his name withdrawn from the list of credits (see Appendix).

1963

63/383

LES MOTS ⟨The Words⟩.

a) Complete version in two parts. *Les Temps modernes*, no. 209 (October, 1963), pp. 577-649; no. 210 (November, 1963), pp. 769-834.

The text does not differ notably from the Gallimard edition and is already dedicated "To Madame Z."

b) Excerpts. "L'Enfance de Sartre" ⟨Sartre's Childhood⟩. *L'Express*, November 28, 1963.

c) Book. Gallimard, [1964]. 213 pages.

Dedication: To Madame Z. 15 copies on Japanese vellum; 45 on Holland vellum and 125 on wood-free vellum.

Printing date: December 30, 1963. Came out in January, 1964, and was published on the same date in the Soleil series.

d) Folio series, no. 24. Gallimard, [1972].

WORDS or THE WORDS.

t1) Excerpt. *Words*, translated by Irene Clephane. *Encounter*, XXII (May, 1964), 3-13.

t2) Excerpt. *Making of a Writer*, translated by Bernard Frechtman. *Harper's Magazine*, October, 1964, pp. 101-4.

t3) WORDS, translated by Irene Clephane. London: Hamish Hamilton, 1964.

t4) Ibid. in paperback. Penguin Books, 1967.

t5) THE WORDS, translated by Bernard Frechtman. New York: George Braziller, 1964.

t6) Ibid. in paperback. Greenwich, Conn.: Fawcett Crest Books, 1966.

It was apparently toward 1953 that Sartre thought about writing an autobiography (see 53/245). He wrote the bulk of the work in 1954, worked on it again at intervals several times afterward, then revised and sharpened it at the beginning of 1963. The shift in reference from 1953 to 1963 accounts for some contradictions in chronology. In an interview he gave to Jacqueline Piatier (see 64/405), Sartre explains why he decided to write an autobiography when he did.

In the light of political events, I became greatly concerned about my relationship to the Communist Party. Immersed as I was in the atmosphere of action, I suddenly got a clear view of the sort of neurosis which had dominated my whole previous existence. I had not been able to see it before: I was inside it. Simone de Beauvoir had guessed the reasons for it before I had. Every neurosis characteristically considers itself natural--I calmly thought that I had been born to write. In my need to justify my existence, I had made an absolute of literature. It had taken me thirty years to rid myself of this state of mind.

When my relations with the Communist Party had given me the necessary distance, I decided to write my autobiography. I wanted to show how a man can move from literature, considered as something sacred, to action, which nevertheless is still the action of an intellectual.

A second interview gives us a more precise idea of Sartre's original intentions and indicates another major concern and another determining event (see 55/267):

It's the story--my own--of a man of fifty, the son of petty bourgeois parents, who was nine on the eve of 1914 and already marked by this first pre-war era. Between the two wars he went pretty far in his studies, yet he lived only by totally deceiving himself about the meaning of life. He was the plaything of a mystification up till the day he discovered that you can become the plaything of circumstances: the day in 1939 when a uniform, a serial number, and the duty to meet a "commitment" that other people have made for you all fall on your shoulders. From that day on he made up his mind to make his own commitments all by himself. . . .

I wanted to avoid everything novelistic, and even everything anecdotal to the extent it was unimportant. Instead, these will be memoirs in which I shall define myself in relation to the historical situation by using a certain sort of psychoanalysis as well as the Marxist method as a system of investigation. It is very important to me to explain what I am writing for. This was what Kafka was concerned with when he said, "I have a mandate, but no one gave it to me." I wanted to explain in this work, into which almost all of me could be put, how it was that I wanted to keep on writing according to a given aesthetic form, but henceforth participating in social events--how I . . . burst.

In a third interview, given to Olivier Todd (see 57/294), Sartre says that what is making him write his autobiography is above all his desire to develop a method:

I have written a certain number of works--on Baudelaire and Genet, and other unpublished essays--in which I tried to determine the meaning of a life and the purpose that fills it. I have been criticized on the grounds that this reconstructing from the outside loses an element of sympathy. Now, no one can blame an author for having a certain amount of sympathy for himself and his purposes: applying my method to myself, I shall profit from a minimum of fellow-feeling.

He adds that a second reason is to show how he went from subjectivity to a certain objectivity:

There are two ways of looking at what one is writing. One may hold that one expresses what no one else feels or thinks. This is literary aristocracy. Or one may hold, on the contrary, that one writes whatever one thinks simply because one is like anyone else. That is my approach--a more democratic one at any rate. . . .

While writing this biography, I am not only concerned with the particular meaning of one life. I want to recall the rather curious evolution of a generation. I was born in 1905 in a circle of petty bourgeois intellectuals. I developed in an age whose masters were, after all, Gide and Proust, indeed an age of subjectivism and aestheticism.

Let us, finally, reprint in conclusion a statement which shows Sartre's development between 1954 and 1963 and explains why the publication of his work was delayed (see 64/405):

63/383

In THE WORDS, *I explain the source of my madness, my neurosis. This analysis may be of help to young people who dream about writing. It is after all an aspiration which is rather strange and cannot help being flawed. . . . In 1954 I was very close to being sorry* [that I had chosen literature]. *I was a neophyte in a different world. I had dreamed my life for almost fifty years. . . . But notice that there are two tones in* THE WORDS*: the echo of this condemnation and an attenuation of its harshness. The reason why I did not publish this autobiography sooner and in its more radical form is that I thought it was excessive. There's no reason to drag a poor guy through the mud because he writes. Furthermore, I came to realize in the interim that action has its problems too, and that one can be led to action by neurosis.*

THE WORDS was very well received by the critics, who saw in it such different things as the author's return to literature, a new manifestation of his bad faith, a low blow struck at childhood, an expression of the blackest pessimism, etc., and who nevertheless unanimously proclaimed the excellence of a work already numbered among the classics of autobiography. The success of THE WORDS was undoubtedly a determining factor in Sartre's being granted the Nobel Prize for Literature in 1964; a good understanding of the work also allows us to see why he refused it.

Let us indicate here that in spite of certain rumors there is not for the moment any completely written and publishable sequel to THE WORDS. It is not impossible, however, that in the rather near future Sartre will devote a volume to his adolescence. But now he envisages the autobiography of his adulthood as a sort of *political testament*.

64/384

Ot avtora ⟨On the Part of the Author⟩, preface to the Russian translation of THE WORDS.

a) Novyi Mir (Moscow), no. 10 (October, 1964), p. 60.

b) Excerpt in *Le Monde*, October, 1964.

This letter from Sartre to his Russian readers precedes the Russian translation of THE WORDS by Lena Zonina and I. Iakhnina and was published in *Novyi Mir* for October and November, 1964. This letter was not reprinted in the publication in book form (*Slova* [Moscow: Izd. Progress, 1966]), in which it is replaced by a long introduction by M. Bazhan.

We reproduce below the complete text of this letter, established according to the manuscript which we owe to the kindness of Madame Lena Zonina:

Thanks to Novyi Mir *I am making my first contact with Soviet readers. I am delighted to do so, and I hope very much that I shan't be the loser by it. All the more so because for years I have been coming to the U.S.S.R. almost every year and think I can say I have good friends here. Nevertheless,* THE WORDS *may not please you: I tell in it about a childhood which will undoubtedly seem very foreign to men my age--that is, to sexagenarians--and really exotic or unimaginable to the young. My Soviet contemporaries were born at the time of the first Russian Revolution; they were twelve years old in 1917. They certainly did not live these first years of their lives, caught up as they were between two mass movements, the first foreshadowing the other, in the same way we did ours. Even today bourgeois France still regretfully calls the period from 1900 to 1914 "la Belle Epoque." And of course it wasn't the good old days at all--not at least for the working classes--but the government and the press hid the real situation and the petty bourgeoisie shut its eyes to it. Now I tell about a bourgeois childhood. Son and grandson of petty- bourgeois intellectuals, I believed I was seeing what I was being shown--an orderly world--and I lived without history, in happiness and boredom, these difficult years which were leading us to the butchery of 1914. Well then, you'll say, why tell about this empty and deceitful dream? For two reasons.*

First, I wanted to go back along the long and sinuous road which Frenchmen my age followed to see what catastrophes and overwhelming events have torn their falsely candid optimism and idealism to shreds. I wanted to say how many among them--me included--came to join the camp of the exploited and the oppressed, to work as well as they could for the advent of socialism. The great event in our lives was your revolution. We did not live through it directly but from a distance and with a time-lag and a certain provincialism; yet that permanent confrontation of Western men with the great events of the U.S.S.R. suffices to show that there is only a single history of the world which shows each of us one or another of its aspects but unites us all to the very extent it divides and opposes us. For this first reason I feel justified in offering my book to the Soviet public: no doubt it stops around 1915, but others which will retrace my whole life will follow. For now it was necessary to show what sort of children the men we have become were made of. The first years count more than the others in a life: one slowly frees oneself from them, but one never does completely leave them.

64/384

The other reason has not always been understood: some critics have reproached me for being too hard on that child I was. People like memoirs to show a little kindness. They want the author, by going easy, to invite his readers to go easy on themselves. The truth is that I am neither hard nor easy, and it is not the little boy I'm dealing with but the milieu and time which shaped him, and above all the myth of childhood as it has been forged by adults. I ask that this little book be taken for what it is: an effort to demystify.

63/385

Doigts et non-doigts ⟨Fingers and Non-Fingers⟩, piece about Wols.

a) Wols (pseudonym of Alfred Otto Wolfgang Schülze, born in Berlin on May 27, 1913, died September 1, 1951). *Wols en personne* ⟨Wols in Person⟩. Watercolors and drawings. Texts by Jean-Paul Sartre, Henri-Pierre Roché, Werner Haftmann. Delpire, [1963]. Pp. 10-21.

b) Reprinted in SITUATIONS, IV.

Fingers and Non-Fingers.

--Wols. *Watercolors, Drawings, Writings,* translated by Norbert Guterman. With an introduction by Werner Haftmann. Essays by Jean-Paul Sartre and Henri-Pierre Roché. New York: H. N. Abrams, 1965.

Excellent piece written especially for volume *(a)*. Sartre came back to Wols again at some length in a 1964 interview: *Today's painter is trying to make others participate by participating himself, throwing himself into the painting so that we will be thrown into it along with him. All of Wols's art derived from this attempt. He looked for ways to compromise the human species in his paintings. He did so by means of the horrible, which suited the world he lived in--especially between 1937 and 1945--and his own life. This horrible world is us at the same time it isn't us. He paints us as other than ourselves to make us see from the outside and the inside (Clarté*, no. 55 [March-April, 1964], p. 46).

Concerning Wols, see also *Force of Circumstance* (p. 237) as well as FACES (48/157) and FOODS (49/181).

63/386

Preface to *La Pensée politique de Patrice Lumumba* ⟨The

Political Thought of Patrice Lumumba⟩.

a) Book of writings collected and introduced by Jean Van Lierde. *Présence africaine* publications, 1963. Pp. I-XLVI.

b) First published as *La Pensée politique de Patrice Lumumba*. *Présence africaine*, no. 47, 3d trimester (July-September, 1963), pp. 18-58.

c) Reprinted under the same title in SITUATIONS, V.

d) Reprinted in IL FILOSOFO E LA POLITICA ⟨The Philosopher and Politics⟩ (1964).

e) Translated by Helen R. Lane in the volume *Lumumba Speaks*. Edited by Jean Van Lierde. Boston and Toronto: Little,Brown, 1972. Pp. 1-52.

In some respects superior to the preface to Frantz Fanon's *The Wretched of the Earth*, this less brilliant, less well known piece is perhaps the best of those Sartre has devoted to the problems of revolution in the Third World and of its contradictions.

63/386 A

Podderzhat' printzipy mirnogo sosuchtchestvovaniia ⟨Uphold the Principles of Peaceful Coexistence⟩, statement.

a) Pravda, [January] 14, 1963, p. 4.

b) Literaturnaia Gazeta, [January] 15, 1963.

c) L'Humanité, January 14, 1963.

Statement made on January 13 after a two-week stay in the U.S.S.R. with Simone de Beauvoir and after several meetings with writers in Moscow and Leningrad. Sartre calls upon men of culture to unite against war *(There is no place for culture in the cemetery of nuclear war)*, and he emphasizes that such unity does not imply abandoning the ideological struggle.

63/387

* *Le Cinéma nous donne sa première tragédie: "Les Abysses."* ⟨The Movies Have Given Us Their First Tragedy, *Les Abysses*⟩.

a) In support of Nico Papatakis' film, Sartre wrote a piece which was reprinted in many advertisements and, along with pieces by Simone de Beauvoir, André Breton, Jean Genet, and Jacques Prévert, in *Le Monde*, April 19, 1963.

b) Reprinted in *Atlas*, VI, no. 2 (August, 1963), 118.

63/388

63/388

Nel sangue di Grimau l'unità della Spagna ⟨Spain Is United in the Blood of Grimau⟩.

a) Rinascita (Rome), April 27, 1963.

b) French text. *Grimau. Libération*, April 27-28, 1963.

Sartre parallels the emigration of Spanish workers and the execution of the Communist leader Julian Grimau (April 21, 1963) as both showing *the imbecilic savagery of the regime. For Franco, there is only one way of solving things--by blood. It must be shed. Increasingly his terror can maintain itself only by growing. Grimau's condemnation is the government's challenge to the country: if the republicans make a move toward unity, I kill. The victim was well-chosen: who in the West is going to cry over a Communist? I still remember a sergeant saying to the cops around him during a recent protest in France, "The only ones left are Communists; you can go get 'em. . . ." They went and killed eight. What I have a deep respect for in every Communist is that he ran all the risks in joining the party, deliberately made himself* the man to kill *in every bourgeois society*. But just as those killed at the "Charonne" subway stop helped bring about greater labor unity, Grimau's assassination will step up the unification of the Resistance in Spain.

63/388 A

Short statement about the C.O.M.E.S. ⟨European Writers' Community⟩ Congress in Leningrad.

-- *Pravda*, [August] 9, 1963, p. 4.

After having taken part in the work of the C.O.M.E.S. Committee (see the resolution published in the August 8 *Literaturnaia Gazeta*), and after having spoken before the congress on August 8 (see below), Sartre says that the meeting has been a success and hopes that the contacts will be kept up.

Taking the floor during a press conference given on August 9 by the participants in the congress, Sartre stresses that he took part as a socialist opposed to bourgeois culture, and says that in the ideological struggle, socialism will win (see *Pravda*, [August] 10, 1963, p. 4).

On August 13, 1963, Sartre and Simone de Beauvoir were received, along with a group of intellectuals

(Giuseppe Ungaretti, Giancarlo Vigorelli, Aleksei Surkov, etc.) by Nikita Khrushchev in his villa at Gagra. At that time Sartre had a discussion with the Soviet statesman and thanked him, during a short speech, for his hospitality (see the August 14 *Pravda* and the August 15 *Literaturnaia Gazeta*, which reproduces a group photo including Khrushchev, Sartre, and Simone de Beauvoir).

63/388 B

"Na Zapade eto bylo by nevozmozhno" ⟨That Would Be Impossible in the West⟩, interview.

-- *Literaturnaia Gazeta*, [August] 20, 1963.

Interview concerning the work of the Leningrad Congress and the Gagra reception. Sartre notes Nikita Khrushchev's interest in literature, and says he is struck by his having asked Andrei Tvardovski to read a poem in public. He says he wants to continue the dialogue, and calls on the *Literaturnaia Gazeta* readers to take part in the discussion of the novel.

63/388 C

Impressions of travel in Armenia.

-- *Kommunist*, [September] 12, 1963.

Unconsulted text. In it Sartre gives his impressions of the trip he made in Armenia after he had taken part in the Leningrad Congress.

63/389

"Coesistenza pacifica e confronto delle idee" ⟨Peaceful Coexistence and the Confrontation of Ideas⟩, interview.

a) Rinascita (Rome), no. 35 (September 7, 1963).

b) Reprinted in IL FILOSOFO E LA POLITICA ⟨The Philosopher and Politics⟩ (1964). Pp. 269-75; pp. 309-16 of the pocket edition (see 64/398).

Interview which takes up, without adding anything especially striking, the themes of the Moscow speech on "the demilitarization of culture" (see 62/379 A and 62/380). For Sartre, the ideological struggle necessarily implies a cultural unity which the cold war has artificially disrupted. Here he elaborates on the idea that competition in the realm of ideology will work to the advantage of Marxism.

63/390

"Pátě pres devátě ⟨The Fifth over the Ninth⟩, interview of Sartre and Simone de Beauvoir by AJL [Antonin J. Liehm].

a) Literární Noviny (Prague), November 23, 1963.

b) Reprinted in Antonin J. Liehm. *Rozhovor* ⟨Conversation⟩. Prague: Ceskoslovenský Spisovatel, 1966. Pp. 71-86.

This volume also includes talks with Georges Lukács, Michel Butor, Robert Merle, etc.

From November 12 to 24 Sartre was the guest of the Czechoslovak Writers' Union. Together with Simone de Beauvoir (who subsequently had had to interrupt her stay), he attended the premiere of THE CONDEMNED OF ALTONA at the Prague National Theater and gave several lectures in Prague, Bratislava, and Brno. His traveling translator was Liehm.

This interview consists of a bird's-eye view of the novel, socialism, Franz Kafka, Gustave Flaubert, THE CONDEMNED OF ALTONA, etc.

63/390 A

"4 otázky Jeanovi Paulovi Sartrovi a jedna odpoved' Simone de Beauvoirovej" ⟨Four Questions for Jean-Paul Sartre and an Answer by Simone de Beauvoir⟩, talk with Ladislav Mnacko, Peter Karvas, Pavol Stevcek, and Tomas Straus.

-- *Kulturni Život* (Prague), November 23, 1963.

Sartre talks about the consequences of the Twentieth Congress and the thaw on Western thinking, the possibilities of East-West rapprochement, especially on the cultural level, and the role that little countries like Czechoslovakia and Poland can play in this rapprochement.

The talk ends with a few comments by Simone de Beauvoir on her memoirs.

63/390 B

"J.-P. Sartre v Bratislave: O románe, politike a intelektuáloch" ⟨Jean-Paul Sartre in Bratislava: On the Novel, Politics, and Intellectuals⟩, conversation by Sartre and Simone de Beauvoir with Alexander Matuska, Pavol Stevcek, and Dominik Tatarka.

-- *Kulturni Život*, [November] 23, 1963.

Held during a stay by Sartre in Bratislava, this talk has to do chiefly with the problems of the novel.

63/390 C

"Jean-Paul Sartre à Prague" ⟨Jean-Paul Sartre in Prague⟩, interview-article by Antonin J. Liehm.

-- *Paris-Prague* (journal of the France-Czechoslovakia Association), no. 19 (November-December, 1963), pp. 22-23.

Antonin J. Liehm briefly describes Sartre's trip to Czechoslovakia and gives excerpts from a lecture on peaceful coexistence:

In order to push back bourgeois thought one has to try to understand it. . . . Today, in peaceful competition, it is no longer a question of rejecting psychoanalysis out of hand but of grasping its kernel of truth and rejecting its errors. . . . It is much more important to show Marxism using psychoanalytic methods and perfecting human understanding than to think that it is closed to this discipline. . . .

I came to see that one's choice of being is not the original source of one's damnation, that it has its own source in one's social conditioning.

Then Sartre talks about THE CONDEMNED OF ALTONA and what he saw in Czechoslovakia: *In all of that I discerned the same traits: the desire for a renewal, an opening up which was still tied systematically to a deep fidelity to the principles of socialism. . . .* [The Czechoslovakians] *can be the mediators between the socialist writers of the East and West.*

64/390 D

"Entretien à Prague sur la notion de décadence" ⟨Talk in Prague on the Concept of Decadence⟩.

a) Plamen (Prague), no. 2 (1964), pp. 16-25.

b) French text. In *La Nouvelle Critique*, nos. 156-57 (June-July, 1964), pp. 71-84.

This talk took place in November, 1963, at the offices of the review *Plamen*. The other participants were the writers Ernst Fischer, Eduard Goldstücker, Jiri Hajek, Adolf Hoffmeister, Milan Kundera, and Petr Pujman.

64/390 D

Sartre, who is obviously being treated with great respect, speaks first and begins by denying that he has any interest in the idea of decadence, which can only be an obstacle to discussion between Eastern intellectuals and Western intellectuals like himself who are openly committed to Marxism. He says: *I think that more than anything else it was my reading of Freud, Kafka, and Joyce (three names I cite because they were so often cited in Leningrad) that led me to Marxism.* When people in the East treat these authors as "decadent," they outlaw the entire personal culture of Western intellectuals. Thus this idea makes dialogue difficult and must be rejected a priori. Furthermore, it is very debatable to say that these authors are decadent because they belong to a decadent society, for even though capitalism is *as inhumane and vile as ever*, it is far from bankrupt. *We Western Leftists cannot let some of the basic authors who shaped us--Proust, Kafka, or Joyce--and whom we do not reject be considered decadent, because that would simultaneously involve the condemnation of our past and the negation of any contribution we might make to the discussion.*

The discussion is polite but gives the impression of a dialogue of deaf-mutes: it is only by relying on very general formulations that the speakers find a common ground.

63/391

Parts of letters and various writings.

-- Simone de Beauvoir. *La Force des choses.* Gallimard, [1963]. ⟨Simone de Beauvoir. *Force of Circumstance,* translated by Richard Howard. New York: Putnam, 1965. The following page references are to the English-language edition.⟩

We point out below the main parts given by Simone de Beauvoir:

	Page
-- Note dated September 14, 1939: *I am now cured of socialism, if I needed to be cured of it.*	5
-- Note on his relations with the Communists.	130
-- Notes on the R.D.R. ⟨Revolutionary Peoples' Assembly⟩.	176-77
-- Letter about Sacha Guitry, May, 1948.	161
-- Note explaining his giving up the "Ethics."	199
-- Letter about the political situation, August, 1950.	225
-- Notes on THE DEVIL AND THE GOOD LORD.	242-43
-- Notes on his discovery of the class struggle.	261-62

For *The Prime of Life*, see 60/354.

63/392

Une Lettre de J.-P. Sartre ⟨A Letter by J.-P. Sartre⟩ (addressed to Maria Craipeau).

-- *France-Observateur*, December 12, 1963, p. 2.

Letter dated "Thursday, December 5, 1963," and followed by a reply from Maria Craipeau.

In an article entitled "Une Vie en marge" ⟨A Marginal Life⟩ and published in *France-Observateur*, Maria Craipeau had made a rather sharp criticism of Simone de Beauvoir in reference to *Force of Circumstance*. Sartre took this criticism very badly and immediately sent Maria Craipeau a biting letter in which he not only challenged the justification for her claims but also attacked her personally. The affair caused some stir and was used against Sartre.

63/393

Un bilancio, un preludio ⟨A Summing Up, a Prelude⟩.

a) *L'Europa Letteraria*, IV, nos. 22-24 (1963), 162-68.

b) Abridged translation in *Inostranaia Literatura*, no. 19 ([November], 1963), pp. 243-45.

c) French text. *Un Bilan, un prélude*. *Esprit*, no. 329 (July, 1964), pp. 80-85.

Remarks at a colloquium on the novel organized in Leningrad on August 5 to 8, 1963, by the Union of Soviet Writers and sponsored by the C.O.M.E.S. ⟨European Writers' Community⟩. The *Esprit* issue also includes remarks by Bernard Pingaud, Nathalie Sarraute, and Alain Robbe-Grillet, preceded by an introduction by Pingaud, "Last Year at Leningrad."

The rather low level of the Russian contributions (also reprinted in *Esprit*) to this confrontation between Eastern and Western writers' conceptions of literature scarcely gives Sartre a chance to express more than relatively commonplace ideas which mainly indicate his desire to conciliate.

63/NOTE 1.

The January 22, 1963, *Monde* and the January 24, 1963, *Express*, in particular, report a press conference held at the home of the former minister François Tanguy-Prigent on January 21, 1963, in which Sartre, Francis Jeanson, and Noël Favrelière (these last two were condemned by default), among others, took part. The purpose of this press

63/NOTE 1.

conference was to announce the creation of a committee for the complete rehabilitation of homeland Frenchmen prosecuted and condemned for helping the F.L.N. ⟨Algerian National Liberation Front⟩. Those taking part declared that they were going to openly aid and comfort the deserters who were still being prosecuted, in order to make the government take a stand.

In his remarks, which we were unable to get the complete text of, Sartre stressed the urgency of a campaign in support of those who were still imprisoned or excluded from public life for having resisted the Algerian War. He shows the inconsistency of the government in signing the Evian agreements and organizing cooperation with Algeria, yet continuing to hold that a Frenchman who acted for Algerian independence had committed a crime. *If they really want cooperation, then they must, in the name of it, liberate and reintegrate this handful of men and women.*

63/NOTE 2.

Le Monde (February 20, 1963), reporting the trial of the "Petit-Clamart Conspirators," quotes a letter to the court from Sartre the gist of which is as follows: *I do not know the facts. I do not know the persons who are having me called nor anyone who knows them. So in terms of the new law, I am forbidden to testify.*

Sartre had in fact been called as a witness by the defense lawyers, who wanted to ask him this question: "You said in 1957 that Ben Sadok's act could not be called a terroristic act. Could you not say the same of Bastien-Thiry's act?" The court ruled definitively that hearing well-known political figures, such as Sartre, whom the defense had called as witnesses, was not necessary.

1964

64/394

SITUATIONS, IV: PORTRAITS.

-- Gallimard, [1964]. 461 pages. Publicity band: "Literature and Painting."

This volume includes fifteen pieces, in French, published from 1948 to 1963 and divided into three sections:

I.	-- *Portrait of a Man Unknown* (on Nathalie Sarraute)	see ## 48/159
	-- *The Artist and His Conscience* (on music)	# 50/195
	-- *Of Rats and Men* (on André Gorz)	# 58/303
II.	-- *The Living Gide*	# 51/214
	-- *Reply to Albert Camus*	# 52/223
	-- *Albert Camus*	# 60/344
	-- *Paul Nizan*	# 60/333
	-- *Merleau-Ponty Alive*	# 61/365
III.	-- *The Prisoner of Venice* (on Tintoretto)	# 57/300
	-- *The Paintings of Giacometti*	# 54/257
	-- *The Unprivileged Painter* (on Lapoujade)	61/356
	-- *Masson*	60/348
	-- *Fingers and Non-Fingers* (on Wols)	63/385
	-- *A Garden of Capucines*	52/222
	-- *Venice from My Window*	53/235

These two last pieces come from the abandoned work "Queen Albermarle and the Last Tourist."

SITUATIONS, IV has been generally considered one of the best volumes published in France in 1964.

Translations of SITUATIONS, IV.

t1) Essays marked # translated by Benita Eisler;

64/394

essay marked ## translated by Maria Jolas. All in SITUATIONS. New York: George Braziller, 1965; London: Hamish Hamilton, 1965.

t2) Ibid. in paperback. Greenwich, Conn.: Fawcett Crest Books, 1966.

t3) The Unprivileged Painter: Lapoujade, and *Venetian Pariah*, translated by Wade Baskin. In ESSAYS IN AESTHETICS (1963).

64/395

SITUATIONS, V: COLONIALISME ET NÉO-COLONIALISME ⟨Situations, V: Colonialism and Neocolonialism⟩.

-- Gallimard, [1964]. 255 pages.

This volume includes thirteen pieces, in French, written from 1954 to 1963 and arranged, with a single exception, in the chronological order of their publication. There are no major changes.

-- *From One China to the Other* (Cartier-Bresson)	see # 54/250
-- *Colonialism Is a System*	56/285
-- *A Portrait of the Colonized, Preceded by "A Portrait of the Colonizer" by Albert Nemmi*	# 57/298
-- *You Are Really Something*	57/293
-- *We Are All Assassins*	58/305
-- *A Victory* (Henri Alleg)	# 58/302
-- *The Pretender*	58/306
-- *The Constitution of Contempt*	58/309
-- *The Frogs Who Wanted a King*	58/310
-- *Analysis of the Referendum*	61/358
-- *The Sleepwalkers*	62/375
-- *The Wretched of the Earth* (Frantz Fanon)	# 61/355
-- *The Political Thought of Patrice Lumumba*	# 63/386

Only essays marked # have been translated so far. See separate entries.

64/396

SITUATIONS, VI: PROBLÈMES DU MARXISME, 1. ⟨Situations, VI: Problems of Marxism⟩.

-- Gallimard, [1964]. 385 pages.

This volume includes five pieces, in French, published from 1950 to 1954 and reprinted without major changes:

-- *Portrait of the Adventurer* (Roger Stéphane) see 50/196
-- *Which Are False, the Wise Men or the Elephants?* (Louis Dalmas) 50/193
-- *Are We in a Democracy?* 52/219
-- *The End of Hope* (Juan Hermanos) 50/194
-- *The Communists and Peace* 52/220, 54/254

For translations of *The Communists and Peace*, see 52/220.

64/397

QU'EST-CE QUE LA LITTÉRATURE? 〈What Is Literature?〉.

-- Idées series. Gallimard, [1964]. 375 pages.

See 47/125.

64/398

IL FILOSOFO E LA POLITICA 〈The Philosopher and Politics〉.

a) Translated by Luciana Trentin and Romano Ledda. Preface by Mario Alicata. Rome: Riuniti, 1964.

b) Pocket edition. Enciclopedia tascabile series, no. 94. Rome: Riuniti, [1965].

This selection of political writings was published in Italy before the French publication of SITUATIONS, IV, V, and VI. It includes an Italian version of the following pieces, two of which have never been published in French:

-- *The Communists and Peace* see 52/220, 54/254
-- *The Ghost of Stalin* 57/291
-- *You Are Really Something* 57/293
-- *We Are All Assassins* 58/305
-- *The Pretender* 58/306
-- *The Constitution of Contempt* 58/309
-- *The Frogs Who Wanted a King* 58/310
-- *Analysis of the Referendum* 61/358
-- *Merleau-Ponty Alive* 61/365
-- *The Sleepwalkers* 62/375
-- *The Demilitarization of Culture* (complete text) 62/379 B
-- *Discussion of the Criticism of "The Childhood of Ivan"* 62/379 D
-- *The Cold War and the Unity of Culture* (not published in French) 62/380
-- *Peaceful Coexistence and the Confrontation of Ideas* (interview not published in French) 63/389
-- *The Political Thought of Patrice Lumumba* 63/386

This volume includes an index of names cited.

64/399

"Incontro con Jean-Paul Sartre" ⟨A Meeting with Jean-Paul Sartre⟩, interview.

-- Interview recorded in March or April, 1964, on the occasion of the publication of IL FILOSOFO E LA POLITICA ⟨The Philosopher and Politics⟩ and published in an unidentified Italian periodical.

64/400

Foreword ⟨prefacing letter in French⟩ to *Reason and Violence: A Decade of Sartre's Philosophy, 1950-1960,* by Ronald D. Laing and David G. Cooper.

a) London: Tavistock Publications, 1964. P. 7.

New edition, 1971.

b) Pocket edition. Vintage Books, 1971. Gives both the French text of the foreword and a translation by A. M. Sheridan Smith.

c) Raison et violence: Dix ans de la philosophie de Sartre (1950-1960), translated by Jean-Pierre Cottereau. Foreword by Jean-Paul Sartre. Payot, Petite Bibliothèque series, no. 202. [1972]. P. 5.

This foreword is dated November 9, 1963.

Laing and Cooper are among the best of the contemporary practitioners and theoreticians of existential psychoanalysis. Both were strongly influenced by Sartre's thinking, and in *Reason and Violence* undertake a study based on SAINT GENET and CRITIQUE OF DIALECTICAL REASON. Cooper is the author of *Psychiatry and Antipsychiatry*, excerpts from which were published in the December, 1967, *Temps modernes*; whereas Laing is the author of *The Divided Self* (Penguin Books, 1965) and several other studies of schizophrenia.

64/401

"La Culture en question" ⟨Culture Challenged⟩, interview.

-- *21 x 27 (L'Etudiant de France)*, no. 5 (February, 1964).

This rather short interview, given to representatives of the U.N.E.F. ⟨National Union of French Students⟩, bears on the problems of culture in the university setting. Sartre gives this definition:

Culture is the critical mirror of the whole man . . . culture is a mirror, and mirrors and cultures make no sense unless man finds in them the possibility of recognizing and challenging himself. Then he criticizes the *cours magistral*, which he sees as the seedbed of all dogmatism. He says that the culture which the university dispenses is a class culture, and in concluding sings the praises of the Russian teaching system.

64/402

"Entretien avec Jean-Paul Sartre" ⟨Conversation with Jean-Paul Sartre⟩, interview by students of philosophy at the Sorbonne.

a) Philo-Observateur, no. 4 (March, 1964).

b) A somewhat different article based on the same interview was published in *21 x 27 (L'Etudiant de France)*, no. 6 (March, 1964).

This interview, which is of little interest, has to do essentially with the teacher-student relationship. Sartre criticizes the present system, especially the *cours magistral* system, which he thinks can be changed only by a total reform. For philosophical studies he recommends above all the critical spirit.

Those who like variant editions will find a meticulous comparison between texts *(a)* and *(b)* in the Dreyfus-Trotignon bibliography.

64/403

"Sartre parle . . ." ⟨Sartre Speaks⟩, interview by Yves Buin.

-- *Clarté*, (monthly of the Union of Communist students), no. 55 (March-April, 1964), pp. 41-47.

Thanks in part to the intelligence of Yves Buin's questions, this is one of Sartre's best discussions of the relationship between politics and art. The two men try to define realism in literature as well as in painting and music and (by means of a series of examples) to establish the bases of a revolutionary art. While he denounces the shortcomings of traditional theories of realism, Sartre says that he is a convinced adherent of Marxist methodology and subsequently sets forth his idea of the task of criticism:

64/403

Modern works call for the development of a modern criticism which can see them as a whole, that is, in terms of their historical conditions and thus their irreducibility, in their intentional meaning and in relation to the hierarchy of their deeper-lying meanings, as a product *both of a man and of an era and an objective surpassing of the conditions under which they were produced, a surpassing which acts retroactively upon them to change them.*

Before speaking at length about Gustave Flaubert, Sartre goes back to the concept of commitment and speaks of it in terms of a formulation already found in Simone de Beauvoir's memoirs: *It seems to me that art is always a representation of the world as it would be if it were rebuilt by free men.*

Let us cite, among the numerous subjects touched on, Franz Kafka, Boris Vian, Ingmar Bergman, Lucien Goldmann, Jean Genet (*Is it provocative to ask why his play,* The Blacks, *is not performed in the U.S.S.R.?*), the painter Georges Mathieu, Jean-Marie-Gustave Le Clézio (concerning the story "The Day Beaumont First Came to Know Pain"), Vladimir Maiakovsky (*The Bedbug*), Wols, Claude Simon (*He writes about time, about memory. When you come right down to it, what does he show us that Proust hasn't already shown?*), Bertolt Brecht, the New Novel and the concept of the *avant garde.*

64/404

Interview by an A.P.S. (Algerian Press Service) man.

-- Excerpts in *Le Monde*, April 15, 1964.

Sartre expresses his satisfaction at the cooperative agreements reached between France and Algeria and says: *I think that having France linked to the "third world" through Algeria is very helpful. Perhaps more helpful to us than to you. . . .* He adds that aid to a country one has *exploited for a hundred years* is an absolute must, and that *"Cartiérism" is only a kind of "Poujadism."*

64/405

"Jean-Paul Sartre s'explique sur *Les Mots*" (Jean-Paul Sartre Explains What He Was Doing in THE WORDS), interview by Jacqueline Piatier.

-- *Le Monde*, April 18, 1964.

"A Long, Bitter, Sweet Madness" or "Jean-Paul Sartre Speaks."

t1)"A Long, Bitter, Sweet Madness," translated by Anthony Hartley. *Encounter*, XXII (June, 1964), 61-63.

t2) "Jean-Paul Sartre Speaks." *Vogue*, January 1, 1965, pp. 94-95, 159.

Very important interview that ought to be reprinted here in its entirety. Sartre not only goes over THE WORDS but also shows how he had changed *within that which has remained unchanged* and how he conceives of literature in 1964. Speaking of the literary *neurosis* which motivated him for forty years, he maintains, *One is no more saved by politics than by literature*. But even though he does not think salvation is to be found anywhere, Sartre does not feel desperate: *I have . . . always been an optimist. Even too optimistic*. Before remarking that he has always been happy, he says:

The universe is still dark. We are disaster-ridden animals. . . . But I discovered abruptly that alienation, man's exploitation by man, and undernourishment relegated metaphysical evil, which is a luxury, to the background. Hunger is an evil, period.

It is in this perspective that he asks, *Do you think that I could read Robbe-Grillet in an underdeveloped country?* and says, *Weighed against a dying child,* NAUSEA *doesn't count*. This sentence, which recalls Leo Tolstoy's famous "All of Shakespeare is not worth a pair of boots," naturally caused a scandal (see the reactions of Yves Berger and Claude Simon in the May 28, 1964, *Express*, as well as the debate "What Can Literature Do?" 65/419). Sartre told us during a conversation that his sentence had been misinterpreted, that he had in no way intended to put a work of fiction like NAUSEA and a child dying of hunger on the same level, but that it was important to raise the question: What does literature mean in a hungry world? (see also 66/449).

Among the other subjects tackled: Samuel Beckett, André Gide, Alain Badiou's *Almagestes*, Stéphane Mallarmé, Gustave Flaubert, etc.

64/406

Jean-Paul Sartre et Zola ⟨Jean-Paul Sartre and Zola⟩, letter to Jacqueline Piatier.

-- *Le Monde*, April 25, 1964, p. 12.

Short clarification of the April 18 interview:

I don't think I said that the hermeticism of Mallarmé's poetry was a stupid mistake. . . .

64/406

In my judgment, hermeticism, as a theory, is a mistake, that's all. . . . I did not say that Zola and Gide had the worst possible attitude.

Sartre will make an additional clarification in the interview he gives to *L'Arc* in 1966 (see 66/449).

64/406 A

"Ein Sartre-Interview anlässlich seines Stücks *Der Teufel und der Liebe Gott*" ⟨An Interview with Sartre concerning his play THE DEVIL AND THE GOOD LORD⟩, by Jean Guitron [Guitton].

a) *Frankfurter Rundschau*, May 23, 1964.

b) Excerpts. In Liselotte Richter. *Jean-Paul Sartre*. New York: Frederick Ungar, 1970. Pp. 86-87.

We have been unable to locate the French text of this interview, which according to the *Frankfurter Rundschau* was done in 1951 in relation to THE DEVIL AND THE GOOD LORD. Here Sartre speaks in a very interesting way of the philosophical and religious content of his play, and deals in a more general way with atheism. He says in particular: *Universalist atheism is not time bound, it is the purely abstract and unhistorical assertion that God is not. The mistake of that ideology is not that it denies God's existence, but that it fails to notice that we today still belong to a religious form of culture in which the vast majority of people are believers, or at least half-believers.*

64/407

* Paper given on May 23, 1964, at the colloquium, "Ethics and Society" organized in Rome by the Gramsci Institute.

a) Summary in *L'Unità*, May 24, 1964.

b) Excerpts in Italian. In *Rinascita*, no. 37 (September 19, 1964).

c) Excerpts. *Determinazione e libertà* ⟨Determinism and Freedom⟩. In the anthology *Morale e Società* ⟨Ethics and Society⟩. Acts of the Rome Convention organized by the Gramsci Institute. Rome: Editori Riuniti-Istituto Gramsci, [1966]. Pp. 31-41.

d) Notes on the relationships between ethics and history. In Francis Jeanson. *Sartre*. Les Ecrivains devant Dieu series. Desclée de Brouwer, [1966] . Pp. 137-38.

These are short excerpts from notes written for Sartre's contribution to the colloquium. The cuts are not indicated.

e) Text *(b)* retranslated from the Italian as *Détermination et liberté*. *Essais* (Bordeaux), special issue, "Sartre notre contemporain" ⟨Sartre, Our Contemporary⟩, nos. 2-3 [spring, 1968], pp. 109-20.

This translation, which we reprint in Vol. II, has not been proofread by Sartre.

With a view to his participation in the international colloquium organized from May 22 to 25, 1964, by the Gramsci Institute on the theme "Ethics and Society," Sartre drew up around two hundred pages of notes which we got a quick glimpse of in manuscript form and which are of the greatest interest. In them he continues, but this time on the basis of the philosophical positions of the CRITIQUE OF DIALECTICAL REASON, the reflection he undertook for the treatise on ethics he abandoned in 1949 (see 49/187).

The published excerpts from his participation in the colloquium consist chiefly in a critique of positivist or neo-positivist conceptions of ethical norms, considered simply as social facts related to inert structures. Thus these pages specify in part Sartre's objections to structuralism and, more particularly here, to *certain Marxists tempted by structuralism* [who] *are trying to muffle the motor of history, that is, the class struggle.*

In 1964-65, Sartre continued to write about ethics. He stopped, not because as in the postwar years he encountered conceptual difficulties, but because he wanted to finish his study of Gustave Flaubert first. Sartre may take up the writing of his "Ethics" again and complete it rather rapidly. As a matter of fact, he told us at the beginning of 1969 that his dialectical ethic was entirely composed in his mind, and that the only remaining problems he foresaw were problems of writing it up.

64/408

Statement made at the death of Maurice Thorez.

a) L'Humanité, July 16, 1964.

b) France nouvelle, July 15-21, 1964.

At the death of Maurice Thorez, which came on July 11, 1964, Sartre, who was in Italy, sent the French Communist Party the following statement:

It isn't necessary to have always agreed with Communist Party policies to recognize in Maurice

64/408

Thorez one of the greatest figures in the international workers' movement. Even his opponents always respected his qualities as a man, his intelligence, his energy, his courage, and his perseverance. It is thanks to him, above all, that the P.C.F. ⟨French Communist Party⟩ *has become France's major party. He struggled untiringly for working-class unity, in France and throughout the world, for socialism, against fascism, and against war. In spite of unavoidable differences which we must work to iron out, these objectives are and must remain those of the whole French Left.*

64/409

Palmiro Togliatti.

a) First published as *Il mio amico Togliatti* ⟨My Friend Togliatti⟩. *L'Unità*, August 30, 1964.

b) French text. In *Les Temps modernes*, no. 221 (October, 1964), pp. 577-87.

c) Reprinted in SITUATIONS, IX.

To see the great distance at this time between Sartre's highly qualified support for P.C.F. ⟨French Communist Party⟩ policy and his deeply sympathetic ties with the Italian Communist Party, we need only compare the tone (not to speak of the length) of the tributes the writer paid to these two Communist leaders who died within a few weeks of one another (see 64/408).

Sartre was in Rome when Togliatti died on August 21, 1964, in Yalta. He attended his burial and wrote for *L'Unità* this piece in which we see an honesty of feeling and even a certain pride in being able to say he was the friend of a man of such worth. For along with a great esteem for Togliatti, he had developed a real friendship. Sartre tells about his first meeting with the Italian leader in a Roman restaurant during the summer of 1959, and in his portrait of the man he draws that of his party and gives his reasons for being sympathetic with the Italian Communist Party, *the most intelligent of parties*. In conclusion, he says: *For that matter, he whose loss I regret is not simply the man who with his own hands forged a party of tough, free men: this party will be able to survive his loss and follow his path. It is above all the old man, calm and powerful, whom I saw last May for the last time. A man I loved. My friend Togliatti.*

TEXTS PERTAINING TO THE REFUSAL OF THE NOBEL PRIZE (October, 1964)

Sartre had forewarned the Swedish Academy that he would refuse the Nobel Prize for Literature (worth 53,000 dollars) if it were awarded to him. The academy disregarded this first refusal and awarded him the prize anyhow. As we are told in an article in *L'Aurore* (October 23, 1964), "it was in confrontation with a bowl of lentil soup, in a peaceful restaurant in the fourteenth *arrondissement* [L'Oriental], that Jean-Paul Sartre, accompanied by Simone de Beauvoir, [learned of] this latest stroke of fate." Sartre immediately drew up a statement which was translated by Carl Gustav Bjurström and read on October 22, 1964, in Stockholm by a representative of his Swedish editor. This statement, retranslated from Swedish but checked by Sartre himself, was subsequently disseminated in its entirety by the France-Presse agency and reprinted in many newspapers, especially *Le Monde* and *Izvestia*.

64/410

L'Ecrivain doit refuser de se laisser transformer en institution ⟨The Writer Should Refuse to Let Himself Be Turned into an Institution⟩.

a) Le Monde, October 24, 1964.

b) Les Lettres françaises, October 29-November 4, 1964.

I Always Refuse Distinctions, or *Sartre on the Nobel Prize*.

t1) I Always Refuse Distinctions. The Times (London), October 23, 1964, p. 12.

t2) Sartre on the Nobel Prize, translated by Richard Howard. *New York Review of Books*, December 17, 1964, pp. 5-6.

Here is the text *in extenso:*

> *I am extremely sorry that this business has taken on an air of scandal: a prize has been awarded and I have refused it. It has all happened simply because I was not told soon enough what was being planned. When I read in the October 15* Figaro littéraire, *in an article by the paper's Swedish correspondent, that the Swedish Academy was inclining toward me but had not yet made up its mind, I thought that by writing the academy a letter, which I mailed the next day, I could straighten things out and that would be the end of it.*

I did not know then that the Nobel Prize is awarded without consulting the person concerned, and I thought there was time to stop it. But I understand that when the Swedish Academy has made a choice it cannot retract it.

My reasons for rejecting the prize, as I explained in my letter to the academy, have nothing to do with the Swedish Academy nor with the Nobel Prize per se. In that letter I offered two sorts of reasons, personal and objective.

These are my personal reasons. My refusal is not an unprecedented act. I have always declined official honors. After the war, in 1945, I was put up for the Legion of Honor. I turned it down, though I had friends in the government. Likewise I never wished to enter the Collège de France as some of my friends suggested.

This attitude is based on my conception of the role of the writer. A writer who takes a position on political, social, or literary questions should rely only on the means which are his--the written word. Any honors he might receive expose his readers to a pressure which I consider undesirable. The signature "Jean-Paul Sartre" is one thing; "Jean-Paul Sartre, Nobel Prizewinner" is something else.

The writer who accepts this sort of honor also involves the association or institution which has honored him. My sympathies for the resistants in Venezuela commit me alone; but if Nobel Prizewinner Jean-Paul Sartre supports the resistance in Venezuela, he drags the whole institution of the Nobel Prize into it with him.

So the writer should refuse to let himself be turned into an institution, even (as at present) under the most honorable circumstances.

This attitude is of course entirely my own and involves no criticism whatsoever of those who have already been crowned. I have great esteem and admiration for several of the laureats I have the honor of knowing.

These are my objective reasons for refusing the prize. The only struggle at present possible on the cultural front is for the peaceful coexistence of the two cultures, East and West. I do not mean that they should fall into each others arms. I am quite aware that their confrontation must take the form of a conflict. But it should be a meeting of men and of cultures, not of institutions.

Personally, I feel the contradiction between the two cultures very deeply. I am made of these contradictions. My sympathies go without question to socialism and to what is called the Eastern bloc, but I was born and brought up in a bourgeois family and culture. This allows me to work with everyone who wants to bring the two cultures together. I nevertheless hope, of course, that "the best man may win." Socialism.

This is why I cannot accept any honor awarded by the cultural authorities, East or West, even though I well understand why they exist. Although all my sympathies are with the socialists, I would be just as unable to accept, for example, the Lenin Prize, should it be offered me, which it hasn't.

I realize that the Nobel Prize is not per se a literary prize offered by the Western bloc; but it is also what people make of it, and things can happen which are beyond the control of the Swedish Academy.

That is why, in the present situation, the Nobel Prize is, objectively speaking, an honor restricted to Western writers or Eastern rebels. It has not, for example, been awarded to Neruda, one of South America's greatest poets. Louis Aragon has never been seriously considered for it, even though he well deserves it. It is regrettable that Pasternak was given the prize before Sholokhov, and that the only Russian work so honored has been published abroad and banned at home. There could have been a compensating gesture to balance things out. I would have been glad to accept the prize during the Algerian War, when we had signed the "Declaration of the 121"; because it would have honored not just me but the freedom we were fighting for. But nobody offered me the prize then, only now, after all the fighting is over.

In the Swedish Academy's citation, they speak of freedom. This is a word that lends itself to numerous interpretations. In the West it is taken to mean abstract freedom. But to me it means a more concrete freedom--the right to have more than one pair of shoes and to eat when one is hungry. To me it seems less dangerous to decline the prize than to accept it. To accept it would be to lend myself to what I would call "an objective salvaging." I read in the Figaro Littéraire *that "my controversial political past would not be held too much against me." I know this article does not express the academy's opinion, but it shows clearly how my acceptance would be interpreted in certain right-wing circles. I consider this "controversial political past" to be still valid, even though I am quite ready to admit, when I am among friends, that I have made certain mistakes in the past.*

This does not mean that the Nobel Prize is a "bourgeois prize," but that is the bourgeois interpretation which circles I know all too well would make.

64/410

Finally, I come to the question of the money. By adding a great sum of money to the honor, the academy places a very heavy burden on the laureat's shoulders, and I have been tormented by this problem. On the one hand, one can accept the prize and with the money he receives support organizations or movements he thinks are important. I thought myself of the Apartheid Committee in London. On the other hand, one can decline the prize as a matter of principle, and then he deprives this movement of support it could have used. But I think this problem is a false one. I am obviously giving up 250,000 kroner *because I do not want to be institutionalized in the East or the West. But you can't be asked either to renounce for 250,000* kroner *principles which are not yours alone but shared by all your comrades.*

This is what made both the awarding of the prize and the refusal I must make so painful for me.

I should like to conclude this statement with an expression of sympathy for the Swedish public.
⟨Translated from the French translation of the Swedish.⟩

64/411

"Sartre nous explique son refus" ⟨Sartre Explains His Refusal⟩, interview by N. L. Kemski.

-- *Paris-Presse-L'Intransigeant*, October 24, 1964.

Constantly chased after by reporters, Sartre finally gets cornered by one at two in the morning and grants him a short interview in which he says:

I want to be read by people who feel like reading my books. Not by celebrity collectors. . . . I refuse honors because they commit me. And it's important to me to stay free. A writer ought to live according to his own lights.

There is also a short statement by Sartre in an article elegantly entitled "J'ai retrouvé Sartre (prix Nobel malgré lui) après une poursuite à 100 à l'heure dans Paris" ⟨I Found Sartre (Nobel Prizewinner in Spite of Himself) after a One-Hundred-Mile-an-Hour Chase through Paris⟩ (Jean-Claude Larrivoire in *France-Soir*, October 23, 1964).

The innumerable reactions to Sartre's refusal would be worth a study in themselves. Let us be satisfied with pointing out three of them:

-- René Maheu. "Sur un refus" ⟨Concerning a Refusal⟩. *Le Figaro*, October 26, 1964. Sartre's old schoolmate and present director of UNESCO makes an interesting comparison between the 1964 Nobel Prizewinner and Socrates.

-- Gabriel Marcel. "Prise de position" <Taking a Stand>. *Nouvelles littéraires*, October 29, 1964. Marcel denounces Sartre as an "inveterate denigrator and systematic blasphemer [who has] spread about him the most pernicious teachings and the most poisonous advice which have ever been bestowed upon young people by an obvious corrupter of the young." And he concludes: "In choosing Sartre the jury has raised high a man who is digging the grave of the West."

-- André Breton [and the Surrealist group]. "Le rappel de Stockholm" <The Reminder of Stockholm>. *La Breche*, no. 7 (December, 1964): "Beneath the mask of an agreeable show of independence, it is quite clearly a matter of a perfectly placed political act, a propaganda operation in support of the *Eastern bloc*. Eight years after Budapest, Sartre is 're-enlisting'! . . . Refusing a prize is not enough; the justifications of this gesture must not negate it. Sartre, by his statement, has seriously *poisoned* the very idea of refusal."

Let us stress, however, that although Sartre's refusal was misunderstood and commented on in various ways by a segment of public opinion, it was, on the other hand, accepted and appreciated by many intellectuals.

In an interview published in *Le Nouvel Observateur* (no. 1 [November 19, 1964]), Sartre goes over again in detail his reasons for refusing and the reactions which followed: *Why did I refuse this prize? Because I think that for sometime now it has had a political coloration. If I had accepted the Nobel Prize--or even if I had made an insolent speech in Stockholm, which would have been ridiculous--I would have been coopted. If I had been a member of a party, for example the Communist Party, the situation would have been different. The prize would have been awarded indirectly to my party or would, in any case, have been of use to it. But when it is a case of a single individual, even one who has "extremist" ideas, he is in a way inevitably coopted by simply being crowned. It's a way of saying, "Finally he's on our side." I could not allow that.*

Most of the papers attributed personal reasons to me: I was upset because Camus had gotten it before I had . . . I was afraid that Simone de Beauvoir might be jealous . . . or I was at best a noble soul who refused all honors out of pride. I have a very simple answer to all this: if we had had a popular front government--as I hope we shall--and it had done

64/411

me the honor of awarding me a prize, I would have accepted with pleasure. . . .

What has troubled me the most in this business has been the letters from poor people. . . . They have written me heartbreaking letters. They all say, "Give me the money you're refusing."

What is really scandalous is that this money has not been spent. . . .

The paradox is that in refusing the prize I did nothing. It was if I had accepted it that I would have done something--I would have let myself be co-opted by the system.

64/412

"L'Alibi" ⟨The Alibi⟩, interview.

a) Le Nouvel Observateur, no. 1 (November 19, 1964), pp. 1-6.

b) Reprinted in SITUATIONS, VIII.

With *France-Observateur* slowing down and *L'Express* about to adopt the commercial formula we know it by today, part of the *France-Observateur* staff and some dissident *Express* editors decided in the fall of 1964 to create a new left-wing weekly. Sartre agreed to show his support for *Le Nouvel Observateur* by contributing a long interview to its first issue to help launch the weekly. He has never stopped supporting it since.

This interview, which made a rather big stir, bears chiefly on the theme of depoliticization. Sartre shows that, contrary to what is often claimed, young people today are only depoliticized in a very relative sense. In comparison to their prewar counterparts, they show a considerably higher level of political consciousness. Generally speaking, moreover, people are much more conscious of the political implications of all problems than they used to be. But this is especially true of young people. *The young people I meet may be less hotheaded than before, but what is most striking to me is that they are often just as politically conscious as I am. They are starting out from the point I have reached. They don't come to ask me for advice but to discuss things as my equal.* Sartre then shows that the need to be fully informed is already a sign of a deepened political consciousness, and that people are no longer unaware of the interdependence of historical events on a worldwide scale. Speaking of politics, he says: *As far as I'm concerned this doesn't mean an* attitude *the individual may adopt or abandon according to circumstance but a* dimension *of the person.* Then he comes back to the problem of the depoliticization of youth to claim: *To say that young people are depoliticized is to want them to be and to work toward making them increasingly so. The fact that young people are less directly interested in political battles serves as an alibi for turning them away even more.* Then he analyzes the economic and ideological pressures on young people which are involved in the "rock and roll" phenomenon. Answering a question about "the end of ideology," he quotes and comments on this sentence Che Guevara said to him one day: "I can't help it if reality is Marxist." He deplores the Eastern Marxists' failure to analyze their own societies according to Marxist methods, but he refutes the argument that all industrial societies, socialist or capitalist, have the same problems. *If there were conflicts in the U.S.S.R., they would have the aspect of reform and not of revolution. There would not be a class to overthrow, but changes could be demanded, which is something very different.* Then Sartre talks about the new content that the revolutionary struggle ought to have (demand for workers' power in management) and shows what the role of a left-wing press might be: *Without falling into Manicheism, we have to stiffen our refusal to compromise. When you come right down to it, every left-wing position is, to the extent that it is contrary to what they try to inculcate in the whole society, "scandalous." This does not mean that we must try to be scandalous, which would be ridiculous and ineffectual, but that we must not be afraid to be. If the position taken is correct, scandal should come crown it like a sign or natural sanction of a left-wing attitude.* To finish, Sartre talks about reactions to his refusal of the Nobel Prize.

64/412 A

"Le Devoir des intellectuels" ⟨The Duty of Intellectuals⟩, interview by Claude Faux.

-- *Libération*, Libé-Spécial supplement, December 2, 1964.

In this interview done by his secretary, Claude Faux, in the presence of the Moroccan Mohamed Tahri, Sartre tells why he refused the 53,000 dollars of Nobel Prize money, defines the role of the intellectual in colonized countries, and above all, analyzes the political situation in Morocco.

64/413

Message from Sartre to the reception in homage to Nazim Hikmet organized by *Les Lettres françaises* at the Salle Pleyel on December 6, 1964.

-- *Les Lettres françaises*, December 10-16, 1964.

Sartre says of Nazim Hikmet that he was *the model of what a man ought to be. He was a faithful friend, a courageous militant, and an enemy without weakness of the enemies of man. And yet he did not want to blind himself about anything or serve everywhere at once. He knew that man is nowhere to be found but is still to be created, and that he had to act unremittingly upon himself at the same time he was fighting the enemy. He knew in short that as Pascal said of the Christian, as we may say today of the militant, and, on this particular occasion, of the militant intellectual, he must "never sleep." And he never did sleep. The admirable thing about him is that death was his first and last sleep. But the works of a man who has unflinchingly kept watch relieve him and continue to keep watch for us after he has gone.*

64/NOTE.

In September, 1964, Sartre sent a message of sympathy to the World Youth Congress, which was going to be held in Moscow and whose goal was to express the solidarity of the young in support of national liberation struggles (see *Sovietskaia Kultura*, [September] 3, 1964, p. 1).

1965

65/414

LES TROYENNES ⟨The Trojan Women⟩, adaptation of Euripides' play.

a) Euripides. *Les Troyennes*. French adaptation by Jean-Paul Sartre. Théâtre National Populaire, [1965]. 79 pages.

Printing date: March 8, 1965. 50 copies on wood-free Lafuma. The volume was sold only at the T.N.P. The buyer could also get a little book of photographic illustrations of the play.

A note specifies: "This edition does not include the changes made in the script during the final rehearsals."

b) Current edition. Gallimard, [1966]. 131 pages.

Printing date: January 14, 1966.

80 copies on Holland vellum and 220 on woodfree vellum.

This volume reprints the text of the preceding edition with a few changes in punctuation as well as in the introduction (pp. 2-8), which consists of the remarks Sartre made in *Bref* (see 65/415).

THE TROJAN WOMEN, free adaptation by Ronald Duncan.

t1) New York: Alfred A. Knopf, 1967; London: Hamish Hamilton, 1967.

t2) In KEAN; NEKRASSOV; THE TROJAN WOMEN. Penguin Books, 1969.

t3) Paperback. New York: Vintage Books, 1972.

65/414

The play was first performed on March 10, 1965, at the Théâtre du Palais de Chaillot by the Théâtre National Populaire.

Produced by Michel Cacoyannis. Stage machinery and costumes by Jean Tsarouchis. Music by Jean Prodromides. Main characters: Jean Martinelli (Poseidon), Françoise Le Bail (Pallas Athena), Eléonore Hirt (Hecuba), Jean-Pierre Bernard (Talthybios), Judith Magre (Cassandra), Nathalie Nerval (Andromacha), Yves Vincent (Menelaus), Françoise Brion (Helen).

The play was written in July-August, 1964, in Rome. There is an 84-page manuscript of it.

65/415

"*Les Troyennes*: Jean-Paul Sartre s'explique" ⟨Jean-Paul Sartre Explains What He Meant in THE TROJAN WOMEN⟩, remarks gathered by Bernard Pingaud.

a) Bref (magazine of the Théâtre National Populaire), no. 83 (February, 1965). On six pages.

b) Reprinted as the introduction to the Gallimard edition (see 65/414).

Sartre says here why and how he adapted THE TROJAN WOMEN. In his view, Euripides' theater is transitional: it marks the close of the tragic cycle and the transition to the comedy of Menander, and becomes, like the theater of Eugène Ionesco and Samuel Beckett, an *elliptical conversation about clichés*. (Here Sartre begins the reflection on the function of clichés and commonplaces which he will take up again in his pieces about Sören Kierkegaard and Georges Michel.) THE TROJAN WOMEN is less a tragedy than an oratorio whose dominant theme is *the condemnation of war in general, and colonial expeditions in particular*.

Sartre dramatizes this war theme by adding Poseidon's final monologue and brings the play up to date by replacing the classical contrast between Barbarian and Greek by one between Troy (a symbol of the Third World) and Europe.

65/416

"Interviu sa Zhan-Pol Sartrom" ⟨Interview with Jean-Paul Sartre⟩, by Gisèle Halimi.

-- *Nin* (Belgrade), [March] 28, 1965.

Interview about THE TROJAN WOMEN. In it Sartre talks about the problems of adaptation Euripides' play gave him, stresses its political context, and shows the role women play in it.

65/417

SITUATIONS, VII: PROBLÈMES DU MARXISME, 2. ⟨Situations, VII: Problems of Marxism⟩.

-- Gallimard, [1965]. 345 pages.

This volume includes eight pieces, in French, published from 1953 to 1962:

-- *Reply to Claude Lefort*	see # 53/238
-- *Operation "Kanapa"*	54/253
-- *Reformism and Fetishes* (Pierre Hervé)	56/283
-- *Reply to Pierre Naville*	56/284
-- *The Ghost of Stalin*	# 57/291
-- *When the Police Give the Three Raps . . .* (on Robert Brasillach)	57/301
-- *The Demilitarization of Culture*	62/379 B
-- *Discussion of the Criticism of "The Childhood of Ivan"*	62/379 D

Only essays marked # have been translated so far. See separate entries.

65/418

LA TRANSCENDANCE DE L'EGO: ESQUISSE D'UNE DESCRIPTION PHÉNOMÉNOLOGIQUE ⟨The Transcendence of the Ego: Outline of a Phenomenological Description⟩. Introduction, notes, and appendix by Sylvie Le Bon.

-- Vrin Philosophical Books, 1965. 134 pages.

For details, see 37/9.

65/419

Que peut la littérature? ⟨What Can Literature Do?⟩, remarks during a debate.

-- Simone de Beauvoir, Yves Berger, Jean-Pierre Faye, Jean Ricardou, Jean-Paul Sartre, Jorge Semprun. *Que peut la littérature?* Introduced by Yves Buin. L'Inédit series of 10/18. Union générale d'éditions, 1965. 128 pages. Sartre's remarks on pp. 107-27.

This volume reproduces a debate held December 9, 1964, at the Mutualité by the staff of the newspaper

65/419

Clarté, organ of the Union of Communist Students. This debate attracted 6,000 people and gave rise to a good number of reactions. *Le Figaro littéraire*, in particular, published in its December 17, 1964, issue the replies fourteen writers gave to the question Sartre and Simone de Beauvoir asked. See also a critical report of the meeting by Mary McCarthy ("Crushing a Butterfly," *Encounter*, March, 1965, pp. 53-55).

Excerpts from the remarks made by the various participants appeared prior to publication in book form in *Clarté* (no. 59 [January, 1965], pp. 17-22).

The debate was above all a confrontation between those who upheld "telquelisme"(Faye and, especially, Ricardou) and those who upheld committed literature (Sartre, Simone de Beauvoir, Semprun). Ricardou criticizes Sartre for preaching "art for the sake of man" (whereas in fact "art is man") and for having said in an interview (see 64/405), *Weighed against a dying child,* NAUSEA *doesn't count.*

In his remarks--which with their repetitiveness and excessive abstractness are certainly not among his best--Sartre defends himself against the attacks which have been made on him by stressing the reader rather than language, and redefines the reader's relationship to the work.

Let us also point out a phrase in his remarks which was said ironically but perhaps prophetically: *I hope the New Novel will culminate in a revolution in France* (p. 108).

65/420

"Pátě pres devátě" ⟨The Fifth over the Ninth⟩.

See 63/390.

65/421

"Sartre non va in U.S.A." ⟨Sartre Is Not Going to the U.S.A.⟩, interview by Maria A. Macciocchi.

a) L'Unità, March 19, 1965.

b) Excerpts. "Pourquoi Sartre a refusé de se rendre aux U.S.A." ⟨Why Sartre Refused to Come to the U.S.⟩. *La Voix ouvrière* (Geneva), March 24, 1965.

Sartre explains why he has decided not to go to the United States and proposes that Italy take the initiative in getting all European intellectuals to act against the war in Vietnam.

65/422

"Pourquoi je refuse d'aller aux Etats-Unis: Il n'y a plus de dialogue possible" ⟨Why I Refuse to Go to the United States: Dialogue Is Not Possible There Anymore⟩, interview.

a) Le Nouvel Observateur, April 1, 1965.

b) Reprinted as *Il n'y a plus de dialogue possible.* In SITUATIONS, VIII.

"Why I Will Not Go to the United States," excerpts translated by Lionel Abel.

t1) With an editorial on Sartre's refusal. *The Nation*, April 19, 1965, pp. 407-11.

t2) Meanjin, XXIV, no. 3 (1965), pp. 340-44.

In 1964, Sartre had agreed to give a series of five lectures on Gustave Flaubert and on philosophy at Cornell University. Shortly before the agreed-upon date (April, 1965), he let the group of professors who had invited him know that he could not come to the United States.

He explains here that his refusal is tied to the escalation of the war and, in particular, to the bombing of the North: *Today it is impossible for a European intellectual to ask the State Department for a visa to go to the United States. If he goes, and no matter what he says when he goes, the people of the Third World will condemn him, because you don't go to the homeland of the enemy. The reaction of my Cuban friends is significant in this respect. A few months ago they said to me, "Sure you should go to the United States, and talk about Cuba." Since the bombings of North Vietnam they all say to me, "What business would you have going there?"*

Sartre also justifies his refusal by the powerlessness of the American Left. *I think . . . that an American Leftist who sees his situation clearly, who sees himself isolated in a country completely conditioned by the myths of imperialism and anticommunism, I think this man, to whom I offer my respect, is one of the wretched of the earth. He totally disapproves of the policy being carried out in his name, yet his action, at least in the short run, is completely ineffectual.*

Sartre does express his hope, however, that the

65/422

United States will evolve and form *a new American thought.*

Sartre's refusal brought many reactions from American university professors and liberals. His estimate of the domestic situation in the United States was often judged to be partial and much too pessimistic.

65/423

Sartre répond ⟨Sartre Replies⟩ (to a letter from David I. Grossvogel).

a) Le Nouvel Observateur, April 8, 1965.

b) Reprinted, with the letter from Grossvogel, in SITUATIONS, VIII.

This text follows a letter in which David I. Grossvogel, a professor at Cornell University, deplores Sartre's refusal to come to the United States and challenges the reasons which he gave to justify his refusal.

In his reply, Sartre says in particular: *It is convenient but absurd to explain this refusal by hatred: I don't feel any for anyone, above all for two hundred million people. That would wear me out.*

65/423 A

Sia l'Europa a imporre agli U.S.A. il negoziato ⟨Europe Should Impose Negotiations on the U.S.A.⟩, message.

-- *L'Unità*, April 18, 1965.

Message addressed to young Italian Socialists, Communists, and United Socialists who were taking part in a march for peace and freedom in Vietnam held in Bologna. Sartre says in particular: *The Vietcong must--no matter what form the negotiations take--be considered a valid representative, just as in the case of Algeria the French government had to deal with the G.P.R.A.* ⟨Provisional Revolutionary Government of Algeria⟩.

65/424

"Culture de poche et culture de masse" ⟨Pocket Culture and Mass Culture⟩, comments collected by Bernard Pingaud.

-- *Les Temps modernes*, no. 228 (May, 1965), pp. 1994-2001.

Sartre's comments bring to a conclusion the section devoted to pocket books which opened in the April and May, 1965, *Temps modernes*. They refer especially to a very good piece by Serge Sautreau and André Velter published in the April issue and entitled "The Pocket Book."

In Sartre's view, the pocket book is one "cultural fact" among others: *So we must not ask, as we too frequently do, if the millions of new readers it reaches have the right or the chance to acquire* culture. *We must, on the contrary, try to define a culture on the basis of this new technique for selling and disseminating, as up till now we've done it on the basis of traditional publishing methods.* Sartre continues by comparing the pros and cons of the socialist countries' state publishing system to those of dissemination through pocket books. *Although state publishing hobbles the production of new culture, it places all the great works of the past at the disposition of a new public. It transmits the "heritage" to all and not just to a few. The Pocket Book, in turn, has, after a period of breaking in and inching along, shown that it could provide a major increase in the dissemination of difficult works and create new contacts between readers and creators. But it has obtained this result only by remaining confined to the traditional reading public.*

65/425

"Playboy Interview: Jean-Paul Sartre: A Candid Conversation With the Charismatic Fountainhead of Existentialism and Rejector of the Nobel Prize," interview by Madeleine Gobeil.

a) Playboy (Chicago), XII, no. 5 (May, 1965), 69-76.

b) Reprinted in *Playboy Interviews*. Chicago: Playboy Press, 1967. Pp. 162-79.

c) Long excerpts. "Nous devons créer nos propres valeurs" ⟨We Must Create Our Own Values⟩. *Magazine littéraire*, no. 56-57 (September, 1971), pp. 10-13.

Important interview made in 1964, before Sartre was chosen for the Nobel Prize. Since it touches on almost every subject, let us reprint a few excerpts here: *I'm twice a traitor--a traitor in the conflict of the generations, and a traitor in the class war. The 1945 generation thinks I've betrayed them because they got to know me through* NO EXIT *and* NAUSEA, *written at a time when I hadn't yet worked out the Marxist implications of my ideas. . . .*

At sixteen, you see, I wanted to be a novelist. But I had to study philosophy in order to enroll in

65/425

École Normale Supérieure. My ambition was to [be]me a professor of literature. . . .

Though [Jean Genet] *has ceased having "myths," [an]d in this sense is perfectly free, the results have [be]en rather grim. He is now completely alone. . . .*

God had nothing to say . . . about the Algerian War. There were priests who behaved like decent folk and others who behaved like swine. . . .

My duty as an intellectual is to think, to think without restriction, even at the risk of blundering. I must set no limits within myself, and I must let no limits be set for *me* . . . (Sartre there defines himself in relation to the Communist Party).

There are no great writers in France today. The practitioners of the "New Novel" are talented, and viewed as experiments in form, their books are interesting. But they bring us absolutely nothing except a justification of our technocratic, politically sterile French social order. . . .

I have always tried to surround myself with women who are at least agreeable to look at. Feminine ugliness is offensive to me. I admit this and I'm ashamed of it. . . . I prefer their company to that of men. As a rule I find men boring. They have specialized sensibilities and they talk shop. But there are qualities in woman that derive from the female predicament, from the fact that she is both a slave and an accomplice. . . . Similarly, what I particularly appreciate in my Jewish friends is a gentleness and subtlety that is certainly an outcome of antisemitism. . . .

I hate to possess. . . . When I like an object, I always want to give it to someone. It isn't generosity--it's only because I want others *to be enslaved by objects, not me. . . .*

I don't think *that one should make a point, as Gide did, of systematically breaking with one's past; but I want always to be accessible to change. I don't feel bound by anything I've written. Nevertheless, I don't disown a word of it, either.*

Sartre gives additional autobiographical information, talks about the problem of alienation and his relations with the Communists, and criticizes General Charles de Gaulle's politics.

Since 1965 *Playboy* has published several things by Sartre.

65/426

"Up All Night."

-- *The Nation*, May 31, 1965, p. 574.

Short article giving excerpts from a long telegram Sartre sent on May 5, 1965, to the organizers of a teach-in on Vietnam at Boston University.

Sartre expresses his sympathy for the American intellectuals fighting against the war in Vietnam and hopes that they will have more success than the French intellectuals who opposed the Algerian War: *I wish you better luck than we had and I dearly hope you will succeed. . . . But even if you don't, your demonstrations will not have been in vain. They are occurring at a time in history when irresponsible men are presenting an odious image of your country to the world, and they help us see that this image is false and that the coming generation is determined to disassociate itself from it completely.*

This telegram marks a certain shift in Sartre's position and constitutes, as the American commentator points out, the most cordial statement he has made of late about the United States.

65/427

"Refusons le chantage" ⟨Let's Refuse to Be Blackmailed⟩, interview.

a) *Le Nouvel Observateur*, June 27, 1965.

b) Reprinted in SITUATIONS, VIII.

65/428

"Achever la gauche, ou la guérir?" ⟨Should the Left Be Killed Or Cured?⟩, interview.

a) *Le Nouvel Observateur*, June 24, 1965.

b) Reprinted in SITUATIONS, VIII.

In the first interview, Sartre takes a stand against the federation, proposed by Gaston Deffere, which was to be formed from an alliance between the S.F.I.O. ⟨French Branch of the Workers International⟩ and the M.R.P. ⟨Peoples' Republican Movement⟩. *Any politics which takes the exclusion of the Communist Party to be a foregone conclusion, which seeks to rob it of its electors and even its militants or reduce it to a supportive role, is inevitably reduced to choosing its supporters from the Right, and to reviving the Third Force under some other name.*

Between the publication of the first and second interviews, Defferre's federation dies before it is ever born. Sartre takes up and extends the analysis he began the week before. He shows that the Left is *moribund* and that it has *no chance of seizing power in the near future*. But this fact does not imply that there is nothing to be done. On the contrary, it shows the politics which could bring the Left closer to power, even while foreseeing that the developments required will be lengthy and may take thirty years. What Sartre wants for now is a single candidate of the Left, including the Communists, in the coming presidential election. Replying to the accusation that he is a defeatist, he says: *The real defeatists are those who--like Defferre--propose to kill the Left under the pretext of curing it. Does recognizing an alarming state of affairs mean being a pessimist? I said it to you, I wrote it, I'm not the only one who thinks it: the Left is sick. But I think it is incapable of dying. The Left is not some "liberal idea" of the intellectuals. An exploitative society may work away at winning out over critical thinking and left-wing movements, and may even, during certain periods of time, render them powerless. But it can never kill them, for it is its own existence which gives rise to them.*

65/428 A

"Sartre, Vilar, François Périer et 'Le Théâtre Vivant': Des projets explosifs" ⟨Sartre, Vilar, and François Périer at "The Living Theater": Some Explosive Projects⟩, interview-article by Colette Godard.

-- *Les Nouvelles littéraires*, July 1, 1965.

Report of the press conference given by Sartre, Jean Vilar, and François Périer on June 23, 1965, at the Théâtre de l'Athénée, to announce the revival of THE CONDEMNED OF ALTONA (see 65/326).

Sartre, who attended all the rehearsals of the play, said in particular:

What I want to do is give people a bad conscience.

THE CONDEMNED OF ALTONA *is the degradation of a man and his entourage through silence. . . . Every act is followed by the positive and negative consequences.* [Here], *it's the negative aspect of the act which is shown, the aspect we must recognize, understand, and assume so that we will be able to act in full awareness and in a positive fashion. . . .*

I have a lot to do. I write for the theater on impulse, when things are going badly.

We also learn that Sartre is planning a play which may be called "Prométhée" ⟨Prometheus⟩, and which will contain everything he has lived through for thirty years.

65/429

"Sartre Talks of Beauvoir," interview by Madeleine Gobeil.

a) Translated by Bernard Frechtman. *Vogue* (American edition), no. 146 (July, 1965), pp. 72-73.

b) French translation. "Entretien avec J.-P. Sartre" ⟨Conversation with J.-P. Sartre⟩. In Serge Julienne-Caffié. *Simone de Beauvoir*. La Bibliothèque idéale series. Gallimard, [1966]. Pp. 38-43.

This is the first time, it seems, that Sartre has ever spoken at such length in an interview about Simone de Beauvoir and his relationship with her. One of the things he points out is especially valuable in a bio-bibliographical context: *When we're both asked a question at the same time, we usually give the same answer. . . . We have such a large stock of common memories that ultimately we react to a situation in the same way--I mean with the same words, words that are conditioned by the same experiences. . . . Once she gives me, as it were, the "imprimatur," I have complete confidence in her.*

Let us recall that Simone de Beauvoir had herself painted a lucid portrait of Sartre in an American magazine (see "Jean-Paul Sartre: Strictly Personal," translated by Malcolm Cowley, *Harper's Bazaar* [January, 1946], pp. 113, 148, 160). Since this piece is little known to French readers, we reproduce below (with Simone de Beauvoir's permission) lengthy excerpts from it:

[Sartre] hates the country. He loathes--it isn't too strong a word--the swarming life of insects and the pullulation of plants. At most he tolerates the level sea, the unbroken desert sand, or the mineral coldness of Alpine peaks: but he feels at home only in cities, in the heart of an artificial universe filled with man-made objects. He doesn't like raw vegetables or milk fresh from the cow or oysters on the half shell, but only cooked foods; and he always asks for preserved fruit instead of the natural product. . . .

. . . Sartre has always felt a violent antipathy for persons swollen with self-importance. He doesn't like doctors, engineers, or cabinet ministers. As a general rule, he avoids the company of successful men, preferring that of women and younger men, because they impress him as having more spontaneity and truth. . . .

From the very beginning, Sartre was fiercely determined to be a free man: he kept clear of everything that might burden him down or chain him to one place. He has never married; he has never acquired any possessions; he doesn't own so much as a bed or a table, a picture, a keepsake, or a book. Nevertheless, he has always spent his money as fast as he earned it, and sometimes a little faster. His adult life has been passed in a series of hotel rooms in which there is never anything of his own, not even a copy of his latest work; visitors are often surprised at their bareness. In the early days, the freedom thus achieved had a negative character. Because he believed that nothing mattered except his work, Sartre was trying not to become involved in life; he took no interest in politics and even refrained from voting.

An evolution in another direction began shortly before the war and continued more rapidly in the German prison camp where he spent nine months. . . .

. . . Short and square (some of his American friends call him "Monsieur Cinq-par-Cinq" ⟨Mr. Five-by-Five⟩) and usually in robust health, he is very little troubled by his body. When it manifests itself by weariness or illness, he refuses to acknowledge that Sartre and his body have any community of interests. He is incapable of sitting back and taking things easy: he has to be active at all times; he makes use of his body, but he doesn't depend on it. He eats and drinks copiously, he smokes to excess, but he doesn't find it difficult to undergo privations. If he happens by chance to fall ill, he is likely to conceal or deny his symptoms, so that the doctor has a hard time making his diagnosis. In the same way, Sartre refuses to admit that he has any identity with his own past life. He seldom indulges in reminiscences; he admits his mistakes with disconcerting candor; he can describe and criticize himself with strict impartiality. The truth is that he has already ceased to recognize himself in the former Sartre of whom he speaks. His real likeness, he thinks, exists in the future; and hence he never feels any vanity about what he has done in the past.

On the other hand, he reveals an immense pride when discussing the things he intends to do. It is the metaphysical and impersonal pride of a liberty that tries to be absolute, that refuses to be chained down by circumstances; and sometimes it has helped him to achieve the nearly impossible. Sometimes, however, it has brought him into collision with facts that couldn't be pushed aside, but Sartre is indifferent to these failures. He launches on new undertakings without hope of success or reward, for he doesn't feel that the world owes him anything whatever. He expects nothing from others, but everything from himself.

He feels no envy, no regrets; he doesn't mourn over the limitations that life imposes on every individual; he finds it enough to be what he is. He hates conversations about ideas, because no idea ever comes to him from the outside. He reads very little, and if he happens to be in a mood for reading, any book at all will fascinate him. The only demand he makes on the printed pages is that they should serve as a springboard for his thoughts and reveries, very much as fortunetellers use tea leaves as a point of departure for their visions of the future. One characteristic that impresses all his friends is Sartre's immense generosity. He gives without reckoning, gives his money, his time, and himself; he is always ready to be interested in others, but he doesn't wish for anything in return; he doesn't need anybody. . . .

. . . He feels that nausea or revulsion in the face of everything contingent and tasteless, and, on the other hand, joy at surmounting the "given" and existing at liberty, are the two phases of a single experience. He isn't even disturbed by the ultimate prospect of death; he thinks about it seldom, and then with a great deal of tranquillity. His death, so it seems to him, is a future event that will still be part of his life; it is the final and necessary limitation by which his life can be defined. Active but never tense; enterprising, but never restless; often passionate in his efforts, but without feeling the anguish and bitterness of disappointed hopes, Sartre is at present a person in perfect harmony with himself, a happy man. Moreover, he feels no qualms about being happy, for he is convinced that other men can discover, more or less readily, in the consciousness of their own liberty, a joy as solid as his own.

65/430

"L'Ecrivain et sa langue" ⟨The Writer and His Language⟩, text put together and transcribed by Pierre Verstraeten.

a) Revue d'Esthétique, XVIII, sections 3-4 (July-December, 1965), 306-34.

b) Reprinted in SITUATIONS, IX.

Pierre Verstraeten is a young Belgian philosopher whom Sartre considers one of the rare *disciples* who have absorbed his thinking in a creative way. This questioner's pertinent questions stimulate Sartre's thinking, and thus the dialogue takes place on an unusually high level for a talk. This results in a very compact philosophical text which complements the pages in *What Is Literature?*, in which Sartre makes his famous distinction between prose and poetry. Because this interview is directed toward specific problems of language, it constitutes an important contribution to the discussion aroused by the investigations of the structuralists.

In analyzing his relationship to language taken as a "practico-inert structure," Sartre is led to redefine his usage of the terms *sense, signification, that which signifies,* and *that which is signified,* to which he gave a different content than the linguists did. He rejects the distinction which the *Tel Quel* group, following Roland Barthes, made between *écrivain* ⟨the writer⟩ and *écrivant* ⟨the one who is writing⟩ because he thinks that the true writer is the one who goes beyond the two practices of writing designated by these terms. His attitude toward language is, in contrast to that of the "literary positivists," a profoundly optimistic one: *Basically, I think that there is nothing inexpressible if we can only invent a way of expressing it.*

To analyze the differences between literary and philosophical language, Sartre gives a philosophical commentary on the very beautiful phrase in the *Confessions* in which Jean-Jacques Rousseau expresses his disaffection toward Mme de Warens: "I was where I was and I went where I went, never any farther."

He also specifies the way in which he adapted German terminology in BEING AND NOTHINGNESS. Elsewhere he reproaches himself for sometimes using in that work an excessively literary language which gave rise to misunderstandings, and he gives as an example of this, *Man is a useless passion.* He thinks that the CRITIQUE OF DIALECTICAL REASON, the writing of which is wholly conceptual, escapes this criticism, but he grants he could have *written it better.* On the other hand, he challenges an objection to this book made by Claude Lévi-Strauss, who says that all writing is analytic, and that consequently Sartre cannot claim to justify the dialectic with analytic writing. After having improvised, in a sentence some twenty lines long, a dazzling definition of dialectical thinking, Sartre replies to this argument by recalling that *dialectic is not the opposite of analysis; dialectic is the controlling of analysis in the name of totality.*

Let us further point out this significant declaration, following the statement *stupidity is a result of oppression,* by one of the most incontestably intelligent authors of our century: *Intelligence has never concerned me as a philosophical problem.*

65/430 A

"Conversación con Jean-Paul Sartre" ⟨Conversation with Jean-Paul Sartre⟩, interview by Jorge Semprun.

-- *Cuadernos de Ruedo iberico*, no. 3 (October-November, 1965), pp. 78-86.

65/431

Avant-garde? De quoi et de qui? ⟨Avant-Garde? What and Whose?⟩.

-- *Le Nouvel Observateur*, October 20-26, 1965, p. 29.

Excerpts from a short speech made in Rome on October 6, 1965, at a Congress of the C.O.M.E.S. ⟨European Writers' Community⟩, whose theme was "The European Avant-Garde, Yesterday and Today" (see report in *Le Monde*, October 16, 1965).

Sartre thinks there is a false avant-garde for which the problem is *simply to exploit all the possibilities of a given language, either through an experimental study of its limits or by introducing a new order into the reading of it.* This avant-garde, made up of James Joyce, Louis-Ferdinand Céline, Alexander Solzhenitsyn, André Breton, Alain Robbe-Grillet, etc., is *traditionalist in spite of itself* and *is carrying on a dialogue with dead men.*

For Sartre *a real avant-garde presupposes that the writer does not limit himself to using language but creates it by writing. Creates the language, instead of playing with it, creates it and in so doing gives it to his country.* An avant-garde writer *is no longer defined by differential variations but by real contradictions. He must create himself in public. He finds before him men prepared to become aware by means of words written from their own* Weltanschauung. And Sartre concludes that the conditions for a real avant-garde exist only *outside Europe.*

65/432

Political interview given in Paris to Mikis Theodorakis.

65/432

a) Published November 9, 1965, in several Athenian dailies.

b) Excerpt. "Jean-Paul Sartre dénonce l'américanisation de la culture" ⟨Jean-Paul Sartre Denounces the Americanization of Culture⟩. *Le Monde*, November 10, 1965. (This article is cut out of the third edition.)

> Addressing himself to the Greek Left, which organized the August, 1965, demonstrations in Athens, Sartre says: *In your opposition to a false front of sovereignty which in fact puts up with and facilitates all sorts of American meddling, you have shown Europeans that on our continent as in Latin America, the reestablishment of a real democracy is inseparable from the reconquest of national sovereignty.* After having denounced the Americanization of daily life in the West and declared that *to permit the imposition of an alien culture is to agree to live someone else's life,* Sartre says that in France *the dictatorship we are struggling against, far from being imposed by the United States, claims, on the contrary, to be liberating us from its grip. But the Americans' investments enable them to control our economy and we suffer, as you do, from the Americanization and depersonalization of culture. . . . For this reason, we share a common struggle. For you as for us, these objectives are tied inseparably to each other: democracy, national sovereignty, autochthonous culture.*

65/432 A

"Sartre, entre Dios y su mamá" ⟨Sartre, between God and His Mama⟩, interview-article by Cesar Tiempo.

-- *La Estafeta Literaria* (Madrid), November 20, 1965.

Part of a series very appropriately named "Encuentros intempestivos" ⟨Off-the-Cuff Encounters⟩, and done, equally appropriately, in a cafe, this interview is conducted in a very journalistic and superficial tone. The questions are asked *a quemarropa* (point-blank), and it is hard to tell whether Sartre is irritated or having fun. Judge for yourselves ⟨from French translation by Rybalka and Contat⟩:

-- How would you define man?

-- *An optical illusion.*

-- What is the worst thing that can happen to a revolutionary?

-- *Become a slave of freedom.*

-- How would you define woman?

-- *The illusion of an illusion.*

-- And Simone de Beauvoir?

-- *A revised, corrected, and improved edition of that illusion.*

-- Why don't you marry her?

-- *You should never marry an illusion. . . .*

-- What do you think of the devil?

-- *He's only a poor underlaborer. He gets the souls, but he isn't the one who condemns them.*

-- Do you think you're one of the elect?

-- *An elect is a man God has up against a wall.*

-- What does existing mean to you?

-- *Toasting yourself without thirst.*

Cesar Tiempo's presentation itself includes a good number of mistakes. Sartre's mother is, we are told, Jewish, which allows Sartre himself to be described as "semijudio, feo y sentimental" ⟨half-Jewish, ugly and sentimental⟩ (according to the famous phrase of Valle Inclan), and to be compared to Montaigne, Marcel Proust, Charlie Chaplin, and a certain David Viñas.

65/433

"Les Circonstances imposent de voter pour François Mitterrand" ⟨The Circumstances Require a Vote for François Mitterrand⟩, statement.

-- *Le Monde*, December 4, 1965, p. 2.

Les Temps modernes (no. 234 [November, 1965], pp. 769-75) had published an editorial entitled "Un Compromis inutile" ⟨A Useless Compromise⟩ in which serious reservations concerning François Mitterrand's candidacy in the presidential elections were expressed. On the eve of these, Sartre nevertheless resigned himself to publishing a statement in which he called for a vote for Mitterrand and said, *To vote Mitterrand is not to vote for him but* against *personal rule and* against *the socialist flight to the Right.*

65/434

"Le Choc en retour" ⟨The Counter-Shock⟩, interview.

65/434

a) Le Nouvel Observateur, December 8-14, 1965.

b) Reprinted in SITUATIONS, VIII.

Interview done the day after the first round of presidential elections had put Charles de Gaulle on the second ballot. Sartre analyzes the election returns, and remarks that Jean Lecanuet is the one who *cut into the Gaullist support* and who in fact caused the runoff. Above all, he calls attention to the fact that the unity of the Left is still a fiction and that, although it is necessary to vote Mitterand on the second ballot, it is important above all to exploit the success of the Left by working to unite it around a precise program. *We are only at the starting point. There is still an enormous amount of work to be done which is scarcely begun and which the Left ought to, to begin with, provide itself with the means of doing.*

For the interview in *Al Ahram*, see 65/457.

65/NOTE 1.

Sartre sent a message to a meeting on the Dominican Republic which took place on June 18, 1965, at the Mutualité.

65/NOTE 2.

Sartre attended the World Peace Congress held in Helsinki from July 10 to 15, 1965, and read a motion calling for "the immediate withdrawal of United States troops and their allies from South Vietnam" (see *Le Monde*, July 17, 1965, p. 3).

65/NOTE 3.

In December, 1965, and in the company of several French and foreign notables on the Committee for the Defense of Ahmed Ben Bella, Sartre registered a complaint with the United Nations Committee for the Rights of Man in order "to draw the attention of the member nations to the threats which the rights of the human person and the guarantees to individuals are presently being subjected to in Algeria" (*Le Monde*, December 17, 1965, p. 9).

1966

66/435

L'Universel singulier ⟨The Singular Universal⟩.

a) In *Kierkegaard vivant* ⟨The Living Kierkegaard⟩. Colloquium organized by UNESCO in Paris from April 21 to 23, 1965. Ideas series. Gallimard, [1966]. Pp. 20-63.

The volume also includes a short speech by René Maheu and pieces by Jean Beaufret, Gabriel Marcel, Lucien Goldmann, Martin Heidegger, Jean Wahl, Karl Jaspers, etc.

b) Excerpt. *Ce philosophe est un anti-philosophe* ⟨This Philosopher Is an Anti-Philosopher⟩. *La Quinzaine littéraire*, no. 7 (June 15, 1966), pp. 4-5.

c) Reprinted in SITUATIONS, IX.

Sartre's lecture was given on April 21, 1964. Short excerpts from it were quoted in an article by Jean d'Ormesson, "Un Colloque à l'UNESCO sur Kierkegaard vivant" ⟨A UNESCO Colloquium on the Living Kierkegaard⟩, *Le Monde*, April 25, 1964.

Sartre had said relatively little about Sören Kierkegaard prior to giving this very important lecture on him. By means of the personality and works of the Danish philosopher, he devotes his chief efforts to defining man's relationships to history: *Kierkegaard was perhaps the first to show that the universal enters singularly into history to the extent that the singular is instituted there as universal* (p. 53).

For the piece published as the preface to Stéphane Mallarmé, *Poésies*, see 53/234.

66/436

"Entretien avec Jean-Paul Sartre" ⟨Talk with Jean-Paul Sartre⟩, by Léonce Peillard.

a) Biblio and *Livres de France*, 17th Year, no. 1 (January, 1966), pp. 14-18.

b) Long excerpts. "Jean-Paul Sartre parle" ⟨Jean-Paul Sartre Speaks⟩. *Le Figaro littéraire*, January 13, 1966.

c) Reprinted in COMMUNISTS ARE AFRAID OF REVOLUTION (see 69/502).

"Communists Are Afraid of Revolution: Two Interviews," translated by Elaine P. Halperin.

-- *Midway*, X, no. 1 (summer, 1969), 53-61.

This issue of *Biblio* and its supplement, *Livres de France*, is devoted to Sartre. Sartre, having refused to fill out the usual stock questionnaire, does his best to answer the questions of an interviewer who, in spite of his good will, is obviously incapable of following Sartre's thinking. In spite of the superficial tone imposed upon him, Sartre somehow or other manages, with his characteristic benevolence, to rescue the talk from banality.

After several biographical and political reflections, the interview goes on to consider bourgeois theater and THE CONDEMNED OF ALTONA and then concludes with an intriguing exchange of views about the way chocolates are wrapped in Russia.

The same issue of *Biblio* contains an unpublished piece by Sartre, a bibliography, an article by Francis Jeanson, and an excellent presentation by André Gorz of the development of Sartre's thinking.

66/437

Letter to *Le Figaro littéraire*.

-- In "Quelques mots de Sartre" ⟨A Few Words by Sartre⟩. *Le Figaro littéraire*, January 27, 1966.

Sartre protests the paper's unauthorized publication of his interview with Léonce Paillard, and specifies: *I have always refused and I shall always refuse to collaborate, in any form whatsoever, with* Le Figaro littéraire. See on this subject 52/NOTE.

The newspaper's editorial staff says that it was all a misunderstanding and reminds Sartre of his previous collaborations with the paper in 1945 and 1949.

66/438

Père et fils ⟨Father and Son⟩, excerpt from "Flaubert."

-- *Biblio* and *Livres de France*, 17th Year, no. 1 (January, 1966), pp. 19-23.

This part was not included in the articles published in *Les Temps modernes* (see 66/439).

66/439

La Conscience de classe chez Flaubert ⟨Class Consciousness in Flaubert⟩.

-- *Les Temps modernes*, no. 240 (May, 1966), pp. 1921-52; no. 241 (June, 1966), pp. 2113-53.

Class Consciousness in Flaubert, first part of study (May), translated by Beth Archer.

-- *Modern Occasions*, I, no. 3 (spring, 1971), 379-89; I, no. 4 (fall, 1971), 587-601.

66/440

Flaubert: Du poète à l'artiste ⟨Flaubert: From Poet to Artist⟩.

-- *Les Temps modernes*, no. 243 (August, 1966), pp. 197-253; no. 244 (September, 1966), pp. 423-81; no. 245 (October, 1966), pp. 598-674.

Gustave Flaubert is without a doubt the writer Sartre has been most concerned with. His interest in him goes back to his childhood, as we know now from the passages in THE WORDS (pp. 55-56) where he speaks of "Charbovary" and says particularly: *I reread the last pages of* Madame Bovary *twenty times and ended by knowing whole paragraphs by heart. . . .*

Later on, NAUSEA sometimes has a certain Flaubertian tone, with its Le Havrian setting and a character like the Autodidact, who is reminiscent of Bouvard and Pécuchet. In the visit to the Bouville museum and other passages of antibourgeois satire, the antiphrasal irony and even the cadence of many lines irresistibly recall Flaubert. And it is in Flaubert's writing, furthermore, that Sartre may have found the name of his main character: "roquentin" is a word found here and there in *L'Education sentimentale* ⟨Sentimental Education⟩ and *Bouvard et Pécuchet* ⟨Bouvard and Pécuchet⟩ which seems to us to have a typically Flaubertian ring.

It is only later that Sartre seems to have planned to write a study of Flaubert. After having used him at length as an example in BEING AND NOTHINGNESS (pp. 558-62) to attack traditional psychology and develop a theory of existential psychoanalysis, he says in this connection: *This psychoanalysis has not yet found its Freud. At most we can find the foreshadowing of it in certain particularly successful biographies. We hope to be able to attempt elsewhere two examples in relation to Flaubert and Dostoevsky* (translated by Hazel E. Barnes [New York: Philosophical Library, 1956], p. 575).

This project will have no immediate effect. As a matter of fact, in a second stage which begins in 1945 (see the pieces collected in SITUATIONS, II, pp. 12-13, 167, 172-73, 198-99, 255), Sartre sees Flaubert as the very image of the bourgeois writer, who just denies without committing himself. He reproaches him for having launched into *vile insults to the workers* (p. 167), and he says, in a phrase which caused a scandal: *I hold Flaubert and Goncourt responsible for the repression which followed the Commune because they didn't write a single line to try and stop it* (p. 13). Arguments similar to those developed in SITUATIONS, II, are already to be found in BAUDELAIRE (Gallimard edition, pp. 160-64).

Then Flaubert seems to drop out of Sartre's immediate concerns until around 1954-55, the period in which he goes back over his own childhood and starts writing his autobiography, and in which he also deepens his understanding of psychoanalysis and Marxism. Let us point out an article from this period by Jean-Baptiste Pontalis, "La Maladie de Flaubert" ⟨Flaubert's Illness⟩, which was published in *Les Temps modernes* for March and April, 1954 (reprinted in *Après Freud* ⟨After Freud⟩, [Gallimard, 1968], pp. 293-329). Around 1956 the Communist philosopher Roger Garaudy is going to give Sartre an opportunity to write a first study of Flaubert. Simone de Beauvoir has this to say about the subject in *Force of Circumstance* (p. 346):

"Garaudy had suggested to him that they take a particular topic and use it to compare the usefulness of the Marxist and Existentialist methods; they had decided that they would both make a study of Flaubert and his works, each in his own way. Sartre wrote a long essay crammed with material, but too carelessly put together for him to think of publishing it."

Beginning in April, 1957, *Les Temps modernes* announces for publication an article entitled "Gustave Flaubert." In the July-August, 1957, issue, this title will become "L'Idiot de la famille" ⟨The Family Idiot⟩ and will continue to be announced until April, 1958, without ever being published. This same issue promises an article, "Existentialism and Marxism," which will become *Search for a Method*. In *Search*, Sartre once again uses Flaubert as an example to show the weaknesses of traditional Marxist interpretations as well as psychoanalytic ones (see pp. 45-48, 71-72, 89-94, and 100 of the Gallimard edition of CRITIQUE OF DIALECTICAL REASON). Sartre gives special weight to the family and childhood, and tries to determine the conditions of what he no longer hesitates to call *Gustave Flaubert's literary commitment* (p. 72).

It was partly to be able to deal with Flaubert that Sartre wrote CRITIQUE OF DIALECTICAL REASON; and conversely, it was in order to continue his reflections on the dialectic that he had recourse to the author of *Madame Bovary*. This point comes out quite clearly in an interview (see 60/334) when he is answering Madeleine Chapsal's question,

-- You needed to write about the Dialectic to be able to talk about Flaubert?

J.-P. S.-- *Yes. The proof of this is that in a Polish article* [Existentialism and Marxism] *I could not help talking about him, and conversely that I put long passages from my book about him into* CRITIQUE OF DIALECTICAL REASON.

Since 1960 Sartre has drawn up several manuscripts on Flaubert and announced more than once that he intended to publish a work which would be a two-part study, stopping with *Madame Bovary*, of the man through the works and the work through the man. The best short account presently available is on the record, *Sartre attiré et repoussé par Flaubert* ⟨Sartre Attracted and Repelled by Flaubert⟩ (Disques culturels français, Français de notre temps series, sponsored by the Alliance française, no. 17. Reference: 17 FT 63. Introduction [rather acidulous] by Marc Blancpain. Recorded, apparently, in 1963 or 1964). In it Sartre says especially that Flaubert is *the most radically uncommitted writer in French literature*, but that his *furious noncommitment* is only *the other side of a total commitment which began in his childhood.* The aim of Sartre's study is, on the one hand, to show *the* oeuvre *becoming singular through the man* and *the man becoming universal through the* oeuvre; and on the other hand, to adapt to this task, *in an order whose fundamental starting point is the Marxist doctrine, all the means of knowing we have at hand today, all the methods of studying a man we have at our disposal.* In a subsequent analysis of the famous "Madame Bovary c'est moi" ⟨I am Madam Bovary⟩, Sartre begins to explain the origins of this *feminizing of experience* in Flaubert's writing.

In an interview given to Jacqueline Piatier (see 64/405), he answers the question "Why Flaubert?" in this way: *Because he is just the opposite of what I am. You have to knock heads with what challenges you.*

66/440

Sartre was not completely satisfied with the two studies published in *Les Temps modernes* in 1966. Completely revised, they are integrated into Vol. III of *The Family Idiot* (Gallimard, 1972).

66/441

"Entretien avec Jean-Paul Sartre: L'Anthropologie" ⟨Discussion with Jean-Paul Sartre: Anthropology⟩.

a) Cahiers de Philosophie (journal of philosophy students at the Sorbonne), nos. 2-3 (February, 1966), pp. 3-12.

b) Reprinted as *L'Anthropologie*. In SITUATIONS, IX.

Important discussion as far as Sartre's objections to structuralism are concerned (see also 65/430, 66/436, and 66/449). Sartre takes up again here the philosophical approach he established in the CRITIQUE OF DIALECTICAL REASON and claims that *it is man who sets the limits of the field of philosophy*. According to him, the concept of structure becomes unintelligible and nondialectical if instead of conceiving of structure as mediation, as a phase of the practico-inert, one studies it as pure contingency, as external constituent, without relating it to the historical *praxis* which constitutes it. The linguistic model is indeed *the clearest structural model*, but it is an abstract model which is based on an inert synthesis and which becomes intelligible only if it is related to the totalizing *praxis* of the act of human speech. For Sartre there are two phases of investigation: conceptual analysis, which bears on static structures (detotalized totalities), and dialectical comprehension, which *puts the object of investigation back into the context of human activity* and integrates *the analytic phase of structural analysis as a fact of the ongoing practical totalization. . . . Any phenomenon investigated is intelligible only in relation to the totalization of other phenomena of the historical world.*

The discussion ends with an answer to a question about psychoanalysis asked by a Lacanian. Sartre once again makes use of the example of Flaubert and specifies the nature of his agreement with Jacques Lacan's formulation, "The unconscious is the discourse of the other," in the following terms: *In my view, Lacan has clarified the meaning of "unconscious" as discourse which separates through language or, if you prefer, as counter-finality of the spoken word in which verbal groupings are structured through the act of speaking into a practico-inert grouping. These verbal groupings express or constitute intentions which determine me without being mine. With these qualifications--and to the extent that I agree with Lacan*--intentionality *has to be considered basic. There is no mental process which is not intentional, nor is there any which is not bogged down, sidetracked, betrayed by language, but we reciprocally are the accomplices of these betrayals which* constitute *our depth.*

66/442

Preface to *La Promenade du dimanche* ⟨Sunday Stroll⟩, by Georges Michel.

a) Piece originally written for the program for *La Promenade du dimanche*. Théâtre du Studio des Champs-Elysées, 1966. Premiere of the play: February 26, 1966.

b) Excerpt. "Le Théâtre de Georges Michel a pour thème principal la lutte de la répétition contre l'histoire: LE LIEU COMMUN" ⟨The Main Theme of Georges Michel's Plays Is the Conflict between Repetition and History: The Commonplace⟩. *Bref* (journal of the T.N.P. ⟨Théâtre National Populaire⟩), no. 99 (October, 1966), p. 25.

c) Reprinted as "Jean-Paul Sartre présente *La Promenade du dimanche*" ⟨Jean-Paul Sartre Introduces *Sunday Stroll*⟩. In Georges Michel. *La Promenade du Dimanche*. Le Manteau d'Arlequin series. Gallimard, [1967]. Pp. 7-10.

Georges Michel (born in 1926) is one of the rare writers of working-class origin in contemporary French literature. Sartre himself took the initiative in contacting him toward 1962, and published his first play, *The Toys*, in *Les Temps modernes*.

This preface not only explains what makes *Sunday Stroll* simultaneously a new and an already classic work; it continues Sartre's reflection on the role of the commonplace and myth in the theater.

Let us recall that Georges Michel is the author of an excellent novel, *The Timid Adventures of a Window Washer*, and that his play *Aggression*, which was performed by the T.N.P. in 1967, was also backed by Sartre (see 67/456).

66/443

Les Mouches ⟨The Flies⟩, short piece written in memory of Charles Dullin.

a) Cahier Charles Dullin, II (1966), 4-5. Printed in an edition of 500 copies on March 31, 1966.

b) Reprinted as *Dullin et "Les Mouches"* ⟨Dullin and *The Flies*⟩. *Le Nouvel Observateur*, December 8-14, 1969, on

66/443

the occasion of the exhibition organized by the Arsenal library in December, 1969, for the twentieth anniversary of Dullin's death.

Sartre comes back here, without adding much that is very new, to the production of THE FLIES and his relationship to Dullin:

It was he whose enthusiastic recommendation, along with Pierre Bost's, saved my first manuscript, which was on the way to being rejected by Gallimard's readers. . . . After the rehearsals of THE FLIES, *the theater never seemed the same to me again.*

66/444

"I poteri dell'intellettuale" ⟨The Powers of the Intellectual⟩, televised interview by Carlo Bo.

-- *L'Approdo Letterario* (journal of the Italian Radio-Television Network), 12th Year, no. 34 (April-June, 1966), pp. 97-110.

This is part of a montage for the television show "Incontri" ⟨Interviews⟩, which includes comments by Sartre, Juliette Gréco, Alain Robbe-Grillet, Jean-Marie Domenach, etc., and reproduces a passage from THE WORDS and one from THE CONDEMNED OF ALTONA.

Sartre's statements (about literature, the New Novel, psychoanalysis, etc.) contain nothing new. As for Jean-Marie Domenach, he sees Sartre as "a sort of Victor Hugo of our time."

66/444 A

"Kazhdyi priezd v Sovietskii Soiuz--radost' dlia menia" ⟨Each Trip to the Soviet Union Is a Joy for Me⟩, interview by A. Matov.

-- *Trud* (Moscow), [May] 26, 1966.

Short interview of no great interest done during a stay by Sartre in Lvov. Sartre points out that he is making his tenth trip to the Soviet Union and says that during his visit to the University of Lvov he was particularly impressed by the excellent French of the students he met and by their knowledge of French literature, classical as well as modern. He notes the great popularity of Gustave Flaubert in the U.S.S.R. and speaks of the study he is writing of him.

66/445

A Message from Jean-Paul Sartre to American Peace-Workers.

-- *PACS News* (published by the Paris American Committee to Stopwar), [no. 1] (summer, 1966).

Formed in 1966 by a group of Americans living in Paris and determined to fight for peace in Vietnam, the Paris American Committee to Stopwar was disbanded in November, 1968, on the order of the French government.

In this message (part of which is reproduced in facsimile), Sartre expresses his solidarity *with all the Americans in the United States who are struggling against the war of aggression their government is waging in Vietnam* and hopes that their *resistance will grow tougher with each new escalation of the war.*

This text was sent to us by Mme Maria Jolas.

66/446

"Samoie glavnoie dlia menia--eto dieistvie" ⟨What Is Most Important to Me Is to Act⟩, interview-article in Russian by L. A.

-- *Inostranaia Literatura* (Moscow), no. 9 ([September], 1966), pp. 243-45.

Interview given by Sartre and Simone de Beauvoir to the staff of *Inostranaia Literatura* during a stay in Moscow. Sartre stresses the importance of Marxism and the October Revolution, but talks above all about his forthcoming "Flaubert" and the Russian adaptation of THE RESPECTFUL PROSTITUTE, in which, he says, he scarcely recognized his own characters (see 46/90). He deplores the fact that people of every stripe have been able to exploit existentialism, and attacks in passing the advocates of the theater of the absurd: *They are not attacking the bourgeois but man himself. . . . To lack faith in man is to go part of the way toward upholding the bourgeois ideology* ⟨from French translation by Rybalka and Contat⟩. In the interview as a whole, the Russian commentator puts the stress on the positive side of Sartre.

Simone de Beauvoir's comments are limited to a few words.

TEXTS RELATED TO SARTRE'S TRIP TO JAPAN, 1966

Sartre had wanted to go to Japan for a long time; as long ago as 1931 he had submitted, unsuccessfully, his

66/446

candidacy for a job as reader in that country. It was only in 1966, however, that he was able to manage, upon the invitation of the University of Keio and in the company of Simone de Beauvoir, a stay which lasted from September 18 to October 16. Sartre's work is widely disseminated in Japan, and there is a certain number of texts in book form in a Japanese translation which are unpublished elsewhere. Let us cite especially FUNNY FRIENDSHIP, which is a reprint of the text published in *Les Temps modernes*; the collection SARTRE IN 1968, which consists of his interviews about the Days of May and Czechoslovakia; and the two volumes A PLEA FOR INTELLECTUALS and CONVERSATIONS WITH SARTRE, listed below. These works are published by Jimbun Shoin Publishers, who in 1971 brought out an excellent bibliography of Sartre done by Takeshi Ebisaka, Michihico Suzuki, and Kinuko Urano; and who are presently readying a partial translation of this volume.

It is, by the way, thanks to Takeshi Ebisaka that we are able to index the following texts:

66/447

A PLEA FOR INTELLECTUALS, Japanese translation of three lectures.

-- Tokyo: Jimbun Shoin Publishers, [February], 1967.

This volume brings together the three lectures about the intellectual which Sartre gave in Japan:

The Situation of the Intellectual, lecture given at Keio University in Tokyo on September 20, 1966; and the two lectures below which have also been reprinted elsewhere.

66/447 A

The Function of the Intellectual, lecture given at Hibiya Hall in Tokyo on September 22, 1966.

-- *Asahi Janaru*, VIII, no. 42 ([October] 9, 1966).

66/447 B

Is the Writer an Intellectual? lecture given at Kyoto House in Kyoto on September 29, 1966.

-- *Chūō Kōron*, [December], 1966.

A summary of these three lectures was published in the daily *Asahi Shimbun*. The main arguments employed are to be found in the talk, "L'Intellectuel face à la révolution" ⟨The Intellectual Confronting Revolution⟩ (68/483). After revision by Sartre, the French text of these three lectures was published as *Plaidoyer pour les intellectuels* ⟨A Plea for Intellectuals⟩ in SITUATIONS, VIII.

66/447 C

Talk with Jean-Paul Sartre, involving Kenzaburo Ohye, Shuishi Katō, Rokuro Hidaka, Yoshikazu Sakamoto, Shunsuke Tsurumi.

-- *Sekai* ([December], 1966).

66/447 D

Statement against the war in Vietnam.

-- *Sekai* ([December], 1966).

This statement was made on October 15, 1966, during a meeting organized by the anti-Vietnamese War organization, "Beheiren," with the participation of Makoto Oda, Ken Kaiko, Osamu Kuno, Yoshimi Takauchi, etc.

66/447 E

Talk with Jean-Paul Sartre, involving Kiroyuki Hirai, Michihiko Suzuki, Kōji Shirai, Takeshi Ebisaka.

a) Bungei, ([December], 1966).

b) Excerpts. Jean-Jacques Brochier. "Sartre Critique Littéraire" ⟨Sartre as a Literary Critic⟩. *Magazine littéraire*, nos. 56-57 (September, 1971), pp. 24-26.

Texts 66/447 C, D, E, were reprinted in:

66/447 F

CONVERSATIONS WITH SARTRE, in Japanese.

-- Tokyo: Jimbun Shoin Publishers, [March], 1967.

Let us also point out that Sartre gave a televised interview on Channel NHK, and that shortly before he left he addressed a letter to the Sohio Union Headquarters approving the order given by the headquarters for a general strike on October 21, 1966, in protest against American policy in Vietnam (see *Le Monde*, October 18, 1966).

66/448

Saint Georges et le dragon ⟨Saint George and the Dragon⟩.

a) L'Arc, no. 30 ([October], 1966), pp. 35-50.

b) Reprinted in SITUATIONS, IX.

Part of the abandoned work on Tintoretto (see 57/300). Sartre's text is preceded by an introduction by Bernard Pingaud and accompanied by a reproduction of a detail from Tintoretto's painting, "St. George Pinning the Dragon." Sartre's commentary, although purely iconographic, throws an extremely revealing light on this famous painting, for it tries to find corroboration in the painting itself for the socio-existential analysis of *The Prisoner of Venice*.

66/449

"Jean-Paul Sartre répond" ⟨Jean-Paul Sartre Replies⟩, interview with Bernard Pingaud.

a) L'Arc, special issue, "Sartre aujourd'hui" ⟨Sartre Today⟩, no. 30 ([October], 1966), pp. 87-96.

b) Long excerpts in *La Quinzaine Littéraire*, no. 14 (October 15-31, 1966).

For some years now, Sartre has been asked constantly to express his views on the most varied topics in interviews. The generosity--the thoughtlessness, some would say--with which he gives in to these requests has sometimes served him badly. This was especially true of the present interview, which had repercussions that Sartre undoubtedly had not foreseen or wanted. What he gives here is not so much a reasoned response to criticisms of his philosophy made by investigators, thinkers, or writers claiming in different ways to be structuralists as a veritable counterattack. Sartre sets forth here, in a sometimes brusque and peremptory fashion, his basic objections to the latent philosophy he detects in the works of Michel Foucault, the structuralist linguists, Claude Lévi-Strauss, Jacques Lacan, Louis Althusser, and the writers of the *Tel Quel* group. To Sartre, these works have in common their *rejection of history* and their participation in a *neo-positivism* against which, in the name of Marxism, he rebels.

Although it is regrettable that Sartre did not engage in a more searching and less polemical discussion which took better account of the notable differences between the authors rather hastily lumped together here, it seems more than likely that such a discussion would not bring any important modifications in the conclusions set forth during this discussion. For in fact, the conflicts between Sartrian philosophy and structuralism, although they have been artificially heightened by journalists and insufficiently studied by investigators, are nonetheless essential and seem to be, up till now, insurmountable, in spite of the interesting attempt Jean Pouillon has made to reconcile the two points of view (see "Présentation: Un Essai de définition" ⟨Introduction: An Attempt at Definition⟩, *Les Temps modernes*, no. 246 [November, 1966], pp. 769-90).

Among the immediate and negative reactions to this interview the following must be pointed out:

-- François Châtelet. "Sartre répond comme un dépossédé" ⟨Sartre Answers Like a Dis-Possessed Man⟩. *Le Nouvel Observateur*, November 2-8, 1966 (this article elicited a response in the same issue from Francis Jeanson, who comes rather clumsily to Sartre's defense; it is entitled "On secoue trop le cocotier. . . ." ⟨They're Shaking the Coconut Tree Too Much⟩);
-- Jean-François Revel. "Sartre en ballottage" ⟨Sartre Adrift⟩. *L'Express*, November 7-13, 1966;
-- Gilles Lapouge. "Sartre contre Lacan" ⟨Sartre versus Lacan⟩. *Le Figaro littéraire*, December 29, 1966 (this article includes an interview of Jacques Lacan);
-- Philippe Sollers. "Un Fantasme de Sartre" ⟨A Fantasy of Sartre's⟩. *Tel Quel*, no. 28 (winter, 1967), pp. 84-87.

Let us recall, finally, that Michel Foucault replied to Sartre, in a tone of esteem and admiration but reproaching him with not having read *The Order of Things*, in an interview broadcast by the O.R.T.F. ⟨French Radio-Television⟩ and reprinted, against his will, in *La Quinzaine littéraire* (no. 46 [March 1-15, 1968] and no. 47 [March 15-31, 1968]).

Sartre's arguments against Foucault were taken up again and elaborated on by Sylvie Le Bon in a study entitled "Un positiviste désespéré: Michel Foucault" ⟨A Desperate Positivist: Michel Foucault⟩ (*Les Temps modernes*, no. 248 [January, 1967], pp. 1299-1319).

Concerning Sartre's objections to structuralism, see also 65/430, 66/436 and 66/441.

For "Le Crime" ⟨The Crime⟩, interview in the *Nouvel Observateur*, see 66/464.

66/450

Un Cancer en Afrique . . . ⟨A Cancer in Africa⟩, text on apartheid.

a) Christianisme social, LXXIV, nos. 11-12 (1966), 423-30. Text consisting of Sartre's remarks at the day organized by the Coordinating Committee against Apartheid on November 9, 1966, in Paris.

b) Published under the title "Ceux qui sont aux prises avec l'apartheid doivent savoir qu'ils ne sont pas seuls" ⟨Those Who Are Fighting Apartheid Should Know They're Not Alone⟩. *Droit et liberté*, no. 257 (December, 1966), pp. 8-9.

c) Excerpts quoted in a short article. Jean Geoffroy. "Sartre et l'apartheid" ⟨Sartre and Apartheid⟩. *Le Nouvel Observateur*, November 16-22, 1966, p. 6.

The Cancer of Apartheid.

-- *London Bulletin* (of the Bertrand Russell Peace Foundation), no. 6 (autumn, 1968), pp. 47-49.

66/NOTE 1.

During his stay in Greece in August, 1966, Sartre made a statement to one of the representatives of the Athenian press. The August 14-15, 1966, *Monde*, which carries a short account of this interview given in an A.F.P. ⟨French Press Agency⟩ wire, reports that in it Sartre came out particularly for the legalization of the Greek Communist Party, without which there could not possibly be a democracy.

66/NOTE 2.

In March, 1966, Sartre formed the Committee for the Defense of Iranian Political Prisoners and beginning on that date signed all the communiques coming out of this committee. Let us select, in particular, the following texts:

-- Appeal in favor of two men condemned to death in Iran (see *Le Monde*, May 13, 1966).

--Protest against the execution of the young patriot Bahman Qashqai (*Le Monde*, November 25, 1966).

-- Protest against the "numerous tortures, summary executions, prison sentences, and death sentences given to professors, students, and other Iranian citizens" (*Le Monde*, November 10, 1968).

-- Communique protesting the repression in Teheran and denouncing more specifically the activities of the Savak, the Iranian secret police (*Le Monde*, April 8, 1970).

-- Communique warning against certain people who claim to speak for the Committee for the Defense of Iranian Political Prisoners (see *Le Nouvel Observateur* [October 18-24, 1971], p. 10).

66/NOTE 3.

In November, 1966, Sartre, Laurent Schwartz, Henri Bartoli, and Alfred Kastler launched an appeal announcing the formation of the National Vietnam Committee. One thing this committee did was to organize on November 23, 1966, a meeting at the Mutualité, "Six Hours of the World for Vietnam," during which Sartre spoke (see excerpts in *Le Monde*, November 25, 1966).

66/NOTE 4.

The December 1, 1966, *Feuille d'avis de Lausanne* published a statement by Sartre, and supported by Simone de Beauvoir, in support of Freddy-Nils Andersson, director of La Cité publications in Lausanne, who had published Henry Alleg's *The Question*, preceded by Sartre's *A Victory*, in Switzerland during the Algerian War. Of Swedish origin, but long a Swiss resident, the publisher had been the target of an act of expulsion which the Swiss government had taken for political reasons. Sartre says that he regrets this action and that Andersson is *a disinterested and sincere man whose presence can only honor his country of residence.* Sartre's declaration, as one might suspect, had no effect on the Swiss government, and Andersson was expelled.

66/NOTE 5.

Colette Audry's useful work, *Sartre* (Seghers, 1966), includes on pp. 115-84, excerpts from Sartre's philosophical works as well as, facing p. 129, a facsimile of a page of the manuscript for the study of Flaubert.

66/NOTE 6.

Michel-Antoine Burnier's study *Choice of Action* gives quite a few excerpts from conversations he had with Sartre in March, 1961 (pp. 8-81), February, 1963 (pp. 131, 143, 144, 152) and in 1965 (pp. 95-96, 168).

66/NOTE 7.

At the beginning of 1966, the German weekly *Europa* (17th Year, no. 13 [January 17, 1966], pp. 51-52) published, under Sartre's signature but without any indication of its source, an article entitled *Macht der Kommunismus Bankrott?* ⟨Is Communism Going Bankrupt?⟩. This article, which undertakes to examine the situation of communism ten years after the Hungarian affair, seems curious to us in many respects. On the one hand, it reprints almost word for word, in its first part, an interview given to *L'Express* in November, 1956 (see 56/289). On the other hand, it attributes remarks to Sartre which he might make today but which seem too pessimistic and anti-Russian for the time. Probably this is a montage which Sartre was in no way responsible for.

1967

67/451

QUESTIONS DE MÉTHODE ⟨Search for a Method⟩.

-- Idées series. Gallimard, [1967]. 251 pages.

This volume, like CRITIQUE OF DIALECTICAL REASON, is dedicated "Au Castor" ⟨To the Beaver⟩ [Simone de Beauvoir]. It reproduces without change pages 15-111 of the Gallimard edition of CRITIQUE.

See 57/296 for first publication and translation.

67/452

UN SOLEIL, UN VIÊT-NAM ⟨One Sun, One Vietnam⟩.

-- Jean Paul Sartre and Matta. UN SOLEIL, UN VIÊT-NAM. Paris, 1967. In-folio 30 x 22, 24 unnumbered pages. Justification: "ONE SUN, ONE VIETNAM was published by the National Vietnam Committee, to support its activities, on the occasion of the soirée, 'One Hundred Artists for Vietnam,' on June 28, 1967, at the Palais de Chaillot, Paris. 2000 copies of the original manuscript by Jean-Paul Sartre and the lithographs by Matta were printed on Arches vellum in Michel Cassé's shop."

This in-folio includes an eleven-page manuscript, entitled "L'Unité" ⟨Unity⟩ and dated June 10, 1967, which is reproduced in lithograph along with six lithographs by Matta.

Rapidly sketching a chronology of events in Vietnam since 1945, Sartre shows that the distinction between South and North Vietnam is arbitrary and imposed by force. He concludes: *And yet through pain and*

67/452

suffering the Unity remains. The heroic war the F.L.N. ⟨National Liberation Front⟩ and the peasants from the bombed-out villages around Hanoi are waging under different circumstances in both South and North is the struggle of one single people *against the aggressor.*

67/453

A qui rêve la demoiselle? ⟨Who Is the Young Girl Dreaming of?⟩, excerpt.

-- In Jean-Paul Leroux and Michel Chrestien. *Le Livre blanc de l'humour noir* ⟨The White Book of Black Humor⟩. La Pensée moderne, 1967. P. 363.

Poem written for Juliette Gréco.

67/453 A

"Sartre parle" ⟨Sartre Speaks⟩, interview by Louis Winitzer.

-- *Le Magazine MacLean* (Montreal), January, 1967, pp. 26-28.

Vivid interview, but scarcely adding anything new. In it Sartre repeats comments about the New Novel, the avant-garde, the Nobel Prize, the political situation in France, etc., that he has made elsewhere. Let us point out, however, the following two passages:

God disappeared from my life when I was eleven. One day I said he doesn't exist *and I never doubted that since. Certain Catholic commentators remind me of certain psychoanalysts, for whom one is still a pederast whether one admits being one or is afraid to admit it. . . .*

There are real differences in wages and standards of living in the U.S.S.R., but money doesn't bring power there, can't be reinvested to become the basis for a class power. Whereas in the U.S.S.R. and other socialist countries there is room to make reforms, *in the capitalist countries revolutions are necessary.*

67/454

Mythe et réalité du théâtre ⟨Myth and Reality in the Theater⟩, text of a lecture.

a) Le Point (Brussels), no. 7 (January, 1967), pp. 20-25.

b) A la Page, no. 40 (October, 1967), pp. 1476-88.

Myth and Reality in the Theatre.

-- *Gambit* (London), III, no. 9 (1967), 55-68.

Part of a lecture given in Bonn on December 4, 1966, and recorded by Jean-Pierre Berckmans and Jean-Claude Garot. In his introduction Sartre deals with relationships between the theater and movies and defines *critical theater*:

Contrary to what is claimed, the motion picture did not throw the theater into a state of crisis, did not hurt the theatrical art. It hurt certain theatrical producers by taking their audiences. It hurt a certain kind of theater, the kind which was performing the function of the motion picture, that is, the bourgeois realistic theater whose goal was to achieve direct expression of reality. . . . From this moment on the theater reflected on its own limits and, like any other art, made of these limits the conditions of its possibility.

After the-death-of-God, as Nietzsche puts it, and of inspiration, which was God-whispering-in-our-ear, we had Flaubert's critical novel and Mallarmé's critical poetry--that is, an art which includes the artist's reflexive attitude toward his art. The appearance of the talking picture and various social factors created, beginning in 1950, what could be called critical theater.

Sartre then shows how the representatives of "critical theater" *want to create means of communicating out of the shortcomings of theater themselves*; and he compares, by contrasting them, Jean Genet (*The Blacks*), Antonin Artaud and Bertolt Brecht; happenings, Peter Brook's *US*, and documentary dramas like *In the Matter of J. Robert Oppenheimer*; the theater of silence (in vogue between the wars), the theater of the unconscious (Antonin Artaud), and Eugène Ionesco's plays.

In conclusion, Sartre sees three essential rejections in contemporary theater: the rejection of psychology, the rejection of plot, and the rejection of all realism; and he explains these terms as follows:

By their rejection of psychology, [the authors] *are rejecting the reign of the bourgeoisie, because psychological theater is basically an ideological theater which signifies that historical and social conditions do not make man, that there is psychological determinism and a human nature which is everywhere the same. They reject the conveniences of plot. There*

67/454

is no plot in the sense of a little well-made anecdote with its own beginning, middle, and end. The reason why there isn't is that they think that having a plot would mean amusing the spectator and distracting him from what is essential. . . . They don't want to give up all construction, but they want to construct their subject strictly. . . . Their aim is not to tell a little story but to construct a temporal object in which time, by its contradictions and structurings, will bring out in a striking way the real subject of the play. Finally, they reject realism simply because when you get right down to it, it involves a whole philosophy that they want nothing to do with. To begin with it is a philosophy which seems bourgeois to them, and then one which believes that reality is realist. . . .

These three rejections of the world show that there is nothing absurd about the new theater, but that it is returning by the way of criticism to the great basic theme of the theater, man as event, as History in the event.

67/455

"Une Structure du langage" ⟨A Structure of Language⟩, interview by Jean-Claude Garot.

-- *Le Point*, no. 8 (February, 1967), pp. 27, 29.

This short interview is part of an investigation of contemporary theater by Jean-Pierre Berckmans which is entitled "La Route de l'hystérie" ⟨The Way of Hysteria⟩ and which also includes interviews by Julian Beck, Jerzy Grotowsky, and Marc'O. Sartre hurriedly expresses his reservations about Peter Brook's efforts, the Living Theater, "happenings," and Jerzy Grotowsky.

67/456

"*L'Agression* de Georges Michel" ⟨Georges Michel's *Aggression*⟩, interview by Nicole Zand.

-- *Bref* (periodical of the Théâtre National Populaire), no. 103 (February-March, 1967), pp. 4-6, 8.

Interview made before the premiere of Georges Michel's play, *Aggression*, in March, 1967. Sartre comments on the play and shows that it expresses the phenomenon of "relative pauperization" in our society, which, in the name of consumer values, creates needs that young people lack the means of satisfying. He praises Georges Michel for his success in going beyond realism in his plays by *skewing them toward the mythical*, and he contrasts these plays to a work like Eugène Ionesco's *Rhinoceros*, which is only symbolic. *I consider Georges Michel a complete man of the theater because he cannot tell the difference between production and the spoken word. . . . From this point of view then, I find his plays wholly original. They are the plays of a solitary man who has not been influenced by anyone. They are essentially protest plays, but they never become plays with a message because that road goes nowhere.*

TEXTS PERTAINING TO THE ISRAELI-ARAB PROBLEM, 1965-67

Sartre had supported Egypt's position during the Suez Crisis in 1956. Toward 1965, judging that Gamal Abdel Nasser's politics had developed in a revolutionary direction, he decided to open a dialogue between the Egyptian Left and the Israeli Left. To help accomplish this he announced that he would go to Egypt and Israel himself, and that *Les Temps modernes* would devote a special number to the Israeli-Arab conflict.

Sartre's and Simone de Beauvoir's trip, first planned for December, 1966, finally took place in February-March, 1967; and the issue of *Les Temps modernes* was sent to press at the end of May, 1967, a few days before Israel attacked.

65/457

Interview given to *Al Ahram* and made by Ali El Samman.

a) Al Ahram (Cairo), [December] 25, 1965.

Unconsulted text.

The interview was also reprinted in the Israeli daily, *Al Hamishmar*.

b) Very short excerpt. "Sartre entre les Arabes et les Juifs" ⟨Sartre among the Arabs and the Jews⟩. *Le Nouvel Observateur*, January 12-18, 1966, p. 4.

c) Excerpts in *Le Monde*, January 21, 1966.

"An Interview with Sartre," translated from Arabic by Amnon Kapeliuk.

-- *New Outlook* (Tel Aviv), IX, no. 2 (77) (February, 1966), 58-62.

Sartre declares his sympathy for the Egyptian revolution, speaks of his coming trip to Egypt

65/457

and Israel, and announces his intention to publish a special issue of *Les Temps modernes* which will confront the two sides but remain *strictly neutral*.

66/458

Interview given to *Al Hamishmar* and gathered by Simha Flapan.

a) *Al Hamishmar* (journal of the Israeli MAPAM), [beginning], 1966.

b) Reprinted in entirety. "Jean-Paul Sartre et les problèmes de notre temps" ⟨Jean-Paul Sartre and the Problems of Our Time⟩. *Cahiers Bernard Lazare*, no. 4 (April, 1966), pp. 4-9.

"Sartre on Israel and Other Matters."

t1) *New Outlook*, IX, no. 4 (79) (May, 1966), 8-11.

t2) Condensed version. "Jean-Paul Sartre on a Jewish-Arab dialogue." *Jewish Digest*, January, 1967, pp. 27-29.

Sartre begins by making clear the reasons which persuaded him to take the initiative for an Israeli-Arab dialogue: *I find that I am torn by contradicting loyalties and friendships. The situation of my Jewish friends during the Occupation revealed the problem of the Jews in Europe to me at the same time that our common resistance to nazism was creating deep-seated bonds between us. After the Liberation came I wrote what I had felt during these years of struggle: as long as one Jew is threatened in this world, not a single Christian can believe he's safe. Consequently, my friends and I followed the Israeli's postwar struggle against the English with great interest. But in a similar fashion the struggle against colonialism led us during the Algerian War to take our stand with the F.L.N.* ⟨National Liberation Front⟩ *freedom fighters and to cement many friendships in the Arab nations. . . . Thus we find ourselves, now that the Arab world and Israel are in conflict, divided so to speak within ourselves, and we are living this conflict as if it were our personal tragedy.*

Sartre then talks about the problems of the Third World, Vietnam, ANTI-SEMITE AND JEW, Marxism, and the chances for socialism in Europe and France.

66/459

Interview given to *Al Ba'ath*.

-- *Al Ba'ath* (Syrian weekly), [February], 1966. We know this text through the short excerpt given in *New Outlook*, X, no. 4 [88] (May, 1967), 32.

The Syrians were opposed to any compromise with Israel. Sartre tries to convince them that a dialogue is necessary.

67/460

Open letter to the newspaper, *Al Ahram*.

a) Al Ahram, [February] 25, 1967.

b) English text. *New Outlook*, X, no. 4 (88), (May, 1967), 29-30.

Short letter published at the outset of Sartre's and Simone de Beauvoir's stay in Egypt, which was to last till March 13, 1967. Sartre was the guest of the newspaper, *Al Ahram*. He expresses his sympathy for the Egyptian revolution and says he came to study the Egyptian way to socialism. No mention of Israel is made.

According to the issue of *New Outlook* cited above, Sartre made additional statements in the March 6, 1967, *Al Anwar* (Beirut) and the March 9 *Al Ahram*.

During his stay in Egypt, Sartre visited the Palestinian refugee camps, had a talk with President Gamal Abdel Nasser and gave several lectures. One of these, given in Cairo on March 6 before more than two thousand people, including the Egyptian minister of culture, had as its subject peaceful coexistence and the Russell tribunal. Sartre said in particular:

One can coexist peacefully with countries whose ideology is different from one's own, but one cannot coexist peacefully with war criminals. . . . If we proved that the Americans are war criminals, that would make peaceful coexistence more difficult. . . . It would be demonstrated that in practice [peaceful coexistence] *is more favorable to the Americans than to the Soviets* (see *Le Monde*, March 7, 1967).

As he was leaving Egypt, Sartre held a press conference at which he praised President Nasser, *a prudent, judicious and far-sighted leader* (see *Le Monde*, March 15, 1967).

67/461

"Jean-Paul Sartre à Guivath-Haviva" ⟨Jean-Paul Sartre in Guivath-Haviva⟩, report of a lecture.

-- *L'Information d'Israël*, March 17, 1967.

Reaching Israel from Athens on March 14, 1967, Sartre and Simone de Beauvoir were welcomed in Tel Aviv by the president of Parliament and a large group of deputies and intellectuals. In the lecture given at Guivath-Haviva, Sartre comments on his trip to Egypt: *The salient point in the Egyptian intellectuals' attitude toward Israel is, of course, their hostility: But there is a difference between the Marxists and the non-Marxists.* He says he was greatly impressed by the realism and good sense of President Gamal Abdel Nasser, and then answers questions about China and philosophy.

On March 18, at the Genossar kibbutz in Galilee, Sartre had a long talk with Yigal Allon, the Israeli labor minister. On March 19, Sartre and Simone de Beauvoir were received by Arab intellectuals and were greeted in the Accra region by demonstrations by Palestinian nationalists hostile to the Israeli government.

On March 24, Sartre gave a public lecture in Tel Aviv on the war in Vietnam and the Russell Tribunal, and Simone de Beauvoir shortly afterward gave a paper at the Hebrew University in Jerusalem on the role of the writer. On March 28, without giving any reason, Sartre cancelled the visit he was to make to the Israeli commander in chief, General Itzhak Rabin, and to units of the Israeli army.

Sartre also met Levi Eshkol and had the following talk and press conference:

67/461 A

Talk with the editors of *New Outlook*.

a) Excerpts in *New Outlook*, X, no. 4 (88) (May, 1967). 24-27.

b) Excerpts in "Jean-Paul Sartre et Simone de Beauvoir en Israël" ⟨Jean-Paul Sartre and Simone de Beauvoir in Israel⟩. *Cahiers Bernard Lazare*, no. 10 (May, 1967), pp. 18-20.

Here Sartre deplores the conditions under which the Arab minority live in Israel.

67/461 B

Press conference given in Tel Aviv on March 29, 1967, by Sartre and Simone de Beauvoir.

a) Excerpts in *L'Information d'Israël*, March 30, 1967; *Le Monde*, March 31, 1967.

b) English text. *New Outlook*, X, no. 4 (88) (May, 1967), 14-23.

One will find in the same issue one of the many editorials evoked by Sartre's trip as well as two articles culling commentaries from the Arab and Israeli press.

c) French text. In "Jean-Paul Sartre et Simone de Beauvoir en Israël." *Cahiers Bernard Lazare*, no. 10 (May, 1967), pp. 16-17.

> Sartre begins by talking about antisemitism and then gives his impressions of Israel and, in particular, the kibbutzim he visited. Before answering the journalists' questions, he concludes:
>
> *If the new Israeli man, the new Israeli Jew, can develop in peace and understand all his contradictions, make them his own, and go beyond them in his actions, he'll be--he is already but he'll be--one of the most superior men to be found in History.*
>
> In his answers to the journalists' questions, Sartre once more insists that he is neutral and declares that he recognizes *without reservation* the two prior conditions for any settlement, Israel's sovereignty and the Palestinian refugees' right to return to Israel. These two conditions seem to him to be for the moment insurmountable obstacles, and he goes so far as to admit: *I am sorry to say so, but in a sense I see no encouraging sign for an Israeli-Arab peace.*

67/462

Interview about Israel by Jigal Arci.

a) First published as "Arabové a Židé" ⟨Arabs and Jews⟩. *Literarni Novini* (Prague), April 15, 1967.

b) Translated into German. "Araber und Juden" ⟨Arabs and Jews⟩. *Volksstimme* (organ of the Austrian Communist Party); *Neues Forum* (Vienna), CLXII-CLXIII (June-July, 1967), 439-41.

c) Excerpts in French. "Impressions israéliennes de Jean-Paul Sartre" ⟨Jean-Paul Sartre's Impressions of Israel⟩. *Cahiers Bernard Lazare*, no. 11 (June-July, 1967), pp. 27-29.

67/462

Interview made before the outbreak of hostilities. Sartre takes up the Israeli-Arab problem again and concludes: *The future of the Israelis and the Arabs depends upon the development of the Left. The European Left owes it to itself to show its confidence in the left-wing forces of the two countries in order that the weight of these forces may enhance the chances of a dialogue.*

Concerning Sartre's position after the Six-Day War broke out, see 69/504.

67/463

Pour la vérité ⟨For the Sake of Truth⟩, preface to the special issue of *Les Temps modernes*, "Le Conflit israélo-arabe" ⟨The Israeli-Arab Conflict⟩.

a) Les Temps modernes, no. 253*a* (June, 1967), pp. 5-11. This issue was translated into German, Catalan, Spanish, Portuguese, and Japanese.

b) Conclusion of the preface reprinted as "Nos exigences contradictoires" ⟨Our Contradictory Requirements⟩. *Le Nouvel Observateur*, June 14-20, 1967.

Sartre explains in this text why the staff of *Les Temps modernes* limited itself to compiling a file in which the Israeli and the Arab points of view coexist in simple "contiguity." He sums up the Left's internal disagreements about the conflict and promises an article in which he will give *not an opinion--which would be pretentious and futile--but some reflections inspired by* [his] *trip* (this article has not so far been published). As Sartre himself specifies, *For the Sake of Truth* was written May 27, 1967, that is, before the Six-Day War broke out. *The neutrality--or, if you like, the noncommitment--that we swore ourselves to, we intend to maintain, in spite of what has happened*, with the exception of one point *which was not in the program. We will not push our discretion to the point of ratifying a war of extermination. This evening still the guns are quiet, but if at dawn tomorrow they began to speak, we feel obligated to say that we condemn aggression in advance no matter what quarter it may come from, and equally condemn the provocation which makes war inevitable.*

On the other hand, at the end of May Sartre signed, together with a certain number of intellectuals, an appeal which reads as follows (see *Le Monde*, June 1, 1967):

"We the undersigned French intellectuals, believing that we have shown that we are friends of the Arab peoples and opponents of American imperialism, and not supporting every stand that the Israeli leaders take, nevertheless take note of the State of Israel's present manifestation of evident restraint and desire for peace.

"Whatever the big powers' game may be, it is incomprehensible that a segment of public opinion should think it obvious that Israel has allied itself with the forces of imperialism and aggression, and the Arabs with the forces of socialism and peace. It is equally incomprehensible that these same people are forgetting that Israel is the only country whose very existence is being challenged, that threatening proclamations come from Arab leaders every day.

"In these conditions, we call upon democratic opinion in France to reaffirm with vigor:

"1. That the security and sovereignty of Israel, including, naturally, freedom to sail in international waters, are a necessary condition and the starting point for peace;

"2. That this peace can be made and ought to be assured and strengthened by direct negotiations between sovereign states in the reciprocal interests of the peoples concerned."

This appeal was interpreted as a stand taken by Sartre. It aroused great satisfaction in Israel and strong reactions in the Arab countries. By its very date, let us stress, it cannot constitute approval of the Six-Day War.

Concerning the position he took later, see 69/504.

TEXTS PERTINENT TO THE "RUSSELL TRIBUNAL"

During the summer of 1966, Lord Bertrand Russell took the initiative in convoking the "International Tribunal against War Crimes in Vietnam." Sartre agreed from the start to take part, and he participated in the founding meeting held in London on November 14 and 15, 1966. He was elected executive president of the tribunal.

66/464

"Le Crime" ⟨The Crime⟩, interview.

a) Le Nouvel Observateur, November 30-December 6, 1966.

b) Reprinted in SITUATIONS, VIII.

"Imperialist Morality," or "Policies May Be Juridically, Objectively Criminal . . . ," anonymous translation with no indication of origin.

t1) "Imperialist Morality." *New Left Review*, no. 41 (January-February, 1967), pp. 3-10.

t2) "Policies May Be Juridically, Objectively Criminal. . . ." With one passage omitted. In Jean-Paul Sartre and Vladimir Dedijer. *War Crimes in Vietnam.* Spokeman Pamphlet, no. 12. Bertrand Russell Peace Foundation, [1970].

After the meeting in London Sartre explains *the scope and meaning of what the "tribunal" intends to do. . . . For us it's not a matter of judging whether American policy is evil--most of us have no doubt about that--but to see whether it falls within the jurisdiction of the laws governing "war crimes."* He then replies to the chief objections which can be made to the very existence of such a tribunal. The tribunal does not pretend to judge the Americans in the name of morality, for: *Imperialist politics is an inevitable historical reality which as such escapes all juridical or moral condemnation. . . . The fact is that although the development of History is not governed by law and morality--which are, on the contrary, produced by it--these two superstructures do have a "retroactive effect" on this development. That is why a society may be judged in terms of its own criteria. . . . Our "tribunal" is only proposing today to apply capitalist imperialism's own laws to it.*

Rejecting the term *idealist*, which has been applied to the tribunal, Sartre specifies: *We are . . . in no way manifesting the indignant condemnation of a group of upright citizens, but are giving a juridical dimension to international political actions in an effort to combat the tendency of the majority of people to make only practical and moral judgments of the behavior of a social group or government. . . . If we wanted to set ourselves up as a real tribunal and pronounce sentences, we would be acting as idealists. But we have the right to assemble as citizens, to give the concept of war crime its force again by showing that every policy may and should be judged objectively in terms of existing juridical criteria.* Explaining why the tribunal will have to investigate only American war crimes, Sartre says: *I refuse to put the action of a group of poor hunted peasants who have had to impose an iron discipline upon their ranks, and that of an immense army supported by an overindustrialized country of 200 million inhabitants, on the same footing.* Thinking of the possible effectiveness of the tribunal, he says: *We have been criticized for engaging in petty-bourgeois legalism. That's true, and I accept the criticism. But who are we trying to convince? . . . The petty-bourgeois masses are the ones who need the waking up and shaking up today, because their alliance with the working class--even on the domestic level--is desirable. And the way to open their eyes is through legalism.* The interview continues with an analysis of the Gaullist policy concerning Vietnam, and with an enumeration of the actions that the Left should take. Sartre concludes by expressing the hope that the tribunal will support the struggle of the young Americans who are opposing the war their government is waging.

NOTE: During a press conference held on February 2, 1967, in Paris, Sartre and Laurent Schwartz presented the report of the first investigating committee sent to Vietnam by the Russell Tribunal (see *Le Monde*, February 4, 1967).

67/465

Lettre au Président de la République ⟨Letter to the President of the Republic⟩.

a) Le Monde, April 25, 1967.

b) Reprinted, with General Charles de Gaulle's reply, in SITUATIONS, VIII.

Having been denied permission by the British Labor government, the Russell Tribunal was getting ready to meet in Paris on April 26, 1967, at the Mutualité.

In this letter, dated April 13, 1967, Sartre asks General de Gaulle whether the refusal of Vladimir Dedijer's request for a visa means that the government intends to forbid the tribunal to hold its sessions in France.

Le Monde published the general's reply at the end of this letter.

67/466

"Sartre à Gaulle" ⟨Sartre to de Gaulle⟩, interview.

a) Le Nouvel Observateur, April 26-May 3, 1967.

b) Reprinted in SITUATIONS, VIII.

Sartre to de Gaulle.

-- In *Against the Crime of Silence*. Pp. 29-36. (See 67/467.)

67/466

The interview follows the letter in which de Gaulle announces the government's official decision to forbid the Russell Tribunal to meet on French soil. De Gaulle having called him "mon cher Maître" ⟨"Dear Master"⟩, Sartre comments: *The reason why he called me that, I think, is to make clear that he is speaking to the writer and not to the president of a tribunal he does not wish to recognize. I am only "maître" to the table waiters who know that I write. The fact of the matter is that de Gaulle is answering the representative of the tribunal.* Then Sartre analyzes the reasons why the government, which had originally given the tribunal an official assurance that its sessions could be held in France, has changed its attitude. Sartre sees the reasons as being American pressure and de Gaulle's desire not to involve the masses in his policy. He once again sets forth the tribunal's aims, announces that if it has to it will hold its sessions on a ship anchored outside French territorial limits, and concludes: *Paradoxically, the trouble they are making for us lends legitimacy to our tribunal, and shows besides, they are afraid of us. Not certainly of Bertrand Russell, who is ninety-four, nor of me, who am sixty-two, nor of our friends. If we were nothing but a dozen intellectual simpletons who were ridiculously claiming to set themselves up as judges, they would leave us in peace.*

Why are they afraid of us? Because we are bringing up a problem--the problem of war crimes--which no Western government wants to see brought up; because they all want, once again, to reserve the right to commit them.

67/467

Opening Speech at the "International Tribunal against War Crimes in Vietnam," made on May 2, 1967, in Stockholm.

a) Excerpts. "C'est aussi pour le peuple américain que nous luttons. . . ." ⟨We're Also Fighting for the American People⟩. *Le Nouvel Observateur*, May 10-16, 1967.

b) Complete text in *Tribunal Russell: Le Jugement de Stockholm* ⟨The Russell Tribunal: The Stockholm Judgment⟩. Idées actuelles series, no. 147. Gallimard, [1967]. Pp. 25-31.

This volume, whose editing was directed by Arlette El Kaïm, contains all the documents pertaining to the first session of the Russell Tribunal. In it there is also Sartre's stinging reply to the statements by the American secretary of state, Dean Rusk (who had said about the tribunal, in the company of newspapermen, that he did not intend to "play games with a ninety-four-year-old Englishman").

c) Reprinted in SITUATIONS, VIII.

Translated, together with a number of documents related to the Stockholm and Copenhagen sessions of the Russell Tribunal, in:

-- John Duffett, ed. *Against the Crime of Silence.* Proceedings of the Russell International War Crimes Tribunal, Stockholm and Copenhagen. Introduction by Bertrand Russell. Foreword by Ralph Schoenman. New York and London: Bertrand Russell Peace Foundation, 1968; Flanders, N.J.: O'Hare Books, 1968.

Most of the translations are by Richard Miller and Judith Duffett. Contents of book as related to Sartre:

-- Sartre to Dean Rusk (May 3, 1967)	pp. 25-26
-- De Gaulle to Sartre (April 19, 1967)	27-28
-- Interview to *Le Nouvel Observateur*	29-36
-- Jean-Paul Sartre concerning Dean Rusk	36-37
-- Jean-Paul Sartre: Inaugural Statement	40-45
-- Verdict of the Stockholm Session (May 10, 1967), signed Jean-Paul Sartre, president of the Tribunal	302-9
-- Opening Address to the Second Session, by Jean-Paul Sartre	315-17
-- On Genocide	612-26

Volume with approximately the same contents:

-- Peter Limqueco; Peter Weiss; and Ken Coates, eds. *Prevent the Crime of Silence.* Reports from the sessions of the Russell International War Crimes Tribunal, London, Stockholm, and Roskilde. Foreword by Noam Chomsky. London: Allen Lane, The Penguin Press, 1971. Texts by Sartre:

-- Inaugural Statement	pp. 63-67
-- Summary and Verdict of the Stockholm Session	177-85
-- On Genocide	350-65

> In this speech, Sartre sets forth the origin, the aims, and the limits of the tribunal, and undertakes *to set forth frankly what* [he thinks] *about the question of what has been called its "legitimacy." . . . The Russell Tribunal was born of this dual and conflicting recognition: the judgments at Nuremberg made it necessary to have an institution to investigate and, if need be, make judgments of war crimes; neither the world's governments nor its peoples are in a position at this time to create such an institution. . . . We are powerless: that's what guarantees our independence.*

67/468

"Douze hommes sans colère" ⟨Twelve Unangry Men⟩, interview by Serge Lafaurie.

67/468

a) Le Nouvel Observateur, May 24-30, 1967.

b) Reprinted in SITUATIONS, VIII.

Interview made after the first session of the Russell International War Crimes Tribunal, at the close of which it was unanimously concluded that the Americans are guilty of aggression in Vietnam, and that they have had recourse to "terrorist" bombings to break the people's will to resist. Sartre specifies that *this unanimity was not at all anticipated*, and proves it by recounting in detail the evolution of the debates. Speaking for himself, he says: *What was important as far as I am concerned was our going from the vague, already unbearable idea, "They're killing women, children, and old people in Vietnam," to the precise and odious one, "They're doing it on purpose."* He then refutes certain claims by the press about alleged disagreements within the tribunal, and announces the questions which will be taken up during the second session (see 67/478-67/481).

NOTES:

The conclusions reached by the first session of the Russell Tribunal were presented by Sartre during a press conference at the Mutualité on May 19, 1967 (see *Le Monde*, May 21-22, 1967).

In his capacity as president of the Russell Tribunal, Sartre sent a telegram to Donald Duncan, defense witness for Captain Levy of the U.S. Army, who was court-martialed for having denounced American war crimes in Vietnam. This telegram offered to send the defense proofs presented before the tribunal and announced that a letter would follow (see *Le Monde*, May 28-29, 1967).

There is a piece on the Russell Tribunal, signed by Sartre, in a June, 1967, Bulgarian periodical.

On October 27, 1967, Sartre gave a lecture in Brussels under the auspices of the Free University Tribunal (see the report by Philippe Schittecatte, "Sartre expose les principes du tribunal sur les crimes de guerre au Vietnam" ⟨Sartre Sets Forth the [Russell] Tribunal's Principles Concerning War Crimes in Vietnam⟩, *La Gauche* [Brussels], November 4, 1967).

67/469

Introduction to the Roger Pic exhibition, "Photographies du Vietnam en guerre" ⟨Photographs of Vietnam at War⟩.

a) Catalogue of the exhibition held on June 22-July 27, 1967, Galerie du Passeur, 90, rue du Bac, Paris.

b) Selection in *Le Nouvel Observateur*, June 28-July 4, 1967.

c) Reprinted as the preface to Roger Pic. *Au Coeur du Vietnam* ⟨In the Heart of Vietnam⟩. Maspero, 1968. Pp. 2-3.

> *What is fascinating here and now in this implacable mirror is the constant affirmation of the future, like a rainbow arched above the present horror. . . .*
>
> *These images are imperious, and we have to choose. This unconquerable Vietnam is our ultimate freedom.*
>
> This text was the inspiration of the composer Henri Tomasi's libretto for a symphonic poem entitled "Song of Vietnam," whose first performance was announced for December, 1969, at the Concerts Pasdeloup.

67/470

"Jean-Paul Sartre," interview in Serbian by Komnen Becirovic.

-- *Nin/Politika* (Belgrade), [July] 2, 1967.

> Subjects discussed: Israeli-Arab conflict, Vietnam, Russell Tribunal, alienation, Marxism, Georges Lukács, Hegel, Dostoevsky, Socrates, DIRTY HANDS, etc.

67/471

Remarks at the meeting for Régis Debray at the Mutualité on May 30, 1967.

a) Excerpts in *Le Monde*, June 1, 1967.

b) Complete text put together by Jean-Claude Garot. "Théoricien en Bolivie!" ⟨Theoretician in Bolivia⟩, *Le Point* (Brussels), no. 10 (July, 1967), p. 23.

c) Text identical to *(b)* but lacking a few lines at the beginning. "Le Crime monstrueux de Régis Debray" ⟨The Monstrous Crime of Régis Debray⟩. In *Liberté pour Régis Debray* ⟨Freedom for Régis Debray⟩. Brochure published by the Committee for the Support and Defense of Régis Debray, 59, rue Raymond-Losserand, Paris, XIVe.

d) Text *(c)* reprinted in *Le Procès de Régis Debray* ⟨The Trial of Régis Debray⟩. Maspero, 1968. Pp. 7-10.

> Sartre maintains that Debray has been imprisoned just because he wrote his book, *Revolution in the Revolution*, whose main themes he summarizes, and that his alleged crime is nothing but a matter of opinion.

67/471

We ought to put pressure on our government, which has already acted slightly although very timidly, and on the Bolivian government, to demand the unconditional release of Régis Debray.

67/472

"Vogliono assassinare Debray. Dobbiamo impedirlo" ⟨They Want to Assassinate Debray. We Ought to Stop It⟩, interview by Adolfo Chiesi.

a) Paese Sera (Rome), September 2, 1967. Text reprinted in the September 3, 1967, issue.

b) Quoted in *Le Monde*, September 5, 1967.

Interview on the Régis Debray trial. Sartre says that world public opinion should stop the Bolivian government from committing the crime it is getting ready to commit--assassinating Debray once the waves the affair has made have died down. He speaks of his relations with Debray and compares his arrest to that of Georges Arnaud at the time of the Francis Jeanson affair. Debray is first of all a journalist, and the reasons why he was arrested were that he saw *the Latin American situation with great intelligence and lucidity* and had a friendly relationship with Cuba. He is really being tried for his political views.

67/473

"Sartre e la De Beauvoir in memoria di Ilja Ehrenburg." ⟨Sartre and de Beauvoir in Memory of Ilya Ehrenburg⟩.

-- *L'Unità*, September 3, 1967.

Short statement by Sartre and Simone de Beauvoir upon the death of Ilya Ehrenburg, which occurred on August 31, 1967. Here is the translation ⟨from the French translation by Rybalka and Contat⟩ *in extenso:*

When the fiftieth anniversary of the Russian Revolution is about to be celebrated, it is profoundly sad to learn about the disappearance of a man who, day by day, was the passionate and lucid witness of these fifty years which changed the world.

We had been his friends since 1947, and with the passage of time, our ties to him had become so close that his death moved us like a personal bereavement. We loved his intelligence, courage, humor, and the charm of his tired old face; and more than as a novelist and essayist, we admired him as what may in the full sense of the term be called a cultured man. But we learned during our trips to the U.S.S.R. that he stood for much more than that in the eyes of the Russian public, above all the young. In reality, perhaps his greatest merit was to have known how to preserve till the end of his days the friendship and confidence of the young.

67/474

"Il faut remplacer la démocratie parlementaire par la démocratie sociale" ⟨Parliamentary Democracy Must Be Replaced by Social Democracy⟩, talk with Françoise Gilles.

-- *Combat*, September 8, 1967.

This is a text retranscribed just as it was from an interview of not any great interest which Sartre granted Radio Luxembourg on the occasion of the coming release of the film, *Le Mur*, and which was broadcast by this station on September 7, 1967. The following are the subjects touched on: fascism in Greece; the need for armed struggle in Latin America; the role of the Russell Tribunal; the present situation in the United States; the need for a common program for the Left; the relationship of the Russian intellectuals; his own political stands (not a one of which he is sorry for); his determination not to take a stand on the Chinese Cultural Revolution in the absence of established information; the public's disaffection for the novel; and the fundamental flaws of parliamentary democracy.

67/475

Excerpt from a letter to Régis Debray.

-- *Le Monde*, October 11, 1967.

Writing to Régis Debray, whose trial is about to begin again in Camiri, Sartre certifies that as editor of *Les Temps modernes*, he sent him in 1963 *to keep a close watch on what was happening* in Latin America.

Let us recall that in January, 1965, *Les Temps modernes* published Régis Debray's article, "Le Castrisme: La Longue Marche de l'Amérique latine" ⟨Castroism: Latin America's Long March⟩.

The November 21, 1967, *Le Monde* (p. 8) publishes this brief comment by Sartre on Régis Debray's condemnation: *Everyone was expecting that this iniquitous sentence would be the upshot of this grotesque trial. We should not give up the struggle*

67/475

for his liberation; but what must be repeated is that if in the years to come we are told that he is dead, no matter what cause his death is attributed to we shall know and say it was an assassination.

67/476

Press conference about the movie *Le Mur* ⟨The Wall⟩, at the Venice Festival on September 5, 1967.

-- *Jeune Cinéma*, no. 25 (October, 1967), pp. 24-28.

Sartre says that although he felt hesitant at first about the project to make a full-length feature from his short story, he subsequently let Serge Roullet convince him that it might be an interesting attempt. He says he is completely satisfied with the result. In answer to a question about the part he played in making the film, Sartre specifies that the dialogue may be considered his since (*with the exception of two or three changes I approved of*) it came completely from the short story, that he discussed the script with Serge Roullet, and that he consequently feels *completely committed* to Roullet's film. *He's the one who made it, but he made it with my complete approval and with the opportunity he always gave me to let him know about my criticisms or objections or to make suggestions.* The theme of the movie, which differs from that of the short story, seems to Sartre to have clearly become *time in relation to death.*

Sartre then gives some information about the circumstances in which he had written the short story, and explains what he wanted it to mean (see 37/10).

A question about the possible analogy between youth movements at the time of the Spanish Civil War and the present admirers of the Chinese Red Guards leads Sartre to say: *From a certain point of view, I find much idealism in a young man who admires the Red Guards--and I am using the word "idealism" in both its good and bad sense.*

Sartre's comments are followed by an interview with Serge Roullet which gives useful information about his adaptation of the short story (see also 67/477).

(For the movie, see Appendix.)

The dialogues and complete breakdown of the movie are published in *L'Avant-Scène Cinéma*, no. 75 (November, 1967), pp. 3-34.

There is also a record which includes the dialogues and score of the movie, and which is published by Adès, L'Avant-Scène series, 33 rpm.

67/477

"Jean-Paul Sartre parle du *Mur*." ⟨Jean-Paul Sartre Talks about *The Wall*⟩.

-- *Le Nouvel Observateur*, November 1-7, 1967.

What we have here are excerpts from the "radio-duplex" which Radio-Television Luxembourg set up on October 23, 1967, on the occasion of the simultaneous New York-Paris premiere of the movie *The Wall* and during which Sartre, at the movie theater " Le Racine" answered questions from French and American students who had attended the screening at the same time. Sartre says in particular: *The flaw in the short story* The Wall *is the general flaw in all writing: it gives you something to think about, it grips you if its author has a little talent, but it leaves you free. In other words, it saves the reader from an experience. The movie makes you go through the experience. In Roullet's film, you see people who do very little, who simply feel their death, and you feel it with them. You can't think anything about death by execution while you are watching the movie. All you should do is feel the uneasiness and even the anguish of it.*

67/478

Déclaration à la séance d'ouverture de la seconde session du tribunal Russell le 20 novembre 1967 à Roskilde (Danemark) ⟨Statement Made at the Opening of the Second Session of the Russell Tribunal on November 20, 1967, in Roskilde (Denmark)⟩.

a) In Arlette El Kaïm, ed. *Tribunal Russell 2: Le Jugement final* ⟨Russell Tribunal 2: The Final Judgment⟩. Publishing director: Jean-Paul Sartre. Idées actuelles series, no. 164. Gallimard, [1968]. Pp. 11-14. Gallimard's publicity layouts include an original short presentation by Sartre (see especially *Le Nouvel Observateur*, June 26-July 2, 1968, p. 36).

b) Italian text. In *Il Ponte*, no. 11 (November 30, 1967), pp. 1396-97.

Jean-Paul Sartre: Inaugural Statement.

-- In *Against the Crime of Silence*. Pp. 40-45. (See 67/467.)

Short statement in which Sartre lists the charges that the tribunal is going to have to consider during its second session.

67/479

"Le Génocide" ⟨Genocide⟩, interview by Serge Lafaurie.

-- *Le Nouvel Observateur*, December 6-12, 1967.

Sartre comments here on the verdict of the Russell Tribunal, which at the close of its second session judged the Americans guilty of the crime of "genocide" in Vietnam. He summarizes the arguments made at Roskilde in justification of this verdict (see 67/480).

67/480

Le Génocide ⟨Genocide⟩.

a) *Les Temps modernes*, no. 259 (December, 1967), pp. 953-71.

b) Reprinted in *Tribunal Russell 2: Le Jugement final* ⟨Russell Tribunal 2: The Final Judgment⟩. Pp. 349-68. (See 67/478.)

c) Reprinted in SITUATIONS, VIII.

On Genocide.

t1) With an introduction by Carl Oglesby, explaining how the text was written. In *Ramparts*, VI, no. 7 (February, 1968), 36-42.

t2) Translated as *Genocide. New Left Review*, no. 48 (March-April, 1968), pp. 13-25.

t3) *Ibid.* In *London Bulletin* (Bertrand Russell Peace Foundation), no. 5 (summer, 1968), pp. 79-81.

t4) Reprinted in Jean-Paul Sartre. ON GENOCIDE. With a summary of the evidence and the judgments of the International War Crimes Tribunal by Arlette El Kaïm-Sartre. Boston: Beacon Press, 1968. Pp. 55-85. In both cloth and paperback.

NOTE: A report on the second session of the International War Crimes Tribunal has been published under the title *We Accuse!* by the Bertrand Russell Peace Foundation.

t5) Reprinted in *Against the Crime of Silence*. Pp. 612-26. (See 67/467.)

At the end of the second session, which was held in Roskilde, near Copenhagen, from November 20 to December 1, 1967, the Russell Tribunal unanimously answered yes to the question, "Is the United States government guilty of the crime of genocide in respect to the Vietnamese people?" Sartre, as executive president of the tribunal, was given the responsibility of drawing up a statement of the reasons for this verdict. His text was discussed and adopted by all the members of the tribunal.

Although this text was written under the most restricted conditions (to draw it up, Sartre took time from the few hours of sleep left the members of the tribunal by its lengthy final sessions), it is nevertheless one of the most striking ones he ever wrote. Using close reasoning, Sartre explains why the war the Americans are waging in Vietnam must be considered genocide, which he defines in this way: *This present genocide, which is the end result of the unequal development of societies, is* total *war being waged to the hilt* by one side only *and* without the slightest reciprocity. He concludes: *Thus the Vietnamese are fighting for all men and the American forces against them all. And not at all figuratively or abstractly. And not simply because genocide is a crime* in Vietnam *which the rights of the world's peoples condemn. But because this genocidal blackmail, basing itself on the blackmail of atomic war, is slowly spreading to the whole human species, and because this crime being committed daily and openly is making all of those who do not denounce it the accomplices of those who are committing it, and in order better to subjugate us, begins by degrading us. In this, imperialist genocide can only radicalize itself: for the group they want to reach and terrorize,* through the Vietnamese nation, *is the whole human group.*

NOTE: On December 2, 1967, upon his return from Denmark, Sartre made a statement to the reporter Jean-Pierre Elkabach which was broadcast by *France-Inter* and in which he spoke of the session of the Russell Tribunal in Roskilde, Che Guevara's death, and Régis Debray's trial.

67/481

De Nuremberg à Stockholm ⟨From Nuremberg to Stockholm⟩.

a) Tricontinental (theoretical organ of the Organization for the Solidarity of the African, Asian, and Latin American Peoples, published in four languages in Havana, Paris, and Milan), no. 3 (November-December, 1967), pp. 7-19. Reprinted in *Tricontinental,* no. 1 (January-February, 1968), pp. 7-19.

b) Reprinted in SITUATIONS, VIII.

This article, written before the second session of the Russell Tribunal, defines and summarizes the action taken by the tribunal and supports its legitimacy. Conclusion: *We have made a judgment* for the masses--*we men of the masses, and there is no denying that we have made it* before *the masses themselves*

67/481

approved of it. But our judgment has not yet received its truth: what we have to do now is present it, with its motives and justifications, to the world's peoples. If they ratify it, it will become their own *and receive whatever objectivity it may have from them. Then we will know that we are completely legitimate, and that the masses, by giving their approval, are manifesting a more profound demand--the demand for the creation of a real tribunal to try the war criminals. A tribunal which comes from them and gives a juridical dimension to their ethical demands. A revolutionary tribunal.*

67/482

L'Universel singulier ⟨The Singular Universal⟩, piece about Carlo Levi.

-- *Galleria* (Caltanissetta, Sicily), 17th Year, nos. 3-6 (May-December, 1967), pp. 256-58.

The French text is followed by an Italian translation by Aldo Marcovecchio, *L'universale singolare*, pp. 259-60.

Sartre is an old friend of Carlo Levi, with whom he participated in numerous politico-cultural meetings. Here he pays tribute to him and at the same time defines in terms of him what he means by *the singular universal:*

*That this man who is so singular should tell you--with that voice, those intonations, those features and that air of malicious detachment which are his alone--about an ephemeral adventure he saw come to be and then die out in an instant is a singularity chosen by another singularity. Yet at the same time Rome is there, all of it, opaque and present--*lived *in its indecomposable totality.*

But "nature" and "culture" are indistinguishable, and the project of writing cannot be distinguished from the project of being a man. For Levi, being himself means making himself a singular universal; writing means communicating the incommunicable, singular universality. What this means is that in his writing he has bound himself into the selfsame knot of contradictions which his life expresses, and which Merleau-Ponty once described in these terms: "Our bodies are enmeshed in the fabric of the world but the world is made from the stuff of my body."

67/NOTE 1.

On April 10, 1967, Sartre participated in a meeting in support of Hugo Blanco which was organized at the Mutualité by the French Committee for Solidarity with the Victims of Repression in Peru (see the account of the meeting in *Solidarité Pérou*, no. 6 [May, 1967]). He subsequently signed two telegrams to the Peruvian president, F. Belaunde Terry, one concerning the disappearance of Enrique Amaya Quintana (see *Le Monde*, July 5, 1967, p. 5), the other protesting the condemnation of Hugo Blanco (see *Le Monde*, October 13, 1967, p. 3).

In another connection, a text addressed to the Venezuelan president, Raul Leoni, and signed by Sartre, Simone de Beauvoir, Alfred Kastler, Daniel Mayer and Jean Dresch expresses concern over the "disappearances" and "suicides" of a sizable number of militants of the Venezuelan Left (see *Le Monde*, July 23-24, 1967, p. 4).

67/NOTE 2.

Jacques L. Salvan, in the preface to his *The Scandalous Ghost: Sartre's Existentialism as Related to Vitalism, Humanism, Mysticism, Marxism* (Detroit: Wayne State University Press, 1967), reports the terms of a discussion that he had with Sartre in 1951 and that he published in a student magazine of the time. Sartre says in particular:
-- *I don't have anything against Bergson. I only criticize him for thinking in the language of* things. *How can his interaction of "states of consciousness" or his "deep-seated self" create freedom? What does he mean by his "duration"?*
-- *I don't have anything against mysticism except that it is seeking beyond consciousness* a unity which does not exist.
-- *I think that* form is important only in relation to demonstration.

67/NOTE 3.

A volume including Sartre's chief plays (THE FLIES, THE VICTORS, THE RESPECTFUL PROSTITUTE, THE DEVIL AND THE GOOD LORD, NEKRASSOV, and THE CONDEMNED OF ALTONA) was published in 1967 by "Isskustvo" publishers in Moscow, in a translation by S. I. Velikovskii and with a printing of 15,000 copies. It is to be noted that this time the title of THE RESPECTFUL PROSTITUTE is translated literally,and that NEKRASSOV is translated as "It's Nothing But the Truth."

67/NOTE 4.

The volume *Dramata* (Prague: Orbis, 1967) gives Antonin J. Liehm's Czech translation of THE VICTORS, DIRTY HANDS, and THE TROJAN WOMEN. It includes a preface by Sartre to DIRTY HANDS (pp. 75-77) and a postscript by

67/NOTE 4.

Milan Kundera on Sartre's plays (pp. 284-95), and reprints the comments Sartre made about THE TROJAN WOMEN in *Bref* (see 65/415).

67/NOTE 5.

A communiqué signed by Sartre, Simone de Beauvoir, Jean-Louis Barrault, Marguerite Duras, Nathalie Sarraute, etc., celebrates the fourteenth anniversary of the attack on the barracks at Moncada by Fidel Castro and his companions on July 26, 1953, and renews in this connection the signers' solidarity with the Cuban Revolution, "as threatened and as full of hope as on its first day."

1968

68/483

"L'Intellectuel face à la révolution" ⟨The Intellectual Confronts Revolution⟩, comments gathered by Jean-Claude Garot.

a) Le Point (Brussels), no. 13 (January, 1968), pp. 18-23.

b) Excerpts. "Jean-Paul Sartre, que pensez-vous de la Chine, Russie, Cuba?" ⟨Jean-Paul Sartre, What Do You Think about China, Russia, Cuba?⟩. *La Gazette de Lausanne*, January 20-21, 1968.

Intellectuals and Revolution, translated by Bruce Rice.

-- *Ramparts*, IX, no. 6 (December, 1970), 52-55.

Long interview which has the interest of giving the theoretical political positions Sartre held some time prior to the events of May in France and the Russian intervention in Czechoslovakia.

Sartre begins by giving a general definition of the intellectual as *singular universal*, whose job, in virtue of the demand for rationality and universality which make an intellectual of him, is always to take the most radical stand, and thus to back the stand of the least favored, who in principle embody the universality to be conquered. Yet radicalism runs the risk of becoming "leftism" (*that is, the demand for immediate and instantaneous realization of the universal*). The two checks on the leftist temptation are the demand for truth, which requires *constant evaluation of the field of possibilities*, and the contradiction peculiar to the intellectual, who must be both disciplined and critical in respect to the party representing the demand for universality.

68/483

Turning next to concrete political options, Sartre says that as an intellectual he cannot possibly declare himself for or against the Chinese, *and this for one reason only: everything I've read so far about the question has not given me any satisfactory universal understanding.* (He mentions in this connection an article by Pierre Verstraeten, as well as the analyses made in the *Marxist-Leninist Notebooks*, which are *admirable, but in the strict sense without foundation.*) In respect to the U.S.S.R., he says there is need for a critique which does not go so far as breaking the tie of *dialectical loyalty.* Here he refers to the positions André Gorz set forth in his *Difficult Socialism.* As far as Cuba is concerned, Sartre shows that the Castroist strategy is completely valid for Latin America but inapplicable to Europe, to whom it does, however, offer *an example of radicalization.*

The intellectual's main job in the developed countries of the West is to do the work of critical analysis. His role is not to make *statements on the level of precise programmatic objectives but to set forth their principles.* In this office, Sartre repeats that works like those of Gorz are indispensible. The primary objective in France should be to *unite the Left around a common program.*

In conclusion, Sartre says that a revolutionary situation can be created by an electoral victory for the Left, because American imperialism no longer tolerates even peaceful reforms, as is shown by the example of Greece.

68/484

Correspondence (reply to a letter from Francis Jeanson).

-- *Les Temps modernes*, no. 260 (January, 1968), pp. 1335-36.

After October, 1967, Francis Jeanson's name disappeared from the list of managing editors of *Les Temps modernes*. In a letter to Sartre, Jeanson gives his reasons for having for some time neglected his functions within the review: his activities as a cultural director in Burgundy have taken up all this time. Sartre acknowledges, in a few lines, Jeanson's resignation.

68/485

Interview on the occasion of the Havana conference on culture in January, 1968.

a) Granma (Havana), [January], 1968. Text we did not consult in the original.

b) Excerpts translated from the Spanish. In, especially, *La Voix ouvrière* (Geneva), January 12, 1968.

Sartre had accepted the Cuban government's invitation to participate in a conference on culture which was held in Havana in January, 1968. Shortly before he was to leave for Cuba, he was afflicted with a painful arterial ailment which compelled him to give up the trip.

A *Granma* writer interviewed him at length by telephone, and Sartre affirmed his complete agreement with the objectives of the cultural conference, expressed his wish that a representative of the Third World be chosen to preside over it, and added, especially, the following: *I think that at the present time, it is in Vietnam, Cuba, and Latin America that a European's own fate is at stake.* A great part of the interview concerns the war in Vietnam and the role of the Russell Tribunal (these are the passages reprinted in *La Voix ouvrière*).

Let us point out that many intellectuals gathered in Havana took Sartre's illness to be a pretext. The insistent rumor was that Sartre had not come to the cultural conference because he had reservations about the new course of the Cuban Revolution and was afraid, after the stand he had taken shortly before the Six-Day War (see 67/462), to confront the intellectuals from the Arab countries.

68/486

Message (to the Havana cultural conference).

-- *Granma* (weekly review) (Havana), January 21, 1968.

This message, addressed to the minister of culture, explains why Sartre cannot attend the cultural conference and expresses his unqualified support for it. Sartre says especially: *I would have liked to question myself before the delegates and ask myself with their help whether our culture--which was detestable and noxious when it was imposed by force--could not, now that a free cultural exchange between sovereign and equal nations is being established, be seen in its proper place, without overestimation or underestimation, as a modest yet perhaps effective means the liberated nations should make use of and surpass as they go toward their own cultural and revolutionary fulfillment.*

68/486 A

Text about Hélène de Beauvoir.

a) Catalogue for an exhibition at "Les Nouvelles Images" Gallery, The Hague, 1968.

b) Catalogue for an exhibition at the Nantenshi Gallery, Tokyo, from February 5 to 15, 1968.

This short text, which has been communicated to us by Takeshi Ebisaka, deals with the paintings and engravings of Simone de Beauvoir's sister. It ends this way: *Just as in a poem the words serve only to surround the silence, offering the reader what they do not say, in Hélène de Beauvoir's works, the colors and the forms are just the other side of an absence: that of the world she makes exist by not representing it.*

For the text *Détermination et liberté* ⟨Determinism and Freedom⟩, which appeared in *Essais* (Bordeaux), nos. 2-3 [(spring, 1968)], see 64/407 and Vol. II.

68/486 B

"Vietnam stavio Ameriku na techku istoriisku probu" ⟨Vietnam Has Put America to a Difficult Historical Test⟩, interview by Aleksandar Prlia.

-- *Politika-Ekspres*, [April] 9, 1968. Excerpts in *Politika*, same date.

During a stay in Dubrovnik in April, 1968, Sartre and Simone de Beauvoir conferred with Vladimir Dedijer about the actions the Russell Tribunal might take and, on April 8, talked to a group of students from Ljubliana. An article published in *Politika-Ekspres* for April 2 ("Sudu pune ruke tuzhbi" ⟨The Tribunal Has Cards on the Table⟩) points out that the tribunal could meet in Bokhin in Yugoslavia to tackle the following problems: apartheid in South Africa, repression in Angola and Greece, the Kurd question, and the return to the Arab countries of the territories occupied by Israel.

In the interview listed above, Sartre replies to questions about Vietnam and the assassination of Martin Luther King. He thinks that there are two Americas, and that the American government is *the world's most conservative*. In a second part, Sartre says he thinks the positions developed in WHAT IS LITERATURE? are still valid and that he is on the side of the young in their conflict with the preceding generations.

68/487

"Le Théâtre de A jusqu'à Z: Jean-Paul Sartre" ⟨Theater from A to Z: Jean-Paul Sartre⟩, interview by Paul-Louis Mignon.

-- *L'Avant-Scène Théâtre*, nos. 402-3 (special issue on Sartre) (May 1-15, 1968), pp. 33-34.

Short interview giving lots of original information: Sartre mentions a "Horatio Coclès" he wrote when he was thirteen and an "Epiméthée" he wrote later. He also goes back to BARIONA, THE FLIES, NO EXIT, and other plays.

The same issue of *L'Avant-Scène Théâtre* includes the complete text of THE RESPECTFUL PROSTITUTE and THE DEVIL AND THE GOOD LORD and provides extensive documentation: a complete analysis of the plays; chronology, bibliography, testimonies (especially one by Robert Chandeau, who was Sartre's student in 1935-36); excerpts from criticisms; photographs; reproductions of playbills; etc. The whole thing is well conceived but includes many errors in dates and details.

INTERVIEWS IN RELATION TO THE EVENTS OF MAY-JUNE, 1968

68/488

Interview by Françoise Gilles on the student rebellion, broadcast by Radio Luxembourg on Sunday, May 12, 1968.

a) The text of this interview was circulated in Paris during the days of May in the form of a tract published by the U.N.E.F. ⟨National Union of French Students⟩.

b) Short quotation in *Le Journal du Dimanche*, May 19, 1968.

c) Excerpt on record. "Les Journées de mai 1968 par les journalistes de Radio-Television-Luxembourg" ⟨The Days of May, 1968, according to the Belgian Radio-Television Newsmen⟩. Philips, B77757 L. (We thank R.T.L. for having sent us the complete recording of this interview.)

The May Movement has sometimes been described as a "Sartrian" revolution, and it has been said that it was "structuralism's death warrant" (see Epistémon, *Ces idées qui ont ébranlé la France* ⟨These Ideas Which Shook France⟩ [Fayard, 1968], p. 76). "How was it possible for a riot to produce, in the brief space of a springtime, this sudden flowering? There is no need to look to Marx and Marcuse for an answer. The effects of it were prophesied eight years ago by a philosopher whom structuralism buried a little too soon. . . . Sartre took his stand immediately and on the fundamental issues with the students. . . . He understood the situation of May, 1968, from within the movement, because he had already described this process in 1960 in CRITIQUE OF DIALECTICAL REASON." The same author said in an interview: "Sartre first described in his book the passive and anonymous forms of individual alienation--this is what he calls the 'practico-inert'--and then he showed how a group introduces negation into history and shapes itself (instead of being shaped), invents itself by breaking with this passive and anonymous society that an American sociologist called 'the lonely crowd.' The students who sparked the outbreak of the revolution of the spring of 1968 were shaped by, if not this second Sartrian philosophy, at least a dialectical philosophy of history. May of 1968 is the historical upsurge of a 'wild-flowering' force of negation. It is the inroad of a 'Sartrian' freedom, not that of the isolated individual but the creative freedom of groups" (*Le Monde*, November 30, 1968).

Although it is obviously absurd to put structuralism--which aims to be no more than a methodology of the human sciences--and an explosion of the class struggle on the same plane, it is nonetheless true that the events of May-June, 1968, gave a new relevance to Sartre's conception of history, and that the descriptions in CRITIQUE OF DIALECTICAL REASON provide the best tools for understanding these events. Yet it must be noted that none of the many French works devoted to the days of May applied, as far as we know, Sartre's method and terminology to the study of this historical crisis. It should also be noted that the students involved who were asked about the authors who had influenced them cited Karl Marx, Leon Trotsky, and Rosa Luxemburg, or Fidel Castro and Che Guevara, more frequently than Sartre (or, moreover, Herbert Marcuse . . .). Let us point out in this connection Daniel Cohn-Bendit's statement: "They wanted to chuck us Marcuse as our model. Joke. None of us read Marcuse. Some read Marx, of course, maybe Bakunin and, among contemporary authors, Althusser, Mao, Guevara, Lefebvre. Almost all the political militants of the March 22 Movement read Sartre. But there isn't any author who can be taken to be the inspiration of the movement" (*The Student Revolt: The Leaders Speak,* Seuil edition, p. 70; see 68/489).

Right after the first days of serious confrontations between the students and the police in the Latin Quarter, Sartre published (along with Simone de Beauvoir, Colette Audry, Michel Leiris, and Daniel

Guérin) a statement calling upon "all workers and intellectuals to give moral and material support to the struggle started by the students and professors" (see *Le Monde*, May 8, 1968, p. 11). On the eve of May 10, a manifesto was published which bore the signatures of (among others) Sartre, Maurice Blanchot, André Gorz, Pierre Klossowski, Jacques Lacan, Henri Lefebvre, Georges Michel, and Maurice Nadeau, and whose text reads as follows:

"The solidarity which we here affirm with the worldwide student movement--this movement which has just suddenly shaken, in some striking hours, the so-called good society so perfectly embodied in the French world--is first of all an answer to the lies by means of which all our institutions and (with few exceptions) all our political organizations, all (with almost no exceptions) our agencies of the press and communications, have tried for a month to change this movement, distort its meaning, or even make it laughable.

"It is scandalous not to recognize what is seeking expression and is at stake in this movement: the wish to escape, in every way, an order which is alien but so strongly structured and integrated that mere confrontation always risks being co-opted by it. And it is scandalous not to understand that the violence which certain forms of this movement are reproached with is their response to the enormous violence which serves to protect and preserve most of today's societies, and which is simply being revealed by the savagery of the police.

"It is this scandal that we mean to denounce without further delay, and we mean at the same time to affirm that it is of capital and perhaps decisive importance that the student movement, without making any promises and, on the contrary, refusing any premature commitments, oppose and keep on opposing the Establishment with a power of refusal which we believe is capable of opening up a future" (*Le Monde*, May 10, 1968).

Finally, on Sunday, May 12, Radio Luxembourg broadcast an interview during which Sartre, following the "night at the rue Gay-Lussac barricades," said particularly: *These young people do not want their fathers' future, that is to say our own, a future which has proved we were cowardly men worn out, exhausted, and used up by our complete obedience, completely victims of a closed system which locks in on the worker from the moment he is old enough to work. . . . Violence is the only thing that's left, no matter what the regime, to students who have not yet become a part of the system that their fathers fashioned for them and who do not want to. In other words, they do not want concessions, they do not*

68/488

want people to arrange *things, to satisfy some minor claim of theirs in order actually to wedge them in and make them go through channels. . . . The only way they can relate to that university is to* break *it, and the only way to break it is to go down into the streets. . . . In our used-up Western countries, the only power to challenge on the Left is made up of students and, soon I hope, of all the young. This power to challenge is violent because at bottom the Left is violent, and it cannot be otherwise because people are doing violence to it. . . . A trait that's common to the young is that we have made them everywhere a bankrupt society. Their real problem is to find a way to attune their fight to the working classes', for even though the motivations differ, the fight is the same. . . . At present it is up to the students, as they, however, are perfectly aware, to decide what form their struggle is to take. It isn't up to us to give them our advice, for even if we have protested all our lives, we're always just a little compromised by this society we've made.*

68/489

"L'Imagination au pouvoir: Entretien de Jean-Paul Sartre avec Daniel Cohn-Bendit" ⟨Put Imagination in Power: Jean-Paul Sartre Questions Daniel Cohn-Bendit⟩. (Text transcribed by Serge Lafaurie.)

a) Le Nouvel Observateur, special supplement, May 20, 1968.

This supplement was sold only in Paris.

b) Excerpts in *Le Monde*, May 22, 1968.

c) Reprinted in Jacques Sauvageot; Alain Geismar; Daniel Cohn-Bendit; and Jean-Pierre Duteuil, *La Révolte étudiante: Les Animateurs parlent* ⟨The Student Revolt: The Leaders Speak⟩. Seuil, [1968]. Pp. 86-97.

"Jean-Paul Sartre Talks to Danny the Red," or "Daniel Cohn-Bendit Interviewed by Jean-Paul Sartre."

t1) "Jean-Paul Sartre Talks to Danny the Red." *Atlas*, XVI, no. 1 (July, 1968), 22.

t2) "Daniel Cohn-Bendit Interviewed by Jean-Paul Sartre," translated by B. R. Brewster. In *The French Student Revolt*. New York: Hill and Wang, 1968. Pp. 73-83.

Sartre's conclusion is omitted from this volume. It reads as follows: *What is interesting about your action is that it is putting imagination in power. You have a limited imagination, just like everyone else, but you have a lot more ideas than your elders.*

We were educated in such a way that we have a precise idea of what is possible and what is not. A professor will say, "Get rid of exams? Never. You can change them, but you can't get rid of them!" Why? Because he has been taking exams for half his life.

The working class has often imagined new ways of struggling, but always in relation to the precise situation it found itself in. In 1936 it invented the occupation of the factories because that was the only weapon it had to consolidate and exploit its victory at the polls. You have a much more fertile imagination, as the slogans we are reading on the Sorbonne walls show. Something has come out of you which is confounding, shaking up, rejecting everything which made our society what it is today. It's what I would call an extension of the field of possibilities.

Sartre's constant attitude throughout those days in May was to throw the weight of his notoriety behind the students and to avoid giving advice which he thought they could very well do without. This talk with the man Jean Genet called the "genius bourgeois-bugger" is so characteristic in this respect that someone could write: "Sartre becomes, in Cohn-Bendit's presence, a modest interviewer for the 'Nouvel Observateur'" (Philippe Labro, *Ce n'est qu'un début* ⟨This Is Only the Beginning⟩, Edition Spéciale series, no. 2 [Editions et Publications Premières, 1968], p. 30). The talk helped a lot to show a section of public opinion that Cohn-Bendit, far from being the muddle-headed, ruddy-complexioned agitator portrayed by the big papers of all stripes, was a conscientious militant capable of analyzing events with coolness and lucidity.

Let us point out that there was a rumor running around Paris that the talk was made up out of the whole cloth because both Sartre and Cohn-Bendit had refused to meet. We need not say that this rumor was completely unfounded.

68/490

Statements made to the students in the main amphitheater of the occupied Sorbonne on May 20, 1968.

a) Quotations in Michel Legris's report. "M. Jean-Paul Sartre à la Sorbonne: Pour l'association du socialisme et de la liberté" ⟨M. Jean-Paul Sartre at the Sorbonne: For the Association of Socialism and Liberty⟩. *Le Monde*, May 22, 1968. Excerpts in Lucien Rioux and René Blackmann. *L'Explosion de mai* ⟨The May Explosion⟩. Laffont, 1968. Pp. 346-48.

68/490

b) The complete text of Sartre's statements was, it seems, disseminated in Paris as a tract.

c) A complete translation of this text was published in the Yugoslav newspaper *Politika* in June, 1968 (exact date not yet determined).

The announcement in the Latin Quarter that Sartre had come to show his wholehearted support for the occupation of the Sorbonne drew quite a crowd. In a lecture hall filled to overflowing where a great many students and curiosity-seekers had been unable to find a place to sit down, Sartre answered the many questions of an audience which began by being noisy but soon established its own rules for keeping order. He said especially: *Cohn-Bendit is keeping the movement on the right level of confrontation where it ought to stay. It is obvious that the strikes taking place now sprang from the student uprising. The C.G.T.* ⟨General Federation of Labor⟩ *has adopted a "me too" position. It had to follow the movement in order to reach it. It wanted more than anything else to avoid this wild-flowering democracy that you've created and that is upsetting all our institutions. Because the C.G.T. is an institution. What is being formed is a new conception of a society based on full democracy, a linking up of socialism and liberty.*

On June 15, Sartre also took part along with student militants in a debate held at the Cité Universitaire (see *Le Monde*, June 29, 1968).

68/491

"Les Bastilles de Raymond Aron" ⟨Raymond Aron's Bastilles⟩, remarks gathered by Serge Lafaurie.

a) Le Nouvel Observateur, June 19-25, 1968.

b) Reprinted in SITUATIONS, VIII.

Talking about the shift in public opinion against the students after the violent demonstrations at the beginning of June, Sartre insists on the fact that student violence is *counter-violence* in response to police provocation. *What has to be explained to people is that "uncontrolled" violence has a meaning, that it does not express a desire for disorder but the yearning for a different order.* Sartre then makes a general criticism of the traditional concept of teaching, refers to his own experience as a student and then as a professor at Laon and the Lycée Pasteur, and makes repeated personal attacks on Raymond Aron (*I'll be willing to bet that Raymond Aron never protested, and that's why in my judgment he isn't worthy of being a professor).* Let us point out this definition: *A man is nothing if he isn't a contester. But he ought to be loyal to something too. To me that's what an intellectual is: someone who's loyal to a political and social order but never stops contesting it. Of course his contestation and his loyalty will contradict each other. But that's good. It's a fruitful contradiction. When there's loyalty without contestation, that's no good. You're not a free man any more.*

68/492

"L'Idée neuve de mai 1968" ⟨What Was New about May, 1968⟩, remarks gathered by Serge Lafaurie.

a) Le Nouvel Observateur, June 26-July 2, 1968.

b) Reprinted in SITUATIONS, VIII.

Sequel to the preceding interview, made after the first round of elections. Sartre draws the moral of the failure of the May Movement. *(In a way the movement did in fact fail. But it only failed for those who thought the revolution was at hand, that the workers were going to go all the way with the students, that the action which began at Nanterre and the Sorbonne would lead to a social and economic apocalypse which would bring about not only the downfall of the regime but the overthrow of the capitalist system. That was a dream.)* He notes that he took part in a debate with students at the Cité Universitaire and says that it should be possible to transcend the conflict between those who want to impose a "critical university" and those who claim it is impossible to establish such a university in a capitalist society by means of the theory of "revolutionary reformism" André Gorz developed.

Replying to the Communists' arguments against the student movement, Sartre says: *What the young revolutionaries, bourgeois or not, are demanding is not anarchy but very precisely democracy, a true socialist democracy which so far has not been established anywhere. . . . What I condemn everyone who insulted the students for is not having seen that they were making a new demand, the demand for sovereignty.*

68/493

"Die Revolution kommt wieder nach Deutschland" ⟨The Revolution Returns to Germany⟩, interview by Gustav Stern, Georg Wolff, and Dieter Wild.

a) Der Spiegel (Hamburg), July 15, 1968, pp. 58-64.

A slight mistake in translation involved a reversal of the order of events in a passage in which Sartre recalls the Popular Front of 1936. *L'Humanité* (July 18, 1968) took advantage of it to accuse Sartre of "falsifying well-known facts" (see "Jean-Paul Sartre et le Front populaire" ⟨Jean-Paul Sartre and the Popular Front⟩, *Le Monde*, July 21-22, 1968).

b) Excerpts. "J.-P. Sartre: Le Parti communiste a trahi la révolution de mai" ⟨J.-P. Sartre: The Communist Party Has Betrayed the May Revolution⟩. *Le Monde*, July 16, 1968.

c) Complete French version. In LES COMMUNISTES ONT PEUR DE LA RÉVOLUTION ⟨Communists Are Afraid of Revolution⟩, pp. 7-32. (See 69/502.)

d) Reprinted as *Les Communistes ont peur de la révolution*. In SITUATIONS, VIII.

"Communists Are Afraid of Revolution: Two Interviews," translated by Elaine P. Halperin.

-- *Midway*, X, no. 1 (summer, 1969), pp. 41-52.

This interview, which was done after the second round of elections had resulted in a strengthening of the Gaullist majority, marks an obvious toughening of Sartre's judgment of the Communist Party's attitude during the events of May. He holds the organizations of the "political" Left responsible for the failure of the "social" Left which rose up in May: *It went as far as it could go and was finally defeated only because its "representatives" deceived it.* Sartre concentrates his attack on the P.C. ⟨Communist Party⟩: *I think that in this crisis the Communist Party adopted an attitude which was in no way revolutionary or even, in fact, reformist.* According to him the Communists resigned themselves in advance to the Left's losing the elections *because they did not want at any price to seize power.* This attitude is explained both by their fear of having to shoulder responsibility for an economic crisis in case the Gaullists fell from power, and by the Stalinist line, laid down since 1945, forbidding them to challenge, through a revolution, the division of the world set up at Yalta.

Sartre also shows that the events in France disconfirmed Herbert Marcuse's *revolutionary pessimism,* produced an *irreversible politicization of the young,* and established ties between students and workers within the action committees; and that finally the gains made by the workers *broke the equilibrium of the French economy.* Speaking of political perspectives for the future, he says: *I am convinced that all the present leaders of the Left will no longer mean anything in ten years, and I don't see what danger there would be in establishing a revolutionary movement independent of the P.C. and its Left. I even think that this is inevitable and the only thing that can "unstop" the P.C.'s politics by letting the real revolutionaries who are left make themselves heard and give the party a new direction.*

You will notice that the radical stands Sartre took during and after the events of May correspond on the whole to those of what is called the "leftist" tendency of the revolutionary movement, and that since 1956 he has never, it seems, been farther from the Communist Party than he is now.

68/494

"I Communisti hanno paura della rivoluzione?" 〈Are the Communists Afraid of Revolution?〉, discussion with Italian students.

-- *L'Espresso* (Milan), August 25, 1968.

In this discussion, which took place in July, 1968, in Bologna, Sartre explains the events of May, 1968, and interprets them from the student point of view.

68/495

"Sartre sulla Mostra di Venezia" 〈Sartre on the Venice Film Festival〉, round-table discussion with Alfredo Angeli, Roberto Faenza, Ugo Gregoretti, and Franco Solinas.

-- *Paese Sera* (Rome), August 21, 1968.

Before the opening of the 1968 Venice Film Festival, a strong movement against it developed in Italy. The newspaper *Paese Sera* and the A.N.A.C. (National Association of Italian Filmmakers) organized a round-table discussion among Sartre and four young filmmakers which was aimed at making known the view of the active minority who were against the festival and its director, Luigi Chiarini.

During the discussion, Sartre says he agrees completely with the document published by the A.N.A.C. The document demanded a total reform of the Venice Film Festival and of the structure of the film industry. So Sartre lines up with the challengers' most radical positions and comes out for the elimination of competitive world festivals in favor of meetings

68/495

which would let film professionals and critics develop a common policy in terms of the requirements of a culture open to the masses. He says especially: *In fact, I have always as a matter of principle been against all festivals and awards, whether they be literary awards or film awards like those in Venice or Cannes; for it's the consumers who are being manipulated through these awards.* Similarly, Sartre thinks the competitive festivals of the Eastern countries are a *symptom of a reformism which is no longer revolutionary.* A competition is in fact intrinsically meaningless, because it has a commercial, and thus quantitative, rather than a qualitative, that is cultural, origin. Sartre rejects the argument that the festivals help noncommercial films become known, and he cites the example of *The Wall*, which was shown in Venice and nevertheless had great difficulty getting shown in France.

As far as criticism is concerned, Sartre says particularly: *I think for example that the critics' function should be solely explanatory and informative, and that they ought not to express value judgments, for that is up to the movie-going masses.* Festival juries are only super-critics and therefore represent just the opposite of what culture could be. . . . *That's why I see no reason at all to keep holding festivals. It's the films which don't win the awards, moreover, which are usually the most interesting.* And Sartre takes Luis Buñuel's *Belle de jour*, which had won an award the year before at Venice, as an example: *a very bad film by an excellent filmmaker who had no success with the two or three very beautiful films he made* ⟨from French translation by Rybalka and Contat⟩.

After having said that he approves of the idea of the state considering movies a public service, Sartre says he does not understand the attitude of filmmakers like François Truffaut, who boycotted the Cannes Festival, but are, on the other hand, supporting the Venice one.

68/496

"Jean-Paul Sartre sui fatti di Praga" ⟨Jean-Paul Sartre's View of What Happened in Prague⟩, interview by Oretta Bongarzoni (on the Russian intervention in Czechoslovakia).

a) Paese Sera (Rome), August 25, 1968.

b) Quoted in *Le Monde*, August 27, 1968.

"Crisis and Hope," excerpts.

-- *The Nation*, September 30, 1968, p. 297.

Sartre had had high hopes for what was called "the Prague spring." In April, 1968, he had given a long interview on Czech television. He heard the news of the Russian invasion in Rome, and immediately denounced it in an interview in the Communist newspaper *Paese Sera. I am a member of the international tribunal which Bertrand Russell established. I do not know what action we'll take, but I think this is clearly a case of aggression, of what is called in international law a war crime. . . . It is because I deeply respect the history of the Soviet Union and am anything but an anti-Communist that I feel it is my duty to condemn without reservation its invasion of Czechoslovakia.*

After having approved of the stands that the Italian and French Communist parties have taken on the Czechoslovakian affair, and then recalled the contradictions between a socialist economy and a bureaucratic management in the U.S.S.R., Sartre goes on to consider the role of intellectuals and students as well as the attitude of the P.C.F. ⟨French Communist Party⟩, which betrayed the May Movement in France but denounced, on the other hand, the Russian intervention in Czechoslovakia. *I'd say we're dealing with two contradictory attitudes. In France ten million people wanted revolution, but the Communist Party turned them down. So you could say that to a certain extent the conflict between Czechoslovakians and Russians is closely analogous to the conflict between students and the P.C.F.*

Sartre says in conclusion: *Today the Soviet model is no longer valid, suffocated as it is by the bureaucracy. The model which was being developed in the new tack Czechoslovakia was taking may, on the other hand, attract many men. In this sense Prague, aside from bearing the highest witness to socialist civilization, offers hope.*

68/496 A

"J.-P. Sartre," conversation with Umberto Silva and Lello Maiello.

-- *Filmcritica* (Rome), September,1968, pp. 395-401.

Interesting interview in which Sartre talks about the use of the concept of structure in film criticism, the possibilities for a revolutionary cinema, and Jean-Luc Godard's films.

68/497

"Sur les sphères d'influence" ⟨On Spheres of Influence⟩, joint letter signed by Bertrand Russell, Laurent Schwartz, Jean-Paul Sartre, and Vladimir Dedijer.

-- *Le Monde*, October 17, 1968.

"On Spheres of Influence."

-- *The Times* (London), October 9, 1968. (First publication.

This letter, which was written after persistent rumors of Russian and Bulgarian threats to Yugoslavia and Albania, denounces the secret agreements which the signers say the American and Russian leaders have reached with the aim of preserving their respective "spheres of influence."

"The secret diplomacy of the leaders of the Soviet Union and the United States is a threat to human liberty and sovereignty everywhere. For the sake and safety of truth, it is essential that this identity of interest between American capitalism and the Soviet bureaucracy be clearly understood and fought."

This letter evoked an official response from the Bulgarian leaders and several reactions in the Soviet press (see *Literaturnaia Gazeta*, October 23 and November 16, 1968).

NOTE: At the end of October, 1968, on the other hand, Sartre signed, along with Bertrand Russell and Herbert Marcuse especially, an appeal calling for the immediate withdrawal of Russian troops from Czechoslovakia and protesting the threats menacing the Czechoslovakian intellectuals and militant workers on black lists (see especially *La Voix ouvrière* [Geneva], December 27, 1968). This appeal announces that an International Conference on Czechoslovakia will be called. Let us point out that this conference, which was organized by the Russell Foundation and not the "International War Crimes Tribunal," was held in Stockholm on February 1 and 2, 1969, and that Sartre did not take part in it.

68/498

Il n'y a pas de bon gaullisme . . . ⟨There Is No Good Gaullism⟩.

a) Le Nouvel Observateur, November 4-10, 1968.

b) Reprinted in SITUATIONS, VIII.

This text was sent by Sartre and read during a meeting held on October 11, 1968, at the Mutualité by the Committee for the Fight against Repression. In it Sartre violently denounces all the forms of repression which followed the May Movement. *The regime is in its very nature an expression of the ruling class we are fighting. . . . Bloody, armed repression, the use of that pack of thieves in uniform they call the forces of order to preserve the existing disorder, is only a particular case of the repressive action which is taken every day against the workers in the society we live in.*

68/499

"J'ai pensé à un pays où on ne pourrait vraiment rien faire d'autre" ⟨I Thought about a Country Where a Person Really Had No Options⟩, remarks gathered by Bernard Pingaud.

-- *Théâtre de la Ville/Journal*, no. 2 (November, 1968), p. 27.

Interview given on the occasion of the French production of IN THE MESH (see 48/156) by the Théâtre de la Ville in February, 1969. Jean Mercure's adaptation for the theater of this 1946 script was rather well received by the public, even though the critics had ripped it to shreds. Most of those who wrote about it said that the very idea of staging this script today was a mistake, a judgment Sartre in retrospect was not so far from sharing. The text of the adaptation was published by the Théâtre de la Ville (1968, 80 pages).

In this interview, Sartre explains the meaning his work had for him in 1946, the changes he had considered making in it as a consequence of the success of Fidel Castro's revolution, and the way in which the Russian intervention in Czechoslovakia had finally persuaded him not to change the dénouement of his plot.

He says in conclusion: *A people's theater should be above all a theater of action, rich in events and poor in words, with the meaning being given off silently, as it were, by the play as a whole, instead of being stated within it. I must add that at the present time I can't conceive of people's theater which doesn't have a political dimension.*

68/500

Interview given in Prague to an A.F.P. ⟨French Press Agency⟩ reporter.

-- Quoted in *Le Monde*, December 3, 1968.

68/500

Sartre went to Prague from November 28 to December 1, 1968, upon the invitation of the Czechoslovakian Writers' Union to attend the premiere of THE FLIES. Another theater in Prague was staging DIRTY HANDS for the first time in Czechoslovakia, but Sartre did not attend this performance.

During this interview, Sartre said in particular: *I have seen great courage here, a justified and reasoned hope which shows itself in temperate, perceptive attitudes. Those who think the Czechoslovaks are downhearted may be making a mistake. . . . In spite of being blocked in August, the way that opened up in January (after being in the making several years) is strictly Marxist and differs from other movements of liberalism or of bourgeois individualism. It offers one model for a more developed form of socialism, which shows its essentially democratic nature.*

NOTE: The day he arrived in Prague, Sartre made a statement which was printed in a morning paper, and during his stay there he gave an interview to Karel Bartosek, who writes for *Politika*, and also spoke on Czechoslovak television. See further 69/506.

68/501

Short statement made to a newspaper in Prague.

-- *Svobodne Slovo*, [November 29, or 30, 1968].

According to the December 1-2, 1968, *Le Monde*, Sartre said in particular: *I don't know a single progressive Frenchman who didn't condemn the arrival of foreign troops in Czechoslovakia. More and more people are realizing that, in spite of all your trials, you have shown that a different way to socialism is possible.*

68/501 A

"Se Sartrem o dnesku" ⟨With Sartre Concerning Today's Problems⟩, interview by Karel Bartosek and Petr Pujman.

-- *Listy* (Prague), December 12, 1968.

Theoretical interview on the role of intellectuals, socialism, and Stalinism; and on the role Czechoslovakia can play in Europe.

68/501 B

"Sartre v Praze" ⟨Sartre in Prague⟩, interview.

-- *Mlady Svet* (Prague), December 13, 1968.

Unconsulted text.

68/NOTE 1.

Sartre signed a personal appeal for the Greek People's Defense Committee, dated January 12, 1968. This appeal was published, along with others, in the program for the world premiere of Nico Papatakis' film "The Herdsmen of Disorder" on February 20, 1968, at the Bobino.

In 1969, Sartre signed another text protesting the prison sentences inflicted on two Italian militants who on November 8, 1968, had hijacked a Boeing from the Greek company, Olympic Airways (see *Le Monde*, March 23-24, 1969).

68/NOTE 2.

The March 20, 1968, *Literaturnaia Gazeta* published an appeal from intellectuals against the American escalation of the war in Vietnam, an appeal signed by, among others, Sartre, Simone de Beauvoir, Louis Aragon, François Mauriac, and Pablo Picasso.

68/NOTE 3.

During a meeting in favor of "Black Power" organized on April 30, 1968, at the Mutualité with James Forman, Aimé Césaire, and Daniel Guérin, Sartre said particularly: *The same aggressor is oppressing thirty million Vietnamese and twenty million blacks in the United States. . . . The Americans have only let a fraction of the "Third World" into their country. I wonder if that other Vietnam that Che Guevara called for is not about to happen in the United States* (see *Le Monde*, May 2, 1968).

68/NOTE 4.

From February 19 to March 1, 1968, the French Department of Security tried eighteen Guadeloupans on the charge of having threatened French territorial integrity by their nationalist activities. Sartre, Aimé Césaire, Michel Leiris, Daniel Guérin, etc., were called as defense witnesses. In the deposition he made on February 27, 1968, Sartre called for a dialogue with the Guadeloupans and stressed the fact that their problems ought to be considered in the broader perspective of Third World problems.

68/NOTE 4.

The complete report of the debates may be found in *The Trial of the Guadeloupans* (Co.GA.SO.D. ⟨The Guadeloupan Committee for Aid and Support of the Guadeloupan Prisoners⟩, 1969), in which Sartre's deposition takes up pp. 351 to 356. See also the February 28, 1968, *Le Monde*.

Sartre had already taken a stand in 1963 in favor of eighteen young Martiniquans accused of plotting against national security. In a letter addressed to Daniel Mayer, he said especially: *The contradictions and the alleged overpopulation of the French West Indies are problems which can only be solved within the framework of West Indian nationalism.*

68/NOTE 5.

The record *Sartre*, published by "L'Encyclopédie sonore," Phares series (33 rpm/30 cm, no. 320 E 869), includes the following ⟨in French⟩:

1. NAUSEA, selection (read by Georges Wilson);

2. THE FLIES, act 2, scene 8 (Nathalie Nerval and Sami Frey);

3. NO EXIT, scene 5 (Michel Vitold, Nathalie Nerval, Simone Vannier);

4. EXISTENTIALISM IS A HUMANISM, selection (Georges Wilson);

5. DIRTY HANDS, tableau 5 (Michel Duchaussoy and Michel Vitold);

6. THE DEVIL AND THE GOOD LORD, act 3, tableau 8, scene 2 (Georges Wilson);

7. THE CONDEMNED OF ALTONA, act 5, scene 1 (Fernand Ledoux and Michel Duchaussoy);

8. THE WORDS, final pages (Georges Wilson).

68/NOTE 6.

A certain number of excerpts from Sartre's philosophical works are given in *Sartre*, texts chosen by Marc Beigbeder and Gérard Deledalle, Sélection-philosophique Bordas series (Bordas [1968]).

Marc Beigbeder's introduction and the bibliography contain several mistakes, which are disturbing in a textbook.

1969

69/502

LES COMMUNISTES ONT PEUR DE LA RÉVOLUTION ⟨Communists Are Afraid of Revolution⟩.

-- Controverses series, no. 5. John Didier, [1969]. 63 pages. Printing date: January 8, 1969.

"Communists Are Afraid of Revolution: Two Interviews," translated by Elaine P. Halperin.

-- *Midway*, X, no. 1 (summer, 1969), 41-61.

This little volume, of which the French edition is subtitled JEAN-PAUL SARTRE'S "J'ACCUSE" ⟨Jean-Paul Sartre's "I Accuse"⟩, consists of the French text of the July, 1968, *Der Spiegel* interview (see 68/493) plus that of the interview published in 1966 in *Biblio* and *Livres de France* (see 66/436). The latter, which is one of the poorest anyone ever got from Sartre, was reprinted without his authorization by an unscrupulous publisher who would have been wiser to replace it with, for example, the August, 1968, *Paese Sera* interview. Although Sartre was very unhappy about the proceedings, he was polite enough not to protest. The brochure also reprints, without updating it, the bibliography that was published in *Livres de France* in 1966.

69/503

"Le Mur" au lycée ⟨*The Wall* in high school⟩.

a) Le Monde, January 18, 1969. Article published in the "Libres opinions" ⟨Free Opinions⟩ section.

b) Reprinted in SITUATIONS, VIII.

69/503

Sartre protests against the transfer of an instructor at the Lycée de Vernon, who was guilty, according to the administration and certain parents, of having suggested to sixteen- to eighteen-year-old students that they write a paper on THE WALL and of having had them write weekly themes based on *Le Monde*.

Sartre thinks this transfer is politically motivated, sees it as an intimidating tactic (*A little terrorism never hurts does it?*), and in closing turns to Edgar Faure to ask him if he intends to go back to *an authoritarian regime which threatens to be worse than all those which preceded it.*

69/503 A

"Sartre: Israël, la Gauche et les Arabes" ⟨Sartre: Israel, the Left, and the Arabs⟩, interview by Arturo Schwarz.

a) Italian translation. In *Quaderni del Medio Oriente* (Milan), 1st Year, nos. 3-4 (January, 1969), pp. 2-11.

b) French version, with some cuts. In *L'Arche*, no. 152 (October 26-November 25, 1969), pp. 32-40, 73, 75.

c) Reprinted in SITUATIONS, VIII.

"Sartre Looks at the Middle East Again."

-- *Midstream*, XV, no. 7 (August-September, 1969), 37-38.

The most complete interview Sartre has given recently on Near Eastern problems.

In the Israeli-Arab conflict, neither side has the whole truth. . . . Today we're loaded to the bursting-point with passion, and I don't see any short-term possibility of defusing these bombs of passion.

69/504

"Un Juif d'Israël a le droit de rester dans sa patrie. En vertu du même principe, un Palestinien a le droit d'y rentrer" ⟨An Israeli-Jew Has the Right to Remain in His Homeland. By the Same Token, a Palestinian Has the Right to Return to His⟩, interview by Claudine Chonez.

a) Le Fait Public, no. 3 (February, 1969), pp. 12-17.

b) Excerpts in *Le Monde*, February 1, 1969.

c) Reprinted as *Interview*. In SITUATIONS, VIII.

Since the Six-Day War in June, 1967, Sartre had refrained from any public expression of his views of the Israeli-Arab problem. In this interview, given to support a magazine founded by the journalists dismissed by the O.R.T.F. ⟨French Radio-Television⟩, he advocates a peace negotiated directly between the Arabs and Israelis on the following bases: return of territory occupied by Israel, recognition of Israeli sovereignty, and settlement of the Palestinian refugee problem. As the title of the interview suggests, Sartre insists above all on the last point: *The expelled Arabs are living in an untenable situation: they have children who were born in very bad conditions, and grandchildren who are obsessed, and rightly so, by the idea of returning to Palestine.* Sartre thinks that Israel has the right to sovereignty but ought to consider the Palestinian problem and not leave the fate of the occupied regions in doubt. Although this stand does not involve a shift in Sartre's position, it does mark a certain rapprochement to the position of the Arab moderates.

Sartre criticizes the French government's embargo policy in passing ([It]*'s really an indefensible caprice which has nothing to do with anything*) and goes on to say: *This decision of General de Gaulle's will be of no consequence, none whatsoever. Let's face it, nothing that General de Gaulle has done in the past several years has ever been of any consequence. Or if it has the consequences have been pernicious. Generally speaking, people ought not to play the great power when they aren't a great power.*

69/505

"La Jeunesse piégée" ⟨Trapped Young People⟩, comments gathered by Serge Lafaurie.

a) Le Nouvel Observateur, March 17-23, 1969.

b) Reprinted in SITUATIONS, VIII.

These comments, in which Sartre justifies his opposition to Edgar Faure's "guidelines" and tries to explain what the cultural revolution means in France, had broad repercussions. In particular, they evoked a reply from Edgar Faure in *Le Nouvel Observateur* for March 31-April 6, 1969, as well as many letters in subsequent issues.

Sartre thinks that *the only justifiable reform--which would in fact be a revolution--would consist in inventing a university whose aim would no longer be to choose an elite but to bring culture to everyone, even those who will not be "cadres."* He gives the following answer to the question, "If you were a philosophy professor today, what would you do?":

69/505

I'd ask my students what they wanted us to talk about, and even whether they wanted me to come or not. If they didn't want a course I wouldn't give them one. But I'd back them up to the hilt in their struggle. I'd try above all to do what, in the present state of isolation they've been thrust into, they often do not have the heart to do. I'd try to explain to people outside the university that they are not petty-bourgeois nihilists but simply trapped young people who refuse to accept an education that's designed to make them slaves. I'd also explain the underlying meaning of the Faure maneuver: to replace the dictatorship of those petty little kings of knowledge, the professors clinging to outmoded power, by an apparent link between the different disciplines and by a collective effort, illusions which are carefully preserved in order to hide the "modernization" of the university which is being carried out in the interest of capitalist monopolies, whose requirements, if they are presented anonymously at the regional or national level, will no longer seem to be private interests, but the dictatorship of rationality.

69/506

"Aujourd'hui plus que jamais--l'engagement" 〈Today More Than Ever--Commitment〉, interview-article on Sartre and Simone de Beauvoir, by Dagmar Steinova.

-- *La Vie tchécoslovaque*, March, 1969, pp. 14-15.

Interview given during a short trip Sartre and Simone de Beauvoir made to Prague at the end of November, 1968. After having stressed the clearly Marxist nature of the positions taken by Czechoslovakian intellectuals and the necessity of a Marxist analysis of the situation in Czechoslovakia, Sartre gives the following definition of commitment:

Commitment for an intellectual means saying what he feels and saying it from the only possible human point of view, which means he must demand, for himself and for everyone, concrete human freedom. Concrete freedom is not just the freedom that the bourgeois give us, but it's not just the suppression of it either. Concrete freedom means that freedom has been given a concrete content, has been turned into a freedom which is both material and formal. So today more than ever it is impossible to avoid commitment. The only thing a writer and a novelist can do as writer and novelist is to show, from this point of view, the struggle for human liberation, the situation human beings live in, the risks they run, and the possibilities for change.

Sartre then tackles the question of the alliance of the intellectuals and the working class, and remarks that this alliance, *which just missed coming about, but didn't during the month of May in France,* is coming about in Czechoslovakia, and that it leaves great hope for the advent of *true socialism* in this country.

69/507

L'Homme au magnétophone ⟨The Man on Tape⟩, text on psychoanalysis.

a) Les Temps modernes, no. 274 (April, 1969), pp. 1813-19. This text is followed by two "replies," one by Jean-Baptiste Pontalis, and one by Bernard Pingaud, as well as by the testimony of A. on which the text is a commentary.

b) All these texts reprinted in SITUATIONS, VIII.

A Psychoanalytic Dialogue, with a Commentary by Jean-Paul Sartre, abridged version of A.'s testimony and of Sartre's text, translated by Paul Augst.

-- *Ramparts*, VIII, no. 4 (October, 1969), 43-49.

Since there was a deep division among the *Temps modernes* staff concerning the advisability of publishing the transcription of a "psychoanalytic dialogue" that a certain A. had offered them, it was decided that Sartre would set forth his reasons for being fascinated by the testimony, and Pontalis and Pingaud would say why they were against it. In spite of the relative brevity of the texts, two important questions are asked. On the one hand, is it possible in psychoanalysis, as Sartre and certain practitioners such as Ronald D. Laing and David G. Cooper would have it, to substitute a therapy based on reciprocity for a therapy based on "violence"? On the other hand, will it not be necessary, as Pontalis would like, to better define Sartre's long-standing but ambiguous relationship to psychoanalysis? Sartre himself says that he is not *a "fair-weather friend" of psychoanalysis but a critical fellow-traveler.* In demanding here that the idea of the subject be reintroduced, he remains faithful to his own ideas and only speaks in a direction which has been evident in his thinking ever since the thirties.

It was following this affair that Pontalis and Pingaud resigned from the editorial committee of *Les Temps modernes*.

69/508

Défendez-vous ⟨Defend Yourselves⟩, text of a short speech.

69/508

-- *Complexe* (Anvers), no. 4 [July, 1969], pp. 69-71.

On December 28, 1968, Sartre stood surrounded by the cast of THE DEVIL AND THE GOOD LORD on the stage of the Palais de Chaillot and spoke to the T.N.P. ⟨Théâtre National Populaire⟩ audience in protest against the banning of Armand Gatti's play, *Passion en violet, jaune et rouge* ⟨Passion in Violet, Yellow and Red⟩. It is this short speech which is reprinted here in its entirety. Sartre tackles the general problem of censorship in the theater and says in particular, concerning the steps taken against Gatti's play:

We're talking about an authoritarian act without any legal justification whatsoever. It's what we quite precisely call le fait du prince. *The law is deliberately violated, and the ban is based* on force alone. *If we do not protest against this absurd step, the state can do anything it wants and will end, like the Vichy government, by banning* Tartuffe. *But above all, this act of force threatens to stupidly destroy the marvelous theater which belongs to no one but you.*

69/509

Introduction (to a set of documents on Greece).

-- *Les Temps moderne*, no. 276a ([August], 1969), pp. 5-6.

Briefly introducing an important set of documents entitled "Aujourd'hui la Grèce . . . ," ⟨Today Greece . . .⟩ Sartre writes in particular: *The same threat weighs on all the peoples of the world together; he who rises up against it anywhere is fighting for us all.*

69/510

"La Luna: Una vittoria o una trappola?" ⟨The Moon: Triumph or Trap⟩, interview by Augusto Marcelli.

-- *Paese Sera* (Rome), August 30, 1969.

Asked what he thinks about the American moon landing, Sartre says in particular:

I'm indignant when I see they keep on writing that the moon landing is the most important moment in history. It's crazy. It's nothing more than a perfect technological achievement. . . .

What I mean especially is that we cannot be proud of conquering the moon unless we are at the same time ashamed of the crimes being committed around us. In Vietnam and elsewhere. It is all inseparably tied together. It would be too easy to say, as unfortunately people are saying, "Man is marvelous because he can go to the moon," without identifying ourselves with the man who is destroying Vietnam. . . .

I'm not at all opposed to this exploit, but I am opposed to the propagandistic uses to which the mass media are still putting it by presenting the fact as a step forward, a turning point, in history. All that is false. It's a matter of a magnificent feat, exactly like Lindbergh's, which is undeniably contributing to the development of the aerospace industry ⟨from French translation by Rybalka and Contat⟩.

Sartre ends by saying that he feels completely in support of youth's attempts to make a fundamental change in human relations, and that he thinks that these attempts, in spite of their setbacks, are more important than the conquest of the moon. He further says that the needed unity of intellectuals and workers would be facilitated if the students simplified their language.

69/511

"Masses, spontanéité, parti" ⟨The Masses, Spontaneity, and the Party⟩, conversation with the staff of *Il Manifesto*.

a) First printed in Italian. "Classe e partito." *Il Manifesto* (Bari), no. 4 (September, 1969), pp. 46-54.

b) French version. In *Les Temps modernes*, no. 282 (January, 1970), pp. 1043-63.

c) Text *(b)* reprinted in *"Il Manifesto": Analyses et thèses de la nouvelle extrême-gauche italienne* ⟨*Il Manifesto:* Analyses and Theses of the Italian New Far Left⟩. With an introduction by Rossana Rossanda. Seuil, [1971]. Pp. 298-317.

d) Text *(b)* reprinted in SITUATIONS, VIII.

The Risk of Spontaneity and the Logic of the Institution.

t1) Telos, [Buffalo], no. 4 (fall, 1969), pp. 191-205.

t2) As *Masses, Spontaneity, Party* in Ralph Miliband and John Saville, eds. *The Socialist Register 1970.* London: Merlin Press, 1970. Pp. 233-49.

This substantial discussion bearing on the theory of the relationship of class and party took place on

69/511

August 27, 1969, in Rome, under the initiative of *Il Manifesto*, a journal of the Left opposition within the Italian Communist Party. It is preceded by a long introductory note by Rossana Rossanda which examines the theory of the party in the main Marxist writings.

Answering a question about *The Communists and Peace*, Sartre once again admits the theoretical shortcomings of this work but tries to situate it historically:

> *In 1952, when I wrote* The Communists and Peace, *the essential political choice was to defend the French Communist Party and above all the U.S.S.R., which had been accused of war imperialism. It was essential to deny these accusations if one didn't want to find oneself on the side of the Americans. Later, it became evident that the Soviet Union, in acting at Budapest in a way that Stalin (whether as a result of political intelligence or for other reasons) had not acted toward Yugoslavia in 1948, and in subsequently relapsing into crime with its intervention in Czechoslovakia, was acting like any imperialist power. I don't mean to make a moral judgment in saying this. I'm simply saying that the external politics of the Soviet Union seem to be primarily and essentially inspired by its rivalry with the United States and not by the principle of respect for equality in its relations with the other socialist states. My 1956 position developed from this observation. Obviously, it is impossible at this stage not to see the contradiction with my 1952 position; and I tried to explain it in my* CRITIQUE OF DIALECTICAL REASON. *Naturally, the solution I gave there was only a formal one which should have been followed by a historical analysis of the U.S.S.R. in the Stalinist era--an analysis which is already blocked out as part of a second volume of the* CRITIQUE, *which will probably never be published.*

69/512

"Itinerary of a Thought," interview by P. A., R. F., Q. H. [Perry Anderson, Ronald Fraser, Quintin Hoare].

a) Complete version in English. In *New Left Review*, no. 58 (November-December, 1969), pp. 43-66.

b) Reprinted in Robert C. Solomon, ed. *Phenomenology and Existentialism*. New York: Harper and Row, 1972.

c) Reprinted as "An Interview with Sartre" and without a long passage concerning the CRITIQUE OF DIALECTICAL REASON. In *New York Review of Books*, March 26, 1970.

d) A French version retranslated from English as "Sartre par Sartre" ⟨Sartre by Sartre⟩ and omitting many important passages, especially concerning Bertolt Brecht and the CRITIQUE OF DIALECTICAL REASON. In *Le Nouvel Observateur*, January 26-February 1, 1970.

e) Text *(d)* reprinted in SITUATIONS, IX.

An interview which, because of its richness and scope, is one of the most important Sartre ever gave. Made when he was completing the first two volumes of his "Flaubert," and thus benefiting from an influx of new ideas, it situates his past works and points out with great clarity and originality what his future work will be like.

69/513

"MM. A. Malraux, F. Mauriac et J.-P. Sartre demandent au général Ovando la libération de Régis Debray" ⟨MM. A. Malraux, F. Mauriac, and J.-P. Sartre Ask General Ovando to Free Régis Debray⟩.

-- *Le Monde*, November 11, 1969.

It was Sartre who took the initiative for this letter dated November 3 which, independently of any propaganda or ideology, had as its only aim helping Régis Debray.

69/514

Televised interview on the Song-My ⟨My Lai⟩ massacre.

a) Excerpts in *Le Monde*, December 13, 1969.

b) Long excerpts. "On tue les Vietnamiens parce qu'ils sont vietnamiens" ⟨They're Killing Vietnamese because They Are Vietnamese⟩. *La Voix ouvrière* (Geneva), December 13, 1969.

c) Complete text in Italian. In *Paese Sera* (Rome), December 14, 1969.

This interview, which was the first Sartre had granted French television since the fifties, was broadcast on December 11, 1969, as part of the news show "Panorama." In it, Sartre answers questions by Olivier Todd for fifteen minutes. He denies that there is any parallel between the American massacres and the alleged massacres committed by the N.L.F. ⟨National Liberation Front⟩ and says that even though this is probably the biggest massacre which has taken place in Vietnam since the beginning of the war, it just goes to show

69/514

that the war is a war against the Vietnamese people.

69/NOTE 1.

Together with Laurent Schwartz, Pierre Vidal-Naquet, and Henri Bartoli, Sartre called for a protest on January, 1969, in Paris, in support of the Czechoslovakian people on the occasion of the death and funeral of Jan Palach (see *Le Monde*, January 29, 1969). On the same occasion Sartre also gave Jacques Séguy a short interview which was broadcast by Radio Luxembourg on January 28, 1969, and in which he said he had observed a *real and solid alliance between students and workers* in Czechoslovakia. Speaking of Jan Palach's suicide, he said that in his judgment as in the Marxists', a spectacular suicide can play the role of *an emotional factor and detonator of the unity of the masses.* And he said finally that the Left ought--for the same reasons which led it to struggle against the war in Indochina, the Algerian War, and American aggression in Vietnam--to protest against the occupation of Czechoslovakia and demand that the Russian troops be withdrawn.

On the other hand, Sartre is one of the 109 French intellectuals and artists who, at the initiative of the Writers' Union, signed an appeal denouncing the repression in Czechoslovakia (see *Le Monde*, November 21, 1969).

69/NOTE 2.

On February 10, 1969, Sartre, along with Michel Foucault in particular, took part in a meeting held at the Mutualité under the aegis of the S.N.E.-Sup ⟨National Union of University Professors⟩ and the U.N.E.F. ⟨National Union of French Students⟩ to protest the expulsion of thirty-four students from the University of Paris. In his remarks, Sartre addressed himself to the students and took a stand against the guidelines for university reform: *The aim of these guidelines is evident. It is to put you in a treacherous position. If you vote, you recognize their legitimacy. If you don't, you isolate yourself from the majority of the students. What they're asking you to do is to recognize the legitimacy of the old established disorder* (*Le Monde*, February 12, 1969).

69/NOTE 3.

In the name of the "Organizing Committee for a Strike against the Vote on April 27," Sartre held a press conference in Paris on March 17, 1969, to ask the French people to refuse the "participation" in government proposed by General Charles de Gaulle. He said especially: *Voting can only contribute to recognizing the regime. What the referendum is hiding is the death of parliamentary government. Today democracy is no more than a myth, for all the decisions are made outside the elected assemblies. . . . It is impossible to conceive of any form of mass struggle which does not use violence* (*Le Monde*, March 19, 1969).

69/NOTE 4.

Les Temps modernes (no. 273 [March, 1969], pp. 1727-28) published an appeal entitled "Pour ouvrir des perspectives révolutionnaires et anti-impérialistes en Grèce" ⟨To Open Revolutionary and Anti-Imperialist Perspectives in Greece⟩ and signed by Jean-Marie Domenach, William Klein, Jean-Paul Sartre, and Laurent Schwartz. See also *Le Monde*, April 8, 1969, p. 5.

69/NOTE 5.

Under the debatable title of "Un Texte de Jean-Paul Sartre" ⟨A Text by Jean-Paul Sartre⟩, the May 10, 1969, *Le Monde* published the following appeal signed by Colette Audry, Simone de Beauvoir, Marguerite Duras, Michel Leiris, Maurice Nadeau, Jean-Paul Sartre, etc.:

" . . . Alain Krivine's candidacy is the occasion for the new forces revealed in May and June of 1968 to make themselves heard by using the means provided by bourgeois legality. The great majority are still unaware of the fate and significance of the May Movement. That is why, independently of any future agreement with the Communist League program and theses presented by Alain Krivine, the undersigned decided to support him."

Sartre, however, did not actively support Alain Krivine and would have preferred to have him withdraw his candidacy prior to the elections.

69/NOTE 6.

In March, 1969, Sartre, Louis Aragon, Simone de Beauvoir, Elsa Triolet, and others signed a text protesting antisemitism in Poland: "Under the pretext of anti-Zionism, an antisemitism has been developing for some months now in Poland with the support of at least a segment of the ruling circles" (*Le Monde*, March 29, 1969).

69/NOTE 7.

On June 12, 1969, Sartre and twelve other left-wing intellectuals formed a group intended to aid American

69/NOTE 7.

deserters and draft dodgers (see *The New York Times*, June 13, 1969).

69/NOTE 8.

Sarajevo television broadcast on October 3, 1969, an interview with Sartre by Eleonora Prohoc on the theme "Marxism Today" (recorded in July in Dubrovnik; fifty minutes duration).

69/NOTE 9.

In November, Sartre lent his name to a statement in which the National Writers' Committee protested Alexander Solzhenitsyn's expulsion from the Soviet Writers' Union ("a monumental error which is not merely damaging to the Soviet Union but helps propagate the view of socialism its enemies propagate" [see *Le Monde*, November 19, 1969]).

Some time later, Sartre was one of the sixteen signers of a letter drawn up for the same purpose by Arthur Miller (see "Sixteen Western Intellectuals Score Soviet Attacks on Solzhenitsyn," *New York Times*, December 5, 1969).

69/NOTE 10.

On December 18, 1969, Sartre sent to General Juan Velasco, president of the Republic of Peru, a telegram supporting Peruvian political prisoners (see *Le Monde*, December 28-29, 1969).

69/NOTE 11.

On December 19, 1969, Sartre presided over a press conference at the Palais d'Orsay in which a young twenty-one-year-old Vietnamese woman told about the Ba Lang An Massacre in which approximately three hundred civilians perished (see *Le Monde*, December 21-22, 1969).

1970

70/515

Le Socialisme qui venait du froid ⟨The Socialism That Came in from the Cold⟩, preface.

a) In Antonin J. Liehm. *Trois générations: Entretiens sur le phénomène culturel tchécoslovaque* ⟨Three Generations: Discussions of the Czechoslovak Cultural Phenomenon⟩, translated from the Czech by Marcel Aymonin. Témoins series. Gallimard, [1970]. Pp. I-XXXI.

b) Reprinted in SITUATIONS, IX.

The Socialism That Came in from the Cold, translated by Helen R. Lane.

t1) Evergreen Review, XIV, no. 84 (November, 1970), 27-32, 65-73.

t2) In Antonin J. Liehm. *The Politics of Culture*, translated by Peter Kussi. New York: Grove Press, 1972.

Sartre's text (pp. 1-37) is followed by an answer by Josef Skvorecky (pp. 177-180), which was first published in *Evergreen Review*, no. 87 (February, 1971).

> Without a doubt one of the most important texts Sartre has written during the past ten years, this text marks an apparently irrevocable break with the U.S.S.R. In it one finds, in a style of striking clarity and strength, a description of bureaucracy and the vices inherent in an imported socialism. In Sartre's view, what the European Left has to do now is answer *the basic question of this era: how can we get together and get rid of the old rigid structures, and how can we produce new ones which will enable the coming revolution to avoid giving birth to* that kind of socialism?

70/516

Je-Tu-Il ⟨I-Thou-He⟩, preface to *L'Inachevé* ⟨The Uncompleted⟩, a novel by André Puig.

a) Excerpt. "Les Déguisements de l'indicible" ⟨The Disguises of the Inexpressible⟩. *Le Nouvel Observateur*, April 20-26, 1970.

b) André Puig. *L'Inachevé*. Gallimard, [1970]. Pp. I-XXXI. Dedicated to Arlette El Kaïm.

c) Reprinted in SITUATIONS, IX.

The theoretical nature of this interesting but difficult preface may have succeeded in putting off some potential readers of this excellent novel by André Puig, who has been Sartre's secretary since 1963. That is why it would undoubtedly have gone better as an afterword. After having defined the novel as *a prose form which aims to develop a singular and fictional temporal unfolding into a unified whole*, Sartre characterizes Puig as one of those *critical novelists* who are showing the *decomposition of realism* and bringing about a *Copernican revolution: up until the time that they began to write, the imaginary* represented *reality; they are trying, on the other hand, to summon up reality within the imaginary, it is no longer the image which aims at reality but reality which reveals itself indirectly by exposing the unreality of the image.*

70/NOTE 1.

On January 10, 1970, Sartre, together with Michel Rocard and Kateb Yacine, in particular, were present at the removal from the Medical-Legal Institute of the bodies of five African workers asphyxiated during the night of January 1 to 2 in their barracks at Aubervilliers. He made a short speech about this to reporters from many television networks.

Sartre did not take part in the other demonstrations (such as the occupation of the main office of the French National Association of Managers) which characterized the victims' funeral rites, but he testified on February 23, 1970, at the trial of Roland Castro, who had been charged at that time with assault and resisting arrest (see the report of the hearing by Jean-Pierre Quélin in *Le Monde*, February 25, 1970).

70/NOTE 2.

At the time Biafra fell, several well-known leftists--including Simone de Beauvoir, Claude Lanzmann, Jean Pouillon, Laurent Schwartz, and Sartre--brought out a piece which establishes responsibilities and says "that after the assassination of Biafran hopes, political gangsterism has spread to the four corners of the earth." The following passage is also worth quoting: "There are no justifications for such shameful behavior except tired old question-begging ones which don't even camouflage the part these unfeeling monsters are playing in this nameless horror in whose name men have already turned Jews into soap and Sudanese blacks into game, slowly killed the Indians of South America, and struck down the Kurds in Iraq or the Indonesian Communists; this horror in whose name men are eliminating the people of Vietnam and their flora and fauna, in whose name the Soviet Union has deported millions of its citizens and sent tanks into Czechoslovakia. The events in Biafra sum all these up and mark the beginning of a decidedly new period in which no matter what established country will be able, in the face of no matter what other country or of all of them put together, to boast that it can do no matter what in the name of no matter which principle. Let the professional killers and ideologists rejoice: their reign has spread to the four corners of the earth." (See *Le Monde*, January 13, 1970, and the excerpts entitled "Sartre on Biafra," *New York Review of Books*, March 26, 1970.)

70/517

Le Peuple brésilien sous le feu croisé des bourgeois ⟨The Brazilian People in the Bourgeois Crossfire⟩, short speech.

a) Complete text in *Témoignage chrétien*, January 29, 1970.

b) Reprinted in SITUATIONS, VIII.

Brazil in Torment, anonymous translation.

-- *The Spokesman* (Nottingham), no. 2 (April, 1970), pp. 9-11.

Short speech given during a meeting to show solidarity with the Brazilian people held at the Mutualité by several Catholic and Protestant publications. In it Sartre gives a historical review of the situation which led to the 1964 coup and stresses the responsibility of the nationalist bourgeoisie in the establishment of the dictatorship.

70/518

Intervention à la conférence de presse du Comité, le 27 janvier 1970 ⟨Words Spoken at the Committee's Press Conference on January 27, 1970⟩.

a) Rouge (Communist League weekly), no. 50 (February, 1970).

b) Reprinted, unfortunately with the same title, in SITUATIONS, VIII.

Text of words spoken at a press conference held on January 27, 1970, by the "Committee for the Liberation of Soldiers in Prison," in which Alain Krivine also participated for the Communist League and Michel Rocard for the P.S.U. ⟨Unified Socialist Party⟩.

Shortly beforehand, this committee had published an appeal (signed especially by Sartre, Rocard, Krivine, Jean Rostand, Aimé Césaire, Simone de Beauvoir, and Marguerite Duras) in which it called for the immediate freeing of four soldiers who had distributed leftist handouts and had been accused of inciting soldiers to disobey and of hurting the morale of the troops (see *Le Monde*, January 28, 1970).

Three of these soldiers were brought before the military tribunal at Rennes and condemned on February 6, 1970, to prison terms. Sartre, who was sick, was unable to testify at the trial but sent a letter in which, on the basis of the premise that the three accused were, above all, French citizens, he protested the very existence and functions of a military tribunal (see report of the hearing by Jean-Pierre Quélin, *Le Monde*, February 8-9, 1970).

70/NOTE 3.

Sartre and the *Temps modernes* staff sent a telegram expressing their solidarity with Piergiorgio Bellocchio, editor of the revolutionary paper *Lotta continua*, who had been hailed before the court of assizes in Milan on fourteen different charges stemming from only four articles (see *Le Monde*, February 28, 1970).

It is interesting to note here that although Bellocchio was legally responsible for the articles in *Lotta continua*, he was not actually responsible but had only lent his name, as Sartre was to do later, to a group of student editors.

Somewhat later, Sartre will publish an appeal to Italian intellectuals for support for *Lotta continua* (see *Tout*, no. 2 [September (actually October) 8, 1970]).

70/519

Message pour la conférence de presse du Comité Israël-Palestine à Paris, le 23 mars 1970 ⟨Message for the Israel-Palestine Committee Press Conference in Paris, March 23, 1970⟩.

a) Excerpts in *Le Monde*, March 25, 1970.

b) *Israël-Palestine* (liaison and information bulletin for the Israel-Palestine committees [Brussels]), no. 2 (July-August, 1970), p. 23.

From March 20 to 22, 1970, on the initiative of young independent leftist revolutionary militants, a conference of the Israel-Palestine committees of ten European countries was held at Choisy-le-Roi. Sartre sent a message to the organizers in which he said especially: *I support the Israel-Palestine Committee because it is a committee formed by members of the revolutionary Left, and because it approaches the Israel-Palestine problem in the unifying perspective of the development of socialist forces in the Near East.*

70/520

"Entretien avec Jean-Paul Sartre" ⟨Conversation with Jean-Paul Sartre⟩, granted to members of the Paris Israel-Palestine Committee.

-- *Israël-Palestine*, no. 1 (March, 1970), pp. 8-11.

In choosing to support the Israel-Palestine Committee, Sartre remains faithful to the position he had taken since before the Six-Day War, which consisted in granting both the Palestinians' rights to Palestine and the Israelis' rights as a nation. In this interview he explains both why a solution which recognizes both sets of rights can only be a revolutionary one, and why *at the present hour there is no purely revolutionary stand.*

Sartre sent a telegram of sympathy to the organizers of a debate on the possibilities for peace in the Near East, in which many Jewish and Israeli-Arab writers took part on April 30, 1970, in Tel Aviv (see *Le Monde*, April 15, 1970).

SARTRE AS EDITOR OF "LA CAUSE DU PEUPLE"

Beginning in April, 1970, Sartre found himself led by the logic of his own personal development and that of repression to assume legal responsibility for several leftist publications and to defend the revolutionary press as a whole in every way he could. This commitment began with *La Cause du peuple* ⟨The Cause of the People⟩ and continued with *Tout!* ⟨What We Want: Everything!⟩, *La Cause du peuple--J'accuse* ⟨The Cause of the People--I Accuse⟩ and *Révolution!* ⟨Revolution!⟩; it brought him several libel suits.

70/520

The newspaper *La Cause du peuple* ran a first series of twenty-one issues in May-June, 1968. Edited at the time by Roland Castro, it was the publication of the Movement in Support of the People's Struggles, mass organization of the U.J.C.M.L. ⟨Union of Young Marxist-Leninist Communists⟩. The title *La Cause du peuple* was taken up again in a first number dated November 1, 1968, by militants in the G.P. ⟨Proletarian Left⟩, an organization which had grown out of the U.J.C.M.L. and, to a lesser extent, the March Twenty-Second Movement. The newspaper has never been, however, the official organ of the Proletarian Left; edited for the most part by militant workers, it was meant above all to be a means of liaison between the factories the G.P. had a base in. In March, 1970, issue no. 18 of *La Cause du peuple* was confiscated and its first editor, Jean-Pierre Le Dantec, run in on charges of provoking crimes against national security and justifying theft, pillage, arson, and murder. On April 18 his successor, Michel Le Bris, was arrested on the same charges.

It was following these arrests and confiscations, and at the request of the people behind the paper, that Sartre decided to take over the editing of *La Cause du peuple* beginning with its issue no. 20. The paper was never banned, but it was constantly confiscated until its no. 31 (November 20, 1970). Beginning with no. 36 (March 4, 1971), Le Dantec and Le Bris appeared as coeditors, and finally the publication stopped coming out with issue no. 39 (May 1, 1971) and merged with *J'accuse*.

Sartre was also designated editor of:

-- Various supplements to *La Cause du peuple: La Cause du mineur* ⟨The Cause of the Miner⟩, *Le Métallo rouge* ⟨The Red Metalworker⟩, *Les Cahiers prolétariens* ⟨Proletarian Notebooks⟩, *Soldats en lutte* ⟨Soldiers in the Struggle⟩, *Vérité Rhône-Alpes* ⟨The Truth about the Rhone-Alps Region⟩.
-- *La Parole au peuple* ⟨The People Speak⟩, Maoist Communist paper published by a splinter group of *L'Humanité rouge* ⟨Red Humanity⟩.
-- *Dossiers P.I.M.*, no. 3 and *Le Bidasse en colère* ⟨The Angry Private⟩, no. 1, published by the bookstore La Commune.
-- Several publications of *Secours rouge* ⟨Red Aid⟩.
-- *Ce que nous voulons: Tout!* ⟨What We Want: Everything!⟩, "fortnightly" with Vive la Révolution ⟨Long Live the Revolution⟩ leanings (16 issues from September, 1970 to July, 1971).
-- *La Cause du peuple--J'accuse* (first number published on May 24, 1971) and its supplements.
-- *Révolution!* (published by a dissident group from the Communist League) starting with issue no. 3 in June, 1971--and its supplements: *Même Combat* ⟨The Same Struggle⟩ and *Cahiers Révolution* ⟨Revolution Notebooks⟩.

On the other hand, Sartre refused to take over the editing of a paper with anarchist tendencies, *Vivre sans temps morts, jouir sans entraves* ⟨To Live without Dull Moments, to Enjoy without Constraints⟩.

70/521

Statement in which Sartre announces that he is assuming the editorship of *La Cause du peuple.*

a) Le Monde, April 28, 1970. Reprinted in almost the entire French press.

b) La Cause du peuple, no. 20 (May 1, 1970). With corrections in no. 21 (May 8, 1970).

c) Rouge, no. 64 (May 18, 1970). With a short letter from Sartre expressing his support for *articles* which *deal with* violence and not with *acts* which *express* violence.

> *After the arrest of Le Dantec and Le Bris, I agreed to assume temporarily the editorship of* La Cause du peuple. *To avoid any misunderstanding, I want to make it clear that this decision does not imply either that the Proletarian Left is changing its line in the slightest or that I am abandoning the positions I have taken in* Les Temps modernes *and elsewhere.*

This new stand of Sartre's caused quite a stir and provided the occasion for a campaign of denigration and insult unlike any he had been subjected to since the time of the Algerian War. François Mauriac, in his bloc-notes in the *Figaro littéraire* (June 15-21), set the tone for a good number of responses in writing, "The thirst for martyrdom Sartre is possessed by is no reason for putting this incurably inoffensive person in prison." In the same paper (May 4-10, 1970), Dominique Jamet did not hesitate to resort to the argument against Sartre, worthy of *Minute*, according to which his action during the Resistance was limited to having THE FLIES staged . . . with the blessing of the German censor. A ponderous evaluation of Sartre's attitude may be found in an article by Raymond Barrillon (*Le Monde*, April 29, 1970): "Doesn't Jean-Paul Sartre bear witness for thousands of the young and not so young, violent or not, who fear for the future and end up no longer expecting anything from it? . . . Sartre's rebellion merits our reflection. One forbids oneself to laugh at a man who commits himself at the very age at which many are borne to the sweet philosophy of 'understanding' of forgetfulness and indifference to what will be tomorrow the suffering of others."

70/522

Statement protesting the confiscation of no. 22 of *La Cause du peuple.*

-- *Le Monde*, May 17-18, 1970.

Sartre justifies the guerilla-type action of the

70/522

Maoists and says, It is a matter of making it possible, through a long labor extending over years, for 97 per cent of the French to be able one day to make a revolution.

70/523

Interview by Pierre Dumayet broadcast by Radio-Television Luxembourg on May 16, 1970.

-- Excerpts in *Le Monde*, May 19, 1970.

About *La Cause du peuple* and the actions of the Proletarian Left.

70/524

"Jean-Paul Sartre fait parler les 'casseurs'" ⟨Jean-Paul Sartre Lets the "Troublemakers" Talk⟩, conversation between Sartre and Alain Geismar, remarks gathered by Serge Lafaurie.

-- *Le Nouvel Observateur*, May 24, 1970.

Just as in May, 1968, he had given Daniel Cohn-Bendit the chance to set forth his analysis of the events, here Sartre intervenes very little and lets Alain Geismar explain the meaning of the actions taken by the Proletarian Left.

70/NOTE 4.

On May 25, 1970, at the Mutualité, Sartre presided at a meeting organized by the leftist groups to demand that the former editors of *La Cause du peuple* be freed. He opened the debates--which were rather lively--by stressing the fact that seventy militants were presently incarcerated and being dealt with according to the rules of the common law, and by noting that this was the first time since 1881--with the exception of the period of the Occupation--that two editors had been imprisoned (see *Le Monde*, May 27, 1970).

It was during this meeting that Sartre was photographed raising his fist (a photo reprinted throughout the world) and that Alain Geismar made the approximately eight-minute speech in which, like other participants, he called for a street demonstration on May 27, which was the pretext for arresting and sentencing him (see the text of his speech in *Minutes du Procès Alain Geismar* ⟨Minutes of the Alain Geismar Trial⟩ [1970], pp. 79-82).

70/525

Toute la vérité ⟨The Whole Truth⟩.

a) Le Monde, May 27, 1970. Text published in the "Libres opinions" ⟨Free Opinions⟩ section.

b) Reprinted in SITUATIONS, VIII.

Published on the eve of Sartre's testimony at the trial of Jean-Pierre Le Dantec and Michel Le Bris, and of the violence this trial brought on in the Latin Quarter, this text denounces the repressive measures coming down on revolutionary militants: *The challenges, searches, and arrests have been increasing in number for several months now. The land of freedom has the world's most conspicuous police force. There is not a day that we don't read in the papers that young people*--always *young people--have been sentenced for violence whose meaning remains obscure to us. So France must be being drowned in a wave of delinquency: the government is framing laws to defend us against the new generation.*

70/NOTE 5.

On May 27, 1970, Sartre testified as a defense witness at the trial of Jean-Pierre Le Dantec and Michel Le Bris. After having stressed the fact that he too should in all justice have been on the bench of the accused, he says in reference to *La Cause du peuple: This paper, as you know, is called the paper of enraged workers. . . . Three articles out of four are drafted by workers. That's what explains the violence of its language. What you are going to condemn here is the violence of the people.* (See the report of the hearing by Jean Lachâtre in *Le Monde*, May 29, 1970; see also a short excerpt from Sartre's testimony in the special supplement to issue no. 2 of *L'Idiot international*, June, 1970.)

70/NOTE 6.

Most of the articles in no. 24 (June 2, 1970) and nos. 26-31 of *La Cause du peuple* are signed Jean-Paul Sartre or Simone de Beauvoir, but they did not write them.

70/NOTE 7.

The tape of a statement Sartre made for *L'Idiot international* was stolen from the newspaper's office, which was ransacked by unknown intruders during the night of June 3-4, 1970.

70/NOTE 8.

On June 4, 1970, Sartre announced during a press conference that an Association of Friends of *La Cause du peuple* had been formed, whose goal was to give moral, material, and legal aid to the paper. This association, whose leading spirits were Simone de Beauvoir and Michel Leiris, got support from a certain number of intellectuals and artists, including Marguerite Duras and Jean-Luc Godard. It had a de facto but not de jure existence after the prefect of police's "refusal to acknowledge" it. This refusal was judged illegal, which led the government to have passed in Parliament, in June, 1971, a law governing associations, which was in turn judged unconstitutional by the Constitutional Council. Without taking part in the editing of *La Cause du peuple*, the association played a very active role in printing and distributing it from June to December, 1970.

70/NOTE 9.

On June 20, 1970, Sartre, accompanied by Simone de Beauvoir and François Truffaut among the notables, distributed *La Cause du peuple* in the marketplace on rue Daguerre without being disturbed (see *Le Monde*, June 23, 1970).

On June 26, this time in the company of Louis Malle, Alexandre Astruc, Sami Frey, etc., Sartre is issued a summons on the *grands boulevards* while he is distributing *La Cause du peuple*. Released after an hour and a half, he says on leaving the police station in the Bonne-Nouvelle section: *Once again I see that there are two weights and two measures for the people handing out* La Cause du peuple. And he concludes: *I'll do it again.*

70/526

Qui sont les terroristes? ⟨Who Are the Terrorists?⟩, excerpts from a press conference.

-- *La Cause du peuple*, no. 26 (July 10, 1970).

On June 18, 1970, Sartre presided over a press conference held at his home to announce the formation of Secours Rouge ⟨Red Aid⟩ and to denounce the government's repressive measures.

On June 11, he had taken part in the founding of Secours Rouge and had signed the appeal published by the promotion committee (see text in *La Cause du peuple*, no. 25 [June 16, 1970]). The goal of this organization, which adopted the name of an organization which had had some importance before the war, was originally "to assure the political and legal defense of victims of oppression, and to give them and their families unqualified material and moral support." But Secours Rouge quickly took on a highly political role in trying to bring together the different leftist groups in favor of concrete movements based among the people and led by them, and in organizing big demonstrations (the Burgos trial, the campaign against the prison system, etc.). In spite of certain successes and a pretty good base in the provinces, the organization suffered from defections and internal dissensions and did not play the role it could have. Sartre himself resigned from the promotion committee in February, 1971.

70/527

"Le Système capitaliste ne peut plus se maintenir sans une répression" 〈The Capitalist System Can No Longer Keep Going without Repression〉, remarks gathered by Jean-Marie Borzeix.

-- *Combat*, July 9, 1970.

Long interview in which Sartre reviews his recent political activity. He begins by stressing the simultaneously general and precise context in which he was led to support *La Cause du peuple (concealed repression, police repression* coupled with *flagrant violation of the law)*, and shows how much his personal position was travestied by the press: *It was frequently said--because that's the bourgeois gimmick--that I wanted to play the martyr and get myself arrested. But I don't have any desire whatsoever to get myself arrested. On the contrary! I want to avoid being arrested, because that way I can show, and my comrades--Louis Malle or someone else--can help me show that there are two weights and two measures. . . . When other people say that I want to get myself arrested because I want to become fashionable again, I think I can truthfully say that I don't have to.*

Next Sartre explains that he hopes the Secours Rouge 〈Red Aid〉 and the Association of Friends of *La Cause du peuple* will bring about a new union between the intellectuals and the masses like the one which existed in the nineteenth century. He would like to have, furthermore, a confrontation with the minister of the interior on the television program "A armes égales" 〈With Matched Weapons〉, in order to discuss the problem of repression. In the July 10, 1970, *Combat*, Raymond Marcellin declined the challenge.

70/528

"Le Tiers monde commence en banlieue" 〈The Third World Begins in Our Suburbs〉, remarks made during a debate.

70/528

a) First published in an article, "Les Pays capitalistes et leurs 'colonies intérieures,'" containing two sets of remarks, one by Sartre and the other by J.-P. N'Diaye, in *Tricontinental* (French edition), no. 2 (July, 1970), pp. 21-23.

b) Reprinted separately in SITUATIONS, VIII.

Text of remarks made during a debate held on June 13, 1970, by the Union of All Senegalese Workers in France on the occasion of the publication of the dossier, *Le Livre des travailleurs africains en France* ⟨The Book of African Workers in France⟩ (F. Maspero, 1970).

Before citing certain precise facts, Sartre says, *The surplus exploitation of the African worker is a necessity for the French capitalist economy. It is often said that the Americans have "internal colonization" at home: well, what France is doing right now is rebuilding at home the colonies she lost overseas.*

70/529

"Jeg er en ydmyk turist!" ⟨I'm Just a Tourist!⟩, interview by Arne Hestenes and Odd Wentzel.

-- *Dagbladet* (Oslo), July 8, 1970.

Interview given on the occasion of a trip to Scandinavia with Vladimir Dedijer. Sartre says this is his third trip to Norway, gives his impressions of the country, and talks about the political situation in France.

70/530

"Die Praxis des Philosophen" ⟨The Philosopher's *Praxis*⟩, excerpts from an interview given on German television.

-- *Theater Heute*, September, 1970, pp. 1-2.

In this interview televised on July 12, 1970, by the First Program of the German Federal Republic, Sartre essentially repeats what he said in *Combat* (see 70/527) and speaks of the role of the intellectual. See notice in *Le Monde*, July 10, 1970.

70/531

Introduction to the dossier *Les Massacres, la guerre chimique en Asie du Sud-Est* ⟨Massacres and Chemical Warfare in Southeast Asia⟩.

-- *Cahiers libres* ⟨Free Notebooks⟩, nos. 179-80. F. Maspero, [September] 1970. P. 7 and on the back cover.

Short introduction to a volume made up of reports by Gisèle Halimi, Francis Kahn, Gabriel Kolko, etc.

70/532

"J.-P. Sartre: L'Ami du peuple" ⟨J.-P. Sartre: The People's Friend⟩, remarks collected by Jean-Edern Hallier and Thomas Savignat.

a) L'Idiot international, no. 10 (September, 1970).

b) Reprinted in *Du rôle de l'intellectuel dans le mouvement révolutionnaire* ⟨The Role of the Intellectual in the Revolutionary Movement⟩. Le Désordre series, no. 12. Eric Losfeld, [1971]. With the responses of Bernard Pingaud and Dionys Mascolo, which had been published in *La Quinzaine littéraire*, no. 104 (October, 1970) and no. 107 (December 1-15, 1970). Pp. 9-31.

c) Reprinted in SITUATIONS, VIII.

Important conversation in which Sartre tries to define the role of the intellectual before and after May, 1968. For him, the intellectual, whom he defines as the *technician of practical knowledge*, is characterized by his consciousness of the contradiction between the universality he aims for in his understanding and the particular interests he submits to in his work. The traditional intellectual *enjoys his role* and derives a good conscience from his bad conscience. The new kind of intellectual has to *eliminate himself as an intellectual*, has to go beyond his contradiction by putting himself *directly in the service of the masses* and in this way being *reeducated*. It seems unlikely to Sartre that intellectuals who are over thirty and have already turned out a book will be reeducated in this way. He puts his hope in the new generation.

Sartre also explains why, in spite of his having been radicalized by what happened in May, 1968, he decided to complete his "Flaubert," at the same time considering himself *available for any politically just task he might be asked to carry out.*

70/532 A

"Parla Monsieur X" ⟨Mr. X Speaks⟩, interview by Giampiero Mughini.

70/532 A

-- *L'Astrolabio* (Rome), September 16, 1970, pp. 27-29.

70/NOTE 10.

On September 18, 1970, Sartre spoke at a meeting held at the Mutualité by Secours Rouge ⟨Red Aid⟩ against repression and attacks on free speech (see *Le Monde*, September 21, 1970).

70/533

Lettre de J.-P. Sartre ⟨A Letter from J.-P. Sartre⟩.

-- *Tout!* ⟨What We Want: Everything!⟩, no. 1 (September 23, 1970).

Letter by which Sartre assumes the editorship of the "fortnightly" *Tout!*, started by militants close to the Vive la Révolution ⟨Long Live the Revolution⟩ group, and in which he states: *I am making myself available to any revolutionary newspaper in order to make the middle class either bring me to a political trial which will be clearly concerned for once with the freedom of the press, or--by not bringing charges against me--reveal the deliberate illegality of its repression.* In May, 1971, issue no. 12 of *Tout!* will be confiscated in the shipping offices because it is devoted to the F.H.A.R. ⟨Homosexual Front for Revolutionary Action⟩, and legal proceedings for offense of public decency will be begun. On the other hand, the deputy mayor of Tours, Jean Royer, will bring charges against Sartre, the editor, for the same reason. (See the statement signed by the staff and Sartre in *Tout!*, no. 14 [June 7, 1971].) In June, 1971, Sartre will be charged, as editor, with slandering the police and the prison administrators because of an article on drugs published in *Tout!*, no. 8 (February 1, 1971). A statement signed by Sartre and the newspaper staff (see *Tout!*, no. 15 [June 30, 1971]) reacts against this charge and says that a trial "will only underline what everyone is aware of, the rottenness of bourgeois customs and the new direction of a revolution which aims to change the whole nature of everyday life."

70/534

"Coexistences," text of the catalogue for a show by Paul Rebeyrolle at the Galerie Maeght, 13, rue de Téhéran.

a) Derrière le miroir, no. 187 (October, 1970). 8 pages.

b) Reprinted in SITUATIONS, IX.

Falling into line with the preface to the 1961 Lapoujade show, this text on political commitment in painting shows no striking development in Sartre's esthetic ideas but tries to give a definition of what he thinks "*leftist* painting" means.

[Rebeyrolle's] guerilleros *are really fighting, without being aware of it, against both capitalism and Russian socialism: because either the revolution will be made against both systems or man has had it.*

70/535

"Sartre on Mexico," interview.

-- *The Spokesman*, no. 6 (October, 1970), pp. 35-38.

This very good text on revolutionary perspectives in Mexico and the Third World apparently was also published in Spanish but not in French. It is the transcription of a filmed interview Sartre granted in February, 1970, to the International Committee in Support of the Struggling Mexican People.

Sartre thinks that the Castroite model does not suit Mexico, and that revolutionary movements ought to be autonomous and ought not to play the big power blocs' game. *Real revolution, revolution which can liberate a country, and real socialism must break completely with all previous models and take directives, orders, and advice from no one.*

70/NOTE 11.

Sartre testified by letter at the first trial of the distributors of *La Cause du peuple* in the court concerned with national security on September 11, 1970: *If they are guilty, I am more guilty than they; if they are innocent, they are more innocent than I (Le Monde,* September 13-14, 1970).

He testified in person at a second trial on September 29, 1970, saying about *La Cause du peuple: I am in no way a straw man but the real editor. It is true, and I will say it one more time, that I don't agree with all the ideas put forth in the paper any more than I agree with all the ones put forth in my journal* Les Temps modernes. *But many of these ideas are the same as mine (Le Monde,* October 1, 1970).

Hailed as a witness on October 21, 1970, in Alain Geismar's trial at the police court in the seventeenth *arrondissement* <ward>, Sartre wrote a letter to the tribunal in which he said in particular: *The tribunal has never considered my testimony. . . . So there doesn't seem to me to be any use at all in my coming into court, because I have become convinced that as far as I am concerned the chips are down and no one would listen to me. . . . So it seems to me that it is more important for me to bear witness this very day in the streets and in the eyes of public opinion (Minutes of the Alain Geismar Trial,* French edition, p. 107).

So on October 21 Sartre went to Boulogne-Billancourt to talk to the workers at the Renault plant during a twenty-minute improvised meeting. The text of his harangue is found in:

70/536

Jean-Paul Sartre à Renault-Billancourt <Jean-Paul Sartre at Renault-Billancourt>, short speech.

-- *L'Idiot international*, no. 11 (November, 1970).

70/536 A

"Aktion statt Druckerschwärze" <Action Instead of Printed Words>, interview by Alice Schwarzer.

-- *Neues Forum* (Vienna), XVII, no. 2-3/II (November, 1970), 1023-25.

70/537

Preface to *Minutes du procès d'Alain Geismar* <Minutes of the Alain Geismar Trial>.

a) In *L'Idiot international* Documents. Volume printed by Editions Hallier on November 5, 1970. Pp. 17-20.

b) Reprinted as "Les Garanties bourgeoises" <The Bourgeois Guarantees>. *Le Nouvel Observateur*, November 9-15, 1970.

c) Reprinted as *L'Affaire Geismar* <The Geismar Affair>. In SITUATIONS, VIII.

The reason why we are publishing [the minutes of the trial] *here is not to ask the bourgeoisie for*

> *any sort of indulgence toward the revolutionaries who are seeking to overthrow it but to show that we cannot become its accomplice in illegality. . . .* [Geismar's sentence] *is not too harsh; it's iniquitous.*

70/NOTE 12.

On October 16, 1970, Sartre, along with several supporters of *La Cause du peuple*, assumed the responsibility of transporting issue no. 29 from the printer's to the bookstore La Joie de Lire. After having distributed the paper in the rue Saint-Séverin, he made a short speech during an impromptu press conference (see *Combat*, October 17-18, 1970).

70/NOTE 13.

A statement from Sartre announces that issue no. 30 of *La Cause du peuple* will be printed on November 6, and that this issue will be distributed by a certain number of bookstores and publishing houses (see *Le Monde*, November 6, 1970). Publicity in the November 10 *Le Monde* indicates sixteen places where the issue is on sale.

70/NOTE 14.

Another announcement from Sartre observes that nos. 32, 32a, and 33 of *La Cause du peuple* have not been confiscated, and announces a second printing of no. 33 for distribution in the kiosks (see *Le Monde*, January 15, 1971).

70/538

Un Procès populaire ⟨A Peoples' Trial⟩, tract distributed by Secours Rouge ⟨Red Aid⟩.

a) Liberté vaincra! (journal of the Secours Rouge in Nord-Pas-de-Calais), no. 1 (December, 1970).

b) Cahiers prolétariens, no. 1 (January, 1971), p. 77.

c) Excerpt in *Le Monde*, December 13-14, 1970.

This tract calls upon the inhabitants of the coal fields at Lens to take part in what will be "the first peoples' tribunal in France," a tribunal which will judge those responsible for the catastrophe at Fouquières-les-Lens (sixteen miners killed by firedamp on February 4, 1970).

70/538

This tribunal was held in Lens on December 12 under the aegis of the Secours Rouge du Nord <Red Aid in the North>, and at it Sartre read an indictment which was subsequently reprinted in the following forms:

70/539

Au peuple des mines <To the Mining People>.

a) Anonymous four-page tract.

b) Reprinted as *Premier procès populaire à Lens: Réquisitoire* <The First People's Trial at Lens: Indictment>. In SITUATIONS, VIII.

In this indictment, Sartre accuses the Coal Bureau of being directly responsible for mining accidents and diseases: *The Boss-State is guilty of the assassination of February 4, 1970. The management and engineers responsible . . . are equally guilty of premeditated murder: they premeditatedly chose profit instead of safety.*

On the other hand, Sartre demands freedom for the militants accused of having, shortly after the catastrophe at Fouquières, set fire to the Coal Bureau offices at Hénin-Liétard in reprisal. On December 14, 1970, these militants appeared before the Internal Security Court and were all, with the exception of Bernard Liscia, acquitted.

NOTE: Joris Ivens made a film of the peoples' tribunal at Lens, and Sartre appears in it at length.

70/NOTE 15.

On the occasion of Marshal Tito's visit to France, Sartre, Lelio Basso, Ernest Mandel, and Laurent Schwartz signed a resolution protesting the repressive measures directed at Yugoslavian students (see *Le Monde*, October 24-25, 1970).

70/NOTE 16.

During a demonstration at the Cité Universitaire in Paris on November 5, 1970, Sartre took part along with several other speakers in demanding that the Maison du Maroc not be allowed to revert to control by the Cherif government (see *Le Monde*, November 7, 1940).

70/NOTE 17.

Sartre was one of the signers of two appeals against decisions by the board of censors, one of which concerned Pierre Guyotat's *Eden, Eden, Eden,* the other William Klein's *Eldridge Cleaver, Black Panther* (see *Politique-Hebdo,* November 12-18, 1970).

1971

71/540

L'IDIOT DE LA FAMILLE: GUSTAVE FLAUBERT DE 1821 À 1857 ⟨The Family Idiot: Gustave Flaubert from 1821 to 1857⟩, Volumes I and II.

a) Preface published as *Sartre présente son Flaubert* ⟨Sartre Introduces His Flaubert⟩. *Le Monde*, May 7, 1971.

b) Bibliothèque de la Philosophie series. Gallimard, [1971]. Two bound volumes, with cover bearing an unsigned Introduction by Jacques Bersani, put on sale on May 12, 1971. Volume I: 1104 pages; printing date, March 15, 1971. Volume II: 1036 pages (1105-2140); printing date, March 20, 1971.

One year after the book was first put on sale, approximately 10,000 copies had been sold. Translations are presently being made into English, German, Spanish, Italian, and Japanese. English translations are now under contract with New Left Books (London) and Pantheon Books (New York).

c) Page 13 was reprinted in "serial" form in *L'Humour rouge*, nos. 2-7 (June, 1971).

> Announced as an event, THE FAMILY IDIOT had, judging by the hundreds of already published reviews and the many comments published in the newspapers, considerable success as a curiosity piece: in September, 1971, the *Times Literary Supplement* went so far as to devote its first three pages to it. Most of the people who commented on it were, however, crushed by the sheer bulk of the work and disoriented by the variety of Sartre's critical insights; it will undoubtedly take several years to recognize and explore what Claude Burgelin calls this "verbal Himalaya" and Serge Doubrovsky this "anthropological saga."

In his first two volumes, by reconstituting through *empathy* a neurotic experience as it was lived through, Sartre describes the way in which Flaubert *was constituted* and *became a person*. We are thus invited to slip into Flaubert's subjective experience in order to relive with him that flight into the imaginary which made a writer out of him. As the unwanted child of a cold mother and an overbearing father who always favored his older brother, Flaubert was constituted as a passive creature with an unfortunate relationship to practical language.

Excluded from the active, positive, and utilitarian universe of the Flauberts, he assumed the familial sentence which condemned him to inertia and, thanks to an intentional and memorable crisis which brought him to his brother's feet one night in January, 1844, at Pont-l'Evêque, avoided the necessity of "taking up a trade" and won the right to devote himself to the passive and quasi-feminine activity which writing will be for him. By means of this writing, he is going to try satanically to make the world unreal by throwing himself and the world headlong into the imaginary, thereby taking the point of view of death on life, of nothingness on being, and adopting a God's-eye view in opposition to science and to his father's triumphant reason.

By presenting Flaubert's neurosis as a passive dynamic (a *choice undergone*) engendered dialectically by a strict familial and sociocultural conditioning (his *constitution*) which was in turn assumed by a trapped freedom (his *becoming a person*), Sartre gives an answer in his first two volumes to the question, How does one become a writer? Or more exactly, What kind of man did Flaubert have to be to write *Madame Bovary*?

For an account of the genesis of THE FAMILY IDIOT, see 66/440, 69/512, and 71/541.

71/541

"J'ai voulu montrer un homme et montrer une méthode" ⟨I Wanted to Present a Man and a Method⟩, interview by Michel Contat and Michel Rybalka.

a) Le Monde, May 14, 1971, pp. 17, 20-21.

b) German and Romanian translations.

In this interview made on May 1, 1971, Sartre comments at length on what he was aiming at in his "Flaubert": to write a "true" novel--which implies constant recourse to the imagination and thus constitutes a sort of "literary" effort even though it is based on

71/541

precise biographical and historical information--and at the same time to develop, on the basis of historical materialism, a method which would give the work its contemporary, committed dimension.

This continuing affirmation of a radical rationalism is to be noted: *The fundamental project in my "Flaubert" is to show that at bottom everything can be communicated. . . , that every human being is perfectly capable of being understood if the appropriate methods are used and the necessary documents are available.*

71/542

Preface to *Le Procès de Burgos* ⟨The Burgos Trial⟩, by Gisèle Halimi.

a) Témoins series. Gallimard, [1971]. Pp. VII-XXX.

b) Excerpts. "Coup de tonnerre en Europe" ⟨Thunder in Europe⟩. *Le Nouvel Observateur*, May 24-30, 1971.

c) Reprinted in *Enbata* (Basque journal),no. 236 (December 30, 1971).

Important text which may be compared to the preface to Antonin J. Liehm's *Three Generations* and which has already been much used by national-group movements. Criticizing centralization and showing the inadequacies of both bourgeois nationalism and the abstract Marxism which believes in a "chemically pure" class struggle, Sartre shows the import of Basque nationalism and, in particular, of culture.

Independence or death: these words spoken yesterday in Cuba and Algeria are being said again today in Euzkadi. Armed struggle for an independent Euzkadi, that's what the present situation really calls for. . . .

For a colonized person speaking his language is already a revolutionary act. . . . Today Basque culture must be above all a counter-culture . . . *the* praxis *which arises from man's oppression by man in the Basque country.*

71/543

Short speech and appeal for the Russian Jews.

-- In *Appeal from the Left for the Russian Jews* (brochure). Paris, June, 1971. Pp. 19-24, 35.

Along with Simone de Beauvoir, Beate Klarsfeld, Artur London, Daniel Mayer, Jean Rostand, etc., Sartre signed "Appeal from the Left for the Russian Jews," which protested the proceedings against the Jews wanting to leave Russia. He took the floor during a meeting held on January 7, 1971, at the Mutualité to show on the basis of historical evidence what the condition of the Jews had been before and after the Revolution of 1917, to call for the liberation of those who had been condemned in Leningrad, and to demand that not only Jews but all Russian citizens who so desired be granted free exit from the U.S.S.R. The speech concludes as follows: *In order for a just policy like this to be established*, the Russian working classes would have to seize the power they have been robbed of!

71/544

La Justice populaire ⟨Peoples' Justice⟩, interview.

-- *J'accuse*, no. 1 (January 15, 1971).

Long interview in which Sartre analyzes the concept of peoples' justice, which he contrasts to class justice, and specifically analyzes what happened during the peoples' tribunal at Lens, trying at the same time to clear up a certain number of misunderstandings about leftist actions and about his own role in them.

There is an interesting criticism of Sartre in a debate about peoples' justice between Michel Foucault and Maoist militants which was published in the dossier *Nouveau fascisme, nouvelle démocratie* ⟨New Fascism, New Democracy⟩ (*Les Temps modernes*, no. 310*a* [May, 1972]).

J'accuse, which was less directly militant, better edited, and more carefully gotten up than *La Cause du peuple*, was designed to reach a mass audience and be the journal of revolutionary democracy. Sartre did not have to assume legal responsibility for it, but he took an active part in its creation and editing. After five numbers, *J'accuse* merged with *La Cause du peuple* in May, 1971.

71/545

"Entretien avec . . . Jean-Paul Sartre" ⟨Interview with . . . Jean-Paul Sartre⟩, by Yvon Toussaint.

-- *Le Soir* (Brussels), January 26, 1971.

71/545

Clear but not very original interview in which Sartre specifies comments he made elsewhere on the political situation in France, the international situation, the peoples' tribunal at Lens, and the role of the intellectual.

71/546

"Conversacion con un militante llamado Jean-Paul Sartre" ⟨Talk with a Militant Named Jean-Paul Sartre⟩, interview by Claude Kiejman and Daniel Waksman Schinca.

-- *Marcha* (Montevideo), February 12, 1971.

Long, interesting interview in which Sartre tells more clearly than elsewhere what his situation is in relation to the different leftist groups, and in which he describes their actions since May, 1968, in contrast to those of the P.C. ⟨Communist Party⟩ and the C.G.T. ⟨General Confederation of Labor⟩.

71/547

Violence et grève de la faim ⟨Violence and the Hunger Strike⟩.

-- *J'accuse*, no. 2 (February 15-March 15, 1971).

Text, dated February 8, 1971, meant to support the strike by imprisoned leftists as well as other hunger strikes, especially the one which began on January 22 in the Saint Bernard chapel in Maine-Montparnasse and which Sartre followed very closely. Sartre reminds us that *a hunger strike in today's France is a violent and revolutionary step*, and insists that it is not a *tactic*.

The totality of the strikers' actions drew attention to the prison system and led the minister of justice to promise reforms.

71/548

Press conference concerning the "occupation" of the Sacré-Coeur.

-- Excerpts in *La Croix* and *Le Monde*, February 17, 1971.

Together with approximately 200 militants, Sartre participated during the evening of February 13, 1971, in an abortive occupation of the Sacré-Coeur. This demonstration was a continuation of the hunger strikers' actions and was intended, as theirs were, to protest recent police brutalities (attack on a young workers' barracks, the mutilation of Richard Deshayes, etc.). The occupation was thwarted by the attitude of the rector of the Basilica and by police intervention inside the Sacré-Coeur (15 people seriously wounded and 70 arrests). Sartre just barely had time to get out before the police got there.

This business caused a big stir (the front-page headline of *L'Aurore* said "They Were Trying to Burn Down the Sacré-Coeur"), and had repercussions it would take too long to specify here: uneasiness in Catholic circles, trials of the protesters, etc.

In a press conference held on February 15 with Jean-Luc Godard, Sartre explained why they tried to occupy the Basilica and what had happened when they did.

71/549

Portes ouvertes à l'Elysée: Les conclusions de Jean-Paul Sartre ⟨Open Doors at the Elysée Palace: What Jean-Paul Sartre Thinks about It⟩.

-- *J'accuse*, no. 3 (March 15, 1971).

This text follows an article in which Mme Espinosa, president of the association for the defense of the victims at Saint-Laurent-du-Pont, expresses her surprise that a gift of twenty-five thousand dollars given by an American has been held up at the Elysée Palace for more than three months and has never reached the families of the 146 victims. Sartre finds the whole business *typical of the Fifth Republic* and decries the *mixture of incompetence and cupidity characteristic of the regime.*

The twenty-five thousand dollars were finally given to the Secours Catholique ⟨Catholic Aid⟩.

71/NOTE 1.

Following the arrest on March 20, 1971, of the Cuban poet Heberto Padilla on the personal decision of Fidel Castro, Sartre was among the signers of a letter of protest addressed to Castro (see *Le Monde*, April 9, 1971). Some time later, after Padilla had signed an autocriticism in which K. S. Karol and René Dumont were accused of being C.I.A. agents, Sartre was among the signers of a new letter to Castro which certainly was to be taken to constitute, as far as he was concerned, a break with the Cuban regime. In very lively terms this letter especially urges Fidel

71/NOTE 1.

Castro "to spare Cuba from the dogmatic obscurantism, the cultural xenophobia, and the repressive system which Stalinism imposed in the socialist countries" (see *Le Monde*, May 22, 1971).

71/550

"J'accuse" et la politique ⟨*J'accuse* and Politics⟩.

-- *J'accuse*, no. 5 (May 1, 1971).

With *J'accuse* Sartre began a period of activist journalism. He reflects on the kind of action the revolutionary press can take: *The present role of* J'accuse *is to unmask the ideology of those in power, their "parliamentary democracy," and to illuminate all action taken by the people. If you toss out what the sympathizing press says (63 per cent of the French are satisfied with Pompidou: how could this be* possible*?), you'll find beneath the "stability" of the electorate the truth of a society on the way toward its revolution.*

71/NOTE 2.

On May 12, 1971, a delegation led by Sartre went to the police station at Ivry-sur-Seine to find out the conditions in which an Algerian worker, Hadj Behar Rehala, had been wounded by the police. This business led to a new dispute between the Communists and Sartre (see *Le Monde*, May 12, 13, 14, and 18, 1971).

71/551

"Sartre Discusses Quebec," interview.

-- *Guardian* (New York), May 19, 1971.

This text bears on the repression in Quebec and must have been published in French-language publications. It is undoubtedly put together from parts of a filmed interview Sartre made with F.L.Q. ⟨Quebec Liberation Front⟩ representatives in December, 1970, for use at a meeting; and since the interviewers ask Sartre questions they ought to be better able to answer than he, it is of poor quality.

71/552

Debate about the movie *Le Chagrin et la pitié* ⟨The Sorrow and the Pity⟩.

-- *La Cause du peuple-J'accuse*, no. 2 (May 31, 1971).

On May 3, 1971, Sartre, together with Maoist militants and two former resistants, attended a screening of the Max Ophuls and André Harris movie *The Sorrow and the Pity*, and took part in the debate which followed. His judgment of the movie is on the whole negative: his chief complaint is that it eliminates the role that the working class played in the Resistance. The other participants generally agree.

71/NOTE 3.

Sartre took on active concern for the case of Alain Jaubert, a journalist worked over in a patrol wagon on May 29, 1971, and joined in the complaint he brought against the police (see *Le Monde*, June 1, 1971, etc.).

71/553

Communiqué ⟨Statement⟩.

-- *Le Monde*, June 4, 1971; *Révolution!*, no. 3 (June, 1971).

Following charges brought against the magazine *Révolution!* (edited by people who had split off from the Communist League) for an article about the police, Sartre assumes the editorship of the publication and its supplements.

71/554

Statement announcing the creation of the "Libération" news service, signed by J.-P. Sartre and Maurice Clavel.

a) Excerpts in *Le Monde*, June 19, 1971.

b) Complete text in several leftist magazines, including *L'Idiot international*, nos. 19-20 (June 30-September 1, 1971).

Following the Jaubert case, a great need for freedom arose in the press. . . . The "Libération" news service seeks to be a new tribune which will provide a forum for journalists who wish to tell all and people who wish to know all.

This service, whose director is Maurice Clavel, has published almost every day since June 30, 1971, two bulletins entitled *A.P.L. Informations*, one for France and the other international.

71/555

Venez tous le 27 juin faire le procès de la police française ⟨Everybody Come Bring the French Police to Trial on June 27⟩.

a) La Cause du peuple-J'accuse, no. 5 (June 21, 1971). Reprinted in a special supplement on the searches in the Latin Quarter entitled *Z Provocation* ⟨Provocation Z⟩ and confiscated by the police.

b) Widely distributed in handouts and on notices.

> *A peoples' tribunal will be held on June 27. It will examine the role of the police in French daily life since January 1, 1971. This tribunal is absolutely necessary: there is a profound conflict between police activities and the masses.*

This text was followed by an appeal, "For a Peoples' Trial of the Police," which stated its solidarity with the planned tribunal and which was signed by 237 intellectuals (see *Le Monde*, June 24, 1971; *La Cause du peuple-J'accuse*, no. 6 [June 28, 1971]).

Scheduled for the Cité Universitaire, the tribunal was banned by police headquarters. After this injunction, which was followed by various searches and by the indictment of Michelle Vian for "calling an undeclared protest," the peoples' tribunal was replaced by a meeting-press conference at the Mutualité on June 30. Sartre, who was sick, was unable to attend, but he sent a letter as well as a recording of an interview which he had granted on June 24 to the R.T.L. ⟨Luxembourg Radio-Television⟩ but which had not been broadcast (see *Le Monde*, July 2, 1972).

71/556

Pourquoi un tribunal populaire contre la police? ⟨Why Hold a Peoples' Tribunal against the Police?⟩, interview.

-- *La Cause du peuple-J'accuse*, no. 6 (June 28, 1971).

Sartre says it will be the police who are on trial at his trial, and specifies--in what is undoubtedly the best thing he has written on the question--what corresponds on the ideological level to the idea of a peoples' tribunal.

NOTE: Under the title "Jean-Paul Sartre répond à M. Roland Boscary-Monsservin, député républicain indépendant" ⟨Jean-Paul Sartre Replies to M. Roland Boscary-Monsservin, Independent Republican Deputy⟩, *La Cause du peuple-J'accuse* (no. 4 [June 13, 1971]) makes use of texts by Sartre published in *J'accuse* (nos. 1 and 2) to put together a serious answer to an ironic question about peoples' tribunals the deputy from the Aveyron had asked the minister of justice.

71/NOTE 4.

In its June 16, 1971, issue, the weekly *Minute*--which pays close and careful attention to everything Sartre does--headed its front page: "Enough of This Indulgence for Those Who Incite Disorder, Pillage, and Hatred: LET'S PUT SARTRE IN JAIL!" A few days later, on June 19, Sartre was summoned to court where he was told that four charges for libel against the police department and the prison system were being brought against him by the ministers Raymond Marcellin and René Pleven as a result of two unsigned articles published in *La Cause du peuple* on May 23 and June 16, 1970, and an article on drugs published in *Tout!* on February 1, 1971. For each charge Sartre risked a maximum prison sentence of one year and a maximum fine of three hundred thousand francs.

In a short statement in the June 21, 1971, *Combat*, Sartre says that he considers these charges *one more instance of repression and trial by force.* It may be recalled in this connection that at the time of the Affair of the 121 in 1970, General Charles de Gaulle intervened personally to prevent charges from being brought against Sartre, and even stated in this connection, "Leave the intellectuals alone," and "You don't arrest Voltaire."

Cn September 24, Sartre was summoned before Judges Pierre-Camille Galmiche and Jean Sablayrolles, and upon his release from questioning made a short statement: *From the moment an article constitutes a problem for the rulers, there is no more freedom in France (Le Monde*, September 26-27, 1971).

The case was not followed up and today it seems that there will be no sequel to the whole affair.

71/557

"Iron in His Soul," interview by John Gerassi.

a) Guardian (Manchester), September 4, 1971.

b) Reprinted in *Guardian Weekly*, September 18, 1971.

c) More complete version. "Sartre Accuses the Intellectuals of Bad Faith." *New York Times Magazine*, October 17, 1971.

Speaking especially to Americans, Sartre asserts that the intellectual's traditional role has become

71/557

outmoded, and that he must now take up unequivocally the role of militant. The forcefulness of Sartre's comments drew a number of responses: see especially the letters to the editor in the *New York Times* for October 21 and November 12 and 21.

John Gerassi is presently writing a political biography of Sartre; he is, by the way, the son of the painter Fernando Gerassi and Stépha Avdicovitch, who were before the war among the best friends of Sartre and Simone de Beauvoir.

71/558

Interventions and appeals on behalf of Iranian political prisoners.

a) "Bulletin de Comité de défense des prisonniers politiques iraniens" ⟨Bulletin of the Iranian Political Prisoners' Defense Committee⟩ (Paris). Mimeographed. Special no., February, 1972.

This bulletin reprints the following texts, all dated 1971:

-- J.-P. Sartre's reply to an article by Eric Rouleau published in *Le Monde*, July 13, 1971.
-- Statement from the Iranian Political Prisoners' Defense Committee (of which Sartre is president) concerning the repression and torture in Teheran.
-- Telegram and letter to the prime minister of Iran expressing concern about the fate of 37 persons arrested in August, 1971.
-- Statement of November 10 expressing solidarity with the Iranian students carrying out a hunger strike at the Cité Universitaire.
-- Telegram to the Iranian ambassador in Paris, dated November 16, on the same subject.
-- Statement of September 22 protesting the festivities in Persepolis.

Sartre also signed an international appeal to oppose these festivities (see *A.P.L. Informations International*, October 15, 1971).

-- Statement of the Defense Committee warning against certain actions taken and specifying that Sartre's secretary, André Puig, is the only one authorized to speak in the committee's name. Also reprinted in *Le Nouvel Observateur*, October 18-24, 1971.
-- Letter of support from Sartre to a round-table discussion set up by the Defense Committee for December 16, 1971.

b) Excerpts in *Le Monde*, December 22, 1971.

71/NOTE 5.

Following the assassination of the Algerian Djellali Ben Ali, Sartre took part in two demonstrations in the Goutte d'Or section, one on November 7, the other on November 27. Together with Gilles Deleuze, Michel Foucault, Jean Genet, Michel Leiris, Claude Mauriac, Yves Montand, etc., he formed a Djellali Committee and sent an appeal from intellectuals to Arab workers (see *La Cause du peuple-J'accuse*, no. 14 [December 13, 1971]).

71/559

Preface to a festival program, "Cinq peuples chantent leur lutte" ⟨Five Peoples Sing Their Struggle⟩.

a) Program for a festival held at the Mutualité in November, 1971.

b) Reprinted in *Enbata* (Bayonne), December 2, 1971.

Short text hailing a meeting of Basque, Breton, Occitan, and other singers. Sartre says in particular: *Whatever the positions of the different groups gathered here, I support them; because I think the way to real internationalism is through the peoples' right to self-determination and not through the false bourgeois, Jacobin, and imperialist universality.*

71/560

La Semence et le scaphandre ⟨The Seed and the Diving Suit⟩, excerpt from a youthful novel.

-- *Magazine littéraire*, no. 59 (December, 1971), pp. 29, 59-64.

These are the first two chapters of an autobiographical novel Sartre must have written in 1923-24 while he was getting ready at the Lycée Louis-le-Grand for the competitive entrance exams for the Ecole normale supérieure. The text, established by Michel Rybalka on the basis of the original manuscript, describes in a scarcely concealed way Sartre's friendship for Paul Nizan.

71/560 A

Statement by J.-P. Sartre and the "Friends of *La Cause du peuple*."

-- *A.P.L. Informations*, December 21, 1971.

71/560 A

This statement asks people to go welcome Alain Geismar when he comes out of Fresnes prison on December 24 after serving eighteen months, and to come talk to him at the theater of the Cité Universitaire. See the report on this meeting in *Le Monde*, December 26-27, 1971.

71/NOTE 6.

In an article ("The Shame of France," *New York Times*, July 19, 1971), Vladimir Dedijer describes a short trip he took to Alsace with Sartre when the latter was recovering from a mild attack he had had on May 25. The two men are thinking of forming an international commission to investigate the activities of the French police, and Sartre talks to Dedijer about his relations with Albert Schweitzer:

He was my uncle and he didn't like my maverick behavior one bit. Later on he tried to make peace with me, saying that even though our methods were different we were both working for the same cause, but I didn't fall for that old jazz.

71/NOTE 7.

We are assembling below a certain number of appeals and odd texts Sartre signed during 1971:

-- Appeals calling upon the Czechoslovak government to free the members of a Trotskyite revolutionary group (*Le Monde*, January 22 and March 17).
-- Petition supporting the strikers at the weekly *Jeune Afrique* (*Bulletin des amis des grévistes de Jeune Afrique*, no. 2 [May, 1971], a newsletter Sartre was designated as *legally responsible for*).
-- Telegram to the prefect of Guadeloupe protesting against the attitude of law enforcement officers during the run-ins which took place on April 21 at Pointe-à-Pitre (*Le Monde*, May 2-3).
-- Appeal calling for a stop to the prosecution of Jean-Edern Hallier, Georges Mury, and Dominique Grange for articles published in *L'Idiot international* (*L'Idiot liberté*, no. 7 [June 15-July 14]).
-- Similar appeal concerning Charles Michaloux, editor of *Rouge* (*Rouge*, July 5).
-- Petition and letter calling for the liberation of the fifteen members of the Living Theater imprisoned in Brazil (*Le Monde*, July 27 and August 4).
-- Statement protesting the prosecution of *Révolution!* (*Révolution!*, no. 5, October).
-- Open letter to the minister of the interior concerning the Lefol business (*A.P.L. Informations*, September 30; *Les Temps modernes*, November).
-- Appeal in opposition to the construction of an international airport at Narita, near Tokyo.

-- An appeal by forty-five intellectuals calling for the granting of emigration rights to Soviet Jews (*Le Monde*, October 28).
-- Appeal in opposition to the death sentence for nineteen Turkish militants accused among other things of kidnaping four American soldiers (*A.P.L. Informations International*, October 29).
-- Appeal made by a committee composed of Sartre, Simone de Beauvoir, Aimé Césaire, Michel Leiris, etc., for the establishment of a Patrice Lumumba African Cultural Center at Nanterre (*A.P.L. Informations*, December 20).
-- Letter signed by Sartre, Noam Chomsky, and Vladimir Dedijer announcing a meeting of a Russell Memorial Symposium in September, 1972, to study the problem of spheres of influence (*New York Review of Books*, December 30, pp. 29-30).

1972

72/561

SITUATIONS, VIII: AUTOUR DE 68 ⟨Situations, VIII: Around 1968⟩.

-- Gallimard, [1971]. 478 pages. Printing date: December 23, 1971. Publicity band: "Politics from 64 to 71."

This volume consists of four parts and includes the following texts, in French:

I. Vietnam: The Russell Tribunal
- -- *Dialogue Is Not Possible There Anymore* see 65/422
- -- *An American Writes to Sartre* 65/423
- -- *Sartre Replies* (to David I. Grossvogel) 65/423
- -- *The Crime* 66/464
- -- *Letter to the President of the Republic and Reply* (Charles de Gaulle) 67/465
- -- *Sartre to de Gaulle* 67/466
- -- *Twelve Unangry Men* 67/468
- -- *Russell Tribunal: Opening Speech* 67/467
- -- *From Nuremberg to Stockholm* 67/481
- -- *Genocide* 67/480

II. France
- -- *The Alibi* 64/412
- -- *Let's Refuse to Be Blackmailed* 65/427
- -- *Should the Left Be Killed or Cured?* 65/428
- -- *The Counter-Shock* 65/434
- -- *Raymond Aron's Bastilles* 68/491
- -- *What Was New about May, 1968?* 68/492
- -- *Communists Are Afraid of Revolution* 68/493
- -- *There Is No Good Gaullism . . .* 68/498
- -- *"The Wall" in high school* 69/503
- -- *Trapped Young People* 69/505
- -- *The Masses, Spontaneity, and the Party* 69/511
- -- *The Brazilian People in the Bourgeois Crossfire* 70/517

-- *The Geismar Affair* 70/537
-- *The Third World Begins in Our Suburbs* 70/528
-- *The Whole Truth* 70/525
-- *Words Spoken at the Committee's Press Conference* (Committee for the Liberation of Soldiers in Prison) 70/518
-- *The First People's Trial at Lens* 70/539

III. Israel--The Arab World
-- *Interview* (with Claudine Chonez) 69/504
-- *Israel, the Left and the Arabs* 69/503 A

IV. Intellectuals
-- *Note* (of introduction; not previously published)
-- *A Plea for Intellectuals* (not published in French) 66/447
-- *The People's Friend* 70/532

Part of SITUATIONS, VIII (pp. 375-455) was published in a separate volume: PLAIDOYER POUR LES INTELLECTUELS ⟨A Plea for Intellectuals⟩. (Gallimard, Collection Idées, [1972]. 117 pages.)

The major interest of this volume undoubtedly lies in the series of three lectures (given in Japan in 1966 but rewritten in 1970) which make up A PLEA FOR INTELLECTUALS. In them Sartre returns brilliantly to the idea of commitment and to the problems he posed in WHAT IS LITERATURE?

An English translation of the volume is planned by New Left Books (London).

72/562

SITUATIONS, IX: MÉLANGES ⟨Situations, IX: Miscellany⟩.

-- Gallimard, [1971]. 365 pages. Printing date: December 23, 1971. Publicity band: "Sartre by Sartre."

The volume consists of three parts and includes the following texts:

I. On Myself
-- *Writers in Person* see 60/334
-- *The Writer and His Language* 65/430
-- *Anthropology* 66/441
-- *Sartre on Sartre* 69/512

II. Texts
-- *Palmiro Togliatti* 64/409
-- *The Singular Universal* (on Kierkegaard) 66/435
-- *Mallarmé (1842-1898)* 53/234
-- *Saint George and the Dragon* 66/448

-- *The Socialism That Came in from the Cold* 70/515
-- *I-Thou-He* (on *The Uncompleted* by André Puig) 70/516
-- *Coexistences* (on Paul Rebeyrolle) 70/534

III.

-- *The Man on Tape* 69/507
-- *Psychoanalytical* Dialogue (document) 69/507
-- *Reply to Sartre, by J.-B. Pontalis* 69/507
-- *Reply to Sartre, by Bernard Pingaud* 69/507

SITUATIONS IX includes no previously unpublished writings but does assemble several essential texts by Sartre.

The interview *Sartre by Sartre* is not given in its entirety but in a version published in *Le Nouvel Observateur*.

An English translation is planned by New Left Books (London).

72/563

L'IDIOT DE LA FAMILLE: GUSTAVE FLAUBERT DE 1821 À 1857 ⟨The Family Idiot: Gustave Flaubert from 1821 to 1857⟩, Volume III.

a) Excerpts published with an introductory article by Michel Contat and Michel Rybalka, in *Le Monde* (of books), June 30, 1972.

b) Bibliothèque de philosophie series. Gallimard, [1972]. Bound volume 667 pages long. Printing date: June 2, 1972; put on sale on June 29.

The unsigned introductory text printed on the jacket and also published in the *Bulletin* of Gallimard publications (spring, 1972, p. 19) was drafted by Sartre. We reprint it below:

The first two volumes of THE FAMILY IDIOT *tried to reconstruct Gustave Flaubert's neurotic experience as he lived it, and thus as a "unique" reality. Volume III interprets Flaubert's neurosis, and certain of its consequences, from the viewpoint of his social environment. Can we speak of a "general" neurosis found in a number of individuals in a given period, in short, of a historical and situation neurosis? This leads us to study the "objective spirit" at the outset of the second half of the nineteenth century. This will also lead us to return to the subjective Flaubert in order to examine his relation to the Second Empire. Then we shall be ready to study, in part four, that "singular universal"*--Madame Bovary.

72/564

Foreword to *Les Maos en France* ⟨The Maoists in France⟩, by Michèle Manceaux.

-- Gallimard, [1972]. Pp. 7-15. Printing date: February 17, 1972.

This volume brings together a dozen conversations with militant Maoists of various sorts, and ends with an estimate of their historical and political significance made by a political leader.

After having said at the outset, *I am not a Maoist*, Sartre tries to explain what Maoist action is based on and what it consists of. He concludes:

Violence, spontaneity, morality: for the Maoists these are the three immediate characteristics of revolutionary action. They are not oversimplifying things by saying, "Theory is practice," but only that it never appears except in practice. This is the source of their skill at inventing and carrying out local actions which always originate among the masses. . . . The traditional Left parties are still back in the nineteenth century, in the era of competitive capitalism. But the Maoists, with their antiauthoritarian praxis, *seem to be the only revolutionary force--although just beginning to build--capable of adapting themselves to the new forms of class struggle in this era of organized capitalism.*

72/565

Déclaration de Jean-Paul Sartre à la conférence de presse du Comité Vérité ⟨Jean-Paul Sartre's Statement to the Truth Committee's Press Conference⟩.

a) La Cause du peuple-J'accuse, no. 15 (January 7, 1972).

b) Excerpts in *Le Monde*, January 7, 1972.

Statement read at Toul on January 5, 1972, during a meeting organized by the Truth Committee about the prison revolt which took place from December 5 to 13, 1971.

While protesting the conditions of imprisonment at the main prison in Toul, *where it is impossible to live and, ordinarily, to die*, Sartre challenges the whole penitentiary system and asks, What is a prisoner? *We are law-abiding citizens only because we have given in and given up; they are prisoners only because they rebelled.* In his view, the revolt

72/565

at Toul is a *model revolt* because it signifies the movement from *individualist rebellion to common action undertaken in a common interest.*

NOTES:

Shortly afterward a group of well-known people--including Sartre, Gilles Deleuze, and Michel Foucault--asked about the possibility of having a committee of the GIP ⟨Prisoners Information Group⟩ investigate the uprising at Nancy (see *A.P.L. Informations*, January 16, 1972).

On January 17, forty people led by Sartre, Deleuze, Foucault, and Claude Mauriac tried to hold a press conference on the grounds of the Ministry of Justice about the penitentiary system as a whole. After having been kicked out, the protesters held a press conference at the A.P.L. ⟨Free Press Agency⟩ agency, during which Foucault and Sartre spoke, the latter in order to tell what had just happened.

A complete report of this conference was published by the A.P.L. and included in no. 132 of *A.P.L. Informations* (January 18, 1972). See also *Le Monde*, January 19.

72/NOTE 1.

On January 17, 1972, Sartre was once again charged with libel upon the complaint of Marcellin, minister of the interior, for an article published in the September issue of *Vérité Rhône-Alpes*, regional supplement to *La Cause du peuple-J'accuse* (see *Le Monde*, January 19, 1971).

On March 14, Sartre was charged, in his capacity as editor of *La Cause du peuple-J'accuse*, with public abuse of a private party upon the complaint of CANCAVA ⟨Independent National Bank for Craftsmen's Old Age Compensation⟩. The charge stems from an article which was relatively harmless but was entitled "Gestapo-Cancava," and which appeared on July 11, 1971 (see *Le Monde*, March 16, 1972).

72/566

"Nous avons vu le fascisme au coeur de la Régie . . ." ⟨"We Saw Fascism Inside the Régie"⟩, statements by Sartre about an incursion into the Renault plant on February 14, 1972.

a) La Cause du peuple-J'accuse, no. 18 (February 17, 1972).

b) Le Monde, February 16, and *Combat*, February 17, 1972.

On February 11, members of the Gacem Ali Committee (named after an Algerian worker killed in October, 1971) had for the first time gotten inside the walls of the Renault plant to protest against the arbitrary firing of Maoist militants and to remind the head of Renault that he had to account "not to the established government but to the collectivity" (according to the terms of a tract signed the Gacem Ali Committee and Sartre).

A new incursion took place on February 14, this time with the participation of Sartre, Michelle Vian, Dominique Grange, and several journalists. After they had all been brutally herded out, Sartre made a short statement, held a press conference on what had happened, and brought a complaint at the police station.

72/567

Appel ⟨Appeal⟩ for the formation of an investigating committee for the death of Pierre Overney, signed by Sartre and Maurice Clavel.

-- *A.P.L. Informations*, February 27, 1972; *La Cause du peuple-J'accuse*, special supplement, no. 19; *Le Monde*, February 29, 1972, etc.

Following the murder of the Maoist militant Pierre Overney while he was handing out broadsides at the Renault plant on February 25, Sartre and Clavel call upon all democratic citizens to go with them to Boulogne-Billancourt on February 28 to investigate.

This investigation did take place, but produced few results (see *Le Monde*, March 1).

On the same day, Sartre took part in a leftist march of more than 30,000 protesters, and on March 4 he attended Pierre Overney's funeral, after taking part in a procession of 120,000 to 200,000 persons.

72/568

Statement about the kidnaping of Robert Nogrette, signed by Sartre and Maurice Clavel.

-- *Le Monde*, March 10, 1972.

This statement is a sequel to the kidnaping of the chief of personnel at the Régie Renault, Robert Nogrette, by members of the New People's Resistance and in reprisal for the murder of Pierre Overney.

72/568

Sartre and Clavel think this action was *foreseeable,* and that it was certainly thought to be *a normal response to the repression rampant at Renault.*

72/NOTE 2.

A certain number of intellectuals, including Sartre, Simone de Beauvoir, and especially Philippe Sollers, signed a statement intended for the members of the P.C.F. ⟨French Communist Party⟩ in which they condemn the party's attitude following Pierre Overney's murder and state: "The real struggle against the capitalist slave system is from this point on inseparable from the struggle against the P.C.F. in its effort to pervert the Communist idea. This struggle is being led today by the movement which grew out of May, 1968" (see *Le Monde*, March 17, 1972, and other publications).

72/569

Justice et Etat ⟨Justice and the State⟩, lecture given in Brussels on February 25, 1972.

-- Excerpts and reports in the February 26 Brussels papers, especially *La Cité, Le Soir,* and *La Libre Belgique.*

Given as part of the Young Barristers of Brussels Lecture Series, this long address followed by debate deals above all with the legitimacy and functioning of peoples' justice. The complete text will undoubtedly be published in the near future.

72/NOTE 3.

On April 11, Sartre took part in a press conference called by the Secours Rouge ⟨Red Aid⟩ and by the Committee for the Struggle for Decent Housing to give a true picture of the occupations of dwellings and to denounce the methods used in expelling squatters. He was also asked to take part in a peoples' meeting on April 16 in Belleville, but it was banned by the police (see *A.P.L. Informations*, April 11; *Combat*, April 12; *Le Monde*, April 15).

72/570

Lynchage ou justice populaire? ⟨Lynching or Peoples' Justice?⟩, article about the Bruay-en-Artois business.

a) La Cause du peuple-J'accuse, no. 24 (May 17, 1972).

b) Excerpts in *Le Monde*, May 26, 1972.

In its issue no. 23, *La Cause du peuple-J'accuse* had let several people who lived in Bruay-en-Artois have their say about the murder of young Brigitte Dewevre on April 5. Sartre thinks that the article was a call for a lynching, and he deplores the fact that it was not followed by a discussion which would have made a distinction between the notary public, Pierre Leroy (the bourgeois, *hateful for the role he plays in our society*), and X, Brigitte's assassin, *equally hateful for obvious reasons*. He thinks that the principle "Every person accused of a crime is to be held innocent until proven guilty" is a *peoples' victory* and ought not to be abandoned by a peoples' justice.

This article is accompanied by a reply which is signed *La Cause du peuple* and which challenges part of Sartre's argument and states: "A principle of 'peoples'' justice which, in the name of rules, stopped the peoples' natural movement for justice before it got started, would be an oppressive principle which would simply be another form of the principle of all judicial mechanisms based on exploitation: it would be external to the masses."

72/571

Ouverture d'un débat sur "La Cause du peuple" ⟨Opening of a Debate about *La Cause du peuple*⟩.

-- *La Cause du peuple-J'accuse*, no. 25 (June 21, 1972).

This text, which was published with the consent of the whole staff of the paper, may mark a turning-point in Sartre's action as a militant. In it, he states his dissatisfaction with the overly didactic and working-class orientation of *La Cause du peuple* and reproaches it for being *less and less democratic* and for not being aware of certain movements of struggle (movements of the young, of women, of intellectuals, of small businessmen): *In 1970 the C.D.P. enabled new voices to be heard. Today it is becoming as edifying as a bosses' newsletter. Furthermore, by making itself too exclusively the sounding board of concerns of militants which are valid* in combat, *it is becoming factional and is reflecting present struggles in a very narrow way. Now even though the struggle for* working-class *democracy may at times take on a necessary narrowness, it is necessary that the paper which is committed to this struggle give evidence, on the contrary, of the greatest possible democracy. For this reason, we have decided to go back to the fundamental project of* La Cause du peuple: *the masses speaking to the masses.* And Sartre calls upon the readers to express their points of view.

72/572

Letter of solidarity with an Israeli conscientious objector.

a) Reprinted in the Israeli press around the middle of June.

b) Excerpts in *Le Monde*, June 18-19, 1972.

This letter is addressed to the mother of the conscientious objector Giora Neumann, prosecuted by Israeli authorities for refusing to serve in the army. It also constitutes a stand on the Israeli-Arab problem. Sartre in fact congratulates the accused man for having carried out successfully *that courageous and concrete act: to refuse to serve in an army which, although originally a defensive one, became an offensive one by establishing itself as an army of occupation.* This act *thereby condemns the policy of the Israeli government, which is for the time being making any concrete steps toward peace impossible.*

Neumann was condemned to eight months in jail.

In June, Sartre gave an interview on the same question which we have not traced yet.

72/573

"Die Werksbullen haben uns verprügelt" ⟨The Factory Guards Have Given Us a Beating⟩, interview.

-- *Der Spiegel*, June 19, 1972, pp. 124-26.

Sartre talks about the situation of leftism in France in the spring of 1972, and of the role of the intellectual.

72/NOTE 4.

In April, 1972, Sartre wrote a letter to Heidelberg therapists which was to serve as a preface to a volume on antipsychiatry. In it he particularly insists upon the fact that the doctor-patient relation should be conceived of as *a dialectical relationship.*

72/NOTE 5.

Beginning on February 14, 1972, France-Culture presented a radio adaptation in twenty-five episodes of

Roads to Freedom by Roger Pillaudin, with François Périer, Jean-Marc Bory, etc.

72/NOTE 6.

Appeals and various texts signed by Sartre through July, 1972:

-- Petition backing civil servants from overseas possessions who are demanding, by means of a hunger strike, that they be named to posts in their native countries (*Le Monde*, January 19).
-- Statement demanding that General Jacques Massu be prosecuted for defending torture (in his memoirs of the Algerian War) (*Le Monde*, January 20).
-- "L'armée face à la population" ⟨The Army against the People⟩, a document disseminated by the pastor René Cruse and denouncing "military repression" (*Le Monde*, February 10).
-- Appeal by the Committee for Aid to the Lads (*Le Monde*, February 23).
-- Petition in favor of getting rid of internment camps in Northern Ireland (*A.P.L. Informations*, March 3; earlier published in *Dossier International*, no. 3 [February 11]).
-- Appeal signed by Sartre, Claude Mauriac, Michel Foucault, Maurice Clavel, and Gilles Deleuze protesting the repression in the Congo Peoples' Republic after the February 22 coup d'état (*A.P.L. Informations International*, March 6; *Le Monde*, March 8).
-- Statement in support of the hunger strike of four Basque political refugees in Paris (*Le Monde*, March 11).
-- Appeals in support of three Turkish students condemned to death (*A.P.L. Informations*, March 17; *Le Monde*, March 23).
-- Statement demanding that the Trotskyite militant Pierre Rousset be provisionally set free (*A.P.L. Informations*, March 22).
-- Appeal in favor of the strikers at the "Joint français" factory in Saint-Brieuc (*Le Monde*, May 6).
-- Appeal against repression and torture in Argentina, and for forming a defense committee for Argentine political prisoners (*A.P.L. Informations International*, May 12).
-- Appeal for opposition to any intervention by the French Army in Madagascar (*A.P.L. Informations International*, May 17).
-- Appeal at a meeting about the Thévenin case (*Le Monde*, May 19).
-- Appeal for the victims of repression in Czechoslovakia (published as an advertisement in *Le Monde*, May 28-29).
-- Protest against repression in Iraq on the occasion of Vice President Sadam Hussein Takriti's visit to France (*A.P.L. Informations International*, June 13).
-- Appeal against televising insignificance, à propos the reform of the ORTF ⟨French Radio-Television Organization⟩ (published as an advertisement in *Le Monde*, June 14 and 17).
-- Letter of support from Sartre to the four members of

the October 20th Movement whose trial was held in Athens (complete text in *A.P.L. Informations International*, June 15).
-- Letter-petition circulated by the editor Pierre Belfond in opposition to the repression on the island of Mauritius and in support of the painter Hervé Masson (*A.P.L. Informations International*, June 27; *Le Monde*, July 18).
-- Appeal in opposition to the bombing of Vietnamese dikes by the U.S. Air Force(published as an advertisement in *Le Monde*, July 9-10).

72/574

"Entrevista con Jean-Paul Sartre" ⟨Interview with Jean-Paul Sartre⟩, interview by Albina du Boisrouvray, Fernando Claudin, Juan Goytisolo, and Plinio Apuleyo Mendoza.

-- *Libre* (Paris), no. 4 (1972), pp. 2-10.

72/575

A propos de Munich ⟨About Munich⟩.

-- *La Cause du peuple-J'accuse*, no. 29, October 15, 1972.

72/576

Nous accusons le Président de la République ⟨We Accuse the President of the Republic⟩.

-- Text against President Georges Pompidou, used as a poster and printed in *La Cause du peuple-J'accuse*, supplement to no. 29 (October 20, 1972).

72/577

"Je ne suis plus réaliste" ⟨I Am No Longer a Realist⟩, interview by Pierre Vertraeten.

-- *Gulliver* (Paris), no. 1 (November, 1972), pp. 38-46.

72/578

"What's Jean-Paul Sartre Thinking Lately," interview by Pierre Bénichou.

-- *Esquire*, LXXVIII, no. 6 (469) (December, 1970), 204-8, 280-86.

72/579

Le Nouveau Racisme ⟨The New Racism⟩.

a) First published as *Appel de 137 intellectuels* ⟨Appeal by 137 Intellectuals⟩. *La Cause du peuple-J'accuse*, no. 35 (December 15, 1972).

b) Le Nouvel Observateur, December 18-22, 1972.

France and a Matter of Racism.

-- *New York Times*, March 11, 1973.

72/580

Mais c'est quand même bien l'Etat que vous mettez en question! ⟨But in Fact You Are Questioning the State!⟩, interview of Gabriel Aranda by Sartre.

-- *La Cause du peuple-J'accuse*, no. 36 (December 22, 1972).

72/NOTE 7.

On December 11, 1972, Sartre, accompanied by other intellectuals, intervened in favor of striking immigrant workers in Clichy (see communiqué in *La Cause du peuple-J'accuse*, no. 35, [December 15, 1972], p. 7).

1973

73/581

Elections, piège à cons ⟨Elections, Trap for Suckers⟩, text about the March elections.

-- *Les Temps modernes*, no. 318 (January, 1973), pp. 1099-1108.

73/582

"Nous accusons" ⟨We Accuse⟩, statement accusing President Richard M. Nixon for his policy in Vietnam and signed by Sartre, Vladimir Dedijer, and Laurent Schwartz.

-- *Le Monde*, January 21-22, 1973, publicity on p. 4.

73/583

"Sartre parle des maos" ⟨Sartre Talks about the Maoists⟩, interview by Michel-Antoine Burnier.

a) *Actuel* (Paris), no. 28 (February, 1973), pp. 73-77.

b) Under the title "Entretien avec Sartre" ⟨Conversation with Sartre⟩. *Tout va bien* (Geneva), no. 4 (February 20-March 20, 1973), pp. 30-35.

c) Excerpts in *Le Monde*, February 3, 1973.

"On Maoism: An Interview with Jean-Paul Sartre," translated by Robert d'Amico.

-- *Telos*, [St. Louis], no. 16 (Summer, 1973), pp. 92-101.

73/584

"Volksfront nicht besser als Gaullisten" ⟨The Union of the Left Is Not Better Than the Gaullists⟩, interview by Dieter Wild, Wolfgang Gust, and Gustav Stern.

-- *Der Spiegel*, February 12, 1973.

73/585

Sartre on Amnesty, letter to American newspapers.

-- *New York Review of Books*, April 19, 1973, p. 45.

73/586

UN THÉÂTRE DE SITUATIONS ⟨A Theater of Situations⟩, texts on theater selected and presented by Michel Contat and Michel Rybalka.

-- Gallimard, coll. Idées, [1973]. 382 pages. Date of printing: July 20, 1973.

This volume is divided into two sections: one dealing with Sartre's general pronouncements on theater (and occasionally cinema), the other giving most of the texts and interviews related to each one of his plays. Among the texts published here for the first time, let us mention:

-- *Le Style dramatique* ⟨Dramatic Style⟩, a lecture given on January 10, 1944, and followed by a discussion with Jean Vilar, Albert Camus, Jean Cocteau, and others.
-- *Théâtre et cinéma* ⟨Theater and Cinema⟩, notes from a lecture given on May 6, 1958.
-- *Théâtre épique et théâtre dramatique* ⟨Epic Theater and Dramatic Theater⟩, complete text of lecture given at the Sorbonne on March 29, 1960, and known heretofore only through excerpts (see *Beyond Bourgeois Theater*, 60/349).

73/NOTE 1.

On January 4, 1973, Sartre took part in a press conference to present the forthcoming leftist daily newspaper *Libération* (see *Le Monde*, January 6, 1973).

73/NOTE 2.

73/NOTE 2.

On February 7, 1973, Sartre was interviewed during one hour by Jacques Chancel on the series "Radioscopie" (France-Inter network) (see *Le Monde*, February 9, 1973). Published in Jacques Chancel, *Radioscopie*, vol. 3 (Laffont, 1973).

73/NOTE 3.

There is a *preface* by Sartre (pp. 7-14) in Olivier Todd's *Les Paumes* ⟨The Lost Ones⟩ (Union Générale d'Editions, 10/18 series, no. 767, 1973).

73/NOTE 4.

The volume by Sartre, POLITICS AND LITERATURE (London: Calder and Boyars, Signature series, 1973; 126 pages) has the following texts translated by J. A. Underwood and John Calder:

-- *A Theoretician in Bolivia*	pp. 7-12	see 67/471
-- *Revolution and the Intellectual*	13-35	68/483
-- *Myth and Reality in the Theatre* (as published in *Gambit*)	37-67	67/454
-- *A Structure of Language*	69-75	67/455
-- *The Writer and His Language*	77-125	65/430

Appendix on the Cinema

Sartre's interest in the movies goes back, as we know, to his childhood. Later, as a young professor, he devoted what seems to be his only graduation-day speech to them (see 31/7). Simone de Beauvoir's memoirs are filled with accounts which indicate the intensity with which they explored a still-new art, and she could write, "There was one medium which Sartre ranked almost as high as literature: the movies" (*The Prime of Life*, p. 44). And yet Sartre's relationships to the movies--which would be worth a more thorough study--have been both ambiguous and unfortunate.

They have been, on the one hand, ambiguous because Sartre never pursued as far as he did in other realms his reflections on an art form whose special characteristics seem in part to have escaped him, and which he judges in terms of literature and the theater, thereby obviously assigning it a place of secondary importance and a lesser aesthetic value. The few film criticisms he has written show, as do certain comments reported in interviews, that he has if not a misunderstanding at least a somewhat dated conception of film art. It is certainly false to say, as some movie-lovers or critics have said, that "Sartre doesn't understand a thing about movies." But it must be granted that although he was before the war a sort of precursor--especially in very quickly recognizing the importance of the great American "social films"--for many years now his curiosity about the new films seems to have been greatly dulled.

His relationships with the movies have been, on the other hand, unfortunate because almost all the adaptations of his works or original scripts have been, according to an expression which is no doubt excessive but is Sartre's own, *lamentable failures*.

Thus the list of films we give details about below, in chronological order, constitutes for Sartre a more or less uninterrupted series of disappointments. We give the complete credits for the ten films which have to our knowledge been made from Sartre's works, either his original scripts or his adaptations, even when, as in two or three cases, his name does not appear, for reasons our commentaries try to make clear.

1947--LES JEUX SONT FAITS ⟨The Chips Are Down⟩.

French film by Jean Delannoy. *Script* by Jean-Paul Sartre. *Adaptation* by Jean Delannoy. *Dialogues* by Jean-Paul Sartre and Jacques-Laurent Bost. *Music* by Georges Auric. *Photography* by Christian Matras. *Cast*: Micheline Presle (Eve), Marcel Pagliero (Pierre), Charles Dullin, Marguerite Moreno, Fernand Fabre, Jacques Erwin, Mouloudji, Robert Dalban, Howard Vernon, etc. *Production*: Gibe-Pathé Films.

In an interview published in the April 15, 1947, *Combat*, Jean Delannoy gives the details about THE CHIPS ARE DOWN and points out that he himself was the one who started Sartre on his script-writing career in 1943: "Discouraged by the mediocrity of the scripts we received every day at Pathé, I went to see Sartre and asked him if he didn't want to work for us." During the years 1943-47, Sartre submitted a number of scripts to Pathé--we do not know exactly how many--among which, in addition to THE CHIPS ARE DOWN were "Typhus," *The False Noses*, IN THE MESH, and a script we know little more about than the title: "La Fin du monde" ⟨The End of the World⟩. Nino Frank, who worked on "Typhus" with Sartre during the winter of 1943-44, mentions an additional script whose title he does not give and which Louis Daquin was to film: "It had to do with a rather melodramatic skit about collaboration and the Resistance whose action took place in Rouen and which we intended to film in Great Britain or, after D-Day, in a port in the North" (*Petit Cinéma Sentimental* ⟨Little Sentimental Cinema⟩ [La Nouvelle Edition, 1950], pp. 170-71). He also says that Sartre had intended to produce films himself later.

Concerning the script of THE CHIPS ARE DOWN, which was published in book form, see 47/118 and 47/119. Jean Delannoy's adaptation closely follows Sartre's text and his production is honest without being either inspired or simply inventive. The film was shown at the 1947 Cannes Festival. Received rather favorably on the whole by the critics, it had a measure of public success. Although it has aged greatly now, as by the way have most of the French movies of the time, all of whose faults it has, the film nevertheless keeps your attention because of the quality of its actors. Among these, Micheline Presle, greatly helped by the superb lighting of Christian Matras, imposes her luminous presence. The realistic scenes, on the other hand, above all those which show militants, make you smile in spite of their intention. Seen at one remove as an aesthetic document from an already distant period, THE CHIPS ARE DOWN takes on a certain nostalgic charm and deserves not to fall into oblivion.

1951--LES MAINS SALES ⟨Dirty Hands⟩.

French film by Fernand Rivers. *Adaptation* by Jacques-Laurent Bost and Fernand Rivers. *Dialogues* by Jean-Paul Sartre. *Music* by Paul Misraki. *Photography* by Jean Berthelot. *Cast*: Pierre Brasseur (Hoederer), Daniel Gélin (Hugo), Claude Nollier (Olga), Jacques Castelot (the Prince), Monique Artur (Jessica), Marcel André, Georges Chamarat, etc. *Production*: Fernand Rivers--Rivers Films. (Paris premiere August 29, 1951.)

Even more than the play, the film provoked violent reactions from the P.C. ⟨Communist Party⟩, which feared, not without reason, that it would feed the anti-Communist campaign. In many theaters, in Paris as well as in the provinces, the film was shown under police protection. And in fact the movie adaptation, quite faithful to the play on the whole, did accentuate its anti-Communist overtones: the militants of the proletarian party, and especially Hoederer's body-guards, are more like gangsters in American movies than workers.

The critics were generally very hard on Fernand Rivers' very conventional filming. The film, which was a rather big commercial success, has no value except that of its leading actors, Pierre Brasseur and, above all, Daniel Gélin, who give a wholly remarkable interpretation of the characters of Hoederer and Hugo.

Given the change in his political position since 1950, Sartre has been bent on publicly disassociating himself from the use which could be made of his film against the Communists, and when he was questioned about it before it was released, he said: *I wash my hands of it. I sold the rights to it twenty days after the premiere of my play. . . . I am not responsible for the date on which it was released or for the film itself, and when the time is right I'll say so. I add that the film is played by excellent actors and that what I'm saying now does not involve them. There was never any question of having the film released in time for the elections. It isn't finished. I don't think it has great "shock value." If it does, the fact that I'll make clear that it is a purely commercial matter which doesn't concern me will greatly weaken that value (Paris-Presse-L'Intransigeant*, June 7, 1951; see 51/210). This is the only statement about the film we have found, and Sartre does not seem to have expressed his opinion of the film itself.

1952--LA P... RESPECTUEUSE (The Respectful Prostitute).

French film by Marcel Pagliero and Charles Brabant. *Adaptation* by Jacques-Laurent Bost and Alexandre Astruc. *Dialogues* by Jean-Paul Sartre and Jacques-Laurent Bost. *Music* by Georges Auric. *Photography* by Eugène Shuftan. *Cast*: Barbara Laage (Lizzie MacKay), Ivan Desny (Fred Clarke), Walter Bryant (Sidney [the Negro]), Marcel Herrand (Senator Clarke), Marie-Olivier, Yolande Laffon, Jacques Hilling, André Valmy, etc. *Production*: Agiman Films and Artès Films, distributed by Marceau Films. (Paris premiere on October 8, 1952.)

The euphemistic version of its title was not enough to guarantee the film against scandal. But this time the scandal was wholly political. At the Venice Festival, where the film was shown in 1952, pro-American circles demanded that the rule against insulting a friendly nation be applied, and the film aroused impassioned debates (see André Bazin's article in *Les Cahiers du cinéma*, no. 16 [October, 1952]).

The movie version, although it follows the play rather closely, is very different from it (see 46/90). Whereas the play was originally conceived of and staged as a "comedy-bouffe," the film, which is not, by the way, without merit, falls into the category of "realistic drama." Certain connecting scenes were shot in the United States, and Marcel Pagliero's production alludes explicitly to the conventions of the American "thriller." The very fine photography of Eugène Shuftan (who was Fritz Lang's cameraman in the United States), the minutely Americanized settings and Barbara Laage's acting all try to create the atmosphere of the American social film, but this attempt at realism makes all the more evident the film's painfully French characteristics, beginning with the disturbing acting of certain main actors.

On the other hand, the film was changed to make it more optimistic: the prostitute Lizzie becomes a completely positive character. Whereas in the play she does not entirely escape being mystified by the right-thinking people and accepts Fred's humiliating proposition, which will make her his weekend amusement, the film ends with a shot showing her complete solidarity with the hunted Black, whom she is getting ready to defend with revolver in hand.

1953--*Les Orgueilleux* ⟨The Beautiful and the Damned⟩.

Franco-Mexican film by Yves Allégret. *Script* by Jean Aurenche and Yves Allégret [based on an original script, "Typhus," by Jean-Paul Sartre]. *Adaptation and dialogues* by Jean Aurenche and Jean Clouzot. *Music* by Paul Misraki. *Photography* by Alex Philips. *Cast*: Michèle Morgan, Gérard Philipe, Victor Manuel Mendoza, Michèle Cordoue, Carlos Lopez Moctezuma, etc. *Production*: C.I.C.C.--Jean Productions (France)--Reforma Films (Mexico), distributed by Columbia. (Paris premiere on November 5, 1953.)

Sartre's name, which is listed in the credits given by the producing firm, no longer appears in the film credits. Sartre himself had it withdrawn because he thought his script was no longer recognizable in the adaptation Jean Aurenche and Yves Allégret made.

To tell what is left of "Typhus" in *The Beautiful and the Damned*, we would have to compare the original text and the film. But we know already that the action of "Typhus" takes place in the Far East, even though Sartre got the inspiration for his script from the account of an epidemic which had raged through Morocco shortly before he went there to spend his vacation with Simone de Beauvoir in 1938 (see *The Prime of Life*, p. 266). An account of the various misadventures the script went through before Yves Allégret revived it may be found in the Nino Frank volume referred to above in connection with THE CHIPS ARE DOWN.

Although *The Beautiful and the Damned* is far from being a success, it is not an unimportant film, and is in any case distinguished from the productions of French moviemaking current at that time. It evokes the Camus of *The Plague* more than Sartre. Jacques Doniol-Valcroze, who sees it as a "phenomenological" film, speaks of it favorably in a criticism in *Les Cahiers du cinéma* (no. 31 [January, 1954]) and summarizes the plot as follows: "A young woman stops over in a little Mexican town with her sick husband. Inflicted with cerebrospinal meningitis, the latter soon dies and the epidemic spreads, requiring the town to be quarantined and making the young woman prisoner of that sort of physical and moral no exit constituted by the cordon sanitaire and the death watch. She is going to discover that she has little sense of loss at the death of her husband, and then that she is increasingly interested in a local derelict, a French ex-doctor who has drowned himself in alcohol after he has been more or less responsible for his wife's death. Redemption through love? Involvement through circumstances? It makes no difference. The man and the woman will remain together to try to break out of the suffocating solitude of despair and confront the world's prejudiced hostility. This ending, which could have been a theatrical trick or a bit of moral sermonizing, is in fact just an incident which in no way stands out from the rest. The film stops there. Just a period. Ten minutes earlier or ten minutes later, nothing would have been changed. In any case, the chips were down without our knowing exactly how."

1954--HUIS CLOS ⟨No Exit⟩.

French film by Jacqueline Audry. *Dialogues* by Jean-Paul Sartre. *Adaptation and additional dialogues* by Pierre Laroche. *Music* by Joseph Kosma. *Photography* by Robert Julliard. *Cast*: Arletty (Inès), Gaby Sylvia (Estelle), Frank Villard (Garcin), Yves Deniaud (le Garçon), Nicole Courcel, Jean Debucourt, Jacques Chabassol, Arlette Thomas, Isabelle Pia, Jacques Duby, etc. *Production*: Marceau Films. (Paris premiere at the end of December, 1954.)

An article prior to the premiere, which includes an interview with Jacqueline Audry as well as excerpts from the script and dialogues of the film, gives the following specification: "Although he did not help make the film, Sartre checked it and said he was satisfied with the script. When Jacqueline Audry came to talk to him about NO EXIT, he wanted to rewrite his work, change it completely, but she didn't give in" (Catherine Valogne, "HUIS CLOS revu par Jacqueline Audry" ⟨NO EXIT reviewed by Jacqueline Audry⟩, *Les Lettres françaises*, September 16, 1954).

The film follows the play very closely. An introductory sequence showing the arrival of a batch of damned souls in the hall of a Kafkaesque palace was added, and the adapters had what seems at first glance to be the ingenious idea of putting a sort of screen in place of the window of the hotel the three characters are shut up in, so that by turns they can see scenes from their past life and observe their next of kin to the extent that the latter have not forgotten them. At the end, the window is shown to be walled up. This idea, which claims to answer to a need in the movies for action and for variety of setting, is actually the main reason for the film's failure. In showing in this way that there is no exit, the adapters took away--without gaining any advantage for the movie--the sense of suffocating promiscuity in eternal confinement which undoubtedly gives the play its essential force. The critics, moreover, justly pointed out the film's weak directing and miscasting of the role of Inès, which does not suit Arletty at all.

1957--*Les Sorcières De Salem* ⟨The Salem Witches⟩.

French film by Raymond Rouleau. *Script and dialogues* by Jean-Paul Sartre based on Arthur Miller's play *The Crucible*. *Music* by Georges Auric. *Photography* by Claude Renoir. *Cast*: Yves Montand (John Proctor), Simone Signoret (Elisabeth Proctor), Mylène Demongeot (Abigail Williams), Raymond Rouleau (Governor Danforth), Jean Debucourt (Reverend Parris), Pierre Larquey, etc. *Production*: Borderie Films--C.I.C.C.--S. N. Pathé Cinéma (France) and Defa (Germany). (Paris premiere on April 26, 1957.)

Concerning the origins of this script, see 56/287.

The changes Sartre made in Arthur Miller's play, which was written to denounce McCarthyism, are generally faithful to its spirit at the same time they accentuate its social implications and its contemporary political significance. Thus Sartre introduces an element of class struggle into the film which explains the social motives of the "witch hunt." The contemporary political significance of the film derives primarily from the increased importance given to the character of Deputy Governor Danforth, which Sartre develops at the expense of Reverend Parris. He also eliminated the role of the sympathetic pastor and filled out that of Abigail Williams, who thereby takes on greater depth and ambiguity than she had in the play.

It is clear that the film bears Sartre's stamp, and the critics have frequently reproached him with having twisted Miller's text in the direction of his own philosophy in order to turn it into nothing but a political demonstration. On the other hand, the film, which lasts for two and one-half hours, has been judged too long, Sartre's dialogues too literary, and Raymond Rouleau's direction too static. The film was nevertheless quite well received on the whole and was rather successful.

1957--KEAN, GENIO E SREGOLATEZZA ⟨Kean, Genius and Disorder⟩.

Italian film in Eastman-color by Vittorio Gassman. Based on the Alexandre Dumas play adapted by Jean-Paul Sartre. *Script* by Suso Cecchi d'Amico, Francesco Rosi, and Vittorio Gassman. *Music* by Roman Vlad. *Photography* by Gianni di Venanzo. *Cast*: Vittorio Gassman (Kean), Eleonora Rossi-Drago (Countess Koefeld), Anna-Maria Ferrero (Anna Damby), etc. *Production*: Franco Cristaldi, Lux Films--Vides, distributed in Italy by Lux Films.

We were unable to see this film, which seems to have never been distributed in France. It was entered at the 1957 Locarno Festival.

Vittorio Gassman had staged the Dumas-Sartre play in Italy, in which his acting of the role of Kean had been much praised. Judging by the articles published at the time of its release, the film follows Sartre's adaptation very closely (Sartre himself has never seen the film). It was favorably received by the Italian critics.

1962--*Freud, The Secret Passion.*

American film by John Huston. *Script* by Charles Kaufmann and Wolfgang Reinhardt. *Music* by Jerry Goldsmith. *Photography* by Douglas Slocombe. *Cast*: Montgomery Clift (Freud), Susannah York (Cecily Koertner), Larry Parks (Dr. Joseph Breuer), Susan Kohner (Martha Freud), Fernand Ledoux (Charcot), etc. *Production*: Wolfgang Reinhardt, Universal.

Having previously made a medium-length film about victims of "shell shock" treated by hypnosis, John Huston had become fascinated by this problem and decided in 1958 to make a film about the period of Freud's life in which he discovered the mechanisms of the unconscious, thanks in part to hypnosis. Huston asked Sartre for a script and got a manuscript from him in 1959 that was almost eight hundred pages long. This script, which inevitably had to be cut, was the basis for work done by new scriptwriters. During a discussion with Kenneth Tynan in 1961 (see 61/363), Sartre gave the following details:

Except in construction, the final script has little resemblance to what I wrote. The fault is partly mine, and partly Freud's. My scenario would have been impossible to shoot; it would have lasted seven or eight hours. . . .

What we tried to do--and this was what interested Huston especially--was to show Freud not when his theories had made him famous, but at the time, around the age of thirty, when he was utterly wrong; when his ideas had led him into hopeless error. You know that at one point he seriously believed that what caused hysteria was fathers raping their daughters. We begin in that period, and follow his career up to the discovery of the Oedipus complex.

That, for me, is the most enthralling time in the life of a great discoverer--when he seems muddled and lost, but has the genius to collect himself and put everything in order. Of course, it is difficult to explain this development to an audience ignorant of Freud. In order to arrive at the right ideas, one must start by explaining the wrong ones, and that is a long process: hence the seven-hour scenario (Tynan Right and Left [New York: Atheneum, 1967], pp. 308-9).

In another interview (62/371), Sartre added: *It was not because of the cuts that I removed my signature--I knew perfectly well that cuts would have to be made--but because of the way in which they were made. It's an honest piece of work. Very honest. But it's not worthwhile for an intellectual to take responsibility for questionable ideas.*

For his part, John Huston told Robert Benayoun, who asked him what part Sartre played in the final version: "The basic idea, the idea of Freud as an adventurer, the explorer of his own unconscious, is mine. I wanted to focus on that episode the way a detective story would. Freud clears up his own case. Sartre had the idea of making Anna O. a composite of several patients. You know that Freud never did in fact meet this Anna O., whose case he knew about only through Breuer. Sartre wrote a script as long as my arm that we couldn't use. But Charles Kaufmann, Wolfgang Reinhardt, and I kept some of his best ideas. Sartre admired Freud, but cut him down a little." (*Positif*, no. 70 [June, 1965]).

It must also be pointed out that the final version of the film was cut by the distributor, who took out almost one-half hour of the original. In spite of a showing which is thus partially disowned by Huston, the film is a great success: not only does it popularize the main themes of psychoanalysis intelligently and fairly, although not strictly, but it also gives Freud's main discoveries their full impact as revelations. The sensitivity of the shots and settings, and the really gripping acting of Montgomery Clift, who gives an intense emotional weight to Freud's relations with his associates and patients, contribute to overcoming the resistances to Freudian theories which are even today often encountered in the uninitiated spectator. This emotional climate, this atmosphere of quivering and contained passion which makes Huston's *Freud* without a doubt and above all a love story in the best sense of the term, may also explain why Sartre preferred to disassociate himself completely from the film.

1963--LES SÉQUESTRÉS D'ALTONA (The Condemned of Altona).

Italo-French film by Vittorio De Sica. Freely adapted from the play by Jean-Paul Sartre. *Script and dialogues* by Abby Mann. *Music*: Shostakovitch's Eleventh Symphony. *Drawings* by Renato Guttoso. Excerpts from *The Great Fear and Misery of the Third Reich* and *The Resistible Rise of Arturo Ui* by Bertolt Brecht (the scene from *Arturo Ui* is played by the Berliner Ensemble). *Cast*: Sophia Loren (Johanna), Maximilien Schell (Frantz), Fredric March (the Father), Françoise Prévost (Leni), Robert Wagner (Werner), etc. *Production*: Carlo Ponti, Titanus Films (Rome) and Société générale de Cinématographie (Paris), distributed by Twentieth Century Fox. (The original version is in English.)

A first adaptation of THE CONDEMNED OF ALTONA had been made, with Sartre's approval, by Jules Dassin. It took great liberties with the play but kept its general spirit as a chronicle of a big German family during the Hitler years. Carlo Ponti, the producer, did not accept this adaptation and called upon Vittorio De Sica, who commissioned his usual scriptwriter, Cesare Zavattini, to write a script. But Carlo Ponti did not like the latter's script any better, so that it was the American liberal scriptwriter Abby Mann who did the definitive reworking of the script and the dialogue. He was considerate enough to ask Sartre what he would like to see preserved in his play from the dismemberment it was being subjected to for both political and commercial reasons (it was necessary in particular to "remodel" each of the roles in terms of the unequal fame of the actors). Sartre replied that the father-son relationship and the clear establishment of their guilt were especially important. But Abby Mann, who was subject to the demands of his producers, did not even succeed in satisfying this nevertheless modest request. Consequently, Sartre demanded that the credits mention that the adaptation was "freely inspired" by his play, and he lost interest in the undertaking to the extent of never wanting to see the completed film.

The chief fault of the film lies less in its betrayal of the play than in its failure to blend into a coherent whole the parts borrowed unchanged from the theater and the changes made to meet the specific needs of the movies. The result is a bastard film in which filmed scenes from the theater, acted in a very debatable way, are juxtaposed in the greatest confusion with realistically shot but unimaginatively staged scenes. Whereas the play rose to the level of a philosophical reflection on the individual's responsibility as historical actor, the film only offers a criticism (sometimes effective, by the way) of post-Nazi Germany.

1967--*Le Mur* ⟨The Wall⟩.

French film by Serge Roullet. From the short story by Jean-Paul Sartre. *Adaptation* by Serge Roullet. *Dialogues* by Jean-Paul Sartre. *Music* by Edgardo Canton. *Photography* by Denis Clerval. *Cast*: Michel de Castillo (Pablo Ibbieta), Denis Mahaffey (Tom Steinbock), Matthieu Klossowski (Juan Mirbal), Bernard Anglade (the doctor), René Darmon (Ramon Gris), Anna Pacheco (Concha), etc.

Production: Procinex--Niepce Films, distributed by Rank. (Paris premiere on October 23, 1967.)

The Wall is the only film based on one of his works that Sartre has said he was satisfied with. He publicly supported it by giving a press conference during its showing at the Venice Film Festival in September, 1967, and he answered questions from the audience during its simultaneous premiere in Paris and New York (see 67/476 and 67/477; see also Sartre's letter to Serge Roullet printed on the back side of the detachable cover of Gallimard's edition of LE MUR).

The critics generally praised the faithfulness of Serge Roullet's adaptation of the short story. Yet it could be pointed out that this literal faithfulness definitely leads to a rather sizable betrayal: Serge Roullet's austere, elegant, and icy production is actually closer to the classical style of Albert Camus's *The Stranger* than to Sartre's own style in *The Wall*. The latter borrows its apparently unpolished and unfinished spontaneity from the American detective story, and would thus seem to call for filming in the style of the American crime movie. Serge Roullet's modesty and wholly "Bressonian" discretion erase the rawest aspects of the story (especially in its description of physical fear) and, added to the "absurdist" theme, help make *The Wall* more a Camusian than a Sartrian film. Which does not keep the film from being a worthy success.

NOTES.

Toward 1943, Sartre worked for a time with Henri-Georges Clouzot on a script which was to be an "epic adaptation" of NO EXIT also partially inspired by Dante's *Inferno*.

Sartre plays himself and speaks one of his own texts in a sequence of the movie by Nicole Védrès, *La Vie commence demain* ⟨Life Begins Tomorrow⟩ (1950). For the text, see Volume II.

In 1955, Alexandre Astruc was supposed to film an original script by Sartre on the life of Kean. The project failed before Sartre had really set to work.

Louis Daquin was supposed to film NEKRASSOV in 1956 (see item in *Paris-Presse*, January 18, 1956).

In 1956 there was a possibility that Sartre might adapt Zola's *Germinal* for, it seems, Julien Duvivier. This project was not followed through.

There is an Argentine film by Pedro Escudero and Tad Danielewski, *No Exit*, which was made in 1962 on the basis of Sartre's NO EXIT and which Sartre knows nothing whatsoever about.

In 1962 Sartre approved of an Italian television film entitled *L'Uomo Sartre* ⟨Sartre, the Man⟩ and made by Leonardo Autera and Gregorio Lo Cascio.

The adaptation of NO EXIT which Michel Mitrani filmed for television, with Michel Auclair, Judith Magre, and Evelyne Rey, was broadcast by the O.R.T.F. ⟨French Radio-Television⟩ in October, 1965.

In 1966, Michel Mitrani also made an excellent adaptation of *The Room* for television, with Michel Auclair and Geneviève Page.

Sartre appears twice, and very briefly, in Jacques Baratier's film about Saint-Germain des Près, *Disorder at Twenty* (1967).

INDEXES

Index of Titles of Sartre's Works

DIRECTIONS FOR USE OF THE INDEX OF TITLES

This index is divided into the following categories: (1) Fiction; (2) Plays; (3) Filmscripts, Films Adapted from Sartre's Works; (4) Nonfiction Books; (5) Articles, Essays, Reviews; (6) Prefaces, Introductions, Forewords, Program Notes; (7) Collections; (8) Statements, Letters, Messages, Appeals, Tracts, Testimony; (9) Interviews, Discussions, Debates, Collected Remarks, Press Conferences; (10) Public Lectures and Speeches; (11) Phonograph Records; (12) Books Containing Substantial Texts by Sartre.

Where two items have similar titles, a date or other distinguishing mark follows each title in parentheses. The *first page number* following a title *refers to the main bibliographical entry for that title*, in those cases in which the item has a main entry.

Titles in each category are listed in alphabetical order, with the following exceptions: items in (8) and (9) are listed in the order of their main bibliographical entries (i.e., generally, in *chronological* order); those in (6) are listed alphabetically according to the name of the writer or artist on whose behalf the item was written (or, when no author is given, according to the title of the publication in which it is contained); and those in (12) are listed alphabetically according to the name of the author or compiler of the book in question.

In (6), the indexed entry for each text is a description. Where Sartre's text has its own title, this title follows the entry in parentheses.

Books listed in (12) are, for the most part, limited to those containing texts by Sartre whose first or only or most readily available appearance is in these books, or where the text does not appear elsewhere in English translation. Their titles appear in the original language, except where there is a published English translation. Other books or articles mentioned in the text can be found by referring to the author's name in the Index of Names.

In general, Sartre's works are indexed under the titles of their best-known U.S. translations. Where the title of the British translation differs from that of the U.S. translation, or where a variant English version has gained wide acceptance, the alternate title is cross-indexed for major works and is included in parentheses following the indexed title of less widely known works. Where no English translation has been published, the translated title given in the main bibliographical entry has been used.

Titles of interviews are followed by the place and year of their original publication. When only the name of the interlocutor is known, an interview or discussion can be found by consulting the Index of Names.

The reader should bear in mind that many of Sartre's works have appeared in more than one format: an article as a book; a preface or speech as an article; and so on. As a rule each item is indexed under the category of its earliest appearance, and major works are cross-indexed under the category of their subsequent publication.

Unpublished or proposed works by Sartre are indicated as such and are included in the category in which they would have fallen had they been published. Published excerpts are listed separately only when they appeared prior to the work from which they were excerpted. Where an item by Sartre is mentioned in the Bibliography but no title is given, it is indexed here under the description with which it appears in the Bibliography (or a shorter form of this description).

Although several items for which there is no main bibliographical entry are included in this index, it has been impossible to include all the appeals, statements, and so on which Sartre has signed or coauthored. Such items can be found by using the Index of Subjects or the Index of Names.

1. FICTION

2. PLAYS

3. FILMSCRIPTS, FILMS ADAPTED FROM SARTRE'S WORKS

4. NONFICTION BOOKS

5. ARTICLES, ESSAYS, REVIEWS

6. PREFACES, INTRODUCTIONS, FOREWORDS, PROGRAM NOTES

7. COLLECTIONS

(For collections of plays published in English, see titles of individual plays.)

8. STATEMENT, LETTERS, MESSAGES, APPEALS, TRACTS, TESTIMONY

9. INTERVIEWS, DISCUSSIONS, DEBATES, COLLECTED REMARKS, PRESS CONFERENCES

10. PUBLIC LECTURES AND SPEECHES

11. PHONOGRAPH RECORDS

(All those mentioned are recorded in the French language.)

12. BOOKS CONTAINING SUBSTANTIAL TEXTS BY SARTRE

Index of Names

Index of Subjects